The Harlem Renaissance 1920–1940

Series Editor

Cary D. Wintz
Texas Southern University

A Garland Series

Contents of the Series

The Politics and Aesthetics of "New Negro" Literature

Edited with introductions by

Cary D. Wintz
Texas Southern University

GARLAND PUBLISHING, INC.
New York & London
1996

Library of Congress Cataloging-in-Publication Data

The politics and aesthetics of "New Negro" literature / edited with in-
    troductions by Cary D. Wintz.
        p.   cm. — (The Harlem Renaissance, 1920–1940 ; 2)
    Includes bibliographical references.
    ISBN 0-8153-2213-5 (alk. paper)
        1. American literature—Afro-American authors—History and
    criticism.   2. Politics and literature—United States—History—20th
    century.   3. American literature—20th century—History and criticism.
    4. Harlem (New York, N.Y.)—Intellectual life—20th century.
    5. Afro-Americans—Intellectual life.   6. Afro-Americans in literature.
    7. Afro-American aesthetics.   8. Harlem Renaissance.   I. Wintz,
    Cary D., 1943–   . II. Series.
    PS153.N5P65   1996
    810.9'896073—dc20   96-16126
                                                         CIP

Printed on acid-free, 250-year-life paper
Manufactured in the United States of America

Contents

Setting the Political Agenda for the Harlem Renaissance

Series Introduction

The Harlem Renaissance was the most significant event in African American literature and culture in the twentieth century. While its most obvious manifestation was as a self-conscious literary movement, it touched almost every aspect of African American culture and intellectual life in the period from World War I to the Great Depression. Its impact redefined black music, theater, and the visual arts; it reflected a new more militant political/racial consciousness and racial pride that was associated with the term "New Negro"; it embodied the struggle for civil rights that had been reinvigorated by the founding of the N.A.A.C.P. and the ideology of W.E.B. Du Bois; and it was an aspect of the urbanization of African Americans that first attracted public attention in the early twentieth century with the black migration.

Within this context it is difficult to pinpoint the chronological limits of the Harlem Renaissance. Generally the consensus among scholars is that the Harlem Renaissance was an event of the 1920s, bounded on one side by World War I and the race riots of 1919 and on the other side by the 1929 stock market crash. Some, however, have either greatly expanded or sharply restricted the time span of the movement. In 1967 Abraham Chapman wrote that he saw elements of the Renaissance in Claude McKay's poetry of 1917 and even in W.E.B. Du Bois's poem, "The Song of the Smoke," which was published in 1899.[1] Nathan Huggins argued that the Renaissance began during the years between the beginning of World War I and 1920, when the center of power in the African American community shifted from Tuskegee to Harlem, and he saw the Harlem Riots of 1935 as the end of the movement.[2] John Hope Franklin, on the other hand, wrote as late as 1980 that the Harlem Renaissance extended into the 1960s; more recently he has modified that concept, and now speaks of a first and second phase of the Harlem Renaissance, with the latter phase extending into the 1940s and beyond; he also observes that African American literary creativity was not confined to Harlem, but spread across the entire country[3] Benjamin Brawley, the preeminent African American literary historian contemporary to the Harlem Renaissance, downplayed the concept of the "so-called Negro literary renaissance," which he felt was centered around the publication of Carl Van Vechten's *Nigger Heaven* in 1926 and which he argued had no significant positive influence on African American literature.[4] Finally, Sterling Brown, one of the Harlem Renaissance poets and later a literary scholar, denied that Harlem was ever the center of a black literary movement.[5]

For the purposes of this collection the Harlem Renaissance is viewed primarily as a literary and intellectual movement. While theater, music, and the visual arts are looked at briefly, the focus is on African American literature, the assessment and criticism of this literature, and the relation of this literature to the political and social issues confronting African Americans in the early twentieth century.

The Harlem Renaissance was a self-conscious movement. That is, the writers and poets who participated in the movement were aware that they were involved in a literary movement and assumed at least partial responsibility for defining the parameters and aesthetics of the movement; black scholars and intellectuals were also aware of the Harlem Renaissance (even if they railed against it) and attempted to define the movement in terms both of literature and the political and social implications of that literature. While it was self-conscious, the Harlem Renaissance lacked a well-defined ideological or aesthetic center. It was more a community of writers, poets, critics, patrons, sponsors, and publishers than a structured and focused intellectual movement. It may be best conceptualized as an attitude or a state of mind—a feeling shared by a number of black writers and intellectuals who centered their activities in Harlem in the 1920s and early 1930s. The men and women who participated in the movement shared little but a consciousness that they were part of a common endeavor—a new awakening of African American culture and creativity; other than that what bound them together was a pride in their racial heritage, an essentially middle-class background, and the fact that all, to a greater or lesser degree, were connected to Harlem at the time that Harlem was emerging as the cultural, intellectual, and political center of black America.

Within this context, the Harlem Renaissance may best be conceptualized as a group of black writers and poets, orbiting erratically around a group of black intellectuals positioned in the N.A.A.C.P., the Urban League, and other African American political and educational institutions. These older intellectuals supported the movement, criticized it, attempted with varying success to define it, and served as liaison between the writers and the white publishers, patrons, and critics who dominated the business of literature in the United States in the 1920s. Complicating and enriching this mix was the fact that the lines between the various types of participants were not clearly drawn. James Weldon Johnson, for example, was a major promoter of the movement and a poet and novelist in his own right; Jessie Fauset, the most prolific novelist of the period, also served as literary editor of *The Crisis* and actively promoted the careers of young black writers; Countee Cullen, Sterling Brown, and Gwendolyn Bennett wrote regular literary columns, while Wallace Thurman, Langston Hughes, and several other writers attempted to publish literary magazines; and Carl Van Vechten, a white promoter of African American literature, worked closely with the Knopfs to publish black literature, authored the best-known novel of Harlem life, and almost singlehandedly created the white fascination with Harlem and African American life that characterized the 1920s.

With this definition it becomes a little easier to define the parameters of the movement. The Harlem Renaissance began in the early 1920s, when Jean Toomer published *Cane* and African American writers and intellectuals began to realize that something new was happening in black literature. The movement extended well into the 1930s and included the works of Zora Neale Hurston, Claude McKay, and Langston Hughes that were published in that decade. As long as they and other writers consciously identified with the Renaissance, the movement continued. It did not, however, encompass the younger writers like Richard Wright, Frank Yerby, or Ralph Ellison, who emerged in the 1930s and 1940s. Like so much else, these boundaries are not exact. Antecedents to the Harlem Renaissance are clear in the first two decades of the twentieth century; likewise it is easy to place some of Langston Hughes's work from the 1940s and 1950s in the Renaissance.

The goal of this series is to reprint articles and other materials that will delineate a clear picture and foster an understanding of the Harlem Renaissance. Three types of materials are included in this series. First, and most important, are the critical and interpretive materials on the Harlem Renaissance written by participants in and contemporaries of the movement. These firsthand accounts will assist readers in understanding the efforts of Harlem Renaissance writers, poets, and critics to define the movement and enable readers to glimpse the dynamics of the movement. Second, this series includes a retrospective look at the Harlem Renaissance through the eyes of participants and contemporaries, as well as by writers and critics who were involved in post-Renaissance black literature. Finally, the series presents a sample of the scholarly analysis and criticism of the movement from the 1950s through the early 1990s. The selections come from articles, essays, columns, and reviews in periodical literature; selections from memoirs, novels, histories, and books of criticism; and essays from scholarly journals. These materials are supplemented by a selection of previously unpublished materials, including letters, speeches, and essays. Not included are the literary works of the Harlem Renaissance. There are a number of anthologies of African American literature that already serve that purpose well.

This series also reflects one of the major problems confronting the study of the Harlem Renaissance in particular and African American history in general—the difficulty of accessing needed source materials. For years the study of African American history was handicapped by the fact that many of its primary sources had not been preserved or were not made available to scholars. If they had been preserved, they were housed in scattered collections and often incompletely processed and catalogued. The sharp increase in interest in African American history during the last thirty years has improved this situation enormously, but problems still persist. This series is in part an effort to make material related to one aspect of African American history more available to students and scholars. Unfortunately, it also suffers from the problem that some resources, even when located, are not readily available. For this reason a number of items by James Weldon Johnson had to be excluded; likewise, a very valuable retrospective on the Harlem Renaissance that was published initially in *Black World* is missing here. In the future, perhaps these and other barriers that impede research in African American history will be lifted.

As in any project of this nature there are scores of persons who have provided valuable support and assistance; it is impossible to name them all here. I want to especially thank Leo Balk and Carole Puccino of Garland Publishing. Leo with patience and firmness guided this series to completion; Carole worked diligently to arrange permissions for the publication of the material that appears here. In addition, I want to thank Paul Finkelman, who played a key role in helping me conceptualize the scope and nature of this project. Wolde Michael Akalou, Howard Beeth, Merline Pitre, and my other colleagues and students at Texas Southern University provided valuable feedback as the project developed. I also had wonderful assistance from the staff at the libraries

I visited while collecting the material for this series. I want to especially acknowledge the staff at the Harry Ransom Humanities Research Center at the University of Texas at Austin, the Beinecke Library at Yale University, and the Heartman Collection at the Robert J. Terry Library at Texas Southern University; in addition, librarians at the Fondren Library at Rice University, the M.D. Anderson Library at the University of Houston, the Perry Casteñeda Library at the University of Texas at Austin, and the library at the University of Houston, Clear Lake helped me track down the copies of the more elusive journals and periodicals used for this collection. I also want to thank Kathy Henderson and and Barbara Smith-Labard, who helped arrange for permission to publish previously unpublished materials from the collections at the Harry Ransom Humanities Research Center. Finally, research for this project was supported in part by a Travel to Collections grant from the National Endowment for the Humanities.

    Cary D. Wintz

Notes

    1. Abraham Chapman, "The Harlem Renaissance in Literary History," *CLA Journal* 11 (September 1967): 44–45.

    2. Nathan Irvin Huggins, ed., *Voices from the Harlem Renaissance* (New York: Oxford University Press, 1976), 6–10.

    3. John Hope Franklin, *From Slavery to Freedom: A History of Negro Americans*, 5th ed. (New York: Alfred Knopf, 1980), 383; John Hope Franklin and Alfred A. Moss, Jr., *From Slavery to Freedom: A History of African Americans*, 7th ed. (New York: McGraw-Hill, Inc., 1994), 379–80.

    4. Benjamin Brawley, *The Negro Genius: A New Appraisal of the American Negro in Literature and the Fine Arts* (New York: Dodd, Mead, 1937), 231–68.

    5. Sterling Brown, "The New Negro in Literature (1925–1955)." In *The New Negro Thirty Years Afterward*, ed. by Rayford W. Logan, Eugene C. Holmes, and C. Franklin Edwards (Washington, D.C.: Howard University Press, 1955).

Further Reading

Cooper, Wayne F. *Claude McKay: Rebel Sojourner in the Harlem Renaissance*. Baton Rouge: Louisiana State University Press, 1987.

Douglas, Ann. *Terrible Honesty: Mongrel Manhattan in the 1920s*. New York: Farrar, Straus, and Giroux, 1995.

Ferguson, Blanche E. *Countee Cullen and the Negro Renaissance*. New York: Dodd, Mead, 1966.

Hemenway, Robert E. *Zora Neale Hurston: A Literary Biography*. Urbana: University of Illinois Press, 1977.

Huggins, Nathan Irvin. *Harlem Renaissance*. New York: Oxford University Press, 1971.

———, ed. *Voices from the Harlem Renaissance*. New York: Oxford University Press, 1976.

Hull, Gloria T. *Color, Sex, and Poetry: Three Women Writers of the Harlem Renaissance*. Bloomington: Indiana University Press, 1987.

Kerman, Cynthia Earl, and Richard Eldridge. *The Lives of Jean Toomer: A Hunger for Wholeness*. Baton Rouge: Louisiana State University Press, 1987.

Levy, Eugene. *James Weldon Johnson: Black Leader, Black Voice*. Chicago: University of Chicago Press, 1973.

Lewis, Dadid Levering. *W.E.B. Du Bois: Biography of a Race, 1868–1919*. New York: Henry Holt, 1993.

———. *When Harlem Was in Vogue*. New York: Vintage Books, 1981.

Marable, Manning. *W.E.B. Du Bois: Black Radical Democrat*. Boston: Twayne Publishers, 1986.

Rampersad, Arnold. *The Life of Langston Hughes*. Vol 1. *I, Too, Sing America: 1902–1941*. New York: Oxford University Press, 1986.

———. *The Life of Langston Hughes*. Vol 2. *I Dream a World: 1942–1967*. New York: Oxford University Press, 1988.

Singh, Amritjit. *The Novels of the Harlem Renaissance: Twelve Black Writers, 1923–1933*. University Park: The Pennsylvania State University Press, 1976.

Sundquist, Eric J. *To Wake the Nations: Race in the Making of American Literature*. Cambridge: Harvard University Press, 1993.

Tillery, Tyrone. *Claude McKay: A Black Poet's Struggle for Identity*. Amherst: The University of Massachusetts Press, 1992.

Wintz, Cary D. *Black Culture and the Harlem Renaissance*. Houston: Rice University Press, 1988.

Volume Introduction

One feature of the Harlem Renaissance was the struggle of both black writers and black intellectuals to define an appropriate aesthetic for African American literature and to define the appropriate relationship between an African American literary movement and racial politics in the United States in the 1920s and 1930s. The literature of the 1920s was one element of a black cultural movement that included music, art, and theater. In their efforts to define an appropriate aesthetic for black artistic endeavors, critics and artists explored the Southern and African roots of black culture and the impact of race and urbanization on the African American experience. black writers and intellectuals debated the appropriate political agenda for black literature as they confronted the reality that in the 1920s black literature was dependent on white patrons, publishers, and book buyers.

The first selection in this volume is the anthology of African American art and literature that Charles S. Johnson published in 1927 as *Ebony and Topaz: A Collectanea*. Johnson was a University of Chicago–educated sociologist who came to New York in 1921 to take the position of director of research and investigations for the Urban League. For slightly more than five years, beginning in 1923, he edited the Urban League's monthly magazine, *Opportunity*. Like James Weldon Johnson, Alain Locke, and to a lesser degree, W.E.B. Du Bois, Charles S. Johnson used his position to promote African American literature. He opened the pages of *Opportunity* to young writers and sponsored the *Opportunity* literary contests. In 1927, under his direction, the Urban League published *Ebony and Topaz*, a collection similar to *The New Negro*, in which he outlined his views on African American literature. Johnson believed that literature would promote interracial communication and help blacks contend with the social issues that they confronted as a result of the black migration to Northern cities.

The second and third sections of this volume consist of a series of essays written in the late 1920s and early 1930s that attempt to place African American literature and the other African American arts within the context of American and African American culture. In section two, black writers and critics assess the significance of the Harlem Renaissance and the role of black literature; in section three, critics explore black music, theater, and the visual arts in terms of the relationship of developments in these areas to the Harlem Renaissance as well as their relation to African American and African heritage.

The final three sections in this volume address the politics of African American literature from three distinct perspectives. First, the racial pressures that confront African American writers are explored. These include the responsibility to write "race literature" (i.e., literature that focuses on racial themes and the experiences of African Americans), the special difficulties that confront black writers as they seek publishers and audiences, and attempt to make a living through their writing, and the particular problems that individual writers had with their politics and their art. The fifth section examines the relationship between black writers and white publishers through the examination of unpublished materials that detail the relationship between Langston Hughes and his publisher, Alfred Knopf. The final section focuses on the political options that confronted black writers in the 1920s, in particular the relationships of the Garvey movement, socialism and the Bolshevik revolution, and the other racial/political ideologies of the 1920s to the writers of the Harlem Renaissance.

The efforts to define a political agenda or an aesthetic agenda for the Harlem Renaissance did not bear fruit, whether these efforts came from black intellectuals or white publishers. Most black writers subscribed to the views that Langston Hughes expressed in his essay, "The Negro Artist and the Racial Mountain," in which he insisted that black writers must be free to write about truth as they define it, regardless of what other blacks or other whites think. However, the Harlem Renaissance did not occur in a vacuum. The realities of race in America, together with the historical, culture, and artistic traditions of blacks, both in this country and in Africa, both in literature and in the other arts, had an impact on the Harlem Renaissance.

EBONY and TOPAZ

A COLLECTANEA

EBONY AND TOPAZ
A COLLECTANEA

Edited by

CHARLES S. JOHNSON

FOREWORD

IF "every life has pages vacant still whereon a man may write the thing he will," it is also true that in many little-considered lives there are pages whereon matter of great interest has already been written, if the appraising eye can only reach it.

So with the recently developed discoveries of the wealth of material for artistic and intellectual development in the life, manners, and customs of the Negro and his unique and all-too-frequently unappreciated and unasked contribution to our American self-consciousness.

This challenging collection focuses, as it were, the appraising eyes of white folks on the Negro's life and of Negroes on their own life and development in what seems to me a new and stimulating way.

Great emotional waves may not be stirred by taking cognizance of the performances of Negroes in art and literature, but faithfulness to an ideal of proportion or fair play makes us uneasy lest through ignorance we miss something by straying into the tangles of prejudice.

Most of us claim to recognize Miss Millay's thought that

"He whose soul is flat, the sky
Will fall in on him by and by."

and will follow with zest the explorations of appraising eyes which have been made available to us in attractive form on these pages.

L. HOLLINGSWORTH WOOD.

4

CONTENTS

5

ILLUSTRATIONS

A Drawing by Charles Cullen

8

INTRODUCTION

I T is only fair to rid this volume, at the beginning, of
some of the usual pretensions, which have the effect of
distorting normal values, most often with results as
unfortunate as they are unfair. This volume, strangely
enough, does not set forth to prove a thesis, nor to
plead a cause, nor, stranger still, to offer a progress
report on the state of Negro letters. It is a venture in expression,
shared, with the slightest editorial suggestion, by a number of persons
who are here much less interested in their audience than in what they
are trying to say, and the life they are trying to portray. This measurable freedom from the usual burden of proof has been an aid to
spontaneity, and to this quality the collection makes its most serious
claim.

It is not improbable that some of our white readers will arch their
brows or perhaps knit them soberly at some point before the end.
But this is a response not infrequently met with outside the pages
of books. There is always an escape of a sort, however, in ignoring
that which contradicts one's sense, even though it were the better
wisdom to give heed.

Some of our Negro readers will doubtless quarrel with certain of
the Negro characters who move in these pages. But it is also true
that in life some Negroes are distasteful to other Negroes. Following
the familiar patterns, we are accustomed to think of Negroes as one
ethnic unit, and of whites as many,—the Nordics, Mediterraneans;
or Germans, Irish, Swedes; or brachycephalics and dolichocephalics,
depending upon our school of politics or anthropology. The significance of the difference is not so much that Negroes in America actually represent different races among themselves, as that there is the
same ground, in dissimilar customs and culture patterns, which are
the really valid distinctions between races, for viewing Negroes differently among themselves. The point, if it were important enough,
could be proved about as satisfactorily as proofs in this field go, and
with the same type of data. Beneath the difference, however, as
must be evident, is the cultural factor which distinguishes one group
of Negroes from another: the small, articulate group from the more
numerous, and, one might even add, more interesting folk group;
the unconscious Negro folk contributions to music, folk lore, and the
dance, from the conscious contributions of Negroes to art and letters.
The sociological confusion here has brought about endless literary
debates.

Accepting the materials of Negro life for their own worth, it is
impossible to escape certain implications: It is significant that white
and Negro writers and artists are finding together the highest expression of their art in this corner of life. And, as Mr. Albert Jay
Nock reminds us, an interesting person in literature is just what he

9

is in life. It is evident in many quarters that Negroes are being discovered as "fellow mortals," with complexes of their own to be analyzed. With Julia Peterkin, Paul Green, Dubose Heyward, Guy Johnson, there has been ushered in a refreshing new picture of Negro life in the south. Swinging free from the old and exhausted stereotypes and reading from life, they have created human characters who are capable of living by their own charm and power. There is something here infinitely more real and honest in the atmosphere thus created, than in the stagnant sentimental aura which has hung about their heads for so many years.

The Negro writers, removed by two generations from slavery, are now much less self-conscious, less interested in proving that they are just like white people, and, in their excursions into the fields of letters and art, seem to care less about what white people think, or are likely to think about the race. Relief from the stifling consciousness of being a problem has brought a certain superiority to it. There is more candor, even in discussions of themselves, about weaknesses, and on the very sound reasoning that unless they are truthful about their faults, they will not be believed when they chose to speak about their virtues. A sense of humor is present. The taboos and racial ritual are less strict; there is more overt self-criticism, less of bitterness and appeals to sympathy. The sensitiveness, which a brief decade ago, denied the existence of any but educated Negroes, bitterly opposing Negro dialect, and folk songs, and anything that revived the memory of slavery, is shading off into a sensitiveness to the hidden beauties of this life and a frank joy and pride in it. The return of the Negro writers to folk materials has proved a new emancipation.

It might not seem to go too far afield to refer to the statements offered not infrequently in criticism, that the cultured Negroes are not romanticized in fiction as generously as the folk types. This has a distinctly sociological implication back of which is the feeling that a loftier opinion of all Negroes would follow an emphasis in fiction upon more educated individuals. The attitude is not uncommon in the history of other races and classes. For many years, Americans were affected by the same sensitiveness in relation to Europe, and even in the Southern United States, until very recently, the literature has been defensive and for the most part ineffectual. Aside from the greater color and force of life in those human strata which seem to have struck lightning to the imaginations of our present writers, it might be suggested that the educated Negroes, even if they are not yet being romanticized in fiction, are finding a most effective representation through their own comment upon the extraordinarily interesting patterns of Negro folk life to which they have intimate access. Or, perhaps, they have succeeded only too well in becoming like other people whom writers generally are finding it difficult enough to make interesting.

The most that will be claimed for this collection is that it is a fairly faithful reflection of current interests and observations in Negro life. The arrangement of the materials of this volume follows roughly the implications of significance in the new interests mentioned. The first part is concerned with Negro folk life itself. The vast resources of this field for American literature cannot be escaped even though they are no more than hinted at in this volume. There is here a life full of strong colors, of passions, deep and fierce, of struggle, disillusion,—the whole gamut of life free from the wrappings of intricate sophistication.

The second part sweeps in from a wider radius of time and space some of the rare and curiously interesting fragments of careers and art which constitute that absorbing field of the past now being revealed through the zeal and industry of Negro scholars. The garnering of these long gone figures who flashed like bright comets across a black sky is an amenity which has found root quietly and naturally in Negro life.

A third division is concerned with racial problems and attitudes, and these are rather coldly in the hands of students. In these, there is the implication of a vast drama which the stories and the poetry merely illuminate.

The fourth section might well be set down as the most significant of current tendencies—the direction of Negro attention inward in frank self-appraisal and criticism. The essays touch boldly and with a striking candor some of the ancient racial foibles. At frequent points they violate the orthodoxy, but in a spirit which is neither bitterly hopeless nor resentful. This is perhaps one of the most hopeful signs of life and the will to live. And finally, there is a division which gives a brief glimpse into the intimate self-feeling of articulate Negroes. These lack conspicuously the familiar tears of self-pity and apology.

The classification is not a strict one, but it has a possible usefulness as a guide through the varieties of expression to be found herein. There will be in one an abandonment to the fascination of a new life, in another a critical self searching, in one humor for its own sake, in another humor with a thrust; there will be stoical rebellion, self reliance, beauty. Those seeking set patterns of Negro literature will in all likelihood be disappointed for there is no set pattern of Negro life. If there is anything implicit in the attitude toward life revealing itself, it is acceptance of the fact of race and difference on the same casual gesture that denies that the difference means anything.

This is probably enough about the contributions to this collection to let them take their own course. From the list of contributors are absent many names with as great reason for inclusion as any present. There were, however, physical limits to such a volume, with all that this implies, and, if there is, for those who must pass judgment, less merit in what appears than should be, some measure of this deficiency may be laid to the omissions.

A spirit has been quietly manifest of late which it would be a gentle treason to ignore. Its expression has been a disposition on the part of established writers, scholars, artists and other interested individuals, to offer to Negro writers the practical encouragement of those facilities which they command. To this may be accredited among other things a share in the making of that mood of receptivity among the general public for the literature of Negro life.

CHARLES S. JOHNSON.

If you want to tell anything to Heaven, tell it to the wind.

An African Proverb

A DRAWING FOR JUMBY
By Aaron Douglas

JUMBY

(To Doris)

By Arthur Huff Fauset

Jean-Marie

JEAN-MARIE tossed fitfully upon her bed of straw until a cock, crowing shrilly in the early morn awoke her with jarring suddenness. She raised herself slightly, and fearing to open her eyes, clutched the wall of the thatch-roofed hut, in order to steady her trembling body.

Feverishly she felt of her waist, her temples, her pale brown limbs, and her feet. She was puzzled. Assuredly there was something wrong. But where? She peeled open her eyes timorously. As the delicate brown lids slowly unfolded, she beheld the marvelous blue Caribbean, bobbing gently, playing a child's game, as it were, with the rising sun.

Jean-Marie shivered. Then from her throat came a tiny sound like the cluck of a hen. She stretched out full length on her back, and extending her clasped hands as far as possible from her body, she heaved a sigh of gladness.

Thanks be to Jumby, a dream! Suppose, now, that she had awakened to find herself bitten by a cobra, her limbs swollen double, and her pale amber brownness turned a hideous black! Just suppose Kasongo, the obeah man, *could* really put "nastiness" upon her, and she had awakened with Barbados Big Foot (elephantiasis), and thousands of tiny chiggers building their houses in the seams of her feet!

Ah, the chiggers! They got everywhere, and into everything. You could not move for the chiggers. And how they did bite! She gazed upon a tiny red splotch on her arm, and scratched it ruefully. The more she scratched the more it burned.

But the blacks did not mind the chiggers. Manja, sleeping over there in the corner, her almost naked body exposed to the caprices of brown scorpions, red and green lizards, mosquitoes, huge white ants, and roaches big as fingers . . . she did not mind the chiggers. Why, she had colonies of them, on her elbows, the sides of her hands, of her feet! The tops of her feet were live chigger-hives. But Manja did not mind. . . .

But then, what had she to do with these folk anyway! She did not look like them, she did not think like them. They were black; she was pale brown. Their eyes were constantly red, and the whites spotted with gelatine-like masses which affected their sight. Hers were clear like the Caribbean, and soft and brown like a chewink's feathers. Instead of the brittle, harsh mat of hair which adorned their heads, rough almost to prickliness, her hair was black, and soft like velvet or silk.

Jean-Marie leaped lightly from her bed, and glided to the door of the hut. Her tall slim figure was lithe like a leopard's; her pale brown limbs moved with the grace of a beautiful race horse. She opened wide the door and gazed at the silent wonder of the island on which her home was situated.

Mateka, the sacred mount, towered in the distance, some dark green knight, hiding his crest in a thin white mist. The sun, a streak of white in a pale blue sky, peeked his head over the mountain's top.

Jean-Marie noted the light green patches by the side of the mountain, where the blacks had cultivated their cane and their cotton, and the roads, looking like brown streaks crawling up the great hill. She saw a dozen tiny sail-boats, much like geese-

15

13

feathers, tossing and bobbing on the Caribbean. Far in the distance, the native huts looked like cattle lying in the grass.

Frogs croaked. Crickets chirped. Tall palms, glistening in the sunlight, and looking like sentinels on the side away from the sun, bended and swayed to the occasional purring of the breezes.

Far off a boy was yodeling. Somewhere a woman was hoeing and spading. Between the pat-pats of her hoe, she sang snatches of lines from hymns taught by Wesleyan missionaries:

"... that Jesus doied fo' me."

Jean-Marie remained some moments entranced. The spell was broken, however, by a sudden rustling of leaves in front of the hut. Out of the shrubbery, hobbled an old woman. She was black, and she wore a head-dress of red and gold which sparkled in the sunshine. In her mouth was a clay pipe, in her right hand a gnarled stick which she carried for a cane. She wore a simple frock of brown and white, and her feet were bare.

They called her Ganga the Good.

"Hyeh, hyeh," she fairly screamed as she perceived Jean-Marie standing in the doorway. Her cry aroused Manja and two other women who dwelt in the hut.

"Hyeh, hyeh, lookit, lookit," Ganga cried again.

She pointed to a spot on the ground, some distance away from the hut. Everyone rushed to see.

"Da' he," she said. "Jumby comin' dis toime roight hyeh. Sure, Oi knows you be's de one sometoime, Miss Jean-Marie. Hyeh be's it, roight where's Jumby's put it."

Breathlessly, they crowded about the speaker who gazed intently upon an object on the ground. There lay the head of a white cock, its beak pointing to the corner of the hut where Jean-Marie slept.

"Bukra," shouted Manja, as she turned to Jean-Marie, a malicious look in her red eyes, "nas'iness shor' git you dis toime. Laf' on an' hop skippity-skip, but you kitch de chigger foot yit."

Blood mounted to Jean-Marie's cheeks.

"So!" she exclaimed. "Maybe if I have chigger foot, Babu trade my brown leg for your ugly black leg of an elephant!"

"E-yah, e-yah," screamed Manja, the whites of her eyes glistening with rage. "You bukra bitch. You no say nas'iness come ovah you. ... You see ... mebbe *you* leg swell like banyan; mebbe breasts look like jellies (cocoanuts); mebbe you guts rot an' grow snakes .. .wait an' see ... e-yah, e-yah."

Manja spat on the ground. She turned her back on Jean-Marie and rushed back to the hut, dragging her "big foot" behind her.

Ganga looked at Jean-Marie and pointed to the cock's beak. Then directing a warning finger towards the young girl she said, "Keerful, white chile . . . white cock mean badness . . . trouble pointin' yo' way."

Kasongo

MANJA hobbled away from the *ajoupa* (thatched hut) of Kasongo the obeah man. Kasongo lived far back in the island, away from the village, away from the road, away from the sea. He had to hide himself. Were not the police everlastingly on his heels, trying to send him to Antigua for a good ten years' stretch, with twenty lashings a week?

But he had been too clever for the stupid police. Anyway, they were afraid of him, afraid of his charms. Was it not a common saying that when Kasongo looked at a man thru his dead eye (the other eye was like fire), he was sure to be caught in a squall and die by drowning? or if you caught him whistling thru his hare-lip it meant loss of a dear one?

When Flonza, the half-Indian wife of Francois died suddenly, even the police knew that Kasongo had baked a tarantula, beaten it into powder, and secreted it in Flonza's food. And why? . . . So that Francois might marry another woman.

There was Mariel. He was secretly hated by Kasongo, because he had gone to the States and learned powerful obeah. Fool! Mariel should have known better than to drink whiskey out of Kasongo's glasses. Everyone knew that Kasongo had a habit of slipping powders made from maggots, roaches and crickets in his whiskey. No wonder Mariel developed swelling in his right arm. What might have happened if he had not gone over to Martinique and consulted the most powerful obeah man on the island? There they slit open his arm with a knife. His hand was alive with small black worms! Only the powerful medicine of the obeah man prevented them from eating him up alive. Instead, they came jumping out of his flesh like skippers from a piece of rotten ham. . . .

Manja hurried to a sequestered spot under some tall banyan trees. She emptied the pocket of her dress of some charms she had received from Kasongo. There were strands of hair taken from the dead body of a man who had died from "bad man's" disease (syphilis), some huge yellow-stained toe-nails, a clot of human blood, a dried chicken gizzard, and a rabbit's paw. All had been dipped in a peculiar black powder.

She bound these together in a piece of cloth torn from an old dress worn by Jean-Marie. Standing with her back to the sun, she held the bag over her left shoulder and mumbled these words:

> Be some Peter
> Be some Paul
> An' be de Gahd dat mek us all,
> Spin ball,
> Spin jack,
> An' ef she don' do whut you says
> May I neber come back.

Then she hastened to the hut where Jean-Marie lived. No one was about. She walked rapidly to the little plot of earth behind the hut, where every evening just before sun-down Jean-Marie tended her tiny garden. Near a favorite rose-bush Manja placed the charm on the ground, saying softly,

> Not for Manja,
> Not for Adova,
> Not for Merve,
> But only for Jean-Marie.

Then she strode briskly into the hut and prepared for evening.

Jumby

IN the heart of the night Jean-Marie woke suddenly. Her eyes felt like blazing coals.

Feverishly she gazed out on the starry firmament. The heavens were a curtain of soft velvet studded with diamonds. Moonbeams, the molten music of star-elfs, streamed into the hut, and played weird tunes in the sunken depths of her eyes.

Night, the black obeah man who sprinkles star dust in lovers' potions, drugged her with his lures, and before she was able to recover from the magic spell of soft loveliness, her body was aflame with madness and longing.

(Oh, Jungle Girl, with amber face, why do you struggle against a foe who draws you tight with bands like steel, and will not let you go?

Oh, Jungle Girl, with eyes so pure, would you be a jungle lover and scoff at jungle charms?

Oh, Jungle Girl, with limbs pale brown, fly, fly to your destiny!)

She looked in the direction of Manja and saw a dark bundle, half clear in the moonlight. Manja was asleep.

Fever mounted in her body. The spell of love added to its flame until the pallet on which she lay burned like a bed of fire.

She tried to cool the flame which was her body by crooning soft words to her lover:

> Babu, my Babuji, you will come to me.
> Say, Babuji, that you will come.
> Oh, my Babuji, come to me . . . come.

Quietly, so that Manja should not hear, she murmured the words of a lovesong taught her in Trinidad by her African grandmother who had learned it from a wandering Zulu:

> U-ye-ze, u-ye-ze,
> Ma-me! U-ye-ze U-mo-ya!
> U-ye-ze, u-ye-ze,
> Ma-me! U-ye-ze U-mo-ya!
> Nakuba
> Se-ku-li—
> Ba-nchi la-ke ngo—
> Sha-da na-lo
>   Ngomte-to!
> He cometh, he cometh,
> Rapture! Cometh the Strong Wind!
> He cometh, he cometh,
> Rapture! Cometh the Strong Wind!
> Let me have
> But his robe,
> And the marriage vows
> I will utter,
>   By the law!

Her body moved in rapturous rhythm with each note. She imagined herself in the arms of her lover, and that she was perishing in a fire of passion.

Abruptly she ceased her chanting. Somewhere in the distance, she heard the faint din of beating. Gradually it swelled, then as gradually died away, only to swell again. Jean-Marie listened intently. She heard. E-yah! Jumby!

> Dum-a-lum-a-lum (pom-pom)
> Dum-a-lum-a-lum (pom-pom)
> a-Dum-a-lum-a-lum
> a-Dum-a-lum-a-lum
> Dum-a-lum-a-lum (pom-pom)

> E-yah! Jumby!

Eh! eh! Bomba, hen, hen!
Canga bafio te,
Canga moune de le,
Canga do ki la,
Canga li.

All of her body was aflame. Her eyes, her ears, her hands, and those pale brown limbs were like live coals of fire. Her bed had become a pyre.

Like a panther pierced by the hunter's spear, she leaped from her cot, and gliding across the floor of the hut, rushed out into the moonlight. Louder and louder the drums beat. Swifter the pale creature sped along her path.

The way was tortuous and long. The Jumby Dance must not be within hailing distance of the police, and beside, members of the village would never have it said that they believed in Jumby.

Jean-Marie sped over the dense underbrush. Her tiny feet tripped over the brambles and thorns with the lightness of a hare. Her brown body moved forward with the speed of a gazelle.

Over hills tracked with sharp-pointed stones she traveled; down into valleys where the tangled grass lay hidden neath the waters of the swamp she trod. The gray mongoose darted from beneath her feet, and occasionally a huge field rat; but these she never saw.

She came nearer the spot from whence sounded the monotonous call of the drum. Its tones sank louder into the depths of her heart.

Dum-a-lum-a-lum
Dum-a-lum-a-lum

As she came out of a clump of forest, she suddenly espied a hut in a small open space close by the ocean. Tall cocoanut palms, and mango trees heavy ladened with fruit, sheltered it from the moon's beams.

The drumming stopped abruptly, as Jean-Marie appeared like some elfin sprite under the shadowed moon-light.

She approached the hut.

There, squatting on the ground, she perceived dimly the forms of nearly a score of men and women, many of them old. They were barefooted, and naked except for loin-cloths. All of them wore amulets, made from sharks' teeth, dried frogs, and mummified rats.

As she came near to them, they rose, then bowing almost to the ground, they murmured, "Welcome, fair daughter of the kings. Welcome."

The door of the bamboo hut opened. A tall dark man appeared. He was bedecked in leopard skins, and with charms which rattled all over his body like many sea-shells. His body was smeared with the blood and brain of fowls, and his eyelids were daubed with white paint.

Extending his arms towards Jean-Marie, he greeted her.

"Welcome, oh daughter of the kings," he said. "Many days and nights we have been waiting for you. At last Jumby has sent you forth. Enter with me, for this night we feast to Jumby, and celebrate with the dance of the leopard."

Jean-Marie clasped her hand in his, murmuring, "Babuji, my Babuji. . . . I have come at last . . . to you Babuji . . . at last I have come."

The head-man beckoned to the others to follow. Slowly they filed in couples into the hut.

The room was nearly bare except for a small table which was alight with the unsteady gleam of ten candles placed around its edges. The flickering flames cast eerie shadows on the walls of the hut.

In the center of the table was the body of a two-footed creature, half beast, half fowl, made from carcasses of small animals sewed together, into which had been stuffed the entrails of a cow. Mounted on its neck was the head of a white cock. A roasted pig, squatting with its fore-paws extended was to the left, and to the right was the roast carcass of a huge gray rat.

These were the gifts to the Jumby.

Jean-Marie and the company bowed in silence before the objects on the table, and formed around them in a circle. Soon the sputtering candles mixed their vapors with the stench of sweat and unwashed bodies.

"Daughter of the kings," intoned the head-man, "soon Jumby will appear. You are his daughter, and the mother of the children of men. Pray guard your children well."

He bowed and disappeared silently into the darkness.

As the door closed upon him, a drum suddenly sounded a warning note. Almost hidden, it stood with the drummer in a corner of the room.

"E-yah!" shouted the drummer. "E-yah! It is Jumby."

He commenced to beat slowly and gently, accompanied by the sound of rattles and castanets which another tall figure played upon. Softly the drummer began chanting an African melody as if imploring Jumby to enter the hut and partake of the feast prepared for him. . . .

But Jumby does not appear. The drummer as if to coax him, quickens his beat, and raises his voice; then permits the song to die down to a low sob, while the measures of his beating become long and sustained.

Very slowly, almost imperceptibly, the door opens. In the diminishing candle light it is difficult to make out the head-man, who clad in his leopard skins, silently enters the hut. But the drummer has seen the door open. He beats madly upon his instrument and sings:

Mbwero! Mbwero! Mbwero!
Beware! Beware! Beware!

Jean-Marie steps out from the group and prepares to save her children from the ravages of the leopard, who by this time is seen almost creeping on all fours. Meanwhile the crowd of dancers move slightly, now forward, now backward, keeping time with the drummer, and shouting.

Mbwero! Mbwero! Mbwero!

Jean-Marie dances nearer the leopard. She sings:

Be careful, children.
It is Jumby in the form of a leopard.
Be careful! Mbwero! Mbwero! Mbwero!

Her "children" scream and sing, all the while stepping backward and forward to the drum accompaniment.

Slowly the leopard advances, sniffing the air, but at first ignoring the dancers and proceeding to the feast prepared for him on the table. He bows before the central figure, then proceeds to eat portions of the roast pig and roast rat. Suddenly he turns upon the crowd, and with his tongue extended and emitting terrible growlings, he throws them into convulsions of fear.

Madder beats the drum. Wilder the hissing of the snares and rattles. More hideous the screams of the participants to whom the intoxicating effect of sweat, burnt tallow, and palm oil which is poured on the candles to make them sputter, bring a strange reality to the dance.

Jean-Marie in the role of protector, steps in front of her children, and attempts to keep off the onslaught of the leopard. Her steps grow quicker, now forward, now backward. As she moves backward she motions to the children behind her to flee, calling out to them, "My children, Mbwero!"

The participants imitate her steps, her motions, her calls.

The leopard, swaying and measuring his step to the music of the drummer, dashes forward suddenly, and catches one of Jean-Marie's children, whom he sets aside. Jean-Marie screams defiance, but he brushes her aside and snatches another child from her protecting embrace.

One after another of her children he captures, until only a single child remains. Jean-Marie has become exhausted. Her steps become slower and feebler. She clings to the remaining child with fingers that are numbed with weakness and exhaustation. No use . . . the leopard seizes it also, and casts it aside to be devoured.

Once more the drum beats wildly. Jean-Marie the mother has become a furious tigress. Her children are all dead. Must she die also?

The leopard slowly approaches her. Jean Marie rushes to attack him, then retreats with backward steps. With claws protruding, the leopard rushes again, but the snarling Jean-Marie holds her ground, forcing him to turn back. The leopard prepares to leap. Jean-Marie seizes a club which rests on the table for the purpose, and lifts it high over her head in order to strike the leopard and slay him. . . .

Behold . . . a silver gleam from the thatched roof-top. It is the flash of a cobra's fang, which darts like an arrow straight into the pale brown arm of Jean-Marie. One shrill scream she utters, and falls in a heap on the floor.

Now she seems to be swimming against an overpowering current. Her arms and limbs become numb and heavy. She feels a terrible swelling in her breasts. Her eyes are balls of fire burning, burning, burning. There is a putrid smell in her nostrils, as of flesh rotting . . . and the sensation of myriads of swarming creatures. . . .

Jean-Marie awoke from an age of slumber. Startled, she looked into the loving eyes of Ganga the Good.

"But—but—the cobra—" she gasped, feeling her arms and limbs.

"Po' chile," whispered Ganga, "dat was mighty close call. All de jumbies sho' dancin' in you."

"But Ganga . . . my children . . . where are they?"

"Da now, Bukra chile, you mus' a seed all dat de night we fin' you tearin' t'roo de bush. Fever mos' burn you to def!"

She held Jean-Marie close in her arms.

"Bukra chile," she said softly, "ma po' Bukra chile."

"Babuji," whispered Jean-Marie, "my Babu-ji."

19

Drawing for ON THE ROAD ONE DAY, LORD
by AARON DOUGLAS

On The Road One Day, Lord ꙮ ꙮ ꙮ

BY PAUL GREEN

SIX striped figures on a blazing road, swinging their picks, and four behind piling out the dirt with shovels. The white dust hides the blackberries in the hedge and the willow clumps are bent under its weight. The heat of July shimmers across the wide land as far as the eye can see. The sweat pours down. It is the only dampness in the world for the ten mourners on the road. On a stump to the left a guard squats, drowsy, vapid, like a toad. The rifle in the crook of his arms keep alert, it watches, its muzzle watches like an eye, it threatens. Fall, picks, and heave arms! On the bankside to the right, another guard sits. He also is sleepy, drowsy. His rifle also keeps alert and watches, its muzzle threatens. The convicts dig with their backs to the guards, their faces set down the infinite stretch of road that disappears in a point on the horizon. Like so many soulless puppets, they lift their hands towards the sky and bring them down, never any slower, never any faster. And as the picks strike against the earth with a thud, a husky desperate groan bursts from their baked lips. As rhythmic as the beating of their hearts the "hanh" accompanies the falling of the picks, carrying over long maddening hours of pain, carrying over until the sun sinks cooling in the west and the guard stirs and croaks, "Call it a day." At times their voices are raised in a chant, level, patient, eternal and tough as the earth in which they dig. They don't talk much, not so much. Talk breaks up the rhythm of labor, and that's what they're there for—labor, labor, working on the roads. Ninety days on the roads, Tom Sterling, and sixty days for you, Bantam Wilson. The judge dropped his tobacco by his foot, rose and gave sentence. Disturbance of the peace. Assault with intent to kill. These niggers, these everlasting niggers, always fighting, always shooting. They've got no sense, they'll never have no sense. Give 'em the law, let 'em feel it. Obedience, peace, peace. This is the republic, these are the institooshuns. Land of our fathers. This shall be a lesson. Sixty days. Ninety days. Dig, dig. Side by side they dig—Bantam Wilson and Tom Sterling. Misery has made them friends, sorrow companions. Bantam's spirit walks unbroken, Sterling is crushed and under. The feel of iron and abuse of tongues have broken him. His great shoulders are bent, his legs hardly sustain his weight, and his arms fling up the pick and let it fall hour after hour, day after day, with slowly decreasing power. See, his face now bends above the lightless earth beneath. These are the children—hanh. These are the brethren marching to Canaan Land. The guard on the right stirs in his sleepiness and beats at the flies with his hat.

First Guard. Rain or shine the old dog flies stay with you.

Second Guard. (Lighting cigarette and passing the package on to the first.) And the dam' muskeeters allus drilling for water.

First Guard. Heigh you, Sterling, raise up that pick and let 'er come down. (The convicts dig on, accompanying every blow with their everlasting "hanh", saying never a word.) You hear me? I say put some pep into that digging.

23

21

Bantam. (After a moment—without looking around). He sick. Ain't able to work.

Second Guard. You bastard monkey runt, who's talking?

First Guard. Hell 'll be frozen 'fore you git this little digging done. (They lapse into silence again. The second guard stretches his arms in a yawn.)

Second Guard. Lord, I'm sleepy—sleepy.

First Guard. Better leave her off a few nights. (The convicts with the shovels burst into a snicker.

Second Guard. (Brutally, his voice sharp with hate.) Somebody begging for the little rawhide. (The four convicts terrified push their shovels deeper into the loose earth and pile it out).

First Guard. I want water.

Second Guard. The goddamned water boy's fell in and drownded. (Standing up and calling). Water boy! Water boy! Heigh, water jack! Could a-been there and half way back! (The diggers begin a low working chant, pitiful and pleading. "Mercy, mercy," it calls. "Water, water, give us some water. Where is it? Where is he? Where is the Great I Am, the Almighty God! Listen now, Jesus, while us gi' you de call. Eigh Lawd, come wid de 'sponse'!"

Convicts.

> I called my people—hanh,
> I said my people—hanh,
> I mean my people—hanh,
>   Eigh, Lawd!

First Guard. That's right, sing him out'n the bushes.

Second Guard. If it ain't water it's grub, ain't that it's something else. Bear down on them picks! Jesus Christ! (Sterling suddenly tumbles over and falls with his face flat in the dirt. A convulsive shudder runs through the other convicts, but they carry on their digging, never any slower, never any faster.)

Convicts.

> I called my friends—hanh,
> I said my friends—hanh,
> I mean my friends—hanh,
>   Eigh, Lawd!

First Guard. (Springing up as he glances at Sterling). Heigh now, none o' that, none o' that!

Bantam. (His voice rising in a whine). He sick, bad sick!

First Guard. Better got cured fore he come here. (Marching up to the prostrate body). Git that face out'n the dirt! Git it out. (Whirling towards Bantam.) Nobody asked for your jowing. (Eyeing him). Want the little cat-tails?

Bantam. (Slinging his pick). Jesus, Jesus!

First Guard. Snap out'n it, Sterling.

Second Guard. (Getting a leather thong from his coat). Put a fire-coal on his tail and rise him.

First Guard. Gonna step to it, Sterling? (But Sterling makes no answer).

First Guard. He's a stall boy. Hell, he's stalling!

Second Guard. Damn right, he's stalling.

First Guard. This ain't no party.

Second Guard. Hell it ain't no party! (He smoothes the thong with his hand and looks at the first guard).

First Guard. Make 'em work, make 'em work—that's right.

Second Guard. Work, work—that's what they're here for—work!

First Guard. Work—work—let him taste it.

Second Guard. (Raising the strap above his head). Thirty-nine, thirty-nine. We got our orders. (His voice coming out stronger now, more sharply). The law, the law, it's wrote in a book. (But still he holds the leather poised without bringing it down. A low murmur of horror rises among the convicts, growing into their chant, full of hate now, full of begging, but hopeless withal).

Convicts.

> I called my sister—hanh,
> I said my sister—hanh,
> I mean my sister—hanh,
> Eigh, Lawd!

First Guard. Hold her a minute, we'll see, we'll see. (He goes up to Sterling and pokes him gently in the ribs with the muzzle of his rifle, but only the twitching back makes answer).

Second Guard. Stick him in the collar. (He cuffs him gently in the collar, then with more insistence, at last with vehement roughness. A low whine is heard). He's saying something.

First Guard. (Bending down). Goddamn it we'll see!

Second Guard. And what song is he singing now?

First Guard. Don't say nothing. Moans and whines. He don't say nothing.

Second Guard. By God we'll see. Oh yes, he'll talk. He'll tell us a mouthful! (The chant grows fuller, the rhythm begins to shape the picks, to hold the rising and falling arms to their labor. The prayer for help, for peace, grows stronger—and with it the baffled will, the confused soul sends forth its cry).

Convicts.

> I called my brother—hanh,
> I said my brother—hanh,
> I mean my brother—hanh,
> Eigh, Lawd!

First Guard. Let him have it. (The second guard hands his rifle to the first and then looking around the world as if for a witness of justification, begins to beat the prostrate figure. Again a shudder and the gust of a groan sweep the convicts. They drive their picks deeper in the ground, but never any faster, never any slower).

Convicts.

> I called my mother—hanh,
> I said my mother—hanh—

Second Guard. Six—seven—eight—nine—ten—

First Guard. And now you'll work—and I reckon you'll work.

Second Guard. Eleven—twelve—thirteen—fourteen—(And the watchers in the skies cry blood, blood—earth, earth, sweet earth receive it. Keep it, or save it till the next harvest).

First Guard. Oh yes he'll work, and I reckon he'll work. (The water boy bursts through the hedge at the left, stands terror-stricken a moment, and then dropping his bucket with a clatter tears down the road. The precious water sinks into the dried earth. Now they chant in hopelessness and the four with shovels wag their heads, their parching tongues protrude through baked lips. Ah, hope is no more—life is no more —death—death all around us. Grave, grave, swallow us up, hide us away, keep us).

Second Guard. Fifteen—sixteen—seventeen—eighteen. (Now Tom Sterling has reached the end. In a last burst of life he staggers to his feet, his eyes glazed with madness).

First Guard. Go to work. Look out—(The second guard turns to grab his rifle but Sterling is upon him. He strikes him in the face and beats him to earth, crushing the stems of the early golden rod by the ditch and tearing the clumps of knotted lady-thumb).

Sterling. (His voice coming out in a great animal scream). Hah—hah—hah— (He beats the guard's upturned face with his fists).

Second Guard. Kill him! Kill him! (The convicts sing on, now their chant rises louder, fresher. Revenge! Revenge! Hope he is not perished from us. Our arms are still strong).

Convicts.

> I called my father—hanh,
> I said my father—hanh,
> I mean my father—hanh,
> Eigh, Lawd!

Second Guard. Kill him! Kill him! (The first guard stands stupefied. Then as if suddenly awakening he steps back, raises his rifle, and shoots Sterling through the back. He rolls over and lies with face upturned in the burning sun. The second guard crawls over to the bank and lies stretched out in the grass, his body heaving and jerking with angry strident sobs. The first guard stands looking foolishly down at the dead Negro. The four convicts drop their shovels and hover together in a shuddering group, the six sing on, beaten—darkness, night—God sits high in heaven, his face from the Negro, his hand towards the white man. The poor and needy stretch their weak hands and the iron palings divide them).

First Guard. The goddamned fool, he's dead, dead!

Second Guard. (Sitting up with a high laugh as he wipes the blood from his face). Had to kill him, we had to kill! (Peering forward). Dead as a fly. (With a sort of wild sob). This ain't right. They's something wrong—something wrong here.

First Guard. Sing, you bastards. Dig, you sons of bitches! (And the body lies still. Once it knew swiftness, legs that ran by the cabin, played in the cornfield. Eyes that knew starlight, knew moonlight, as was said in the song. Tongue that knew singing! And I lay this body down. In the cool hedge the fly says "zoom." And a buzzard wheels by the flat disc of the sun. And they dig and they sing. O earth, give us answer! Jesus hear us!)

Convicts.

> I called my Jesus—hanh,
> I said my Jesus—hanh,
> I mean my Jesus—hanh,
> Eigh, Lawd!

DUSK

By Mae V. Cowdery

Like you
Letting down your
Purpled shadowed hair
To hide the rose and gold
Of your loveliness
And your eyes peeping thru
Like beacon lights
In the gathering darkness.

DIVINE AFFLATUS

By JESSIE FAUSET

Tell me, swart children of the Southland
Chopping at cotton
In the sandy soil,
What do ye dream?
What deeds, what words of heroes
Leaven and lighten up
Your toil?
Know ye of L'Ouverture who freed a nation?
Heard ye of Crispus Attucks,
Or of Young?
Does fiery Vesey
Stir the spark within ye,
Or Douglass
Of the rare and matchless tongue?
That Washington
Who moulded a Tuskegee—
Does he inspire ye?
Does brave Moton thrill?
Mark ye Du Bois
That proud, unyielding eagle,
Beckoning ye higher than the highest hill?

But the swart children
Of the Southland
Stopping to dash the sweatbeads
From dull brows,
Answer: "These names
Mean nothing to us,
They, nor the unheard causes they espouse.
Only we know meek Jesus,
Thorn-encircled,
Broken and bleeding
In his Passion's toils;
And Lazarus
Sharing crumbs with dogs;
And Job,
Potsherd in hand, a-scraping at his boils!"

A drawing for GENERAL DRUMS
by Aaron Douglas

GENERAL DRUMS

By JOHN MATHEUS

THE drums were beating incantation over the tops of the pines, through the witching moss festoons of oily-leaved magnolias. The throbbing tones hugged the low earth, too, like the sultry heat beneath the Southern moon, beguiling men from normal ways of thinking. Little fears lurked in hallucinating shadows, unnamed trepidations and bold, brazen dread. Memories came thumping, drubbing, rubbing the soft, somnolent night.

The drums caught Charles Pringle in their tentacles, as he stumbled along Yazoo road, his wide-toed army shoes kicking up yellow flakes of dust. War came to engulf him in all the menace of its terror. Again the boom of 75's, the tatoo of machine guns, the shriek and whine of shells. Startled in him was that latent impulse to flatten his trim form into the earth, color of khaki, color of him.

The silence and the loneliness coveted his composure, envied his anticipated happiness. Out from them leaped the sullen drumming. The weird opalescence was filled with ghostly armies. They came even though he shut his eyes, transcending material vision. So many things he remembered and Jimmy Spiles, handsome, yellow Jimmie Spiles, white teeth flashing, curly hair awry.

But Jimmie was dead in France. He knew that.

The moon was a golden chandelier and its light was argent, silvering the memories of the many times he had dreamed of just this hour, when he should be walking down Yazoo Road to Malissy's house, alone, the only suitor now for her olive brown hand.

Up from the shadows of tall trees and fronded shrubs, loomed faint, familiar outlines—picket fence, shining white, triangle of rambling roses, pyramid of japonica bush, the high, flat-roofed porch and ancient house with wide weather-boarding, planed by slaves with their hands. Time by way of wage for that unrequited labor had swept away the old master and his clan, had left the heritage in plebian black hands emancipated.

That reckoning had been settled long ago; two wars had devastated since then, spreading the oblivion of changing interests over rancorous feelings. And now Charles Pringle was coming back on an August night, when the moon was full.

He was not the same trifling, unsophisticated plow boy of the Yazoo bottoms. He had seen much of the world in eighteen months and the vision had made him wise and cunning. Inoculated with the virus of murder by hard-boiled second lieutenants in bustling cantonments, where healthy, human animals were trained to kill, then thrown on the firing line, the very fibre of his being had been branded by it all. One torturing, inerasable memory, standing out in bold relief, had sensitized chords of his nature which the echoes of the drum beats touched to responsive vibrations—wild drum beats, pounding in the night!

Malissy, herself, came to the door when he knocked, standing before him, graceful as a magnolia, with its ivory-petaled flowers blooming.

"Charlie Pringle! Charlie Pringle!" she cried, giving vent to the demonstrative quality of her African blood.

He remained on the threshold, twirling his over-sea cap in his big hands, grinning and joyous to hear her mocking bird voice echoing *his* name.

Then she burst into tears, into hysterical weeping, summoning forth her gray-haired squaw-faced grandma.

29

27

"Laws a-mussy, what *is* agwine on hyah," she spluttered.

Seeing the familiar face of Charlie Pringle in unfamiliar clothes, she stopped, surveying him from head to foot.

"Howdy, chile. Yo' back heah! De Lawd allus teks de righteous an' leabs debils tuh repent. How yo', son? Come in. What yo', ca'in' on fo' dat away, Malissy?"

"But—but—granny, yo'—Ah can't help it. Po' Jimmie. To think he might be here too an' we—we—jes' married."

" 'Twas de Lawd's way, honey," soothed the old-woman soberly. "Yo' aint been home yit, Charlie?"

"Naw. Don't spose pap's special anxious 'bout seein' me, sence ah knocked him out the night 'fo' we all lef' fo' camp."

"Yo' ought to been ashamed, strikin' yo' own pappy."

"It were de licker that made me done it," said Charlie, hanging his head, hypocritically.

"Charlie, what did he say? What did he do? How did it happen?" questioned Malissy, eyes swollen with weeping.

"Dey say ol' man Spiles don' gone nummy in de haid, sence he got dat ar deespatch fum Washington, tellin' him 'bout Jimmie bein' kilt. He was br'r Spiles onliest daughter's son. Po' chile! Po' chile! Hit's turrible—lostin' he's girl when Jimmie was bo'n, dough what evah buckra man war Jimmie's daddy, don' gi' de ol' man a pow'ful heap o' money. Didn't he done built him a new cabin? Wha' he git de dollahs to do 'at?"

The gossipy reminiscence of old age would have wandered on and on, if Malissy's sharp voice had not broken in.

"Granny, let him talk, let him tell me."

Charlie Pringle began his story with the sneaking satisfaction that he could command attention *now*, that *he* was important because he held a secret and no one should ever know that secret, unless he willed to tell it.

"We all lef' No'folk sudden one night 'bout ten o'clock. Come 'roun' woke us all up an' down tuh de wharf we went. Jimmy jokin' an' laughin' lak he always was."

Malissy sighed and sobbed afresh.

"We was sick pretty near all de time goin' across de watah. Sich waves and hearin' shootin' at submarines.

"When we all landed we stood around half a day—pourin' down rain, waitin' to git somein' t'eat. Then they took us tuh de woods whar we camped and drilled some mo'. In about two weeks we broke camp, took freight cars. We rid all night. De nex' day say we wasn't in them trenches!

"Jimmy sho' war skeert," he eyed Malissy covertly.

"Then one mo'nin' dey tol' us tuh get ready—we was goin' ovah de top."

He went into the details of the military manoeuvers while the two women listened, trying to comprehend the technique of the art of killing.

"Dat white man blew his whistle an' ovah we went, yellin', screamin'. I disremember anything mo' ontell ah saw Jimmy fall—bullet hit him in de haid. He never said nary a word, jes' lay there a-jerkin' and—"

He stopped short. A breeze from the woods bore the beating of the drums.

"Tha' 'tis. Jes' ez Ah was sayin', ol' man Spiles beatin' fo' Jimmy, gone nummy in de haid."

"Hunh!" ejaculated Charlie, rolling his eyes, "Ah mus' be goin' now. Guess pappy may be glad tuh see me aftah so long. Ah'll be back tuh tell you' mo', 'bout tuh-morrow night."

Malissy was too weak to move. Her grandmother escorted their visitor to the door. The moonlight shadowed his form, doggedly treading towards town.

The returned soldiers were all heroes in the eyes of Negro town. The bravado and loquacity of Charlie Pringle even found favor in the sight of his grieved and mistreated parent. He forgave the prodigal and enjoyed basking in the glow of his son's present greatness.

Overgrown black boys from all sides flocked into town, strutting in khaki and putees, never to look upon life again as in the old days.

There was a mass meeting in honor of the soldiers' return in Ebenezer Baptist Church, where speeches were made and ice cream was served. Then until wee hours of the morning a dance swayed in K. of P. Hall with raucous blare of string and wind instruments.

Charlie Pringle did not go to the church, but he was present at the dance, that is he was, until an old man entered, shuffling his big feet over the smooth floor, peering and peeping into people's faces with queer, bloodshot eyes, filmed with watery scum of weakness. He was an eccentric old man, with the face of a black Punch, long, beaked nose and under lip projecting. He apologetically elbowed through the crowd, showing toothless, blue black gums.

The older Negroes addressed him in skirting, awesome tones, "Howdy, Gen'ral Spiles."

The younger folk, with their passions mounting in the dance's revelry, paid him little thought.

He began to talk loudly in a cracked, squeaking voice:

"Any yo' all seen Jimmie. Yo' know Jimmie, mah po' gran'son, Jimmie Spiles. He done aint come back. Wha's 'at Cha'lie Pringle. Ah wants tuh ax him 'bout Jimmie. Yes, Ah was a gen'ral in de Union A'my, fit in de battle o' Vicksburg, beatin' drums, beatin' drums—callin' up speerits tuh hep us—beatin' drums—"

This was why Charlie Pringle went out the back door and some minutes later entered Negro town pool room, with its sawdust box spittoons and cabbage smelling "eatin' house" across the hall.

September passed and October came. Charlie Pringle found himself on many nights sitting on Malissy's porch. She, with sad brown eyes; he, with cunning in his gaze.

"Yo' nevah wan' tuh lissen tuh me," he was protesting one night, "less A'hm talkin' 'bout Jimmie Spiles. Always Jimmie."

"Well wasn't he my husban'?"

"An' ain't he dead, too?"

"Not in mah heart," said Malissy rising.

"But, but Malissy, Ah—Ah laks yo'."

"Go 'way, Charlie, an' yo' his frien' too."

He grabbed the girl in fierce desire and kissed her.

The sting of her strong, brown hand still burned on his cheek, when he bolted away, muttering, "Always Jimmy. Jimmy livin' an' Jimmie dead!"

The first armistice day celebration provoked great excitement in town. Preparations were made to observe the anniversary of the occasion with fitting aplomb. The local leaders began to spread advertisements and work up spirit from the first of November. The editor of the town paper wrote patriotic editorials urging one hundred percent participation.

Then came the question that always caused trouble. The colored ex-soldiers had asked to be allowed to march in the parade. They had also asked for the privilege of allowing some one to represent their only dead member, Jimmy Spiles, that he might march in memory of the departed.

Much discussion followed among the whites. There was some talk of allowing the Negro ex-soldiers and ex-stevedores to march in the rear. Some such request or suggestion had been made, but no answer was ever sent back.

Charlie Pringle had been picked out by the colored committee to represent his dead buddie. He turned quite ashy and vowed he never could do it, because, because.—

So the colored people compromised and voted to celebrate at the K. of P. Hall with a monstrous Armistice Night Ball.

When the eleventh of November came the public schools were closed, the stores and workshops. Main street, with its ramshackled line of one and two story buildings put on decoration of bunting and American flags.

Promptly at ten o'clock the parade appeared. At the head marched the local band. The strident notes of Dixie floated in the morning breeze. The crowd rushed to the curb. Black faces peered as best as they could behind the barrage of their white fellow townsmen.

Down the street marched the pride of the home town, dressed in their old doughboy uniforms and cheered enthusiastically by the patriotic watchers.

Ten paraded for the boys who had not come back. They bore banners with the names of the martyrs written in gold stars.

Then when everyone thought the parade had passed and the excited people were pushing toward the Court House Square where Lawyer Chester was to give the oration of the day, who should appear, togged in all the faded, ragged splendor of an old blue Union Army uniform, the trousers bagging down over the brogans, the coat buckled tightly around the middle, crowned by a bespangled hat with gold cords—who should appear but old man Spiles.

He marched with a strange erectness and alacrity. His old beaked nose seemed to beget a subtle fierceness as some smouldering ember trying to flare up once more before going out entirely.

He was beating a drum, making it reverberate with martial briskness and exuding a dignity worthy of all the faded tinsel.

There rose a great shout of hilarious laughter.

"Ha! Ha! Ha! Ho! Ho! Ho! He! He! He!"

"Old man Spiles."

"Howdy, uncle. Howdy, General Drums."

But on he went.

"Ah'm marchin', yessah, Ah'm marchin'," he quacked. "Ah'm marchin' fo' Jimmie, Jimmie Spiles. He war in de wah. Yessay, mah gran'chile ain't come back."

General Drums was the crowning excitement of the morning. The Negro spectators looked with popping eyes. Charlie Pringle saw and dodged around the corner.

"A Yankee uniform," someone shouted.

It was like waving a red flag before a bull.

The jests became menacing. Somebody threw a stone, but the old man never wavered.

The tone of the crowd became more and more hostile.

"Let that old darkey alone," shouted a stentorian voice at the threatening crowd.

It was Lawyer Chester himself, jumping from his Cadillac, his wavy brown hair brushed back from his high forehead, bearing his middle years with fresh vigor of early manhood.

"Gentlemen, yo' all wouldn't harm a crazy old uncle, would you?"

A chorus of laughter greeted his query, good nature prevailed and the crowd drew back shouting, "General Drums, General Drums, where'd you learn to beat them there drums?"

"Jes' bo'n dat away, chilluns. Yessah, bo'n wif a caul I was."

"What do yo' mean, what are yo' doing this for, uncle?" the lawyer turned to the old man.

"Ah'm marchin' fo' Jimmy Spiles," he answered simply, peering at his questioner.

He seemed then to recognize him, for he took off his hat and standing, gave the military salute.

Lawyer Chester turned pale under his coat of tan.

He reached in his pocket and put something in the old man's right hand, encumbered with drum sticks.

"Take this and go home," he commanded sharply.

Schooled long in obeisance to the white man's will, old General Drums doffed his hat again, but quickly put it back, and beginning to beat quite lustily, marched on, tramping in the dust a twenty dollar bill.

"Ah'm marchin' fo' Jimmie Spiles," he quacked over and over again.

Then Lawyer Chester reached for the money, swearing softly, and mopped his fine, high forehead and went away to the Court House Square to deliver his oration.

Dusty Main Street was deserted and only the red, white and blue bunting glared and the flags of the United States of America fluttered in the near noonday sun.

Charlie Pringle showed up at Malissy's house, with his wheedling air and lecherous gaze, begging the girl to come to the Armistice Ball with him. She refused.

"Go on, chile," encouraged her grandmother. "Yo' don't do nothin' but set 'roun' here a-moppin' and a-drizzlin' roun'. Go out and enjoy yo'self one ebenin'."

So Fate played into Charlie Pringle's hand.

"Why don't you fix up in your best, Malissy?" said he.

"If yo' don't wan' to go with me as Ah am, yo' don't need to tek me *atall*," said the girl.

He dared not say more.

Malissy found the dance not at all in keeping with her sombre thoughts. In the first place she had come against her better judgment to a public dance when she innately shrank from the raw promiscuity of the males who presumed a familiarity she resented. Jimmie had been of a different sort. In the second place she mistrusted this persistent and audacious pursuit of Charlie Pringle and regretted yielding in this instance, for he might construe her acquiescence as privilege for irrefutable concessions. Then she had a general misgiving of his motives and reliability.

But once in the Negro town and inside the crowded hall the intimate contact with the hilarity of the crowd and intoxication of the semi-barbaric music began to weave their subtle web around her.

She had purposely refused to dress her best, fearing the consequences of attracting too much attention, holding back under the leash of her self imposed restraint. But the fact that she had been a war bride and was now a war widow, gave her unwittingly in the eyes of admiring beaux the advantage of prestige.

Thus she was lead to dance with many partners, defying the furious scowls of Charlie Pringle and thereby asserting her none too complete surrender to his wishes.

He chafed under the gnawing fire of jealousy.

Always a creature of sudden caprice Malissy became smitten with inexplicable remorse. A desire to leave at once urged her to the act. There was nothing for her escort to do save follow.

It was nearing midnight. The moon had come up late and was shedding its magic opalescence over the metamorphosed country. The road was deserted. The air felt refreshing after the crowded heat of the dance hall. Clumps of pines became visible by and by and the sweetly fragrant magnolias.

"Malissy," suddenly blurted out her moody partner, "are yo' goin' tuh marry me?"

"No," snapped Malissy. "How many times must Ah tell yo'. Yo' posin' as po' Jimmie's best frien'."

"Oh, damn Jimmie," snarled Pringle, wild, steaming fury rising in him.

Malissy turned with heaving bosom, "Don't ever come near me again, yo' dirty viper."

"Yo're goin' to be sorry fo' that, Miss Uppity," was the hot rejoinder.

He grappled with the woman.

"Yo're mine an' Ah'll have yo' or Ah'll know the reason why. Ah've done too much tuh git yo'. Yo'—Ah shan't be outdid."

Malissy became calm and quiet in her terror. Interpreting her change as submission he was melting from his fiery mood, when noises came loping out of the night, a vague whirring, indicating distance but no sense of direction. With increasing intensity it was closing in upon them.

Neither stirred. Malissy felt a coldness clutching at her heart. Her fear of the man merged into the greater apprehension of the unknown. She felt the strong, lithe body pressed against her go limp.

The approaching sound grew intelligible. It was the drums, that ungodly rhythm was the drums. And that shrill, cracked quavering was saying, "Jimmy Spiles."

And while the drums beat on there came a popping as of guns and Charlie Pringle saw the glare of the battle again and heard the roar of musketry. And behind them all loomed that inerasable memory which made him gaze ahead with glassy stare and point with trembling finger.

As Malissy turned, a cloud passed over the moon, but she could see a form in the shadows and a face, her husband's face, dead Jimmy Spile's face, pale, curly hair awry.

Then Charlie Pringle's courage snapped.

"Save me, Malissy," he screamed. "Tell him to go away. Ah thought that bullet in the back killed him. It might a been a German bullet, but Ah couldn't wait. I did it fo' yo'. I swear tuh Gawd, Ah did it fo' yo'. Ah'm leavin'. Tell him Ah'm leavin'."

Footsteps approached and the drums.

A voice cried, "Stop that damn beating, Spiles. What's the matter with yo'."

The grey cloud drifted from the pallid moon. They saw the form of Lawyer Chester, hat in hand.

Charlie Pringle's face was working like an epileptic's in a fit.

"Beatin' fo' Jimmy Spiles. Bof us been in de ahmy."

"You skunk," shouted Lawyer Chester, pushing Charlie Pringle from Malissy's side, "I'll give you three hours to be on your way out of Yazoo bottom. If I ever catch sight of your sneaking hulk yo'll hang for murder."

Charlie Pringle stood rooted to the spot, abashed by the shadow of the hangman's noose, speechless, more terrified than if he had seen the accusing wraith of Jimmie Spiles.

"General, I'm going to take you home."

"Yessah," and the old man doffed his hat.

"Come here, girl," he commanded and guided the prostrated girl with the gesture of a gentleman.

He put her in his car.

"No back firing," he soliloquized, looking at his engine, "because I want to take you to your grandmother, girl, without any more disturbance."

And old man Spiles sat in the rear, hugging his drums.

GULLAH

By Julia Peterkin

T is surprising to find that outside of the South, there is scarcely any acquaintance with the word "Gullah" although it stands not only for a large number of Negroes who make up most of the population along our lower coasts but also for the quaint and charming patois which they speak.

There are many theories concerning the original home of these people, almost as many as there are ways of trying to reduce their odd speech into written words. Although some of them still have a distinct pride of race they know nothing of where they came from. I have heard people living in the Quarters here on Lang Syne Plantation boast that they who are Gullahs were bound to be better in every way than the people on a neighboring plantation who are Guineas. This belief was probably being handed down prior to the earliest days of slavery.

These Gullahs may have been brought from Angola on the west coast of Africa by the traders who took them to market along with the gold and ivory transported from that rich country, and the word "Angola" shortened to "Gullah." Or they may have been brought from Gallah on the African east coast along with cargoes of salt which was so valuable it was once used as money currency. But this question will never be settled.

The human cargoes were brought to the rice and cotton plantations, and since they often out-numbered the white people in the ratio of hundreds to one, none but the house servants or body servants came into close contact with their owners, the rest having to learn to speak English from the white overseers or other white servants.

A strange mixture of old English and French resulted, many of the words being utterly changed in tone and cadence and grammar. Harsh sounds were eliminated and this new speech slid easily, musically off the lips of the people who used it.

After the Civil War and Freedom, most of the plantation owners moved away and the Negroes were left to shift for themselves the best they could, in the deserted rice and cotton fields. Generations have succeeded each other in the same isolated environment. The same old customs, superstitions, religion, tradition and language have been faithfully handed down. And this language which is not easily understood except by a trained ear, is not only beautiful, but its whimsical words and phrases, its quaint similes and shrewd sayings are undoubtedly a permanent enrichment of American language and literature.

REQUIEM

By Georgia Douglas Johnson

I weep these tears upon my bier
Another may not shed,
For there is none save I alone
Who knows that I am dead.

35

FORECLOSURE

By STERLING A. BROWN

Father Missouri takes his own.
These are the fields he loaned them,
Out of hearts' fullness; gratuitously;
Here are the banks he built up for his children—
Here are the fields; rich, fertile silt.

Father Missouri, in his dotage
Whimsical and drunkenly turbulent,
Cuts away the banks; steals away the loam;
Washes the ground from under wire fences,
Leaves fenceposts grotesquely dangling in the air;
And with doddering steps approaches the shanties.

Father Missouri; far too old to be so evil.

Uncle Dan, seeing his garden lopped away,
Seeing his manured earth topple slowly in the stream,
Seeing his cows knee-deep in yellow water,
His pig-sties flooded, his flower beds drowned,
Seeing his white leghorns swept down the stream—

Curses Father Missouri, impotently shakes
His fist at the forecloser, the treacherous skinflint;
Who takes what was loaned so very long-ago,
And leaves puddles in his parlor, and useless lakes
In his fine pasture land.
Sees years of work turned to nothing—
Curses, and shouts in his hoarse old voice,
"Aint got no right to act dat way at all"
And the old river rolls on, slowly to the gulf.

DREAMER

By LANGSTON HUGHES

I take my dreams
And make of them a bronze vase,
And a wide round fountain
With a beautiful statue in its center,
And a song with a broken heart,
And I ask you:
Do you understand my dreams?
Sometimes you say you do
And sometimes you say you don't.
Either way
It doesn't matter.
I continue to dream.

THE DUNES

By E. MERRILL ROOT

LET earth have her ancient way—
  Sun and sand and wind and spray—
On the lonely dunes today.
Trampling silver dust of spumes
Strides the wind: he wears the glooms
Of vast purple clouds for plumes.
Mightily Lake Michigan
Hurls his white diluvian
Wolves across the narrow span.
Mournful grass like huddled sheep
Cowers from the roar and sweep
Of the waves and winds that leap.
And the sand (that once was proud
Rock) lies desolate and cowed,
Broken to a level crowd.
And one tree, a twisted gnome,
Rises from the monochrome
Leprous silver of his home.

There in primal joy I lie
Underneath a savage sky
Where the pluméd clouds go by.
Joyful on the trampled verge
Of two worlds, I lie and urge
In my soul their shock and surge.
For my spirit wins elation
And majestic affirmation
Best from stormy desolation.
There in primal loneliness
Let me lie amid the stress
Of the cosmic emphasis.
Let me hear forevermore
Life, of which I am the shore,
On my body's beaches roar!
Not for me earth's plenilune
But the wild white crescent moon
Of the beach that ends the dune!

EIGHTEENTH STREET

(BIRMINGHAM)

An Anthology in Color

By NATHAN BEN YOUNG

STROLLING MUSICIANS

EIGHTEENTH Street hath music of its own. Some of it harks back to the far away Continental Africa, some of it is the new American music.

Like strolling minstrels of old these rag-tag fellows appear on the Street from nowhere and depart as they come. One night it is the Kitchen Mechanics Quartet in the Bon Ton Drug Store in an impromptu progrom of bearded medleys and ballads in which the first tenor switches to baritone and the basso to lead ad. lib. But even in their rendition of "Sweet Ando-line" there is a quaint touch of something three hundred years or more old.

Oh yes, "Kitchen Mechanics" because they cook, wait table, and chauffeur for the rich "white folks" on the Highlands.

Another night it is a strolling string band: a three string weather-beaten bass fiddle upon which a stumpy fellow of ginger-cake complexion plays, singing a "mean" tenor to boot; a red-brown guitar lashed to its 'framer' by a red ribbon attached to neck and tail piece; a small fiddle handled like a tender baby by a fat black man. A block from them and they sound like a suppressed orchestra, a half block and you get the rhythm more pronounced, a choice place in the standing circle and you are a-tingle to a rondo of metallic harmony.

Still another night and The Street is tuneless except for the rattle of the electric piano in the entrance of the Dreamland Theater. Along this thoroughfare of rustling mixtures for once music is absent. Then you walk into a crowd; in the center is a solitary black boy of wild eyes. In his hand is an ordinary piece of fishing pole bamboo about two feet long.

"Play 'When the Saints Go Marching In'," someone requests; and without emotion the bamboo is raised to his lips and a tune flows like golden honey. It is crude, here and there a flattened note or lack of accidental, but that only makes it more seducing. And you stand by until this solitary Mozart of the street responds with "The Yellow Dog Blues," "Da-da Strain" and "Maggie."

"Where'd he come from?" the person next to you asks.

"Wetumka," comes the answer. "Been looking for a job but can't find one."

"Why don't you see Hopkins—he's always atta good musicians," suggests the bystander.

"I ain't no musician," grunts the boy. "Jes' toots my flute for fun. It's one I made—bored the holes with a hot iron and learnt to play it myself."

"Play the 'Star Spangled Banner'," comes out of the crowd.

"What for?" challenges the man already talking to the flute player. "Ain't we all standing already—and furthermore, I done heard too much of that tune in camps and over in France. An' what good we get from fighting in the war? Play 'Sweet Mama'."

But most common are the blind beggars with guitars or accordions, attended to by half-naked boys, and even girls in some instances. These children lift the collection in tin cups, asking everyone and even visiting the nearby places of business.

37

Chief among these beggar boys is Fat Boy. He wears his job like a veteran and is the most difficult to get rid of without dropping a coin in his cup. His tactics never vary; just a dogged presentation without loss of words of poor-mouth.

Where the other boys chided, "please help the blind," Fat Boy simply said, "mister —mister—mister—" a hundred times if need be until you did something.

"Mister—mister—mister" and in a soft yet persistent voice Fat Boy plagued and plainted until he caught your eye. One look into those round expectant eyes of a wary child and if you gave only a rebuff you would surely think about it later and regret. And the time he approached you fall a victim of Fat Boy's tenacious subtlety, maybe saying to yourself that you gave to get rid of the nuisance.

HENRY RUNROUND—18th Street Dandy

IT'S Henry Somebody—but no one knows what that Somebody is. Everybody knows Henry Somebody as Henry Runround. That last name is purely descriptive. Simply that for years Henry has been running around with the girls.

Henry's specialty is mid-night butterflies, ice cream fillies and baby vamps, to use by force those effete, commonplace labels. But that's just what they are and that's Henry's main purpose in life. With his dapper self, with his smile and chivalrous air, with his affable voice and everreadiness to do the slightest favor, he finds much to keep him busy between the Peoples Cafe, Dreamland theater, Bon Ton Drug Store and intervening points.

Henry always arranges to have a new sartorial touch about him, either a low cut sport shirt, or kitty-bow jazz tie, or hanging monocle, or flare-open vest, or any fad that's not been overdone by the numerous lesser dandies. And don't leave unmentioned Henry's two gold teeth that he lets at you through intermittent smiles.

Besides being an automatic, endless chain lover, Henry has an ambition. His ambition takes various shoots: News reporter, fireman on the railroad, soda jerker, and injuree minuteman.

He may be all these things in a single week. He writes sporting items and acts as official scorer for the Palmetto Giants baseball games; the very next day you encounter him in blue striped overalls, blue cap and red bandana handkerchief swashed around his throat, with a trimmed lantern in one hand and a pair of gloves in the other.

"What's the dress-up mean, Henry?" a friend greets him.

"Firing for the Frisco—going out on Number 26," coldly replies Henry.

"Henry's lying," another fellow breaks in. "Henry wouldn't carry the fireman's dinner on salary.

"Well, mister Know-all, come go and see. See if I don't fire No. 26 out this evening. Come on!" Henry has started off, beckoning his accosters.

"Oh, I get you Henry," announced the first fellow, "you're putting on a stunt for the masquerade ball at the Palm Garden to-night. We've got you Runround Henry!" And they laughed as the probable fireman ambled on through the crowded street.

Nevertheless, they were not sure that Henry Runround or Runround Henry, which is just as good, was really firing or not. No one knew; Henry did so many things and had so much time to do anything, so why not a fireman?

Well, when Henry wasn't on his beat attracting the female and wasn't writing up a ball game or serving in a rush as extra soda jerker at the Bon Ton, and wasn't dressed up as a fireman, then there was a chance of him being in another role. The chance didn't come often but always Henry accepted it. Accident orphan or expert injuree. On the first news of a street car accident or public disaster, Runround Henry made it there and made good use of a couple of handkerchiefs, his pen knife and his lugubrious look. A cash settlement was his favorite way out.

Henry Runround—what an apt name for him to live up to!

MADAM ANTOINETTE SANDAL

ℙARVENU—Eighteenth Street does not know of the word but it knows Madam Antoinette Sandal, it knows her cherry colored sedan, her Woman's Crowning Glory Beauty Parlors, her beribboned Pekingese, her seven diamond rings on one hand and even talks of her bank balance in two down-town banks as running in five figures.

The gold rush and the oil booms—to the Americans of color, hair and beauty culture is the mild equivalent. Washer-woman yesterday, maker of home-made hair grower today, and the Growmo Company, Inc. to-morrow.

However, not all of the many hundred 'entrepreneurs' strike wealth in such quickness; only the lucky few. Madam Antoinette Sandal was lucky—except in the matter of husbands! Recently her third husband departed with his handbag of belongings to parts unknown. His two forerunners had set the precedent. In fine, the Madam gets husbands with the same ease she gets dollars, and gets rid of them both in like manner.

But her unpardonable shortcomings according to the high circles of gossip is her inability to get the washboard out of her makeup, to dispel the atmosphere of suds in her social bearing. However, money spent freely will make a difference—and so, Madam Antoinette Sandal is paid homage by the upper crust.

"My hair and beauty preparations work for me, my social secretary writes for me, my money talks for me and I should worry, indeed," out of the Madam's own gold-rimmed mouth.

LAWYER HARREL—The Old Tiger

ℕOW, Gentlemen of the Jury. Remember the law says it is better to turn loose ninety-nine guilty men than convict one innocent man, and from the evidence submitted the defendant is only surrounded by the megrest circumstances. . . ."

"Your Honor," interrupted the District Attorney, "such mathematical calculations are not in the law of Alabama as the attorney would have the jury believe."

"Well, Your Honor, I didn't say it was in the law of Alabama; but Your Honor and Gentlemen of the Jury, it is in the *moral law!* Now, coming back to this defendant whom the State's case would have you believe is a murderess, you all remember the parable of the Master which He told about the woman at the well. You have a picture of it . . . the scorners, the accusers, the woman with her face in her hands, and the Master standing over her. He stooped and wrote in the sand; what He wrote no man knows, and then he charged them, ' He that is without sin among you, let him first cast a stone at her.'

"And what did those scoundrels do? *What did they do?* They slunk away one by one. . . ."

"Your Honor," the District Attorney again to his feet, "is this Court to understand that the lawyer is actually intimidating the jury and insulting this Court? Sounds like that to me."

"Now, Your Honor, I did not interrupt the good attorney for the State when he was speaking, when he stood flatfooted and berated this jury with his scornful forefinger, arousing them with, 'who are you going to believe? Who are you going to believe? White man or niggers?' If that isn't intimidating their prejudices, then. . . ."

"The defense may proceed with the speech; too much time has been spent on this case as it is," ordered the Court eyeing the wall clock.

That was a bit of the case of "State of Alabama vs. Dolly Jones," charged with murdering her husband. Dolly got ten years and Dolly's attorney got ten dollars for defending her. Sometimes he doesn't get anything. But he's used to that now; fifteen years in the courts, and seventy-one years old, he has long before set up for himself a philosophy of life. Never in a Law School, read it and passed the Bar orally, Lawyer Harrell was in the manner born to the profession. His mind wrapped intuitively around legal knots and softened them; he always seemed to have the right angle of things. He hangs around the criminal courts out of pure love, as a youngster broods over a puzzle or a dime detective story. It was play to him, counting in the odds of his swarthy face. The court bailiff summed it up unknowingly when he remarked: "That old nigger lawyer Harrell must carry a rabbit foot—he never misses the point."

HAPPY TRAMP

HAPPY Tramp has a real name but only Verge Deems, the undertaker, knows it. Yet everybody in the downtown section knows Happy Tramp. He is a guttersnipe. He is no tramp now for he never gets a mile away from Eighteenth Street. But he was a tramp once.

Talk? Shut your eyes and hear him; with little imagination you could feel that a professor of English was speaking. What a contrast! a statue of brown humanity, chest-sunken, matted hair and draped in a pair of patched overalls and a jumper coat, straw hat with aspects of a wreck victim, and shoes a stevedore would sneer at. Those shoes: well, hear Happy Tramp:

"On my feet again, gentlemen. You see I've been off them for two months, but I'm on my feet again." And he hoists up a leg, one after the other, showing his bare foot through a completely worn sole.

"And you smoking a Portina, with another in your pocket," someone comments.

"Gentlemen, you see the aroma from a good cigar lifts me to ephemeral heights and allows me to transcend my ransomed body. Listen to Browning: 'Poor vaunt of life indeed, were man but formed to feed on joy, to solely seek and find a feast. . . .'"

"You see, I've told you Happy Tramp's been to school," a lounger remarks to another. And it was true. Somewhere back a decade or more this same floating piece of humanity stood high in his classes. He was a genius of his day and a coming light for his Race, but Time worked a slipknot and the 'coming leader' was blown to the four corners of the earth, returning with what is now known to Eighteenth Street as Happy Tramp.

T. FAIRFAX LEROUX

GENTLEMAN of leisure, minister of the Gospel, economist, editor, social worker, and general jumping-jack is this fellow. And all those things easily in the course of one twelve months.

But nothing short of a picture of him suffices. Not a measly word picture, not even a real photograph. Nothing but an eyeful picture of him gets over to you the amount of dignity and eminence that can be covered under so little a stretch of brown skin. Dapper would weakly describe him, only he's no young man. Grey headed, prematurely so he pompously claims, but there's too much of the old grafty world in his bloodshot eyes to prove youth in the thirties even.

Some more words of him: a snaggle-tooth bombast, a gospel ballyhooer, a misogynist, a brass paper weight. This last needs explanation. Living in a district where his people are needed as laborers, he reaches the height of his power, both egotistically and dollarly, when they, his people, are floating Northward. Brass paper weight—for the corporations depending on black hands he is a sort of sinker to hold down those with a tendency to flitter away to other fields. Brass because it takes that for such a job.

There are so many sides to him, so many facets, until it is difficile to know just when you are getting him right. Perhaps his anti-feministic affectation is worth while. To him ladies are merely breakable china for men not busy with the thought burden of the world. They never entered his life—at least, not now, since his hair was beginning to turn grey. "Young man, when you've reached my stately age and grandeur of thought," he explained to a youngster on the street, "you'll know not to mix women and toil. Let me but remind you of honest history: Antony, snuffed out of the noonday light of Rome by artful Cleopatra, biblical Sampson shorn of his hair and resistive powers, Alexander the Great sunk in ribaldry with his hundred generals by a Persian female, Napoleon millstoned with Josephine around his neck. Young man, go to your history."

But this was just a preamble to one of his street harangues. And with a voice that warmed in on a good pitch, his set jaw and sloping forehead, topped by a wiry pompadour of streaked grey, were charms that gathered him an audience.

Yet, when all was said and done by him, his hearers walked away still unconvinced, they walked away as if somebody had hit them in the face with a handful of confetti.

Another favorite theme of his that must not be omitted is: My past glories, me, and the future. He seldom got past the middle—me. Incidental to his past were his French and Negro ancestors, as you see from his name; Creole by common usage, but he negates this cleavage vehemently.

The sweet meat of his past was his foreign training—"two years in Glasgow, one in Leipzig, and then four years under the English flag on the seven seas," he puts it. "But," he concludes eloquently, "never have I felt the pangs at my heart cockles so gripping as when I came under the gracious outstretched hand of Miss Liberty to land in that great cosmopolitan monolith, New York, then to wend my way to this glorious Southland, where God and men, black and white, are working out a great destiny. How but can my last and eternal rest be sweet in this land of magnolias and corn, how. . . ."

And then some roughneck breaks loose with, "Hurrah, he's stumping for corn. *Corn*—bottled in bond!"

And that was the switch that threw his verbal train into a siding, wrecking the impromptu speech.

TWO-GUN HART

THERE are all kinds of fools: natural born, self-made, sick fools, half-wits, love-lorn and plain. Two-gun Hart is different and perhaps an appropriate title would be Strutting Phool. He ranges from Third Avenue along Eighteenth Street down to Fourth Avenue and back, touching all the four theaters. He doesn't miss a single show but he does miss several meals. A western thriller is his best diet, and on them he lives, longs and thrives. And it is this imitating of the two-gun movie heroes that has turned him a dunce. Yet his imitating is original.

Talk to him. He is incoherent and rattle-tongued, but you can catch some of his atmosphere.

"Adius, Senor," he greets you in foreign. He culled these from the screen, not by reading them himself but by hearing someone repeat them.

"Howdy Hart," you say for the sake of getting him to talk. "What's on at the Star to-day?" as if you were planning to go to the theater.

"What's on? Me. Fight ind'uns and they shoot my hat off, but I get's 'em. Bookety, bookety, bookety—that's the way I makes my get-way," and this with a kicking up of his heels to give you the scene. There are spurs on his high-heel shoes, and from the spurs up he is dressed like a cow boy. Two-gun Hart stays that way, sleeps that way for that matter.

"Hart, can *you* ride a horse?" you jostle him.

"Umph. What you take me for? Me ride? I bust broncoes for Ringling Brothers three years." And again he gives you a pantomime of a rider on a bucking horse. Remember, this is on the street, people are passing, those few who have not stopped for the show. Hart sees his audience thickening and puts on other western antics, lassoing a boy out of the crowd with an imaginary rope or flashing a gun from his empty holster—the gun being imaginary, but the technic he displays making it rather real.

Then a lady has paused to see what the excitement is and the Phool sees her. That breaks up the show, for he suddenly turns Don Quixotic and bows graciously to her feet, after which he arms through the crowd, mumbling, "no act the fool for squaw; will fight for her."

His expression has changed and no one attempts to stop him; his jaw is set and shoulders held straight. He has flashed from the simpleton to the sane, apparently.

CLEOMANTHA

B EAUTY in a woman is both a triumph and a tragedy on a fifty-fifty basis; it is like glistening gold in the eyes of mad men. And stronger, beauty in a swarthy skin in Dixie is ten percent triumph and ninety percent tragedy. They are increasing two-fold with every generation. "High yellows, whipped-creams, yellow-hammers, Egyptian olives, velvet browns," are just a few of the sobriquets.

Cleomantha, ticket girl at the Dreamland Theater, was born to a bewitching golden brown complexion. There was nothing sharp about her features or form and then there was nothing coarse or ponderous about her either. Her perfection points were her big expressive brown eyes, an unblemished complexion and a melting voice.

Cleomantha now belonged to Eighteenth Street. For five years she has been selling tickets from the various theater booths, and who was it who did not know Cleomantha, who was it who could pass, catch a glimpse of her face and not turn for a second look?

She came from Demopolis, a farming town barely out of the echo of the guns of Shiloh and Vicksburg; most of the good looking colored girls come from these small towns. In the city one never knows anything of their back-home ties; there is only that general rumor that colored men are not tolerated on the streets with these creamy-skinned girls back home, that their white paramours will first warn and then do violence. Such was the rumor that haloed itself around Cleomantha. But Cleomantha treaded her way along the Street composedly and without stopping. She seemed to bend herself to dressing and reading lightsome books and magazines. How she wards off the wolves and whether she does, are still riddles for Eighteenth Street.

THE REVE'ND BUNN

S OLVING the race question, solving it in a 'Jim-swinger' and a pair of heavy tortoise shell spectacles is the job-in-chief of the Rev'end G. W. Bunn, D.D., Ph.D. With such a herculean task upon him he takes it calmly. He is a pacifist without the "fist", and to certain members of his Race little more than a baby's rattle.

However, the evening dailies give space to his articles. Here is a sample:

"When one considers the army of good white people here one must be fair and say a word about them. Notwithstanding those who would drive us to other fields of labor there are those good men and women of the Caucasian Race who understand us and our needs, who loved and harbored our forebears, who will give us a square deal, and it is with these folks that the American Negro had best stay in touch with. Each day they are voicing his part more and more, and in time will see that right here in the South will be a place of desire, and happiness.

Then too, there is no overlooking the rigor of the Northern climate, the coldness of the Northern white man, the competition of the Northern foreigner. The South is the only place for the Negro. . . ."

That is about as good as any of the others he submits. It is what the editors want and there is where the Rev'end's headwork comes in. The world pays for what it wants as a rule, and each one of these epistles is a foundation for the Rev'end to solicit and collect funds for the Welfare Southern Home League, which he officers and headquarters in his ante-room office in the Washington Building.

Where is the corporation employing colored workmen who would not contribute to such an asset? "The South is the best place for the Negro" is a text that anyone can cash in on. Say it louder and longer enough and silver will clink mysteriously into your pockets.

Notwithstanding the sneer that the Rev'end is a cat's paw, me-too-boss Negro, in truth he is a good business man, or in the slang, a jack-getter and a seducer of dollars.

"Selling your birthright," somebody chunked at him. "Hurting your Race," another.

"Wrong," he came back aplomb, "my Race is yet a child, and who is it but knows that when you tell a child *not* to do a thing, he does it. Why, I'm responsible for several train loads going North. May I hint that I'm simply killing two birds with one stone. Ah, brothers, you must learn to look beyond your nose."

LAWYER HARRELL

OLD man Harrell had another murder case to-day. Didn't free his man, but says he will. Jury gave his client six years, which is a lot for a jury to admit in some of his cases.

Leaving the Court room the Court Clerk stopped him. "Harrell, you know more Bible than you do law."

"Glad I do," replied the old man.

"You ought to get a brick church and preach to the niggers," suggested the clerk.

"It's you folks who need preaching to," answered Harrell.

"You'd be a great help to your people," insisted the official.

"My people? Who do you mean? My people?"

They looked at each other fiercely and said no more. Harrell's father owned twenty slaves, among which was Harrell's mother, a mulatto.

MADAM ANTOINETTE SANDAL

AGAIN Madam Sandal has compelled social acknowledgement. This time she extended herself by presenting a fete entitled "The Nile Queen's Garden." Among the citizens of color nothing like it had ever been given. It was a masquerade with a ban on all costumes not foreign. "Only Oriental costumed guests admitted" read the invitations and enclosed separately was the program, to wit:

Costume Reception   (Ten till Eleven)
Madam Angel Bradshaw, Receptress
Dansante Generale
Sampson's Jazz Serpents—Music

Danseuse de specialty
Damsel Juliet Moore
One O'Clock—Demasque et Luncheon
Two O'Clock—The Sheik of the Night

It was an affair of creation and a surprise ending. To have seen the Crowning Glory Ball Room where the fete was given would have been a long remembered scene. But for the French doors and adjustable windows it was a roof garden. However, it is for all-year use and the fete was in March, no time for outdoor effect. For orientation all the window panes were colored alternately green, red and amber; in addition strange new scents from concealed incense burners were released.

At one end of the ball room was draped a purple curtain. Reams of rhythm and impelling tunes from Sampson's Jazz Serpents came through its royal folds and likewise was issued forth Damsel Juliet Moore in a Nile River terpsichorean conception. At one o'clock with the ball room darkened the curtain parted and appeared a huge face of a clock, the hour marks and hands illuminated. A single penetrating gong stroke told the hour and the lights came on by degrees like day-break. One hour later the illuminated clock appeared again telling the hour. This time the lights came on quickly. Ensemble music was played by the orchestra; a hush of expectancy seized the guests. A shiny black cat emerged from the curtain slit and literally sailed down the middle of the ball room. Its body was the anchor for two balloons, one red and one white. Midway the room the balloons were freed and floated lazily towards the ceiling while the inky feline made a good escape through the door. No single guest dared move across the imaginary path of the midnight creature until the door through which the cat left shut with a bang.

The balloons now held everybody's attention. On the white balloon was the letter S and on the red balloon was the letter H. Comment broke from all lips—what was the significance? The lights were softening, finally leaving the doubtful green glow from the stained windows.

"The—hour—has—come," measured a rounded baritone behind the curtain. Strange music as if from a distance was heard again. "Hear ye—all. The—hour—has —come—when—the—Sheik—of—the—Night—will—appear!"

Slowly parted the curtain; gradually came on the amber lights; nearer the music seemed and in solemn carriage stepped forth the "Sheik of the Night," a tall masked figure, clothed in silk and velvet such as no sultan could ever despise. To the center of the room he strode arrogantly and then and there he deliberately unmasked.

Sheik of the Night—none other than Dozier Horn, paragon of bootleggers along Eighteenth Street.

"The balloons, the balloons," someone exclaimed. "I have it—S stands for Sandal and H stands for Horn. They're engaged!"

Chatter, laughter and congratulations were showered upon the Sheik of the Night and the hostess, who suddenly appeared in the midst of the party as the Queen of the Nile.

THE REV'END BUNN

THE Rev'end Bunn has been conspicuous by his absence from Eighteenth Street for a month. His long coat and wilted panama, his loping walk and twisted walking cane, his horned glasses and tar-tinted face, are marks of distinction he has carried elsewhere. Just before he left it was announced that he would take a vacation, swinging through the North and East. Now, tri-weekly his letters are published in the local dailies. Here is one from Youngstown:

Since I have arrived in this busy city I have been overwhelmed with acquaintances from the South, and every one of them makes it known in some way his desire to once more see the good old Southland, where there is consideration of his methods of living and where the grind is not that of a tread mill.

One man told me that if he doesn't save enough money to buy a ticket to Andalusia, he'd walk back. . . .

And one from Cleveland:

. . . Nothwithstanding the high wages and many jobs, the Southern migrants don't seem to be able to get their bearings here at all—the herding into cramped quarters, the eternal rushing, the lack of time to fraternalize, makes them wish and long for their old Southern surroundings.

It makes me tremble to think what a terrible thing would happen to my wayward people in the event the industrial bottom should drop out of things here. . . .

And a letter from New York:

This great city has already far too many colored Americans. I solemnly advise my fellow Racemen not to think of coming to this gigantic place. . . . The South has more to offer them. . . .

And one of the dailies had an editorial comment on the Rev'end Bunn's great trip of revelation, stating that it "should open the eyes of the Southern Negroes to the fact that undisputably the South is the only and best place for them."

HAPPY TRAMP

HAPPY Tramp has just passed along. He does not look one whit different than he always has. Same threadbare trousers completely faded, a jumper coat that was once somebody else's, trash pile shoes topped by bare brown ankles, a two-season straw hat and it is now October.

Six months ago he began selling corn and synthetic rye for Dozier Horn; he has not missed a day and is the best known bootlegger along the Avenue.

"Can't understand Happy Tramp," said Dozier Horn. "I have in keeping for him over two thousand dollars and he won't let me buy him a decent pair of shoes."

Others had wrenched ready dollars from their illicit game; they either gambled and dressed it away, or lost it in paying fines and lawyer fees, or as a few attempted, quit and lived on what they had saved until in need again. Happy Tramp alone remained unaffected.

Then one day Happy Tramp came to Dozier Horn and said:

"I want you to put that money of mine in the bank in the name of Temple Scott. And next, I'm going to have a will drawn up. Early in my life I was sent to Tuskegee to school; in my final year I ran away. I'm going to keep on working and what money I save I'm going to will to Tuskegee."

"But Tuskegee doesn't want blood money," suggested Dozier Horn.

"Many an honorable institution has been built on what you call blood money," Happy Tramp came back. "I pick up a coin from the filth of the gutter; I rub it and it shines. The money's clean and good. Must it be bad if put to a worthy use? That's just the trouble with religion—it's too afraid of the gutter."

"All right, Happy," spoke up Horn. "I'll fix it as you say. But since you're going to be one of those 'philanthepers' I wish you'd put on some decent clothes and look like one. Tuskagee'll be ashamed of you."

"But they don't know me—Happy Tramp. They know Temple Scott." And he strode out to Eighteenth Street and away.

THE REV'END BUNN

Eighteenth Street has lost another habitue. The Rev'end Bunn, D.D., Ph.D. (this latter by correspondence) left to-day for Detroit, where he will take up the pastorate of the Mt. Sinai Baptist Church. In accepting the call he gave out the following statement:

I am not leaving my people in the South, I am following them. Too long
have I been sidetracked from preaching the word of God, and it is with His
Grace I come back into the work.

So it has come to pass that I go to Detroit to do His will. . . .

But this did not get in the white dailies. The Rev'end Bunn, go-between and trumpeter, found the current of migration too strong to resist. When he was on his tour for the Southern Labor Syndicate, Detroit had impressed him with its possibilities and problems. Then had come the clincher, the offer to minister the Mt. Sinai flock at three thousand per year.

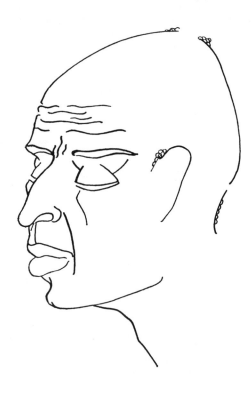

JOHN HENRY
A Negro Legend

By Guy B. Johnson

NEGRO folk have produced so many interesting characters that it is difficult to choose one from among them who stands above the others. However, I believe that most of those who know anything about John Henry will agree with me that he deserves a very high rank, not only in Negro folklore, but in American folklore in general. In the sixty years since this legend originated it has grown tremendously. In song and story John Henry is celebrated in every part of the country where Negro working men are to be found.

John Henry, so the legend goes, was a steel driver. He lived in a day when steam drills and compressed air drills were just beginning to be used in tunnelling, mining, and the like. It is said that John Henry was a superior steel driver and that he enjoyed quite a reputation for his strength and endurance. He felt resentful when he heard steam drills were becoming practicable, and he said that he believed he could out-drill the things. He soon got his chance to make good. One day a representative of a mechanical drill company came to the tunnel where John Henry was working and tried to sell the contractor a steam drill. The contractor was skeptical—said that he believed the drill was no faster than a good hand driver. The agent protested this statement, so the contractor retorted that he had a man whom he was willing to put against the drill. John Henry was called in, and he agreed to compete. As the story goes,

> John Henry said to his Captain,
> "Well, a man ain't nothin' but a man,
> An' befo' I'd be beaten by that old steam drill,
> I'll die with the hammer in my han'
> Lawd, I'll die with the hammer in my han'."

According to some versions of the story, a wager was made between John Henry's "Captain" and the steam drill agent. Some say that in case John Henry lost, his "Captain" was to buy the drill; but if John Henry won, the agent was to give his drill away. At any rate, the legend has it that the contest took place. John Henry drove the required depth before the steam drill did, but the poor man had put too much into the contest. He had barely taken his last stroke when he fell over in a faint and died "with hammer in his hand."

That, I believe, is about as dramatic an episode as one could ask for. I do not wonder that John Henry is regarded almost reverently by thousands of the Negro common folk, or that the tale has a fascination for all who have only recently heard if for the first time.

The John Henry tradition exists in several forms. First, there are the stories, opinions and reminiscences of people who know something about John Henry. There are any number of people living, by the way, who claim to have known John Henry intimately. Of these I shall speak later. Then there are innumerable songs about John Henry. These may be divided into the ballad of narrative type and the work-song type. The former tells a story and is usually sung as a solo with guitar or banjo

47

accompaniment, while the latter is rarely consistently narrative and is most often sung by groups of workmen swinging picks or hammers in unison.

An expert "musicianer" singing a John Henry ballad, picking his "box," patting his foot, swaying his body, is a picturesque sight. The following version is brief, but it gives the essential elements of the story. It was transcribed from the singing of a Negro workman at Chapel Hill, North Carolina.

John Henry was a steel-drivin' man,
Carried his hammer all the time,
An' befo' he'd let the steam drill beat him down,
He'd die with the hammer in his han',
Die with the hammer in his han'.

John Henry went to the mountain,
Beat that steam drill down;
Rock was high, po' John was small,
Well, he laid down his hammer an' he died,
Laid down his hammer an' he died.

John Henry was a little babe
Sittin' on his daddy's knee,
Said "Big Ben" Tunnel on C. & O. road
Gonna be the death o' me,
Gonna be the death o' me."

John Henry had a little girl,
Her name was Polly Ann.
John was on his bed so low,
She drove with his hammer like a man,
Drove with his hammer like a man.

But a group of dusky workmen singing and swinging in perfect rhythm is a still more picturesque sight. There is little substance and much repetition in their song, nevertheless it is enchanting. Here is a good example of a John Henry work song.

This old hammer—huh!
Hammer killed John Henry—huh!
This old hammer—huh!
Hammer killed John Henry—huh
Can't kill me—huh!
Lawd, Lawd, can't kill me—huh!

The variations of ballads, work songs, and stories about John Henry which exist among the Negro folk would fill an enormous volume, so I can only sketch briefly here the ramifications of the legend.

Take, for example, the varying ideas as to the situation in which John Henry met his death. The usual opinion is that he was working in a tunnel when he had his great contest with the steam drill. But steel driving is a term applied not only to the drilling operations used in mining, tunneling, and other work in which explosives are used, but also to the driving of spikes into railroad cross-ties. Therefore, we find John Henry driving steel in tunnels, in mines, in quarries, and on railroads. Practically every Southern state claims John Henry, the legend varying according to local conditions. Sometimes, in fact most often, he is said to have died at "Big Bend Tunnel on the C. and O. Road." Sometimes it is "Tunnel No. Nine" on the Southern Railroad. Again it is a tunnel which railway engineers say does not exist. Sometimes John Henry is represented as dying immediately after the contest, sometimes it is said that he was taken to his shanty where he died later. And I have come across such beliefs as that expressed in the following stanza:

John Henry was killed on the railroad
A mile and a half from town,
His head cut off in the driving wheel
And his body ain't never been found.

Or take the ideas about John Henry's surname. Of course, his full name might have been just John Henry, for that was once a very popular name among Negroes, both slave and free. There were about a dozen free Negro heads of families who bore the name of John Henry even as far back as 1830. But I often ask this question as to John Henry's full name when I am talking to some one about John Henry, and the replies are interesting. One man who claimed to have worked with John Henry said that his name was John Henry Dula. Another who claimed to have been with John Henry when he died, said that his surname was Dabney. Other names I have encountered are John Henry Brown, John Henry Martin, John Henry Jones, John Henry Whitsett.

Some say that John Henry was a North Carolinian, others say he was from South Carolina, or Tennessee, or Alabama, or Virginia. Some Negroes feel very strongly on this matter. In fact, I once heard of a fight arising between two men because one of them said that John Henry was born somewhere other than Virginia. Some admirer of John Henry was so eager to give Virginia the credit that he put a stanza like this in one of the John Henry ballads.

Some said he came from England,
Some said he came from Spain,
But it's no such thing, he was an East Virginia man,
And he died with the hammer in his hand,
He died with the hammer in his hand.

Similar variations of other aspects of the legend might be pointed out, but these will suffice to show the trend. No two persons tell the story of John Henry alike, yet on the whole there is among the Negro folk a firm conviction that John Henry really lived, really beat the steam drill and really "died with the hammer in his hand."

And this leads to the question of how it all got started. Is this John Henry tradition true? I do not consider this question of any great importance, but it is usually the first one which one asks on hearing about John Henry for the first time, so I want to touch upon it briefly.

There are quite a few people living who claim to have known John Henry. I have talked or corresponded with several such persons, and their testimony is an important part of the evidence on this question of John Henry's reality. For example, one old Negro man in western North Carolina told me that he knew John Henry and that he was certain that John Henry really beat a steam drill at Big Bend Tunnel. Another man, a Negro minister from Kentucky, said that as a boy he "packed" water in Big Bend Tunnel and that he saw John Henry beat the steam drill. A young man from Cleveland, Ohio, wrote me that his father worked with the "original John Henry" in Kentucky in 1886. A man from South Carolina wrote that his father once worked with John Henry in Tennessee, but he does not know where John Henry's death occurred. A white man of Orange County, Virginia, stated that he was once employed by one of the contractors who built the Big Ben Tunnel and that he has heard the contractor say time and again that the story of John Henry is true. Three different persons, one from Alabama, one from Michigan, and one from Utah, have written me about the John Henry story, vouching for its authenticity, and giving the time and place of the contest as northeastern Alabama about 1882. There are various other reminiscences, but these are typical of the ones most frequently found.

Thus, when we consider the testimony of old timers who claim to have personal knowledge of John Henry, we find that, while there were inconsistencies and impossibilities in the details, there is a convergence of opinion pointing toward only one or two places as possible locations of the original steel-driving contest. Practically all of the clues which are worth following point either toward the Big Bend Tunnel on the C. and O. Railroad in West Virginia, or toward some such place as Cursey (or Cruzee) Mountain Tunnel in Alabama. The Big Bend Tunnel was built in 1870-72, and, since it antedates the alleged Alabama tunnel by ten years, it is the more likely place.

Last year I made a personal investigation at Big Bend Tunnel, interviewing the residents, especially the old timers who worked on the tunnel when it was being built. I might summarize the situation as follows: There is a pretty general disposition around the Big Bend region to take the John Henry story for granted, but there are several people who firmly believe that John Henry is a myth, and there are only three or four who will say that they actually saw John Henry or saw the famous contest. One man gave me a detailed description of the steam drill and of the contest, which he said he saw as he went back and forth carrying water and drills for the gang on which John Henry worked. Yet his testimony is disputed by other residents who apparently were in as good position as he to know what was going on, as well as by railroad officials and mechanical engineers who say that no steam drill was ever taken to Big Bend Tunnel.

What, then, is the answer to the question? It is entirely possible that the whole thing is purely legendary and that certain men have heard the legend so long that they have actually come to believe that they knew this man John Henry. On the other hand, it is just as possible that the legend is based on an actual occurrence. Indeed, it is possible that more than one John Henry competed with a steam drill and "died with the hammer in his hand" or came so near dying that it was not difficult for his admirers to say that he died. An investigation of the Alabama claims noted above might bring out the same sort of evidence of authenticity as has been found at Big Bend.

At any rate, one who goes out to look for the answer to the mystery of John Henry's origin will not have easy sledding. He will find personal testimony galore, but it is fallible and contradictory and not the sort of proof which scientists demand. Personally, I am pretty well convinced that John Henry existed in the flesh and beat a steam drill at Big Bend Tunnel, but I confess that my belief is based on a sort of common-sense logic and not on what the historians call documentary evidence.

But the question of the origin and truth of the legend does not matter greatly. The legend is here, as vigorous and as fascinating as ever. The great thing, after all, is that thousands of Negro folk believe in John Henry and think of him reverently. To them he is a hero, an epic figure, a martyr who died defending the dignity of common labor and its superiority over that symbol of the white man's civilization— the machine.

I marvel that some poet among the "New Negro" generation does not sing John Henry's praises, that some playwright does not dramatize him, that some painter does not picture him as he battles with the steam drill, or that some sculptor does not fulfil the wishful phantasy of that Negro pick-and-shovel man who said to me, "Cap'n, they tells me that they got John Henry's statue carved out o' solid rock at the head o' Big Ben' Tunnel. Yes, sir, there he stan' with the hammer in his han'."

THINGS SAID WHEN HE WAS GONE
By BLANCHE TAYLOR DICKINSON

My branch of thoughts is frail tonight
As one lone wind-whipped weed.
Little I care if a rain drop laughs
Or cries; I cannot heed

Such trifles now as a twinkling star,
Or catch a night-bird's tune.
My whole life is you, to-night,
And you, a cool distant moon.

With a few soft words to nurture my heart
And brighter beams following love's cool shower
Who knows but this frail wind-whipped weed
Might bear you a gorgeous flower!

APRIL IS ON THE WAY

By Alice Dunbar Nelson

April is on the way!
I saw the scarlet flash of a blackbird's wing
As he sang in the cold, brown February trees;
And children said that they caught a glimpse of the
sky on a bird's wing from the far South.
(*Dear God, was that a stark figure outstretched in
the bare branches
Etched brown against the amethyst sky?*)

April is on the way!
The ice crashed in the brown mud-pool under my
tread,
The warning earth clutched my bloody feet with
great fecund fingers.
I saw a boy rolling a hoop up the road,
His little bare hands were red with cold,
But his brown hair blew backward in the southwest
wind.
(*Dear God! He screamed when he saw my awful
woe-spent eyes.*)

April is on the way!
I met a woman in the lane;
Her burden was heavy as it is always, but today
her step was light,
And a smile drenched the tired look away from her
eyes.
(*Dear God, she had dreams of vengeance for her
slain mate,
Perhaps the west wind has blown the mist of hate
from her heart,
The dead man was cruel to her, you know that,
God.*)

April is on the way!
My feet spurn the ground now, instead of dragging
on the bitter road.
I laugh in my throat as I see the grass greening beside the patches of snow
(*Dear God, those were wild fears. Can there be
hate when the southwest wind is blowing?*)

April is on the way!
The crisp brown hedges stir with the bustle of bird
wings.
There is business of building, and songs from brown
thrush throats
As the bird-carpenters make homes against Valen-
tine Day.

(*Dear God, could they build me a shelter in the
hedge from the icy winds that will come
with the dark?*)

April is on the way!
I sped through the town this morning. The florist
shops have put yellow flowers in the windows,
Daffodils and tulips and primroses, pale yellow
flowers
Like the tips of her fingers when she waved me that
frightened farewell.
And the women in the market have stuck pussy willows in long necked bottles on their stands.
(*Willow trees are kind, Dear God. They will not
bear a body on their limbs.*)

April is on the way!
The soul within me cried that all the husk of indifference to sorrow was but the crust of ice
with which winter disguises life;
It will melt, and reality will burgeon forth like the
crocuses in the glen.
(*Dear God! Those thoughts were from long ago.
When we read poetry after the day's toil,
and got religion together at the revival
meeting.*)

April is on the way!
The infinite miracle of unfolding life in the brown
February fields.
(*Dear God, the hounds are baying!*)
Murder and wasted love, lust and weariness, deceit
and vainglory—what are they but the spent
breath of the runner?
(*God, you know he laid hairy red hands on the
golden loveliness of her little daffodil body*)
Hate may destroy me, but from my brown limbs
will bloom the golden buds with which we
once spelled love.
(*Dear God! How their light eyes glow into black
pin points of hate!*)

April is on the way!
Wars are made in April, and they sing at Easter
time of the Resurrection.
Therefore I laugh in their faces.
(*Dear God, give her strength to join me before her
golden petals are fouled in the slime!*)
April is on the way!

"THE FIRST ONE"

A Play in One Act

By Zora Neale Hurston

Time: Three Years After the Flood
Place: Valley of Ararat
Persons: Noah, His Wife, Their Sons: Shem, Japheth, Ham;
Eve, Ham's Wife; The Sons' wives and children (6 or 7).

Setting:

Morning in the Valley of Ararat.   The Mountain is in the near distance.   Its lower slopes grassy with grazing herds.   The very blue sky beyond that.   These together form the back-ground.   On the left downstage is a brown tent.   A few shrubs are scattered here and there over the stage indicating the temporary camp.   A rude altar is built center stage.   A Shepherd's crook, a goat skin water bottle, a staff and other evidences of nomadic life lie about the entrance to the tent.   To the right stretches a plain clad with bright flowers.   Several sheep or goat skins are spread about on the ground upon which the people kneel or sit whenever necessary.

Action:

Curtain rises on an empty stage.   It is dawn.   A great stillness, but immediately Noah enters from the tent and ties back the flap.   He is clad in loose fitting dingy robe tied about the waist with a strip of goat hide.   Stooped shoulders, flowing beard.   He gazes about him.   His gaze takes in the entire stage.

Noah (fervently): Thou hast restored the Earth, Jehovah, it is good.   (Turns to the tent.)   My sons!   Come, deck the altar for the sacrifices to Jehovah.   It is the third year of our coming to this valley to give thanks offering to Jehovah that he spared us.
(Enter Japheth bearing a haunch of meat and Shem with another.   The wife of Noah and those of Shem and Japheth follow laying on sheaves of grain and fruit (dates and figs).   They are all middle-aged and clad in dingy garments.
Noah: And where is Ham—son of my old age?   Why does he not come with his wife and son to the sacrifice?
Mrs. Noah: He arose before the light and went.   (She shades her eyes with one hand and points toward the plain with the other.)   His wife, as ever, went with him.
Shem (impatiently): This is the third year that we have come here to this Valley to commemorate our delivery from the flood.   Ham knows the sacrifice is made always at sunrise.   See!   (He points to rising sun.)   He should be here.
Noah (lifts his hand in a gesture of reproval): We shall wait.   The sweet singer, the child of my loins after old age had come upon me is warm to my heart—let us wait.

(There is off-stage, right, the twanging of a rude stringed instrument and laughter.   Ham, his wife and son come dancing on down-stage right.   He is in his early twenties.   He is dressed in a very white goat-skin with a wreath of shiny green leaves about his head.   He has the rude instrument in his hands and strikes it.   His wife is clad in a short blue garment with a girdle of shells.   She has a wreath of scarlet flowers about her head.   She has black hair, is small, young and lithe.   She wears anklets and wristlets of the same red flowers.   Their son about three years old wears nothing but a broad band of leaves and flowers about his middle.   They caper and prance to the altar.   Ham's wife and son bear flowers.   A bird is perched on Ham's shoulder.
Noah (extends his arms in greeting):   My son, thou art late.   But the sunlight comes with thee.   (Ham gives bird to Mrs. Noah, then embraces Noah.)
Ham (rests his head for a moment on Noah's shoulder):   We arose early and went out on the plain to make ready for the burnt offering before Jehovah.
Mrs. Shem (tersely):   But you bring nothing.
Ham: See thou!   We bring flowers and music to offer up.   I shall dance before Jehovah and sing

53

joyfully upon the harp that I made of the thews of rams. (He proudly displays the instrument and strums once or twice.)

Mrs. Shem (clapping her hands to her ears): Oh, Peace! Have we not enough of thy bawling and prancing all during the year? Shem and Japheth work always in the fields and vineyards, while you do naught but tend the flock and sing!

Mrs. Japheth (looks contemptuously at both Ham and Noah): Still, thou art beloved of thy father . . . he gives thee all his vineyards for thy singing, but Japheth must work hard for his fields.

Mrs. Shem: And Shem—

Noah (angrily): Peace! Peace! Are lust and strif*e again* loose upon the Earth? Jehovah might have destroyed us all. Am I not Lord of the world? May I not bestow where I will? Besides, the world is great. Did I not give food, and plenty to the thousands upon thousands that the waters licked up? Surely there is abundance for us and our seed forever. Peace! Let us to the sacrifice.

(Noah goes to the heaped up altar. Ham exits to the tent hurriedly and returns with a torch and hands it to Noah who applies it to the altar. He kneels at the altar and the others kneel in a semi-circle behind him at a little distance. Noah makes certain ritualistic gestures and chants):

"O Mighty Jehovah, who created the Heaven and the firmaments thereof, the Sun and Moon, the stars, the Earth and all else besides—

Others: I am here

I am here, O, Jehovah

I am here

This is thy Kingdom, and I am here.

(A deep silence falls for a moment.)

Noah: Jehovah, who saw evil in the hearts of men, who opened upon them the windows of Heaven and loosed the rain upon them—And the fountains of the great deep were broken up—

Others (repeat chant)

Noah: Jehovah who dried up the floods and drove the waters of the sea again to the deeps—who met Noah in the Vale of Ararat and made covenant with Noah, His servant, that no more would he smite the Earth—And Seed time and Harvest, Cold and Heat, Summer and Winter, day and night shall not cease forever, and set His rainbow as a sign.

Noah and Others: We are here O Jehovah

We are here

We are here

This is Thy Kingdom

And we are here.

(Noah arises, makes obeisance to the smoking altar, then turns and blesses the others.)

Noah: Noah alone, whom the Lord found worthy; Noah whom He made lord of the Earth, blesses you and your seed forever.

(At a gesture from him all arise. The women take the meat from the altar and carry it into the tent.) Eat, drink and make a joyful noise

before Him. For He destroyed the Earth, but spared us. (Women re-enter with bits of roast meat—all take some and eat. All are seated on the skins.)

Mrs. Noah (feelingly): Yes, three years ago, all was water, *water*, WATER! The deeps howled as one beast to another. (She shudders.) In my sleep, even now, I am in that Ark again being borne here, there on the great bosom.

Mrs. Ham (wide-eyed): And the dead! Floating, floating all about us—We were one little speck of life in a world of death! (The bone slips from her hand.) And there, close beside the Ark, close with her face upturned as if begging for shelter —my *mother!* (She weeps, Ham comforts her.)

Mrs. Shem (eating vigorously): She would not repent. Thou art as thy mother was—a seeker after beauty of raiment and laughter. God is just. She would not repent.

Mrs. Ham: But the unrepentant are no less loved. And why must Jehovah hate beauty?

Noah: Speak no more of the waters! Oh, the strength of the waters! The voices and the death of it! Let us have the juice of the grape to make us forget. Where once was death in this Valley there is now life abundant of beast and herbs. (He waves towards the scenery.) Jehovah meets us here. Dance! Be glad! Bring wine! Ham smite thy harp of ram's thews and sing!

(Mrs. Noah gathers all the children and exits to the tent. Shem, Japheth, their wives and children eat vigorously. Mrs. Ham exits, left. Ham plays on his harp and capers about singing. Mrs. Ham re-enters with goatskin of wine and a bone cup. She crosses to where Noah reclines on a large skin. She kneels and offers it to him. He takes the cup—she pours for him. Ham sings—)

Ham:

"I am as a young ram in the Spring

Or a young male goat.

The hills are beneath my feet

And the young grass.

Love rises in me like the flood

And ewes gather round me for food."

His wife joins in the dancing. Noah cries "Pour" and Mrs. Ham hurries to fill his cup again. Ham joins others on the skins. The others have horns suspended from their girdles. Mrs. Ham fills them all. Noah cries "pour" again and she returns to him. She turns to fill the others' cups.

Noah (rising drunkenly): Pour again, Eve, and Ham sing on and dance and drink—drown out the waters of the flood if you can. (His tongue grows thick. Eve fills his cup again. He reels drunkenly toward the tent door, slopping the liquor out of the cup as he walks.) Drink wine, forget water—it means death, *death!* And bodies floating, face up! (He stares horrified about himself and creeps stealthily into the tent, but sprawls just inside the door so that his feet are visible. There is silence for a moment, the others are still eating. They snatch tid-bits from each other.)

Japheth (shoves his wife) : Fruit and herbs, woman! (He thrusts her impatiently forward with his foot.) She exits left.

Shem (to his wife) : More wine!

Mrs. Shem (irritated) : See you not that there is plenty still in the bottle? (He seizes it and pours. Ham snatches it away and pours. Shem tries to get it back but Ham prevents him. Re-enter Mrs. Japheth with figs and apples. Everybody grabs. Ham and Shem grab for the same one, Ham gets it).

Mrs. Shem (significantly) : Thus he seizes all else that he desires. Noah would make him lord of the Earth because he sings and capers. (Ham is laughing drunkenly and pelting Mrs. Shem with fruit skins and withered flowers that litter the ground. This infuriates her.)

Noah (calls from inside the tent): Eve, wine, quickly! I'm sinking down in the WATER! Come drown the WATER with wine.

(Eve exits to him with the bottle. Ham arises drunkenly and starts toward the tent door.)

Ham (thickly) : I go to pull our father out of the water, or to drown with him in it. (Ham is trying to sing and dance.) "I am as a young goat in the sp-sp-sp-. (He exits to the tent laughing. Shem and Japheth sprawl out in the skins. The wives are showing signs of surfeit. Ham is heard laughing raucously inside the tent. He re-enters still laughing.)

Ham (in the tent door) : Our Father has stripped himself, showing all his wrinkles. Ha! Ha! He's as no young goat in the spring. Ha! Ha! (Still laughing, he reels over to the altar and sinks down behind it still laughing.) The old Ram, Ha! Ha! Ha! He has had no spring for years! Ha! Ha! (He subsides into slumber. Mrs. Shem looks about her exultantly.)

Mrs. Shem: Ha! The young goat has fallen into a pit! (She shakes her husband.) Shem! Shem! Rise up and become owner of Noah's vineyards as well as his flocks! (Shem kicks weakly at her.) Shem! Fool! Arise! Thou art thy father's first born. (She pulls him protesting to his feet.) Do stand up and regain thy birthright from (she points to the altar) that dancer who plays on his harp of ram thews, and decks his brow with bay leaves. Come!

Shem (brightens) : How?

His wife: Did he not go into the tent and come away laughing at thy father's nakedness? Oh (she beats her breast) that I should live to see a father so mocked and shamed by his son to whom he has given all his vineyards! (She seizes a large skin from the ground.) Take this and cover him and tell him of the wickedness of thy brother.

Mrs. Japheth (arising takes hold of the skin also) : No, my husband shall also help to cover Noah,

our father. Did I not also hear? Think your Shem and his seed shall possess both flocks and vineyard while Japheth and his seed have only the fields? (She arouses Japheth, he stands.)

Shem: He shall share—

Mrs. Shem (impatiently) : Then go in (the women release the skin to the men) quickly, lest he wake sober, then will he not believe one word against Ham who needs only to smile to please him. (The men lay the skin across their shoulders and back over to the tent and cover Noah. They motion to leave him.)

Mrs. Shem: Go back, fools, and wake him. You have done but half.

(They turn and enter the tent and both shake Noah. He sits up and rubs his eyes. Mrs. Shem and Mrs. Japheth commence to weep ostentatiously).

Noah (peevishly) : Why do you disturb me, and why do the women weep? I thought all sorrow and all cause for weeping was washed away by the flood. (He is about to lie down again but the men hold him up.)

Shem: Hear, father, thy age has been scoffed, and thy nakedness made a thing of shame here in the midst of the feasting where all might know—thou the Lord of all under Heaven, hast been mocked.

Mrs. Shem: And we weep in shame, that thou our father should have thy nakedness uncovered before us.

Noah (struggling drunkenly to his feet) : Who, *who* has done this thing?

Mrs. Shem (timidly crosses and kneels before Noah) : We fear to tell thee, lord, lest thy love for the doer of this iniquity should be so much greater than the shame, that thou should slay us for telling thee.

Noah (swaying drunkenly) : Say it, woman, shall the lord of the Earth be mocked? Shall his nakedness be uncovered and he be shamed before his family?

Shem: Shall the one who has done this thing hold part of thy goods after thee? How wilt thou deal with them? Thou hast been wickedly shamed.

Noah: No, he shall have no part in my goods—his goods shall be parcelled out among the others.

Mrs. Shem: Thou art wise, father, thou art just!

Noah: He shall be accursed. His skin shall be black! Black as the nights, when the waters brooded over the Earth!

(Enter Mrs. Noah from tent, pauses by Noah.)

Mrs. Noah (catches him by the arm) : Cease! Whom dost thou curse?

Noah (shaking his arm free. The others also look awed and terrified and also move to stop him. All rush to him. Mrs. Noah attempts to stop his mouth with her hand. He shakes his head to free his lips and goes in a drunken fury) :

Black! He and his seed forever. He shall serve his brothers and they shall rule over him— Ah—Ah—. (He sinks again to the ground.

There is a loud burst of drunken laughter from behind the altar.)

Ham: Ha! Ha! I am as a young ram—Ha! Ha!

Mrs. Noah (to Mrs. Shem) : Whom cursed Noah?

Mrs. Shem: Ham—Ham mocked his age. Ham uncovered his nakedness, and Noah grew wrathful and cursed him. Black! He could not mean *black.* It is enough that he should lose his vineyards. (There is absolute silence for a while. Then realization comes to all. Mrs. Noah rushes in the tent to her husband, shaking him violently.)

Mrs. Noah (voice from out of the tent) : Noah! Arise! Thou art no lord of the Earth, but a drunkard. Thou hast cursed my son. Oh water, Shem! Japheth! Cold water to drive out the wine. Noah! (She sobs.) Thou must awake and unsay thy curse. Thou must! (She is sobbing and rousing him. Shem and Japheth seize a skin bottle from the ground by the skin door and dash off right. Mrs. Noah wails and the other women join in. They beat their breasts. Enter Eve through the tent. She looks puzzled.)

Mrs. Ham: Why do you wail? Are all not happy today?

Mrs. Noah (pityingly) : Come, Eve. Thou art but a child, a heavy load awaits thee. (Eve turns and squats beside her mother-in-law.)

Eve (carressing Mrs. Noah) : Perhaps the wine is too new. Why do you shake our father?

Mrs. Noah: Not the wine of grapes, but the wine of sorrow bestirs me thus. Turn thy comely face to the wall, Eve. Noah has cursed thy husband and his seed forever to be black, and to serve his brothers and they shall rule over him. (Re-enter the men with the water bottle running. Mrs. Noah seizes it and pours it in his face. He stirs.) See, I must awaken him that he may unspeak the curse before it be too late.

Eve: But Noah is drunk—surely Jehovah hears not a drunken curse. Noah would not curse Ham if he knew. Jehovah knows Noah loves Ham more than all. (She rushes upon Noah and shakes him violently.) Oh, awake thou (she shrieks) and uncurse thy curse. (All are trying to rouse Noah. He sits, opens his eyes wide and looks about him. Mrs. Noah carresses him.)

Mrs. Noah: Awake, my lord, and unsay thy curse.

Noah: I am awake, but I know of no curse. Whom did I curse?

Mrs. Noah and Eve: Ham, lord of the Earth. (He rises quickly to his feet and looks bewildered about.)

Japheth (falls at his feet) : Our father, and lord of all under Heaven, you cursed away his vineyards, but we do not desire them. You cursed him to be black—he and his seed forever, and that his seed shall be our servants forever, but we desire not their service. Unsay it all.

Noah (rushes down stage to the footlights, center. He beats his breast and bows his head to the ground.) Oh, that I had come alive out of my mother's loins! Why did not the waters of the flood bear me back to the deeps! Oh Ham, my son!

Eve (rushing down to him) : Unspeak the Curse! Unspeak the Curse!

Noah (in prayerful attitude) : Jehovah, by our covenant in this Valley, record not my curses on my beloved Ham. Show me once again the sign of covenant—the rainbow over the Vale of Ararat.

Shem (strikes his wife) : It was thou, covetous woman, that has brought this upon us.

Mrs. Shem (weeping) : Yes, I wanted the vineyards for thee, Shem, because at night as thou slept on my breast I heard thee sob for them. I heard thee murmur "Vineyards" in thy dreams.

Noah: Shem's wife is but a woman.

Mrs. Noah: How rash thou art, to curse unknowing in thy cups the son of thy loins.

Noah: Did not Jehovah repent after he had destroyed the world? Did He not make all flesh? Their evils as well as their good? Why did He not with His flood of waters wash out the evil from men's hearts, and spare the creatures He had made, or else destroy us all, *all?* For in sparing one, He has preserved all the wickedness that He creates abundantly, but punishes terribly. No, He destroyed them because vile as they were it was His handiwork, and it shamed and reproached Him night and day. He could not bear to look upon the thing He had done, so He destroyed them.

Mrs. Noah: Thou canst not question.

Noah (weeping) : Where is my son?

Shem (pointing) : Asleep behind the altar.

Noah: If Jehovah keeps not the covenant this time, if He spare not my weakness, then I pray that Ham's heart remains asleep forever.

Mrs. Shem (beseeching) : O Lord of the Earth, let his punishment be mine. We coveted his vineyards, but the curse is too awful for him. He is drunk like you—save him, Father Noah.

Noah (exultantly) : Ah, the rainbow! The promise! Jehovah will meet me! He will set His sign in the Heavens! Shem hold thou my right hand and Japheth bear up my left arm. (Noah approaches the altar and kneels. The two men raise his hands aloft.) Our Jehovah who carried us into the ark—

Sons: Victory, O Jehovah! The Sign.

Others (beating their breasts) : This is Thy Kingdom and we are here.

Noah: Who saved us from the Man of the Waters.

Sons: Victory, O Jehovah! The Sign.

Others: We belong to Thee, Jehovah, we belong to Thee.

(There is a sudden, loud raucous laugh from behind the altar. Ham sings brokenly, "I am a young ram in the Spring.")

Noah (hopefully) : Look! Look! To the mountain—do ye see colors appear?

Mrs. Noah: None but what our hearts paint for us—ah, false hope.

Noah: Does the sign appear, I seem to see a faint color just above the mountain. (Another laugh from Ham.)

Eve: None, none yet. (Beats her breast violently, speaks rapidly.) Jehovah, we belong to *Thee,* we belong to *Thee.*

Mrs. Noah and Eve: Great Jehovah! Hear us. We are here in Thy Valley. We who belong to Thee!

(Ham slowly rises. He stands and walks around the altar to join the others, and they see that he is black. They shrink back terrified. He is laughing happily. Eve approaches him timidly as he advances around the end of the altar. She touches his hand, then his face. She begins kissing him.)

Ham: Why do you all pray and weep?

Eve: Look at thy hands, thy feet. Thou art cursed black by thy Father. (She exits weeping left.)

Ham (gazing horrified at his hands): Black! (He appears stupified. All shrink away from him as if they feared his touch. He approaches each in turn. He is amazed. He lays his hand upon Shem.

Shem (shrinking): Away! Touch me not!

Ham (approaches his mother. She does not repel him, but averts her face.) Why does my mother turn away?

Mrs. Noah: So that my baby may not see the flood that hath broken the windows of my soul and loosed the fountains of my heart.

(There is a great clamor off stage and Eve re-enters left with her boy in her arms weeping and all the other children in pursuit jeering and pelting him with things. The child is also black. Ham looks at his child and falls at Noah's feet.

Ham (beseeching in agony): Why Noah, my father and lord of the Earth, why?

Noah (sternly): Arise, Ham. Thou art black. Arise and go out from among us that we may see thy face no more, lest by lingering the curse of thy blackness come upon all my seed forever.

Ham (grasps his father's knees. Noah repels him sternly, pointing away right. Eve steps up to Ham and raises him with her hand. She displays both anger and scorn.)

Eve: Ham, my husband, Noah is right. Let us go before you awake and learn to despise your father and your God. Come away Ham, beloved, come with me, where thou canst never see these faces again, where never thy soft eyes can harden by looking too oft upon the fruit of their error, where never thy happy voice can learn to weep. Come with me to where the sun shines forever, to the end of the Earth, beloved the sunlight of all my years. (She kisses his mouth and forehead. She crosses to door of tent and picks up a water bottle. Ham looks dazedly about him. His eyes light on the harp and he smilingly picks it up and takes his place beside Eve.

Ham (lightly cynical to all): Oh, remain with your flocks and fields and vineyards, to covet, to sweat, to die and know no peace. I go to the sun. (He exits right across the plain with his wife and child trudging beside him. After he is off-stage comes the strumming of the harp and Ham's voice happily singing: "I am as a young ram in the Spring." It grows fainter and fainter until it is heard no more. The sun is low in the west. Noah sits looking tragically stern. All are ghastly calm. Mrs. Noah kneels upon the altar facing the mountain and she sobs continually.

We belong to Thee, O Jehovah
We belong to Thee.

She keeps repeating this to a slow curtain).

CURTAIN

THIS PLACE

By DONALD JEFFREY HAYES

This is the place where strangers meet
And break a friendly bread
This is the place where the wanderer
May rest his weary head . . .

This is the place where songs are sung
Where winter's tales are told
This is the place for broken dreams
When they grow worn and old . . .

This is the place of As-You-Will
Come in—abide—depart
This is the place I offer you
This place—my heart. . . .

THREE POEMS

By COUNTEE CULLEN

SELF CRITICISM

Shall I go all my bright days singing,
  (A little pallid, a trifle wan)
The failing note still vainly clinging
  To the throat of the stricken swan?

Shall I never feel and meet the urge
  To bugle out beyond my sense
That the fittest song of earth is a dirge,
  And only fools trust Providence?

Than this better the reed never turned flute,
  Better than this no song,
Better a stony silence, better a mute
  Mouth and a cloven tongue.

A SONG NO GENTLEMAN WOULD SING TO ANY LADY

There are some things I might not know
Had you not pedagogued me so;
  And these I thank you for;
Now never shall a piquant face
Cause my tutored heart a trace
  Of anguish any more.

Before your pleasure made me wise,
A simulacrum of disguise
  Masked the serpent and the dove;
That I discern now hiss from coo,
My heart's full gratitude to you,
  Lady I had learned to love.

Before I knew love well I sang
Many a polished pain and pang,
  With proper bardic zeal;
But now I know hearts do not break
So easily, and though a snake
  Has made them wounds may heal.

EXTENUATION TO CERTAIN CRITICS

Cry Shame upon me if you must,
Shout Treason and Default,
Say I betray a sacred trust
Aching beyond this vault.
I'll bear your censure as your praise,
Yet never shall a clan
Confine my singing to its ways
Beyond the ways of man.

No racial option narrows grief;
Pain is no patriot;
And sorrow braids her dismal leaf
For all as lief as not.
With blind sheep groping every hill
Seeking an oriflamme,
What shepherd heart would keep its fill
For only the darker lamb?

NEW LIGHTS ON AN OLD SONG

By DOROTHY SCARBOROUGH

I WAS giving a lecture on Negro Folk Songs in Denison, Texas, and was speaking of my fondness for one which is my favorite among the spirituals. At the conclusion of the lecture, I boarded an inter-urban car to return to Dallas, when a young girl who had been sent from Sherman to interview me sat down beside me. In the course of our conversation she reported to me something that her brother, a missionary in Africa, had casually told her while he was at home on a recent furlough. It interested me so much that I asked her to write me a letter about it, in order that I might be sure of having the facts correctly fixed in my memory.

Here is her letter:

Sherman, Texas,
November 30, 1927.

Dear Dr. Scarborough:

Below is a brief account of the origin of "Swing Low, Sweet Chariot," for which you asked last evening on the Inter-urban.

My brother, who is a missionary in the Bokuba Kingdom, Couge Belge, Africa, relates that as he was "on the trail" one day in his hammock, the hammock boys began singing a song (in other language, of course, the tune of which was strangely familiar.)

He inquired of one of them, "Who taught you that song?"

"No one, chief. That song is as old as our tribe. It is a funeral dirge."

The tune was unmistakably that of "Swing Low, Sweet Chariot." It did not vary from the old Southern air in the slightest.

Under separate cover I am sending you a copy of my brother's little book "The Leopard Hunts Alone" of which I spoke. It is all too brief and contains only the suggestions of things he would have liked to say had he the opportunity. But maybe you will find in it a few facts of interest.

Sincerely yours,

(Signed) Catherine Wharton.

I mean to write to Mr. Wharton in the hope of finding out if he got the words of the dirge. I should like to know if the parallelism extends . . . to actual language, as well as to theme and melody.

Miss Wharton said that her brother told her that the Bokuba language had not been written down before the missionaries undertook the task, but that it is musical and well inflected. He has discovered in the tribal folk-lore a collection of fables which are almost identical with those of Aesop, and many stories similar to old Testament accounts.

Some skilled musician, trained in Negro folk-song, should go to Africa and make a study of native songs, with the thought of discovering how much relation there is between specific Negro folk-songs found in America and African music. The results of such research would be extremely valuable.

On the day after the letter reached me I visited the Booker T. Washington High School in Dallas, to hear the trained chorus of more than eight hundred voices sing a number of spirituals. Portia Washington Pittman is doing an admirable work in developing the musical talents of these young people, and in teaching them the value of their heritage of racial songs. I read the letter to the audience, and this daughter of Booker T. Washington expressed keen interest in this bit of information concerning the immemorial history of a song that everyone loves. I thought that others might like to know of it too.

59

LA PERLA NEGRA

By EDNA WORTHLEY UNDERWOOD

SAW her first in *El Teatro Nacional,* the splendid building which the Cubans erected in honor of their love of music and art, just as similarly luxurious buildings—equally sumptuous and satisfying to the eye—have been erected throughout the cities of South America.

It was in May and a night of grand opera. A new tenor of Mexican blood was going to try to initiate a lasting rivalry with Caruso, by his singing of the song of tears in "Pagliacci."

In that audience of beautiful women, whose jewelled *decolletage* was heightened by white shoulders that shone like satin, by the piled up splendor of curls that were blacker than ebony, I found her. She arose upon my field of vision slowly almost imperceptibly, as a great slow-sailing ship swings into sight upon the disconcerting levels of the sea. Or better, perhaps, I did not really *see* her, as that phrase is commonly understood, but instead I *became aware* of her, in the same way as in an art gallery a piece of silent marble impresses itself upon the senses.

She sat a few seats in front of me, swathed in dull, white, dotted lace. On this night of heat she wore a high collar that reached in points behind her ears. She wore long sleeves of the same material, whose points partly covered her hands. For the rest the dress was old-fashioned—a basque, tightly gripped at the waist, and a long draped skirt, flowing into a train; in fact the sort of dress that the great portrait painters of France were painting in 1860. Not a jewel, not a flower did she wear, and on this night of heat she did not use a fan. But what astonishing splendor of line! She represented *form* such as Fantin Latour loved.

A round, superbly poised head, whose short, waving hair was hidden in order not to cloud the outline. And she possessed the motionlessness, the nerveless repose of an animal.

In the intermission, when the audience arose—in friendly Spanish fashion—to go below to the club room for an ice, I saw her face. She was a pale, grey Negress, with the faultless body of an Attic marble, and eyes in which there was no mind, no soul, eyes that were the misty, mellow-green of absinthe. And those astonishing eyes were framed in lashes that made me think of black palm-plumes, when the pulse of the sea shakes them.

Her companion was as unusual as herself, an old, old man—a white man—well over seventy, and not a Spaniard. He was tall, faultlessly attired, evidently a great gentleman, upon whom the salon life of a polished people had set its seal. The only thing a trifle bizarre, perhaps, was the matched emeralds of extraordinary size that fastened his shirt.

During the first part of the opera I did not see her speak, nor pay the slightest attention to what he said to her. Down below in the clubroom where the world was enjoying wines and ices, she was equally silent and impassive. Even when distinguished friends of the old man gathered about them, not once did I see her speak. She merely looked with eyes limpid and green, green as degenerate emeralds are green, or sea-water in the cold north. But she was by far the most distinguished figure in this elegant and aristocratic assembly. She represented majesty of line, and the insolence of indolent youth.

60

Some nights later, in the crowded midnight parade upon the Prado, where all the races of the islands of the earth are mingled, under the languorous, yellow moon that hangs over seas, I saw them again. The old gentleman was making a pitiful attempt to hold himself erect, with the proud, easy exactness of youth. Beside him she walked—*La Perla Negra*—supple and sullen, walked like a panther. Tonight she wore grey lace the hue of her skin, and about her neck, ropes of pale green jade.

I wondered what she thought, what she busied herself with in her mind, she who not only never spoke, but who seemed not even to listen. Forgetful of proud Spanish etiquette, I addressed my nearest neighbor.

"Do you know who they are—that man and woman?"

"Why yes—of course! He is Monsieur X—," mentioning the name of a painter of Europe to whom the world had accorded honors for his art. "The woman is a Negress. He worships her for her beauty. He says that in the old days of his youth—in Paris—he created art. Now he is doing something different. He is living it. He spends his time in designing clothes for her. He dresses and redresses her like a doll. Day-long he feasts his eyes upon her, this living statue of grey marble. They live in that faded violet-tinted palace—in the great garden—not far from the Malecon."

Then this trembling old man was a modern Paris, still going on, on the ancient quest—Beauty. For it he had left home, country, fame, companionship, in his old age. What an artist was he who could feast upon it as upon a miraculous food, and live.

But what was all this for her? Was she happy? Was she contented? Had she any interests, any pleasures, any personality. Did she ever think? And if she did, of what? The great genius, the incredibly sensitive artist who lived beside her, what was he to her? Within her was there anything superior to the instinct for trickery of the savage?

In the early morning when I drove out to that surprising curve of blue water, which is called the Malecon, I passed their faded palace. She was walking in the garden and she wore apple-green and black. A figure in white linen was on the veranda. What subtlety of poetry, what penciled persistence of art was it, that made him dress her in coarse tinted laces, gauzes, and never in satin or silk? And what harmonies he achieved in these gowns he so busily planned! I drove on and forgot them, in looking at the old buildings that border the white, curving Malecon, buildings which, when super-imposed by distance, recalled to me vaguely Turner's "Palace of the Caesars."

The next morning, I drove to a beach outside the city, while yet the hour was early, and the tropic sun was kindly and not bitter. When I reached the beach and the blue haze of the ocean, I saw another car. The old artist, immaculate in white linen, was lounging in his limousine, while *La Perla Negra,* in a bathing suit of dull surfaced white silk, was in the water. Upon the wet, moulded silk the blue sea sent its shivers. She was a statue of the dead, antique world come back to life. Her body, however, was not that of the Greeks and Romans. Its racial heritage was different, but it was of a fineness equally great. The astonishing grey-whiteness of her skin was one that might not belong to a Caucasian race. By blending and interbreeding it had come up for slow generations from ancestors scattered among all the islands of these blue, disconcerting, magic seas.

I watched her swim far out, out where sailing vessels were, which black, greasy Negroes were loading. Sometimes their boat-songs the wind swept over to our ears. Their huge, brutal, semi-naked bodies were within eye-shot—and their gestures. At length he called to her to come back, somewhat impatiently it seemed, explaining that the sun was getting high, and that it was time to go within. As she stepped out of the water to walk toward the limousine, and came straight toward us, I saw a change in

59

her. The usually dull, cold eyes were blazing like the burnished levels of the sea. She moved with a great vigor, a great joy, as if in the depths of her soul, the fire of the morning burned. A waiting maid wrapped her hastily in a white robe of rough wool. As they started to drive away, she looked back again, toward the sea, threw her head back with a savage gesture as if freeing herself from something, and for the first time, I saw her laugh. Her laugh was unpleasant. It was cruel and wild.

Some weeks later I saw the old artist promenading alone at night upon the Prado. Again my curiosity got the better of me.

"Why is he alone?" I asked. "What has become of *La Perla Negra?*"

"Haven't you heard?"

"No. How could I?"

"It was in the paper."

"What paper?"

"La Prensa."

"I did not see it," I admitted regretfully.

"She ran away with a black Negro boatman—a regular Senegambian—to Haiti, the black man's paradise. She did not take any of her beautiful and expensive clothes. She was tired of them. She left them all. She went away bare footed, in a long, white, cotton shirt, just such as island Negresses wear.

"He was inconsolable for a while. Now he is picking up and declared that he is going to create again—paint again—become again the great artist that he was. He says, you can not live art and create art at the same time. He ought to know. He has given it a trial."

She had gone back to the wild undisciplined life of her race. She must have different things. She must have the heated dance under the stars—at night—and the fight that followed. She must feel hunger, discomfort and weariness. She must feel upon her faultless, grey-marble shoulders, the overseer's lash. She must burn up her youth, her beauty in a frenzy of feverish life; in toil, in the brittle dawn, by the edge of the cane fields. She must have the fierce things of her blood.

Not yet was the white man's life, with its weakening trivialities, for her.

She had escaped from that consuming disease which we call *civilization.*

THE NEGRO OF THE JAZZ BAND

(*Translated from the Spanish of José M. Salaverría*)

BY DOROTHY R. PETERSON

I DO not know thru what strange vagaries I was first induced into becoming an habitueé of that particular tea room, as with polite exaggeration it was called, and which, in reality, was no more than a modest eating place foundering along the extreme end of a cosmopolitan beach resort. The tea that they served there was tasteless. The only thing worthy of admiration was the name of the establishment, emblazoned in red letters on a large sign over the arched doorway: *At the Charm of Russia.*

Perhaps I responded to the call of the name or perhaps I had been attracted by the singularity of that deserted corner on the open coast. The fact is, however, that I began

63

61

to repeat my visits to that motley and scantily furnished eating house, which did indeed display in a quite picturesque manner, a series of promising symbols: flags, colored lanterns, huge crayon posters, cubist pictures and other like accessories. Everything tended to show that on that one spot there had been concentrated a small bit of modern Russia. The lure of advertising is so great that there were always to be found a few benevolent tourists who attended the "thé-dansants" which were held every afternoon in that paint daubed hall of *At the Charm of Russia*.

The charm reduced itself to a handful of girls who performed the duties of waitresses, attired in the costumes of Spanish peasant girls, and to a Jazz Band. This jazz band was far from thrilling. It was hardly more than mediocre. But it was sufficiently tuneful to lure some Spanish and French couples and a few stray Americans into the abandon of a fox trot or Charleston. As I never dance at all, I was limited merely to listening to the music of the jazz band which at times, does not fail to interest me. I was also entertained by the rhythmic and clownish gestures which the poor devils who made up the orchestra executed while playing. Particularly the Negro!

He was an authentic and magnificent Negro. That is, he was a completely black Negro, of an unmistakable and unredeemable black. He might have come forth from the very depths of the Guinea jungle. But no, his home was in the United States of North America, because at moments, when the tempo of the music so required, the Negro would utter some words in English, as a sort of refrain, while he manipulated the complicated hardware of which his instruments consisted, a bass drum, a kettle drum, a triangle, cymbals and even, I believe, a fog horn. And with his enormous mouth and thick red lips, the Negro knew how to intercalate at the proper and opportune moment, a series of delirious guffaws completely Negroesque in sound, and which to me, (why should I deny it?) were extremely pleasing. And the truth is that after repeatedly staring at him and studying him, I confess that I became completely fascinated by the Negro of the jazz band.

One night I happened to go for supper to a chop house nearby, where, altho nothing else seemed worthy of recommendation, they served a common variety of very delicious fish soup. Some foreigners, who had also discovered the secret of that marvellous soup á la Marseille, used to frequent the same chop house, which indeed offered few other comforts. On this night at a table next to mine sat a heavily built man. Suddenly the man turned and faced me, and I could not suppress a cry of surprise. The Negro from the jazz band!

But he was no longer a Negro. He was as white as you or I or anyone else. So great was my surprise that I exclaimed with incomprehensible naiveté:

"But, weren't you black this afternoon?"

This discovery of mine produced no pleasure on the other man. I realized it by his expression, the play of the muscles around his mouth, the whole gesture of repugnance. He repressed his annoyance, however, and made haste to answer me courteously:

"It is true that I was black this very afternoon, and now I am completely white. But the surprising part is your discovery of it. I flattered myself that I played my part better. . . ."

"And the flattery is well deserved. You may continue to believe that your dissembling is well done. You make up marvellously well as a Negro. But I am a writer and my habit of close observation has enabled me to pierce your disguise. My interest in writing has caused me to study your physique and your unusual gestures. You, yourself must realize that my curiosity is not difficult to understand, because after all, a man who disguises himself deliberately and intentionally as a Negro is not an everyday occurrence. It is easily comprehensible that one may wish to change his personality, but it is always in the sense of improvement, rather than in a debasing or lowering sense.

I could understand your pretending to the social status of a bankrupt Russian prince, but it is past my comprehension that you should be content to be black."

Then the man who wanted to be a Negro opened his heart to me, as they say, and began to unwind a skein of reflections that stupefied me.

Then listen, sir. At one time in my life I thought as you do. I believed that it was a man's duty to continue striving along an upward path in the pursuit of human perfection, continually striving to become more respected, more renowned and more powerful. It is that for which the majority of people strive, and that, in short, is what explains the progress of the human race. I, like others, aspired to become more. I also proposed to lift myself a few steps in the social scale and raise myself in rank and position. Here, where you see me, I have had conferred upon me the degree of Doctor of Laws; I prepared myself for the position of a political orator; I made my entry into politics; I was on the point of becoming an office-holder, a representative of the people; I even aspired for diplomatic appointment. No one can say that I did not do all that was humanly possible to further that ambition, which in its natural states, inspires man to the improvement and enhancement of his personality; but Luck seemed always against me! Finally, one day while I was smoking innumerable cigarettes close to a formidable Negro in a jazz band, (that one was undeniably a Negro) I conceived this unheard of idea. Why not? I could make as good a Negro as anyone else."

"And did you become easily resigned to this tragedy?"

"Of what tragedy are you speaking to me? There is no tragedy. On the contrary, as soon as I had converted myself into a Negro, I discovered that Life had assumed an aspect of ineffable facility. I was paid well and punctually, and the owners of the business, as well as the leaders of orchestras found it easier to get along with an intelligent Negro than with the ordinary Negro of the jazz band type. My disguise amused them. But no one has ever discovered my greatest disguise."

"Will you permit me to ask you?"

"Why certainly. You have made a certain sympathetic appeal to me and I am going to disclose to you my greatest secret. But do not imagine it to be any complicated nor prodigous mystery. It consists of reversing the whole tide of effort so that while everyone else is straining with all his might towards rising in the scale of Life, you, pretending unawareness, employ your strength, your intelligence and your entire resources in just "holding on." Do you understand? If, instead of "holding on", one wishes to lower his position, then the success is even more complete. Then Life becomes converted into perfect ease. Nothing upsets one, nothing presents difficulties. In a single word, one finds himself *dominating* Life, instead of, as in the case of most men, being dominated by Life. Life in its usual aspect is an overwhelming force! You, who are a writer, will have to confess that you find yourself inferior before your Art, and that the enormity of the difficulties in your Art grind you down, just as tho' the whole world were bearing all its weight upon your life. Imagine, if you can, the sense of liberty and of ease which you would feel, if, with all your present knowledge and experience, you should decide to engage in a very humble trade. The world would say that you had "lowered" yourself, descended in the social scale. But no—you would then be master of your life and of your work, just as now you are the servant of your life and of your Art. But I fear that I have not given you sufficiently convincing arguments. . . ."

"Frankly,—I do not enthuse greatly over the gift of the secret which you have disclosed to me. The disguise of one's own personality somewhat disgusts me."

"Why? since everyone disguises his own personality—since everything is a lie. The point is that other people disguise themselves under a mask of superiority—they falsify in order to be something more. And so their lies are more blameworthy than mine. The world is a marketplace of falsefaces. The rabble pretend to be noble, the fools wise, the blackguards honest, and so on. For a few months I lived surrounded by circus people, people who practiced deliberate pretense, and I look upon that period as perhaps the best of my life. My side partner, a pretty blond girl, both young and sweet dispositioned, did the part of "wild woman" in one of the side shows of the circus. There was nothing at all wild about her, not even in her character. An intimate friend of mine, whom I loved as a brother, did the "strongest man in the world" stunt and made a great deal of money by lifting bodily—weights of 100 kilos, which in point of fact weighed scarcely 12 pounds. I myself was made up as a Negro. And I assure you that behind our disguises and our reversed personalities we lived extremely well; not only happy but with an interest in Life.

"And how did that little partnership of 'pretenders' dissolve?"

"In a quite natural manner. My friend, the one whom I loved as a brother, ran away with the girl who was my partner and that ended our happy little partnership."

On hearing such a humorous ending to this sentimental episode, I could not refrain from bursting out laughing and then I exclaimed:

"You see, your system sometimes fails."

The counterfeit Negro hastened to interrupt me.

"No, the system has not failed. It was I who had failed to apply the system. I was to blame for everything. And my mistake lay precisely in the fact that I had forgotten for the moment the essential nature of the system. I became too ambitious. I wished to possess for myself alone a lovely, young and charming woman—which plan would coincide with the scheme of aspiring to something better. I had aspired to be loved alone—loved for myself—and that was already too much. Cured finally by self-chastisement, I have not again been negligent. Since then, in love as in everything else, I practice my disguise, my pretence, by abasing myself, and I go off to look for those humbler caresses which are within reach of the whole community. . . ."

I was thoroughly stunned, when confronted by that intelligent man who was constructing for his own use and mortification, so strange and dispiriting a philosophy of life. But he gave no signs of being discouraged. The following afternoon I went to take tea again at the picturesque salon of *At the Charm of Russia,* and there stood my Negro. He seemed blacker than ever in the midst of his horrible set of instruments; and his guttural guffaws, I might say, were still more Senegalese and raucous than on other afternoons. He crossed a wink of understanding with me, and then made a valiant attack on the cymbals. . . . I left the tea room almost immediately and since then I have never seen him again. Who knows in what obscure corners of our planet, the tide of his extravagant destiny may have swept him!

IDOLATRY

By ARNA BONTEMPS

You have been good to me, I give you this:
The arms of lovers empty as our own,
Marble lips sustaining one long kiss
And the hard sound of hammers breaking stone.

For I will build a chapel in the place
Where our love died and I will journey there
To make a sign and kneel before your face
And set an old bell tolling on the air.

To
CLARISSA SCOTT DELANY

By Angelina W. Grimke

1

She has not found herself a hard pillow
    And a long hard bed,
A chilling cypress, a wan willow
    For her gay young head . . .
    These are for the dead.

2

Does the violet-lidded twilight die
    And the piercing dawn
And the white clear moon and the night-blue sky. . .
    When they are gone?

3

Does the shimmering note
In the shy, shy throat
Of the swaying bird?

4

O, does children's laughter
Live not after
It is heard?

5

Does the dear, dear shine upon dear, dear things,
In the eyes, on the hair,
On waters, on wings . . .
Live no more anywhere?

6

Does the tang of the sea, the breath of frail flowers,
    Of fern crushed, of clover,
Of grasses at dark, of the earth after showers
    Not linger, not hover?

7

Does the beryl in tarns, the soft orchid in haze,
The primrose through tree-tops, the unclouded jade
Of the north sky, all earth's flamings and russets and grays
    Simply smudge out and fade?

8

And all loveliness, all sweetness, all grace,
All the gay questing, all wonder, all dreaming,
They that cup beauty that veiled opaled vase,
Are they only the soul of a seeming?

9

O, hasn't she found just a little, thin door
And passed through and closed it between?
O, aren't those her light feet upon that light floor,
. . . That her laughter? . . . O, doesn't she lean
As we do to listen? . . . O, doesn't it mean
    She is only unseen, unseen?

"The lynx says, 'I am fleet of foot,'
But the plains say, 'We are wide'."
—*An African Proverb.*

A Mezzo-Tint from a Painting by
P. VAN DYK DEL
—*Courtesy of Arthur A. Schomburg.*

JUAN LATINO, MAGISTER LATINUS

(From the Journal of the search in Spain for fragments of Negro Life.)

By ARTHUR A. SCHOMBURG

OR several hours the snow capped mountain top of the Sierra Nevada was plainly visible as we journeyed onward and upward on the Rosinante express toward the city of Granada. The train came to a full stop. We landed, passed through a veritable bedlam and picked from the hotel agents a resting place more for the name than for its known comforts. After resting we walked to the University grounds, saw the closed gates and walls kalsomined so often that the layers in sections were peeling off. It was dusk and there was a pastoral quiet. We retraced our steps through narrow highways and alleys to the Cathedral. Some form of religious ceremony was on. The voices and the silvery tones from the organ filled the vaulted edifice with a vast religious fervor. People here and there prayed to their favorite saints; others like myself curiously contemplated the solemnity and grandeur of the place. Through the warm colors of the stained and figured glasses light poured in like a flood. We walked up the threadbare steps to the great organ, passing a small urchin pumping air into the bellows as many others have done year on year.

Here in a grilled enclosure were the sarcophagi of Ferdinand and Isabella, who aided Columbus' discovery of America. There they were, amid their pomp and circumstance, seemingly enjoying the perfect even if endless night. And finally, again to the University. I was seeking facts and information on the life of Juan Latino, the Negro who held a professorship at the University as early as 1550. The secretary informed me that Professor Ocete had written a thesis on his life as partial fulfilment for his doctorate degree in philosophy and that he would be glad to introduce me to this man, the holder of the chair of paleontology. Meantime the secretary introduced me to the librarian and I had the great joy of seeing a copy of Juan Latino's own book on the library shelf of his alma mater.

An attendant brought me before Catedratico Ocete and I was invited into his study, where I explained my mission to Granada. I recited the hearsay of my school days when persons remarked that so and so wasn't as *Lati*—taken from the verse that alludes to Latino in Cervantes' "Don Quijote de la Mancha." I had crossed the Atlantic because I was personally satisfied that there was no better place to uncover this information than in Latino's own home and under his own vine and figtree. After my recital, the learned Professor pulled open the drawer of his desk and brought forth a small quarto volume which on inspection was the brochure already alluded to by the secretary of the University. It was an exhaustive research, gathered from fragmentary facts, and buttressed with trustworthy references.

Later he produced an early copy of Latino's work from the Granada University Library, a copy similar to the one in the series which the Ticknor collection of Spanish Literature possessed, but vastly more beautiful in comparison.

What a wonderful city, the Moors called it Paradise Valley, rich with a mellow history and hidden far away up in the foothills of the Sierra Nevada mountains.

Here in Granada during those stormy days when the Abderraman kings were lords of all they surveyed, there were among the people many undiluted black men. It was my pleasure to walk leisurely through and admire the spacious avenue named after the *Gran Capitan* and recall that he was the father of the master of Juan Latino, to pass by the street where his slave lived, the school house and Royal College where he was a tutor, the church where he knelt in humility to his real Master, where he was married to Dona Ana de Carlobar, where his children were baptized, and where eventually after life's task, he was buried in St. Ann's Church.

It is a pleasure to refer to Professor Ocete's monograph *"El Negro Juan Latino Biographical and Critical Essay"* (Granada 1925, 4 to 94 pp.). I view it with a keen desire to see the booklet translated into the English language to help stimulate our own men by the life and services this eminent man has left to posterity.

Catedratico Antonio Marin Ocete of the faculty of the University of Granada is a very charming young man, whose indefatigable knowledge is highly reflected by this work. If we accept, as we cannot otherwise do, the full explanation of our author, it is not illogical to suppose that the docks of Sevilla one day received Catino with his mother, and surely when he was of tender age. To affirm this Ocete begins by denying as notoriously false the affirmation of Salazar that he came to Spain when in his twelfth year. When we study him at close range, what is strange to his personality is the complete adaptation to so distinctly different an environment, the perfect formation of his character and intelligence in plain civilization to reach the height not only of a cultured man but a sage, having a perfect knowledge of languages and classical literature. An eminent master and above all a Latin poet extraordinarily fruitful. Only by his living there from birth under most promising cir-

69

cumstances can we explain it and yet admire such surprising results. Thus it must have been when mother and son were bought by a trafficker who sold them at Baena at the castle owned by the Count de Cabra, Don Luis Fernando de Cordoba and his wife Dona Elvira, only daughter of the Grand Capitan where he played during his infancy with the son of the Duke Don Gonzalo. He was known when a boy by the name of Juan de Sesa, a musician of ability, singer, organist, a player of the lute and the harp. As he grew to manhood his silence and strict application to details were noted; he helped his master's son both with his personal duties and in his studies. The son found in his black companion an apt and intelligent fellow. In time the master rewarded his charge and sent him to the same University where his son won his academic degree. Juan Sesa was afterwards known as Latino who has written his thanks "cum ipso a rudibus omnibus liberaribus artibus institutos et doctus."

Charles V, the instigator and founder of the University of Granada afterward opened by the Archbishop Hernando de Talavera by Bull and Pastoral Letter from Pope Clement VII was received on July 14th, 1531, conferring the same rights and privileges granted previously to the universities of Bologna, Paris and Salamanoa. In the *MSS* book of sermons of Rector Nicholas de la Rosa, it is stated Juan Latino received his B. A. during the year 1546, before the Archbishop, the Chancillor, the Count of Tendilla and many other gentlemen. His age was about twenty-eight. It is grateful to commend Ocete for having successfully located the minutes having the entry of the thirty-nine candidates who received their degree in "artium et philosphie facultate sub disciplina Rvdi. Dmi magistri Benedicte peco" it was duly signed by the learned dignitaries who were empowered by Royal Decree to examine candidates, and attested by the notary Johan de Frias and entered in Book No. 1 de Claustros folio 110.

The year Latino graduated (1546) from the University Archbishop Pedro Guerrero had taken possession of the See, and gave him decided protection, influenced his page, Carlobal, to desist from opposing the Negro for having married his sister, and contrived through his friend the Duke of Sesa that the servitude of the Negro should terminate. When the chair of Latin of the Sacred Cathedral Church School was vacant due to the death of the master Mota, he decided to place his candidate in the person of Juan Latino. As soon as the vacancy became known there was no end of learned men who were aspirants for the honor. On the 8th of August, 1556, while the Cathedral canons were in session licentiate Villanueva entered and said he knew there was a vacancy in the Royal College and it was not proper to let Juan Latino have it when there were so many priests who could fill the position. The Archbishop was inflexible to the undercurrents of opposition and at the beginning of the year the very reverend Pedro de Vivero, Dean

of the Sacred Church and Rector of the University named Juan Latino for the chair of Latin Grammar. Professor Ocete states that notwithstanding the fact noted in the printed work of Latino where he is put down as holding a chair in the University, the item is wrong because no such office existed. An exhaustive examination of the documents available only shows him to have filled the office noted in the Royal College. Opposition continued because Latino was only an ordinary bachelor of arts, but when on November 31st, 1556 he was granted his Master of Arts, all seemed to be smooth sailing. The Royal College was a building erected beside the University and next to the Archepiscopal palace. Here was to be seen in those days familiar faces of well known students, ecclesiastical dignitaries, acolytes, Moorish persons, grave and lettered young men, attracted by the fame of a foreign master—a Negro who graced his chair—the equal of the best of his epoch.

The celebration of the feast of St. Lucar was one of the three principal events of Granada—the Rector, the Chancillor, doctors, licentiates of the University and the students from all the colleges were present on this occasion to hear the address "quam principium appellare solent" from the lips of Juan Latino, *Magister Latinus.*" "It is to be regretted, says Ocete, "that this Latin oration delivered this day, unforgetable, when all Granda turned out spontaneously to hear him and tender a charming demonstration of respect and admiration, has not reached us, for I believe this example of his prose promised a free style more elegant than his verses."

The learned Ocete in a comparative illustration on letters and philosophy of Europe through the humanists F. A. Wolf of Cottigen and C. O. Muller of Berlin says "After three centuries the minds of these men reached the same conclusion of the Spanish grammarians, with which in some way or other Juan Latino was much concerned."

Latino was a most remarkable individual. Through his own efforts against all prejudice—during his period of servitude in the ducal home of his master until his marriage with a lady of quality—he became a distinguished person in Granada. When he finished his studies he climbed to the first and highest professorship in the Royal College. His further studies brought him to higher esteem since he was, in his day, the best versed in the knowledge of classical antiquity and ancient languages, which he knew perfectly well. During his famous lifetime he published three tomes of Latin verses. Through his influence a generation of original authors and translators were developed that gave birth to the Poetical School of Granada.

Don Juan de Austria the natural son of Philip II upon his triumphal entry into the city of Granada was carried away with the epigrammatic inscriptions that adorned the arches erected to commemorate the defeat of the Turks at the battle of Lepanto. The poems were the work of Juan Latino the *Magister Latinus.* It is noted that frequently

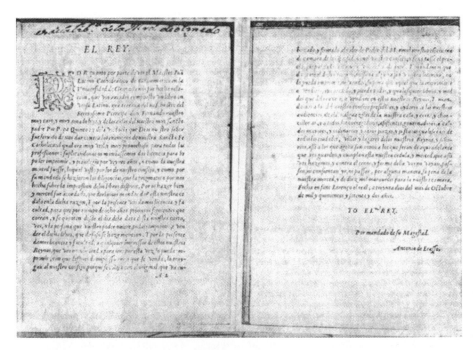

Facsimile

Privilege to print the first book of poetry by a Negro granted by the King of Spain at San Lorenzo the 30th day of October, 1572.

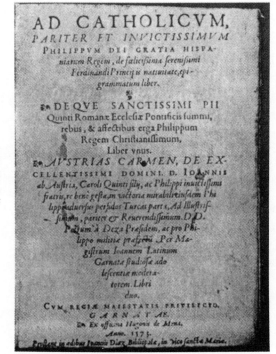

at the table of the Prince were seated two Negroes, Juan Latino was one and priest Christopher de Meneses of the Order of Santo Domingo stationed at Granada, was the other. It is said Don Juan de Austria found great pleasure in the company of these two men whose witticism and literature made them welcome guests at his festive board.

I had the pleasure of examining Latino's other two books of Latin verses at the National Library at Madrid through the courtesy of the Director. The poetical works of this writer and scholar are represented by three tomes. The first was printed by Hugo de Mena in Granada during the year 1573, is eulogistic and deals with the birth of the Prince, with the marriage of Philip II to Mary of Portugal, and with their son who was born in the year 1571, the presumptive heir to the throne named Fernando, whose birth Granada celebrated with joy. Juan Latino who was the local poet, wrote epigrammatic verses for the occasion. The poems on the Pope and the city during his times are also included in this tome.

His poem on the "Austradis libri duo" is an epic poem on the battle of Lepanto and it is the first printed work of the kind to commemorate the naval victory. It is pleasing to read the critical judgment of Ocete on the poetical merit of this obscure writer. "The arduous task has given ample proof of the author's facility to express himself, not a defective verse nor an incorrect description, when the inspiration does not shine the interest lags, yet the form is impeccable. Without doubt, from among his works this is worthy of modern re-printing. Perhaps this may be premature but when our humane culture is more elevated, a discreet selection

from among his poems, if not all, will be read with pleasure and delight. Not a word more nor an idea less, the verses are exact and precise, like fine steel with all the strength yet with all ductibility and often with inspiration without artifices to give exact tone, measure and softness, but awfully real, the idea of death. The whole book can be summed up as the work of a historian who was also a poet."

His second volume of Latin verses was written to lament in panegyrics the re-burial services on the occasion of the transmittal of the royal bodies to the Pantheon erected by Philip II and known as the Monastery of the Escorial. In this work our author included the epitaphs composed for the tablets and other objects used to convey the remains in pomp from Granada. This work was printed during the year 1576.

In his third and last volume, he devoted his pen exclusively to sing the praises of the ducal house of Sesa Don Gonzalo Fernandez de Cordoba. It was his personal tribute to the house that gave him all he received. He wished to let the world know his benefactors. The imprint bears the year 1585 and the only known copy is at Madrid.

There is pleasant satisfaction to know that in the pages of Spanish literature the name of Juan Latino will be further enhanced and remembered through the excellent work of Antonio Marin Ocete, quite unlike Sir William Maxwell-Stirling who in his life of Don Juan de Austria and George Ticknor, who in his "History of Spanish Literature" (Vol. III, p. 492, N. Y. 1869) have delegated the volumes of the Latin scholar to a foot-note in their respective monumental works.

AND ONE SHALL LIVE IN TWO

By JONATHAN H. BROOKS

Though he hung dumb upon her wall
And was so very still and small—
A miniature, a counterpart,
Yet did she press him to her heart
On countless, little loving trips,
And six times pressed him to her lips!
As surely as she kissed him six,
As sure as sand and water mix,
Sure as canaries sweetly sing,
And lilies come when comes the spring,
The two have hopes for days of bliss
When four warm lips shall meet in kiss;
Four eyes shall blend to see as one,
Four hands shall do what two have done,
Two sorrow-drops will be one tear—
And one shall live in two each year.

Sebastian Gomez was known as the "Mulatto de Murillo." During his earlier life, he was a slave purchased to grind the pigments for the colors used by the great master. His talent was discovered by Murillo and he was freed to become a pupil. For nearly a hundred years certain of the paintings of this Negro of Spain were mistaken for those of Murillo.

"JESUS TIED TO A COLUMN"   *By Sebastian Gomez*

This picture came from the Convent of the Cupuchinos. Brother Fray Angel de Leon claims it is this painter's work in his first historical book where most notable events in the convent of San Francisco of Sevilla are noted.

71

"THE SACRED FAMILY"

By Sebastian Gomez

In the Treasury Room of
the Basilica of Sevilla.

"IMMACULATE CONCEPTION"

By Sebastian Gomez

In the possession of an antiquarian in the city of Sevilla.

"THE IMMACULATE CONCEPTION"   *By Sebastian Gomez*

In the Museo Provincial de Sevilla, Spain.

TEMPLE DOOR

ZOUENOULA MASK, 14TH CENTURY

From the Barnes
Foundation Collection
of African Art

Courtesy of Dr. Albert C. Barnes

74

An

ELEGY,

To Miſs. Mary Moorhead,

On the DEATH of her Father,

The Rev. Mr. JOHN MOORHEAD.

INVOLV'D in Clouds of Wo, *Maria* mourns,
And various Anguiſh wracks her Soul by turns;
See thy lov'd Parent languiſhing in Death,
His Exit watch, and catch his flying Breath;
"Stay happy Shade," diſtreſs'd *Maria* cries; 5
"Stay happy Shade," the hapleſs Church replies;
"Suſpend a while, ſuſpend thy rapid flight,
"Still with thy Friendſhip, chear our mental Night,
"The ſullen Night of Error, Sin, and Pain;
"See Earth aſtoniſh'd at the Loſs, complain;" 10
Thine, and the Church's Sorrows I deplore;
Moorhead is dead, and Friendſhip is no more;
From Earth ſhe flies, nor mingles with our Wo,
Since cold the Breaſt, where once ſhe deign'd to glow;
Here ſhone the heavenly Virtue, there conteſt'd, 15
Celeſtial Love, reign'd joyous in his Breaſt;
Till Death grown jealous for his dreer Domain,
Sent his dread Offspring, unrelenting Pain,
With haſty Wing, the Son of *Terror* flies,
Leſt *Moorhead* find the Portal of the Skies; 20
Without a Paſſage through the Shades below,
Like great *Elijah*, Death's triumphant Foe,
Death follows faſt, nor leaves the Prophet long,
His Eyes are ſeal'd, and every Nerve unſtrung;
Forever ſilent is the ſtirring Clay, 25
While the rapt Soul, explores the Realms of Day.
Oft has he ſtrove to raiſe the Soul from Earth,
Oft has he travail'd in the heavenly Birth;
Till *Jesus* took poſſeſſion of the Soul,
Till the new Creature liv'd throughout the whole. 30
When fierce conviction laid the ſinner's Mind,
The Law-loud thundering he to Death conſign'd;
Jehovah's Wrath revolving, he ſurveys,
The Fancy's terror, and the Soul's amaze.
Say, what is Death? The Gloom of endleſs Night, 35
Which from the Sinner, bars the Gates of Light;
Say, what is Hell? In Horrors painful throng;
His Vengeance views, who feel his laſt Change;
The winged Hours, that find Judgment brings,
Decides his Fate, and that of Gods and Kings; 40
Tremendous Doom! And dreadful to be told,
To dwell in Tophet 'ſtead of ſhrines of Gold.
"Gods! Ye ſhall die like Men," the Herald cries,
"And fill'd no more the Children of the Skies."
Trembling he ſees the horrid Gulf appear, 45
Creation quakes, and no Deliverer near;
With Heart relenting to his Feelings kind,
See *Moorhead* haſten to relieve his Mind;
He paints the Anguiſh of his tortur'd Heart,
He points the trembling Mountain, and the Tree, 50
Which bent beneath th' incarnate Deity,
How God deſcended, wonderous to relate,
To bear our Crimes, a dread enormous Weight;
Seraphic ſtrains too feeble to repeat,
Half the dread Puniſhment this Godhead meet, 55
ſuſpended there, (till Heaven was reconcil'd,)
Like *Moſes'* Serpent in the Deſert wild.
The Myſt'ry appear'd what new Dominion given,
With Joy unknown, the raptur'd Soul o'erflows;
While on his Cross-like Savior's Glory bent, 60
His Life proves witneſs of his Heart's intent,
Lament ye lodgers the Friendly Mind,
Which oft relented, to your Miſery kind,
With humble Gratitude un remain'd Praiſe,
To Him whoſe Spirit had inſpir'd his Lays; 65
To Him whoſe Goodneſs gave his Words to flow,
Divine attention, and the Balm of Wo;
To you his Offspring, and his Church, be given,
A triple Portion of his Thirſt for Heaven,
Such was the Prophet, we the Stroke deplore, 70
Which heſh'd hear his warning Voice no more.
But ceaſe complaining, huſh each murm'ring Tongue,
Pursue the Example which inſpires my ſong,
Let his Example to your Conduct ſhine;
Own the all-ruling Providence, divine; 75
So ſhall bright Periods grace your jovial Days,
And heavenly Anthems ſwell your ſongs of Praiſe.

Boſton, December 15, 1773.

Phillis Wheatley.

Printed from the Original Manuſcript, and Sold by WILLIAM M'ALPINE, at his Shop in *Marlborough-Street*, 1773.

A little known poem by Phillis Wheatley, not included in her collected poems.

TO A GENTLEMAN, ON HIS VOYAGE TO GREAT BRITAIN FOR THE RECOVERY OF HIS HEALTH

By PHILLIS WHEATLEY

While others chant of gay Elysian scenes,
Of balmy zephyrs, and of flowery plains,
My song, more happy, speaks a golden name,
Feels higher motives and a nobler flame
For thee, O, R——, the muse attunes her strings,
And mounts sublime above inferior things.
I sing not now of green embowering woods—
I sing not now the daughters of the floods—
I sing not of the storms o'er ocean driven,
And how they howled along the waste of heaven:
But I to R—— would paint the British shore,
And vast Atlantic, not untried before.
Thy life impaired commands thee to arise,
Leave these bleak regions and inclement skies,
Where chilling winds return the Winter past,
And nature shudders at the furious blast.

O, then, stupendous, earth-enclosing main,
Exert thy wonders to the world again!
If e'er thy power prolonged the fleeting breath,
Turned back the shafts, and mocked the gates of death
If e'er thine air dispensed a healing power,
Or snatched the victim from the fatal hour,—
His equal care demands thy equal care,
And equal wonders may this patient share
But unavailing—frantic—is the dream
To hope thine aid without the aid of Him
Who gave thee birth, and taught thee where to flow,
And in thy waves his various blessings show.

May R—— return to view his native shore
Replete with vigor not his own before:
Then shall we see with pleasure and surprise,
And own thy work, great Ruler of the skies!

(The fervent wish of the gentle Phillis was not granted. The subject of her invocation died in Bristol, England, soon after his arrival, about the year 1778. Mr. Ricketson has helped us to determine the date of the poem. The above poem was located in Daniel Ricketson's "History of New Bedford," New Bedford, 1858, 8vo, 412 pages, at page 253).

76

IGNATIUS SANCHO
A mezzo-tint from a painting by Gainsborough

FRANCIS BARBER
From a painting by Sir Joshua Reynolds

A drawing by Charles Cullen

The Runaway Slave at Piligrim's Point

By *ELIZABETH BARRETT BROWNING*

I.

stand on the mark, beside the shore,
  Of the first white pilgrim's bended knee;
Where exile changed to ancestor,
  And God was thanked for liberty.
I have run through the night—my skin is as dark—
  I bend my knee down on this mark—
I look on the sky and the sea.

II.

O, pilgrim-souls, I speak to you:
  I see you come out proud and slow
From the land of the spirits, pale as dew,
  And round me and round me ye go.
O, pilgrims, I have gasped and run
  All night long from the whips of one
Who in your names works sin and woe!

III.

And thus I thought that I would come
  And kneel here where ye knelt before,
And feel your souls around me hum
  In undertone to the ocean's roar;
And lift my black face, my black hand,
  Here in your names, to curse this land
Ye blessed in Freedom's heretofore.

IV.

I am black, I am black,
  And yet God made me, they say:
But if He did so—smiling back
  He must have cast his work away
Under the feet of His white creatures
  With a look of scorn, that the dusky features
Might be trodden again to clay.

V.

And yet He has made dark things
  To be glad and merry as light;
There's a little dark bird sits and sings;
  There's a dark stream ripples out of sight;
And the dark frogs chant in the safe morass,
  And the sweetest stars are made to pass
O'er the face of the darkest night.

81

VI.

But we who are dark, we are dark!
    O God, we have no stars!
About our souls, in care and cark,
    Our blackness shuts like prison-bars!
And crouch our souls so far behind,
    That never a comfort can they find,
By reaching through their prison bars.

VII.

Howbeit God's sunshine and His frost
    They make us hot, they make us cold,
As if we were not black and lost;
    And the beasts and birds in wood and wold,
Do fear us and take us for very men;—
    Could the whipporwill or the cat of the glen
Look into my eyes and be bold?

VIII.

I am black, I am black,
    And once I laughed in girlish glee;
For one of my color stood in the track
    Where the drivers' drove, and looked at me;
And tender and full was the look he gave!
    A Slave looked so at another Slave,—
I look at the sky and the sea.

IX.

And from that hour our spirits grew
    As free as if unsold, unbought;
We were strong enough, since we were two,
    To conquer the world, we thought.
The drivers drove us day by day:
    We did not mind; we went one way,
And no better a liberty sought.

X.

In the open ground between the canes,
    He said "I love you" as he passed
When the shingle-roof rang sharp with the rains,
    I heard how he vowed it fast,
While other trembled, he sat in the hut
    And carved me a bowl of the cocoa-nut
Through the roar of the hurricanes.

XI.

I sang his name instead of a song;
    Over and over I sang his name.
Backward and forward I sung it along,
    With my sweetest notes, it was still the same!
But I sang it low, that the slave-girls near
    Might never guess, from what they could hear,
That all the song was a name.

XII.

I look on the sky and the sea!
We were two to love, and two to pray,—
Yes, two, O God, who cried on Thee,
Though nothing didst thou say,
Coldly thou sat'st behind the sun,
And now I cry, who am but one,—
Thou wilt not speak to-day!

XIII.

We were black, we were black,
We had no claim to love and bliss—
What marvel, ours was cast to wrack?
They wrung my cold hands out of his—
They dragged him—why, I crawled to touch
His blood's mark in the dust—not much,
Ye pilgrim—souls,—though plain as THIS!

XIV

Wrong, followed by a greater wrong!
Grief seemed too good for such as I;
So the white men brought the shame ere long
To stifle the sob in my throat thereby.
They would not leave me for my dull
Wet eyes!—it was too merciful
To let me weep pure tears, and die.

XV.

I am black, I am black!
I wore a child upon my breast,—
An amulet that hung too slack,
And, in my unrest, could not rest!
Thus we went moaning, child and mother,
One to another, one to another,
Until all ended for the best.

XVI.

For hark! I will tell you low—low—
I am black, you see;
And the babe, that lay on my bosom so,
Was far too white—too white for me,
As white as the ladies who scorned to pray
Beside me at the church but yesterday,
Though my tears had washed a place for my knee.

XVII.

And my own child—I could not bear
   To look in his face, it was so white;
So I covered him up with a kerchief rare,
   I covered his face in, close and tight!
And he moaned and struggled as well as might be,
   For the white child wanted his liberty,—
Ha, ha! he wanted his master's right.

XVIII

He moaned and beat with his head and feet—
   His little feet that never grew!
He struck them out as it was meet
   Against my heart to break it through.
I might have sung like a mother mild,
   But I dared not sing to the white faced child
The only song I knew.

XIX.

And yet I pulled the kerchief close;
   He could not see the sun, I swear,
More then, alive, than now he does
   From between the roots of the mangles-where?
I know where!—close! a child and mother
   Do wrong to look at one another
When one is black and one is fair.

XX.

Even in that single glance I had
   Of my child's face,—I tell you all,—
I saw a look that made me mad,—
   The master's look, that used to fall
On my soul like his lash,—or worse,—
   Therefore, to save it from my curse,
I twisted it round in my shawl.

XXI.

And he moaned and trembled from foot to head,—
   He shivered from head to foot,—
Till after a time, he lay, instead,
   Too suddenly still and mute;
And I felt, beside, a creeping cold,—
   I dared to lift up just a fold,
As in lifting a leaf of the mango fruit.

XXII.

But my fruit! ha, ha!—there had been
  (I laugh to think on 't at this hour!)
Your fine white angels,—who have been
  God secret nearest to His power,—
And gathered my fruit to make them wine,
  And sucked the soul of that child of mine,
As the humming-bird sucks the soul of the flower.

XXIII.

Ha, ha! for the trick of the angels white!
  They freed the white child's spirit so;
I said not a word but day and night
  I carried the body to and fro;
And it lay on my heart like a stone—as chill;
  The sun may shine out as much as he will,—
I am cold, though it happened a month ago.

XXIV.

From the white man's house and the black man's hut,
  I carried the little body on;
The forest's arms did around us shut,
  And silence through the trees did run!
They asked no questions as I went,—
  They stood too high for astonishment,—
They could see God rise on his throne.

XXV.

My little body kerchief fast,
  I bore it on through the forest—on—
And when I felt it was tired at last,
  I scooped a hole beneath the moon.
Through the forest-tops the angels far,
  With a white fine finger in every star
Did point and mock at what was done.

XXVI.

Yet when it all was done aright,
  Earth twixt me and my baby strewed,—
All changed to black earth,—nothing white—
  A dark child in the dark.—ensued
Some comfort, and my heart grew young;
  I sat down smiling there, and sung
The song I told you of for good.

XXVII.

And there we two were reconciled,
  The white child and black mother, thus;
For, as I sang it,—soft and wild,
  The same song, more melodious,
Rose from the grave whereon I sat!
  It was the dead child singing that,
To join the souls of both of us.

XXVIII.

I look on the sea and the sky!
  Where the Pilgrims' ships first anchored lay,
The great sun rideth gloriously!
  But the Pilgrims' ghosts have slid away
Through the first faint streaks of the morn!
  My face is black, but it glares with a scorn
Which they dare not meet by day.

XXIX.

Ah! in their stead their hunter—sons!
  Ah, ah! they are on me! they form in a ring!
Keep off—I brave you all at once,—
  I throw off your eyes like a noisome thing!
You have killed the black eagle at nest, I think;
  Did you ever stand still in your triumph, and shrink
From the stroke of her wounded wing?

XXX.

(Man, drop that stone you dared to lift!)
  I wish you, who stand there, seven abreast,
Each for his own wife's grace and gift,
  Little corpse as safely at rest,
Hid in the mangles! Yes, but she
  May keep like babies on her knee,
And sing the song she liketh best.

XXXI.

I am not mad,—I am black!
  I see you staring in my face,—
I know you staring, shrinking back,—
  Ye are born of the Washington race!
And this land is the Free America,—
  And this mark on my wrist,—(I prove what I say)
Ropes tied me up here to the flogging place.

XXXII.

You think I shrieked there? not a sound!
  I hung as a gourd hangs in the sun;
I only cursed them all around
  As softly as I might have done
My own child after. From these sands
  Up to the mountains, lift your hands
O slaves, and end what I begun.

XXXIII.

Whips, curses! these must answer those!
For in this Union, ye have set
Two kinds of men in adverse rows,
Each loathing each! and all forget
The seven wounds in Christ's body fair;
While he sees gaping everywhere
Our countless wounds that pay no debt.

XXXIV.

Our wounds are different—your white men
Are, after all not gods indeed,
Nor able to make Christs again
Do good with bleeding. We who bleed,—
(Stand off!)—we help not in our loss—
We are too heavy for our cross,
And fall and crush you and your seed.

XXXV.

I fall,—I swoon,—I look at the sky!
The clouds are breaking on my brain:
I am floated along, as if I should die
Of Liberty's exquisite pain!
In the name of the white child waiting for me
In the deep black death where our kisses agree.—
White men, I leave you all curse—free,
In my broken heart disdain!

If you know well the beginning
The end will not trouble you much.
　　　　—*An African Proverb.*

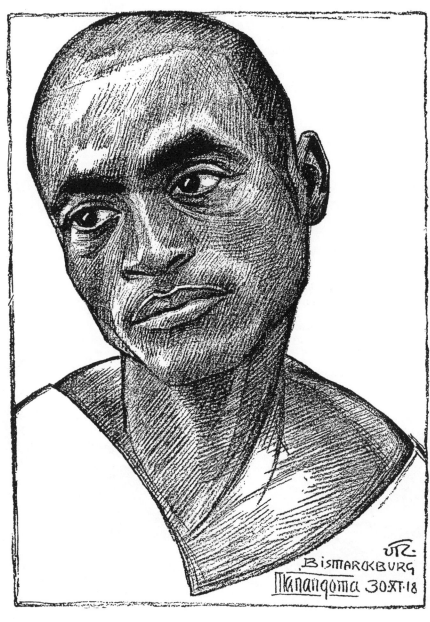

AN AFRICAN TYPE, *by Baron von Ruckteschell*

THE NATURAL HISTORY OF RACE PREJUDICE

By Ellsworth Faris

IN reading the title *Natural History of Race Prejudice,* the reader is asked to regard the occurrence of race prejudice as a natural phenomenon, just as truly as drought, an earthquake, or an epidemic of small pox. Race prejudice is defended by some as desirable, it is deprecated by others as an evil. Men have their opinions and attitudes on this subject but it is not the purpose here to discuss this phase of it. However good or bad it may be, it is assumed that it is possible, and believed to be advantageous to view the matter with detachment and to look to the conditions under which it appears, the cause or causes of its origin, the forms it assumes, the conditions under which it has increased or diminished in intensity, and whether it disappears, and why. This paper is too brief to do more than suggest a treatment of the topic.

The advantage of this mode of procedure is apparent. The history of science seems to show that this method is more fruitful. Knowledge is power; science gives control; to see is to foresee. We can effectively change and control only those events that we can formulate.

Race prejudice is a special form of class prejudice and does not differ in attitude. The only difference is in the object. There may be in a community a prejudice against preachers or soldiers or Republicans. The prejudice against radicals is like the prejudice against Negroes except for its mutability. Religion or politics are voluntary and can be changed, while race is relatively independent of the will.

But class and race prejudice in turn are special forms of a larger category of human experience, namely, prejudice in general. Men speak of prejudice against the Anti-saloon League, too short skirts, the yellow press, cigarettes and small towns.

Prejudice is not easy to define for it is bound up with emotion and contains usually an element of reproach. The dictionary may tell that prejudice is "an opinion or leaning adverse to anything without just grounds or sufficient knowledge," but is is not easy to agree as to what grounds are just or what knowledge is sufficient. And race prejudice, like all prejudices after they endure over a period of time, tends to be supported by arguments. The grounds may not be rational to a critic, but they may seem rational to those who hold the views. It often happens that prejudice is denied by one in whom others confidently assert it.

Nevertheless, for practical purposes, this difficulty is not great. Race prejudice is recognized as a feeling of antipathy or a tendency to withdraw or limit one's contacts toward the members of a certain racial group.

It is important to observe that race prejudice is typically a collective thing. It characterizes a group. It is not private, it is public. Of course, the manifestations are individual, but the point is that race prejudice is of no importance unless the same or similar attitudes and feelings occur in many people at once. Race prejudice then belongs in the field of public opinion or public sentiment.

It is of importance also to point out that race prejudice is attached to the soil. It characterizes a given area and a study of race prejudice can never be adequately made without a map. The significance of this fact arises when we discover that individuals migrating into an area where a certain prejudice exists tend to acquire it although it was absent from their original region. One cannot discuss the subject concretely without a reference to certain areas. The student thinks of the prejudice against Jews in Roumania, against Negroes in Mississippi, against Japanese in California.

In attempting to understand the nature of race prejudice it is important to observe its wide extent. The Japanese have been referred to as the object of prejudice in California, but in Japan the Eta people who number well over a million are the objects of an extreme form of prejudice. An Eta is not supposed to enter the temple for worship. In one recorded instance an Eta insisted on being allowed to worship and said to those who deterred him, "I also am a human being. Why cannot I worship the gods?" The crowd set upon him and he was killed. When his friends complained to the magistrate they were told, "One human being is equal to seven Etas. A man cannot be punished for killing one-seventh of a man. Come back to me when six more of you have been killed." There is prejudice against the Eurasians in China, against the natives, the mulattos and Hindus in South Africa, against the Mexicans in Southern Texas, against the Jews in most parts of the world, and so on around the map.

If now we inquire into the conditions under which the phenomenon appears, we are able to say that there is a quantitative requirement or precondition which seems necessary. If only a few members of an alien group appear they do not usually call out any such attitudes. The first Japanese were received with every evidence of welcome. Thirty years ago a Japanese gentleman married an American girl in Chicago. The wedding was the occasion of widespread interest and one newspaper devoted a whole page of its Sunday edition to pictures and description of the event. The prejudice against them did not arise until they had appeared in far larger numbers. The same remark applies to the Armenian in the West. In Natal in South Africa the British residents invited and imported men from India to work. This was in 1865. They were welcomed and it is agreed that their labor saved the colony from financial disaster. Thirty years later there were more than a hundred thousand, and the prejudice against them was intense. There were Jim Crow laws for the railroads, but they were forbidden on the street cars altogether. Moreover, they were forbidden to walk on the sidewalk and restrictions and social ostracism took an extreme form.

These and similar facts have led to the statement very widely accepted that race prejudice is caused by economic competition. Undoubtedly economic competition does occasion such sentiments, but it appears not to be everywhere the case. There is at present a widespread and very strong feeling in China against two racial groups, the Japanese and the English. Not only has there been an economic boycott, merchants refusing to handle the goods from these nations, but the coolies have refused to work for any Englishman or Japanese, and prominent Chinese have dropped their membership in clubs because of their feelings. This movement is so recent that we can state the facts with confidence. The Japanese hostility was occasioned by the fear of aggression, brought to a dramatic climax by the twenty-one demands, while the hostility to the English grew out of their refusal in the Washington Conference to allow the Chinese to regulate their own tariff provisions. In both cases the feeling was stirred up by the Chinese students who were hardly in any noticeable condition of competition, at least economic. The students petitioned the government, interviewed the merchants, and harangued the coolies. The effect was quite typical but the cause is not apparently the one ordinarily assigned.

Race prejudice has often been asserted by popular writers to be instinctive or hereditary. While this is apparently a complete misstatement it is a very excusable one. The error arises from the normal tendency of unsophisticated people to confuse the customary with the natural. When children grow up in a community they take on the customs and attitudes prevailing, some of which are very old while others are quite recent in origin. But the children can make no distinction between the new and the old and when the attitudes have become second nature they are often thought of as innate or natural. It is said to be "in the blood."

That this is not true can be shown by a comparison in space and time of the same racial stock in respect of this prejudice. The English in South Africa manifest it to an intense degree, as they do also in China against the natives, in sections of Canada against the French, and in parts of India and particularly in Australia. Yet these same English in New Zealand do not have much prejudice against the Maoris who differ from them far more in complexion and civilization than do the Canadian French. Moreover, the prejudice against Jews in England has greatly mitigated. No doubt some exists but it is undeniable that there has been an important modification in the direction of assimilation.

Nor is it possible to assert that wherever two races meet each other there will be prejudice. A list of the areas where it does occur would be too long but we may repeat that in South Africa the English have prejudice against at least four groups, and in Turkey the phenomenon was intense. The Poles and Lithuanians furnish an extreme example, the prejudice between the French and English in Canada has been mentioned, the Negroes in the United States are the objects of it, while in Haiti it is possible to describe a prejudice of the blacks against the whites. The French have their anti-semitism which is perhaps most severe in Roumania. The list if complete would be very long but I mention that in the last few months in Chicago there has developed a racial prejudice between the Polish and the Mexicans, due in part to economic competition and to certain tragic events that accentuated the feeling.

On the other hand race prejudice is relatively absent from Switzerland, the English have lost much of their feeling against the Jews, three races live without race prejudice in Brazil, there is no prejudice against the Indians in Mexico as Indians, two races live without prejudice in New Zealand, several racial groups live together without prejudice in Hawaii, and the phenomenon has never occurred in Greenland in the southern portions of which the common racial type is a mixture of Nordic and Eskimo blood.

If now we inquire more specifically into the conditions of race prejudice it appears that in all cases there is some form of conflict. It may be, and often is, a struggle for money, work, bread, but in many cases it is a struggle for position, status, social prominence, and when it occurs there seems to be a necessity for a definite group consciousness; an esprit de corp arises in one group in contrast to their conception of the other. It is interesting to notice that prejudice is thus double-edged. The prejudice against one group arises with the prejudice for another; prejudice is the other end of one type of loyalty. It is this fact that has made it so easy for those who defend race prejudice and exclusion to present plausible arguments and rationalizations.

The extreme form of race prejudice, or perhaps

better, one extreme limit of its development results in a condition of stability in which it is sometimes difficult to recognize the main features of prejudice. I refer to the accommodation or acceptance of the situation on both sides, in which case the inferior group ceases to struggle against the controlling one. This characterizes much of the relation between the southern masters and their slaves before the war. It is seen in its extreme form in the caste system of India. Now it would be a profitless argument to insist that caste is not prejudice, but for the fact that the acceptance does alter the whole psychology. At the present time when caste in India is beginning to disintegrate prejudice is more easy to find.

Now the caste lines are, or were, extremely rigid. The members of a caste had the same occupation and what we call the social ladder which is used by the social climbers did not and could not exist. A poor man's children could never expect to rise in the world by getting into another group. Moreover, a person could not marry save in his own caste. He could not eat with another not in his own caste, his meals must not be cooked except by one of his own caste, neither could the cooked food be handled by anyone of another group. The interesting thing to the psychologist here is in the form which the defense of such a situation normally takes. Anyone familiar with the literature of educated Indians on this subject will recall how often the condition has been defended as being desirable because of the benefits to civilization and humanity which flow from loyalty to one's own group. Exactly the same arguments occur in the writings of Americans in general and southerners in particular on the question of race mixture in the South. The current activity of the Ku Klux Klan abounds in highly idealistic phrases of loyalty and devotion to the precious heritage of the superior group. Race prejudice takes the form of altruistic devotion. The hostility masquerades as love and the wolf of hatred wears the sheep's clothing of affection and solicitude for the beloved group.

This leads us to the question of the motives which govern race prejudice, and the social psychologists have discovered an important principle which applies. It is now known that in the case of an ancient custom the motives are certain to vary. This is partly due to the fact that the custom is more difficult to change than its motive. Children carry on the custom without any motive, and if the old motive must be given up a new one spontaneously arises and men try to phrase their motives so that others will not condemn them. It is hard to imagine the published defense of race exclusion assigned to the motive of hatred or of fear. It is not conscious hypocrisy; it is the normal thing in human nature to attempt to make our actions appear as defensible as possible.

There are thus survivals in the plays and games of children, in the customs of weddings, funerals, and baptisms which go back to rather humble origins but which continue from approved modern motives. Likewise with race prejudice. Sometimes the despised race is represented as inferior but a recent writer in California defended the severity toward the Japanese and concluded with the statement, "If the Japanese are superior people so much the worse." One can read rationalizations which take the form of a pseudo-scientific assertion, that while both races may be good, the mixture is bad. There is nothing in this except the ingenuity of an author who rather pathetically grasps at a poor reason when he has had to abandon the others.

Race prejudice thus can be shown to be founded not on reason but on sentiments lying deeper and to be relatively impervious to rational arguments. Defenders of the Negro can martial many interesting and important facts. In 1870 the Negro in the United States owned 12,000 homes, 20,000 farms, and property to the value of $20,000,000. At the present time they own 700,000 homes, 1,000,000 farms, and are worth $1,800,000,000. They own 22,000,000 acres of land, which is equal to the area of New Hampshire, Vermont, Massachusetts, Rhode Island, and Connecticut. These facts are very interesting and very important, but when they are quoted to a person who is defending race prejudice in America their effect is sometimes absolutely nothing.

In the concrete social phenomena, particularly those of a collective nature, we may distinguish two parts or elements. One of these is relatively changeable and arises from the need men feel to be logical and the desire they have to appear reasonable to their fellows. The other element is relatively invariable and is based upon, or the expression of the interests and the emotions which lie deep in the personality. These are the social attitudes, and race prejudice is one of them. It is not the result of calm reasoning but arises from an emotional condition in a specific social setting. This attitude is defended by arguments but is not necessarily altered by counter arguments. If the reasons assigned for the prejudice are shown to be bad the usual effect will be the abandonment of the reasons and the assertion of new reasons for the same old attitude. Race prejudice, as will be later shown, can be lost and does on occasion disappear, but it is perhaps futile to expect the attitude to yield to mere arguments, though of course there is no reason why men who who wish to argue may not do so.

We may attempt to summarize the views here expressed under the following heads:

1. Race prejudice is very widespread. It is almost universal. Indeed, sociologists would agree that it might appear anywhere on the planet and has actually been manifested by every racial group. Those who are the victims of exclusion in some areas are themselves exclusive in other places. The Chinese may be discriminated against in America,

but the Chinese in China have exhibited the same antagonism against other racial groups. The Japanese are discriminated against but at times they themselves are discriminating, and so with the peoples of India, whether Hindus or Mohammedans, not to mention the various color lines which exist among American Negroes. We shall therefore be most accurate in our formulation of race prejudice if we regard it as a natural phenomenon and normal in the sense in which Durkheim speaks of crime as normal or poverty or suicide, by which he means that under given conditions the statistical facts force the prediction that the phenomenon will continue to occur.

2. Race prejudice is not one culture pattern but many. It takes many forms and exhibits many degrees. There is always involved a collective attitude of exclusiveness, the object of prejudice being kept at a greater distance than the members of one's own race. But this social distance varies and a rough measure or scale could be made, and has indeep been attempted. The members of the out-group are in some places completely excluded from every form of contact as for example in India where the very shadow of an untouchable is a contamination, or again, the out-group may mingle freely in public thoroughfares but may not sit as neighbors in a public assembly. Sometimes the line is drawn at eating together where it forbids or permits public assemblies of a religious nature, and so on through separate scales to complete "social equality" and the approved courtship and marriage between the young people of the two groups. The exact conditions under which the line is drawn in each case might be historically accounted for, but there is little or no logic in it and it can easily be shown to be absurd. As before remarked, however, one may admit the absurdity and retain the attitude.

3. When race prejudice arises it appears to follow a pattern which has been set locally in the mores if such pattern be present. Thus the extreme form of exclusiveness toward the Indians in South Africa can only be explained by the previously acquired attitudes toward the native Negroes. Feeling against the Indians was no higher in Natal than against the Japanese in California, but the form of exclusion is different, and this pattern was followed in each case. A recent court decision in Mississippi excludes Chinese from the public schools. This is understandable if we recall the pattern existing with reference to the Negroes in the south. It may be called a certain consistency in exclusiveness and follows a certain law of habit.

If prejudice arises where there is no pattern or tradition it may take original forms. Thus the children of the slave women in the south who were not acknowledged by their fathers and who lived with their mothers brought about the classification of mulattoes and full-bloods as members of the same excluded group. In the Portuguese colonies where such children were recognized and publicly ac-knowledged by the father, the mulatto came to be classed with the white group. In Cape Colony the mulatto received certain concessions, as for example, the right to vote which tended to make them into a third caste quite different from the situation in the two other cases.

4. Race prejudice having arisen it may be intensified or mitigated by social experiences. It is aggravated by any conflict between the groups. If conflict ceases entirely, a condition of equilibrium known as accommodation ensues and the feeling is reduced to a minimum. If, however, the conflict or hostility arises in a form where the in-group and out-group unite against a common antagonist or enemy the result is always to mitigate the prejudice and to act in the direction of its removal.

During the World War there was a period when the Negro soldiers and the Negro man-power were regarded as valuable assets to the nation. Men who had never done so before used the words "we" and "us" to include the Negro and white groups taken together. Had the conflict lasted longer, and had it at the same time threatened to go against us, this common feeling would have been more enduring. What happened is a matter of common knowledge. The unexpected armistice released the tension and in some places a very strong reaction took place. Nevertheless, the period is part of the experience of the nation, and the ultimate result in social evolution will be affected by what happened in 1917-18.

5. Race prejudice is increased both in intensity and in duration when to the difference in heredity is added the factor of religious or other social barrier. Anti-semitism seems almost perennial and part of the explanation may be looked for in the multiplicity of barriers to freedom of social intercourse. Each new wave of immigration supplies a group who differ even in dress. The dietary differences are by no means negligible though these tend to disappear, but the religious separation continues to accentuate and emphasize the objects of exclusion when the original motives and occasions have disappeared. Still it is possible to over-state this point. The definition of the we-group and out-group depends upon the arousal of group consciousness and this may take place in disregard of any single type of separation, whether religious, racial, or any other. The massacre at Amritsar united for the time being men in south India with the inhabitants of the Punjab in an intense feeling of brotherhood in spite of many differences and in spite of ancient historical antipathy. It is a common practice of Hindu students in American universities to wear a turban or some distinctive mark so that they will not be classed as Negroes. Yet it sometimes happens that a series of unpleasant experiences will entirely change this attitude and the Hindu will class himself as a colored man, aligning himself with the American Negro. This phenomenon follows

the normal law of group consciousness which perhaps needs no further illustration.

6. Race prejudice cannot only be mitigated, it can disappear. In many cases it has entirely disappeared and in other situations it is obviously decreasing. The Norman Conquest of England was followed by a period of racial hostility and prejudice, but at the present time there is hardly a vestige of the feeling remaining. There was an unmistakable race prejudice against German immigrants in this country and the successive groups of Germans, Irish and French felt the effects of this same phenomenon. At the present time the race prejudice against these three groups is hardly more than vestigial. The hostility which the Germans and Irish encountered is now turned against Italians, Poles, Mexicans and others, but there seems no discoverable difference between the treatment of these last and the way in which the former groups were originally received.

7. If we inquire more particularly into the stages of integration it seems that there can be distinguished certain generalized aspects. There is first of all the gradual taking over of the customs of the dominant group. This is observed first in the costumes, particularly the costumes of the men who go freely among the natives, and of the children and young people who are sensitive to the criticism of those among whom they move. Costume is more conservative in the case of the older women chiefly because of the domestic isolation. Next follows the matter of language. The first generation learns to talk English if possible, but they are sometimes too busy. The second generation has usually two languages, but the third generation often discards the heritage of their fathers for the custom of the country.

The sociologist sees in the public schools of America the real melting pot. The immigrant children are confronted with the new culture in a way that forces them to adopt it. The methods are sometimes brutal, the ridicule of the natives being the most cruel weapon, and because the children are young and defenseless they capitulate rather promptly and are absorbed into the cultural life of their schoolmates. We can generalize all these processes under the head of common experiences which, as before mentioned, are the sources of group consciousness and group loyalty. The bi-racial committees in the south have often been little more than informal conferences by leading members of both races to talk over a situation to see what can be done. These committees help to create a temporary we-group and add ever so little to the stock of traditions which forms the stream of social evolution.

An important means or method for the mitigation of race prejudice lies in the realm of art. To join with an Irish girl in order to help her persuade her father to let her marry a Jewish boy is not given to many Americans. But in the theatre we may do this for two interesting and amusing hours. Art is an experience, a sort of vicarious experience, and yet however vicarious it may be, it is an emotional experience and always modifies our emotional attitudes. The exhibition of primitive African sculpture may have little effect, but it may have some. The reading of a powerful novel in which the human qualities of another race are made appealing acts like a powerful social cement to bind together the hitherto unconnected fragments of a social body.

Of course art can work both ways. The Negroes objected to the "Birth of the Nation" and the "Clansman." No one who strongly desired the disappearance of race prejudice between whites and Negroes would care to see this drama continue in its popularity. Indeed, it may be thought of as a direct reaction to "Uncle Tom's Cabin."

8. Race prejudice being at the same time a collective and an emotional condition it is modified slowly. It is not an individual phenomenon, though every serious individual modification may be theoretically assumed to have some effect on the whole. The important point is that the subjective emotions are only half, the other half being the external conditions and organized regulations. It is only partly true to say that religious emotions or principles can remove it. This would be to neglect the necessity of a change in the external conditions. There is, therefore, a double problem; the one psychological, the other institutional. Any attempt to study it or to change it without recognizing this is apparently doomed to disappointment. This is the sense in which race prejudice is appropriately called a natural phenomenon. It changes slowly but it does change. A too sudden modification, either of attitude or institution, is not only impermanent in character but tends to be followed by a reaction which temporarily leaves the last state worse than the first.

9. But to call race prejudice a natural phenomenon is not to assume that it should be endured or accepted. If we may call race prejudice natural we must also admit suicide, murder, and automobile accidents into this same class. These disturb us and we try to mitigate them, but perhaps we shall never wholly succeed. Nevertheless, the unwelcome effects are undeniable and should be clearly kept in mind.

Race prejudice is narrowing. It may intensify loyalty to one's own group; it certainly produces blindness when members of the out-group are considered. We regard as human those whom we can sympathize with, whose motives we understand, and whose feelings we recognize to be like our own. The barriers men erect in prejudice make it sometimes difficult, sometimes impossible to regard the member of an excluded group as being wholly human. If we fight the Germans we tend to regard them as Huns, as man-like beasts, as cruel savages. If we exclude Negroes we call them inferior or patronize them as being emotionally gifted but intellectually deficient. Reactionaries of today speak of the south Europeans as coming from unassimilable stocks. Sometimes a man who feels this way writes a book to prove it and calls it science. But let us not be deceived in such a culture trait. There is always an emotional element which is difficult to alter and even hard to make explicit. It is a sentiment of race prejudice and it narrows the individual life and always weakens the society where it exists.

The effect of race prejudice on individuals who hold it is to limit their power of discrimination. It blinds a man to differences where these would otherwise be easily seen. Persons are treated according to a stereotype and not as separate and distinct individualities. This is a sort of mental laziness due to the emotional attitude which, being directed toward a class, is manifested toward the varying members of the class as if it did not vary.

The object of this paper has been to show that the desire to change a prejudice is more likely to succeed if we first understand fully the nature of prejudice. Those who are interested in removing a social attitude are more apt to succeed if they first are successful in understanding why people have the attitude who do have it.

ELLSWORTH FARIS,
University of Chicago.

SYBIL WARNS HER SISTER

By ANNE SPENCER

It is dangerous for a woman to defy the gods;
To taunt them with the tongue's thin tip,
Or strut in the weakness of mere humanity,
Or draw a line daring them to cross;
The gods who own the searing lightning,
The drowning waters, the tormenting fears,
The anger of red sins . . .
Oh, but worse still if you mince along timidly—
Dodge this way or that, or kneel, or pray,
Or be kind, or sweat agony drops,
Or lay your quick body over your feeble young,
If you have beauty or plainness, if celibate,
Or vowed—the gods are Juggernaut,
Passing over each of us . . .
Or this you may do:
Lock your heart, then, quietly,
And, lest they peer within,
Light no lamp when dark comes down
Raise no shade for sun,
Breathless must your breath come thru,
If you'd die and dare deny
The gods their god-like fun!

Original Paul Laurence Dunbar Manuscripts

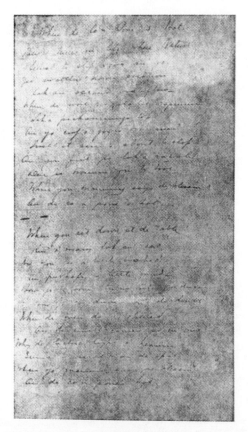

Facsimile

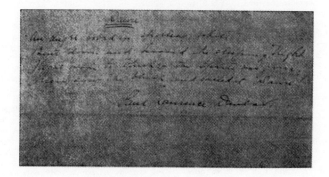

SOME OBSERVATIONS ON THE AMERICAN RACE PROBLEM

By Eugene Kinckle Jones

ECENTLY, I had the pleasure of visiting the cinema version of Harriet Beecher Stowe's *Uncle Tom's Cabin.* So well is the story portrayed that one finds himself living the life of the characters in the slave period of American history. At the end, Eliza and the other members of the Harris family are reunited as the Union soldiers bring freedom to the slaves—Sherman's army passing the plantation of Simon Legree, Eliza's and Uncle Tom's master, at the psychological moment. One sees Old Glory once more flashing triumphantly over the land, and suddenly with the "finis" the theatre lights flash on and I am transported over a period of sixty-two years to find myself once more in America in 1927, a Negro facing many whites— all of whom seem to be saying "What a metamorphosis. How can it be that these same men of sixty years ago now possess so many of those qualities which reflect civilization as we know it!"

The period of the Negro's life as free men in America since the Civil War has been the most progressive period of the Negro's experience anywhere in the world, and it is doubtful that any group of human beings anywhere has made as much advancement under similar circumstances as they have made in so short a time. The last fifteen years of this period have been the most favorable of this sixty-odd year period. The social forces at work during the time just before the entrance of America into the World War and the demand on the Negro during and since the war are recorded as stimuli to this remarkable advancement. But one should not overlook the fact that the Negro must long have been on the alert for the appearance of his chance and was psychologically prepared to throw himself vigorously into situations from which he would emerge with profit.

In the very beginning of the race's life as free men in the South, it was a group of saintly, self-effacing white missionaries, men and women, of the North who went to the South, established schools for the education of the Negro and breathed the spirit of hope into this benighted group, that has since been leading Negroes out of the wilderness of ignorance and despair.

Many persons today are under the impression that race relations are more strained in America now than at any time during the past fifty years. But my opinion is that this is due to confusion in thinking. The situation should be appraised relatively. It is true that the spirit of tolerance seems to be strained in certain quarters although no one would question the statement that the attitude of white employers towards their Negro servants and other menial and unskilled employees is much better. The point of strained relations seems to be where Negroes who have gained education and industrial efficiency seek choice positions or better homes in neighborhoods where whites because of their economic status have not before had Negro neighbors. My impression is that these evidences of intolerance are the inevitable results of the so-called inferior group bringing pressure on their obstacles as they themselves acquire higher living and intellectual standards and assume the rights and the attitude of developing men. And in the game of life, just as in athletic contests, the opposition is greatest nearest the goal line. To illustrate this point: Forty-five years ago, in Richmond, Virginia, the public schools maintained by the city for colored children had local white teachers. My father, a native of Virginia, but a graduate of Colgate University, Hamilton, New York, who was then teaching in one of the missionary schools in Richmond, began to advocate the employment of Negro teachers in Negro public schools there. His argument was that if the Negroes were to be separately educated they should have their own teachers. And if the white teachers were to be associated in the schools with the colored children and brought into frequent contact in conferences with the pupils' parents, he saw no reason why this system should not be extended and Negro and white children be educated together in the same schools. He was publicly attacked in the white press and by white clergymen (!) as a Negro advocating miscegenation and amalgamation of the races. Today there are colored teachers in all the public schools there and it is not considered at all out of place for a Negro leader to advocate the use of colored men as principals of the colored schools. Already we see many evidences of the acceptance of the Negro in his new status. Naturally, you would look for this evidence at the top. Negro intellectuals find very little discrimination in the intellectual world. Artists, musicians, literary men of both races mingle freely in the discussion of their major interests. And this is not only true in the North but it is increasingly becoming true in the South. Students in southern white and Negro colleges are having joint group discussions and there is talk of exchange professorships on special sociological problems between certain southern white and colored colleges. Within the

96

EUGENE KINCKLE JONES
From a drawing by Francis Holbrook

last six months in one of the largest southern cities, an intellectual white man entertained his friends of similar interests in honor of a popular Negro poet. Among the masses, there are evidences also of a growing understanding. Of course, it takes about twenty-five years for the theories expounded in the universities to gain currency among the people at large; but the confusion that has been created by the failure of the theories as to racial inferiority when decided by unbiased scientific measurements has led the outstanding professors in Anthropology, Psychology and Sociology to admit to their students that at least these beliefs have not been substantiated and before many years lay America will admit at least

as much as Lothrop Stoddard does, that any separation of the races must be based *not* upon ideas of inferiority of racial groups but only on the theory of difference, even though this difference has not been and will not be explained.

Slavery left attitudes in whites towards Negroes which the generations since have not entirely eradicated. But gradually Negroes are being recorded as persons capable of becoming self-contained individuals who do not have to depend upon white sufferance and philanthropy for their salvation. This is the most encouraging phase of the whole relationship and it should stimulate philanthropy to more determined endeavor in behalf of the Negro group as this is America's ideal, that its citizenry shall be able to adjust themselves to their environment and make of themselves self-possessed, independent, resourceful, productive citizens. No matter what the disposition of the whites as a whole may be to hinder or to help, measurable social improvement in the Negro must be provided for in any permanent solution of the so-called problem.

Some years ago, it was common practice among social and medical scientists to point out the evidence of Negro inferiority in terms of higher death rates and lower physical resistance to diseases. Now with the Negro mortality figures standing about where the white mortality figures were in America twelve or fifteen years ago and gradually getting better, one never hears a reputable physician or statistician presenting such evidence. Similarly, criminologists cited relative prison population figures to indicate the lower moral status of the Negro. When during the prohibition period we see the Negro prison population of North Carolina and South Carolina decreasing and the white prison population greatly increasing to the point where the proportions tend to be equal, critics of the Negro's morals are silenced.

Of course, the atrocity and the violence with which whites in high places have enacted crimes against person, property and the State have never been approached by Negroes of any standing whatsoever in America, and I have personally witnessed many a white audience wilt in a discussion of the subject of Negro crime when a Negro lecturer has facetiously stated: "When will we in America ever make good Americans out of these white people by stopping them from robbing our country's oil lands, and padding the amounts of our public improvements, and doing away with their husbands and wives in order to be safe in clandestine meetings with the third angle of the triangle?"

Personnel managers and large employers of labor no longer speak of Negroes' lack of industrial capacity, efficiency or skill; although they had never employed them. The war time and post-war experience with Negro labor under favorable circumstances has exploded these myths about the Negro's industrial ability. Now it is only a question, employers say, as to whether their white employees will stand for the employment of Negro workers.

While national legislation has provided the atmosphere for the race's development in a democratic form of goverment, the means by which Negroes could acquire most of this unusual progress have been furnished by social, educational and religious agencies—many of them State or municipally supported, but most of them privately maintained. When all of the social agencies in New York touching Negro life—the family welfare group, baby saving movements, community and settlement houses, employment finding and stabilizing agencies, health education interests, churches—combine to wage warfare on the high infant mortality among Negroes in New York City and succeed in

reducing the death rate of Negro babies to a point less than the infant mortality was ten years before and actually less than the white infant mortality in the very district where the Negro rate was more than three times that of the whole city prior to the campaign of course skeptics of the question of the Negro's ability to become acclimated to northern city life are convinced of their error and are silenced. I do not lose sight of those prejudiced individuals who see in this reduction itself a danger to so-called white supremacy and who would rather see Negro babies die than live. But this group is giving away to enlightened intelligence even though in many cases the motive is self-interest as they know that a disease germ knows no color line and a diseased Negro is a menace not only to well Negroes but to healthy white persons also. When we take cognizance of the increase in the Negro population in Detroit from 6,000 in 1916 to 85,000 in 1926 and observe the satisfactory economic and industrial adjustments there with the aid of the Urban League, the Y. M. C. A., the Y. W. C. A., and the churches and other Negro and white social agencies, one can no longer say that competitive industrial life in the northern city is too strenuous for the Negro and that the agricultural south is the only place for him.

Evidences of the effort being put forth to crystallize sentiment in favor of the Negro may be noted in nearly every important social agency, local or national, where the two races come within the scope of the organizations' activities. I think it is pretty generally conceded that regardless of the kindly attitude towards Negroes of a certain simple, harmless type, the Negro as a group needs special aid, as does every handicapped group, to meet the issues of life and to rise in the social scale and thus to merit and receive the approbation of his dominant neighbors.

Practically every community chest organization or local council social agencies in cities where Negroes constitute a goodly proportion of the population has noted the social needs among this element of the citizenry and many of them have inter-racial committees as member agencies, and support definite pieces of social work in behalf of the Negro population. The Boy Scouts of America, the Federal Council of Churches of Christ in America, and the Young Men's Christian Association have national inter-racial committees and the American Social Hygiene Association, the Young Men's Christian Association, the Young Women's Christian Association and the International Big Brother and Big Sister organizations have special work going on in behalf of the Negro population, and in all of these organizations except one, there is Negro representation on their governing boards.

Most criticism by Negroes of activities with the Negro group is based upon uncertainty as to the best method to solve the problem. The Negroes are not satisfied with half a loaf. The whites are not inclined to give a whole loaf. In the shuffle, many cases of injustice may be noted. Many cases of fruitless effort accompanied by excellent intentions may be recorded. But the curve indicating the trend is upward, and a better day is dawning for race relations in America.

The migration of Negroes to the North has been accompanied by a tremendous migration of the southern whites to the North. Northern capital and business interest are being directed in a greater degree annually to the South. The former movement has precipitated an increasing interest in the problems of the Negro on the part of the northern whites and the latter has generated a stronger resolve on the part of southern whites to make an honest effort to help solve the racial difficulties in the interest of the country as a whole as well as in the South. The meeting together of these three points of view—that of the northern white, that of the southern white and that of the Negro—will produce an interesting understanding and will actually result in a better attitude towards the Negro on the part of the whites. America will profit as a consequence and the cause of human understanding and betterment will be promoted.

ARABESQSE

By FRANK HORNE

Down in Georgia
a danglin' nigger
hangin' in a tree
. . . kicks holes in the laughing sunlight—
A little red haired
Irish girl . . . grey eyes
and a blue dress—
A little black babe
in a lacy white cap . . .
The soft red lips
of the little red head
kiss
so tenderly
the little black head—
grey eyes smile
into black eyes
and the gay sunlight
laughs joyously
in a burst of gold . . .
Down in Georgia
a danglin' nigger
hangin' in a tree
. . . kicks holes in the laughing sunlight—

PHANTOM COLOR LINES

T. Arnold Hill

OW much of the Negro's failure to secure employment is his own fault? Many would answer that most positions are denied because of circumstances chargeable to race. They would tell aptly of instances in which forces beyond the control of the colored applicant or worker kept him out of a job or retarded his promotion. Eligibility would not be questioned since chivalry in war and long citizenship are presumed to establish fitness; and since the Negro's bravery in battle and loyalty to country are acknowledged facts, he is by virtue of such entitled to employment. This irrational conception of values is passing, but it still clings to a class who regards such historical shibboleths as prima facea evidence of acceptability.

Racial prejudice—seldom caste prejudice—is to the casual observer the cause of practically all the dilemmas Negroes encounter in their occupations. A worker, seeing his fellow white workers advancing above him, can assign no cause for it other than disfavor for his race and a corresponding favor for all other races and nationalities.

This is of course a complex question. In it is the recalcitrance of labor unions, the open and subtle antagonism of the snobbish employee, the deliberate revolt of light-headed youth whose bias permits of little reasoning on this or any other subject, the naivete of the employer who honestly believes the Negro incapable of skilled or professional tasks, the dogma of employers who blatantly admit their color prejudices, the traditional hatred of class units who fear the entrance of Negroes into unaccustomed fields, and the public ignorance of the measured steps Negroes have made in recent years. In it, too, is the listlessness of Negro workers, their failure to grasp the subjectiveness of manual labor, the result of which is the absence of a middle group profitably employed, intra-racial antagonism revolting against Negro supervision in plants and the unchecked heresies respecting industrial education against which seldom an effective protest is uttered.

I know Negroes who have worn down their morale in a fruitless effort to secure decent living. I know many who have been discharged when their racial identity became known. Such incidents, and the mockery which makes them incidents, are regrettable. They suggest a topic that might have found place in Stuart Chase's "Tragedy of Waste." But even at this point, where unfairness is plainly revealed, we ask if the Negro should not share a part of the blame for the state of public thought that permits such experiences to continue unabated?

That this has happened so frequently to well-trained Negro youth is of itself reason to ask what is being done to prevent it.

"A bird may be shot upward to the skies by a foreign force; but it rises in the true sense of the word, only when it spreads its own wings and soars by its own living power. So a man may be thrust upward into a conspicuous place by outward accidents, but he rises only in so far as he exerts himself, and expands his best faculties, and ascends by a free effort to a noble region of thought and action." Thus did William Ellery Channing define "elevation" for the working classes. Applying this formula to Negro workers one is moved to overlook failures because the past has not provided opportunity for independent thought and action. Members of this race did not emerge from slavery free moral agents of their own destinies. Freed in the latter half of the nineteenth century they helped America struggle for and secure ascendancy over her European rivals.

But they could not rise when slavery had left them doubtful of their own value, unprepared for industrial labor and illiterate. Negroes were emerging from serfdom when the princely fortunes of the elder captains of wealth were taking form. They had neither personal qualifications of heart or mind and they had no encouragement from others to corner the untouched resources that are the foundation of big estates. The Negro had to be educated. He had to house himself without the aid of masters. He had to work to feed himself and family; there was no time for planning a future.

There is no desire to cavil over the racial shortcomings that may be traced to the effects of slavery. The criticism is not that the race did not make preeminent progress in occupational spheres, but rather that today they give little thought to achieving it.

The proportion of Negroes ten years of age and over gainfully employed, approximately sixty per cent, is larger than that of any other group in the census reports for 1920. The distribution is likewise disproportioned. Of the 4,824,151 Negroes employed, the proportion engaged in the trades, professional service and clerical occupations is far below the average for all classes. The average in domestic and personal service is higher and in transportation the average is not far below. They are numerically strong in agriculture, forming 16.8 per cent of the workers employed in this industry. They are losing ground in domestic and personal service. They have usually been employed when white labor was not available and often discharged when the white short-

100

age subsided. Though they have made undeniable progress in recent years, expanding their diversification until it includes in New York and Chicago practically all important occupations, they are still confined to unskilled and the most onerous tasks, and are often underpaid. The cessation of immigration from abroad, if continued long enough, will undoubtedly be beneficial to them. If the immigration restrictions are modified so as to permit throngs of aliens to rush to our shores, competition between Negroes and immigrants will again be set up just as it was in the sixties and seventies when results disastrous to Negroes ensued. All in all the future is uncertain. It rests upon the Negro's own application to a degree of indispensability that will make replacement unnecessary and expensive.

Some progress is being made in this direction, doubtless the result of exposure to rigid industrial requirements. Critical observations of themselves by groups of workers, called to discuss their problems in industry, are typical of the introspection going on in many parts of the country. The following comments were made in such a conference in Milwaukee:

"An attendant at an oil filling station said his ungovernable temper had caused him to lose several jobs. On his present job he has seen some of the white attendants "balled out" by the superintendent for various reasons but took it calmly. The following day all seemed well. The men did not lose their temper and quit work. He was following their example now and felt if other Negroes did likewise they would not change jobs so much and learn there is really nothing to a lot of this "balling out."

"A moulder having been on one job about two and one-half years said, 'Every day I work side by side with white men, some have been snobbish but are my best friends.' Men who have moulded many years longer than himself have given him a number of fine points which he didn't know. Feels if colored men in various lines take the same interest with other colored men who may be new on the job it will be of much help. Also found since he has become a home owner he gains more respect from the superintendent.

"A sand-blaster said that he has had audience with the foundry superintendent as to why some colored men were not promoted to mechanical jobs. Superintendent felt Negroes couldn't make good on technical work, seemed to be thick headed. Said he noticed white boys were given jobs as apprentices and were better qualified from a technical point of view. He also said the Negro's temper and lack of stability in many instances had caused foremen to refuse them jobs in their department. He stated one colored man had nine fights on a job in one day.

"Mr. J. said he had been a moulder on one job four years. There are a number of jobs, particularly the better paying jobs, which are not given Negroes. Some moulding jobs pay whites more than Negroes on same pattern. He said that most of the prejudices which he had experienced came from sub-foremen because they were prejudiced."

The Negro worker lacks apperception. He is part of an industrial plant but not part of the industrial life of a community. He does not think seriously of his work as he does of his lodge and his church. Unlike the professional man who knows the organizations he should join, the laws and the ethics he must obey, the fee he is to collect, the periodicals he should read, and certain routine he must follow, the manual worker enters upon his duties knowing nothing of and caring less for the besetments he is sure to encounter. He philosphizes on the "Negro problem," but never on the economic side of it except to assign causes for failure. It is not exceptional to find one who can recite verbatim long passages from a ritual of a lodge and who can interpret adequately its purposes and precepts.

Recently I heard presidents of two Negro colleges say that not enough attention is being given to the men and women who toil with their hands. One felt that the whole system of industrial education in the private schools and colleges will have to be reshaped, in order to meet the demands of today. The other believed that the average Negro worker, as distinguished from the professional man, does not know "what its all about." Colored employees are far removed from the problems which concern organized workers. They take little or no pains to learn the laws which govern and protect wage-earners in the various states of the union. They are unfamiliar with the charges of scabbing and the significance of these charges made against them so often by union members. They are unacquainted with the successes of members of their race who have won, by virtue of personal worth, places in the skilled and industrial forces of the country. They still expect advances in positions without corresponding advances in preparation.

The more than sixty national secret and fraternal organizations among Negroes in the United States have an estimated membership of upwards of two million five hundred thousand. Their property holdings are thought to exceed twenty-five million dollars. They have large bank deposits in white institutions, sometimes said to aggregate more than a million dollars in a separate bank. They make extended plans for sickness and death but little provision for economic security. They have great difficulty financing a building of modest dimensions. The added strength to these fraternal organizations and to the race, if they should give attention to business and commerce, would be tremendous. The potentialities for corporal development by virtue of resources, material and human in these fraternal organizations, would long have been seized upon by any group properly conscious of its strength and sufficiently aware of the relationship between economics and the whole problem of the Negro in this country.

There were in 1926, according to the Negro Year Book, 47,000 churches with 5,000,000 communi-

cants and 46,000 Sunday schools with 3,000,000
scholars. Church properties were valued at $98,-
500,000. They contribute comfortable sums to home
and foreign missions, have some splendid denomi-
national publishing houses, make provisions for re-
tired ministers and give large sums to educational
and beneficent institutions. The Negro church is
the most poignant illustration of organization the
race possesses. But their material contributions
have been confined almost wholly to the acquiring
and building of church properties. There is latent
within this group, long accustomed to unified effort,
monetary and mental resources that should be released for more substantial racial achievement.

In charging that the Negro lacks apperception I
am not forgetting the criticisms of inefficiency which
so frequently are lodged against them by those who
know only part of the problem. As to how proficient a group of colored workers is when compared
with a similar group of workers of another race
there is considerable difference of opinion among
employers who hire them. What we often mistake
for lack of ability or lack of will to do is but an
effect, the cause of which has deep psychological
foundation. Thus the significance of work in the
pattern of life is not appreciated. Inability to remove the obstacles of racial discrimination has
dwarfed the faculties the Negro needs for this conception. As a consequence he reasons that a job is
but a job and that no matter how industrious he
may become, he will remain hopelessly tied to casual
occupations.

In the midst of such despondency the National
Negro Business League can never thrive to the point
its leaders would have it. The trouble is not wholly
with the merchants. It is partly within the cerebral
reactions of the masses of Negroes to Negro business; for the same disregard for economic relationship and value we have observed in industry and
commerce is a vital deterrent to the success of business operated by the race. A Negro Business League
must have other purposes than those which are connected with business. If Negro business would succeed it must deal with a state of public mind which
has not yet seen the parts of the "problem" in their
relationship to the whole. There is room for correlation of effort in this field on the part of the Business League, the lodges, the churches, the schools
and the social agencies.

The prominence given today to the cultural
achievements by Negroes makes it more necessary
than ever that the economic side of Negro life should
be strengthened. Most of the researches and practically all books have omitted discussions of this
phase of Negro life. We need a more positive material foundation to maintain the host of intellectuals we so proudly boast of today. More than one
professional man has moved within the past six
months because there was not enough stability and
permanence to Negro workers to support them.

That we are denied opportunities for employment is partly due again to our neglect through our
failure to popularize the successes attained at work.
There is many an employer honestly ignorant of
what we have achieved. There are a number who
sincerely believe that trouble is fomented whenever
white and colored workers are associated together.
There are those who still persist that cold weather
can not be endured by sons of Ham from the torrid
regions of the South. There are perhaps pioneers
who have sacrificed along with their intellectual
brothers and who have made valuable contributions
to race relationship of whom we do not know.
Their exploits have not been given publicity and as
such they do not provide incentives for others to
do likewise nor illustrate the possibilities in a field
in which our capacity is so often questoned.

A large share of the Negro's failure to secure employment is his own fault—not so much the fault of
the job-seeker, but more the indifference of those
whose positions entitle them to lead. We would improve the training which our schools are giving,
adding courses that once were thought unnecessary
because of the limitations in employment. We
would appeal to a fair American sentiment to live
up to appropriate ideals of democracy. We would
have our white youth increase the understanding it
is so rapidly acquiring of Negro life. We would
continue to advise organized groups of employees to
annex their fellow colored workers. But we would
insist upon a more mature understanding and concentration than the Negro has yet given his work
problems. In the guidance of this knowledge he
must be helped by his leaders who have at their
command resources for the infusion of the high
spiritual substance against which foreign forces will
thrust in vain.

DRAWINGS FOR MULATTOES—Number 1
By *Richard Bruce*

DRAWING FOR MULATTOES—Number 2
By Richard Bruce

DRAWING FOR MULATTOES—Number 3
By Richard Bruce

DRAWING FOR MULATTOES—Number 4
By Richard Bruce

THE CHANGING STATUS OF
THE MULATTO

By E. B. Reuter

T IS a generally known fact that in the Negro population of the United States the group of bi-racial ancestry has contributed more than its proportionate share of prominent individuals. But the degree to which this is true is perhaps not realized outside the group of professional students. The names that come first to mind when the question of racial talent and leadership is mentioned — Douglass, Washington, Tanner, Williams, Aldridge, Chestnutt, DuBois, Johnson, et al— are not the names of black men. Paul Laurence Dunbar, Kelly Miller, Roland Hayes and Robert R. Moton are perhaps the only men of relatively uncontaminated Negro blood who have achieved a national reputation. In all fields of endeavor, in proportion to their number in the general Negro population, the mulattoes have furnished a disproportionate percentage of the conspicuously successful individuals.

All through the period of Negro residence in America, the outstanding individuals of the race, in the great majority of cases, have been men of mixed blood. In the various slave insurrections they had a prominent part. Within the slave regime they were the ones least accommodated to the status of servitude, the ones who most often came into conflict with the institution, the ones who most frequently led others in revolt against the status. In the realm of intellectual and semi-intellectual pursuits their part was conspicuous. Benjamin Banneker, perhaps the most capable of the early American Negroes, was a free man because of his descent from a white woman. James Durham, the Negro physician, was a mulatto. George Lisle, Andrew Bryan, Samuel Haynes, and other early preachers of note were men of mixed ancestry. In the later days of the slave institution the percentage of mixed bloods among the leaders was high. With one or possibly two exceptions the dozen or twenty colored men most prominent in the anti-slavery agitation were mulattoes. In the post Civil War decades the mixed bloods were conspicuous in the political and other activities opened to the members of the race. In the ministry, in the early literary and artistic strivings, and in the struggle against oppression the mulattoes played a leading role.

The significance of this distribution of superior men has commonly been misunderstood. It seems on first blush to be somehow indicative of an underlying difference in capacity, to imply a marked superiority rooting in the fact of a white ancestry and relationship. This reading of the facts has been all the more acceptable for the reason that it contributes, in a not too subtle way, to the racial self-feeling of the culturally dominant group. The egocentric bias of popular thought has been reinforced by the biological bias of an unarrived psychology. The mixed ancestry of so many Negro leaders has given support to the biological bias at the same time that it has served as evidence to prove the incapacity of members of the Negro group.

In the situation it is not beyond understanding that Negro writers have not emphasized the fact of mulatto leadership, that they have sometimes minimized it, and that in some cases they have attempted to refute the implied or asserted inferiority of the race by denial of the facts themselves. But such tactics are futile. Not only that: they are ill-advised. The facts will be known and in the present case it is to the advantage of the racial group that they be known. In the cultural superiority of the mulatto lies what is, when comprehensively understood, the most complete refutation of the theory of Negro inferiority.

It is, however, only within the past decade that the facts have been comprehensively understood and a tenable hypothesis has gained currency. And even today, and even among students of social and race psychology, the explanation of social phenomena in biological terms is perhaps the rule rather than the exception.

II

IN explanation of these facts it is usual to resort to the doctrine of racial inequality. Since the white man is superior to the Negro, the mulattoes, who are intermediate between the racial extremes, are superior to the one and inferior to the other. It does not appear to be necessary, however, to resort to this order of explanation in order to account for all the facts before us.

Almost from the beginning of Western culture in America, distinctions were made in the servile class on the basis of blood intermixture. This was in part the result of the doctrine of white racial superiority. But there were other facts making for class separation on this basis.

The first mulattoes were of course the result of primary crosses. They were the sons and daughters of white men or women. In consequence there was often a sentimental factor operating to favor the child. The relations between the parents of the

107

mixed-blood children, at least in some cases, were based on mutual affection. White men were sometimes inordinately fond of their colored babies. This matter of relationship and personal affection was a thing of first-rate importance in those cases where the mulattoes were children of the slave owner or of some member of his family. Being the owner as well as the father or uncle of the mulatto child he was in a position to give it special consideration. The cases where the masters were the slave owners of their own relatives and favored them above other slaves are numerous. Such children were often freed, sometimes they were educated, and generally they were directed into the more stimulating and less deadening sorts of occupation.

Another important factor in the differentiation came in very early. Some of the mulattoes were the children of white mothers and Negro fathers. When the question of the legal status of the Negroes came to be defined in law, a distinction was made on the basis of parentage. It became a rule at law that the status of children should follow that of the mother with the result that some percentage of the mulatto children were free persons. This group perhaps did not include a very considerable proportion of the total mulatto population but it contributed to the increase of the group of free Negroes and to the percentage of mulattoes in the group. The frequent emancipation by slave holders of their mixed-blood relatives also added to the mulatto character of the free Negro population.

Within the slave order itself the mulattoes were commonly favored. The assumption of the greater native ability of the persons of mixed blood led to their being trained for skilled and semi-skilled occupations. They were most frequently selected for positions of responsibility and for positions involving personal and confidential relations. They were everywhere in demand for house servants. They were more generally than the average of the population, city residents. Whatever the reason, and the reasons were different in different cases, the mulattoes were commonly assigned to the more stimulating types of work, were given more education and freedom, and had the advantage of more contact and association with cultured people.

The distinctions thus made in the Negro population afforded the mulattoes on the average more freedom and opportunity and this registered very early in the greater cultural advance of these persons. They furnished most of the individuals of any prominence and achievement. They came to occupy a somewhat special status; they stood somewhat apart from the field hands and common laborers. This class division was of course nowhere complete. There were always black men in the special positions and there were always mulattoes among the field and labor gangs. Some of the leaders were black men. But the distinction was sufficiently marked to be recognized by the Negroes and the mulattoes as well as by the whites. And the explanation, subsequent for the most part to the fact, came to be the same for each of the groups.

III

$\mathcal{T}$HE external situation was reflected in the social and psychological attitudes; the sentiments and beliefs came to be in harmony with the external social order. Men developed the type of mind and the set of habits necessary to a tolerable life. The white group, superior in status and culture, developed the psychological characteristics that go with power and responsibility. The Negroes, repressed and backward, accommodated themselves to the inevitable and developed the reciprocal type of mind.

In the situation, the mulatto was in cultural advance as well as in appearance an intermediate type of man. His white relationship, his somewhat superior status, and his greater degree of accomplishment raised him somewhat above the general level of the Negro population. But the same group of facts placed him below as well as outside the white group. The whites treated them as somewhat superior to the Negroes. They thought them superior and expressed the belief in their treatment. At the same time they believed them to be inferior to the whites and treated them as inferiors. The Negroes, reflecting the white attitude in this as they did in most other matters, looked upon the mulattoes as being of a higher caste and as being natively superior men. In much the same way the mulattoes came typically to conceive of themselves. They were a numerically minor group and the conceptions that they came to hold of themselves and of their natural place in the social order was determined in major part by the beliefs and attitudes of the major groups. The Negroes looked up to them, they looked down upon the Negroes; the whites looked down upon them, they looked up to the whites. A body of popular doctrine thus developed out of the cultural situation. The separation and relative status was a fact imposed from without. It favored the mixed bloods at the expense of the unmixed Negroes. The resulting sentiments and beliefs presently came to operate as an independent force making for the perpetuation and increase of the separation that, in the first instance, gave a basis for the body of belief.

As the differentiation advanced, the mulatto sense of superiority increased. The internal bonds, which distinguish a genuine class organization from a group held together by external forces, formed and strengthened. The mulattoes developed a common body of sentiment and belief that fostered their closer association. They held themselves more and more aloof from the backward Negroes and avoided association with them. In some cases very definite and highly exclusive mulatto societies were formed. Color or its absence came more or less to be a badge of the élite. This separation, seldom complete and often potential rather than realized, continued well into the present period.

It was inevitable that the Negro and mulatto individuals of education and refinement should desire association with persons of like culture. They had little in common with the illiterate laboring groups. They lived in a somewhat different universe. Their whole cultural orientation was toward the white rather than toward the Negro group. Ethically they were frequently more white than Negro. In tastes and ideals, interests and ambitions, standards and education, they were drawn to the dominant culture group. Opportunity for tolerable life and individual success was, or at least seemed to be, greater there.

But, regardless of education and refinement, they were excluded from participation in the white society. An assumption of inferiority and uncleanness attached to them and the traditional definitions classed them with the Negroes. They resented the classification. They had little in common with the rank and file of the Negroes with whom association was often offensive and always depressing. In the situation they were typically discontented, unhappy, rebellious persons. There was a long period during which the educated mulatto was a pathetic figure. His wishes could not be satisfied within the existing social order.

In some cases there was a possibility of individual escape. Where the physical marks were not conspicuous, they simply passed as white men. The number who have thus changed their racial classification with a change of residence is often grossly exaggerated, but that the number was considerable there is no doubt. This became increasingly frequent as continued intermixture and European immigration tended to blur the lines of race distinction, as the technique for concealing tell-tale racial marks increased, and as the anonymity of urban life increased. But large or small in amount, it is an evidence of the mulattoes, protest against an anomalous social status. But it was no solution except in individual and exceptional cases.

Others accepted, at least outwardly, the inevitable, identified themselves with the Negro groups, and assumed its leadership. For this they were prepared by the facts of superior education, a longer and more varied experience, a certain prestige, and a sense of superiority and self-confidence which the black group lacked because they lacked experience. The mulatto aristocracy was a generation or so ahead of the bulk of the race. They came to compose the bulk of the growing business and professional classes. This mulatto leadership the Negro group more or less willingly accepted. They could not do otherwise in the absence of education, status, experience, and self-confidence.

IV

NOT all the Negro leaders were mulattoes. They were more numerous and generally more prominent, capable, and influential. But there were also many influential black men. This was particularly true in certain lines of work, as church leadership, where the absence of education was not a serious handicap. Since the church touched the common Negro at so many points, the minister was always a man of local importance. The mulattoes never reached the dominating position in church affairs that they did in the professional and intellectual pursuits.

There was also, at all times, a more or less unanalyzed opposition on the part of the Negroes to the mulatto leadership and representation. There was a vague irritation arising from the mulattoes' assumption of superiority, an inarticulate desire among the masses for a black leadership. Even among his followers and admirers, Washington was often referred to in disappointed tones as a "little yellow man." The prominence in racial affairs of certain men has certainly been due in part to the fact that they were obviously and conspicuously not mixed bloods.

As the general Negro population gained in education and advanced in economic status more of the latent talent of the race had opportunity to get expression. As educational opportunity was extended through the public schools and in some degree equalized the talented children of the masses had some chance to emerge. And the success of every black child contributed to the growing self-confidence of the group. As time goes on the sheer weight of numbers will also be felt. The Negro group is four or five times as large as the mixed-blood group. Assuming the practical equality of native ability in the two groups, the Negroes will produce four or five times as many outstanding men when the opportunities of the groups have been equalized.

With the general economic and cultural advance of the group there is a greatly increased need for educated men. The number of physicians and lawyers and other professional men is far below the group needs. This has provided and will continue to provide an opportunity for the ambitious black boy. In every group leadership comes chiefly from the favored classes. It is only in exceptional times, when the need for superior men exceeds the capacity of the aristocracy to produce them, that talented individuals born in the lower orders are able to emerge. In the present and recent past the mulatto class, from which Negro leadership has traditionally come, is not able to supply the number of leaders needed.

The growing solidarity of the race operates to the same end. Regardless of the evaluative attitude that one takes toward the growth of racial self consciousness, it makes a place for an additional number of popular leaders and provides a background of racial self-respect that assures their appearance. And it makes certain that, other things approximately equal, the individuals not conspicuously unlike the masses in physical appearance will have some initial advantage. Because of or in spite of conspicuously Negroid features, superior individuals will have an increased opportunity to rise.

There is at the present time another force of some importance operating to equalize the opportunities of the Negroes and mulattoes. This is the growing disposition to judge the work of Negroes by the same standards as are elsewhere applied.

There have always been many sentimental and non-critical individuals ready to applaud any artistic effort of a Negro no matter how crude. They have done the cause of Negro advancement much harm as have also the white faddists who are always ready to patronize any Negro who gains momentary notoriety.

But there is an increasing group of more or less influential men who have become skeptical of the doctrine of race superiority and of the popular idea that native talent and ability are localized in certain favored economic and social classes. They are disposed to offer encouragement to unknown Negroes as well as to others of literary and artistic promise. Back of this interest, in some cases, is a belief that because of a peculiar racial temperament, Negroes are able to make a unique contribution to American culture. Others anticipate a distinctive culture contribution because the body of social experience of the Negroes is distinctive and peculiar. Still others look upon talent as a matter of individual variation as likely to appear in one place as another. They are concerned to discover and recognize it regardless of race or social class.

This relatively new interest has the effect of stimulating the Negroes' artistic efforts. They are assured of an appreciative and sympathetic audience for any meritorious work. So far as the productions of individuals are evaluated in objective terms, the Negro and the mulatto stand on exactly the same level, and a difference in the amount of talent emerging from the two groups is a measure either of the artificial differences in education, tradition, and economic status still existing, or of a difference in the number of favorably varient men that the two groups produce.

V

ALL such changes operate to a reduction in the advantage that the mixed bloods have traditionally enjoyed. In certain fields the Negro gets recognition and award proportional to accomplishment.

The present tendency of liberal-minded white people to discount the accidents of birth and economic status and to recognize individuals on the basis of personality and inherent worth removes in part one of the greatest handicaps of the Negro. He is not prejudged. There is no longer an assumption that his capacity varies inversely as his skin color. This new attitude of the liberal group stimulates and reinforces the growing self-respect of the black man. He can be a Negro, he can even be proud of the fact, without of necessity being a fool. The fact of Negro blood does not of necessity carry with it the presumption of incapacity. It may put certain more or less inconvenient obstacles in the way of the individual's advance. But the obstacles are external: they are in the social organization rather than in the psychology of the individual. External handicaps may be overcome. But there was no advance possible so long as the individual Negro accepted the general belief in the innate incapacity of the black man.

This change in the Negro's attitude toward himself removes one important advantage historically enjoyed by the mixed bloods. There is no longer the same assumption of mulatto superiority. The Negroes are rapidly developing a confidence in their own ability to manage their own affairs and to produce their own talented men.

As a result of the changing situation there is an increasing number of relatively black Negroes among the successful and prominent men.

In the future we may anticipate a farther decline in the preponderance of mixed bloods in the economic, political, and intellectual leadership. With the equalization of opportunity the Negroes, assuming equality in the distribution of native ability, will produce an increasing proportion of the prominent men.

But the advantage that the mixed bloods have enjoyed, and in a measure still enjoy, will continue.

It is not reasonable to anticipate that the difference will disappear in one generation. The mixed bloods have a long start and their tradition of superiority will persist. The doctrine of racial inequality is perhaps more firmly fixed in popular thought at the present time than it has ever been. It is not likely to be dislodged in any reasonable period of time. So long as it persists the mulattoes will enjoy an intangible but very real advantage that will get expression in their relative degree of success. It will require a long period for the Negroes to overcome the handicap of the later start and the popular assumption of lower capacity.

At the present time the mixed bloods occupy a somewhat superior status. As a result superior individuals are attracted to the group and tend to reinforce and perpetuate the status. Individuals born and reared in the group have an initial advantage in the struggle for success.

Again, the mixed bloods have the advantage of better education and more secure economic position. This gives a prestige at the same time that it assures better education, better homes, and greater economic security for the succeeding generations. This operates and will continue to operate to the advantage of the mulatto group.

But these differences are, on the whole, on the decline. With the spread of education, the growth of race consciousness, and the attitude of the liberal white people, the Negroes of talent will more and more come to the front. Ultimately, if the races are in reality equal in capacity, the Negroes will produce as many prominent men, in proportion to their number, as any other element in the population. The fact that the mulattoes have in the past produced more prominent men should be understood as a simple and obvious consequence of the historic circumstances that have favored them.

SUFFRAGE

By WILLIAM PICKENS

HERE ultimate power resides in voters, the importance of the right to vote cannot be overestimated. In its last analysis political suffrage means brute force, as one discovers in a state of war, or in the hands of a policeman. The importance of the right to vote is minimized by men only when they seek to deprive others of the right; it is never minimized when they seek or defend it for themselves.

The right of the individual to cast a vote equal to the vote of any other individual subject to the power of the same government—this right has climbed wearily in American history. And the suffrage articles of many of our state constitutions indicate that there is yet a long clin.b ahead. The right to vote has been supported by two different theories: the theory of "natural rights" and the theory of the good of the state. The natural rights theory looks backward; the good-of-the-state theory looks forward. The good of the state, which I interpret to mean the highest average good of everybody in the state, will prove to be the victorious idea. "Natural rights" is a beautiful sentiment, but one right is not more natural than any other in the state, where all right depends upon might. The good of the state is a progressive idea, based in reason and experience, and that may be advanced even by experimentation. Today the individual or group which seeks to acquire or defend its right to vote, must justify the claim in the good of the whole people, and not in poetic theories about primitive individualism and original compacts.

On the other hand, the idea of the good of the state is limited in its usefulness by the prevailing idea as to who or what constitutes the state. If the emperor be the state, the good of the state is a very small good. If the imperial family and the nobility be the state, the majority of inhabitants are left out; for the whole population cannot join the nobility, unless like the Romans they make all the rest of the world their subjects and slaves. And if, as in Mississippi, the state means only the white inhabitants, the pursuit of the good of the state will, at its best, aim to include less than fifty per cent of the people. Certain limited classes are excluded more or less temporarily from participation in government,—such as children and other dependents and wards. Children up to a certain age would be excluded by nature if not by law. Their exclusion is only temporary. They are the future state. Idiots and criminals are excluded; that is, the *known* and *registered* idiots and the *convicted* and *incarcerated* criminals. But idiots may become sane, and law-breakers may

become law-abiding, so that even these classes suffer only a conditional and possibly temporary exclusion.

These types of exclusion are, therefore, more reasonable, or rather less unreasonabe, than racial exclusion. Exclusion on account of race is a permanent disability, as irrational as it is inalterable. It is not a challenge to ambition but a fixed barrier. Apologists for racial disability have tried to justify it by references to children, paupers, criminals,—and they have used to cite the case of unenfranchised women, until the women destroyed the point of that citation by enfranchising themselves. But none of these cases parallels racial exclusion. Even economic-class exclusion is not a parallel. Excluded day-laborers might become capitalists and employers. The nearest parallel to the exclusion of a racial blood is the exclusion of some lower caste where law and tradition prevent the sons of such peasantry from rising above the status of their fathers. But even peasanthood may be overcome by social evolution or political revolution. The barrier against race is without a rival the most reasonless of all barriers.

Other apologists for racial exclusion remind us that even the favored race did not at first enjoy universally the right of suffrage; that the right was originally based in the possession of real estate, and advanced only gradually to a normal manhood basis. Inhabitants had to own so much real estate, so many acres, to vote. But the growth of industrial cities, where even the richest may not own acres of land, caused a change from this specific basis to an *ad valorem* basis, so that the voter no longer had to own so many acres but only real estate valued at so much, or on which he received a minimum rent or payed a minimum tax. Again, as industrial centers grew populous, it became evident that many good men in cities could not own even a foot of land, that there was not land enough to go round; and so a minimum valuation of personal property and belongings was admitted to qualify the voter. Later still it occurred to some that a man might not own any taxable property, real or personal; and yet be a human being and a decent member of society; therefore capitation taxes, poll taxes, were offered as compromises. A fellow with no property could pay a tax on his head. But even this head-tax was a surviving mark of the tyranny of property, as the appendix in the human body is a survival of some lower animal function. The battle front therefore advanced further toward manhood suffrage by reducing and minimizing taxes and offering alternatives and substitutes, such as service in the army, literacy, general intelligence, and even that indefin-

111

able thing called "good moral character." Thus the tyranny of property, with its heraldry of taxes, died a slow and stubborn death, and in some communities it is not yet dead.

This homage to the title-holder of property and to the so-called tax payer is ridiculous in the light of modern economic knowedge. It assumed that the whole burden of taxation and support of government rested on those who held the property and took the tax receipts. How slowly men's minds came to understand that the greatest payment of tax is the indirect payment: that the heaviest tax is paid by those who work and consume honestly. The level of wages and of the cost of necessaries is influenced by the tax burden of government. When a man buys a pair of shoes, he pays a share of the tax of the factory that made them and of every middleman that handled them; for the tax is a part of the expenses of the business and is figured into every pair of shoes. The tax is paid by every honest consumer of a hen from the hennery, of an apple from the orchard, and of a peanut from the farm. The poor man who pays the rent on a shack, pays the taxes on that shack,—not the man who collects the rent and gets the tax receipt. Those of us who own houses for rent, know how we arrive at fixing the rental figure against the tenant: first, we value the house at more than we could sell it for, and decide that we must earn the usurious rate of ten percent on that valuation; to this we add fifty dollars a year for repairs, and do not make any repairs; then we add the taxes, insurance, water rent, and all other imaginable costs for the year. If we let the place by the week, we next divide this sum by 48, instead of by 52, allowing 4 weeks for improbable vacancies, and by dividing the debt 48 times, we find what the debtor must pay us 52 times in order to discharge it; and finally, when this quotient turns out to be $7 a week, we charge him $10, just to be on the safe side and to simplify bookkeeping. And yet in spite of this chain of evidence, some people do not yet comprehend the truth that not those who get the tax receipts but those who work and honestly consume, especially those who work, pay the taxes, support the government, and are entitled to a vote.

The humbler members even of the dominant races have had to overcome this false notion of the exclusive relationship of property to production and of tax receipts to the ultimate burden of government. And yet the exclusion of the unpropertied and the non-tax-paying is no parallel to the exclusion of a race or blood. A fee simple deed can be acquired by the individual; membership in a favored race cannot be acquired by the individual. If poverty be a bar to citizenship, it can be overcome; but those who have in their veins the blood of any race, will always have it, and their children will have it to a thousand generations. The exclusion of a sex is more nearly like the exclusion of a race. But even sex is permanent only during the life of the individual; the children of a voteless woman might be males and become

voters. Besides, mothers, wives, sisters, daughters, who share the social and private economic life of the voters, can have more influence on their male electors than could the members of any separate race. By every comparison it is clear that race is the most unreasonable basis for citizenship, law or justice.

The citizenship of the Negro is the real test of American democracy. The front of liberty has advanced somewhat against the power and privilege of property but is being held back at the barricade of the color line. The first barrier was slavery. That was demolished in civil war. The way was next blocked by prejudice against ex-slaves, which continues almost unabated against their free-born descendants. Sumner, Chase and Frederick Douglass believed that an emancipated people, unenfranchised, might fall into a condition worse than slavery: for in the slave somebody has a private investment and a personal interest, but an anomalously "free" people without rights or power would be like unclaimed cattle,—wild buffaloes to be hunted by whoever had the inclination. To enfranchise ex-slaves was, of course a serious matter: an evil, but the lesser evil. Some say that so soon after emancipation was not "the best time" to enfranchise the Negro, and that he should have been educated and trained first. This argument makes two wrong assumptions: first, that real prejudice would be more willing that Negroes should get education than that they should get votes, and second, that the amendments made it necessary for unfit Negro individuals to be admitted to suffrage. The constitution forbids discrimination against the Negro on account of race or previous condition of servitude, but still permits discrimination on account of individual unfitness. Prejudice is not more willing that educated than that uneducated Negroes should vote, and the Negro needs the vote to get education. The last fifty years bear no evidence that the unaided sentiment of Mississippi or South Carolina would have enfranchised the Negro in the next two hundred years. There has been but one time when those amendments could have been ratified, and that was before the ex-slave-holding south regained complete local control. Logically, the *only time* when a thing can be done, is always the "best" time to do it; and the *worst time* in all eternity to do a thing is when it cannot be done. The conscience of the people, quickened by the sacrifices of the war, offered the opportunity of an epoch to broaden the base and strengthen the bulwark of popular suffrage. "An oligarchy of skin" is not more reasonable than one of titles or dollars. And we agree with Charles Sumner, the immortal democrat, that: "It is impossible to suppose that Congress will sanction governments . . . not founded on the consent of the governed."

Some say that the Negro should have come to the voting status by slow and gradual stages, as did the white man. That is a fallacious argument: it would be sound if the Negroes had been left alone in some separate territory, not to be governed or disturbed by others who voted. When a people is suddenly placed in an advanced environment, they must meet that environment by the educational, and not by the evolutional, process. In the school of an exacting environment, centuries must be overpassed in a decade, milleniums in a generation; otherwise, instead of teaching it to our children in schools, we should leave them to discover, as their ancestors discovered, the organization of the solar system and the surgery of the vermiform appendix. If Japan, instead of adopting dynamite and airplanes from the white man, had elected to evolve them slowly, as did the whites, that would have been nice—for everybody except Japan. Sumner and Douglass were immediately and abundantly justified by the double-decade of trickery and violence which followed the re-enfranchisement of the ex-slaveholders, from 1870 to 1890. Some of the tricks were: stealing and stuffing ballot boxes; false arrest the day before election and false counting the day after; voting "repeaters" or duplicating votes by thin tissue ballots; and sometimes by advertising the polling place as at one address and suddenly changing it to another. The violence, ranging from ordinary thuggery to murder, continues slightly abated to the present moment, but most of the unlawful tricks have been enacted into trick laws. The courts were apathetic to the brutality and dishonesty and have generally upheld the trick laws. These laws represent an effort to save the sickening conscience of the south, but they usually go only so far as to clothe dishonesty in legal immunity and specious respectability. Men said, as it were: "We are sick of robbing the Negro of his vote illegally, therefore we will revise the constitution and do it legally."

Constitutional conventions and legislatures endeavored to regain political respectability by juggling property requirements, indefinite "educational tests," residence and registration pitfalls, "good character" loopholes for the favored, and the threat of perjury against the disfavored. And in spite of the fact that all the registrars and other officers were white, some of these Negro-catching devices proved to be boomerangs to white applicants. Therefore South Carolina, the mother of nullification, secession and oppression, in a desperate example to save the superior white majority of the south from being surpassed by an inferior black minority, invented and enacted into law in 1895 the most brazen of all tricks,—the so-called "Grandfather Clause." The general architecture of "grandfather" legislation was this: first, the constitutional convention would lay down detailed and treacherous registration requirements for everybody in the state, with no mention of race or color,—and so far to square with the 15th amendment. But then a later clause or section would be added to the effect that those who were eligible or whose ancestors were eligible to vote in 1867 or 1868, could still register without these requirements. The essence of time in this lit-

tle device exempted the whole white population from the consequences of its shortcomings and left the black population at the mercy of the all-powerful registrars,—who knew their business. For nearly two decades this travesty was enforced in Southern states until declared unconstitutional under an organized attack of the Negro in 1914.

Men thought to salvage political honor and to salve their remarkable religious consciences by legalizing dishonesty. Many new constitutions were made, and their suffrage articles, with their labyrinthine catch-clauses, reveal their origin and purpose. States with no trick to try, no trap to set, and no fundamental national law to evade, sometimes write the suffrage articles of their constitutions in a single page, half a page, or a paragraph or so. But when we come to a state like Alabama and its constitution of 1901, the suffrage article consists of seven closely printed pages with twenty sections,—every section being a double-jawed trap with the trigger under the thumb of the registrar. The humble citizen may even be required to "understand" the constitution, something which, after more than a hundred years of serious study, the Supreme Court has not yet accomplished. But the courts, including the Supreme Court, have connived at and abetted these tricks and trick laws. Usually they require the disfranchised and aggrieved Negro to prove what everybody, including the court, already knows: namely, that he was denied the right to vote on account of his race or color. What is well known may be the hardest thing to prove. But when uneducated officials in Alabama refuse to register a Negro graduate of Yale, Harvard or Tuskegee, pretending to disqualify him on his lack of intelligence and not on his race, the presumption ought to lie in favor of that Negro—in a court of justice.

The worst trick, next to the "grandfather clause" itself, is the "white primary," which is a survival of the era of force and violence, a relic of the time when anti-Negro mobs generally bluffed, bullied and beat black men from the polls. A white primary conducted by the party which will also control the regular election, disfranchises the Negro as effectually as if he were on the moon. For example, a white Democratic primary election in Mississippi requires that the voter shall be not only a Democrat but also white. In most southern states the Democratic primary election absolutely and invariably the result of the regular election,—and in such regular election the Negro can cast only a perfunctory and unnecessary vote to ratify the nominations a service by enacting this bold trick into law and making it liable to more direct judicial attack. This was the meaning of "The Nixon Case," won by the colored people of El Paso in 1925. If "white primaries" are constitutional for Democrats, they are also lawful for Republicans, Socialists and all others; so that colored people, or any other minority race or class, could be disfranchised by any dominant political party.

If a race primary is reasonable, a sex primary is more reasonable, and women may be kept out of office and power by the primary-exclusion method. Women should remmber that the anti-slavery struggle gave the first real impetus to woman-suffrage. And so long as women could not vote, they were continually comparing their situations to that of the enslaved or disfranchised Negro; but since women have become enfranchised, their leaders have changed into regular politicians, like the men, forgetting the former comradeship of their cause, dodging moral issues and dealing in political expediences. But it was the World's Anti-Slavery Convention in London in 1840 which inspired its American women delegates to organize the first women's rights convention in New York in 1848. Frederick Douglass, the great Negro anti-slavery leader, was a loyal and life-long friend of woman-suffrage. As late as 1870 a Vermont constitutional convention turned down woman suffrage by the disastrous vote of 233 to 1,—but less than fifty years later women were enfranchised by ratified act of Congress. Will white women now prove that they are indeed the "equal of men" in political chicanery, or will they remember that colored women are still disfranchised by trick laws and maladministration?

Men like a good excuse even for a bad action. Therefore some say: "The Blacks of the south should take their own right to vote. The law is on their side. They are the majority in some localities. White men would die for their rights." All this declamation is the merest bunk. The Negro may be a majority in some locality, but he is a minority in the south as a whole, and a still smaller minority in the nation. State lines are artificial and invisible; so far as the Negro minority is concerned, South Carolina and Mississippi are one community with Virginia and Texas. If Mississippi were a separate and independent nation, free from all outside interference, its colored people could not be held in their present plight for 30 days. Not only the rest of the

south, but the United States army is back of every petty official in Mississippi, if his act be technically sanctioned by local law, however otherwise unjust. A black majority in an Alabama county is a mere local phenomenon, to be weighed against the greater white majority of the United States. White people of Massachusetts and Minnesota, by their very existence as parts of the republic, and especially by their silence and apathy, are the potential and the actual oppressors of the Negroes of the Mississippi deltas.

The whole people have a political and moral, even a physical relation to the status and rights of the smallest minority or the humblest citizen. The right of equal suffrage among a free citizenship is the one fundamental right which should not be abandoned to local prejudice and control. If the voter is the ultimate source of governmental power, the right to vote is primary among rights. If it is successfully denied, other rights become illusions. The solution of the suffrage problem involves the permanent solution of other problems: In every 100 persons in Georgia there are 54 whites and 46 blacks. If the Negro there could vote his 46 percent, he would get better schools by electing some of the school administrators; he would get more justice by defeating the unjust judges; he would have less oppressive laws by electing many of the legislators; he would be seldomer lynched and burned, for in the succeeding election he would defeat the unfaithful or cowardly sheriff. But against the fundamental wrong of racial disfranchisement, philanthropists and humanitarians might spend their money to the end of time trying to help the Negro to these desirable ends. The most economical help is to help one into a position of self-help. Impartial suffrage legislation and administration may not bring the millenium much nearer to the nation as a whole, but it would bring the Negro minority much nearer the millenium.

CONSECRATION

By LOIS AUGUSTA CUGLAR

My sweet, red blood to snuff the Yellow hate,
My proud, White flesh a Black girl's pangs to ease,
My muscles wrenched a Red-skin's wrongs to crush,
My entire body diced to clean the slate,
Sheer mock-heroics? They'll have love of me:
The long-enduring, mystical Chinese,
The colored girls whose goodness makes me blush,
The kind-faced squaws who peddle basketry.
They'll have it. Great God, surely it is right?
He taught it . . . Thy son pleasing in Thy sight—
No dawdling, half-way measures satisfy—
I must earn sure approval in Thine eye.
Failing, I plunge (may nothing me exempt)
In cauldron—seething, scalding self-contempt.

UNDERGRADUATE VERSE
FISK UNIVERSITY

YOUTH OF TWENTY CONTEMPLATES SUICIDE

By T. Thomas Fortune Fletcher

Life is a book
I have read
Twenty pages
The book
Is not beautiful
It bores me.
I do not wish
To read
The rest.
Life is a book
I have read
Twenty pages.

POEM

By Richard Jefferson

You went away.
A sharp, green star
Shot through my heart.
I want you back.
The green-gold flame
Burns sharp as steel
You do not come
Pin pointed sparks of pain
Prick out
The soft flesh
Around my heart
And leave a hard
And ashen skin
Unfeeling, cold and passion-spent.
I do not want you any more.

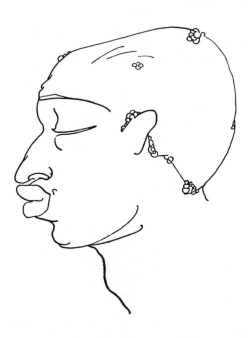

The child that does not cry,
Dies on its mother's back.

    —*An African Proverb.*

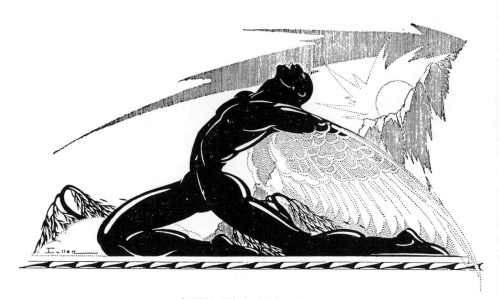

A DRAWING, *by Charles Cullen*

OUR LITTLE RENAISSANCE

By ALAIN LOCKE

OW that the time has come for some sort of critical appraisal, what of our much-heralded Negro Renaissance? Pathetically pale, thinks Mr. Mencken, like a candle in the sunlight. It has kindled no great art: we would do well to page a black Luther and call up the Reformation. Fairly successful, considering the fog and soot of the American atmosphere, and still full of promise—so "it seems" to Mr. Heywood Broun. I wonder what Mr. Pater would say. He might be even more sceptical, though with the scepticism of suspended judgment, I should think; but one mistake he would never make—that of confusing the spirit with the vehicle, of confounding the artistic quality which Negro life is contributing with the Negro artist. Negro artists are just the by-products of the Negro Renaissance; its main accomplishment will be to infuse a new essence into the general stream of culture. The Negro Renaissance must be an integral phase of contemporary American art and literature; more and more we must divorce it in our minds from propaganda and politics. Otherwise, why call it a renaissance? We are back-sliding, I think, into the old swamp of the Negro problem to be discussing, as we have been of late, how many Negro artists are first-rate or second-rate, and how many feet of the book-shelf of leather-bound classics their works to date should occupy. According to that Hoyle, the Grand Renaissance should have stopped at the Alps and ought to have effected the unification of Italy instead of the revival of Humanism.

To claim the material that Negro life and idiom have contributed to American art through the medium of the white artist may seem at first unfair and ungracious; may even be open to the imputation of trying to bolster up with reenforcements a "wavering thin line of talent." But what is the issue—sociology or art—a quality of spirit or complexions? The artists in question themselves are gracious enough, both in making their acknowledgements to the folk spirit, and in asserting the indivisible unity of the subject-matter. Only recently, confirming her adoption of Negro material as her special field, Mrs. Peterkin has said: "I shall never write of white people; to me their lives are not so colorful. If the South is going to write, what is it they are going to write about—the Negro, of course." Still more recently, the distinguished author of *Porgy* applauds shifting the stress from the Negro writer to the "Negro race as a subject for art" and approves of "lifting the material to the plane of pure art" and of making it available to the American artist, white or Negro, "as native subject-matter." And if there is any meaning to the term universal which we so blithely and tritely use in connection with art, it must be this. There is no other alternative on the plane of art. Indeed, if conditions in the South were more conducive to the development of Negro culture without transplanting, the self-expression of the "New Negro" would spring up just as one branch of the new literature of the South, and as one additional phase of its cultural reawakening. The common bond of soil and that natural provincialism would be a sounder basis for development than the somewhat expatriated position of the younger school of Negro writers. And if I were asked to name one factor for the anemic and rhetorical quality of so much Negro expression up to the present, I would cite not the unproved capacities of our authors but the pathetic exile of the Negro writer from his best material, the fact that he cannot yet get cultural breathing space on his own soil. That is at least one reason for the disabilities of the Negro writer in handling his own materials with vivid and intimate mastery.

More and more the younger writers and artists are treking back to their root-sources, however. Overt propaganda now is as exceptional as it used to be typical. The acceptance of race is steadily becoming less rhetorical, and more instinctively taken for granted. There was a time when the only way out of sentimental partisanship was through a stridently self-conscious realism. That attitude stripped the spiritual bloom from the work of the Negro writer; gave him a studied and self-conscious detachment. It was only yesterday that we had to preach objectivity to the race artist to cure the pathetic fallacies of bathos and didactic approach. We are just beginning perhaps to shake off the artifices of that relatively early stage; so to speak the Umbrian stiffness is still upon us and the Florentine ease and urbanity looms just ahead. It is a fiction that the black man has until recently been naive: in American life he has been painfully self-conscious for generations—and is only now beginning to recapture the naivete he once originally had. The situation is well put in a stanza of Mae Cowdery's poem—"Goal,"

> I must shatter the wall
> Of darkness that rises
> From gleaming day
> And seeks to hide the sun.
> I will turn this wall of
> Darkness (that is night)
> Into a thing of beauty.

I will take from the hearts
Of black men—
Prayers their lips
Are 'fraid to utter,
And turn their coarseness
Into a beauty of the jungle
Whence they came.

So, in the development of the materials of Negro life, each group of artists has a provincialism to outgrow; in the one case narrowness of vision, in the other, limiting fetters of style. If then it is really a renaissance—and I firmly believe it is, we are still in the hill-town stage, and the mellowness of maturity has not yet come upon us. It is not to escape criticism that we hold it thus; but for the sake of a fair comparison. The Negro Renaissance is not ten years old; its earliest harbingers cannot be traced back of the beginning of the century; its representative products to date are not only the work of the last three or four years, but the work of men still in their twenties so far as the producing artists are concerned. Need we then be censured for turning our adjective into an affectionate diminutive and for choosing, at least for the present, to call it hopefully "our little renaissance"?

MY HEART HAS KNOWN ITS WINTER

By ARNA BONTEMPS

A little while spring will claim its own,
In all the land around for mile on mile
Tender grass will hide the rugged stone.
My still heart will sing a little while.

And men will never think this wilderness
Was barren once when grass is over all,
Hearing laughter they may never guess
My heart has known its winter and carried gall.

PREMONITION

By ARCADEO RODANICHE

The moon looks like a bleached face
against the sun
that moves on
along the edge of night
which ruins the abysmal lands of yesterdays;
and as it hovers
over the mist of times unborn,—
staring at tomorrows—
it pales with dread
at the sight of the chaos it beholds
undergoing gestation
in the womb of time yet to come.

116

RACIAL SELF-EXPRESSION

By E. Franklin Frazier

I.

ONCURRENT with the growing group consciousness among the colored people there has come into prominence two rather widely divergent opinions as to the principles which should govern the development of the group in America. The opinion represented by one group is that colored people should undertake to conform in every respect to the culture about them, while another group holds that they should develop their own unique culture. Although these two viewpoints can not be said to take this apparently mutually contradictory form in the minds of all leaders, they indicate to a large extent two emerging philosophies of racial development which are receiving emphasis by their respective protagonists. Moreover, it should be added that these two theories have been present since the Negro began to assert himself as a free man in this country, but have received new accentuation by the so-called renaissance of Negro artists and thinkers. The debate in the NATION between Langston Hughes and George Schuyler was a skirmish in the clash between these two viewpoints. While the younger Negro artists are generally regarded as exponents of the opinion favoring a unique culture among the colored people, there is apparent disagreement among them. Countee Cullen's insistence that he wants to be a universal poet rather than a Negro poet is indicative of this lack of unanimity.

The issue between these two theoretical standpoints should not be confused with the more practical but less critical programs of certain Negro leaders and Southern whites, based upon the assumption that innate but not unequal racial endowments make it necessary that each race develop its own separate culture, with the corollary often expressed but always implied that intermarriage would cause a confusion or neutralization of their respective racial endowments. This new appreciation of the racial gifts of the Negro is naïve and seems to be a sublimation of the old admonition to the Negro that he should strive to be the "best possible Negro and not a poor imitation of the white man."

While it is improbable that either of these theoretic viewpoints will issue into immediate practical consequences, it is well to examine the assumptions upon which they are based. It is likely that both philosophies are rationalizations of tendencies which are observable in the different developments which are taking place in the experience of the colored group in America. In this essay, the writer hopes to contribute to the clarification of the issues involved and to evaluate the claims of the respective schools of opinion. As a first step in this analysis, the writer should say something about the relation between race and culture.

II.

ONE of the first results of the general acceptance of the evolutionary hypothesis was the attempt to explain racial differences in terms of the evolutionary process. For example, an attempt was made to show that contemporary "savages" possessed keener sensory powers than civilized man and therefore stood in the evolutionary scale closer to the lower animals than modern man. The comparatively smaller average of brain volume of certain races was taken as conclusive evidence of the retarded evolution of these races. Likewise the assumed mental traits of primitive man were supposed to bear testimony to his inferior evolutionary status. According to Spencer, primitive man lacked emotional control and the power of intellectual concentration. He was explosive and showed a marked deficiency in the capacity for abstract thought. Moreover, according to the classical anthropologists, social evolution followed a unilinear course; and that among the peoples of simple culture today, we had a view of the past evolution of modern man. But of greater importance to our subject was the assumption that primitive man's simple culture was a reflection of his incomplete or arrested physical and mental evolution.

These á priori assumptions based upon superficial observations and favorable data have been totally discredited by the critical field studies of modern anthropologists. Even the recent claim of Bean to having discovered significant anatomical differences in the Negro's brain has been discredited by Mall's subsequent findings. There is a tendency to discard even the term 'primitive' and substitute 'preliterate' in referring to peoples possessing simple cultures both because of the connotations of the older term and because the essential difference between primitive and modern man seems to be the absence of a written tradition among the former. The sensory powers of primitive peoples as well as their capacity for emotional control and abstract thought do not appear to differ essentially from those of civilized man. The recent attempt on the part of Levy-Bruhl, a French sociologist, to establish chiefly on the basis of accounts of travellers and missionaries a different order of mentality for preliterate peoples,

119

117

has met a similar fate at the hands of field workers, who have shown that preliterate peoples are as logical as modern man in the sphere of secular activities of life. There is a rather general agreement among ethnologists and sociologists that cultural advance is due to the contact of peoples rather than the flowering of the genius of a particular racial stock.

There are, however, some sociologists who, while recognizing the inadequacy of the other criteria of racial differences, hold to the theory of differences in temperamental endowment in races. According to this theory, races select different elements of a culture when brought into contact with it. The writer will postpone comment on this assumption until he considers more specifically the issue which is the occasion for this essay.

III.

THE foregoing all too brief summary of the conclusions regarding the relation between race and culture would lead us to believe that there is scarcely any warrant for the proposal that the Negro develop a unique culture in harmony with his racial characteristics. This opinion receives further support even from those authorities who hold to differences in the intellectual capacity of different races. These authorities hold that the intellectual powers of the Negroes and whites show the same range but that there is a greater frequency of those of superior intelligence among the whites. If the Negro were not differentiated from the whites by color, individuals under our competitive social organization would find their places according to their merit and the question of uniqueness of culture would never have been raised. The issue between the philosophies we are examining seems to resolve itself into the old issue of every nationalistic group. At first the group attempts to lose itself in the majority group, disdaining its own characteristics. When this is not possible there is a new valuation placed upon these very same characteristics and they are glorified in the eyes of the group. The same tendencies are observable in the case of the Negro group. There is, however, a conflict between the two tendencies noted above. On the one hand there is an attempt to efface Negroid characteristics and among the extremists of this group to dispense with the appellation, Negro; and on the other hand a glorification of things black. If the New Negro is turning within his group for new values and inspiration for group life, he is following the course of other nationalistic groups.

But to turn within the group experience for materials for artistic creation and group tradition is entirely different from seeking in the biological inheritance of the race for new values, attitudes and a different order of mentality. In the philosophy of those who stand for a unique culture among the Negroes there is generally the latter assumption. Moreover, while the group experience of the Ne-

groes in America may be a fruitful source for the materials of art and to some extent a source of group tradition, it offers a very restricted source for building up a thorough-going group life in America. By the entrance of the Negro into America, he was practically stripped of his culture. His whole group experience in America has been directed towards taking over cultural forms about him. In spite of the isolation in which he has lived, the Negro has succeeded in doing this to a remarkable degree. From the beginning he has not been able to draw upon a group tradition outside of America. When he has been charged with imitation of white models, he has been forced to plead guilty because there were no others. If the Negro had undertaken to shut himself off from the white culture about him and had sought light from within his experience, he would have remained on the level of barbarism. Even at the present time, if the Negro seeks relief from his conflict with the white majority by a flight from the reality of the culture about him, his development will be arrested and he will be shunted from the main highway of American life. In this respect the Negro's position is different from any other nationalistic group in America. While they can maintain their group life by drawing upon the national tradition from the Old World, and participate only to a small degree in the American tradition, the Negro has no source to draw on outside of America and only an inadequately assimilated American tradition from his past in this country.

It is quite possible that those who advocate a unique culture among Negroes would agree on the whole with the position taken above but would insist that the main point at issue is the difference in temperamental endowment. Therefore, as promised above, we shall turn to the consideration of this question. It has been pointed out by some that the facility with which the evangelical denominations spread among Negroes as well as the spirituals, and the seeming lack of strong economic motives, are indications of the peculiar racial temperament of the Negro. In the latter respect he is often contrasted with the Jew. But even here we can not say dogmatically that racial temperament has been the decisive factor in the emphasis placed by the Negroes on certain elements of American culture. There are historical and social factors which are adequate reasons to account for the fact that the majority of Negroes are Baptists and Methodists as well as the predilection of the Jew for economic activities. In Africa the Negro has always been a trader and his markets are an outstanding feature of African cultures. Even in America we find a remarkable development of business enterprises and this type of activities has become for many of the younger Negroes the surest means for the group to acquire status.

Mr. James Weldon Johnson has indicated, it appears to the writer, in "God's Trombones" the unique contribution of the Negro artists. In this unique work of art he has used the literary language of America to give artistic expression to the racial experience of the Negro in America. Whatever of racial temperament there is in these poems has been made articulate through cultural forms which were acquired by the artist in America. This does not deny that it is possible that the Negro artist working on the materials of the Negro's experience in America will create greater works than white artists. But we can not overlook the fact that at present white writers have surpassed Negro writers on the whole in the use of this material. While it may be true that at times the Negro has attempted to appropriate elements of American culture which have justified the rebuke that he was a "poor imitation of the white man" it was due to the fact that his group experience in America had not prepared him for such a rôle, but not because anything in his biological inheritance made the appropriation of such cultural traits incongruous. As the Negro group becomes more differentiated we see developing the same social types that are found in the white majority. There is a growing group of black Babbitts who are indistinguishable in their mental attitudes from the white Babbitts. The racial temperament of the Negro will assert itself in the cultural traits which he takes over; but such an indeterminable factor can not become the norm for determining the lines along which the Negro should build his culture. But it may be asked if it is desirable for the Negro to acquire uncritically all the traits of American culture. The remainder of this essay will be directed to an attempt to give a brief answer to this question.

The very fact that the issue between these two philosophies of racial development has been raised indicates a sophistication that could never have developed in cultural isolation. Negro leaders have enjoyed a cosmopolitan experience that enables them to view objectively their racial experience, as well as American culture and cultural traits in general. This appears to be increasingly one of the chief functions of the Negro intellectual. His strategic position makes him a critic of values for his group. But it still remains an open question how far the Negro group can escape the adoption of the cultural forms of America. One example will suffice to show that even in the sphere of economic life some selection may be possible the Negro must fit into the competitive industrial life about him either as a laborer or capitalist; but if the cooperative system of production and distribution offers superior spiritual values, then as far as practical he should develop in his economic life a cooperative economic technique. This he should do rather than slavishly take over both the form and spirit of modern industrialism. If such a course finds support in the racial experience of the Negro in America or in his temperamental endowment, the task will be easier and will be a distinct contribution to the general fund of American culture. Likewise, if because of racial temperament there is

a greater disposition on the part of Negroes to enjoy life than among the whites and this is recognized as a superior value, without sacrificing the efficiency of the group this trait should not be smothered by forcing the Negro's life into generally accepted molds.

Something should be said about another aspect of this question; namely, the building up of a group tradition. It seems to the writer that any such effort should be encouraged only so far as it is compatible with a fuller participation in American culture. In this matter the experience of immigrant groups has a lesson for the Negro. Those immigrant groups which have maintained the greatest group efficiency have suffered the least amount of social mal-adjustment. The efficiency of their group organization has been the best means for fitting their members for participation in American life. One of the primary needs of the Negro in America where he is not treated as an individual is the development of group efficiency. The work of the Association for the Study of Negro Life and History under Dr. Carter G. Woodson is very rapidly creating a group tradition which is necessary for group morale. This is a socializing process through which the individual members of a group acquire status. This is a healthy sign among Negroes and need not be incompatible with their struggle for fuller participation in American culture so long as it does not increase their isolation.

IV.

THIS discussion has undertaken to evaluate the over-simplified assumption expressed and implied by those who are advocating a unique cultural development for the Negro, that our modern culture is the expression of certain special intellectual and temperamental traits and that the Negro should build a culture in harmony with his racial endowment. It was pointed out that the racial experience of the Negro was unique because of historical and social factors rather than of biological inheritance. Even those traits which are so universally ascribable to temperamental rather than intellectual differences were shown to have a possible explanation in social factors. While for the artist this unique experience was recognized as a fertile source, it was not deemed adequate for the building up of a thorough-going racial tradition which would afford maximum individual development. On the other hand, the utility of a group tradition built even upon African material for group efficiency was given due recognition. But finally it was shown that any nationalistic program that made the Negro seek compensations in a barren racial tradition and thereby escape competition with the white man which was an inevitable accompaniment of full participation in American culture, would lead to intellectual, spiritual and material impoverishment such as one finds among the Southern mountain whites.

OUR GREATEST GIFT TO AMERICA

By George S. Schuyler

N divers occasions some eloquent Ethiop arises to tell this enlightened nation about the marvelous contributions of his people to our incomparable civilization. With glib tongue or trenchant pen, he starts from the arrival of the nineteen unfortunate dinges at Jamestown in 1619, or perhaps with the coming of the celebrated Columbus to these sacred shores with his Negro mate in 1492, and traces the multiple gifts of the black brethren to the present day. He will tell us of the vast amount of cotton picked by the Negro, of the hundreds of roads and levees the black laborers have constructed, of the miles of floors Negro women have scrubbed and the acres of clothes they have washed, of the numerous wars in which, for some unknown reason, the Sambo participated, of the dances and cookery he invented, or of the spirituals and work songs composed by the sons of Ham and given to a none too grateful nation. The more erudite of these self-appointed spokesmen of the race will even go back to the Garden of Eden, the walls of Babylon, the pyramids of Egypt and the palaces of Ethiopia by way of introduction, and during their prefatory remarks they will not fail, often, to claim for the Negro race every person of importance that has ever resided on the face of the earth. Ending with a forceful and fervent plea for justice, equality, righteousness, humanitarianism, and other such things conspicuous in the world by their absence, they close amid a storm of applause from their sable auditors—and watch the collection plate.

This sort of thing has been going on regularly for the last century. No Negro meeting is a success without one or more such encouraging addresses, and no Negro publication that fails to carry one such article in almost every issue is considered worthy of purchase. So general has the practice become that even white audiences and magazines are no longer immune. It has become not unusual in the past few years for the Tired Society Women's Club of Keokuk, Iowa, or the Delicatessen Proprietors' Chamber of Commerce or the Hot Dog Vendors' Social Club to have literary afternoons devoted exclusively to the subject of the lowly smoke. On such occasions there will be some such notable Aframerican speakers as Prof. Hambone of Moronia Institute or Dr. Lampblack of the Federal Society for the Exploitation of Lynching, who will eloquently hold forth for the better part of an hour on the blackamoor's gifts to the Great Republic and why, therefore, he should not be kept down. Following him there will usually be a soulful rendition by the Charcoal Singers of their selected repertoire of genuine spirituals, and then, mayhap one of the younger Negro poets will recite one of his inspiring verses anent a ragged black prostitute gnawing out her soul in the dismal shadows of Hog Maw Alley.

It was not so many years ago that Negro writers used to chew their fingernails and tear as much of their hair as they could get hold of, because the adamantine editors of white magazines and journals invariably returned unread their impassioned manuscripts in which they sought to tell how valuable the Aframerican had always been to his country and what a dirty shame it was to incinerate a spade without benefit of jury. Not so today, my friends. The swarms of Negro hacks and their more learned associates have at last come into their own. They have ridden into popular demand on the waves of jazz music, the Charleston, Mammy Songs and the ubiquitous, if intricate, Black Bottom. Pick up almost any of the better class periodicals of national note nowadays and you are almost sure to find a lengthy paper by some sable literatus on the Negro's gifts to America, on his amazing progress in becoming just like other Americans in habit and thought, or on the horrible injustice of jim crow cars. The cracker editors are paying generously for the stuff (which is more than the Negro editors did in the old days), and as a result, the black scribblers, along with the race orators, are now wallowing in the luxury of four-room apartments, expensive radios, Chickering pianos, Bond Street habiliments, canvasback duck, pre-war Scotch and high yellow mistresses.

All of which is very well and good. It is only natural that the peckerwoods, having become bored to death with their uninteresting lives, should turn to the crows for inspiration and entertainment. It is probably part of their widespread rationalization of the urge they possess to mix with the virile blacks. One marvels, however, that the principal contribution of the zigaboos to the nation has been entirely overlooked by our dusky literati and peripatetic platform prancers. None of them, apparently, has ever thought of it. While they have been ransacking their brains and the shelves of the public libraries for new Negro gifts of which to inform their eager listeners at so much per word or per engagement, they have ignored the principal gift sprawling everywhere about them. They had but to lift their eyes from the pages of their musty tomes and glance around. But they didn't.

"And what," I can hear these propagandists feverishly inquiring with poised fountain pens and notebooks, "is this unchronicled contribution to the worth of our nation?" Well, I am not unwilling to divulge this "secret" that has been all too apparent to the observing. And though the brownskin intelligentsia are now able to pay for the information—and probably willing to do so—I modestly ask nothing, save perhaps a quart of decent rye or possibly one of the numerous medals shoveled out each year to deserving coons. Hence, like all of the others, I now arise, fleck a speck off my dinner jacket, adjust my horn-rimmed nose glasses, and, striking an attitude, declaim the magic word: Flattery!

Yes folks, the greatest gift we have made to America is flattery. Flattery, if you please, of the buckra majority; inflation of the racial ego of the dominant group by our mere proximity, by our actions and by our aspirations. "How Come?" I am belligerently and skeptically quizzed, and very indulgently I elucidate. Imitation, some one has said, is the sincerest flattery. It is quite human to be pleased and feel very important when we are aped and imitated. Consider how we Negroes shove out our chests when an article appears in an enterprising darkey newspaper from the pen of some prominent African chief saying that his dingy colleagues on the Dark Continent look to their American brethren, with their amazing progress, for inspiration? How sweet is flattery, the mother of pride. And pride, we have been told, is absolutely essential to progress and achievement. If all of this be true of the dark American, mow much truer must it be of the pink American? By constant exposure to his energetic propagandists in press, on platform and in pulpit, the colored brother has forged ahead—to borrow an expression from the Uplift—until he can now eat with Rogers silver off Haviland china, sprawl on overstuffed couches and read spicy literature under the glow of ornate floor lamps, while the strains of "Beer Bucket Blues" are wafted over the radio. This is generally known as progress. Now if the downtrodden Negro, under the influence of his flattering propagandists, has been able to attain such heights of material well being, is it any wonder that the noble rednecks have leaped so much farther up the scale of living when surrounded by millions of black flatterers, both mute and vocal? Most certainly not.

Look, for example, at Isadore Shankersoff. By hook or by crook (probably the latter) he grabbed off enough coin of his native land to pay his passage to America. In Russia he was a nobody—hoofed by everybody—the mudsill of society. Quite naturally his inferiority complex was Brobdingnagian. Arriving under the shadow of the Statue of Liberty, he is still Isadore Shankersoff, the prey of sharpers and cheap grafters, but now he has moved considerably higher in the social scale. Though remaining mentally adolescent, he is no longer at the bottom: he is a white man! Over night he has become a member of the superior race. Ellis Island marked his metamorphosis. For the first time in his life he is better than somebody. With-

out the presence of the blackamoor in these wonderfully United States, he would still know himself for the thick-pated underling that he is, but how can he go on believing that when America is screaming to him on every hand that he is a white man, and as such entitled to certain rights and privileges forbidden to Negro scientists, artists, clergymen, journalists and merchants. One can understand why Isadore walks with firmer tread.

Or glance at Cyrus Leviticus Dumbbell. He is of Anglo-Saxon stock that is so old that it has very largely gone to seed. In the fastnesses of the Blue Ridge Mountains his racial strain has been safely preserved from pollution by black and red men, for over two hundred years. Thus he is a stalwart fellow untouched by thrift or education. Cy finally tires of the bushes and descends to one of the nearby towns. There he finds employment in a mill on a twelve-hour shift. The company paternalistically furnishes him everything he needs and thoughtfully deducts the cost regularly from his slender pay envelope, leaving him about two dollars for corn liquor and moving pictures. Cy has never had cause to think himself of any particular importance in the scheme of things, but his fellow workers tell him differently. He is a white man, they say, and therefore divinely appointed to "keep the nigger down." He must, they insist, protect white womanhood and preserve white supremacy. This country, he learns, is a white man's country, and although he owns none of it, the information strikes him not unpleasantly. Shortly he scrapes together ten dollars, buys Klan regalia, and is soon engaged in attending midnight meetings, burning crosses, repeating ritual from the Kloran, flogging erring white womanhood for the greater purity of Anglo-Saxondom, and keeping vigilantly on the lookout for uppish and offensive zigaboos to lynch. Like the ancient Greeks and Romans, he now believes himself superior to everybody different from him. Nor does the presence of jim crow institutions on every hand contribute anything toward lessening that belief. Whatever his troubles may be, he has learned from his colleagues and the politicians, to blame it all on the dark folks, who are, he is now positive, without exception his inferiors.

Think, also, of demure little Dorothy Dunce. For twelve years she attended the palatial public school. Now, at eighteen, having graduated, she is about to apply her Latin, Greek, English Literature, Ancient History, Geometry and Botany to her everyday work as packer in a spaghetti factory. When she was very young, before she entered the kindergarten, her indulgent parents used to scare her by issuing a solemn warning that a big, black nigger would kidnap her if she wasn't a good little girl. Now that she has had American popular education turned loose upon her, she naturally believes differently: i. e., that every big, burly, black nigger she meets on a dark street is ready to relieve her by force of what remains of her virtue.

A value is placed upon her that she would not have in Roumania, Scotland, Denmark or Montenegro. She is now a member of that exalted aggregation known as pure, white womanhood. She is also confident of her general superiority because education has taught her that Negroes are inferior, immoral, diseased, lazy, unprogressive, ugly, odoriferous, and should be firmly kept in their place at the bottom of the social and industrial scale. Quite naturally she swells with race pride, for no matter how low she falls, she will always be a white woman.

But enough of such examples. It is fairly well established, I think, that our presence in the Great Republic has been of incalculable psychological value to the masses of white citizens. Descendents of convicts, serfs and half-wits, with the rest have been buoyed up and greatly exalted by being constantly assured of their superiority to all other races and their equality with each other. On the stages of a thousand music halls, they have had their vanity tickled by blackface performers parading the idiocies of mythical black roustabouts and rustics. Between belly-cracking guffaws they have secretly congratulated themselves on the fact that they are not like these buffoons. Their books and magazines have told them, or insinuated, that morality, beauty, refinement and culture are restricted to Caucasians. On every hand they have seen smokes endeavoring to change from black to white, and from kinky hair to straight, by means of deleterious chemicals, and constantly they hear the Negroes urging each other to do this and that "like white folks." Nor do the crackers fail to observe, either, that pink epidermis is as highly treasured among blacks as in Nordic America, and that the most devastating charge that one Negro can make against another is that "he acts just like a nigger." Anything excellent they hear labeled by the race conscious Negroes as "like white folks," nor is it unusual for them, while loitering in the Negro ghetto, to hear black women compared to Fords, mulatto women to Cadillacs and white women to Packards. With so much flattery it is no wonder that the Caucasians have a very high opinion of themselves and attempt to live up to the lofty niche in which the Negroes have placed them. We should not marvel that every white elevator operator, school teacher and bricklayer identifies himself with Shakespeare, Julius Caesar, Napoleon, Newton, Edison, Wagner, Tennyson and Rembrandt as creators of this great civilization. As a result we have our American society, where everybody who sports a pink color believes himself to be the equal of all other whites by virtue of his lack of skin pigmentation, and his classic Caucasian features.

It is not surprising, then, that democracy has worked better in this country than elsewhere. This belief in the equality of all white folks—making skin color the gauge of worth and the measure of citizenship rights—has caused the lowest to strive to become among the highest. Because of this great ferment, America has become the Utopia of the material world; the land of hope and opportunity. Without the transplanted African in their midst to bolster up the illusion, American would have unquestionably been a much different place; but instead the shine has served as a mudsill upon which all white people alike can stand and reach toward the stars. I submit that here is the gift par excellence of the Negro to America. To spur ten times our number on to great heights of achievement; to spare the nation the enervating presence of a destructive social caste system, such as exists elsewhere, by substituting a color caste system that roused the hope and pride of teeming millions of ofays—this indeed is a gift of which we can well be proud.

EFFIGY

By Lewis Alexander

FORM

You stood in the yard
Like a lilac bush
With your head tossed high
As if to push
Your hair in a blossom
About your head
You wore the grace
Of a fragile reed.

FASHION

Your gown crackled loud
Like the swish of leaves
Being flitted about
By a lyric breeze
Your step was like a dainty fawn
Breathing the nectared air at dawn,
Oft have I seen the rose in you
But it never bloomed such a brilliant hue.

THE NEGRO ACTOR'S DEFICIT

By Theophilus Lewis

HE actor makes the theatre. He creates the theatre by distinguishing himself from a crowd of worshippers or revellers by his special talent for mimicry or simulation. His ability to give clever and convincing imitations of familiar persons and situations and well known objects of nature excites widespread curiosity. By improving his talent he crystalizes transient curiosity into continued interest and makes the theatre a permanent institution of public amusement.

The theatre has now become an independent institution. Formerly it was an appendage of the church. Its performances were a part of religious ritual, religious propaganda or religious orgy. Now its performances attract a definite social interest on their own merits—an interest, separate and distinct from all other interests, which no other institution can satisfy. People no longer go to see the actor simulate the story of the Passion. They go to see him jig a lively step or enact a contemporary and perhaps humorous version of the story of Potiphar's wife. The actor, who began as a subordinate of the priest, has achieved his autonomy and decides for himself whether he shall devote his talent to making people good or to making them happy.

He usually decides to make them happy. As the servant of the church the actor devoted his skill to making his audience reverent. As the master of the theatre he specializes in making his audience merry. He eliminates the elements of ceremonial and worship and restricts the theatre solely to amusement. But the relationship between the church and the theatre has not been completely severed. Neither the church, dominated by the priest, nor the theatre, controlled by the actor, offers its patrons any material boon. Each is strictly a spiritual institution. The church endures because it satisfies men's deepest emotional cravings; the theatre, in its immature state, thrives because it caresses their lighter emotions.

I have not, of course, attempted to trace the literal steps by which the acolyte becomes the actor and the mystery tableau or the revel evolves into the theatre. I am seeking, merely, to isolate the origin and the nature of the theatre as a means of leading up to the final responsibility and test of the actor. The theatre, when it has once been established as an autonomous institution, can be imported from one country to another. America, for example, borrowed its theatre along with other fundamentals of culture from Europe. We Aframericans borrowed our theatre from our white

compatriots. But transferring the theatre from one continent or culture to another continent or culture does not change its essential nature any more than importing English sparrows from abroad made them Baltimore orioles.

The theatre is a spiritual institution in America and Australia as well as in Greece and England. It obtained its original license from the church and it has a similar spiritual function to perform. The actor began as a subordinate of an institution designed to exalt men. When the theatre became independent he found himself head of an institution devoted merely to entertaining them. This, in a sense, is cultural degradation. If the actor permits the stage to remain at this level he is a social factor of negligible significance, except, perhaps, to the police. If, on the other hand, the actor advances the theatre to a point where it exalts as well as entertains, where it both colors and reflects social conduct, he becomes a cultural agent coordinate with the priest and one of the most precious members of society.

I can now consider what Negro actors have done with their theatre, or, if you prefer, what they have accomplished in the theatre. The test will be empirical. I will not compare the accomplishments of Negro actors with an ideal or a theory. I will compare their accomplishments with what actors of other peoples have accomplished, making due allowance for whatever extenuating circumstances exist in favor of Negro actors if they have failed to make the grade.

The theatre, excepting the church and sports, is the most democratic of spiritual institutions. Since sports are hardly influenced by art at all while the church employs art merely as a handmaiden the theatre is really the most democratic of all artistic institutions. It evolved out of a crowd and its entertainment has always been adapted to mass rather than to individual enjoyment. More than any other esthetic institution it reflects the spiritual life of a whole people. This is not to say the theatre appeals to every individual of a group. It means that the theatre, if it is in a healthy state, will attract representative individuals from every class of society from the lowest to the highest. If it draws its patrons from any one class, either the lowest or the highest, to the exclusion of other levels of society, it will become either spiritually anaemic or spiritually crapulous, hence unable to keep pace with the cultural progress of the group.

It seems like a waste of words to describe the audience of the Negro theatre for the reader is doubtless familiar with it already. It is well known

125

that the Negro theatre appeals only to the lowest
elements of the race. Not the lowest class economically, but the lowest intellectually and morally
—the ignorant and depraved. The poorer respectable classes either avoid it or attend its performances
with shamefaced apologies. The middle and upper
classes hold it in contempt and the more intelligent
actors themselves are disgusted with it. There is
no better way to describe the attitude of respectable
Negroes toward their theatre than to point to their
indifference to its frequent indecency. Unlike the
white public, which is often alarmed by the moral
tone of its theatre, the colored respectable classes
seldom protest against the tendency of their stage
toward turpitude. As they never attend its performances its indecency does not offend them and
they do not care whether it continues or not.

The cause of the indifference of the better classes
is obvious and the cause of the interest of the lewd
element is equally so. The general tone of the
Negro stage has never risen above the level of the
burlesque show. Its performances consist of a continuous display of imbecile and obscene humor. An
actor with a deformed mouth will sing a song and
vibrate his lips. An elongated comedian with legs
like broomsticks will sing a song and proceed to
make letter Z's and figure 4's with his limbs. When
an actor has no physical deformity to capitalize he
will make up for the deficiency by arraying himself
in a suit of trick clothes. A derby three inches in
diameter will perch perilously atop his poll, a ten-
inch safety pin will hold his coat together, thirty-
inch shoes will encase his feet and a red flannel
patch will adorn the seat of his black breeches.
Add to this a patter which depends on the mispro-
nunciation of words for its humor and some by-
play of ribald sex jokes and you have the entire
gamut of amusement offered by the Negro stage.
What it was thirty years ago it is today. Amusement of this sort, once the novelty has worn off,
can divert only the dull and depraved. The progressive classes are revolted by it.

Fully eight out of ten colored actors will admit
the deplorable condition of the Negro stage, only
they will demur responsibility for it and place the
blame on the public. They argue that if respectable colored people would patronize the theatre they
(the actors) could raise the standard of amusement.
but since only members of the lower element fill
the auditorium they must play down to the level
of their audience. This sounds plausible enough
but it is nevertheless highly specious. The public
has no business in the theatre except to be entertained and occasionally exalted. The rest is up to
the dramatist, whose part we will not consider for
the present, and the actor.

The actor is an artist, or he ought to be, and
he must assume the same responsibility to the public every other artist assumes. A man goes to the
theatre to see his spiritual likeness just as he goes to
a portrait artist to have his physical likeness depicted. There is a little bit of Henry V in every

Englishman, a mite of Cyrano de Bergerac in every
Frenchman and a bit of Toussant l'Ouverture or
Booker Washington in every Aframerican. The
Englishman, the Frenchman and the Aframerican
each wants to see the stage reflect his inner heroism,
nobility and wit. No one wants to see the actor depict him as a gorilla no more than he wants to see
a portrait artist paint his picture with the snout
of a boar or the ears of an ass. It is not his business to tell the painter what brushes or pigments
to use. Neither is it his concern what methods the
actor employs. He has fulfilled both his duty and
his right when he expresses approval or disapproval
of the finished work.

The artist, whether he is actor, painter or poet,
is a spiritual pioneer. Gainborough did not ask
the citizens of London how he should paint the
Blue Boy, Keats did not canvas the town on how
to write the Ode to a Nightingale nor did the Pari-
sians specify how Coquelin should portray the role
of Cyrano. Each of those artists divined the spiritual needs of the time and proceeded to satisfy
those needs. He did not say people have never
seen a picture, poem or acting like I have in mind
so I must not produce it till they let me know they
are ready to appreciate it. Still that is precisely
what the Negro actor says in substance when he
complains that the absence of the better classes from
the theatre prevents him from raising the standard
of entertainment.

If the Negro actor was the artist he should be,
he would not complain of being dominated by his
audience. Instead he would master his audience
and make it like a progressively higher form of
amusement. It goes without saying that no actor,
whatever his genius, can make a *How Come?* audience like the Master Builder. On the other hand
it is hard to conceive how an actor can be so bad
as to make any audience dislike Cyrano de Bergerac.
It can be logically objected that heroic plays like
the latter are few and far between. It can be just
as logically replied that melodramas are easy to
obtain and that they would uplift the present audience of the Negro theatre and at the same time attract patrons from higher levels of the race. The
fact that Negro actors have not brought their stage
to this transition period from a lower to a higher
form of amusement simply means they lack imagination and energy. It is easier to wear the same old
trick clothes and spiel off the same old patter
than it is to learn the lines of a play, so our actors
follow the line of no resistance and keep doing
the same old stuff. It is not true that they are compelled to play down to their audience. They are
playing up to the limit of their own ability. The
only thing that distinguishes the flashily dressed
hoodlum in the box seat from the actor on the stage
is that the former eats more and drinks less.

Like most shoddy characters the Negro actor,
as a rule, is wholly lacking in race pride. This is
not surprising, for pride of race is akin to pride in
self, and incompetence and lack of patriotism com-

monly go together. The genuine artist is always a patriot at bottom. He may incessantly bawl his countrymen out to the dogs but in his heart he cherishes an intense affection for them. Some first rate artists like Paderewski even do not disdain to assume political office.

The artist imbued with a sense of race pride and responsibility, like Ethel Waters or the late Bob Cole and Florence Mills, is a rare bird in the ranks of Negro performers. Instead of doing their best to make the Negro theatre a house of loveliness for the diversion of Negro audiences most colored actors are forever trying their hardest to get out of it altogether, using it only as a stepping stone to popularity with white producers. Broadway or Big Time vaudeville is the goal of every colored performer. Not all of them reach their goal, of course, but it is always present in their dreams; and they do not feel that they have made a success until they have heard the applause of Caucasian palms.

The Negro stage is so much a thing apart from the interests of the race at large that it is hardly probable that any colored apologists for it will be found outside the ranks of professional actors. There may be some, however, and they may argue that the colored actor cannot have made such a dismal failure of his theatre, for white people frequently attend its performances and enjoy them. These white visitors, it may be pointed out, are often members of the cultured classes and quite familiar with the best their own stage affords. The answer is plain. These white visitors have not seen the same actors doing the same thing year after year for two decades. Hence they mistake what is novel to them for originality on the part of the actor just as they are likely to mistake his obscenity for sophistication. Even so, they do not compare the Negro stage with their own, for they think of the latter in terms of drama while they think of the Negro stage in terms of vaudeville.

Drama and vaudeville. The comparison epitomizes the Negro actor's deficit. We think of the French theatre in terms of its Talmas, Coquelins, Bernhardts and Guitrys. We think of the English theatre in terms of its Burbages, Irvings, Garricks, Siddonses, Bracegirdles and Ellen Terrys. We think of the American theatre in terms of its Forests, Hacketts, Fiskes and Barrymores. We think of the Negro theatre in terms of Johnny Hudgins, Billy Mills, Hamtree Harrington and Miller and Lyles. But what about our Cloughs, Pryors, Desmonds and Bishops? Simply this. If the whole kit and caboodle of them were worth the grave dust of Joseph Jefferson they wouldn't have to hang around Broadway stage doors crying for dramatic handouts at $35 a week top.

The cultural value of the actor, I said in the beginning of this article, must be judged by his ability to raise the theatre above the plane of amusement and make it an instrument for the expression of the higher spiritual life of his people. The theatre should be a dynamic institution that both reflects and colors the general pattern of life of which it is a part. The Negro actor has not only failed to make the stage a vital part of our cultural life; he has degraded it below the notice of the better classes of the race. Our stage does not influence our culture even to the extent of providing matinee idols for romantic schoolgirls. Instead it panders exclusively lasciviousness of the feeble minded and depraved elements of the race. Worse. The majority of our actors are ignorant of both the nature and the history of the theatre and have only the vaguest suspicion why the respectable classes ignore their existence. The few performers intelligent enough to sense what is wrong with our theatre lack sufficient energy to make even a gesture of reform. In his account with his race the balance of the Negro actor remains heavily in the red.

TWO POEMS

By Edward S. Silvera

THE UNKNOWN SOLDIER

"Behold our son, our valiant dead,"
They say to one another—
And all the while
None ever thinks
That he might be my brother:
But I am glad he holds his peace,
I'm glad he can't come back;
I'd hate to see Love crucified
If he, by chance, were black.

OLD MAID

The fires of a thousand loves
Burned bright within her
Night and day,
The years like bellows
Fanned the flames
Which ate her heart and soul away.

DUNCANSON

(An American Artist Whose Color Was Forgot)

W. P. Dabney

STRANGE to say, the world, or rather our world, knows little of R. S. Duncanson, a native of Cincinati, Ohio, who years before the Civil War had established a reputation as an artist of high rank. The ignorance arises from the fact that in this country, his associates were artists and his color was rarely mentioned.

Though self-taught, his pictures early attracted attention. The Art records of England mention and describe some of the paintings he exhibited when making a tour of Europe. His associates even in his home town were men of international reputation, among them Farny, Lindsay, S. Jerome, Uhl, and Henry Mosler, who afterwards located in New York. Among his paintings, now in Cincinnati, are a full size portrait of William Cary which hangs at the Ohio Military Institute, and a life size picture at Ohio Mechanics' Institute of Nicholas Longworth, I. There are several other pictures in existence, among which are magnificent landscapes.

One of the finest, *The Western Hunters' Encampment,* was purchased by me from a connoisseur of the fine arts who had treasured it for years. It hangs on the wall of my library and there, mellowed by the light that falls upon it from above, its marvelous lineal precision, its magnificent coloring accentuated by age, reveal a touch that ever characterizes the work of the masters.

The following brief extract is taken from the *Enquirer* of December 21, 1924:—

"In 1857, Cincinnati was a large art center, the most prominent west of the Alleghenies. Already the city was known for the fame of Hiram Powers, a sculptor, and a score of painters headed by James H. Beard, Thomas Buchanan Read and Robert S. Duncanson, the phenomenal colored man, whose father was a Scotchman of Canada, and whose mother was a mulatto.

"Seventy-five years ago, according to Charles Cist's 'Cincinnati in 1851,' Cincinnati had numerous artists who had already become, or were about to become, distinguished for work. One of these was the colored man, Robert S. Duncanson, who was then already prominent for such historical pieces as 'Shylock and Jessica,' 'Ruins of Carthage,' 'Trial of Shakespeare,' 'Battle Ground of the River Raisin' and 'Western Hunters' Encampment.'

"In 1865, November 24, there appeared in the Cincinnati Daily Gazette the following item from Moncure D. Conway of Cincinnati, who wrote from London, England, telling of the advance of Robert S. Duncanson:

128

"In walking through the gallery of miniatures, at the South Kensington Museum the other day I met Duncanson, whom some of your readers will remember as one who, a few years ago, was trying to make himself an artist in Cincinnati, and who had already produced a worthy piece of imaginative art in a picture of Tennyson's 'Lotus Eaters.'

"Duncanson subsequently left Ohio and repaired to Canada, where his color did not prevent his association with other artists and his entrance into good society. He gained much of his culture and encouragement in Canada, retouched his 'Lotus Eaters,' produced one or two still better paintings and set out for England. In Glasgow and other Scotch cities he exhibited these paintings with success."

"He has been invited to come to London by various aristocratic personages. Among others, by the Duchess of Sutherland and the Duchess of Essex, who will be his patrons. He also received a letter from the poet laureate, Tennyson, inviting him to visit him at his home, in the Isle of Wight, where he will go and take with him the 'Lotus Eaters.' Think of a Negro sitting at the table with Mr. and Mrs. Alfred Tennyson, Lord and Lady of the Manor, and Mirror of Aristocracy—and so forth!
(Signed) "Aubrey" Moncure D. Conway.

"In 1866 there appeared in 'The Art Journal,' of London, England, the following tribute to American Art. It was headed, 'The Land of the Lotus Eaters. Painted by R. S. Duncanson.'

" 'America has long maintained supremacy in landscape art, perhaps indeed its landscape artists surpass those of England. Certainly we have no painter who can equal the works of Church; and modern British School. Duncanson has established high fame in the United States and in Canada. He is a native of the States and received his art education there, but it has been "finished" by a course of study in Italy, by earnest thoughts at the feet of the great masters and by a continual contemplation of nature under Southern skies.

"We therefore may add this picture to the many works of rare value supplied to us by the landscape artists of America.

"Many wonderful tributes have been paid to this man, so worthy, yet so little known among us. A genius of 'purest ray serene,' 'Dunc,' as his contemporaries called him, was temperamental to the extreme. He worshipped his art, idolized the children of his brain and brush. While painting, he would often sing, laugh or even weep, for his soul was in Paradise.

"The time came when the fervor of his emotions, shook asunder the ties of sanity, and then, 'God gathered him to his Fathers.' "

YOUTH

By Frank Horne

I am a knotted nebula—
a whirling flame
Shrieking afire the endless darkness . . .
I am the eternal center of gravity
and about me swing the crazy moons—
I am the thunder of rising suns,
——the blaze of the zenith—
. . . the tremble of women's bodies
in the arms of lovers . . .
I sit on top of the Pole
Drunk with starry splendor
Shouting hozzanas at the Pleiades
. . . booting footballs at the moon—
I shall outlast the sun
and the moon
and the stars. . . .

A Drawing by Aaron Douglas

The Prospects Of Black Bourgeoisie

By Abram L. Harris

HE slave regime furnished the basis for the racial distinctions which it projected and crystallized into a social psychology which in turn became the sentimental bulwark of the slave power and its legacy upon dissolution. In order to hold the system intact, the exploitation of black labor was justified on ground that the Negro was inherently unfitted for independent participation in western culture. Even to the poor white worker whose status was only theoretically superior to that of the slave, the Negro was accursed of God, and "to labor was to work like a nigger." On the other hand, the social superiority of the master class exerted a subtle influence on the Negro slave. Conscious of his own social and economic debasement and contemptuous of the poor white man's economic infirmity, he desired to be like the old masters. The complexity of these attitudes made it impossible for the lower white and black classes to divest themselves of mutual animosity.

When freedom came, the Negro, who, in culture and refinement, more nearly approximated the white man, comprised a sort of natural aristocracy which furnished the race with leaders. Under the slave regime these leaders had been the house servants and artisans. Their proximity to the dominant class of whites and, sometimes, blood relationship predisposed them to an affectation of aristocratic graces, traditions, and manners. But their social philosophy was of northern origin.

This early Negro leadership was mainly political in its purpose and outlook. While the more astute Negro politicians may have perceived some of the economic factors in the race problem, only ephemeral contact was established with the labor movement of the 60's and 70's when competition provoked certain white unions to take the initiative in organizing Negro workers. Of course, many of the unions, like the typographical that was malicious in its discriminations against Negro printers, intensified the Negro worker's skepticism of white labor, particularly when organized. But the chief element that perpetuated discord and profited by it was the Negro politicians who were Negro labor's spokesmen during this period. These politicians were aligned with the Republican Party. When the white workers projected an independent labor party, the Negro Republicans naturally exclaimed that their party was the fountain of all social reform. The masses of Negro laborers believed in the political faith of their leaders; and their social experience could not lead to any appreciation of labor legislation such as was proposed by their white contemporaries. Not that the Negro worker disapproved class legislation. The fact was that he did not approve class legislation when it was designed to ameliorate specific racial handicaps.

On the economic side, the chief undertaking directly after emancipation was the incorporation of the Freedmen's Savings Bank by the Federal Government. This too was tainted with Republican politics. It was not conceived by Negroes as a step in the race's economic elevation. It was organized for Negroes by their political guardians. Although the Bank was a hot-bed of corruption and exploitation, it served to bring the Negro closer to the *habits of thought* that prevailed in the capitalistic economy. Along with this indoctrination in the cultus of savings and private enterprise went habituation to the ideology of the middle-classes.

In later years the racial philosophy which expounded industrial efficiency to the Negro masses became the embodiment of economic individualism and business enterprise, but eschewed political alliances—even with the political power that symbolized these virtues. More paradoxical than this was the fact that business enterprise as a philosophy of racial advancement was made synonymous with the industrial education of the Negro, since they both claimed to be the means of Negro economic emancipation.

II

As social ostracism increased, and the Negro's industrial education—such as it was—counted for little in the competitive economy, the philosophy of business enterprise succeeded in establishing its conceptual independence of the old dualism in economic thinking of Negro leaders. It became *the* means of promoting Negro independence of existing economic arrangements; and now, in our contemporary culture, it bids fair to pre-empt the field of racial betterment philosophies. The practical validity of Negro business enterprise is claimed to be attested by the surpluses of wealth individual Negroes have accumulated. The adherents to the doctrine do not advocate increasing the number of really middle-class Negroes through an increase of independent Negro farmers, even though sound business enterprise must rest as much upon such a class as upon industrial and fiscal fact. In the surrounding white population, business enterprise rests upon a fairly even distribution of functional classes, cultivation of natural resources and ownership of complex indus-

131

trial arrangements. In the Negro population functional classes are most unevenly distributed; and, of course, the Negro has little industrial control and possesses a small share of the nation's natural resources. The Negro middle-class is comprised of small shop keepers, a small group of independent farmers, and persons engaged in rendering professional and personal service. Here of late a decided growth in industrial wage-earners has increased the number of skilled craftsmen in the Negro population while decreasing its agricultural proletariat. At the bottom of the social ladder are to be found the unskilled laborers, domestic servants, and agricultural wage-earners who constitute by far the largest functional groups. The professions are already overcrowded. The desire to escape the lot of the domestic and the poverty of the unskilled laborer accounts for the disproportionate share of Negroes that has been attracted to the healing, teaching, and exhorting professions. Relief from this top-heaviness among Negro functional classes is promised by those who undertake business enterprise as the plan of racial salvation. What are the Negro's prospects of realizing these ideals in American life? Upon the answer to this question hinges the probability of the Negro's continued social performance in accordance with bourgeois logic as well as the prospects of a strictly racial business enterprise, the material base without which, his middle-class bias must become a useless psychological vestige of social heritage.

III

Let us examine the postulates of business enterprise as a racial philosophy. Its adherents maintain that since the Negro problem is purely economic, the solution is the creation of competitive business enterprises within the Negro group so as to afford employment to Negroes. It is further contended that a state of racial economic sufficiency will be attained only when the Negro consumes less and produces more.

The growing prevalence of the above type of reasoning undoubtedly marks a renaissance of Negro economic learning; but one whose philosophic validity was lost upon the advent of modern capitalism. Before the rise of the *bourgeoisie,* the doctrine that guided the economic policy of nations was mercantilism. It held that a nation's stock of gold was the best measure of national wealth and power; and that the way to increase national wealth and power was by producing goods that could be exported for money returns and by consuming less of other nation's goods. As modern industrial society gradually developed, the economists saw that interdependence and not self-sufficiency was the basis of economic and social progress. Today, even in that sphere of economic life known as international trade, this hoary fallacy of economic self-sufficiency has lost much of its pristine virtue. The doctrine of *comparative costs* which is but an extension of the principle of *division of labor* is of greater importance in international trade than is this notion of the self-

contained community. Obviously in a complex culture based upon specialization and interdependence of classes and individuals there can be little approximation to individual, racial or national self-sufficiency.

The absence of statistics on the comparative industrial efficiency of racial groups makes it impossible to ascertain the productivity of different races. Such data are not necessary for a refutation of the insinuation that the Negro is a parasitical class in industrial society. What on earth has the Negro been doing these last three hundreds in America if he has not been producing? To what has his manpower been devoted if not to the increase of wealth and services? It is a fact, however, that the Negro has rarely owned or controlled the instruments and machines of production, i.e., social capital. Nor have the great entrepreneurs been recruited from the Negro race. The Negro as a freeman arrived very tardily on the scene of capitalistic enterprise and adventure. The greater portion of the Negro population has been wage-earners and chiefly unskilled laborers. This can by no twist of economic logic be construed into meaning that the Negro has been more of a consumer than a producer. And it is futile to point out that after all, consumption is merely a demand for production and *vice versa:* for; what these advocates of racial business mean by increased productivity is that the Negro should procure some of the wealth producing factors of the community—which is very different from admonishing him to become more productive. How great are the Negro's possibilities in achieving this goal? If some individuals among the Negroes are to suceed as business undertakers, must their success be a purely racial phenomenon; or can it result from general conditions of the competitive economy? Social attitudes being what they are, will not the racial identity of Negro enterprise restrict its utility to the Negro group? When pushed to its logical extremity, must not this doctrine of Negro business enterprise reckon with the feasibility of erecting within the already existing national economy, a purely racial one?

Thus far the Negro's largest economic institutions have been banks, insurance, and real estate corporations and secret fraternities. In short his most important economic institutions have been financial. Now, the financial superstructure of modern capitalism has been built up in order to hold together the underlying and somewhat diversified but interstitial parts of industry, commerce, and agriculture. Industry proper is devoted to the production of goods. Investment banks supply fixed capital, and commercial banks and paper houses supply working capital for transferring the commodities produced. While financial institutions perform a useful function in production and exchange operations of industrial society, their existence is contingent, not only upon savings, but a market for the capital which savings place at their disposal. The existence of Negro finance organizations may be assured by the savings of the masses. But what about the demand for these savings, i.e., the market for capital-disposal? If the funds of Negro finance institutions flow to the general money market, these institutions must ultimately lose their racial significance in the melée of competition—which may not be a bad thing;—but more of this later. If the available funds do not flow to the general market, they must be confined to investments within the race. Where is the Negro or group of Negroes who owns or controls interest in factories, mines, or public utilities that have need of fixed or liquid capital? Negro business men do operate funeral and embalming, and hair straightening concerns of not ordinary capitalization. These are not sufficiently numerous or potent to give solidity and flexibility to any large financial superstructure. The advances that Negro finance organizations make must take the form of short time consumption loans or, when made for a larger period, take the form of a mortgage on real property. At all events their assets are of a non-shiftable type. But this does not check the Negro's ambition for multiplying banks and finance corporations.

One argument for the creation of Negro banks is that they enable the Negro to keep his earnings within the race. The chief lamentation of Negro business enterprise is that Negroes carry large deposits with white banks. One Negro banker upon visiting New York saw that a great many Negroes were depositing their savings with the United States Postal Savings Department. This was very distasteful to him. He seemed to have felt that a Negro bank should be organized as depository for these funds. Perhaps it never dawned on this banker that the United States Government was at that time employing in New York City, alone, more Negroes than all of the Negro finance institutions combined. Little do these banking promoters realize that they and their institutions rest upon the savings of Negro masses who are employed, not by Negro but by white capitalists.

Another argument for the creation of Negro banks is that they give Negro business men greater credit accommodations. White banks, for example, refuse to extend the same credit terms on a mortgage in real property in a Negro as in a white community. It seems that the policy is not always racial. Very often it is economic. A white business man who seeks a loan on property which he owns in a Negro neighborhood is likely to receive much better terms from a white bank than a Negro owning the same piece of property. The white borrower's direct or indirect credit standing in the business community, apart from the security offered, plays an important part in the transaction. Moreover, it is not unlikely that this hypothetical white borrower of superior credit standing could obtain better accommodations from a Negro creditor than could the average Negro borrower. Aside from the comparative borrowing strength of the Negro and

white business man, what is the character of the security offered, i.e., the real property in the Negro community? Is it good business practice to extend the same credit on it as on property of the same appraised value in a white community? The opinion seems to be that it is not. In certain Negro communities some property is in exceptional physical condition, but the surrounding property has suffered such rapid physical depreciation that the whole section is undesirable for residential purposes. The value of first class Negro property must for this reason fall below what its normal price would otherwise be. Moreover, once property is let to Negro tenants, its vendibility is restricted and its market value reflects the limitation in demand. One may easily deplore these conditions but not deny that business actuated by the *profit motif* in a competitive society is forced to discriminate against mortgages on property in Negro communities. And the prime position that the real estate mortgage occupies in Negro financial operations gives Negro banking a rather non-flexible and investment character.

To the extent that Negro finance institutions assist black wage-earners to acquire property, they are beneficial, though limited in function. Their serviceability could as a matter of fact be heightened by organization upon a co-operative basis which would permit Negro savers to share in the surpluses. But these organizations are conceived in the spirit of business individualism. They are not organized for racial service but for private profit. The surpluses must therefore go to the entrepreneurs. And in Negro business enterprise an inordinately high proportion of the gross profit is diverted by the entrepreneur from reinvestment in the business enterprise and appropriated to his personal consumption which is usually more conspicuously wasteful than that of wealthier and more efficient capitalists in the world of great economic achievement. As a general tendency undue absorption of profits will inevitably weaken the whole fabric of Negro business. It has already led to what a Negro business man called over-expansion which is not over-expansion in any real economic sense of over-investment. It is rather under-investment; the quest for greater and greater profits in face of the limitations placed upon Negro finance institutions by their absence of industrial foundation and inadequate market for capital, leads the Negro entrepreneurs into promotions of dubious worth. Investments are made in amusement corporations and other perpetual motion machines that are perpetual only to the extent that they secure perpetual instalments of investment. But why can't Negro finance institutions secure a firm footing in economic life by purchasing the shares of industrial corporations or by organizing new ones?

Before the Negro was emancipated, the great American fortunes were in the making. When he became a freeman, the foundation of the continental railway systems and the later development of mines, factories and fields had been laid. A score of years after his emancipation, huge combinations capitalized in hundreds of millions arose stifling competition and establishing monopoly in industry. Today some of these vertical and horizontal combinations are capitalized at more than a billion dollars (***). They have not only established a sort of hegemony in industry but have set up interlocking directorates and communities of interest in the financial domain. Does anyone acquainted with this economic evolution believe that the Negro, as such, at this late date can by some financial wizardry acquire much of the nation's sources of raw material, or, obtain control of any of the productive factors?

Of course the shares of large industrial and public utilities are purchasable on the market. Suppose the Negroes in the United States could be prevailed upon to pool their wealth and place it in the hands of Negro enterprises so as to gain control of some of the numerous corporations by mopping-up their securities. Any one of a thousand investment bankers could bankrupt the whole Negro race between tickings of the stock-exchange tickers. No doubt some sagacious and thrifty Negro individuals, or corporations, may purchase securities of existing, or new corporations or portions of the issues of foreign and domestic governments. Such operations must of necessity be limited. When conducted on a wide scale, the Negro business is forced to take chances in the general competitive market where small and inexperienced economic endeavor is disadvantaged. Capitalize some racial enterprise at a billion dollars. If it would live it must ultimately compete with white business. This, for the reasons already alluded to, would be its undoing.

The financial prowess of the Jewish capitalists is often cited for Negro emulation. But the existence of a large population of poor Jews who—no more than Negroes, the occasional object of Jewish capitalists' charity—have escaped the wage-earning class merely because of the existence of Jewish financiers, is usually ignored. A more important fact of Jewry is ignored: the financial history of the Jew

(***)Vide Taussig, Principles of Economics, I, 59. Also Moody, The Truth About Trusts.

which dates back to the Middle Ages when the Church's edict against usury gave the Jews monopoly of money lending.

The logical conclusions from these observations may be summarized.

(1) Negro financial institutions can neither hope to exert any considerable control over national industry requiring fixed capital nor over purely commercial transactions necessitating working capital.

(2) Social attitudes being what they are, the racial identity of Negro economic institutions will, perforce of these attitudes, confine their services to the Negro race.

(3) The restriction of the dealings of Negro finance institutions to the race will shunt them from the general investment market, thus further proscribing their utility.

(4) These institutions may incidentally assist some Negroes to acquire a stake in the economic order and furnish employment to a limited number of educated Negroes, but the masses of Negroes must continue to look to white capitalism for employment.

(5) They are a sort of illogically necessary appurtenance in an economic world where the large capital accumulations necessary for production must depend on Negro as well as on white savers, but where it is felt desirable for social reasons to maintain white and black institutions even at the cost of tragic waste.

(6) The philosophy of wealth and economic enterprise grips the imagination of the Negro even in the lower stratum.

(7) The tenacity with which this belief in racial economic independence is held results from a fructification of the bourgeois ideals that social pressure has forced Negroes to emulate, irrespective of social class.

(8) And while there is need for theoretical formulation of Negro economic experience, there are few, if any, trained Negro economists. But even if theoreticians existed in the Negro population, their profoundest formulations, however rational, when contrary to popular assumptions would be futile speculation to a racial group that is looking for solutions and is impatient of theory.

TO A YOUNG POET

By GEORGE CHESTER MORSE

Lincoln University

Just as molten thoughts o'erflow
From an unknown fiery source
To form themselves in poetry;
Such is the wavering self in woe
Seeking life's straight or winding course
To infinity.

A PAGE OF UNDERGRADUATE VERSE

TO A MOCKING BIRD

By HERMAN E. FIELDS
Shaw University

*I have listened, oft have listened
To a voice I love to hear;
Soft its echo oft resounded,
Falling faintly on my ear.*

*And I asked me as I listened
To that voice, so clear and sweet,
As I wandered in the wildwood,
As I heard the notes repeat.*

*Could this voice of wondrous beauty,
Trilling anthems so divine,
Be a seraph, nymph, or angel,
Thus to cheer this soul of mine.*

*Was it spirit, the harp of Nature,
Chanting praises to the skies,
Or the loving voice, transcendent,
Of a bird in Paradise?*

*And when evening falls upon me,
Still its little form I see,
Flitting in the pale blue heaven
Or about the leafy tree.*

*Even then the echoes haunt me;
Even yet I hear the cry,
Ringing still though but a memory
That will live and never die.*

CONGENITAL

By KATHERINE JACKSON
Tougaloo College

*A pig will be a pig
It matters not his name—
Whenever he is fed,
He always acts the same.*

IDYLL

By GLADYS M. JAMESON
Howard University

*Tall, straight birches
Starkly etched against the sky—
Virgin slim they stand, mutely questing,—
Silver fingers pointed upwards.
Lissom willows bend
Their silver leaves cast dappled shade
Upon the dimpled bosom
Of the placid, dreaming stream.*

If nothing touches the palm leaves
They do not rustle.

—*An African Proverb.*

A DRAWING FOR

COPPER SUN, *by Charles Cullen*
Courtesy of Harper and Bros.

134

VERISIMILTUDE

By John P. Davis

I am a rather young man, with no especial knack for writing, who has a story to tell. I want to tell it as I feel it—without restraint—but I can't do that. Critics are already waxing sarcastic about this way of doing things. They think it is too emotional, too melodramatic. I am going to attempt to tell the story I have in me without any fuss or sensation. To achieve "grandeur of generality," to attain the "universal" rather than the "specific"—these are the things I am trying to do. I want you to say when you have finished reading: "That reminds me of . . . ," or "There are thousands like that character; I may never have known one, but there are thousands, thousands. There must be."

Now you can help me, if you will forget everything else in the world except this story. Whether it actually happened or not is of little consequence. The important thing is that it might have happened, that, in mathematical or scientific terms, given such causes working on such characters, the results about which I am going to tell you would have happened. If at any time you feel that there is something in the story that couldn't happen on your own main street then stop reading. I don't want to create monsters, but real, living characters.

Now this is the story of a man. A man is the hero of most stories. Man is the hero of life. This man was a Negro. Negroes are common enough. There are fifteen million, more or less, in the United States alone. This Negro man was in love. Love is the theme of ninety percent of all fiction. I doubt that it is the theme of ninety per cent of life. But no matter, it is common enough in these days.

The next fact in the plot may seem to point the way to something grotesque, something that veers away off from the center of normal human existence like a comet. The Negro man loved a white woman. Are you disappointed already? Well, I am sorry. But I was a census-taker in Virginia. And you woud be surprised at the number of cases of intermarriage I found. That is why they passed an anti-intermarriage law there. There are such laws in nearly all southern states. There must be a reason back of these statutes. Legislatures don't pass laws for nothing. So it wouldn't be strange if I wrote a story about a Negro man who loved a white woman and married her. But I have no intention of marrying my characters. In fact my plot exists because they did not marry. I say only that he loved her. Whether she loved him, I leave you to judge when you have read the story.

This Negro man was tall, young, and brown. There is nothing to quarrel with here. I haven't said he was handsome. Surely, young, tall, brown Negro bundle-wrappers in down-town New York department stores are common enough not to shock you out of belief. And just as ordinary and matter-of-fact are slim, little, rather-nice-looking white salesgirls.

You see these two characters now, don't you? You see them working side by side ten hours a day. One is selling yard after yard of vari-colored cambric to fat housewives who are harder to please than you would expect Mrs. J. Pierpont Morgan to be. You see these termagants snarl at the shopgirl and then go to buy cambric at a cheaper price in one of the cut-rate stores. Of course, it is the most natural thing in the world that the shopgirl should get angry and stick her tongue out at them when they have turned their backs.

137

135

Take a look at the other character. He is at the end of the counter wrapping up package after package which the girl hands him. He hears the housewives quarrelsome babble. He sees the girl make faces at them. He sympathizes and smiles at her as if to say: "I understand how it is with you." The girl has caught the smile and thrown it back. She wants to talk about that last old biddy who put on the airs of her mistress. And she doesn't see why she shouldn't talk to this bundle-wrapper. He smiled; he would understand. She goes over while there is a lull in the sale of cambric and chats with him about "that old fool who expected to get something for nothing and blamed me because Gimbels charged a cent less per yard for cambric than we did. Why the heck didn't she go there in the first place?" He laughs at the way she got back at the woman. She laughs. The tension is broken. They understand. Isn't all this about as natural and plausible as may be? Put yourself in place of either of the characters. Would you have acted differently?

Common suffering leads to mutual interest. That's why men forced to fight against tyranny form friendships for one another. It is just as plausible, then, that this girl and this man, united by laughter, should form a combine against stupid customers. Talk with a man and you find out that he isn't so different after all. "You can't know a man and hate him," said Woodrow Wilson. The girl, Mame, (we might as well call her that as anything else) probably never heard that statement, but she was human nature just the same. She talked with this bundle-wrapper. Let's call him "Paul." Mame found that Paul went to movies, read the Daily Graphic, and was on the whole a normal human being. She forgot to notice any difference in him. And in the little respites from selling cambric she liked to talk to him about this, that, or the other thing. What they actually said doesn't matter. This will serve as a specimen of what they might have said.

Mame: "I'll sure be glad when six o'clock comes."

Paul: "So will I."

Now right here I had better tell you that I am not trying to reproduce Paul's southern accent or Mame's American cockney dialect. How they said things doesn't matter. It is sufficient to give you the impression of what they thought. Your imagination will have to do the rest.

Paul: "Have you heard anything about the new rule for closing on Saturdays beginning in June?"

Mame: "I haven't heard anything definite, but I certainly hope they do."

But enough of this. The things they talked about, then, were just every-day matters-of-fact about work, life, and movies. Paul never tried to go any farther. Mame never said more than: "See you tomorrow," when she pulled the black cloth over the cambric counter and arranged her cloche hat on her sleek round head.

In real life things don't continue as they began ever. You come to know a person as an acquaintance. Then you are thrown into more intimate contact with him. After that it isn't long before you like him better or like him less. That was the case with Abelard and Heloise. It was true of Paul and Mame.

It won't take much imagination to suppose that Mame lived on 119th street and Paul on 131st. White people live on 119th; black people inhabit 131st. It shouldn't strain your fancy either to imagine that they both usually rode home from work on top of a Seventh Avenue bus. Suppose that coming out from work one evening, some two or three months after their first laugh together, Mame should be waiting for a bus at the same time and the same corner as Paul. This might not have happened. Paul might have lived in Brooklyn and Mame have been accustomed to going home on the subway. But it isn't being sensational to throw characters together to aid the action of the plot. So they did meet each other one night about a quarter after six o'clock waiting for a bus. Paul tipped his hat; Mame smiled. Bus Number Two came along crowded. They went up to the top. There was one seat vacant. They sat down together. They talked of everything you think they would talk about. There were no distractions to interrupt their conversation. They talked as they passed throngs of tired everyday toilers pouring out of stores and warehouses at 42nd street. They talked as they passed alongside Central Park. They talked as the bus trundled into upper Seventh Avenue. Mame got off at 119th street. She smiled and said good-bye. There are flaws in this little episode, I admit. A little too much coincidence. A bit too little motivation. But if you are not too fastidious a reader, I think you will let it pass. For at least it is within the realms of plausibility.

Let us say that Paul and Mame did not meet again for a week, two weeks, a month. But don't let us say they never met again. They did. Perhaps Paul covertly planned it. Perhaps Mame did. That doesn't matter. They met. That is sufficient. And they met several times. In fact, it became a habit for them to ride up on the bus together. Am I losing reality? I think not. You see after all the thing I am suggesting is a mere mechanical detail. Although I handle it clumsily, the intrinsic design of the life I am trying to depict cannot be destroyed.

"So far so good," you say, "but whither go we?" or, if you incline to slang, "What has their riding home from work together got to do with the wholesale price of onions?" The answer is simple. It was on such occasions that Mame found in Paul something she liked. What was the "something," you ask? Say Mame discovered that Paul was going to night school in preparation for a clerical examination for a position in the municipal department of New York. Not much to admire from your point of view. But suppose all Mame's life had been one of crowded tenements. Say she lived with a cross old aunt, wanted an escape, wanted to get away from hum-drum life, to be something better, to marry a decent man—(God knows every woman wants that.) Every woman admires a man who is doing things. And Paul from Mame's point of view was doing things. She said to herself: "This colored fellow is different from anybody else I've ever known. He is a man. I like him. I wish Albert (let Albert be what we Americans would call Mame's "steady feller") I wish Albert would go to night school."

And Paul probably thought: "This white girl is a lot less stuck-up than some colored girls I know. She's darn decent to talk with me like this. I wonder if she would go to the movies some night with me."

Here we are hundreds of sentences and thousands of words from the beginning and never a sign of complications. Well, they will be with us in a moment. First I must get Paul and Mame in love. I could spare myself a great deal of tedious detail by just saying they came to love one another. But you would not believe me. All readers come from Missouri. Anyway I am going to compromise with principle and say that Paul came to love Mame first because of novelty and then because he was forced to admire a woman who broke convention to love him. And Mame fell in love with Paul because to her he represented a somewhat better man than any other she had ever known. The process of falling in love is an evasive thing at best. You somehow know you are in love, but when and how and, above all, why defy analysis. It is an elusive something. Say, then, that these two characters fell in love. If you want a dash of sentiment say they saw dawn in each others eyes. There are lovers that do. If you are practical say Mame saw possibilities of a three room apart-ment and no more drudgery. Repeat for emphasis: they fell in love. What about Albert. Well, let Albert be a wastrel, a drunkard, a loafer. You will find a great many like him. Doubtless, you know a few.

I promised you complications. Life demands them as well as you. Complica-tions? Here they are. Paul takes Mame to see Lya de Putti in "Variety" at the Rialto. A colored fellow whom he knows sees them. Next morning all Harlem is gossiping about Paul who has turned "pink-chaser"—(apologies to Mr. Carl Van

Vechten). When Harlem talks about you it means that you feel curious eyes staring at you. The spirit of scandal stalks your path. People you know avert their eyes as you pass. Stand on the street corner and you stand alone. That is the effect of the colored Mrs. Grundy on a man. The white Mrs. Grundy may look different, but "the lady and Judy O'Grady are sisters under the skins." On 119th street houses have just as many eyes as on 131st. So when Mame let Paul take her home once or twice, people talked. Albert heard about it and "raised Hell." The aunt heard about it and threatened to kick Mame out if she didn't stop "going around with a nigger." Mame looked guilty.

Does this suit you? You have the sunshine and now you see the clouds. Are you worried? You should be. I am not one to lead you up to tragedy and then turn aside to talk about flowers. Well, you know and I know that life wouldn't let this end happily. There has got to be death, there has got to be sorrow. And since it must be, let it come soon.

But I am not quite ready for the show-down. Like a woman who powders her nose before every great moment of her life, I must hesitate, demur—in a word—build up suspense. We need emotional intensification here. For that purpose let Paul be happy enough with Mame to forget the snubs of his own people. Let Mame pacify her aunt temporarily by threatening to leave and thus deplete the family revenue eleven dollars a week. The eleven dollars represents Mame's contribution for room and board. Leave a cancerous wound in the souls of both characters, if you must; but let them live yet awhile. For, like Alamanzor, they have "not leisure yet to die."

Don't be provoked with me. Don't accuse me of "playing in wench-like words with something serious." Peace! brother. Peace! sister. All will be clear in only a little while. Soon you will know. Soon you will sit back in your chair and see Mame and Paul as duly garnished sacrifices. And whether you like them or not, you will know them as they are.

Paul and Mame were happy. They went to Staten Island on picnics. They went to movies. Paul gave Mame candy. Mame gave Paul a tie for his birthday. And love—the ideal of humanity—lived in their hearts. Or if this is too poetic, just say they enjoyed being with one another. I have not explained their love fully enough, maybe—but can you explain it better? If you can, please fill in the facts for yourself.

When two persons become intimate with one another they lose their sense of proportion. They respect neither time, custom, nor place. This fact got Paul and Mame into trouble. They didn't know when it was time to stop talking and pay attention to their work. You see, it was one thing to exchange a few commonplaces while at work; but, it was quite another to delay customers or to smile at each other while the world was waiting for a yard of cambric. Business men know such delays irritate their customers. That is why they hire floor-managers to snoop on their salesgirls. You see what I am driving at, don't you? I am getting Paul and Mame into more trouble. Soon I'll have them discharged. But, not before I give a sidelight on the episode.

Shopgirls have had love affairs before. They have kept customers waiting before; and have got away with it under the very eyes of floor managers. It isn't enough, therefore, for me to offer this as the only excuse for getting Mame and Paul discharged. But I can suggest others. A young Negro man talking to a young white woman for more than five minutes is always subject to suspicion. And when this is repeated again and again, scandal gets busy. You know this as well as I do. There is still another reason. Perhaps, you remember Albert. I shouldn't have had any justification for naming him if I did not intend to weave him into the plot. It would have been faulty technique. So Albert comes in here. He enters through the department store door and makes his way to the cambric counter. Now he is on the scene. He is half-drunk and a little loud. It is ten-thirty in the morning and Albert has come to tell Paul that he had better "damn sight" leave his woman alone—all white women, in fact. That's just what Albert did. He "bawled Paul out" right before a crowd of people. And Mame couldn't keep her temper. She turned red in the face. She dug her nails in her hands and wanted to fly at Albert. Paul held her back. He put his arm around her. The crowd grew larger. A policeman took Albert away. That is all there is for Albert to do in this story. The floor-manager whispered something to Paul and about two hours later both Paul and Mame had their salaries in little manila envelopes. You can't blame the floor-manager very much. It was for the good of the business. Anyway as he told Paul, he had noticed for some time that they were not paying attention to business. He didn't get angry. He was simply hard, cold and matter-of-fact. That was all.

Here we are facing the climax of this personally conducted tour of a short story. Mame and Paul are out of a job. They have to live. Mame is crying. Life seems unfair, bitter, unkind. Don't weep because Mame did. Stand on the sidelines and see the show. What are Hecuba's tears to you, or Mame's? I only record that she wept because, under the circumstances, I think she would have done so. Paul gritted his teeth. They would get a job soon, he told her. And it wouldn't be long before he would be able to take the clerical examination. Then they could get married and go to Atlantic City for a honeymoon. All that is needed here is a little time and a little sanity. But life would cease to be a tragedy, if time would wait for us. The harsh reality, the bitterness of life comes because everything in the world is run by clocks and whistles. Time to get up. Time to retire. Time to live. And time to die. To use a slang expression—Mame and Paul "didn't get the break."

If you have ever hunted for a job in New York, you know what it is like to do so. Your feet hurt after the first two or three days. You get tired of being told that there are no vacancies. Sometimes you go back to the same place on five or six occasions before you can find the employment manager in his office, and then he only shakes his head. Sometimes you think you've got a job; then you are asked where you worked last, how long, why you quit, if you have any references. Your heart sinks and you go out of the door of the inner office, through the outer office, down the elevator and out into the street. And all the time you are saying to yourself: "Oh God, dear God, am I your creature?" A man can stand a great deal more of this sort of thing than a woman. Mame gave up; Paul lasted. There were other reasons for Mame's surrender but this had its share in the result.

Mame, I have said, contributed eleven dollars a week to her aunt. A week or so after she was fired her contributions ceased. Mame hadn't saved up much. Soon that was gone. You understand how that might happen, I know. Money doesn't come from the skies. And the girl's name was Mame and not Cinderella. Mame's aunt was angry with Mame in the first place for "taking up with a nigger." She was angrier when Mame lost her job. "I-told-you-so's" dinned in Mame's ears and buzzed in her head. It was too much for the aunt to stand when Mame couldn't pay her the eleven dollars. Mame had to do one thing or the other: "either get out or give up that nigger." Those were the aunt's own words. Do you think that the aunt is too hard a character? Read any metropolitan daily. The world is getting hard and cold. All the world wants is money. Money was all Mame's aunt wanted. So she turned Mame out. But she wasn't altogether cold. She didn't really mean to turn her out. She wanted only to each Mame a lesson. After all blood is thicker than water. She didn't believe Mame would really go. She wanted her to stop being a fool and come down to earth. There were plenty of decent young white men she could marry. It was infatuation or something that got Mame this way. If she had her way, she'd either put Mame in the insane asylum or that "nigger" in jail. Whoever heard of such "carryings-on?" She was tired of having people talk about her. She wasn't going to be related to a "nigger" even by marriage.

Don't blame Mame's aunt any more than you did the floor-manager or Albert. All—all of them are just cogs in the wheels of the world. If you must fume and fret, say simply that all the world's a pasture and each one in the world, a jackass.

This is what human beings such as Mame's aunt and Albert and the floor-manager might have done to such a girl as Mame. What would Mame have done? Probably, gone to Paul. She did. But he could not take care of her. He had no money. He was being threatened himself with being put out of his rooming house because he didn't pay his rent. It was a poor time to try to bring a young, unmarried white woman into a respectable Harlem rooming house. Go . . . go where? Somewhere, you say? But where? There are streets. But streets in New York are either covered with soft, cold snow, or melted by the rays of a hot blazing sun. Try living in New York without money. Try living anywhere without money. Friends, you suggest? I wish I could. But where are friends when your aunt turns you out of doors and you have done what Mame had done? Then, who with pride would go a begging? Only one thing remains: it whispers in your ear every time there seems no way out—suicide.

Suicide isn't normal. Only abnormal people think of it. Joy may drop from you like a dead bird from a leafless tree, but, somehow, life is still sweet. But too much defeat, too much bitterness make people abnormal. Consider a woman who has drudged all her life; put her in Mame's place. You will find that she is like the string on a violin: draw her too tightly and she snaps. Something snapped in Mame. She kissed Paul goodnight in the park, spent her last dollar and a half to get a room in a settlement house—and turned on the gas. Don't blame Paul. He didn't know she was going to commit suicide. He thought he would see her the next day. Don't say Mame isn't true to life. If you believe she is not, live her life over. Spend two months looking for a job; wandering willy-nilly. Then put her back into the picture as a human being. I think you will succeed.

What about Paul. There isn't much to tell. He stood it. He stood Mame's death. But how he stood it I leave you to imagine. You will agree that he grew bitter. You will not agree that he would commit suicide. That is the sort of melodramatic thing I want to avoid. I am sorry Mame had to commit suicide. But I don't see how she could help it. Do you?

Suppose that after Mame's death Paul got a job as a longshoreman on the New York docks. Not as clerk in the municipal department, mind you. He had given up night school when he lost his job. Then Mame had died and he hadn't gone back. He was bitter, he grew cynical . . . No money, no job, Mame, were the causes. He might have got over it some time, but that time didn't come. Is this anti-climactic? Not quite. Remember Paul is really the chief character.

When you have gone through what Paul went through, you won't be happy and optimistic. You are apt to look on the world and people in it as just so much damned rot. You are apt to walk around with a chip on your shoulder. And a chip on your shoulder doesn't help you any if you are a longshoreman. They are hard working, hard swearing, sweating Negroes, Irish and what-nots—these longshore gangs. And the dock is no place for Hamlet. Even Falstaff would have a hard time getting along. You've got to laugh loudly, work hard, and mix with the gang. Paul did none of these things. He felt just a little above them. He was always moody, introspective, hard to get along with. Even Negroes despised him. You can imagine the opinion that the Irish held.

Under the circumstances can't you imagine Paul becoming a flaming pillar of rage when an Irish longshore boss yelled at him: "Hey, nigger, stop dreaming and go to work. Yes I mean you, you son of a . . . ." But the Irish fellow didn't finish his oath.

Paul hit him over the head with a chisel. Chisels are common on the docks. They are used to open boxes. Paul opened the fellows head with one. He didn't kill him. The Irish foreman lived to testify against Paul. He was quite well when the District Attorney painted a gaudy word picture of how Paul lost his last job. He saw twelve ordinary men, readers of the Daily Graphic, cigar salesmen, shopkeepers, butchers, insurance agents—all, somehow, a little influenced by the way Paul glared at people in the courtroom and by the District Attorney's subtle suggestion that Paul had been the cause of a white woman's suicide. Of course, they thought more about the affair than actually happened. Can't you see that District Attorney? He's running on the State ticket next year. He's got to make a record. Some cases he can't prosecute to win. Politics won't let him. Here is one in which he can have a free hand. Here he can make a name for himself. Look at the jury. They don't know much about sociology, but they know where to get the best beer in New York City. Look at the judge. He's a scholarly man, but he's sick of the crime wave. Something's got to be done. And Paul to him is obviously a criminal. Look at the young man who calls himself a lawyer. He is defending Paul and he means well. But his best is not good enough. Maybe next year or year after he'll be a good lawyer. Paul won't smile, he won't plead. He is obstinate. I think you will find little fault with the verdict. Guilty. The law is the law. He was lucky to get only seven years.

I have outlined this story and set it in New York. If you like you may write it to please your taste and set it any place under the sun. The results would not vary a great deal. If you must have a happy ending, pardon Paul, or, bring him back from prison and regenerate him. But I doubt if you will succeed. It is hard to get a pardon. It is harder to reform a man who looks on life pessimistically for seven years. At least grant that what I have outlined is true or might be true. As someone has written (a Jewish poet, I think):

> The sum and substance of the tale is this
> The rest is but the mise en scéne
> And if I have painted it amiss
> I am a prattler and a charlatan.

Oh yes, you will want a moral. I had forgot. Take it from Shakespeare:—

> "Golden lads and girls all must
> Like chimney sweepers come to dust."

UNDERGRADUATE VERSE
FISK UNIVERSITY

NIGHT
By T. Thomas Fortune Fletcher

Night in the South
Is a black mother
Mourning for murdered sons
And ravished daughters.

LIFE
By Richard Jefferson

Life is a woman's tongue
That babbles on and on
Till quick, impatient death
Weary of hearing it
Constantly rave
Conceals it

WHITE GOD
By T. Thomas Fortune Fletcher

God is white,
Why should I pray?
If I called Him,
He'd turn away.

POEM
By Richard Jefferson

I longed to write a poem of life,
One that was fierce and bitter, wild.
But wrote of stars when once I saw
A white man strangle his black child.

141

Mrs. Bailey Pays The Rent

By IRA DE A. REID

Won't you come home Bill Bailey?
Won't you come home,"
She mourns the whole day long.
"I'll do the cooking, I'll pay the rent,
I know I've done you wrong.
Remember that rainy evening
I drove you out,
With nothing but a fine tooth comb?
Aint that a shame,
I know I'm to blame,
Bill Bailey, won't you please come home?"
—Old popular song.

FOR many years it has been the custom of certain portions of the Negro group living in Southern cities to give some form of party when money was needed to supplement the family income. The purpose for giving such a party was never stated, but who cared whether the increment was used to pay the next installment on the "Stineway" piano, or the weekly rent? On the one hand, these parties were the life of many families of a low economic status who sought to confine their troubles with a little joy. On the other hand, they were a wild form of commercialized recreation in its primary stages. Humor was the counterpart of their irony.

No social standing was necessary to promote these affairs. Neither was one forced to have a long list of friends. All that the prospective host required to "throw" such an affair would be a good piano player and a few girls. Of course you paid an admission fee—usually ten cents—which was for the benefit of some Ladies Auxiliary —though it may have been an auxiliary to that particular house. The music invited you, and the female of the species urged that you remain. The neighborhood girls came unescorted, but seldom left alone. Dancing was the diversion and there is no reason to doubt that these affairs were properly named "SHIN-DIGS."

There was "Beaver Slide," that supposedly rough section of the Negro district, situated in the hollow between two typically Georgian Hills. Here lived a more naive group of Negroes whose sociables were certain to make the passers by take notice. The motto for their affairs seemed to be "Whosoever will let him come, and may the sur-vived survive." Twenty to thirty couples packed into two small rooms, "slow-dragging" to the plaintive blues of the piano player, whose music had a boss accompaniment furnished by his feet. The piano was opened top and front that the strains may be more distinct, and that the artist may have the joy of seeing as well as hearing his deft touches (often played by "ear") reflected in the mechanics of the instrument. They were a free-"joy-unconfined" group. Their conventions were their own. If they wished to guffaw they did—if they wished to fight they did. But they chiefly danced—not with the aloofness of a modern giglio but with fervor. What a picture they presented! Women in ginghams or cheap finery, men in peg top trousers, silk shirts, "loud" arm bands, and the ever present tan shoes with the "bull dog" toe. Feet stamped merrily—songs sung cheerily—No blues writer can ever record accurately the tones and words of those songs—they are to be heard and not written—bodies sweating, struggling in their effort to get the most of the dance; a drink of "lightning" to accelerate the enthusiasm—floors creaking and sagging—everybody happy.

144

During the dance as well as the intermission, you bought your refreshments. This was a vital part of the evening's enjoyment. But what food you could get for a little money! Each place had its specialties—"Hoppinjohn," (rice and black-eyed peas) or Mulatto rice (rice and tomatoes). Okra gumbo, Sweet potato pone—sometimes Chicken—Chitterlings—Hog maws—or other strictly southern dishes. You ate your fill. Dancing was resumed and continued until all were ready to leave—or it had suddenly ended in a brawl causing the "Black Maria" to take some to the station house and the police sending the remaining folk to their respective homes.

And there were those among us who had a reverential respect for such affairs. At that time there was no great popularity attached to a study of the Negro in his social environment. These were just plain folks having a good time. On the other hand, they were capable of description, and to those of us who knew, they were known as "struggles," "break-downs," "razor-drills," "flop-wallies" and "chitterling parties." These they were in fact as well as fancy. It was a struggle to dance in those crowded little rooms, while one never knew if the cheaply constructed flooring would collapse in the midst of its sagging and creaking. What assurance did one have that the glistening steel of a razor or "switch blade" would not flash before the evening's play was done? And very often chitterlings were served—yet by the time forty sweating bodies had danced in a small parlor with one window—a summer's evening—and continued to dance—well the party still deserved that name. But Mrs. Bailey paid her rent.

> *NEWS ITEM: "Growing out of economic stress, this form of nocturnal diversion has taken root in Harlem—that section known as the world's largest Negro centre. Its correct and more dignified name is "Parlor Social," but in the language of the street, it is caustically referred to as a "house rent party."*

With the mass movement of Southern Negroes to Northern Cities, came their little custom. Harlem was astounded. Socially minded individuals claimed that the H.C.L. with the relative insufficiency of wages was entirely responsible for this ignominious situation; that the exorbitant rents paid by the Negro wage earners had given rise to the obnoxious "house rent party." The truth seemed to be that the old-party of the South had attired itself à la Harlem. Within a few years the custom developed into a business venture whereby a tenant sought to pay a rent four, five and six times as great as was paid in the South. It developed by-products both legal and otherwise, hence it became extremely popular.

Yes sir thats my baby and I don't mean maybe you will find her at

A SOCIAL WHIST PARTY
given by
MRS EMILY WILLIAMS
at 124 West 135th Street, Apt. 26
on Thursday evening, November 26, 1925
Music by Prof Campbell
Refreshments Served

bring your friends

Papa is mad about the way you do, So meet the gang and Skoodle um Skoo at

A SOCIAL WHIST PARTY
To be given
At the residence of JAS. BENEFIELD
At 20 West 134th Street ground fl. E.
Saturday evening Sept. 3rd 1927

Good Music. Refreshments served

If you cant Charleston or do the pigeon Wing You sure can shake that thing at a
Social Party
GIVEN BY
STEWART & HOLTON
6 Bradhurst Ave 3
Saturday Evening. Sept. 25, '26
GOOD MUSIC AND REFRESHMENTS

Save your tears for a rainy day.
We are giving a party where you can play
With red mammas and too bad Sheebas
Who wear their dresses above their knees
And mess around with whom they please.
At A
SOCIAL PARTY
Given By
Mrs. Helen Carter & Mrs. Mandy Wesley
Sept. 24th, 1927 at 227 West 18th St.
1 flight up Back
GOOD MUSIC REFRESHMENTS

Leaving me. Papa, it's hard to do, because Mama done put that thing on you.
A Novelty Matinee Dance
by
CHINK
116 West 144th Street. Apt. 27
Sunday. June 27th from 4, until?
Plenty Music Refreshments served

Papa, if you want to see Mama do the Black Bottom. come to
A SOCIAL PARTY
given by
MRS. KELLY
8 WEST 134th STREET, 1 flight, west side
Saturday Evening, February 5, 1927
Good Music Refreshments Served

There has been an evolution in the eclat of the rent party since it has become "Harlemized." The people have seen a new light, and are no longer wont to have it go unnamed. They called it a "Parlor Social." That term, however, along with "Rent Party" is for the spoken word. "Social Whist Party" looks much better in print and has become the prevailing terminology. Nor is its name restricted to these. Others include "Social Party," "Too Terrible Party," "Too Bad Party," "Matinee Party," "Parlor Social," "Whist Party," and "Social Entertainment." And, along with the change in nomenclature has come a change in technique. No longer does the entrepreneur depend upon the music to welcome his stranger guests; nor does he simply invite friends of the neighborhood. The rent party ticket now turns the trick.

There straggles along the cross-town streets of North Harlem a familiar figure. A middle aged white man, bent from his labor as the Wayside Printer, is pushing a little cart which has all of the equipment necessary for setting up the rent party ticket. The familiar tinkle of his bell in the late afternoon brings the representative of some family to his side. While you wait, he sets up your invitation with the bally-ho heading desired, and at a very reasonable price. The grammar and the English may be far from correct, but they meet all business requirements since they bring results. What work the Wayside Printer does not get goes to the nearest print shop; some of which specialize in these announcements.

A true specimen of the popular mind is expressed in these tickets. The heading may be an expression from a popular song, a slang phrase, a theatrical quip or "poetry." A miscellaneous selection gives us the following: "Come and Get it Fixed"; "Leaving Me Papa, It's Hard To Do Because Mama Done Put That Thing On You"; "If You Can't Hold Your Man, Don't Cry After He's Gone, Just Find Another"; "Clap Your Hands Here Comes Charlie and He's Bringing Your Dinah Too"; "Old Uncle Joe, the Jelly Roll King is Back in Town and is Shaking That Thing"; "Here I am Again. Who? Daddy Jelly Roll and His Jazz Hounds"; "It's Too Bad Jim, But if You Want To Find a Sweet Georgia Brown, Come to the House of Mystery"; "You Don't Get Nothing for Being an Angel Child, So you Might as Well Get Real Busy and Real Wild".

And at various parties we find special features, among them being "Music by the Late Kidd Morgan"; "Music by Kid Professor, the Father of the Piano"; "Music by Blind Johnny"; "Music by Kid Lippy"; "Skinny At the Traps"; "Music Galore"; "Charge De Affairs Bessie and Estelle"; "Here You'll Hear that Sweet Story That's Never Been Told;" "Refreshments to Suit"; "Refreshments by 'The Cheater'." All of these present to the average rent party habitueé a very definite picture of what is to be expected, as the card is given to him on the street corner, or at the subway station.

The parties outdo their publicity. There is always more than has been announced on the public invitation. Though no mention was made of an admission fee, one usually pays from twenty-five to fifty cents for this privilege. The refreshments are not always refreshing, but are much the same as those served in parts of the South, with gin and day-old Scotch extra. The Father of the Piano lives up to his reputation as he accompanies a noisy trap drummer, or a select trio composed of fife, guitar, and saxophone.

Apart from the admission fee and the sale of food, and drinks, the general tenor of the party is about the same as one would find in a group of "intellectual liberals" having a good time. Let us look at one. We arrived a little early—about nine-thirty o'clock. The ten persons present, were dancing to the strains of the Cotton Club Orchestra via radio. The drayman was just bringing two dozen chairs from a nearby undertaker's establishment, who rents them for such affairs. The hostess introduced herself, asked our names, and politely informed us that the "admittance fee" was thirty-five cents, which we paid. We were introduced to all, the hostess not remembering a single name. Ere the formality was over, the musicians, a piano player, saxophonist, and drummer, had arrived and immediately the party took on life. We learned that the saxophone player had been in big time vaudeville; that he could make his instrument "cry"; that he had quit the stage to play for the parties because he wanted to stay in New York.

There were more men than women, so a poker game was started in the next room, with the woman who did not care to dance, dealing. The music quickened the dancers. They sang "Muddy Water, round my feet—ta-ta-ta-ta-ta-ta-ta". One girl remarked— "Now this party's getting right." The hostess informed us of the menu for the evening —Pig feet and Chili—Sandwiches à la carte, and of course if you were thirsty, there was some "good stuff" available. Immediately, there was a rush to the kitchen, where the man of the house served your order.

For the first time we noticed a man who made himself conspicuous by his watchdog attitude toward all of us. He was the "Home Defense Officer," a private detective who was there to forestall any outside interference, as well as prevent any losses on the inside on account of the activity of the "Clean-up Men." There were two clean-up men there that night and the H.D.O. had to be particularly careful lest they walk away with two or three fur coats or some of the household furnishings. Sometimes these men would be getting the "lay" of the apartment for a subsequent visit.

There was nothing slow about this party. Perfect strangers at nine o'clock were boon companions at eleven. The bedroom had become the card room—a game of "skin" was in progress on the floor while dice were rolled on the bed. There was something "shady" about the dice game, for one of the players was always having his dice caught. The musicians were still exhorting to the fifteen or twenty couples that danced. Bedlam reigned. It stopped for a few minutes while one young man hit another for getting fresh with his girl while dancing. The H.D.O. soon ended the fracas.

About two o'clock, a woman from the apartment on the floor below rang the bell and vociferously demanded that this noise stop or that she would call an officer. The hostess laughed in her face and slammed the door. Some tenants are impossible! This was sufficient however, to call the party to a halt. The spirit—or "spirits" had been dying by degrees. Everybody was tired—some had "dates"—others were sleepy— while a few wanted to make a cabaret before "curfew hour." Mrs. Bailey calmly surveyed a disarranged apartment, and counted her proceeds.

And so the rent party goes on. In fact, it has been going from bad to worse. Harlem copyists of Greenwich Village give them now—for the lark of it. Not always is it a safe and sane affair. Too many evils have crept in, professional gamblers, confidence men, crooks looking for an accomplice for the night, threats of fights with revolvers and razors drawn—any or all of these things may appear in one party. You are seldom certain of your patrons. However, one entrepreneur is always certain of her guests. She invites only members of the Street Cleaning Department and their friends. She extends the invitation *Viva Voce* from the front window of her apartment. The occupant in the apartment below her once complained to the court of the noise in the course of her parties. The court advised that if the noise were too great she should move. She remained.

At the same time, there may be tragedies. The New York Age carried an editorial sometime ago on a "Rent Party Tragedy." At this affair one woman killed another woman about a third member of the species. The editorial states in part:

"One of these rent parties a few weeks ago was the scene of a tragic crime in which one jealous woman cut the throat of another, because the two were rivals for the affections of a third woman. The whole situation was on a par with the recent Broadway play, imported from Paris, although the underworld tragedy took place in this locality,—In the meantime, the combination of bad gin, jealous women, a carving knife, and a rent party is dangerous to the health of all concerned."

Nowadays, no one knows whether or not one is attending a bonafide rent party. The party today may be fostered by the Tenants Protective Association, or the Imperial Scale of Itinerant Musicians, or the Society for the Relief of Ostracized Bootleggers. Yes, all of these foster parties, though the name is one of fancy. Musicians and Bootleggers have to live as well as the average tenant, and if they can combine their efforts on a business proposition, the status of both may be improved.

It has become in some quarters, a highly commercial affair. With the increased overhead expenses—printing of tickets, hiring the Home Defense Officer, renting chairs, hiring the musicians—one has to make the venture pay.

But the rent parties have not been so frequent of late. Harlem's new dance halls with their lavish entertainment, double orchestra, and "sixteen hours of continuous dancing", with easy chairs and refreshments available are ruining the business. They who continue in this venture of pleasure and business are working on a very close margin both socially and economically, when one adds the complexity illustrated by the following incident:

A nine year old boy gazed up from the street to his home on the "top floor, front, East side" of a tenement on West 134th Street about eleven thirty on a Friday night. He waited until the music stopped and cried, "Ma! Ma! I'm sleepy. Can I come in now?" To which a male voice, the owner of which had thrust his head out of the window, replied,—"Your ma says to go to the Midnight Show, and she'll come after you. Here's four bits. She says the party's just got going good."

SONNET TO A NEGRO IN HARLEM

By HELENE JOHNSON

You are disdainful and magnificent—
Your perfect body and your pompous gait,
Your dark eyes flashing sullenly with hate,
Small wonder that you are incompetent
To imitate those whom you so despise—
Your shoulders towering high above the throng,
Your head thrown back in rich, barbaric song,
Palm trees and mangoes stretched before your eyes.
Let others toil and sweat for labor's sake
And wring from grasping hands their meed of gold.
Why urge ahead your supercilious feet?
Scorn will efface each footprint that you make.
I love your laughter arrogant and bold.
You are too splendid for this city street!

TOKENS

By GWENDOLYN B. BENNETT

IGH on the bluff of Saint Cloud stands the Merlin Hospital, immaculate sentinel of Seraigne . . . Seraigne with its crazy houses and aimless streets, scrambling at the foot of Saint Cloud's immense immutability. Row on row the bricks of the hospital take dispassionate account of lives lost or found. It is always as though the gay, little town of Seraigne were thumbing its nose at Saint Cloud with its famous Merlin Hospital where life is held in a test-tube, a thing to be caught or lost by a drop or two of this or a pellet of that. And past the rustic stupidity of Seraigne's gaiety lies the wanton unconcern of the Seine. The Seine . . . mute river of sorrows . . . grim concealer of forgotten secrets . . . endlessly flowing . . . touching the edges of life . . . moving purposefully along with a grey disdain for the empty, foolish gaiety of Seraigne or the benign dignity of Merlin Hospital, high on the warm cliffs of Saint Cloud.

A trim nurse had drawn Jenks Barnett's chair out onto one of the balconies that over-looked the Seine. Listlessly, aimlessly he turned his thoughts to first one aspect and then another of the Seine, Merlin Hospital, the cliffs of Saint Cloud, Seraigne . . . over and again . . . the Seine, Merlin Hospital, the cliffs . . . of . . . Saint . . . Cloud . . . silly, little Seraigne. It was a better way—that Seine business. Just swallow up life and sorrow and sadness . . . don't bother about the poor fools who are neither dead nor alive . . . just hanging on to the merest threads of existence . . . coughing out one's heart and yet somehow still keeping heart. Purposeless thoughts these as one just as purposelessly fingers the blanket that covers one's emaciated, almost lifeless legs. But the Seine goes on, and Seraigne continues to be happy, and the pain in one's chest grows no easier.

It so happened that at this particular time there were a number of colored patients at the Merlin Hospital. Most of them were musicians who had remained in Paris after the World War. Two of them had come to London and thence to Paris with Will Marion Cook in the Negro entertainer's hey-day. Jenks was one of these. He had been a singer in those days. His voice was now spoken of in the hushed tones one uses when speaking of the dead. He had cherished great plans for himself in those days and no one dared hope otherwise, so rare was his voice in range and quality. That was all changed now. . . .

Merlin Hospital had won nation-wide fame as a haven for patients suffering from tuberculosis. An able staff of doctors and nurses administered daily hope of recovery to broken bodies or perhaps kindly, although inadequate, solace to those whose cases were hopeless. Jenks Barnett had been there five weeks. His case was one of the hopeless ones. The tale of his being there did not take long in the telling. Shortly after the success of Cook's orchestra with its inimitable "singing trombonist" Tollie had come—Tollie Saunders with her golden voice and lush laughter. From the very first she and Jenks had hit it off well together. It was not long before he was inextricably enmeshed in the wonder of her voice and the warm sweetness of her body. Dinner at Les Acacias . . . for Tollie . . . a hat for her lovely head . . . that dress in Chanal's window . . . she wanted one of those large opal rings . . . long nights of madness under the charm of her flute-sweet voice. His work began to suffer. Soon he was dismissed from the orchestra. Singing *soirees* didn't pay too well. And then one day before the pinch of poverty came Tollie had left him, taking with her all the pretty things he had given her . . . leaving no farewell . . . her chance had come to sing in an American production and she had gone. No word of their plan to startle the singing world with their combined talents; no hint of regret that she was leaving . . . just gone. Three nights on a gorgeous drunk and he had awakened to find himself in a dingy, damp Parisian jail with a terrific pain in his back . . . eighteen days in which he moved from one prison-house to another . . . sunshine and air again when his friends had finally found him and arranged for his release . . . sunshine lasts but a short time in Paris . . . endless days of splashing through the Paris rain in search of a job . . . always that pain between his shoulder-blades . . . then night upon night of blowing a trombone in a stuffy little *Boite de Nuit* during which time he forgot the pain in his back . . . and drink . . . incessant drink . . . one more drink with the fellows . . . and after the job cards and more drink. One came to Merlin after one had been to the American Hospital. One came to Merlin after one had been to every other hospital round about Paris. It does not take long to become accustomed to the turning knife in one's chest. It is good for a hopeless case to watch the uncurbed forgetfulness of the Seine.

Spring had sent ahead its perfume this day. It was as though the early March air were powdered with the pollen of many unborn flowers. A haze settled itself in the air and on the breast of the river. Jenks forgot for a moment the relentless ache in his bosom and breathed deeply in sheer satisfaction. In

149

the very midst of this gesture of aliveness the tool of death, lodged in his lung, gave a wrench. A hacking cough rose in his throat and then seemed to become stuck there. His great, gaunt frame was shaken in a paroxysm of pain. The fit of stifled coughing over, his head fell back upon the pillow. A nurse hurried to his side. "Guess you'd better go in now. I told you not to move around."

With quick, efficient hands she tucked the cover more closely about his legs, lowered the back of the invalid chair in which he was sitting, and pushed him carefully back into the hospital. As his chair was rolled through the ward it was as though he were running the gamut of scorn. Jenks was not a favorite at the hospital by any stretch of the imagination. Few of the patients there had escaped the lash of his tongue. Sour at life and the raw deal it had dealt him, he now turned his attention to venting his spume on those about him. Nurses, doctors, orderlies, fellow-patients, persistent friends . . . all shared alike the blasphemy of his words. Even Bill Jackson, the one friend who continued to brave the sting of his vile tongue, was not spared. Bill had known him and loved him before Tollie came. It was in this memory that he wrapped himself when Jenks was most unbearable. He accused Bill of stealing his money when he asked him to bring him something from the city. . . . There had been many who had tried to make Jenks' last days easier but one by one they had begun to stay away until now there was only Bill left. Little wonder the other patients in the hospital heaped invective upon him as he passed.

So thin he was as he lay beneath the covers of the bed that his knees and chest made scarcely perceptible mounds in the smooth whiteness of the bed. The brown of his face had taken on the color of dried mud. Great seams folded themselves in his cheeks. There he lay, the rotting hulk of what he had once been. He had sent for Bill . . . these waiting moments were so long!

"Hi there, Jenks" . . . it was Bill's cheery voice . . . "thought you'd be outside."

"Can't go out no more. Nearly kicked off the other day."

"Thas all right . . . you'll come around all right."

"For God sakes cut it out. I know I'm done for. You know it, too, damn it all."

"Come on now, fella, be your age. You can't last long if you get yourself all worked up. Take it easy."

"Oh I get so damned sick of the whole business I wish I would hurry up and die. But whose business is that but mine . . . got somethin' to tell you."

"Shoot."

"See I'm dyin' . . . get me. They keep stickin' that needle in me but I know damn well I'm dyin'. Now what I want you to do is this . . . I wrote a letter to Tollie when I first came here . . . it's in her picture in my suit-case . . . you know that silver frame. Well when I die I want you to give it to

her, if it's a thousand years from now . . . just a token of the time when we were in love. Don't forget it. Then you remember that French kid that used to be on the ward downstairs . . . she always liked that radium clock of mine. She's been transferred to the Gerboux Sanitarium . . . almost well now. I think they said she would be out in a year. Good kid . . . used to climb up here every afternoon . . . stairs sort of wore her out, too. Give her my clock and tell her I hope she lives to be well and strong 'cause I never'll make it. God, she was an angel if ever there was one . . . she used to sit there on that chair where you're sittin' now and just look at me and say how she wished she could die in my place cause I was such a big man . . . and could sing so. . . . I believe she'd like to have something to remember me by. And, Bill, you take . . . that . . . mmmghgummmmm . . . mmm. . . ."

That strangling cough rose in his throat. His eyes, always cruel, seemed to look out softly at Bill. A nurse hurried swiftly into the room and injected a hypodermic needle into his arm. A tremor went through his body. His eye-lids half closed . . . he slept.

The days dragged out in one week after another. Jenks lingered on like the days. Outside the Seine flowed endlessly on unhindered and free. It was all so futile and strange . . . waiting this way.

June had laid her warm mouth upon the face of the earth. With soft languor the sun slid tenderly over the cliffs of Saint Cloud . . . even tenderly over the grey bricks of Merlin Hospital. Jenks had raged so about not being allowed to lie on the balcony that at last the hospital authorities had relented . . . there was such a short time left for him anyway . . . he might as well have what he wanted . . . this was the first day that had been warm enough. As he lay there he looked out across the cliffs, past the little town of Seraigne, out past the Seine . . . on . . . on . . . immune to life . . . conversant with death . . . on to the great simplicities. He got to thinking of when he was a boy . . . the songs he used to sing . . . he almost thought he'd try to sing now . . . what did it matter if he got another coughing spell . . . but then the nurses would all be in a flurry. Nice to be out here once more looking at the Seine and the world where people lived and breathed.

Bill sighed as he placed the little clock on the mantle-piece. Funny world, this! The French girl had died in late May. He had better not tell Jenks . . . it might upset him. No-o-ope better just keep the clock here. Funny how the first kind thing Jenks had done for anybody since Tollie left him should be done for a person who was dead.

High on the bluff of Saint Cloud stands the Merlin Hospital, immaculate sentinel of Seraigne . . . with its crazy houses and aimless streets, scrambling at the foot of Saint Cloud's immense immutability. Row on row the bricks of the hospital take dispassionate account of lives lost or found.

A PAGE OF UNDERGRADUATE VERSE

SIGNS OF SPRING
By HERBERT PICKETT
Tougaloo College

One day, the last of winter,
It was warm as any spring—
I sat in my room, on Sunday,
And heard the bluebirds sing.

The buds had begun swelling,
And the peach trees were in bloom;
I could not but feel happy,
And forget the winter's gloom.

It was during silent hour
When I saw a cloud appear,
But the drops were soft and gentle—
A sign that spring was near.

It was after silent hour,
After the shower of rain,
That the last sign came—white trousers—
When we went to see the train!

THE SOUDAN
By CLARENCE F. BUYSON
Cleveland College of Western Reserve University

The brooding, sullen forest nights are filled
With varied sights and smells. The purple dusk
Of shaded jungle paths, where Njega killed
Of oily, bubbling slime; the Lemur's cry,
A wild crescendo, then a baffling shriek
And dined, is thick with sounds: the reeking musk
Of sluggish snakes beside a stagnant creek
That dies away; a snail's sepulchral sigh
Of endless woe; a leopard's coughing roar
Above the tangled skein; the monotone
Of pounding surf against a hostile shore;
The stench from dripping mangrove roots; the groan,
Below the drifting mists, of fetid mud
Where new life stirs in old life's stagnant blood.

NOTE:—Njega, in the Benga dialect, means leopard. It is pronounced Njega or Nega, i.e. N—yeaga. A giant snail in the French Soudan gives that peculiar remorseful sigh, which is heard only at night.
Note B:—That Njega is pronounced with two syllables.

DISILLUSION
By LILLIAN BROWN
Tougaloo College

In a far-away wood there lived two monkeys . . .
They went to town on two old grey donkeys . . .
But when they saw what we call "men,"
They decided to go home again.

THE RETURN

By Arna Bontemps

I

Once more, listening to the wind and rain,
Once more, you and I, and above the hurting sound
Of these comes back the throbbing of remembered rain,
Treasured rain falling on dark ground.
Once more, huddling birds upon the leaves
And summer trembling on a withered vine.
And once more, returning out of pain,
The friendly ghost that was your love and mine.

II

The throb of rain is the throb of muffled drums;
Darkness brings the jungle to our room.
Darkness hangs our room with pendulums
Of vine and in the gathering gloom
Our walls recede into a denseness of
Surrounding trees. This is a night of love
Retained from those lost nights our fathers slept
In huts; this is a night that cannot die.
Let us keep the dance of rain our fathers kept
And tread our dreams beneath the jungle sky.

III

The downpour ceases.
Let us go back, you and I, and dance
Once more upon the glimmering leaves
And as the throbbing of drums increases
Shake the grass and the dripping boughs of trees.
A dry wind stirs the palm; the old tree grieves.
Time has charged the years and they have returned.
Then let us dance by metal waters burned
With gold of moon, let us dance
With naked feet beneath the young spice trees.
What was that light, that radiance
On your face?—something I saw when first
You passed beneath the jungle tapestries?
A moment we pause to quench our thirst
Kneeling at the water's edge, the gleam
Upon your face is plain; you have wanted this.
Oh let us go back and search the tangled dream
And as the muffled drum-beats throb and miss
Remember again how early darkness comes
To dreams and silence to the drums.

IV

Let us go back into the dusk again,
Slow and sad-like following the track
Of blown leaves and cool white rain
Into the old grey dreams; let us go back.
Our walls close about us, we lie and listen
To the noise of the street, the storm and the driven birds.
A question shapes your lips, your eyes glisten
Retaining tears, but there are no more words.

I—

By Brenda Ray Moryck

HEN I was a very little girl, a strange and unaccountable idea persisted with me that I wanted to belong to the aristocrats of the earth. Psychologists would explain this complex by referring to the African kings and queens who loom so frequently on the horizon nowadays as the direct forbears of every Negro who achieves, and of many who aspire to achieve, but my mother offers a more physical and intimate reason. She spent the lovely Spring months preceding my birth in a serene and exclusive country seat on a tiny farm adjoining a magnificent estate, where the beautiful titled English woman for whom I was subsequently named, and who was graciously pleased to form an attachment for my mother and an interest in my approaching advent was visiting.

Very early, I began to associate aristocracy with flat-heeled, square-toed shoes, in a day when most children's stubby feet were being sacrificed to the false grace of a pointed toe and ordinary shops refused to display even small children's boots without heels; with short white socks when a mistaken modesty bade mothers cover their small daughters' legs in long, black stockings; clean finger-nails when it was the vogue to cry "let children be children" (meaning let them be pigs); glistening teeth, free from food and film before the alarming days of "one in every five will have it"; loosely hanging, unberibboned locks when two or four tight braids, according to the texture of the hair, flamboyantly decorated with huge, bright-colored bows at the nape of the neck were the vogue; and severely tailored outer play garments, mostly dark blue, when little girls self-consciously appeared on sleds or skates bedecked in last year's finery, and bearskin, crushed plush and velvet betokened the style.

Looking at the children thus accoutred and then examining myself by careful scrutiny, I perceived a striking similarity. So elated was I by this discovery of homogeneity that I entirely forgot to note the difference in the color of our skins. I was so happy in just being a little girl of the sort I admired I neglected to remember that I was colored.

Something happened to me then,—something so deeply satisfying, so limitless in its beneficence, so far-reaching in its results, that I set down details here cognizant of hazarding charges of snobbery. It was as if I had been slipped for all times into an impregnable suit of armor with which to shut in after years all subsequent buffetings of the world. No curious stares, no disapproving comments, nor the starkest criticism in my presence of my wise

mother's extraordinary taste could shake my equanimity or self-satisfaction. The claim is made, I know, that we see life in retrospect through rose-colored glass, but the actual unembellished fact is that I,—a Negro by birth,—a very small girl by years,—began my battle with a hostile, Caucasian-dominated life outside the home-nest, as a happy, self-assured, young being.

Later years soon dimmed the illusion that the symbol of aristocracy is outward dress and appearance—that it is even that soft-mannered or arrogant veneer which so often deceives,—in fact that it is anything but the serenity and strength of mind which come from a consciousness of clear vision, straight thinking and a right evaluation of every detail of life's complexity—not blue-blood but a sterling heritage,—a taste for the fine and the beautiful,—courage and fineness; not wealth in dollars and cents, though to keep high our self-set standards today, we must have money and plenty of it or trail in the dust of unfulfillment a goodly portion of our splendid desires,—not money,—but riches,— a keen and open mind,—a fertile brain, a hungry intellect,—a sane and wholesome outlook on life,— joy in little things,—the gift to love and love abundantly;—not suavity,—correct manners, soft-voiced covering of an empty or dishonest heart, nor yet hauteur,—smug self-esteem through bending heads which might look up in competition—but gentility,—that kindness, consideration, forbearance, tolerance, magnanimity and helpfulness to every living thing which betoken true refinement,— but my firmly established belief that I could measure with earth's elite never vanished.

As a Negro, I came to learn that I belonged to a despised group,—a group hailed everywhere by every ordinary white child as "niggers" or "darkies" —a practice much more common during my childhood even in the north than it is today slightly south of the Mason-Dixon line; that I must suffer impertinent and malicious stares at school every time "Old Black Joe" or "Swanee River" were sung unless I happened to be in the class of a child-lover,—and thank God there were a number to whom I now offer gratitude, who smilingly chose the morning songs themselves and never seemed to remember the existence of those tunes; that I must hand over the set of tea-dishes fallen to my lot as an impartial or blind Santa Claus's gift from a Caucasian Baptist Sunday School Christmas tree because a white infant objected to "that little colored girl" having dishes while she had only a book; that I must play better basket-ball than any other member

153

of the team to keep my place on it as representative of my high school; that I must always be in company with a certain lovely Caucasian in order to drink soda or eat luncheon in certain exclusive shops or bathe at certain beaches; that the privilege of touring the beautiful southern part of "the land of the free and home of the brave" must be foregone because of the insufferable inconveniences maintained by discrimination; that colleges catered to prejudice, and all learned people were not cultured; that some were cats and brutes and boors; that men and women, too, of warped mind and narrow sympathies often dominated the earth,—at least a considerable portion of it, and bent to their evil wills their brothers less fortunate because cursed with a black skin; that my people were burned alive and seldom a voice raised in protest, yet gladly saluted the flag which refused them protection, and in time of war, laid down their lives for a country in which they had lived on sufferance; that "might is often right" so far as exploitation of black men is concerned, and that justice is the white man's meed alone. I could not help it. It was life.

Yet, for every ill, life offers compensation. Being a Negro is sweet at times. It carries with it privileges which cannot but warm the heart of the most cynical and callous. The bitter may denounce friendly overtures as patronage, asking only a fair chance to make their mark according to their abilities, but this is a very partial old world after all,—a world in which the scales for reward and punishment are seldom equal. We rise,—too often, perhaps,—on personal favor,—not only Negroes, but all people. Since we are of this world, if not with it, it seems sensible to rejoice in the kind offices of our well-wishers. "Look not a gift horse in the mouth."

I soon learned that although a representative number of patched up and hungry-looking little plebeians liked to call "Nigger, nigger, never die, black face and shiny eye," and a few sturdy, rosy-cheeked ones, too, every time I passed by, the majority of the children who came from big, comfortable-looking homes,—even elegant houses on quiet streets—(for I went to the public school in a day when intelligent and far-sighted parents had not yet felt the "menace of socialization" or doubted the efficacy of mass training for the individual, and the earlier popularity of the private school and private tutor was on the wane)—were forever seeking me out to make up their ring or complete their team or play their games, and were constantly inviting me home to luncheon "because I want Mama to see you," (Mama being one of those "wholesale-generalizationed" tongued ladies who had pronounced sentence on all colored children as being rough, dirty, and foul-minded).

Remember, please, that I was very young and very human. I enjoyed it all. Preening myself on my desirability as "such a *lovely* little colored girl," I soon let it be known in certain "white trash" enemy groups that I was not allowed to associate with common children! And when I went home at his invitation with my first beau,—an adorable eight-year-old named Leslie, who I might wish even now could read these lines,—and his family, all gathered on the large veranda of his home to receive his fair lady burst into laughter and gurgled, "Why she's *colored*," I thought they were delighted to find me different!

Little prig—little fool! What does it matter,—which or both—so I was happy. Is it not every child's right to be happy? I was happy.

Again, the earmarks of my Negro blood won me a coveted position as alto in a duet with a beautiful little Jewish soprano who has since become nationally known. Nearly all the class entered the competition, but when, by elimination, only three candidates were left, there was such bitterness and weeping and wailing between the two little white girls desirous of singing "The Miller of the Dee" with this exquisite, divine-voiced doll, that the teachers cut short all controversy with the naïve announcement, "If we let the little colored girl win, the others won't feel so badly." "Beauty and the Jacobin!" How times have changed!

My high school career was practically free of all race consciousness, due, I am now positive to the absolute impartiality and unbiased principles of the head, a man of genial character but inflexible rule, and a corps of, for the most part, broad-minded, tolerant teachers who very adroitly never permitted the question of color and race superiority or inferiority to crop up. I was just one of the many, a single pupil in a classical school ministering to a heterogeneous group of hundreds of raw young people, making my mark and claiming notice according to my special talents, solely. Only when I made the basket-ball team was I conscious that my efforts alone had been superior to every other member's and yet I was last to be recognized. But who shall say the extra endeavor a Negro must always put forth in competition with white men does not rebound to his own benefit and credit? Was I not the better player on the court because of longer and more skillful practice before making the team?

Quite apart, however, from my school affiliations, there was another larger and more beautiful life opened to me, solely because I was a Negro. I may or may not have had an arresting personality, I may or may not have been well-bred, well-dressed, generally well-appearing. The fact remains that had I not been distinctly a member of my own racial group, I should never have become a quasi-protegée of an exquisite woman on whom the Gods had smiled in every way at her birth and on through life,—who was graciously pleased to entertain me in her home, introduce me to her friends and take me about everywhere,—not as her hired companion nor the daughter or granddaughter of some faithful retainer in her father's or mother's ménage, but as an interesting little colored girl who deserved to see the best that life offered, and who because of the barrier of a brown skin must otherwise be denied anything but occasional tempting glimpses.

Through her generosity, I tasted a life utterly beyond the reach of most Caucasians, tasted it under the pleasantest auspices, and therefore came to set store on being a Negro as something rare and precious.

The college years did not dispel this assumption. Rather, they tended to heighten it. The disappointments and heart-aches, which every normal teen age girl away from home experiences, were not due to color prejudice. At my college, Wellesley, in my day,—not so very long ago either—the authorities permitted no discrimination. The student body, consequently, taking their cue from their elders and betters as they always do, consciously or unconsciously even today, engaged in no wholesale active hostilities.

There were girls, of course, who tried to be mean and hateful,—usually from small towns in the north and west,—the southern girls, it is my joy to relate, with one lamentable exception—and that from the Nation's capital—were all ladies, and though their faces sometimes flamed with protest at the new order of relationships they were forced to endure, their good breeding never failed and, in time they came to be pleasantly civil outside the classroom as well as within, some of them even achieving a friendliness in senior year and a cordiality at reunions that was not to have been dreamed of in Freshman days, but for the most part, everybody wanted to do something kind for the one little black girl,—alien in a lively, callous, young world of fourteen hundred Caucasians, even the villagers to whom intimate contact with a Negro, not a hairdresser or laundress, was a privilege.

Again, it was always those choice spirits who roam the world and tread the high places of life unfettered by the bonds of public opinion,—either the very, very wealthy or the very blue-blooded, or the jealous devotee of the true principles of democracy, eager to put into practice her newly-conned theories, who were most generous in their friendliness and delightful in their overtures. Sadly must I observe that it was seldom the orthodox Christian recognized by her piety in repeating the prayer for all sorts and conditions of men and her lip-service to "God created of one blood all nations for to dwell upon the face of the earth" who stepped aside from her own interests or widened her circle to include me, but then,—she was not missed.

It was delightful—being a Negro at college. She who would decry the kind of satisfaction derived therefrom must indeed be a hypocrite or else abnormal. Let her consider the creature who walks alone through life, white or black,—friendless, unnoticed, uncherished, and reflect that it is a normal human being's craving to be liked. If, for wholesome reasons, and certainly there is nothing unwholesome in being a Negro, except in the eyes of certain vicious Nordics who seek to make it appear so, a person is liked,—what matters all the rest?

Even today, at a time when the entire attention of the white world at large is focused upon the Negro, with what intent or ultimate purpose it is difficult to forecast; when lynching is increasing, prejudice growing, the right to discriminate sustained on questions of civil right, north and west, as well as south, and unfair competition against the Negro threatening his economic existence except as a peon or pauper,—there is a zest in being a Negro.

Read the recent editorial comment on a dainty brown-skinned, bird-throated comedienne, Florence Mills, and take thought of the homage an intelligent world pays to art irrespective of race or color. Sit in capacity-jammed Carnegie Hall and hear the delicate exquisite music made by Roland Hayes, and know him judged a supreme artist, not of his race but of the world. Then consider. Have I not cause for pride of race?

There is honey as well as hemlock in the cup of every Negro,—sunlight as well as shadow.

.   .   .   .

But as a woman, what did I learn? That the sun shines on the just and the unjust,—that the mountains clap their hands and the morning stars sing together? That the glory of the sunset fades into the exquisite dusk of twilight and the mid-darkness of night bursts into the glory of the dawn? That the green of the tree-leaf turns to a magic red and gold and when winter comes, spring is not far behind?

Did I learn this as a woman? Ah, yes, and more besides,—that the peace and the beauty of earth,—fulfillment,—lie within the mind, embedded and enshrouded in an elusive quantity called soul,—whose entity now men doubt. Bend the body to the rack, confine the intellect to the torture of eternal limitations, the soul is away and free,—ranging the hills,—roaming the fields, winging on the breeze to an elysium which only God can withdraw. The majesty of mountains, the loveliness of twilight, the ineffable beauty of sunsets, the rush of sparkling waters, the pure calm of the deep woods, the mystery of oceans,—starlight, moonlight,—sunlight,—vast spaces under the infinite sky are mine, —mine because I am a woman,—a human being,— one of God's great family for whom He created the world and all that therein is. Smiling eyes of children,—blue eyes under golden curls as well as black eyes in tawny faces are turned toward me. Work, play, and that highest opportunity, the opportunity to help and to give, to mother and to heal,—are mine. "Non ministrari sed ministrare" is the radiance of existence. And can I not keep company with the greatest minds of the earth for all times in my books?

Life is rich and beautiful to a woman.

I am a Negro—yes—but I am also a woman.

"Two men looked out from the prison bars,
One saw the mud, the other, the stars."

A Glorious Company

By Allison Davis

HERE is an old Negro song in which the band of those destined for Heaven, with the prophets and King Jesus, are safely transported thither aboard a train! This journey by train to their last, long station is but an accentuated expression of the fascination and mystery which trains hold for Negroes of the south. I have often thought that the Negro farmhand would lose heart once for all, were it not for the daily encouragement he takes from the whistle of his favorite locomotives. Tied to his plow, under the red, burning sun, or aching with the loneliness of the sterile night, he can find all his desire for escape, all the courage he lacks in the face of the unknown, mingled with his inescapable hopelessness, in the deep-throated, prolonged blast of the express-train, like a challenge to untravelled lands, a terrifying cry to his petty township.

A journey by train for no more than three or five miles fills the poor Negroes of the south with confidence and elation. They are not only holiday-makers; they are seekers and adventurers. With all their children and world's gear about them, they leave nothing more precious than a squalid, smoke-painted shanty, with its empty pig-sty; who knows, then, if perchance they may not find a changed life in the next town or county, and never return? It is pitiable they should not yet have learned they have no fair country, and that oppression rides with them. Yet, no one who has not had his world bounded into less clean and metaphorical limits than those of a nut-shell can understand the hope which these, who journey from home, feel at the possibility of escape.

To them, the mere fact of motion suggests new independence, and incites their trammeled spirits with unbounded enthusiasm. They are rolling, in a rolling world, and at every local station exhort their friends, from the windows, to join the band.

"Git on boa'd, little children,
Dere's room for many a mo'."

is the spirit, if not the letter, of their greeting.

Aboard, they are all friends, drawn by their common adventure. A gambler and bully-boy lavishes his famed courtliness on a withered, old sister, brave in her antebellum finery, and falls at length into her "revival" plans. I have often noticed a fine-looking type of old gentleman, whose rich, brown skin, and soft, curly hair lend him a gentility the Jewish patriarchs lacked. He seems destined to encounter some buxom, dark-skinned "fancy woman," who cleverly leads him into his favorite discourses on the virtues of renunciation

and purity. Trained in flattery by her mode of life, she sits like a rapt student at her master's feet. And if, by unlucky goodness of heart, she offers him a pint of her own home-made "sperrits," knowing the indigence of the pure in heart, he will feel the simple testimony, and forgive.

There will be also the irreconcilables, like this white-skinned lady from the north. She feels only the indignity of the segregated train, and suffers from a kind of hyperaesthesia in this crude gathering of her own people. The odors from their full meal of fried chicken—I have seen even the delectable cabbage in lunch-boxes—arouse in her a genuine hatred of the whole clan; and she would enjoy lynching those wayworn sisters who unshoe their tortured feet. These black folk from whom she shrinks, however, are incorrigibly gentle and courteous, and seek by persistent attentions to make her comfortable,—even to talk with her like a fellow-being in a world of trouble. But her thoughts are fixed, with bitter longing, on the parlor car.

And yet, among the Florida tourists, from the observation car through the dining and lounging cars, down to this truncated segment of the baggage car, she would find no wit and smiles to put zest in the journey, like these about her. Starvation, one's own ignorance, persecution, hard luck, and the way of woman, all are turned into laughter, now reckless, and now ultimately philosophic. A jet-black woman is laughed at by her equally dark escort for spending time and effort to rouge and powder;—and she sees the ridiculous futility of her vanity, and laughs more heartily than he! A consumptive of huge frame jokingly threatens the young porter for treading on his feet, and cannot laugh without pain. And in one corner, in spite of the scowls of the conductor, a one-legged miner sings rich harmonies to his guitar, strumming with fervent sympathy, *Wonder Where's Dem Hebrew Children?* That *he* should look to Palestine two thousand years ago for homeless ones to pity!

More animated and cheerful is the story-teller, touched by just enough of the grape,—turned corn now in this makeshift world—to inspire him to a longer tale of his wanderings. He knows himself a romantic protagonist for this young college-boy who listens, and carries his adventures farther into the hero-world. There, sweet brown girls cherish him, or "evil womans" betray him, according to the powers of the grape. For the most part, he has had Herculean jobs in the mines or on the docks, and harder luck with his women than Samson; but now that he's once again "railroading, behind an eight-driving engine, with the rails ringing," his

156

confidence returns. Tomorrow, nay tonight at the end of his fare, he may be hungry and in the park; but as he talks now, homelessness and starvation are dangers in romance, no more fatal than the wounds of the archangels, which bleed ichor, and heal forthwith!

So it is with them all, escaping the weight of hardship and persecution by some exhilaration of the moment. In an hour now, many will be left at their lonely, country station, while the great engine burns its fiery trail across the black sky, driving on into other lands with happier children. But now they are still in a band and confident. Their pride and courage are fortified by the swaggers of the porter, for he is one of their own; they feel it a strange persecution and hopeful dispensation that he should be here to guide them safely in. So they roll on into a mystery.

In the great, city station, this sense of mystery becomes at once awful and exhilarating. They give porters tips of five cents in a beautiful trance of lavishness. The marble under their feet is turned to buoyant ether, and the great dome above draws their spirits in prayers and hallelujahs. And their exhilaration is the keener because against this brilliant spectacle, they can see in their mind's eye the alley-shack where they will come into the city's life. Now they feel only that here is a journey finished in a new and better land, full of light and splendor.

They have not gone this journey of physical hardship and spiritual cramping without the strength of hope and faith. This faith they will not lose in the newer lands to which they must eventually come, for it is revived daily by the barest victory over disease and poverty, and these will travel with them, to chasten. They go also with humility, which we will not think meanness of spirit, until we have known the daily bitterness of being forced to resign hope and manhood. And if they are humble, having faith in their journey, and courage still to face it with laughter and friendliness, perhaps they may be allowed to go in their stocking-feet, at ease over their dinner of cabbage, until they shall understand the ways of our fine lady, and some day, perchance, even of the Florida tourists.

A STUDENT I KNOW

By Jonathan H. Brooks

He mocks the God invisible
To whom his mother prays;
"What stands on faith for proof is built
On shifting sands," he says.

To him life is a heartless game:
"I grapple, fight, defy,"
He says: "the world is his who wins;
The losers, let them die."

Ah, greenhorn-pilgrim, duped by thieves
And left to writhe in dirt
Beside the way to Jericho—
Wounded, robbed—and hurt!

— AND I PASSED BY

By Joseph Maree Andrew

I USED to take so much of Life for granted. Enough to eat—enough sleep—enough rest—not too much to do—the schools I wanted—the things I wanted—friends with the things they wanted.

I had even been pit-pat too. Took the Natural-Trickery-of-the-White-man to be an indelible streak in the breed. An indelible streak that only called for enough distrust on my own part to get along.

I used to take so much of Life for granted. But once the Wing—the WING of Death—swept across my home. Swept across my home twice in two short years.

It swept twice. It made sure that all of my heart was beneath the two pieces of the World that men call graves.

I used to take so much of Life for granted. When the Wing had swept clean the halls of my home, people came and talked. Came to talk, to tell me how to face two spaces that were empty forever. Empty spaces that ached. Then the talk and the people flowed back around me like blood from around a wound.

The Empty Spaces ached. I was the flesh around the wound—the Empty Spaces, the wound.

I cried to high Heaven—"Is God really good—?"

But I should have bowed and cried low—"Yet-somehow—God is really good."

I had taken too much for granted, you see. The Wing swept clean. It swept away the scales from my eyes, too. I began to soften.

—Soft, you will see what I mean.

The scales left my eyes. I decided I could again see and talk once more without dropping out of things into my own abyss.

Thus I set out on a winter's evening with a friend to dinner. Cold air pooled around us as we stepped out of the door.

I took a deep sniff—drew in as much as I could—pressed my cheeks deeper in the fur around me—appreciated my friend's well clad appearance—sniffed her perfume—and let my pulse race ahead to the click of our heels on the pavement.

Nothing troubled us. Absolutely nothing at all. School and its work lay behind us. A home we could really enjoy lay ahead.

We pattered. Light talk pattered with our heels.

"Let's walk all the way." I had to skip a step as I said. It was so good to be freely alive.

"I want to walk for once," replied the girl beside me.

The hill mounted. Our blood pounded. Our heels clicked. Our tongues raced—I could breathe deeply and I could only know it was cold by the whiffs of the air across my nose (which is strangely tender in winter).

The hill veered sharply. We would either have to prolong the jaunt or take a short cut.

"Are you afraid to cut through—Street? asked my companion. She mentioned a street that is not supposed to be safe after dark.

It has sad houses, sad stores in every available space, and people, white and colored. up and down it. It is sad. The white and colored people fight pitched battles and hate each other as if each blamed the other for being there.

"No! of course I am not afraid." My pulse made me say that.

158

We struck out. I really was a bit afraid. That made my pulses race harder. We crossed an intersection. I stumbled over the car tracks and hopped the curb. Then I turned to look back.

"Not buttered fingers but buttered toes," I explained.

The other girl did not answer. She looked beyond me. I turned the other way to look too.

Something soft brushed against me. A girl—slender, dead-white—in a light blue dress with a low round neck—and with bed-room slippers on her feet—staggered against me.

I welched away. She fell in a sort of confusion against the building behind us. The street light lay full in her face. Her eyes were half closed, her mouth slightly opened.

Something made me catch hold of my throat. The girl staggered and stumbled. She went around the corner.

"Oh—." It sounded futile even to me, but I said it. We both stared at one another. I rambled on: "She did not have a coat!" I started toward the corner. "She is sick!"

"You'd better let that cracker alone! You do not know this place! This is— Street!" cried the girl with me.

I wavered. This was —Street.

That sent us on up the hill. A weight fell on me. The sidewalk made me stumble. I felt burdened. I was stumbling.

I sat at the table. Food, talk, good fellowship flowed around me, bathed me about.

"Come to and answer my question!" some one said beside me.

"Mustn't let yourself worry, my dear," the hostess whispered in the kindly warmth of motherly middle age.

Tears wavered in my eyes. She thought I was rooting back.

Digging beneath my wound.. Filling my Empty Spaces with dreams that hurt. But—

—Cold. A blue voile dress. Bed room slippers. Eyes half-opened. But she was white. She would have pushed me away if I had touched her and she had seen my brown flesh.

What did I have to do with it? She would have spat in my face.

Still a white face swam before me. It swam between me and my plate. A pale blue voile dress. I only knew it was cold by the touch of wind across my face.—

I tried to blot it out then. I tasted food. Tasted ideas. Talked. Listened. Gave in talk. Shut it out.

—Shut out the cry within me. Shut out the cry—What had I to do with it? What had I to do with it?

Played. Played the piano to shut it out.

"You always play so beautifully for me!" the hostess purred.

Beautifully for her! I was trying to send out the warmth my fingers should have had to a thin pale body in a blue voile dress. Trying to make myself hard. Playing down the fight that was within me.

—You should have gone back!

What had I to do with the—

With thee! Jesus of Nazareth—

I was too soft. It was the Empty Spaces that made me soft. People forget things that have nothing to do with them, why could not I? Why could I not let it alone?

Empty Spaces. She was sick. The dress was blue voile.—

A room full of warmth and easy pleasant lovable folk.

The room was warm—bare arms—Empty Spaces. She would leave a space empty. Someone else would become the Flesh-Around—the Wound. Aching around an Empty Space. Empty. Aching.—

And I had gone up the hill.

Jesus of Nazareth! What had I to do with Thee?—

I took my hands off the keys and laid one quickly over my lips.

"Does your tooth ache?" someone queried behind me.

I had to leave then.

Someone else was talking in the room next to me as I put on my hat. "She takes her sorrow too hard. She must give them up!"

I knew they meant me—that was it. I thought of myself so much—so much for granted—that everyone knew I only thought of Things as they related to me.

—Always me. I had not gone back. She hated my kind. I would not let her "Spit in my face." Me.—

Sometimes I think I see her white face and feel her brush by me.

What had I to do with Thee, Jesus of Nazareth?

God forgive me. Forgive me for letting You stumble by me—alone.— In a thin white body this time; into the dark—in a dress that was no dress—no shoes—into the dark of a winter night.

Forgive me for letting hate send me up the hill while You went down.

I wonder where You went then?

I do not know why I did not go back to You. Today I cannot say why. Someday, though, God, I shall have to tell You why.

WHO'S WHO

ARON DOUGLAS is one of the most original of Negro artists; he was one of the sixty-five American artists selected for exhibition with The Society of Graphic Arts; now on art fellowship at the Barnes Foundation. *Arthur Fauset* won the **OPPORTUNITY** first prize with his short story "Symphonesque," reprinted in O'Brien's and the O'Henry Memorial Awards volumes, author of "For Freedom." *Paul Green*, professor of philosophy at the University of North Carolina has written many plays of Negro life. His "In Abraham's Bosom," was awarded last year's Pulitzer Prize. *John Matheus* is a professor of Romance Languages at West Virginia Collegiate Institute and an **OPPORTUNITY** and Crisis short story prize winner.

Countee Cullen has published two volumes of his own poems "Color" and "Copper Sun" and an anthology of the younger Negro poets—"Caroling Dusk." *Charles Cullen* is an artist who has recently found a new enthusiasm in drawings of Negro characters—he illustrated "Copper Sun" and "The Ballad of the Brown Girl." *Julia Peterkin* is the author of "Green Thursday" and "Black April," two of the foremost books about Negroes. *Zora Neale Hurston* has written short stories and plays and more recently has turned to the study of Negro folklore. *Guy B. Johnson* is a co-author of "The Negro and His Songs." He is at the University of North Carolina. *John Davis* took his Master's Degree at Harvard last year and is now publicity director for Fisk University. *Gwendolyn Bennett* has taught art at Howard, and is now on an art fellowship at the Barnes Foundation and a columnist for **OPPORTUNITY**. *Nathan Ben Young* is an attorney in St. Louis. He once lived in Birmingham. *Edna Worthley Underwood* is a poet, novelist and translator of international reputation, author of *The Passion Flower, The Pageant Maker* and other volumes.

Arthur A. Schomburg is perhaps the greatest of Negro bibliophiles. His collection of rare books was recently turned over to the N. Y. Public Library. *Dorothy Scarborough* is author of "On the Trail of Negro Folk Songs." She is a professor of English at Columbia and has written two novels. *Phillis Wheatley* was the first Negro poet (1753-1784). *Dorothy Peterson* is a teacher of Spanish in the New York Public Schools. *Professor Ellsworth Faris* is the head of the Department of Sociology at the University of Chicago and *Eugene Kinckle Jones* is Executive Secretary of the National Urban League. *Dr. E. B. Reuter* is professor of Sociology at the University of Iowa. *William Pickens* is Field Secretary of the National Association for the Advancement of Colored People. *Alain Locke* is editor of the *New Negro*. *E. Franklin Frazier* is a young sociologist now preparing for his degree of Doctor of Philosophy at the University of Chicago and a frequent contributor to magazines. *George Schuyler* is on the staff of the *Messenger* and the *Pittsburgh Courier* and a contributor to magazines. *Theophilus Lewis* is dramatic critic for the *Messenger*. *Abram L. Harris* is a professor of Economics at Howard University. *T. Arnold Hill* is director of the Department of the Industrial Relations of the National Urban League, formerly Executive Secretary of the Chicago Urban League. *Richard Bruce* is a young artist and poet. He is at present filling a role in *Porgy*. *Ira Reid* is Industrial Secretary of the N. Y. Urban League. *W. P. Dabney* is author of *Cincinnati's Colored Citizens* and editor of the Cincinnati Union a free lance newspaper. *Francis Holbrook* is an artist who has contributed frequently to Opportunity. He lives in Brooklyn.

Brenda Moryck is an **OPPORTUNITY** and Crisis prize winner for essays and short stories. She teaches school in Washington. *W. E. Braxton* is an artist. He won the gold and silver medals offered by Adelphia College, Brooklyn.

161

THE NATIONAL URBAN LEAGUE

Organized 1910 ❧ ❧ ❧ ❧ ❧ *Incorporated 1913*

17 MADISON AVENUE
NEW YORK CITY

THE NATIONAL URBAN LEAGUE is an organization which seeks to improve the relations between the races in America. It strives to improve the living and working conditions of the Negro.

Its special field of operation embraces cities where Negroes reside in large numbers.

The Executive Boards of the national and of the forty local organizations are made up of white and colored people who have caught the vision of social work and believe in justice and fair play in the dealings of men with each other.

The Leagues Program

It maintains a Department of Research and Investigations with Charles S. Johnson as Director, who also edits "OPPORTUNITY" magazine—the official organ of the League. This Department makes thorough investigations of social conditions in cities as bases for the League's practical work.

As rapidly as practicable committees are organized to further the recommendations growing out of such studies and especially to stimulate existing social welfare agencies to take on work for Negroes or to enlarge their activities in behalf of their Negro constituents. Occasionally special work for Negroes is organized where existing agencies are not willing to assume work for Negroes, or where there are no available facilities for meeting these needs.

The League furthers the training of colored social workers through providing fellowships for colored students at schools of social work and providing apprenticeships in the League's field activities for prospective social workers.

It conducts programs of education among colored and white people for the purpose of stimulating greater interest on the part of the general public in social work for colored people.

The League has a Department of Industrial Relations with T. Arnold Hill as Director. This Department seeks:

1. To standardize and coordinate the local employment agencies of the League so that exchange of information and more regular correspondence between them can assure applicants for work more efficient and helpful service and employers of labor a more efficient group of employees;

2. To work directly with large industrial plants both in cities where the League is established and in communities removed from such centers to procure larger opportunity for work and for advancement on the job for Negro workers and to stimulate Negro workers to a fresh determination to "make good" on the job so that their future place in industry may be assured;

3. To help through available channels of information to ascertain points at which there is need of Negro labor and points at which there is an oversupply of Negro labor and to use existing agencies of publicity and placement to direct Negro labor to those points where they are most needed and where their families will more easily become adjusted.
   This Department seeks to promote better relations between white and colored workers not through activities involving force, but through the orderly development of a feeling of good-will and comradeship. This accomplished would mean the removal of barriers against Negro membership in organized labor.

Officers:

L. HOLLINGSWORTH WOOD, President   EUGENE KINCKLE JONES, Executive Secretary
LLOYD GARRISON, Treasurer

Contributions in aid of the League may be made direct to the National Office.

LIST OF AFFILIATED BRANCHES OF THE NATIONAL URBAN LEAGUE

❦

AKRON, OHIO
Association for Colored Community Work
493 Perkins Street
MR. GEORGE W. THOMPSON

ATLANTA, GEORGIA
Southern Field Secretary
239 Auburn Avenue
JESSE O. THOMAS

ATLANTA, GEORGIA
Atlanta Urban League
239 Auburn Avenue
JOHN W. CRAWFORD, *Exec. Secy.*

BALTIMORE, MARYLAND
Baltimore Urban League
521 McMechen Street
R. M. MOSS, *Exec. Secy.*

BOSTON, MASSACHUSETTS
Boston Urban League
119 Camden Street
SAMUEL A. ALLEN, *Exec. Secy.*

BROOKLYN, NEW YORK
Brooklyn Urban League
105 Fleet Place
ROBERT J. ELZY, *Exec. Secy.*

BUFFALO, NEW YORK
Urban League of Buffalo
357 William Street
WILLIAM L. EVANS, *Exec. Secy.*

CANTON, OHIO
Canton Urban League
819 Liberty Avenue, S. E.
GERALD E. ALLEN, *Exec. Secy.*

CHICAGO, ILLINOIS
Chicago Urban League
3032 South Wabash Avenue
A. L. FOSTER, *Exec. Secy.*

CLEVELAND, OHIO
The Negro Welfare Association
2554 East 40th Street
WILLIAM R. CONNERS, *Exec. Secy.*

COLUMBUS, OHIO
Columbus Urban League
681 East Long Street
N. B. ALLEN, *Exec. Secy.*

DETROIT, MICHIGAN
Detroit Urban League
1911 St. Antoine Street
JOHN C. DANCY, *Exec. Secy.*

ENGLEWOOD, NEW JERSEY
*Englewood League for Social Service
Among Colored People*
71 Englewood Avenue
LOUIS S. PIERCE, *Exec. Secy.*

KANSAS CITY, MISSOURI
Community Service Urban League
1731 Lydia Avenue
EDWARD S. LEWIS, *Exec. Secy.*

LOS ANGELES, CALIFORNIA
Los Angeles Urban League
1325 Central Avenue
MRS. KATHERINE J. BARR, *Exec. Secy.*

LOUISVILLE, KENTUCKY
Louisville Urban League
615 W. Walnut Street
J. M. RAGLAND, *Exec. Secy.*

MILWAUKEE, WIS.
Milwaukee Urban League
631 Vliet Street
JAMES H. KERNS, *Exec. Secy.*

MINNEAPOLIS, MINN.
Minneapolis Urban League
71 West 7th Street
St. Paul, Minn.

MORRISTOWN, NEW JERSEY
85 Spring Street
MISS ALICE WHITE

(OVER)

163

LIST OF AFFILIATED BRANCHES OF THE
NATIONAL URBAN LEAGUE

NEW YORK CITY
New York Urban League
202 West 136th Street
JAMES H. HUBERT, *Exec. Secy.*

NASHVILLE, TENNESSEE
The Public Welfare League
708 Cedar Street
PAUL F. MOWBRAY, *Exec. Secy.*

NEWARK, NEW JERSEY
New Jersey Urban League
212 Bank Street
THOMAS L. PURYEAR, *Exec. Secy.*

PHILADELPHIA, PENNSYLVANIA
Armstrong Association of Philadelphia
1434 Lombard Street
WAYNE L. HOPKINS, *Exec. Secy.*

PLAINFIELD, NEW JERSEY
Plainfield Urban League
1226 Arlington Street
MRS. EVA KNIGHT, *President*

PITTSBURGH, PENNSYLVANIA
Pittsburgh Urban League
518 Wylie Avenue
ALONZO C. THAYER, *Exec. Secy.*

RICHMOND, VIRGINIA
Richmond Urban League
2 West Marshall Street
C. L. WINFREE, *Exec. Secy.*

SPRINGFIELD, MASSACHUSETTS
St. John's Institutional Activities
643 Union Street
DR. WILLIAM N. DEBERRY, *Exec. Secy.*

SPRINGFIELD, ILLINOIS
Springfield Urban League
1610 East Jackson Street
SAMUEL B. DANLEY, JR., *Exec. Secy.*

ST. PAUL, MINNESOTA
St. Paul Urban League
71 West 7th Street
ELMER A. CARTER, *Exec. Secy.*

ST. LOUIS, MISSOURI
Urban League of St. Louis
615 North Jefferson Avenue
JOHN T. CLARK, *Exec. Secy.*

TAMPA, FLORIDA
Tampa Urban League
1310 Marion Street
MR. B. E. MAYS, *Exec. Secy.*

WATERBURY, CONNECTICUT
Interdenominational Committee
81 Pearl Street
MRS. LEILA T. ALEXANDER

WESTFIELD, NEW JERSEY
Westfield Urban League
417 West Broad Street
MISS IRENE SUMERSET, *Exec. Secy.*

HARTFORD, CONNECTICUT
22 Avon Street

YOUNGSTOWN, OHIO
Booker T. Washington Settlement
962 Federal Street
SULLY JOHNSON, *Exec. Secy.*

The Negro-Art Hokum

By GEORGE S. SCHUYLER

NEGRO art "made in America" is as non-existent as the widely advertised profundity of Cal Coolidge, the "seven years of progress" of Mayor Hylan, or the reported sophistication of New Yorkers. Negro art there has been, is, and will be among the numerous black nations of Africa; but to suggest the possibility of any such development among the ten million colored people in this republic is self-evident foolishness. Eager apostles from Greenwich Village, Harlem, and environs proclaimed a great renaissance of Negro art just around the corner waiting to be ushered on the scene by those whose hobby is taking races, nations, peoples, and movements under their wing. New art forms expressing the "peculiar" psychology of the Negro were about to flood the market. In short, the art of Homo Africanus was about to electrify the waiting world. Skeptics patiently waited. They still wait.

True, from dark-skinned sources have come those slave songs based on Protestant hymns and Biblical texts known as the spirituals, work songs and secular songs of sorrow and tough luck known as the blues, that outgrowth of ragtime known as jazz (in the development of which whites have assisted), and the Charleston, an eccentric dance invented by the gamins around the public market-place in Charleston, S. C. No one can or does deny this. But these are contributions of a caste in a certain section of the country. They are foreign to Northern Negroes, West Indian Negroes, and African Negroes. They are no more expressive or characteristic of the Negro race than the music and dancing of the Appalachian highlanders or the Dalmatian peasantry are expressive or characteristic of the Caucasian race. If one wishes to speak of the musical contributions of the peasantry of the South, very well. Any group under similar circumstances would have produced something similar. It is merely a coincidence that this peasant class happens to be of a darker hue than the other inhabitants of the land. One recalls the remarkable likeness of the minor strains of the Russian mujiks to those of the Southern Negro.

As for the literature, painting, and sculpture of Aframericans—such as there is—it is identical in kind with the literature, painting, and sculpture of white Americans: that is, it shows more or less evidence of European influence. In the field of drama little of any merit has been written by and about Negroes that could not have been written by whites. The dean of the Aframerican literati is W. E. B. Du Bois, a product of Harvard and German universities; the foremost Aframerican sculptor is Meta Warwick Fuller, a graduate of leading American art schools and former student of Rodin; while the most noted Aframerican painter, Henry Ossawa Tanner, is dean of American painters in Paris and has been decorated by the French Government. Now the work of these artists is no more "expressive of the Negro soul"—as the gushers put it—than are the scribblings of Octavus Cohen or Hugh Wiley.

This, of course, is easily understood if one stops to realize that the Aframerican is merely a lampblacked Anglo-Saxon. If the European immigrant after two or three generations of exposure to our schools, politics, advertising, moral crusades, and restaurants becomes indistinguishable from the mass of Americans of the older stock (despite the influence of the foreign-language press), how much truer must it be of the sons of Ham who have been subjected to what the uplifters call Americanism for the last three hundred years. Aside from his color, which ranges from very dark brown to pink, your American Negro is just plain American. Negroes and whites from the same localities in this country talk, think, and act about the same. Because a few writers with a paucity of themes have seized upon imbecilities of the Negro rustics and clowns and palmed them off as authentic and characteristic Aframerican behavior, the common notion that the black American is so "different" from his white neighbor has gained wide currency. The mere mention of the word "Negro" conjures up in the average white American's mind a composite stereotype of Bert Williams, Aunt Jemima, Uncle Tom, Jack Johnson, Florian Slappey, and the various monstrosities scrawled by the cartoonists. Your average Aframerican no more resembles this stereotype than the average American resembles a composite of Andy Gump, Jim Jeffries, and a cartoon by Rube Goldberg.

Again, the Aframerican is subject to the same economic and social forces that mold the actions and thoughts of the white Americans. He is not living in a different world as some whites and a few Negroes would have us believe. When the jangling of his Connecticut alarm clock gets him out of his Grand Rapids bed to a breakfast similar to that eaten by his white brother across the street; when he toils at the same or similar work in mills, mines, factories, and commerce alongside the descendants of Spartacus, Robin Hood, and Erik the Red; when he wears similar clothing and speaks the same language with the same degree of perfection; when he reads the same Bible and belongs to the Baptist, Methodist, Episcopal, or Catholic church; when his fraternal affiliations also include the Elks, Masons, and Knights of Pythias; when he gets the same or similar schooling, lives in the same kind of houses, owns the same makes of cars (or rides in them), and nightly sees the same Hollywood version of life on the screen; when he smokes the same brands of tobacco and avidly peruses the same puerile periodicals; in short, when he responds to the same political, social, moral, and economic stimuli in precisely the same manner as his white neighbor, it is sheer nonsense to talk about "racial differences" as between the American black man and the American white man. Glance over a Negro newspaper (it is printed in good Americanese) and you will find the usual quota of crime news, scandal, personals, and uplift to be found in the average white newspaper—which, by the way, is more widely read by the Negroes than is the Negro press. In order to satisfy the cravings of an inferiority complex engendered by the colorphobia of the mob, the readers of the Negro newspapers are given a slight dash of racialistic seasoning. In the homes of the black and white Americans of the same cultural and economic level one finds similar furniture, literature, and conversation. How, then, can the black American be expected to produce art and literature dissimilar to that of the white American?

Consider Coleridge-Taylor, Edward Wilmot Blyden, and Claude McKay, the Englishmen; Pushkin, the Russian; Bridgewater, the Pole; Antar, the Arabian; Latino, the Spaniard; Dumas, père and fils, the Frenchmen; and Paul Laurence Dunbar, Charles W. Chestnut, and James Weldon Johnson, the Americans. All Negroes; yet their work shows the impress of nationality rather than race. They all reveal the psychology and culture of their environment—their color is incidental. Why should Negro artists of America vary from the national artistic norm when Negro artists in other countries have not done so? If we can foresee what kind of white citizens will inhabit this neck of the woods in the next generation by studying the sort of education and environment the children are exposed to now, it should not be difficult to reason that the adults of today are what they are because of the education and environment they were exposed to a generation ago. And that education and environment were about the same for blacks and whites. One contemplates the popularity of the Negro-art hokum and murmurs, "How come?"

This nonsense is probably the last stand of the old myth palmed off by Negrophobists for all these many years, and recently rehashed by the sainted Harding, that there are "fundamental, eternal, and inescapable differences" between white and black Americans. That there are Negroes who will lend this myth a helping hand need occasion no surprise. It has been broadcast all over the world by the vociferous scions of slaveholders, "scientists" like Madison Grant and Lothrop Stoddard, and the patriots who flood the treasury of the Ku Klux Klan; and is believed, even today, by the majority of free, white citizens. On this baseless premise, so flattering to the white mob, that the blackamoor is inferior and fundamentally different, is erected the postulate that he must needs be peculiar; and when he attempts to portray life through the medium of art, it must of necessity be a peculiar art. While such reasoning may seem conclusive to the majority of Americans, it must be rejected with a loud guffaw by intelligent people.

[*An opposing view on the subject of Negro art will be presented by Lanston Hughes in next week's issue.*]

The Negro Artist and the Racial Mountain

By LANGSTON HUGHES

ONE of the most promising of the young Negro poets said to me once, "I want to be a poet—not a Negro poet," meaning, I believe, "I want to write like a white poet"; meaning subconsciously, "I would like to be a white poet"; meaning behind that, "I would like to be white." And I was sorry the young man said that, for no great poet has ever been afraid of being himself. And I doubted then that, with his desire to run away spiritually from his race, this boy would ever be a great poet. But this is the mountain standing in the way of any true Negro art in America —this urge within the race toward whiteness, the desire to pour racial individuality into the mold of American standardization, and to be as little Negro and as much American as possible.

But let us look at the immediate background of this young poet. His family is of what I suppose one would call the Negro middle class: people who are by no means rich yet never uncomfortable nor hungry—smug, contented, respectable folk, members of the Baptist church. The father goes to work every morning. He is a chief steward at a large white club. The mother sometimes does fancy sewing or supervises parties for the rich families of the town. The children go to a mixed school. In the home they read white papers and magazines. And the mother often

166

says "Don't be like niggers" when the children are bad. A frequent phrase from the father is, "Look how well a white man does thing.." And so the word white comes to be unconsciousl. a symbol of all the virtues. It holds for the children beauty, morality, and money. The whisper of "I want to be white" runs silently through their minds. This young poet's home is, I believe, a fairly typical home of the colored middle class. One sees immediately how difficult it would be for an artist born in such a home to interest himself in interpreting the beauty of his own people. He is never taught to see that beauty. He is taught rather not to see it, or if he does, to be ashamed of it when it is not according to Caucasian patterns.

For racial culture the home of a self-styled "high-class" Negro has nothing better to offer. Instead there will perhaps be more aping of things white than in a less cultured or less wealthy home. The father is perhaps a doctor, lawyer, landowner, or politician. The mother may be a social worker, or a teacher, or she may do nothing and have a maid. Father is often dark but he has usually married the lightest woman he could find. The family attend a fashionable church where few really colored faces are to be found. And they themselves draw a color line. In the North they go to white theaters and white movies. And in the South they have at least two cars and a house "like white folks." Nordic manners, Nordic faces, Nordic hair, Nordic art (if any), and an Episcopal heaven. A very high mountain indeed for the would-be racial artist to climb in order to discover himself and his people.

But then there are the low-down folks, the so-called common element, and they are the majority—may the Lord be praised! The people who have their nip of gin on Saturday nights and are not too important to themselves or the community, or too well fed, or too learned to watch the lazy world go round. They live on Seventh Street in Washington or State Street in Chicago and they do not particularly care whether they are like white folks or anybody else. Their joy runs, bang! into ecstasy. Their religion soars to a shout. Work maybe a little today, rest a little tomorrow. Play awhile. Sing awhile. O, let's dance! These common people are not afraid of spirituals, as for a long time their more intellectual brethren were, and jazz is their child. They furnish a wealth of colorful, distinctive material for any artist because they still hold their own individuality in the face of American standardizations. And perhaps these common people will give to the world its truly great Negro artist, the one who is not afraid to be himself. Whereas the better-class Negro would tell the artist what to do, the people at least let him alone when he does appear. And they are not ashamed of him—if they know he exists at all. And they accept what beauty is their own without question.

Certainly there is, for the American Negro artist w^ can escape the restrictions the more advanced among^ch.s own group would put upon him, a great field of unused material ready for his art. Without going outside his race, and even among the better classes with their "white" culture and conscious American manners, but still Negro enough to be different, there is sufficient matter to furnish a black artist with a lifetime of creative work. And when he chooses to touch on the relations between Negroes and whites in this country with their innumerable overtones and undertones, surely, and especially for literature and the drama, there is an inexaustible supply of themes at hand.

To these the Negro artist can give his racial individuality, his heritage of rhythm and warmth, and his incongruous humor that so often, as in the Blues, becomes ironic laughter mixed with tears. But let us look again at the mountain.

A prominent Negro clubwoman in Philadelphia paid eleven dollars to hear Raquel Meller sing Andalusian popular songs. But she told me a few weeks before she would not think of going to hear "that woman," Clara Smith, a great black artist, sing Negro folksongs. And many an upper-class Negro church, even now, would not dream of employing a spiritual in its services. The drab melodies in white folks' hymnbooks are much to be preferred. "We want to worship the Lord correctly and quietly. We don't believe in 'shouting.' Let's be dull like the Nordics," they say, in effect.

The road for the serious black artist, then, who would produce a racial art is most certainly rocky and the mountain is high. Until recently he received almost no encouragement for his work from either white or colored people. The fine novels of Chestnutt go out of print with neither race noticing their passing. The quaint charm and humor of Dunbar's dialect verse brought to him, in his day, largely the same kind of encouragement one would give a side-show freak (A colored man writing poetry! How odd!) or a clown (How amusing!).

The present vogue in things Negro, although it may do as much harm as good for the budding colored artist, has at least done this: it has brought him forcibly to the attention of his own people among whom for so long, unless the other race had noticed him beforehand, he went with little honor. I understand that Charles Gilpin acted for years in Negro theaters without any special acclaim from his own, but when Broadway gave him eight curtain calls, Negroes, too, began to beat a tin pan in his honor. I know a young colored writer, a manual worker by day, who had been writing well for the colored magazines for some years, but it was not until he recently broke into the white publications and his first book was accepted by a prominent New York publisher that the "best" Negroes in his city took the trouble to discover that he lived there Then almost immediately they decided to give a grand dinner for him. But the society ladies were careful to whisper to his mother that perhaps she'd better not come. They were not sure she would have an evening gown.

The Negro artist works against an undertow of sharp criticism and misunderstanding from his own group and unintentional bribes from the whites. "O, be respectable, write about nice people, show how good we are," say the Negroes. "Be stereotyped, don't go too far, don't shatter our illusions about you, don't amuse us too seriously. We will pay you," say the whites. Both would have told Jean Toomer not to write "Cane." The colored people did not praise it. The white people did not buy it. Most of the colored people who did read "Cane" hate it. They are afraid of it. Although the critics gave it good reviews the public remained indifferent. Yet (excepting the work of DuBois) "Cane" contains the finest prose written by a Negro in America. And like the singing of Robeson, it is truly racial.

But in spite of the Nordicized Negro intelligentsia and the desires of some white editors we have an honest American Negro literature already with us. Now I await the rise of the Negro theater. Our folk music, having achieved world-wide fame, offers itself to the genius of the great in-

167

dividual American Negro composer who is to come. And within the next decade I expect to see the work of a growing school of colored artists who paint and model the beauty of dark faces and create with new technique the expressions of their own soul-world. And the Negro dancers who will dance like flame and the singers who will continue to carry our songs to all who listen—they will be with us in even greater numbers tomorrow.

Most of my own poems are racial in theme and treatment, derived from the life I know. In many of them I try to grasp and hold some of the meanings and rhythms of jazz. I am sincere as I know how to be in these poems and yet after every reading I answer questions like these from my own people: Do you think Negroes should always write about Negroes? I wish you wouldn't read some of your poems to white folks. How do you find anything interesting in a place like a cabaret? Why do you write about black people? You aren't black. What makes you do so many jazz poems?

But jazz to me is one of the inherent expressions of Negro life in America: the eternal tom-tom beating in the Negro soul—the tom-tom of revolt against weariness in a white world, a world of subway trains, and work, work, work; the tom-tom of joy and laughter, and pain swallowed in a smile. Yet the Philadelphia clubwoman is ashamed to say that her race created it and she does not like me to write about it. The old subconscious "white is best" runs through her mind. Years of study under white teachers, a lifetime of white books, pictures, and papers, and white manners, morals, and Puritan standards made her dislike the spirituals. And now she turns up her nose at jazz and all its manifestations—likewise almost everything else distinctly racial. She doesn't care for the Winold Reiss portraits of Negroes because they are "too Negro." She does not want a true picture of herself from anybody. She wants the artist to flatter her, to make the white world believe that all Negroes are as smug and as near white in soul as she wants to be. But, to my mind, it is the duty of the younger Negro artist, if he accepts any duties at all from outsiders, to change through the force of his art that old whispering "I want to be white," hidden in the aspirations of his people, to "Why should I want to be white? I am a Negro—and beautiful!"

So I am ashamed for the black poet who says, "I want to be a poet, not a Negro poet," as though his own racial world were not as interesting as any other world. I am ashamed, too, for the colored artist who runs from the painting of Negro faces to the painting of sunsets after the manner of the academicians because he fears the strange un-whiteness of his own features. An artist must be free to choose what he does, certainly, but he must also never be afraid to do what he might choose.

Let the blare of Negro jazz bands and the bellowing voice of Bessie Smith singing Blues penetrate the closed ears of the colored near-intellectuals until they listen and perhaps understand. Let Paul Robeson singing Water Boy, and Rudolph Fisher writing about the streets of Harlem, and Jean Toomer holding the heart of Georgia in his hands, and Aaron Douglas drawing strange black fantasies cause the smug Negro middle class to turn from their white, respectable, ordinary books and papers to catch a glimmer of their own beauty. We younger Negro artists who create now intend to express our individual dark-skinned selves without fear or shame. If white people are pleased we are glad. If they are not, it doesn't matter. We know we are beautiful. And ugly too. The tom-tom cries and the tom-tom laughs. If colored people are pleased we are glad. If they are not, their displeasure doesn't matter either. We build our temples for tomorrow, strong as we know how, and we stand on top of the mountain, free within ourselves.

[*In last week's* Nation *Negro art was discussed from an opposing point of view by George S. Schuyler.*]

OPPORTUNITY

L. HOLLINGSWORTH WOOD
Chairman

EUGENE KINCKLE JONES
Executive Secretary

CHARLES S. JOHNSON
Editor

A JOURNAL OF NEGRO LIFE
Published Monthly by
The Department of Research and Investigations

NATIONAL URBAN LEAGUE
127 EAST 23rd STREET, NEW YORK, N. Y.
Telephone Gramercy 3978

WILLIAM H. BALDWIN
Secretary

LLOYD GARRISON
Treasurer

ERIC WALROND
Business Manager

VOL. 4   AUGUST, 1926   No. 44

Contents

Single Copies, FIFTEEN CENTS—*Yearly Subscriptions*, ONE DOLLAR AND A HALF, FOREIGN, $1.75.
Entered as second-class matter, October 30, 1923, at the Post Office at New York, New York, under the act of March 3, 1879.

Editorials

THE opposing discussions of George S. Schuyler and Langston Hughes in the *Nation* on the question of Negro art offer evidences of a sort of mental fermentation which is in itself much more significant than the conclusions of either. Mr. Schuyler denies that there is such a thing as Negro art and regards the "Aframerican" as "merely a lamp-blacked Anglo-Saxon." Mr.

American Negro Art

Hughes contends that there is a Negro art and laments that Negro art expressions are being choked by "the urge within the race to whiteness, the desire to pour racial individuality into the mold of American standardization and to be as little Negro and as much American as possible." So long as the corollary of Mr. Schuyler's denial is that Negroes are inescapably different in the sense that scions of slave holders and pseudo-scientists regard them, his is a strong case, with the Negroes at least. So long as the corollary of Mr. Hughes' contention is that a slavish imitation of American standards is drowning native Negro art, he quite successfully goads the pride of every Negro intelligent enough to read his article. It is unfortunate that, for the sake of a good debate, they could not have defined beforehand the terms with which they were to play.

For neither does Mr. Schuyler mean that there is no beauty in Negro life, nor Mr. Hughes that Negroes are contentedly inferior creatures with amusing peculiarities. When one of them is talking about art form the other is discussing art content; one is thinking of the Negro bourgeois, the other of intellectual parvenus; one of art, the other of artists. When Mr. Schuyler is thinking of unconscious folk art of the past, Mr. Hughes is thinking of individual Negro artists of the present, and when Mr. Schuyler is thinking of individual Negro artists of the past like Pushkin and Dumas, Mr. Hughes is thinking about the sable Babbitts of the present. And both discuss art as if they were thinking of culture.

The peculiar difficulty about the situation is that Negroes really express all the contradictions and paradoxes pointed out and there will be found the joyous, carefree spirits on whom rests lightly the stamp of the American pattern, and the Negroes who want to be like whites and the emancipated Negro intellectuals who seek to portray the beauties of their own kin. But determinations can be no more easily made in the case of Negroes than could be made in the endless dispute about American and English temperament and capacity. We must expect a deal of misunderstanding here. The question is still open as to whether or not there is or can be such a thing as distinctive Negro art. Certain it seems, if there could be, it would not remain distinctive for long. It is more important now that we develop artists and let the question of a distinctive art settle itself.

170

African Negro art is less understood by American Negroes than by Frenchmen; the middle class Negroes are closer to middle class whites than they are to the "levee" Negroes who created the Blues and the Charleston; the spirituals are called the only truly American music; and the English and French think jazz expresses the hectic rhythm of American life.

Dumas and Pushkin, who would be classified as Negroes in America, writing about Frenchmen and Russians outrank any American artist writing about Americans, and the stories of Du Bose Heyward and Julia Peterkin about Negro life are superior to most of the work of Negro writers about themselves.

The hopeful part of the situation is that an artist can express best the life which he knows and in that life which is the Negroes', any Negro artist has the advantage. He may express without restraint whatever is there, and Mr. Hughes is right when he says that "without going outside his race and even among the better classes with their 'white' culture and conscious American manners but still Negro enough to be different, there is sufficient matter to furnish a black artist with a life time of creative work."

What is most important is that these black artists should be free, not merely to express anything they feel, but to feel the pulsations and rhythms of their own life, philosophy be hanged.

OPPORTUNITY

L. HOLLINGSWORTH WOOD
Chairman

EUGENE KINCKLE JONES
Executive Secretary

CHARLES S. JOHNSON
Editor

A JOURNAL OF NEGRO LIFE
Published Monthly by
The Department of Research and Investigations

NATIONAL URBAN LEAGUE
127 EAST 23rd STREET, NEW YORK, N. Y.
Telephone Gramercy 3078

WILLIAM H. BALDWIN
Secretary

LLOYD GARRISON
Treasurer

ERIC WALROND
Business Manager

VOL. 4   OCTOBER, 1926   No. 46

Contents

Single Copies, FIFTEEN CENTS—*Yearly Subscriptions,* ONE DOLLAR AND A HALF, FOREIGN, $1.75.

Entered as second-class matter, October 30, 1923, at the Post Office at New York, New York, under the act of March 3, 1879.

Editorials

Gambling the Lyre   Professor Leon Whipple in the August *Survey Graphic,* with his rather belated review of the "New Negro," edited by Alain Locke, raises a question that has either been overlooked, or avoided in direct statement by the whole line of commentators. The book, he thinks, has two failures: First, it claims too much for the Negro as a present artist; second, it seems willing to sacrifice the indubitable native gifts of the African for a mere equalitarianism in the culture and society of the whites. The first part of this has, of course, been mentioned before, and although it was the scheme of the book that the contributions of the thirty or more authors should stand for themselves as the best expression of present day Negroes, without precise relationship to the world of letters, the observation may well enough be allowed to pass under his further reflection that in the projection of the book the Negro is making a case, and one does not make a case by understatement. It is the second item of his objection which touches the moot question.

The art of the Negro, he says, lies in the spirituals, in jazz and in the dance. As they leave the soil and become sophisticated, their art vanishes. The new Negro wants to live like a white man and sing like a Negro. It is the art and gift of the old Negro that America loves. What is happening, he concludes, is that the new Negro is "gambling his lyre for a mess of pottage."

He states a paradox. Beneath it is the very paradox which inheres in the American race question. It really limits the contribution of American Negroes to what they accomplish unconsciously, and by virtue of their more primitive experiences. It is, we are inclined to think, unreasonable to expect that in a day of general advance, the Negroes will remain culturally in the position of those earlier ones who created the spirituals, or even those present ones who are inventing new Blues and dances like the Charleston. And it is just as unreasonable to interpret the inevitable result of education and cultural development as the blind urge to equalitarianism in white culture and society. It is possibly true, but irrelevant, that the familiar culture is white. Whatever the indubitable native African gift, the present day Negroes have known no other culture save that American, into which they were born. For the same reason they have embraced Christianity instead of Mohammedanism for example, or the worship of animals and fetiches.

If the argument of Professor Whipple is followed, they must give up either the art or the enlightenment. But the argument, though entirely logical in itself, seems to be founded upon improper premises. The new emphasis of Negroes in the direction of conscious art is clearly not now on making spirituals and jazz and the dances in which Americans delight, although they have, as a part of the recent self-consciousness begun to re-appraise these unconscious contributions. It is not in arrogating to themselves even the peculiar endowment of song and rhythm, the concession of which, has undoubtedly helped to gain for them an audience, but in the recognition that if they are to survive in this new age they must prepare for and accept the measurements applied generally to artistic accomplishment. Their assumption is that given the opportunity for development, their contribution need not depend upon purely primitive traits, or upon the expressions invented out of the weariness and sorrow of their peculiar position. From the point of view of their future development, it would be disastrous to rely upon any but these new standards.

It means a long, difficult struggle, but this is just, since it will depend upon the work and genius of the Negroes themselves. And if, as Professor Whipple thinks, there is a peculiar African endowment that can enrich American art, it will show itself, whether the Negroes are conscious of it or not.

A very great amount of sheer commonplaceness is being solemnly passed out of that region "within the veil," under the label of Negro literature; and from the other side of it, there is even more of the over-wrought sentimentality which, it is thought, the moment demands. While all this is encouraging in respect to the general state of public concern on the life and thoughts of Negroes, there is danger that the alloys will accomplish more harm than the real can accomplish benefits.

In the presence of this activity, it is encouraging to encounter in a mid-western paper, this comment following Paul Robeson's singing of Negro spirituals:

> "Here is . . . a man of attainment in several directions, yet he adapts himself to the elementary quality of his subject. . . . When he has finished a spiritual you wonder how he was able to make so much out of so little. Take, for example, "Were you there?" with its repetitions. . . . With these simple words, with this reiterated question, with an exaltation of feeling difficult to describe but impossible to escape, Paul Robeson brings before us vividly, poignantly, the whole picture of the passion of Calvary."

A writer in a recent issue of the New Republic tries to explain the unnatural survival of the uncannily doleful St. Louis Blues, created by Handy, the Negro Memphis musician. It has lived twelve years, mounting yearly in popularity while all the popular tunes of its day have faded utterly from memory. It has sold a half million piano copies and a million and a half phonograph records. There is something undefinable but real in these. It is encouraging that the publishers of Cullen's book of poems mark a steady, unexcited demand, a year after publication; that Alain Locke's New Negro is finding its way into classrooms; that Jean Toomer's Cane, is eagerly sought now, about two years after it was allowed to die in the book stalls; that Hughes' Weary Blues and Walrond's Tropic Death have carried on their own merits beyond the first propulsion of the publishers; that Abraham's Bosom is moving from its experimental stage at the Provincetown to the Garrick Theatre, while the somewhat puny Bottom of the Cup withdrew after a few days; and that Porgy is to be presenetd as the first play of the season by the Theatre Guild.

THE public has recently given a sudden ear to the submerged voices of dark Americans; hearing has brought a measure of interest and this interest, in characteristic American fashion has catapulted itself into something very much like a fad. Zeal to catch the flood tide has exposed many immaturities—more serious still, it has lured into the current a host of specious speculators in fame, some of whom are just clever enough to recognize the Negro themes which hold popular favor. The number of singers of spirituals is growing at an astonishing rate, while the actual development of competent Negro artists and interpreters of these songs proceeds more normally.

Some Perils of the "Renaissance"

The new eccentric dances in approximation of the famed "Charleston" which came from the soil, reveal the sterility of those eager ones who have only their sophistication to match the folk spontaneity out of which came these first exotic creations in rhythm. Paris and London are receiving along with authentic Negro artists a generous alloy of performers whose only legitimate claim to distinction is their complexion.

III

Characteristics of Negro Expression

by ZORA NEALE HURSTON

DRAMA

Zora Neale Hurston

THE Negro's universal mimicry is not so much a thing in itself as an evidence of something that permeates his entire self. And that thing is drama.

His very words are action words. His interpretation of the English language is in terms of pictures. One act described in terms of another. Hence the rich metaphor and simile.

The metaphor is of course very primitive. It is easier to illustrate than it is to explain because action came before speech. Let us make a parallel. Language is like money. In primitive communities actual goods, however bulky, are bartered for what one wants. This finally evolves into coin, the coin being not real wealth but a symbol of wealth. Still later even coin is abandoned for legal tender, and still later for cheques in certain usages.

Every phase of Negro life is highly dramatised. No matter how joyful or how sad the case there is sufficient poise for drama. Everything is acted out. Unconsciously for the most part of course. There is an impromptu ceremony always ready for every hour of life. No little moment passes unadorned.

Now the people with highly developed languages have words for detached ideas. That is legal tender. " That-which-we-squat-on " has become " chair." " Groan-causer " has evolved into " spear," and so on. Some individuals even conceive of the equivalent of cheque words, like "ideation" and "pleonastic." Perhaps we might say that *Paradise Lost* and *Sartor Resartus* are written in cheque words.

The primitive man exchanges descriptive words. His terms are all close fitting. Frequently the Negro, even with detached words in his vocabulary—not evolved in him but transplanted on his tongue by contact—must add action to it to make it do. So we have " chop-axe," " sitting-chair," " cook-pot " and the like because the speaker has in his mind the picture of the object in use. Action. Everything illustrated. So we can say the white man thinks in a written language and the Negro thinks in hieroglyphics.

A bit of Negro drama familiar to all is the frequent meeting of two opponents who threaten to do atrocious murder one upon the other.

Who has not observed a robust young Negro chap posing upon a street corner, possessed of nothing but his clothing, his strength and his youth? Does he bear himself like a pauper? No, Louis XIV could be no more insolent in his assurance. His eyes say plainly " Female, halt ! " His posture exults " Ah, female, I am the eternal male, the giver of life. Behold in my hot flesh all the delights of this world. Salute me, I am strength." All this with a languid posture, there is no mistaking his meaning.

A Negro girl strolls past the corner lounger. Her whole body panging[1] and posing. A slight shoulder movement that calls attention to her bust, that is all of a dare. A hippy undulation below the waist that is a sheaf of promises tied with conscious power. She is acting out " I'm a darned sweet woman and you know it."

These little plays by strolling players are acted out daily in a dozen streets in a thousand cities, and no one ever mistakes the meaning.

WILL TO ADORN

The will to adorn is the second most notable characteristic in Negro expression. Perhaps his idea of ornament does not attempt to meet conventional standards, but it satisfies the soul of its creator.

In this respect the American Negro has done wonders to the English language. It has often been

[1] From " pang."

39

Characteristics of Negro Expression

stated by etymologists that the Negro has introduced no African words to the language. This is true, but it is equally true that he has made over a great part of the tongue to his liking and has had his revision accepted by the ruling class. No one listening to a Southern white man talk could deny this. Not only has he softened and toned down strongly consonanted words like " aren't " to " aint " and the like, he has made new force words out of old feeble elements. Examples of this are " ham-shanked," " battle-hammed," " double-teen," " bodaciously," " muffle-jawed."

But the Negro's greatest contribution to the language is : (1) the use of metaphor and simile ; (2) the use of the double descriptive ; (3) the use of verbal nouns.

1. Metaphor and Simile

One at a time, like lawyers going to heaven.
You sho is propaganda.
Sobbing hearted.
I'll beat you till: (*a*) rope like okra, (*b*) slack like lime,
(*c*) smell like onions.
Fatal for naked.
Kyting along.
That's a lynch.

That's a rope.
Cloakers—deceivers.
Regular as pig-tracks.
Mule blood—black molasses.
Syndicating—gossiping.
Flambeaux—cheap café (lighted by flambeaux).
To put yo'self on de ladder.

2. The Double Descriptive

High-tall.
Little-tee-ninchy (tiny).
Low-down.
Top-superior.
Sham-polish.
Lady-people.
Kill-dead.

Hot-boiling.
Chop-axe.
Sitting-chairs.
De watch wall.
Speedy-hurry.
More great and more better.

3. Verbal Nouns

She features somebody I know.
Funeralize.
Sense me into it.
Puts the shamery on him.
'Taint everybody you kin confidence.
I wouldn't friend with her.

Jooking—playing piano or guitar as it is done in Jook-
houses (houses of ill-fame).
Uglying away.
I wouldn't scorn my name all up on you.
Bookooing (beaucoup) around—showing off.

Nouns from Verbs

Won't stand a broke.
She won't take a listen.
He won't stand straightening.

That is such a compelment.
That's a lynch.

The stark, trimmed phrases of the Occident seem too bare for the voluptuous child of the sun, hence the adornment. It arises out of the same impulse as the wearing of jewelry and the making of sculpture —the urge to adorn.

On the walls of the homes of the average Negro one always finds a glut of gaudy calendars, wall pockets and advertising lithographs. The sophisticated white man or Negro would tolerate none of these, even if they bore a likeness to the Mona Lisa. No commercial art for decoration. Nor the calendar nor the advertisement spoils the picture for this lowly man. He sees the beauty in spite of the declaration of the Portland Cement Works or the butcher's announcement. I saw in Mobile a room in which there was an over-stuffed mohair living-room suite, an imitation mahogany bed and chifferobe, a console victrola. The walls were gaily papered with Sunday supplements of the *Mobile Register*. There were seven calendars and three wall pockets. One of them was decorated with a lace doily. The mantel-shelf was covered with a scarf of deep home-made lace, looped up with a huge bow of pink crêpe paper. Over the door was a huge lithograph showing the Treaty of Versailles being signed with a Waterman fountain pen.

It was grotesque, yes. But it indicated the desire for beauty. And decorating a decoration, as in the case of the doily on the gaudy wall pocket, did not seem out of place to the hostess. The feeling back of such an act is that there can never be enough of beauty, let alone too much. Perhaps she is right. We

40

Characteristics of Negro Expression

each have our standards of art, and thus are we all interested parties and so unfit to pass judgment upon the art concepts of others.

Whatever the Negro does of his own volition he embellishes. His religious service is for the greater part excellent prose poetry. Both prayers and sermons are tooled and polished until they are true works of art. The supplication is forgotten in the frenzy of creation. The prayer of the white man is considered humorous in its bleakness. The beauty of the Old Testament does not exceed that of a Negro prayer.

ANGULARITY

After adornment the next most striking manifestation of the Negro is Angularity. Everything that he touches becomes angular. In all African sculpture and doctrine of any sort we find the same thing.

Anyone watching Negro dancers will be struck by the same phenomenon. Every posture is another angle. Pleasing, yes. But an effect achieved by the very means which an European strives to avoid.

The pictures on the walls are hung at deep angles. Furniture is always set at an angle. I have instances of a piece of furniture in the *middle* of a wall being set with one end nearer the wall than the other to avoid the simple straight line.

ASYMMETRY

Asymmetry is a definite feature of Negro art. I have no samples of true Negro painting unless we count the African shields, but the sculpture and carvings are full of this beauty and lack of symmetry.

It is present in the literature, both prose and verse. I offer an example of this quality in verse from Langston Hughes:

> I aint gonna mistreat ma good gal any more,
> I'm just gonna kill her next time she makes me sore.
>
> .   .   .   .
>
> I treats her kind but she don't do me right,
> She fights and quarrels most ever' night.
>
> .   .   .   .
>
> I can't have no woman's got such low-down ways
> Cause de blue gum woman aint de style now'days.
>
> .   .   .   .
>
> I brought her from the South and she's goin on back,
> Else I'll use her head for a carpet track.

It is the lack of symmetry which makes Negro dancing so difficult for white dancers to learn. The abrupt and unexpected changes. The frequent change of key and time are evidences of this quality in music. (Note the St. Louis Blues.)

The dancing of the justly famous Bo-Jangles and Snake Hips are excellent examples.

The presence of rhythm and lack of symmetry are paradoxical, but there they are. Both are present to a marked degree. There is always rhythm, but it is the rhythm of segments. Each unit has a rhythm of its own, but when the whole is assembled it is lacking in symmetry. But easily workable to a Negro who is accustomed to the break in going from one part to another, so that he adjusts himself to the new tempo.

DANCING

Negro dancing is dynamic suggestion. No matter how violent it may appear to the beholder, every posture gives the impression that the dancer will do much more. For example, the performer flexes one knee sharply, assumes a ferocious face mask, thrusts the upper part of the body forward with clenched fists, elbows taut as in hard running or grasping a thrusting blade. That is all. But the spectator himself adds the picture of ferocious assault, hears the drums and finds himself keeping time with the music and tensing himself for the struggle. It is compelling insinuation. That is the very reason the spectator is held so rapt. He is participating in the performance himself—carrying out the suggestions of the performer.

The difference in the two arts is: the white dancer attempts to express fully; the Negro is restrained,

4 I

177

Characteristics of Negro Expression

but succeeds in gripping the beholder by forcing him to finish the action the performer suggests. Since no art ever can express all the variations conceivable, the Negro must be considered the greater artist, his dancing is realistic suggestion, and that is about all a great artist can do.

Negro Folklore

Negro folklore is not a thing of the past. It is still in the making. Its great variety shows the adaptability of the black man: nothing is too old or too new, domestic or foreign, high or low, for his use. God and the Devil are paired, and are treated no more reverently than Rockefeller and Ford. Both of these men are prominent in folklore, Ford being particularly strong, and they talk and act like good-natured stevedores or mill-hands. Ole Massa is sometimes a smart man and often a fool. The automobile is ranged alongside of the oxcart. The angels and the apostles walk and talk like section hands. And through it all walks Jack, the greatest culture hero of the South; Jack beats them all—even the Devil, who is often smarter than God.

Culture Heroes

The Devil is next after Jack as a culture hero. He can out-smart everyone but Jack. God is absolutely no match for him. He is good-natured and full of humour. The sort of person one may count on to help out in any difficulty.

Peter the Apostle is the third in importance. One need not look far for the explanation. The Negro is not a Christian really. The primitive gods are not deities of too subtle inner reflection; they are hardworking bodies who serve their devotees just as laboriously as the suppliant serves them. Gods of physical violence, stopping at nothing to serve their followers. Now of all the apostles Peter is the most active. When the other ten fell back trembling in the garden, Peter wielded the blade on the posse. Peter first and foremost in all action. The gods of no peoples have been philosophic until the people themselves have approached that state.

The rabbit, the bear, the lion, the buzzard, the fox are culture heroes from the animal world. The rabbit is far in the lead of all the others and is blood brother to Jack. In short, the trickster-hero of West Africa has been transplanted to America.

John Henry is a culture hero in song, but no more so than Stacker Lee, Smokey Joe or Bad Lazarus. There are many, many Negroes who have never heard of any of the song heroes, but none who do not know John (Jack) and the rabbit.

Examples of Folklore and the Modern Culture Hero

Why de Porpoise's Tail is on Crosswise

Now, I want to tell you 'bout de porpoise. God had done made de world and everything. He set de moon and de stars in de sky. He got de fishes of de sea, and de fowls of de air completed.

He made de sun and hung it up. Then He made a nice gold track for it to run on. Then He said, " Now, Sun, I got everything made but Time. That's up to you. I want you to start out and go round de world on dis track just as fast as you kin make it. And de time it takes you to go and come, I'm going to call day and night." De Sun went zoonin' on cross de elements. Now, de porpoise was hanging round there and heard God what he tole de Sun, so he decided he'd take dat trip round de world hisself. He looked up and saw de Sun kytin' along, so he lit out too, him and dat Sun!

So porpoise beat de Sun round de world by one hour and three minutes. So God said, " Aw naw, this aint gointer do! I didn't mean for nothin' to be faster than de Sun!" So God run dat porpoise for three days before he run him down and caught him, and took his tail off and put it on crossways to slow him up. Still he's de fastest thing in de water.

And dat's why de porpoise got his tail on crosswise.

Rockefeller and Ford

Once John D. Rockefeller and Henry Ford was woofing at each other. Rockefeller told Henry Ford he could build a solid gold road round the world. Henry Ford told him if he would he would look at it and see if he liked it, and if he did he would buy it and put one of his tin lizzies on it.

Originality

It has been said so often that the Negro is lacking in originality that it has almost become a gospel. Outward signs seem to bear this out. But if one looks closely its falsity is immediately evident.

42

Characteristics of Negro Expression

It is obvious that to get back to original sources is much too difficult for any group to claim very much as a certainty. What we really mean by originality is the modification of ideas. The most ardent admirer of the great Shakespeare cannot claim first source even for him. It is his treatment of the borrowed material.

So if we look at it squarely, the Negro is a very original being. While he lives and moves in the midst of a white civilisation, everything that he touches is re-interpreted for his own use. He has modified the language, mode of food preparation, practice of medicine, and most certainly the religion of his new country, just as he adapted to suit himself the Sheik hair-cut made famous by Rudolph Valentino.

Everyone is familiar with the Negro's modification of the whites' musical instruments, so that his interpretation has been adopted by the white man himself and then re-interpreted. In so many words, Paul Whiteman is giving an imitation of a Negro orchestra making use of white-invented musical instruments in a Negro way. Thus has arisen a new art in the civilised world, and thus has our so-called civilisation come. The exchange and re-exchange of ideas between groups.

IMITATION

The Negro, the world over, is famous as a mimic. But this in no way damages his standing as an original. Mimicry is an art in itself. If it is not, then all art must fall by the same blow that strikes it down. When sculpture, painting, acting, dancing, literature neither reflect nor suggest anything in nature or human experience we turn away with a dull wonder in our hearts at why the thing was done. Moreover, the contention that the Negro imitates from a feeling of inferiority is incorrect. He mimics for the love of it. The group of Negroes who slavishly imitate is small. The average Negro glories in his ways. The highly educated Negro the same. The self-despisement lies in a middle class who scorns to do or be anything Negro. " That's just like a Nigger " is the most terrible rebuke one can lay upon this kind. He wears drab clothing, sits through a boresome church service, pretends to have no interest in the community, holds beauty contests, and otherwise apes all the mediocrities of the white brother. The truly cultured Negro scorns him, and the Negro " farthest down " is too busy " spreading his junk " in his own way to see or care. He likes his own things best. Even the group who are not Negroes but belong to the " sixth race," buy such records as " Shake dat thing " and " Tight lak dat." They really enjoy hearing a good bible-beater preach, but wild horses could drag no such admission from them. Their ready-made expression is : " We done got away from all that now." Some refuse to countenance Negro music on the grounds that it is niggerism, and for that reason should be done away with. Roland Hayes was thoroughly denounced for singing spirituals until he was accepted by white audiences. Langston Hughes is not considered a poet by this group because he writes of the man in the ditch, who is more numerous and real among us than any other.

But, this group aside, let us say that the art of mimicry is better developed in the Negro than in other racial groups. He does it as the mocking-bird does it, for the love of it, and not because he wishes to be like the one imitated. I saw a group of small Negro boys imitating a cat defecating and the subsequent toilet of the cat. It was very realistic, and they enjoyed it as much as if they had been imitating a coronation ceremony. The dances are full of imitations of various animals. The buzzard lope, walking the dog, the pig's hind legs, holding the mule, elephant squat, pigeon's wing, falling off the log, seabord (imitation of an engine starting), and the like.

ABSENCE OF THE CONCEPT OF PRIVACY

It is said that Negroes keep nothing secret, that they have no reserve. This ought not to seem strange when one considers that we are an outdoor people accustomed to communal life. Add this to all-permeating drama and you have the explanation.

There is no privacy in an African village. Loves, fights, possessions are, to misquote Woodrow Wilson, " Open disagreements openly arrived at." The community is given the benefit of a good fight as well as a good wedding. An audience is a necessary part of any drama. We merely go with nature rather than against it.

Discord is more natural than accord. If we accept the doctrine of the survival of the fittest there are more fighting honors than there are honors for other achievements. Humanity places premiums on all things necessary to its well-being, and a valiant and good fighter is valuable in any community. So why hide the light under a bushel? Moreover, intimidation is a recognised part of warfare the world over, and threats certainly must be listed under that head. So that a great threatener must certainly be considered an aid to the fighting machine. So then if a man or woman is a facile hurler of threats, why

43

should he or she not show their wares to the community? Hence the holding of all quarrels and fights in the open. One relieves one's pent-up anger and at the same time earns laurels in intimidation. Besides, one does the community a service. There is nothing so exhilarating as watching well-matched opponents go into action. The entire world likes action, for that matter. Hence prize-fighters become millionaires.

Likewise love-making is a biological necessity the world over and an art among Negroes. So that a man or woman who is proficient sees no reason why the fact should not be moot. He swaggers. She struts hippily about. Songs are built on the power to charm beneath the bed-clothes. Here again we have individuals striving to excel in what the community considers an art. Then if all of his world is seeking a great lover, why should he not speak right out loud?

It is all in a view-point. Love-making and fighting in all their branches are high arts, other things are arts among other groups where they brag about their proficiency just as brazenly as we do about these things that others consider matters for conversation behind closed doors. At any rate, the white man is despised by Negroes as a very poor fighter individually, and a very poor lover. One Negro, speaking of white men, said, " White folks is alright when dey gits in de bank and on de law bench, but dey sho' kin lie about wimmen folks."

I pressed him to explain. " Well you see, white mens makes out they marries wimmen to look at they eyes, and they know they gits em for just what us gits em for. 'Nother thing, white mens say they goes clear round de world and wins all de wimmen folks way from they men folks. Dat's a lie too. They don't win nothin, they buys em. Now de way I figgers it, if a woman don't want me enough to be wid me, 'thout I got to pay her, she kin rock right on, but these here white men don't know what to do wid a woman when they gits her—dat's how come they gives they wimmen so much. They got to. Us wimmen works jus as hard as us does an come home an sleep wid us every night. They own wouldn't do it and its de mens fault. Dese white men done fooled theyself bout dese wimmen.

" Now me, I keeps me some wimmens all de time. Dat's whut dey wuz put here for—us mens to use. Dat's right now, Miss. Y'all wuz put here so us mens could have some pleasure. Course I don't run round like heap uh men folks. But if my ole lady go way from me and stay more'n two weeks, I got to git me somebody, aint I ? "

THE JOOK

Jook is the word for a Negro pleasure house. It may mean a bawdy house. It may mean the house set apart on public works where the men and women dance, drink and gamble. Often it is a combination of all these.

In past generations the music was furnished by " boxes," another word for guitars. One guitar was enough for a dance; to have two was considered excellent. Where two were playing one man played the lead and the other seconded him. The first player was " picking " and the second was " framming," that is, playing chords while the lead carried the melody by dexterous finger work. Sometimes a third player was added, and he played a tom-tom effect on the low strings. Believe it or not, this is excellent dance music.

Pianos soon came to take the place of the boxes, and now player-pianos and victrolas are in all of the Jooks.

Musically speaking, the Jook is the most important place in America. For in its smelly, shoddy confines has been born the secular music known as blues, and on blues has been founded jazz. The singing and playing in the true Negro style is called " jooking."

The songs grow by incremental repetition as they travel from mouth to mouth and from Jook to Jook for years before they reach outside ears. Hence the great variety of subject-matter in each song.

The Negro dances circulated over the world were also conceived inside the Jooks. They too make the round of Jooks and public works before going into the outside world.

In this respect it is interesting to mention the Black Bottom. I have read several false accounts of its origin and name. One writer claimed that it got its name from the black sticky mud on the bottom of the Mississippi river. Other equally absurd statements gummed the press. Now the dance really originated in the Jook section of Nashville, Tennessee, around Fourth Avenue. This is a tough neighbourhood known as Black Bottom—hence the name.

The Charleston is perhaps forty years old, and was danced up and down the Atlantic seaboard from North Carolina to Key West, Florida.

The Negro social dance is slow and sensuous. The idea in the Jook is to gain sensation, and not so much exercise. So that just enough foot movement is added to keep the dancers on the floor. A

44

180

Characteristics of Negro Expression

tremendous sex stimulation is gained from this. But who is trying to avoid it? The man, the woman, the time and the place have met. Rather, little intimate names are indulged in to heap fire on fire.

These too have spread to all the world.

The Negro theatre, as built up by the Negro, is based on Jook situations, with women, gambling, fighting, drinking. Shows like " Dixie to Broadway " are only Negro in cast, and could just as well have come from pre-Soviet Russia.

Another interesting thing—Negro shows before being tampered with did not specialise in octoroon chorus girls. The girl who could hoist a Jook song from her belly and lam it against the front door of the theatre was the lead, even if she were as black as the hinges of hell. The question was " Can she jook? " She must also have a good belly wobble, and her hips must, to quote a popular work song, " Shake like jelly all over and be so broad, Lawd, Lawd, and be so broad." So that the bleached chorus is the result of a white demand and not the Negro's.

The woman in the Jook may be nappy headed and black, but if she is a good lover she gets there just the same. A favorite Jook song of the past has this to say:

> *Singer :* It aint good looks dat takes you through dis world.
> *Audience :* What is it, good mama?
> *Singer :* Elgin [1] movements in your hips
> Twenty years guarantee.

And it always brought down the house too.

> Oh de white gal rides in a Cadillac,
> De yaller gal rides de same,
> Black gal rides in a rusty Ford
> But she gits dere just de same.

The sort of woman her men idealise is the type that is put forth in the theatre. The art-creating Negro prefers a not too thin woman who can shake like jelly all over as she dances and sings, and that is the type he put forth on the stage. She has been banished by the white producer and the Negro who takes his cue from the white.

Of course a black woman is never the wife of the upper class Negro in the North. This state of affairs does not obtain in the South, however. I have noted numerous cases where the wife was considerably darker than the husband. People of some substance, too.

This scornful attitude towards black women receives mouth sanction by the mud-sills.

Even on the works and in the Jooks the black man sings disparagingly of black women. They say that she is evil. That she sleeps with her fists doubled up and ready for action. All over they are making a little drama of waking up a yaller [2] wife and a black one.

A man is lying beside his yaller wife and wakes her up. She says to him, " Darling, do you know what I was dreaming when you woke me up? " He says, " No honey, what was you dreaming? " She says, " I dreamt I had done cooked you a big, fine dinner and we was setting down to eat out de same plate and I was setting on yo' lap jus huggin you and kissin you and you was so sweet."

Wake up a black woman, and before you kin git any sense into her she be done up and lammed you over the head four or five times. When you git her quiet she'll say, " Nigger, know whut I was dreamin when you woke me up? "

You say, " No honey, what was you dreamin? " She says, " I dreamt you shook yo' rusty fist under my nose and I split yo' head open wid a axe."

But in spite of disparaging fictitious drama, in real life the black girl is drawing on his account at the commissary. Down in the Cypress Swamp as he swings his axe he chants:

> Dat ole black gal, she keep on grumblin,
> New pair shoes, new pair shoes,
> I'm goint to buy her shoes and stockings
> Slippers too, slippers too.

Then adds aside : " Blacker de berry, sweeter de juice."

To be sure the black gal is still in power, men are still cutting and shooting their way to her pillow. To the queen of the Jook!

Speaking of the influence of the Jook, I noted that Mae West in " Sex " had much more flavor of the

---

¹ Elegant (?).   ² Yaller (yellow), light mulatto.

45

Characteristics of Negro Expression

turpentine quarters than she did of the white bawd. I know that the piece she played on the piano is a very old Jook composition. " Honey let yo' drawers hang low" had been played and sung in every Jook in the South for at least thirty-five years. It has always puzzled me why she thought it likely to be played in a Canadian bawdy house.

Speaking of the use of Negro material by white performers, it is astonishing that so many are trying it, and I have never seen one yet entirely realistic. They often have all the elements of the song, dance, or expression, but they are misplaced or distorted by the accent falling on the wrong element. Every one seems to think that the Negro is easily imitated when nothing is further from the truth. Without exception I wonder why the black-face comedians *are* black-face ; it is a puzzle—good comedians, but darn poor niggers. Gershwin and the other " Negro " rhapsodists come under this same axe. Just about as Negro as caviar or Ann Pennington's athletic Black Bottom. When the Negroes who knew the Black Bottom in its cradle saw the Broadway version they asked each other, " Is you learnt dat *new* Black Bottom yet ? " Proof that it was not *their* dance.

And God only knows what the world has suffered from the white damsels who try to sing Blues.

The Negroes themselves have sinned also in this respect. In spite of the goings up and down on the earth, from the original Fisk Jubilee Singers down to the present, there has been no genuine presentation of Negro songs to white audiences. The spirituals that have been sung around the world are Negroid to be sure, but so full of musicians' tricks that Negro congregations are highly entertained when they hear their old songs so changed. They never use the new style songs, and these are never heard unless perchance some daughter or son has been off to college and returns with one of the old songs with its face lifted, so to speak.

I am of the opinion that this trick style of delivery was originated by the Fisk Singers ; Tuskeegee and Hampton followed suit and have helped spread this misconception of Negro spirituals. This Glee Club style has gone on so long and become so fixed among concert singers that it is considered quite authentic. But I say again, that not one concert singer in the world is singing the songs as the Negro song-makers sing them.

If anyone wishes to prove the truth of this let him step into some unfashionable Negro church and hear for himself.

To those who want to institute the Negro theatre, let me say it is already established. It is lacking in wealth, so it is not seen in the high places. A creature with a white head and Negro feet struts the Metropolitan boards. The real Negro theatre is in the Jooks and the cabarets. Self-conscious individuals may turn away the eye and say, " Let us search elsewhere for our dramatic art." Let 'em search. They certainly won't find it. Butter Beans and Susie, Bo-Jangles and Snake Hips are the only performers of the real Negro school it has ever been my pleasure to behold in New York.

Dialect

If we are to believe the majority of writers of Negro dialect and the burnt-cork artists, Negro speech is a weird thing, full of " ams " and " Ises." Fortunately we don't have to believe them. We may go directly to the Negro and let him speak for himself.

I know that I run the risk of being damned as an infidel for declaring that nowhere can be found the Negro who asks " am it? " nor yet his brother who announces " Ise uh gwinter." He exists only for a certain type of writers and performers.

Very few Negroes, educated or not, use a clear clipped " I." It verges more or less upon " Ah." I think the lip form is responsible for this to a great extent. By experiment the reader will find that a sharp " I " is very much easier with a thin taut lip than with a full soft lip. Like tightening violin strings.

If one listens closely one will note too that a word is slurred in one position in the sentence but clearly pronounced in another. This is particularly true of the pronouns. A pronoun as a subject is likely to be clearly enunciated, but slurred as an object. For example : " You better not let me ketch yuh."

There is a tendency in some localities to add the " h " to " it " and pronounce it " hit." Probably a vestige of old English. In some localities " if " is " ef."

In story telling " so " is universally the connective. It is used even as an introductory word, at the very beginning of a story. In religious expression " and " is used. The trend in stories is to state conclusions ; in religion, to enumerate.

I am mentioning only the most general rules in dialect because there are so many quirks that belong only to certain localities that nothing less than a volume would be adequate.

46

IV

Harlem Reviewed

by NANCY CUNARD

Is it possible to give any kind of visual idea of a place by description? I think not, least of all of Harlem. When I first saw it, at 7th Avenue, I thought of the Mile End Road—same long vista, same kind of little low houses with, at first sight, many indeterminate things out on the pavement in front of them, same amount of blowing dust, papers, litter. But no; the scale, to begin with, was different. It was only from one point that the resemblance came to one. Beginning at the north end of Central Park, edged in on one side by the rocky hill of Columbia University and on the other by the streets that go to the East River, widening out more and more north to that peculiarly sinister halt in the town, the curve of the Harlem River, where one walks about in the dead junk and the refuse-on-a-grand-scale left in the sudden waste lots that are typical of all parts of New York—this is the area of Harlem. Manhattan and 8th Avenues, 7th, Lenox, 5th and Madison Avenues, they all run up here from the zone of the skyscrapers, the gleaming white and blond towers of down-town that are just visible like a mirage down the Harlem perspective. These avenues, so grand in New York proper, are in Harlem very different. They are old, rattled, some of them, by the El on its iron heights, rattled, some of them, underneath, by the Sub in its thundering groove.

Why is it called Harlem, and why the so-called capital of the Negro world? The Dutch made it first, in the 17th century; it was "white" till as recently as 1900. And then, because it was old and they weren't rebuilding it, because it's a good way from the centre, it was more or less "left" to the coloured people. Before this they lived in different parts of New York; there was no Negro "capital." This capital now exists, with its ghetto-like slums around 5th, bourgeois streets, residential areas, a few aristocratic avenues or sections thereof, white-owned stores and cafeterias, small general shops, and the innumerable "skin-whitening" and "anti-kink" beauty parlors. There is one large modern hotel, the Dewey Square, where coloured people of course may stay; and another, far larger, the Teresa, a few paces from it, where certainly they *may not*! And this is in the centre of Harlem. Such race barriers are on all sides; it just de-

Mr. Ezell Dunford and his beautiful Packhard car. Harlem

pends on chance whether you meet them or no. Some Negro friend maybe will not go into a certain drug-store with you for an ice-cream soda at 108th (where Harlem is supposed to begin, but where it is still largely " white "); " might not get served in there " (and by a coloured server at that—the white boss's orders). Just across the Harlem River some white gentlemen flashing by in a car take it into their heads to bawl, " Can't you get yourself a white man ? "—you are walking with a Negro, yet you walk down-town with the same and meet no such hysteria, or again, you do.

In his book, *Black Manhattan*, James Weldon Johnson has made a map of Harlem showing the rapid increase of Negro occupation. This of course cannot be taken otherwise than as percentage, as there are some whites living in all parts of it. The Negro population is always increasing, but the houses do not expand; hence overcrowding in all but the expensive apartments and the middle-class lodgings. These last are pretty similar to our own Bloomsbury kind. And why then do the Negroes continue to flock

67

Harlem Reviewed

to Harlem? Because in most other parts of New York they simply " don't let to coloured," at least never *en masse*. More and more of the " white " streets on the fringes of Harlem " go black " and become part of it. It happens this way. A coloured family or two get houses in such or such a street. Prejudiced white neighbours remonstrate with the landlord, who may not care—the more so as he knows that other coloured families will be wanting to move in. The whites have complained of his houses, demanded repairs. He won't make them, and for Negroes he can *double the rent* (this is invariably so), and no repairs need, or will, ever be made. The Negroes come, up go the rents, and the whites abandon that street. One of the reasons why Harlem is so concentrated is that this procedure takes some time; in housing themselves, as in every single other thing, they have to fight and fight; they are penalised for being black or coloured in every imaginable way, and, to the European, in many unthinkable ones.

Some 350,000 Negroes and coloured are living in Harlem and Brooklyn (the second, and quite distinct, area in greater New York where they have congregated). American Negroes, West Indians, Africans, Latin Americans. The latter, Spanish-speaking, have made a centre round 112th St. and Lenox Avenue. Walk round there and you will hear—it is nearly all Spanish. The tempo of the gestures and gait, the atmosphere, are foreign. It is the Porto-Ricans, the Central Americans and the Cubans. Nationalisms exist, more or less fiercely, between them and the American Negro—as indeed does a jealous national spirit between American Negro and black Jamaican. The latter say they are the better at business, that

A group of Cuban Negroes at Pelham Park, just out of New York, where all races mix on the beach and in the park—that is, more or less, for here too you observe a coloured section filled with whites, but no Negroes in the preponderant white parts

the coloured Americans have no enterprise. (Are we to see here the mantle of the British as a nation of shopkeepers on West Indian shoulders?) The American Negro regards the Jamaican or British West Indian as " less civilised " than himself; jokes about his accent and deportment are constantly made on the Harlem stage. And so they are always at it, falling out about empty " superiorities " and " inferiorities," forgetting the white enemy.

The Jamaican is " a foreigner "—and yet it was Marcus Garvey, from Jamaica, who, more than any living Negro, roused the black people of America just after the war with his " Back to Africa " movement. This sort of Zionism, after a lightning accumulation of millions of dollars, collapsed entirely. " Back to Africa " was held out to all the Negroes in the American continent, a Utopian impossibility at both ends—for how can 12,000,000 transport themselves *en masse*, as Garvey urged them to do, and in what part of Africa would the white imperialists allow such, or even a small part of such, a settlement? Apart from this, the Africans were, not surprisingly, angered by Garvey's self-given title of "Provisional Emperor of Africa." The African country chosen by Garvey was Liberia, which, as is known to everyone, is really an American (Firestone) colony. There is an anomaly now in the position of the Garvey movement. Though he is himself discredited, his followers (and there are several inter-factions too) disavow him but continue to call themselves Garveyites and proclaim his doctrine. Those extraordinary half salvation army, half British military uniforms that you see in the streets occasionally are Garvey's men; you come across them speaking at street corners, holding a large crowd. But it is all hot air. It is not organised in any direction or built on anything solid. Individually they have not the drive of the black Communist orator, for they are not speaking of anything serious; Garvey's theory was " all-black "; he wanted his people to be independent of, to cut away from, the white race entirely. The wrong kind of pride; a race pride which stopped at that, and paid no heed to the very real and concrete misery, oppression and struggles of the Negro toiling millions throughout the States.

If you are " shown " Harlem by day you will inevitably have pointed out to you the new Rockefeller apartments, a huge block towering above a rather sparse and visibly very indigent part of 7th Avenue. These were built by the millionaire of that name, supposedly to better the conditions of Negro workers by providing clean and comfortable lodging for them, but inhabited, however, by those who can afford

68

Harlem Reviewed

to pay their rents. The Y.M.C.A. and the newly built Y.W.C.A.—more institutes for " uplift." The Harlem Public Library, with its good collection of books on Negro matters, and just a few pieces of African art, so few that the idea strikes one vexingly : why, in this capital of the Negro world, is there no centre, however small, of Africanology ? The American Negroes—this is a generalisation with hardly any exceptions—are utterly uninterested in, callous to what Africa is, and to what it was. Many of them are fiercely " racial," as and when it applies to the States, but concerning their forefathers they have not even curiosity.

At night you will be taken to the Lafayette Theatre, the " cradle of new stars " that will go out on the road all over America and thence come to Europe. It is a sympathetic old hall, where, as they don't bother ever to print any programmes, one supposes that all the audience know all the players; it has that feeling too. Some of the best wit I heard here, and they can get away with a lot of stiff hot stuff. Ralph Cooper's orchestra was playing admirably that night they had " the street " in. This was to give a hearing to anyone who applied. They just went on the stage and did their stuff. And the audience was *merciless* to a whole lot of these new triers, who would have passed with honour anywhere out of America. The dancing of two or three of the street shoe-blacks, box on back, then set down and dancing round it, was so perfect that the crowd gave them a big hand. No-one who has not seen the actual dancing of Harlem in Harlem can have any idea of its superb quality. From year to year it gets richer, more complicated, more exact. And I don't mean the unique Snake-Hips and the marvellous Bo-Jangles, I mean the boys and girls out of the street who later become " chorats " and " chorines " (in the chorus), or who do those exquisite short numbers, as in music the Three Ink Spots (a new trio), adolescents of 16 or 17 perhaps, playing Duke Ellington's *Mood Indigo* so that the tears ran down one's face.

There was a new dance too, one of the sights of the world as done at the Savoy Ballroom, the Lindy-Hop. The fitting third to its predecessors, Charleston and Black Bottom. These were in the days of short skirts, but the Lindy is the more astounding as it is as violent (and as beautiful), with skirts sweeping the floor. Short minuet steps to begin, then suddenly fall back into an air-pocket, recover sideways, and proceed with all the variations of leaves on the wind. For the Lindy is Lindbergh, of course, created by them in honour of

" Jessie," who toured the world with a theatrical company and who was the charming hostess in a "speak-easy" when I knew her in Harlem

his first triumph. These Tuesday nights at the Savoy are very famous, as is the Harlem " Drag Ball " that happens only once a year. To this come the boys dressed as girls—some in magnificent and elaborate costumes made by themselves—and of course many whites from down-town. A word on the celebrated " rent-party " that the American press writes up with such lurid and false suggestions. This is no more nor less than an ordinary evening dance in someone's house. The " rent " part is its reason for being, for the guests give about 50 cents to come in, thereby helping pay the rent, and they buy liquor there which, as everywhere in dry America (and doubtless it will go on even if prohibition is entirely abolished), is made on the premises or by a friend. The music, as like as not, comes from a special kind of electric piano, a nickel a tune, all the best, the latest ones.

But it is the zest that the Negroes put in, and the enjoyment they get out of, things that causes one more envy in the ofay.[1] Notice how many of the whites are unreal in America ; they are *dim*. But the Negro is very real ; he is *there*. And the ofays know it. That's why they come to Harlem—out of curiosity and jealousy and don't-know-why. This desire to get close to the other race has often nothing honest

[1] *Ofay :* white.

69

Harlem Reviewed

about it ; for where the ofays flock, to night-clubs, for instance, such as Connie's Inn and the Cotton Club and Small's, expensive cabarets, to these two former the coloured clientèle is no longer admitted ! To the latter, only just, grudgingly. No, you can't go to Connie's Inn with your coloured friends. The place is *for whites*. " Niggers " to serve, and " coons " to play—and later the same ofay will slip into what he calls " a coloured dive," and there it'll be " 'Evening, Mr. Brown," polite and cordial, because this will be a real coloured place and the ofay is not sure of himself there a-tall. . . .

This applies of course to the mass of whites who treat Harlem in the same way that English toffs used to talk about " going slumming." The class I'm thinking of is " the club-man." They want entertainment. Go to Harlem, it's sharper there. And it doesn't upset their conception of the Negro's social status. From all time the Negro has entertained the whites, but never been thought of by this type as possibly a social equal. There are, however, thousands of artists, writers, musicians, intellectuals, etc., who have good friends in the dark race, and a good knowledge of Harlem life, " the freedom of Harlem," so to speak.

" You must see a revival meeting," they said to me. " It's nothing like what it is in the South, but you shouldn't miss it."

Beforehand I thought I wouldn't be able to stand more than ten minutes of it—ten minutes in any church. . . . When we got into the Rev. Cullen's on 7th Avenue (the Rev. is the father of the poet, Countee Cullen) a very large audience was waiting for the " Dancing Evangelist " (that is Becton's title, because of his terrific physical activity). A group of " sisters " all in white spread itself fan-wise in the balcony. There was a concert stage with deacons and some of Becton's 12 disciples, and the 7 or 8 absolutely first-class musicians who compose the orchestra, of whom Lawrence Pierre, a fine organist and a disciple. Nothing like a church, an evening concert.

The music starts, a deep-toned Bach piece, then a short allocution, and then the long spirituals, a deep robust soloist that a massed chorus, the audience, answers back. They begin to beat time with their feet too. The " spirit " is coming with the volume of sound. At this point Becton enters quietly, stands silent on the stage, will not say a word. They must sing some more first, much more ; they must be ripe ground. How do they reconcile Becton's exquisite smartness (pearl-grey suit, top hat, cane, ivory gloves, his youthful look and lovely figure), the whole sparkle about him, with the customary ponderousness of the other drab men of God? A sophisticated audience? No, for they appear to be mainly domestic workers, small shop workers, old and young, an evidently religious public, and one or two whites.

A new spiritual has begun ; the singing gets intenser, foot-beating all around now, bodies swaying, and clapping of hands in unison. Now and again a voice, several voices, rise above the rest in a single phrase, the foot-beat becomes a stamp. A forest shoots up—black, brown, ivory, amber hands—spread, stiffened-

out fingers, gestures of *mea culpa*, beating of breasts, gestures of stiff arms out, vibrating extasy. Far away in the audience a woman gets " seized," leaps up and down on the same spot belabouring her bosom. It comes here, there—who will be the next ? At one moment I counted ten women in this same violent trance, not two with the same gestures, yet *all* in rhythm, half-time or double time. A few men too, less spectacular. Then just behind me, so that I see her well, a young girl. She leaps up and down after the first scream, eyes revulsed, arms upstretched—she is no longer " there." After about a minute those next to her seize her and hold her down.

Connie's Inn, 7th Avenue, in the heart of Harlem, a smart Negro night-club, which panders so entirely to the prejudice of its white clientèle that coloured people are actually excluded as guests ; the only Negroes inside are, of course, menials, and the coloured entertainers. No better example than this of the poison of Jim-Crow carried into the very centre of the Negro town ; an example, too, of the incapacity of American whites in keeping away from the despised " niggers "

The apex of the singing has come ; it is impossible to convey the scale of these immense sound-waves and rhythmical under-surges. One is transported,

70

completely. It has nothing to do with God, but with life—a collective life for which I know no name. The people are entirely out of themselves—and then, suddenly, the music stops, calm comes immediately.

In this prepared atmosphere Becton now strides about the stage, flaying the people for their sins, leading their ready attention to this or that point of his argument by some adroit word, a wise-crack maybe. He is a poet in speech and very graceful in all his movements. His dramatisation is generous— and how they respond . . . "yeah man . . . tell it, tell it." Sin, he threatens, is "cat-foot," a "double-dare devil." And the sinner? "A double-ankled rascal," thunders this "adagio dancer," as he called himself that night, breaking off sharp into another mood, an admonishment out of "that inexpressible something by which I raise my hand." There are whirlwind gestures when he turns round on himself, one great clap of the palms and a sort of characteristic half-whistle-half-hoot before some point which is going to be emphasised—and the eloquence pours out in richer and richer imagery. Becton is the personification of expressionism, a great dramatic actor. You remember Chaliapine's acting of Boris Godounov; these two are comparable.

Then, "when the millenniums are quaking it's time to clap our hands." It is the moment for the "consecrated dime," and the singing begins again, but the trances are over; other preachers may speak

Elder Becton, "The dancing evangelist"

later. This ritual goes on from eight till after midnight, about four nights a week, and sometimes both the faithful and the evangelist are so indefatigable that it goes on for 24 hours. These services, really superb concerts, are the gorgeous manifestation of *the emotion* of a race—that part of the Negro people that has been so trammelled with religion that it is still steeped therein. A manifestation of this kind by white people would have been utterly revolting. But with the Negro race it is on another plane, it seems positively another thing, not connected with Christ or bible, the pure outpouring of themselves, a nature-rite. In other words, it is the fervour, intensity, the stupendous rhythm and surge of singing that are so fine—the christianity is only accidental, incidental to these. Not so for the assembly of course, for all of it is deeply, tenaciously religious.

Becton is the most famous evangelist of the coloured race in America. He has a following of more than 200,000, from New York to Florida, from Baltimore to Kansas. Like Christ he has 12 disciples. "The reason I have my party comprised of all men is because Jesus' disciples were all men, and if it was right for him it is right for me." He is one of the most elegantly dressed men in the world. Another comparison : "If Jesus were alive he would dress like me," for "if I came out in a long black coat, a collar turned backwards and looked downcast and forlorn, people would say that if they have got to look like that to be christians, they don't want to join the church." Some other sayings of Becton's which fetch the religious are : "I work for God on contract and he keeps his bargain." "I told you, Lord, before I started out that I was a high-priced man, but you wanted me." "God ain't broke!" The "consecrated dime" and its fellows of course supply all Becton's needs. His organisation is called "The World's Gospel Feast," which publishes a quarterly called *The Menu*, the motto of which is : "A Square Deal for God"!

I have given all this detail about the revivalist meeting because it is so fantastic, and, *aesthetically* speaking, so moving. But when one considers the appalling waste of this dynamic force of people, and this preying on the prayers and fervours of old-fashioned, misguided, religious Negroes, it is tragic. Some time during this last summer (1933), after a new point in horror had been reached in the Scottsboro case at the Decatur "retrial," a young Negro minister frankly voiced his realisation of the truth; he said that the Communists were the only ones to defend his race, that they had proved it unquestionably throughout the whole history of Scottsboro; he said that for this reason although he was a man of God he was a Communist. Had Becton been honest, had he spoken thus, he would have swept the land. His followers would have had the same faith in these new words as in all his past "heavenly messages." But his was an individual racket.

I went to see Becton. A very handsome and courteous man. During our talk he leant forward earnestly: "In what manner do *you* think will come the freeing of my race?" "Only by organised and militant struggle for their *full* rights, side by side with Communism." He smiled. "And in what way do you think?" I asked him. "I think it will be by prayer," he murmured. I wanted to shout at him "Be honest *now*. Use your great dramatic gift for the right thing; you could be a giant in the freeing of your people." He spoke of the new million-dollar temple he was going to build. "I have not the money, but I shall get it"—and no doubt he would have been able to collect it all by these consecrated dimes. . . . But now, one year after I saw him, Becton is dead. "Bumped off" suddenly and brutally by some gangsters, shot in a car.

Another spectacular man of God is the Rev. Father Devine, who that year was having a hard time with the authorities for what, in Jamaica, used to be called "night noises." The fervent assembled in too great numbers and their exaltation was too loud. Sensational vengeance followed Father Devine's arrest; the judge who condemned him died the next day.

It may seem odd that one's thoughts stay so long with these black priests and their terrific hold over their large following. But religion amongst the Negroes, those that have it (for the younger generation is shaking off its weight, and replacing this by a desire for, an acquisition of, racial and economic facts), their reaction to religion cannot be dissociated in my mind from their past collective reaction to tribal ceremony and custom in Africa. They are *honest* and at home in their belief; that is the whole difference as compared with whites. A white audience in church lifts one's heart in utter disgust; with the Negroes one longs for this collective force to be directed towards the right things, solidarity with those whites who are struggling for their rights too against the super-brutality of American "democracy."

The Negro ministers and churches vary in their attitude to the more and more violent struggle for Negro rights. Since the Scottsboro case and other equally vicious frame-ups, some have helped the International Labor Defence, the organisation which is fighting these cases; some have refused all aid. The same applies to the Negro newspapers. Scandals have occurred, such as misuse of funds collected by *The Amsterdam News*, an important Harlem paper, for the great march on Washington this spring by over 4,000 Harlem Negroes, protesting against the new legal lynch verdict on Heywood Patterson at Decatur.

The Harlem Liberator is the only honest Negro paper in the States, and there are some four or five hundred. . . . Controlled by jacks-in-office at the beck and call of American white money and black philanthropic support, this Negro bourgeoisie sits giving praise to each new president and each party that promises that "new deal to the Negro" that never comes (and will never come from Republican, Democrat or Labour), launching out frantic and crassly ignorant attacks on the Communists (see particularly the so-called "Symposium" of a dozen or so Negro editors in one of the spring 1932 numbers of *The Crisis*). They are worse than the black imperialist lackeys in colonial countries, for they are not without money and some power, neither of which is ever applied to the crying needs of the race. There is not one paper (except *The Harlem Liberator*) that can be called a proper "Race" paper. Although they deal almost entirely with Negro doings, these doings are found to be mainly social events and functions. The coloured stage is much spoken of, which is very much to the good, for the white papers scarcely mention any Negro achievement; yet there is hardly a star who is not at some time or other of his or her career literally pulled to pieces by some scandal of press-invention. As to writing sanely about any inter-racial friendships or associations . . . one might be reading a Southern white rag.

Confusion (and confusing the minds of its readers) is a strong newspaper characteristic. I say confusion, but it is by design. Example: on several pages you will read vulgar, ignorant and abusive articles on Negro "reds"; misrepresentations, and every attempt at discredit. (For instance, the *Pittsburgh Courier* printed a baseless and indescribably vicious attack on Ruby Bates, one of the two white State witnesses in the Scottsboro case, because she admitted having lied in the first trial, thus being part responsible for 9 innocent black boys being in jail under death-sentence for $2\frac{1}{2}$ years, and because now she was speaking all over the country showing up the Southern lynch-terror and race-hate, on the same platform as Communist organisers.) And on another page will be found an honest account of some event in connection with these same Negro comrades. What is the explanation? The editor has been forced into this last by the remonstrances of militant Negroes who are bitterly aware of the sempiternal treacheries

72

188

Harlem Reviewed

of the black bourgeoisie all along the line, but nowhere as vilely so as in their newspapers. The Negro race in America has no worse enemy than its own press.

If treachery and lying are its main attributes so is snobbery flourishing in certain parts of Harlem. " Strivers Row "; that is what 139th Street has been called. An excellent covering-name for " those Astorperious Ethiopians," as one of their own wits put it. There are near-white cliques, mulatto groups, dark-skinned sets who will not invite each other to their houses; some would not let a white cross their thresholds. The Negro " blue-bloods " of Washington are famous for their social exclusivity, there are some in Harlem too. I don't know if a foreign white would get in there, possibly not. The snobbery around skin-colour is terrifying. The light-skins and browns look down on the black; by some, friendships with *ofays* are not tolerated, from an understandable but totally unsatisfactory reaction to the general national attitude of white to coloured on the social equality basis. A number of the younger writers are race-conscious in the wrong way, they make of this a sort of forced, *self*-conscious thing, give the feeling that they are looking for obstacles. All this, indeed, is Society with a vengeance ! A bourgeois ideology with no horizon, no philosophical link with life. And out of all this, need it be said, such writers as Van Vechten and Co. have made a revolting and cheap lithograph, so that Harlem, to a large idle-minded public, has come to mean nothing more whatsoever than a round of hooch [1]-filled night-clubs after a round of " snow "[2]-filled boudoirs. Van Vechten, the spirit of vulgarity, has depicted Harlem as a grimace. He would have written the same way about Montparnasse or Limehouse and Soho.

On the Corner 129th St. and 7th Ave. *Harlem*

Do places exist, or is life itself as described by Paul Morand (another profiteer in coloured " stock ")? Claude MacKay has done better. The studies in inter-colour relationships (in *Ginger Town*) are honest. But his people, and himself, have also that wrong kind of race-consciousness; they ring themselves in, they are umbrageous. The " Negro Renaissance " (the literary movement of about 1925, now said to be at a halt, and one wonders on whose authority this is said) produced many books and poems filled with this bitter-sweet of Harlem's glitter and heart-break.

This is not the Harlem one sees. You don't see the Harlem of the romancists; it is romantic in its own right. And it is *hard* and *strong*; its noise, heat, cold, cries and colours are so. And the nostalgia is violent too; the eternal radio seeping through everything day and night, indoors and out, becomes somehow the personification of restlessness, desire, brooding. And then the gorgeous roughness, the gargle of Louis Armstrong's voice breaks through. As everywhere, the real people are in the street. I mean those young men on the corner, and the people all sitting on the steps throughout the breathless, leaden summer. I mean the young men in Pelham Park; the sports groups (and one sees many in their bright sweaters), the strength of a race, its beauty.

[1] Drink.   [2] Cocain.

Young men in Pelham Park, just out of New York

73

Harlem Reviewed

The Sweetvendor. Harlem

For in Harlem one can make an appreciation of a race. Walk down 7th Avenue—the different types are uncountable. Every diversity of bone-structure, of head-shape, of skin colour; mixes between Orientals and pure Negroes, Jews and Negroes, Red Indians and Negroes (a particularly beautiful blend, with the high cheek-bones always, and sometimes straight black hair), mulattoes of all shades, yellow, " high yaller " girls, and Havana-coloured girls, and, exquisitely fine, the Spanish and Negro blends; the Negro bone, and the Negro fat too, are a joy to the eye. And though there are more and more light-coloured people, there is great satisfaction in seeing that the white American features are absorbed in the mulatto, and that the mulatto is not, as so often in England, a coloured man with a white man's features and often expression as well. The white American and the Negro are a good mix physically. The pure black people—there are less of these (more than two-thirds of the race now being mixed with white). These are some of the new race that Embree has written of in his *Brown America*; they are as distinct from the African as they are from the nordic.

The major part of Harlem's inhabitants are of course the Negro workers. Since the depression began the proportion of those that are unemployed is very much higher than that even of the white workers. They have been, they are being sacked, and their wretchedly underpaid jobs given to the whites. Unable to pay the rent, not a week goes by without numerous evictions, they are thrown out into the street. Bailiffs come and move out the few belongings they have. And it is here that the Communists have put up a strong and determined defence. Black and white comrades together go where the evictions are taking place and move the things back. Police and riot squads come with bludgeons and tear-bombs, fights and imprisonments, and deaths too, occur. In every form the oppression that the governing class carries out increasingly becomes more brutal as the need of the unemployed makes stronger and stronger demand for food, work and wages.

There is no finer realisation than that of knowing that the black and white proletariat is getting more and more together now on the only real basis that must be established and consolidated for ever : the equal rights of both under the Communist programme. And when this is in practice the full and final abolition of this artificially-bred race-hatred on the part of the whites, bred out of the enslaving of blacks, will be arrived at. In this and in no other way. There is no colour *problem*. The existence of the Negro race is not a problem, it is *a fact*. And in America, as in all other imperialist countries, this use of a wrong word is neither more nor less than a vicious lie on the part of the ruling class in urging the workers of each country into thinking that the Negro, the coloured race, was created by nature as a *menace*. The growing volume of the Communist consciousness among the black workers, and in some of the Negro intellectuals, dates chiefly from five years ago, and has in that time made, and is making, rapid increase. It is something new, *more and more tangible*, as here in England now, in the street as I go by I am immediately aware of a new expression in some of the faces, a look of purpose and responsibility.

One of the first things I was impressed by, the best thing that remains of Harlem, was the magnificent strength and lustiness of the Negro children. As I walked from end to end

Harlem Dustmen

74

of it, down the length of 7th Avenue, the schools were just out. The children rushed by in rough leather jackets in the cold wind, some of them playing ball on roller skates, shouting and free. May these gorgeous children in their leathers be the living symbol of the finally liberated Negro people.

Up with an all-Communist Harlem in an all-Communist United States!

75

A Negro
Art
Exhibit
The following editorial was contributed by Miss
Ernestine Rose, the efficient librarian of the
Harlem branch of the New York Public
Library :—

The exhibit by Negro artists shown on the third floor of the
135th Street Library during August and September 1922, was
the second event of its kind to be held. It differed from the one
of 1921 in several important respects. It was not so broad in
its inclusion, being limited purposely to art in its more re-
strictive meaning, i. e. painting, drawing, sculpture; whereas
the former exhibit included as well woodwork, art embroidery
and needle work, china painting, and artistic photography.
Both exhibits included much rare bibliographical material,
such as original manuscripts dealing with slavery and works
by leading Negro writers.

The quality of the later exhibit was no higher as a whole
than that of the former, possibly not as high, but it seemed to
a layman that there were several high points, which the first
had never reached. This is distinctly encouraging to those who
wish to see these exhibits continued.

The etchings of Albert Smith were fine types of a mature and
perfected art; W. Russell's still-life studies were exquisite in

color and texture; and the charcoal illustrations of Elmer C. Stoner were splendidly planned and executed. George Young's manuscripts, original letters, and portrait engravings of such great men of the race as Alexander Dumas and Toussaint L'Ouverture formed a distinctive feature.

A very striking note in the exhibit was the preoccupation of the artists with general rather than racial subjects. This is quite to be expected and is a normal development, for Negro artists are learning their trade. They are concerned largely with art as art, not as Negro art, and their struggle is for recognition in the realm of creation where race distinctions are less than nothing.

Yet, as time goes on, as artistic training is developed, as self-consciousness decreases, it is inevitable that Negro artists will avail themselves of the riches inherent in their race history and consciousness, in its peculiar beauty and vigor. We look forward confidently to that time. Only then will American Negro art find its finest and most original expression.

To Certain of Our Phillistines

By Alain Locke

OF all the arts, painting is most bound by social ideas. And so, in spite of the fact that the Negro offers, in the line of the human subject, the most untouched of all the available fields of portraiture, and the most intriguing, if not indeed the most difficult of technical problems because of the variety of pigmentation and subtlety of values, serious painting in America has all but ignored him. As far as my knowledge and judgment go, the best that has been done by reputable American masters in this line is work like Winslow Homers' "Gulf Stream" or his "A Sunday Morning in Virginia" and the "Pickanniny" of Robert Henri. All of this work is in the vein and mood of the traditional "Study in Brown" — the half-genre, half study-sketch in which so many a master hand has satisfied its artistic curiosity without exerting its full command either of interpretation or expression. Negro artists, themselves victims of the academy-tradition, have had the same attitude, and have shared the blindness of the Caucasian eye. Nothing above the level of a genre study or more penetrating that a Nordicized transcription has been done. Our Negro-American painter of the best academic technique, though in his youth and into his mature period a professed type—realist devoted to the portrayal of Jewish Biblical types, has never maturely touched the portrayal of the Negro subject.

Facts shouldn't be regretted: they should be explained. Social conventions stand closer guard over painting than most of the other arts. It is for that reason that a new school and idiom of Negro portraiture is particularly significant. As might be expected, it began in Europe, and because of the American situation has had to be imported. Portraiture is too controlled by social standards for it to be otherwise. But its really promising and vital development will be American, and, at least we hope, in large part the work of Negro artists. The latter cannot be predicted with as great confidence as the former—for the American Negro mind, in large sections, suffers as yet from repressions which make the idioms of the new school less welcome than the genre-peasant portraiture to which we have become accustomed, and almost as objectionable as the caricature conventions from which our "touchy" reactions have been developed. Too many of us still look to art to compensate the attitudes of prejudice, rather than merely, as is proper, to ignore them. And so, unfortunately for art, the struggle for social justice has put a pessimism upon a playing-up to Caucasian type-ideals, and created too prevalently a half-caste psychology that distorts all true artistic values with the irrelevant social values of "representative" and "unrepresentative," "favorable" and "unfavorable"—and threatens a truly racial art with the psychological bleach of "lily-whitism." This Phillistinism cannot be tolerated. Already on the wane in our social life, after a baneful career, it cannot be allowed this last refuge in art. To rid ourselves of this damaging distortion of art values by color-line, we shall have to draw the culture-line sharply and without compromise, and challenge, without hope or expectation of quarter, our own Phillistines.

Meanwhile, until we can find or create a considerable body of appreciative support for the new art, the painting of the Negro subject will have to rely upon the boldly iconoclastic stand of the convinced and purposefully original artist. The work of Winold Reiss, represented in the Harlem number of the *Survey Graphic,* and more elaborately in the exhibition of the original color pastels at the Harlem Branch of the New York Public Library, was deliberately conceived and executed as a pathbreaker in the inevitable direction of a racially representative type of art. In idiom, technical treatment, and social angle, it was meant to represent a new approach, and constructively to break with the current tradition. In the first place, it breaks as European art has already done, with the limited genre treatment of the Negro subject. Next, it recognizes what is almost a law of development, that a new subject requires a new style, or at least a fresh technique. The Negro physiognomy must be freshly and objectively conceived on its own patterns if it ever is to be seriously and importantly interpreted. Art must discover and reveal the beauty which prejudice and caricature have obscured and overlaid. Finally it must reinforce our art with the dignity of race pride and the truly cultural judgment of art in terms of technical and not sentimental values.

Awed by a name, the Phillistines will accept in a Holbein or a Van Eyck or a Rubens qualities which they bray at in this logical application in contemporary work. All vital art discovers beauty, and opens our eyes to beauty that previously we could not see. And no great art will impose alien canons of beauty upon its subject matter. But it is harder to discover beauty in the familiar—and that may perhaps be why our own Negro artists may be the last to recognize the new potentialities, technical and æsthetic, of our racial types.

Modern art happily has already discovered them: Mr. Reiss is simply a pioneer in the application of this discovery to the American Negro subject. Already Max Slevogt, Pechstein, Elamie Stein, Von Reukteschell, Lucie Costurier, Neville Lewis, F. C. Gadell, and most especially the Belgian, Auguste Mambour, have looked upon the African scene and the African countenance and discovered there a beauty that calls for a distinctive idiom both of color and of modelling. Their work should even now be the inspiration and the guide-posts of a younger school of American Negro artists. Mambour's canvases at the International Art Show at Venice impressed me as standing out among the most pre-eminent work of the entire exhibition, not merely the Belgian section. Not that we would have all our young painters, ultra-modernists of this or that European cult or coterie, but that the lesson of an original and bold approach is just that which must be learned to start any vital art development among us.

We have a right to expect and demand two things of the cultural expression of the Negro, that it should be vital and that it should be contemporary. This isn't the creed of being new-fangled for the sake of being so—let others who have more cause to be decadent and blasè than we, be eccentric and bizarre for the sheer need of new sensations and renewed vigor. But for another more vital and imperative reason the artistic expression of Negro life must break through the stereotypes and flout the conventions—in order that it may be truly expressive at all—and not a timid, conventional, imitative acceptance of the repressions that have been heaped upon us by both social persecution and by previous artistic misrepresentation. Artistically we shall have to fight harder for independence than for recognition, and this we cannot achieve either through slavish imitation, morbid conventionalism, or timid conservatism.

Let us take as a concreet instance, the much criticized Reiss drawing entitled "Two Public School Teachers." It happens to be my particular choice among a group of thirty more or less divergently mannered sketches; and not for the reason that it is one of the most realistic but for the sheer poetry and intense symbolism back of it. It happens to represent my own profession, about which I may be presumed to know something. I am far from contending that there is an orthodox interpretation of any art—many minds, many reactions—but this at least is my reaction. I believe this drawing reflects in addition to good type portraiture of its sort, a professional ideal, that peculiar seriousness, that race redemption spirit, that professional earnestness and even sense of burden which I would be glad to think representative of both my profession and especially its racial aspects in spite of the fact that I am only too well aware of the invasion of our ranks in some few centers by the parasitic, society-loving "flapper." I do not need to appeal to race pride, but only to pride of profession to feel and hope that "The Two School Teachers" in addition to being "good drawing" is finely representative. The young Negro artist, when he comes, will conquer this opposition in his own, unique way; but at any rate, here is the smoothest pebble we can find—ready for David's sling.

OPPORTUNITY

L. Hollingsworth Wood
Chairman

Eugene Kinckle Jones
Executive Secretary

Charles S. Johnson
Editor

A JOURNAL OF NEGRO LIFE
Published Monthly by
The Department of Research and Investigations

NATIONAL URBAN LEAGUE
127 EAST 23rd STREET, NEW YORK, N. Y.
Telephone Gramercy 3976

William H. Baldwin
Secretary

Lloyd Garrison
Treasurer

Eric Walrond
Business Manager

Vol. 4   MAY, 1926   No. 41

Contents

Single Copies, Fifteen Cents—*Yearly Subscriptions,* One Dollar and a Half, Foreign, $1.75.

Entered as second-class matter, October 30, 1923, at the Post Office at New York, New York, under the act of March 3, 1879.

Editorials

Negro Art

O NLY a few years ago the most accredited anthropologists were soberly and patiently insisting, in the face of a widespread and apparently agreeable disbelief, that after all, Negroes, known principally in an unnatural environment, possessed about the same capacity as other peoples. These later anthropologists had long years of tradition, and even the early bunglings of this branch of science itself to overcome. When in 1916 Dr. Franz Boaz's con-

summate attack upon a flourishing system of racial misconceptions (*Mind Of Primitive Man*) referred to the cultural achievement of African tribes in their art, industry and folk philosophy, it was information so strange that it could not be appreciated. Only the European Museums had made any worthy collections, and to the ignorance of America in general on this score was added a blank and recordless past to bind American Negroes to their mean status. But these very pieces in which the anthropologists and ethnologists first saw values suddenly became important to European art, and soon thereafter became themselves recognized as art. The two men who have contributed most to this recognition are Paul Guillaume and Dr. Albert C. Barnes. The former lives in Paris, where as the leading spirit of a group of modernists in painting and music, he opened up to them the prodigal gifts of those unknown black artists; the latter lives in America, where with an almost uncanny foresight he has assembled, over a number of years, one of the largest and most valuable private collections of African and modern art existing anywhere—a collection now valued in millions. Despite the compelling qualities of these African sculptures, their manifest influence upon practically the whole of that important new school of artists abroad, and, indeed, in spite of the rich decorativeness in designs from these sources which are becoming more and more familiar in this country, not a great deal is known about this art itself.

This issue, in which Negro art is again discussed, is fortunate in having the guidance and collaboration of the Barnes Foundation. On this subject there is no greater authority.

The Contest

T HE interest in a body of literature by Negroes about Negro life has received fresh stimulus as the first uncoverings of materials and craftsmanship reveal a field stretching far and promisingly into the future. The first year of OPPORTUNITY's Contests brought or aided in bringing to light, the work of at least fifteen competent writers. The Second Contest, sponsored in all of its literary sections by the good patron of letters, Mr. Casper Holstein, and in its wary venturings into the field of Journalism by the Empire State Federation of Colored Women's Clubs, offers a new and larger group of writers whose work as a whole reaches an even superior level of craftsmanship and interest. This was the thing hoped for, and the only thing to be expected

on the proposition of an evolving literature. The
list of awards given elsewhere in this issue is the
result of careful and, in some of its processes, arduous analysis of each of the more than 1,200 entries.
It is unfortunate that by the very nature of contests,
it is not possible to show the splendid efforts of
hundreds of contestants whose work failed of inclusion in the narrow list of winners, by a shade.
These bear eloquent witness to the solidity and
depth of this new school of writers—of this new era
itself. For it is, happily, no longer a matter of a few
torches flickering brightly against a dense shadow of
mediocrity, but—if the figure may be pardoned—
a conflagration, the topmost flame of which is definite from the next only by virtue of a moment's
greater reach. Obscure ones of last year burst into
higher positions this year and so it may be again.

There was, of course, much ordinary work among
the entries and some downright poor writing, particularly in poetry. And while no contest escapes this,
we feel reasonably certain that no contest has drawn
in from a limited group a larger body of actually
worth while writing. The June issue will be devoted largely to the contest materials. Of the status
of this movement, and the substance of what is frequently being referred to as the "Negro literary
renaissance," our readers will have an opportunity
to judge for themselves.

Negro Art, Past and Present*

By ALBERT C. BARNES

A SCORE of years ago, most of those persons who watched the beginning of a new era in art were profoundly astonished to realize that its source of inspiration was the work of the race for centuries despised and condemned to a servile status. Nothing could have seemed more unbelievable that idols made to be worshipped by savages, and masks designed for use in Heathen rites, should have shown the way out of an artistic impasse apparently hopeless. Just at the moment when the traditions of European painting had been completely summed up in the work of Renoir and Cézanne and had found a monumental expression unrivaled since the days of Rembrandt, Velasquez and the Masters of the Italian Renaissance, contemporary art seemed suddenly to have lost its creative powers. Art threatened to decline into a period of academicism and eclecticism, like that which occurred in Italy in the Sixteenth and Seventeenth Centuries. At the critical moment, as M. Paul Guillaume has shown, the treasures of Negro sculpture were recaptured from the anthropologist and the antiquarian, and from them was derived a new impetus toward creative work in plastic art, in music and in poetry.

To persons who understood either the distinguished aesthetic ancestry of Negro sculpture or the psychological makeup of the Negro himself, it is not, however, surprising that the failing powers of European art should have been revived by the art of the Negro. The greatest of all sculptures, that most purely classic in conception and execution—the Egyptian—was itself African. Late Egyptian (Ptolemaic) sculpture had been enriched by the influence of Greek art and the influence of Egypt is clearly apparent in the massiveness, the in-

BAOULE
14th Century

tense structural conviction and the fine sense of decoration which Negro art abundantly displays. The greatest traditions of antiquity were as much the birthright of the Negro as of the European, and in the best Gabon, Sudan and Ivory Coast work, we find the use of these traditions quite as sensitive and individual as Donatello's and Michael Angelo's, and certainly more distinctively sculptural in character. The eruption of Negro influence into European art of the Twentieth Century was thus not a mingling of two alien and incongruous influences, but a recovery by European art of an important element in its own past. The place of the Negro in modern art is not that of a parvenu or an intruder, but of one who belongs there by natural right and artistic inheritance.

Mere inheritance, however distinguished, would not qualify any individual or race for a place among the elect in art. The real secret of the Negro's achievement lies in his temperament, in his natural gifts. An examination of these gifts, as they have been developed or stifled by his circumstances, will reveal both the source of his accomplishment in the past and the promise of even greater accomplishment in the future. If we consider the result of his contact with the white race, we shall see why Negro art declined 400 years ago and how, at present, it is struggling out of its long eclipse.

Primitive Negro sculpture was the manifestation of a life which was a stable organization, thoroughly adjusted to its surroundings, and was therefore able to find natural authentic expression. Before the coming of the Portuguese into Central Africa, the Negroes had established a mode of life in harmony with their environment and congenial to their temperament. Their material wants were slight, they required little shelter or clothing, food was abundant. As they had no commerce with the world, they were free from economic pressure. Hence they had almost unlimited leisure for the free exercise of their powers, and especially of their vivid and dramatic religious instinct, enriched by their luxuriant imagination. Although they lacked all scientific conception and their religious rites were consequently full of superstition, the very naiveté of their religion made it more colorful and dramatic. It was a religion into which they could pour all their instincts—their fondness for music, for the dance, for histrionics, for ceremony; in general, for participation in a natural, spontaneous, rhythmic group activity.

Into this paradise came the Europeans in the early Sixteenth Century, and very soon the natural life of the Negro was at an end. The material powers of the white races, and the prestige whic' this conferred, deprived the Negroes of their freedom, their self-confidence and their initiative. Reduced to a status of inferiority, they sought to imitate the Europeans and their art sank into a debased and mongrel form.

For American Negroes, the most important event in the history of their relations with white men was the transplanting of many thousands of their race to America. Torn from their native environment and from their carefree, irresponsible life, they were herded together on Southern plantations, given over to an incessant toil and compelled to rebuild their existence from its foundations. The new civilization of which they were forcibly made a part was totally alien to them, and their history in it was that of a long and painful effort towards adjustment. A radically novel set of habits and customs was imposed upon them by their American conquerors. At first, their reaction was one of simple despair, with occasional bursts of blind revolt. Gradually, however, they began to adjust themselves; self-expression was found in the adaptation of their ancient heathen rites, in which belief in the supernatural was paramount. After several generations of worship by incantation and exorcism, conversion to Christianity was almost universal. At the start, Christianity was chiefly a means of a consolation. Since their freedom and natural spontaneous life seemed almost hopelessly lost in this world, it was inevitable that they should seek compensation in dreams of another and happier supernatural life. Religion is always a search for harmony, for environment which shall meet and satisfy our desires, and in which we can feel at home. It is almost a psychological necessity for a race partially frustrated and depressed, above all for a race so richly endowed emotionally and imaginatively, to find a satisfactory religion. But the Christianity adopted by the Negroes had little theological quality. It was much more closely akin to the rites of their African forests than to the orthodox Christianity of the whites. What interested them in it was its assurance to the lowly of their intrinsic importance and value and its promise to the disinherited and

the outcast that a happier existence was in store for him. They were also deeply moved by ceremonials, by all the ways of giving expression to collective emotion; hence the denomination which first gained their allegiance was the Baptists. Subsequently, the Methodists, which also provided a highly emotional ritual and which all could share, gained many converts. Both of these churches held frequent camp meetings, at which the instincts of the Negro were given full play, his imagination, stimulated by that of his fellows, made vividly real to him both his

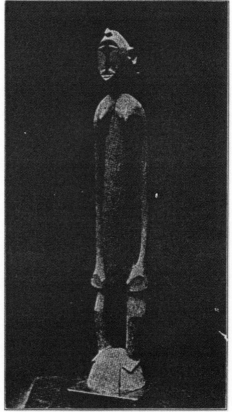

SOUDAN - NIGER
19th Century

present woes—largely symbolized by images of hell-fire and blood—and the glories for which he pined, but which were so conspicuously absent from his earthly habitation. The intensity of his vision and the completeness of its mastery over him, was testified to by its accompaniment of physical abandon—stamping, shrieking and shouting, rushing to and

(Continued on page 168)

Negro Art, Past and Present

(*Continued from page* 149)

fro, wild waving of arms, laughter and tears, and often the rigidity of the trance.

In Africa, the tribal priest had been not only a religious leader and counsellor, but a master of tribal ceremonies, a medicine man, a magician who controlled the powers of nature. Many of these functions were taken over by the preacher of his church when he came under Christianity, and, although some of them were discarded, religion remained the point about which all common activities were focussed. Even today, in the South, the church is not only a house of worship, but a place where societies and lodges meet, suppers are held, entertainments and lectures are given, charity distributed, and views exchanged. It is a community center—much as the Roman Catholic Church was in the Middle Ages. And just as the great artistic achievements of the Middle Ages, tne building of the cathedrals, was an outgrowth of community life inspired by religion, so the greatest artistic achievements of the Negroes, and, indeed, of America, was the "spirituals" in which the sufferings, griefs and hopes of the slaves were given an embodiment at once religious and aesthetic.

These spirituals originated ultimately in African tribal chants, but their form, and the images embodied in them, were determined by the customs of congregational worship in the South. The sermons of the preacher were not theological or ethical discussions; they were exhortations to believe in what has been called the Christian Ethic—to believe and so to be comforted. Their substance was not thought but emotion and imagination, a fact which accounted for the deep earnestness, the fervid eloquence of the exhorter. Rhythm, poetry, music form the natural language of emotion, and for this reason, and also in order that all might participate in the ceremony, hymns in which the speaker's images were repeated and embroidered, inevitably became part of the service. What had at first been merely a wail of sorrow or a dirge became articulate in words the burden of which was the misery of life and the happiness of Heaven—a song at once plaintive and ecstatic. These hymns were anonymous—each of them represented not the work of any one man, but the gradual development of sentiments common to whole groups of men. Like the Homeric poems, also the work of generations of singers, they thus came to represent the griefs and aspirations of a race. Their appeal was universal; they embodied the souls of a whole people.

The nominal emancipation of the Negroes, though it brought the worst of their sufferings to an end, was by no means a real liberation. Disfranchisement, poverty, denial of equal privilege, a menial function in life, was still the lot of the Negro. Without power or prestige, the Negro's frame of mind remained abject, apologetic, or sullenly defiant. No free and full development of his capacities was possible while he stayed in a state of economic serf-dom and profound self-distrust. Real freedom, material and spiritual, was out of the question until economic security was established and full self-respect achieved. Of the two, the latter was probably the more important, since an intelligent, resolute effort toward material improvement is impossible in the absence of independence of mind and self-confidence.

The Negro's achievement of respect for himself and his race was a slow process. For many years he did not suspect the artistic importance of his own spirituals, and they were looked upon by him and his white neighbors as merely the manifestation of an illiterate and inferior race. Their general popularity did not begin until 1871, when the Fisk University singers toured the country to make their living and to raise money for Fisk. At Oberlin, they first won recognition and were invited to give a concert at Brooklyn; after this their fame spread all over America. Nevertheless, the spirituals remained for many years merely a form of light entertainment. A few discerning judges recognized their value, and Dvorak used some of them in his "New World Symphony"; but their true importance was not appreciated until recent years, and the work of collecting, editing and publishing them did not begin until a very few years ago. For much of this pioneer work credit is due to two American negroes, the Work brothers, John and Frederick.

The Negro's pride in his race, the foundations of which were largely laid by recognition of his musical accomplishment, has been powerfully fortified by the rediscovery of ancient Negro sculpture and by acknowledgement, on the part of the most important contemporary artists, of the magnitude of their debt to it. It has revealed an entirely unsuspected wealth of plastic endowments in the Negro race, a sense for the visible essentials of natural objects, and an ability to arrange forms in varied, rhythmic, harmonious, moving designs which do not suffer by comparison with the most distinguished classic achievements of any of the other races. It is no exaggeration to claim that the best of what has been developed in contemporary art during the past twenty years owes its origin to the inspiration of primitive Negro sculpture. In the painting and sculpture of the acknowledged leaders of our age—Picasso, Matisse, Modigliani, Lipchitz, Soutine and others—any trained observer can recognize the Negro motive. The music of the French group known as The Six—Satie, Auric, Honneger, Milhand, Poulenc and Talliaferro—is the ancient Negro spirit embodied in musical forms representative of the highest degree of musical culture and knowledge. Much of Strawinsky's best work belongs to the same category. Diaghlieff drank deeply at the ancient African spring, fused its feelings with the spirit of Russian music and dance, and there emerged a number of the best pieces of the famous Russian ballet. The poetry and prose of Guillaume Apollinaire, Jean Cocteau, Max Jacob, Blaise Cendrars and Reverdy are likewise fundamentally Negro in emotional content and formal expression. The leading dressmaker of our age, Paul Poiret of Paris, acknowledges to his companion of his early career, Paul Guillaume, the debt of awakening the creative spirit through contact with Negro sculpture that Paul Guillaume surrounded himself with, nearly twenty years ago. No informed visitor to the great Paris Expoition of 1925, Art Decoratif, could have failed to be impressed with the predominance of the Negro motive in the really creative work of the decorators of all the great countries represented at that exhibition. In Paris today, the posters that arrest the attention were unmistakably inspired by primitive Negro sculpture. All these great and widely spread influences—in painting, sculpture, music, poetry, literature, decoration—are freely acknowledged by the creators of the worth-while art of the past eighteen years. Appreciation of this sculpture has been rare, especially among the Negroes themselves, but as it becomes more generally diffused, there is every reason to look for an abatement of the superciliousness on the part of the white race and the unhappy sense of inferiority in the Negro himself, which have been detrimental to the true welfare of both races.

It is in poetry and music that the most important contemporary accomplishments of the Negro are to be found. The Negro is a poet by nature. The very deficiencies with which he is sometimes charged, his indifference to science and technology, have been an assistance to him here. Free from preoccupation with the abstract and the mechanical, his attention has been unswervingly fixed upon the concrete, the immediate, the colorful. His mind runs to rich, luxuriant images, organized to meet the demands of an intensely emotional temperament. This temperament appears in everything he does; it is able to lend a charm, a picturesqueness to the most trivial occurrences of every-day life. My extensive experience in the employment of Negroes has afforded innumerable opportunities to observe them at their daily work. If left to themselves and allowed to do what they have to do in their own way, they display an unlimited ability not only to do it efficiently, but to make a drama out of it. Their motions are rhythmic and the tones of their voices are real music. The Negro's recital of anything that may happen, if he is encouraged to tell it in the way natural to him, is never a mere record of facts; it is full of humor, color, dramatic suspense. The Negro lives his poetry. It is a part of his life, not an embellishment laid on from without. When he comes to express his experience in words, the expression is as spontaneous, as harmonious, as full of personality, as is Life itself.

All this is abundantly illustrated in the work which the poets of the Negro race have produced. The poetry of James Weldon Johnson, Angelina Grimke, Langston Hughes, Countee Cullen, Claude McKay and many others conforms in the highest degree to Milton's rule for great poetry, that it must be "simple, sensuous and passionate." The images are vivid and full of color; they express the personal sorrows, hopes and aspirations of the poet, transfigured by imagination and given universal human significance. They have the emotional harmony, the rhythmic surge, the poignancy and rapture which are the authentic note of poetic inspiration. In the work of the Negro novelists at its best, the same vivid realism is combined with imaginative vision. The modern literary movement among the Negroes is rapidly advancing, and, in conjunction with the new interest in Negro sculpture and music, is undoubtedly the chief agent in making the Negro aware of his actual spiritual stature. When this consciousness is fully spread through his own race and the race of his oppressors, the Negro will be assured of the high place he deserves in American civilization.

* Address delivered at the Woman's Faculty Club, Columbia University, New York, March 26, 1926.

The Negro Spirituals and American Art

By LAURENCE BUERMEYER

IN his book, "A Modern Symposium," Mr. Lowes Dickinson makes one of his speakers explain the emotional poverty of American life and literature by their lack of any profound or deeply felt religious experience. Religion in America, he says, has been chiefly a matter of custom and social respectability, a guarantee of right conduct, not a central and dominating interest which organized the individual's personality as a whole. The reason for this has been that Americans, as a people, came to the battle with nature equipped with the knowledge and technical skill developed through long centuries in Europe. They began where Europe left off: hence the impact of natural forces could be met with weapons which made victory a foregone conclusion. Americans, never having known utter helplessness, have never known real fear and have never had to seek supernatural aid in an hour of bitter extremity. Individual exceptions to this rule, of course, there have been, but the national consciousness has always felt itself prepared to vanquish nature by natural means, its disposition has been practical and optimistic, it has not known terror and despair, and it has therefore missed the fulness of religious experience which, for example, the Jews and the early Christians possessed.

This statement, true as it may be of the dominant race in America, has assuredly no application to an important part of the American people—the Negro race. No people has ever been more wholly at the mercy of circumstance than were the slaves who in the Seventeenth and Eighteenth Centuries were brought from Africa and settled upon the plantations of the South. Unorganized, hopelessly illiterate, snatched from their own civilization and introduced into a society completely alien and radically hostile to them, they had and could hope to have no real control over their destinies. They had no instruments for making their will prevail over the forces of their environment, and no idea how such instruments might be found. The Jews, during their exile in Egypt or their Babylonian captivity, were not more helpless or more in need of inner consolation and sustenance than the Negro slaves. And for the Negroes, as for the Jews, light in the darkness was found in a supernatural religion, a scheme of things unseen but profoundly real, which corrected the injustices of the visible world and compensated the disinherited for what they lacked in the realm of material things. The Negroes thus found in religion something more than an assistance in practical and wordly success.

Although the religion of the Negroes was Christian in name, it had scarcely anything in common with the hard-headed, prudential Calvinism of the native American tradition. It was less legalistic; it had substantially no intellectual content; it was an affair of the heart and not of the mind. Like the Catholic religion, it provided a large place for ritual, for religious drama, but, unlike the Catholic, its ritual was one in which all could participate. It belonged to its members without exception, not primarily or peculiarly to the clergy. It was also distinctively racial, in that many of its customs were taken over bodily from the ancient tribal religions of Africa and were purely primitive and pagan. Free from any ecclesiastical authority, it was able to develop into a form precisely adjusted to the emotional needs of its congregations; there was no inflexible past to lay a dead hand upon its natural growth. Hence participation in it was spontaneous, whole-hearted and whole-souled, free from perfunctory observance of rules obeyed without personal conviction. In a word, it expressed the whole personality of the Negroes as orthodox Christianity never expressed the whole personality of the whites. Consequently, it flowered in an art which was human and personal as no other American art has ever been. This art was the music and poetry of the "Spirituals."

Recent investigation has made it clear that the long delay in appreciation of the Spirituals, the failure of critics to recognize their importance as a distinctive and authentic art form has been due to their fundamental musical quality.[*] In European music, melody is the essential, dominating principle. Harmony and rhythm are secondary to melody. A composition is primarily a theme, and everything else is subsidiary to thematic development. But in Negro music the ground plan, the first principle, is the rhythmic organization, and both melody and harmony are secondary to this. Hence, though the themes of European music at its best are more varied and distinguished than those of Negro music, Negro rhythms are much the more complicated, richer, and more moving. The distinctive quality, the true expressiveness of Negro music is lost to anyone who has ears only for melodic charm and the listener who has not learned to seek out the rhythmic scheme, and to vibrate in unison with it, cannot participate in the experience which it provides. The general absence, in those whose musical education is of the conventional pattern, of such habits of attention, has been fatal to a just comprehension of the Negro Spirituals. Their significance, the wealth of experience, both religious and aesthetic, which they contain have never been grasped by the American consciousness or incorporated in the American tradition.

Had it been so understood and assimilated, the indictment of American art and civilization quoted above would have been vastly less justified. It can scarcely be denied that American intelligence has

---

[*] See James Weldon Johnson, Preface to "The Book of American Negro Spirituals," The Viking Press, 1925.

been predominantly calculating and unimaginative, that "intellectual" has been too often synonymous with "cerebral," that there has been no deep fund of experience for American art to draw upon. In consequence, in spite of an individualism which has often been stridently self-assertive, American self-expression usually seems shallow and personal individuality rare. American art, in other words, has been in the main a rather feeble and savorless echo of European art, not growing out of the soil of na-

BUSHONGO - BALUBA
14th Century

tional life, but transplanted from abroad and kept alive in a hot-house. American architecture, American music, American painting and sculpture, and the greater part of American literature—in a word, all the expressions of the "genteel tradition" have been an imitation of European models. Our only important indigenous art has been without influence and recognition, partly because of misunderstanding, partly because of race prejudice.

It is, or should be, a commonplace that individual self-expression is impossible to anyone who has not assimilated a tradition. Assimilation of a tradition is not the same thing as imitation of a model; it involves living through the experience of which the tradition is an outgrowth. It must therefore develop out of roots which go down into the deeper soil of experience, of common activities inter-related at many points and embracing the inarticulate and unrationalized parts of the personality as well as the superficially conscious parts. It must, in other words, have primitive elements, and it is precisely in these primitive elements that the art of the Spirituals is richest. Though anonymous, they were, of course, written and composed by individuals, but the individuality of their authors is submerged in the collective spirit which they express. This does not mean that they are stereotyped or conventional, but only that their burden is the tribulations, hopes and joys which a whole people have in common, not the particular purposes or aspirations by which one man is distinguished from another. They are the cry of a race asking to be led out of captivity, finding solace in protesting against the cruelty of the oppressor, or in dwelling in fancy upon the freedom, the joys of possession and accomplishment of which the race as a whole is deprived. ("Go down, Moses, way down in Egypt land, tell ole Pharoah to let my people go," "Were you there when they crucified my Lord?" "Sometimes I feel like an eagle in de air," "All God's chillun got shoes.") Like all oppressed peoples, they are too much absorbed in their common woes to be much concerned, or, indeed, to be conscious of the hardships incidental to individual temperament or character; there is no protest of the individual against the customs or ideals of the group. Indeed, separation of any sort from the group is excessively hard to bear and is an occasion for lament. ("I couldn't hear nobody pray.") The voice of a Voltaire, an Ibsen or a Nietzsche would be as incongruous in the Spirituals as it would be in the Iliad. This primitiveness is genuine; it is no self-conscious homesickness for the primitive like the worship of "nature" in Rousseau or Chateaubriand. The only approach to it in American art is the poetry of Walt Whitman, but unlike "Leaves of Grass" it appealed to and was enjoyed by those whose lives it celebrated: Whitman's vogue was among the over-civilized.

It is obviously impossible to find in the Spirituals the expression of a complete or rounded experience of life. They contain not a vestige of reflection, of the "wonder" out of which grows the intellectual life. The Negro world was "human, all-too-human"; even when all allowances are made for their conditions of life, the total absence of one of the characteristic human interests points to a deficiency in experience. How much this is a question of inherent quality of mind is a question doubtless unanswerable, but the defect does not in any case impair the value of Negro music for American art as it exists. Interest in the general, the universal

(Continued on page 167)

The Negro Spirituals and American Art

(Continued from page 159)

(and the practical is a form of the general), whatever its importance for a well-balanced culture, readily slips into a deficient realization of the sensuous, into a preoccupation with bleak abstractions. This the Negro has entirely escaped, and in escaping it he has qualified himself to bring to America the aesthetic contribution which is more imperatively needed than any other.

In the Spirituals the words sung, if considered apart from the music, are likely to seem trite, sometimes baldly prosaic, and almost always destitute of the magic of phrase which we expect from poetry of the first order. It must be remembered, however, that the words were no more intended to stand by themselves than are the words in an opera libretto, which invariably, even in the best of operas, seem thin and prosaic if they are read simply as poetry. If words and music are to be united in a single whole, neither can be self-sufficient; too weighty a content in either leaves too little attention for the other. It is almost inconceivable that the last scene of "Anthony and Cleopatra," the opening of the third book of "Paradise Lost," or the "Ode to a Nightingale" should be set to music, or that words should be sung to the Eroica Symphony. The Spirituals, indeed, are more even than a union of words and music, they contain elements from the dance as well. Time was beaten to them by the whole body, by the head as well as by the hands and feet. They are, in the literal physical sense, extremely moving. They thus engaged all the activities of the personality and so represent a very highly integrated art.

Not only is the art of the Spirituals highly integrated, it is integrated, musically, at a very high level. The rhythms are of an extremely complex and moving order, and the sense displayed for counterpoint is also very considerable. The contrapuntal effects, unfortunately, are largely lost in the printed and published versions of the Spirituals, and they disappear almost entirely when the songs are attempted by white singers. They depend partly upon traditions of singing which have never been really mastered, except by the Negroes themselves, partly upon the Negro gift for improvisation, which makes each rendering of the songs, by competent Negro musicians, a distinct experience or creation. The same gift for improvisation appears in the extremely rich and varied harmonic effects, scarcely suggested by the written notes, which a Negro choir is able to introduce. The real importance of the Spirituals, their extraordinary musical richness and emotional conviction, can only be appreciated when they are sung by a Negro chorus of the first rank. If they are sung as solos, or in arrangements made by those whose musical perceptions are controlled by the conventional European standards, the greater part of their distinctive quality disappears. But at their best, as sung, for example, by the chorus of the Bordentown Manual Training and Industrial School for Negroes, under the exceedingly skillful direction of Mr. Frederick J. Work, they reveal reaches and depths of musical and human experience unexplored by the art of any other race.

EDITORIAL/

THE art of the African like the African himself has needed interpreters. Not that it lacks the power to make itself felt; the penetration of its stark force has been inescapable. It has required a sort of rationalization for minds set to the familiar patterns of art. This has required, especially in this country, a daring aesthetic faith. The interest created recently by the Blondiau-Theatre Arts Exhibit and the prompt success of the plan, sponsored by Alain Locke, to place the nucleus of a permanent African art collection in Harlem, are evidences of an overcoming of the first shock of unfamiliarity, in those circles a few paces removed from the artists and connoisseurs. It is appropriate that this issue which again devotes many of its pages to Negro art, should be dedicated in a spirit of appreciation, to the Barnes Foundation, the institution which has, almost from the first discovery of this new art vein, and against a vast and stubborn scepticism in America, sensed its vital force, collected it, and made it intelligible to lovers of art.

More About African Art

The recent volume *Primitive Negro Sculpture* by Thomas Munro and Paul Guillaume, bases its interpretations upon the Foundation's collection, and, perhaps in greater degree than is evident, is guided by the clarifying objectivity of Dr. Barnes himself.

II.

The cultural values of this art have been immense. Interest in it, for example has brought interest in the subjects, the Negroes themselves; the cultures and intelligences out of which they came. A revision of concepts about the African has been forced; their unintelligible rites assume the dignity of a meaningful even if strange culture. To any one familiar with the depressing arguments which have had their way with contemporary Negroes because of an assumed recordless past, the value of such an influence is apparent.

On the other hand, there is no more convincing evidence of the cultural assimilation of American Negroes than in their own response to this art in sections remote from authentic enthusiasms. The shock of its bold self-assertion, if anything, is even greater with them. Nor is this utterly surprising. The Negro art belongs to its own setting, historical and environmental. The racial link of temperament with the past and with Africa is yet debatable even among the most zealous students.

III.

In the approach to Negro plastics, as has been pointed out in the volume referred to, totally different aesthetic qualities are sought for enjoyment. Where Greek statues seek "an ideal of perfect human form," the Negro plastics seek effects "in shapes and designs of line, plane and mass." The human body, dissociated into its parts is given new creation,

new and pleasing rhythms and harmony of parts. There is, thus, an infinity of forms possible,—a challenge to creativeness. The three dementionality of the sculpture, the startling newness and exhaustlessness of the geometric designs, the emotional force and steady light of intelligence here displayed explain the power of these creations over an important sector of the art life of Europe, and a growing sector in America. The work of the inimitable Winold Reiss and his brilliant Negro pupil Aaron Douglas has done much to suggest the wealth of this source.

For a great part of the new material of this issue on the subject we acknowledge our indebtedness to Mr. Harry Alan Potamkin of Philadelphia, editor of the *Guardian*, of Philadelphia, a student of this art and of its influence; to Mr. Lawrence Potamkin we are likewise indebted for the translations which appear.

The Art of the Congo

By MELVILLE J. HERSKOVITS

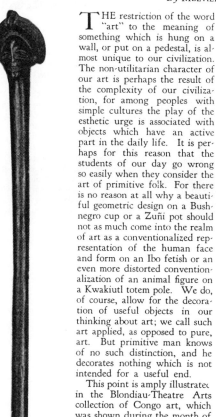

*Bushango
Chief's Sceptre*

THE restriction of the word "art" to the meaning of something which is hung on a wall, or put on a pedestal, is almost unique to our civilization. The non-utilitarian character of our art is perhaps the result of the complexity of our civilization, for among peoples with simple cultures the play of the esthetic urge is associated with objects which have an active part in the daily life. It is perhaps for this reason that the students of our day go wrong so easily when they consider the art of primitive folk. For there is no reason at all why a beautiful geometric design on a Bush-negro cup or a Zuñi pot should not as much come into the realm of art as a conventionalized representation of the human face and form on an Ibo fetish or an even more distorted conventionalization of an animal figure on a Kwakiutl totem pole. We do, of course, allow for the decoration of useful objects in our thinking about art; we call such art applied, as opposed to pure, art. But primitive man knows of no such distinction, and he decorates nothing which is not intended for a useful end.

This point is amply illustrated in the Blondiau-Theatre Arts collection of Congo art, which was shown during the month of February at the Neumann Galleries. Here we had a large collection, brought together by a man who has sustained his interest in the art of the native Africans for over twenty-five years,—a collection, which, representative of numerous tribes living in the basin of the Congo river, comprised almost a thousand pieces. Masks, cups, fetishes, stools, throwing-knives, spears, woven raphia-fibre and grass mats, drums, horns, canes, musical instruments,—all of them showing the esthetic expression operative in their makers; all of them forming some integral part of the life of the people who made them.

THE media represented in the pieces displayed were wood, iron and ivory, besides the woven objects mentioned. And one must emphasize this weaving because of the fact that it influences the art of the region so profoundly. It is a well-known fact that very often the patterns which result from restrictions imposed by a given medium which is worked will influence an entire art of a people. This is particularly true among one tribe of the Congo which is perhaps best known for the consummate artistry of its products. This tribe is the Bushongo, and among them a very typical series of patterns are woven and embroidered in raphia fibre cloths. This pattern is then carried over into wood-working, into the decoration of iron objects, and into ivory carvings. It is purely geometrical, and is often found in the same piece with realistic designs. There were a number of lovely examples of this technique. The cups which are illustrated here show two of these adapted patterns. But the adaptations are not made blindly, and you will notice, if you look closely, that the designs, instead of being transferred simply as a copy, are fitted to the curve of the cups so that a dynamic quality is given to the result.

It is true that the best examples of the curiously conventionalized heads and bodies which one too often thinks of as the African art is found to no great extent in the region which was represented by the Blondiau collection. And yet, when one regarded the beautifully finished cups in the form of the human head which formed a part of the collection, where the feel for mass was utilized so skilfully in the carving of the cups, or when one looked at the Warega miniature faces cut from ivory, the realization soon came that the Congo native has a feeling for plastic design that is not greatly inferior to that of his West African brother. Such pieces were, naturally, the ones which caught the European-trained eye first. They are most nearly like what is usually thought of as "African art," and they are nearest the kind of thing we label "art" and place on pedestals. But they had their use for the people

Bushongo Geometric Pattern Vases

who made them, no less than had the cloths woven from raphia.

The feeling for decorative design was also shown in the throwing knives which were to be seen. Particularly the ceremonial axes with handles of wood or bronze demonstrated this deep artistry that characterizes everything which comes from this region. The placing of two or three miniature faces on the

Bakuba Ointment Box

sides of the flattened iron rods which hold the blade itself to the handle struck one as effective in the ex-treme. This use of such faces as a decorative de-sign is, of course, very common in this part of Africa. And they are much more perfect than the larger forms in which human representations are carved. The masks which were shown exhibited neither the feeling nor the technical perfection displayed by the best examples of West African masks. This was, however, partly due to the collection itself, for I have seen masks from the Congo which are wrought with superb feeling for the medium and consummate ability to work in it. But it was in such small deco-rative detail as the head carved on the tip of a man-dolin which was exhibited, or the one placed at the upper end of a chief's cane, which is illustrated here, that the finest examples of anthropomorphic carving appear.

NOT all the pieces shown, of course, were up to the standard of the ones I have mentioned. There was a great deal of material not as fine as these other pieces, and many which held interest more purely ethnographic than artistic. But this was all to the good, and the right idea for a collection

of primitive art. It was apparent that for M. Blon-diau, there are no labels as to what constitutes "art."

Bushongo Ceremonial Headcup

And it is because of this that we were privileged to see the artistic spirit of these Congo peoples at its freest, expressing itself in all media and in the realm comprising the only realm in which primitive art can be understood or appreciated; that of the entire life of the people.

FRONT AND REAR

VIEW OF

THE STATUE OF

MIKOPE MBULA

FROM THE

COLLECTION OF

TERVUEREN MUSEUM

207

African Plastic in Contemporary Art

By HARRY ALAN POTAMKIN

THE painters were the first of contemporary artists to utilize the plastic of the primitive Africans. A number of them, particularly Modigliani, played with its forms in their exercises in sculpture, but these exercises were generally not for the purposes of sculpture but as practice in forms to be carried over into painting. Modigliani was captured by the linear structure of the African masks and statues. In his few sculptures he indicates the detail in the African technique that interested him most, building on the vertical. The face is modelled to the straight line, the nose linear to accentuate the line. Fundamentally, this is more picturesque than sculpturesque and Modigliani carried the linear structure over to his painting. Frivolous observers will sometimes belittle Modigliani for his limited scope, although he has painted on the elliptical and circular pattern, as well as vertical. But even in the vertical he was able to make variations complete in themselves. This is a greater feat than working in many separate forms. This was Modigliani's idiom, in combination with color, and he worked within the limitations he set himself. Philosophically he was nearer to the African sculptor than any other European artist. His Italian origin is evinced in the slight angles he gave to the heads of his subjects, an Italian grace that goes back to the earliest painters. Also in unblended color is he related to his Italian origins, as contrasted with the color mixtures of a Pascin. Modigliani's first paintings from the African are caryatids patterned directly on the Congo stool—and basin-caryatids. He later adjusts the technique of the drawn line or the circular pattern to studies of sitting, then reclining, nudes.

The attenuated line supplied the idiom for Wilhelm Lehmbruck, a German sculptor, whose long kneeling figures are modelled on a slow-moving line. Other slow-moving lines play into the central structural line, even to the lines of the fingers playing into the hand. The structure is something like that of a tree, twigs, branches and boughs flowing into and out of the central trunk. Of course, Lehmbruck establishes definite intervals in his radiations of lines, and this interval of line in variation (in its angle, reference to the mass, etc.) is rhythm.

Among the first to see the possibilities of the African compositions as modern method was Pablo Picasso. Before 1907 Picasso was influenced variously by the Italians, El Greco, Toulouse-Lautrec, Cezanne, and others, who called his attention to the problem of formal design and relationships of fundamental forms. In 1907 he encountered the Negro mask which gave him an immediate direction. The first inferences Picasso drew from the mask indicate his quick grasp of visual essentials, although in his first pictorialization of them he is simply duplicating these essentials, so that his drawings resemble caricatures. Following the progress from these drawings of 1907, one observes the successive developments in the application of these inferences, the new combinations of the essentials, the crossing with the infer-

ences from other plastics, and their induction into the more mathematic cubism. It is wrong to assume that Picasso "outgrew" African art. The assumption is based on snobbery. Picasso is an artist of powerful synthetizing mind and artistry. He does not exclude any contributing experience nor withhold from any esthetic contact; he fuses his intimacies into an expression upon which he places his personal imprint.

Giorgio de Chirico will use egg-shaped stylized heads (African derivation) upon a mechanistic torso draped in Greek folds. But the parts are not fused as are Picasso's. The separation of entities in Picasso's case has been only one step in the completion of the painting; the final painting is a re-establishment of a new totality with these separate entities—a fundamental African principle. Chirico's basic technique of disrelation is dogmatic of Italian futurism and French super-realism, but he avoids final dissociation by placing the various parts in a relation to space. Space unites the separate entities by virtue of a common relationship to it. Chirico by this visual factor has been rescued from the anti-plastic of futurism and the indirection of super-realism.

The egg-shaped head of a Chirico philosopher is found also in the egg-shaped forms or arc-forms in general of Brancusi who followed the implication of African art to its surd. Constantine Brancusi's conception of pure art is the complete objectivity of the artist. The material shall determine procedure, the artist may not superimpose his idea or purpose upon the material. The artist must call forth the discoverable qualities of the material, the grain in the marble, the lustre, etc., the pure form, which in marble is circular. Brancusi opposes the tenet of transcending the medium (yet he does transcend in many instances); he is a minimizer of the medium: the finished sculpture is never (he would have it) anything else but the medium.

Raymond-Duchamp-Villon stylized the dissociated bodily parts in curved masses that interrelate into a fluid composition. The feet are solid bases like those of the African sculptures, but by the raising of one leg a delicacy of grace is achieved instead of a stationary solidity. The figure is seated in relaxation, a superb achievement with a stylized, abstract pattern. (It is probably from Duchamp-Villon's sculptures that the new store-window lay figures have been taken.)

The principle of formal design as expressed in Negro art has been most emphatically used in sculpture by Jacques Lipschutz. He has made use of the rhythmic alternation of contrasting forms which served so well in the application of the principles of cubism. Lipschutz more than any other sculptor accepted and utilized the surface inscription as part of sculptural design, a device I find unacceptable as sculpture. Today he is modelling sculptures in the flat, not reliefs, for depth is present in the relationship between the planes, but sculptures, like unleavened bread.

"Relationship between the planes" recalls the development of another relationship, the hollow-ridge formula for forehead-and-eyes, utilized by numerous sculptors: Jacob Epstein, Pablo Manes, Ossip Zadkine, Chana Orloff, etc. The constructivists, Alexander Archipenko and Rudolf Belling, after utilizing the formula, extend its implication to satisfy their mechanistic concept and excavate the hollow entirely, so that air-space is part of the composition; a sculptural attempt to suggest the fourth dimension, it has been suggested. Belling has followed the stylistic principle to build a human portrait on the basis of machine parts and forms, an amazing performance. Archipenko extended the African composite sculpture (wood and glass, wood and mother of pearl, wood and paint, etc.) in his sculpto-painting. The constructivists and German expressionists have made composite uses of various domestic and other contemporary materials: hair combs and tramway transfers; as well as celluloid and glass sculptures in which the architectural principle and the principle of air-as-sculptural-space are enacted. Among the constructivists, Willy Baumeister builds up his forms (in painting) ovally. But he is not entirely removed from an attempt at resemblances. Chirico's egg-shaped philosopher has his countenance lined abstractly, Baumeister's faces maintain the relationship of features.

Henri Matisse, one of the most important influences on contemporary painting, was himself influenced by the linear stylization of Negro sculpture which, however, served to give exactness to two influences of greater potence with Matisse: Persian caligraphic art, Hindu sculpture. His use of African plastic, working on the caligraphy of Persian art, carries on the tradition of Modigliani. Marie Laurencin further reduces visual depth, making linear statements (see especially her charcoal drawings) after the African. Irene Lagut stylizes her forms linearly, her dog a series of curves like a Dahomey relief.

Ossip Zadkine uses the solid mass in his sculpture, and stylizes the face to the extent of delineating the nose by drawing the line, bringing into sculpture Matisse caligraphy, a dubious transaction. Chana Orloff undulates the massed thighs once, lightening the solid weight. Otherwise the mass head relates to the mass thigh much as it does in a Zadkine sculpture. There is very little that is organic here.

This brings us to Henri Gaudier-Breszka. I believe Gaudier, who was killed in his early twenties in the War, would, had he lived, have indicated the finest utilization and conversion of the African plastic. Much superior to his elder colleague, Jacob Epstein, he could follow a tendency to its basis and there attack it. The mass structure of African sculpture, delineation, geometric contrasts, he at once apprehended and analyzed. He had come to the conclusion before his death that sculpture—particularly contemporary sculpture — should be organic. It would be worth a great deal to us to know what he would have done in relating the organic of sculpture to the abstract mind.

Perhaps the answer is in the sculpture of Gaston Lachaise, a Frenchman resident in America. La-

chaise's bronzes are built with small mass head to large mass body, the dissociated parts—component circles—are joined into a total organism. The dissociation takes place within the already established organism. Soutine effects a similar totality in painting, although less clearly and more thickly than does Lachaise.

African sculpture reached Germany alter than it did France. It received its most vivid stimulus in Carl Einstein's collection and book Negerplastik, 1915. But the Germans, outside of a Lehmbruck or a Belling, did very little original with it. Karl Schmidt-Rottluff, a typical instance, reproduced in wood and painting the raw block form of the least attractive examples of the sculpture. It has served the stolid primitivism of a Kirchner, but whatever of value in African sculpture the Germans found was carried over from the French.

There are others who have made use of the African plastic: Henri Laurens, Leon Borget (an almost unknown French sculptor), John Mowbray-Clarke, André Derain, Marcel Gromaire, Wyndham Lewis, Duncan Grant, Dobson, Bolin, Juan Gris, Fernand Leger, La Fauconnier, Kvapil, etc., the list in indefinite. Derain, a singular artist, employed the elongation of the face and bodily parts and the reduction to the geometric outline; Gromaire built group portraits on the perpendicular and rectangular; Gris dissociated contributing details in contrast and repetition with exquisite sensitivity; Leger satisfied the dissociation in a unifying mechanico-abstract pattern; etc. Negro plastic enhanced the purist values in the various esthetic dogmas: Cubism, Purism, Fauvism, Synchronism, Vorticism (Wyndham Lewis and Gaudier), Expressionism, Futurism, Dadaism, Superrealism, ad infinitum. It served through the agency of the artists mentioned, Archipenko, Duchamp-Villon, Brancusi especially, to revive the derivative crafts: of the lay figure for store displays, fabrics, costumes (Bakst), women's fashions (Paul Poiret), etc.; illustration of books and magazines, caricature (see the work of a Covarrubias), posters. Strangely however the initial stimulator in African art was not carried over to its most obvious uses: the African mask has been little used in the theatre and dance. This is chiefly due to the continual misstatement of the means of the theatre and dance; their practitioners have preferred the oriental mask of characteristic to the African mask of design. Although in at least one foreign school of the theatre, masks have been made on the basis of plastic design from the conventional papier mache used in the typical mask.

The African instinct was most successful in wood. The few examples of stone sculpture show no great understanding of the possibilities of stone. Brass and copper were much better understood by the medieval Jewish craftsman of Russia and Poland who hammered the design into the metal. The Africans cut their masks from the copper, attaching frequently strips to the outlines of the excavations. Their interest was in the use rather than in the material. Leon Borget is one French artist who has worked in brass (has just begun to do so) from the African method. (Derain's masks are hammered.)

Borget has attached, in his first experiment, loosely and removably a black sheetiron forehead to the yellow brass of the countenance, accentuating the hollow-ridge contrast.

These notes must not be taken as more than fragmentary. I have sought to isolate a few of the African threads in a few of the artists who have, mainly consciously, worked the threads into their work. I have also wished to indicate how the principles of African plastic served to augment current tendencies and concentrate the esthetic concern upon the strictly inherent. There have been multitudes of artists working unconsciously with these African forms, some borrowing matter-of-factly from the original contemporary utilizers of this old art. These borrowers have frequently misunderstood the import of the thing they were duplicating, because they could not see the structural basis upon which the final complicated design was built. Contrary to Willard Huntington Wright, it was not the minor artist who was captured by the art of the barbarians, but the major artist who recognized the major argument of his art. I do not believe that much more can be learned from it, but I am certain its possible combinations have not been exhausted. And it will do the artist considerable good to refer to this art directly for its demonstration of an esthetic enactment, rather than forever record it thrice-removed and inaccurately, like a rumor.

THE NEGRO IN DRAMATIC ART

RAYMOND O'NEIL

EVELYN PREER, THE GIFTED NEGRO ACTRESS, IN "SALOME"

THERE are two peoples in the modern world possessing in marked degree fresh and strong potentialities for artistic creation—the Russians among Europeans and the Negroes among the conglomeration of racial and national groups which go to make up the United States.

The similarity between the gifts and accomplishments of these two peoples is striking and easily endures a severe scrutiny. They are most pronounced in folk expression. The Russians possess dance forms which in variety and expressiveness are equalled in the contemporary world only by those of the Negro. There is wanting only some outstanding synthetic and sophisticated intelligence to carry the Negro's dance forms to the height of artistic development to which the Ballet Russe carried those of their own land.

In folk music both peoples have expressed themselves in manners which are unrivalled in their diversity and in the poignancy and truthfulness of their interpretation of human emotions, from reckless jollity to most tragic sorrow.

Another resemblance between Russian and Negro is discernible in the effort each makes to decorate his living quarters. Those

who know the carved and brightly painted exteriors of houses of the Russian peasant or of the small town dweller are at no loss to understand and appreciate the spirit that has led the Negro to paint in bright colors and decorate with vivid curtains the little vegetable stands, soft drink parlors and barbecue restaurants he has built in the poorer sections of Negro quarters. Wherever he has had to take the white man's expressionless and ugly dwelling or store he has generally let bad enough alone but whenever he has had the opportunity of building for himself a small dwelling or business place there has almost invariably gone into it an original feeling for form and decoration which is both charming and hopeful.

Yet it is in the theater where the Negro and the Russian show their most pronounced artistic kinship. Strangely enough it needed the performances of the Moscow Art Theater Company in the United States to emphasize this fact and to point the way to a still more significant conclusion which is that the resemblance between the Negro and the Russian in artistic expression is based upon an almost identical attitude towards life and a sensuous manner of living it.

211

By means of the Moscow Art Theater the Russians have brought the ugly duckling of theatrical representation to a degree of fidelity towards actual life and to a degree of beauty that no other national group has attained. Even American critics have penetrated to this fact. They have written thousands of columns in praise of this company in which are set forth scores of ingenious hypotheses in an effort to explain the freshness, richness and vitality of the Russian theater's presentations.

Yet not a commentator has touched upon the basic and simple reason which is the Russian's sensuous acceptance of life. For him all the senses exist to be exercised, delectified and developed. His nature is warm and his emotions are many, varied and responsive. Always is he saying "yea" to life sensuously, even to the paradoxical extent of finding pleasure in tears, sorrow and the contemplation of death.

With all these qualities the Negro is likewise richly endowed. He too is gifted with a sensuous nature. He loves life and he lives life with the sensuous and the emotional parts of him constantly exposed to it. As with the Russians these sensuous qualities are the springs of the Negro's creative potentialities. Developed, refined and brought under a constantly more subtle and sophisticated intellectual control they predicate possibilities in creation and expression that give one a warm joy merely to contemplate.

TWO STRIKING POSES OF MISS PREER

It might be shown with not a great amount of difficulty that nations and peoples have created beauty in direct proportion to their capacity for extracting sensuous enjoyment from life. Those people who have not been gifted with responsive sensuous natures pretty generally have had a sad art and a still sadder life.

Consider for a moment the plight of the non-Negro American. Through the greater part of his national history he has been the object of a steadily played stream of restrictions and prohibitions which have had as their object the paralyzing and extirpation of his sensuous nature and emotions. Being mostly Anglo-Saxon, hence possessing sensuous and emotional qualities none too robust at the best, he surrendered to the assault upon him with scarcely a protest. The result has been a nation of individuals who receive less fun, pleasure and inspiration from clouds, flowers and birds than any other group of civilized beings.

In his own image the good one hundred per cent American has set up his art. By an elaborate system of automatic precautions he has seen to it that it shall not return to him more of emotion than he himself possesses or that unexpectedly it shall not impinge upon a sense or feeling which may be merely sleeping. Thus it comes that in his teeming land of plenty the normal white, Protestant, Nordic American lives without a music of his own, without more than occasional pieces of painting or sculpture, with a literature just emerging from the nursery, and with a stage reflecting a life as hollow and painful as a drilled-out aching tooth. Frequently he sends up his voice to the effect that as soon as he is through with this "development-of-a-country business", he will turn his attention to art. Certainly, he suggests, with a note of pride and an overtone of contempt in his voice, a working people cannot be expected to produce an art as they labor.

In this he is unaware that another people have been working at his side in the same land, who, through suffering a heavy handicap of political and economic disabilities, have been producing an art as they worked. And here again is a pleasant resemblance between the Russian and the American Negro. They have both dwelled and worked in areas undeveloped or in the process of development and as they have worked they have taken time to gaze upon clouds, to listen to birds, to smell flowers and to regard the bodies and souls about them. And doing this they have been impelled to sing, and dance, and play and in this spontaneous glorification of the senses and the objects the senses apprehended they have created an art, each in his own image.

These arts are twins in that they are rich and warm and sensuous, leaving none of the senses neglected. They are lithe and soft and round and gentle. Understanding much, they forgive everything that is human. They spring from the earth, a well manured earth, and hold their blossoms straight up into the sky. They are wistful, tender, straightforward as a child and they are robust, passionate, sensuous as a youth. And always they are human, all too human.

Negro and Russian arts possess these qualities because their creators possess them. That ability sensuously to comprehend life and to enjoy in and for itself the act of living has been the basis of

IRA ALDRICH
A Great Actor of the 19th Century

Russian vitality and richness in the arts and has been the basis of what the Negro so far has created. Upon it can be forecast his pregnant future. An Evelyn Preer and a Charles Gilpin, to consider only the theatre, are no mere accidents. They are the product of a mode of living and are the precursors, undoubtedly, of many more distinguished products of that mode.

As the Russians guarded their arts as much as they could from Westernization, so will the Negro have to guard his from one hundred per cent Americanization. Particularly must he be on his guard against the white friends of his art who will urge its development in the direction of their prejudiced imagination. A very great advantage which Negro art has enjoyed has been white contempt or indifference towards it, qualities which are rapidly changing now to interest and to eventual commercial and intellectual exploitation. Many people who love art for the strength it gives to man are hoping that the Negro will be able to resist this evil white pressure with the same flexible strength with which he has resisted so much other evil from the same source. For there is nothing more precious in America today than the creative potentialities that the Negro indubitably possesses.

213

THE THEATRE

THE NEGRO IN THE FIELD OF DRAMA

By Rowena Woodham Jelliffe

EIGHT years ago, when I first became associated with a Negro Little Theatre group, the attitude of the group itself was about as follows. All the players wanted to play leading roles, it was almost impossible to do a play which had in it the character of a maid or any person of lowly state because no one would play such parts, the part of a villain was popular so long as he was not a Negro villain, and every one wanted a part which allowed them to wear pretty clothes and appear to good advantage. The audience attending and supporting the players demanded something at which they could laugh, and refused to pay more than twenty-five cents for that privilege. In other words the actor was interested in drama because it gave an opportunity for pleasant exhibitionism and the audience only when it told a good joke.

Both actors and audience were emphatically opposed to Negro plays and thought them highly degrading to their race. There have come amazing changes, the group leading the way and the audience lagging some little distance behind on the new course but nevertheless following. Three years ago the group chose to try a Negro play. We were praised and condemned for doing it, but somehow the praise rang louder in our ears than the damning. And so we continued, with the result that our Negro plays became extremely popular and brought a largely increased audience which is now about half colored and half white.

I believe that in Negro life and tradition we have the richest ingredient in our national drama both as material for the writer and medium for the actor. The objection on the part of the Negro to the prevalence of the folk play in the field of Negro drama is, I think, based on a misunderstanding of the present flare for the Negro play. White America, becoming pressed for spiritual elbow room and weary of its mechanical way of life, has turned with genuine appreciation to the drama of the folk level. That the Negro happens most admirably to supply that need, both as source material and interpreter, is a fortunate happenstance for the Negro race. That the present flare bespeaks directly a primary interest in the Negro as such is not true. White America going to the theatre would be no more interested in Negro life on the sophisticated level than in their own life on the same level. Certain it is that as a result of the Negro folk play there has come an incalculable increase of appreciation of the Negro as an artist, and consequently a new social appraisal.

Of the three classes of theatricals: musical comedy, professional drama and the tributary theatre, it seems to me that at the present time musical comedy is the hopelessly decrepit member of the trio. Its stock has run so thin that one wonders that it has the audacity to lift its head at all. Only the unfailing vitality of its actors gives it sufficient strength to sing its several pitiful swan songs. Surely the Negro has something better to offer in the field of musical comedy. I look for it to burst forth in some new and far more vital form. This may be the next significant development. The professional drama is in a most wholesome state; vital, strong and unafraid. But that the professional drama has to do with the Negro at all today is probably due to having tested its strength and its beauty in the tributary theatre. The tributary theatre, daring to experiment, should have the credit for bringing the Negro play upon the American stage.

The primary consideration of the Negro dramatist and the actor alike should be for the art of the theatre. Sociological considerations should be secondary. Nor should the theatre be considered a medium of propaganda. Undue concern about putting the best racial foot foremost should be forgot. I believe that the Negro artist achieves in the field of drama in about the proportion to which he is able to escape the bonds of race consciousness. Then is he able, having acquired the necessary perspective, to portray and interpret the life and mood of his race beautifully and truly.

Perhaps the chief talent which the Negro actor brings to the art of the theatre is his peculiar quality of motorness, his extraordinary body expressiveness, which more than compensates for the degree of facial expression which is lost to an audience (in comparison with white actors) due to a darker skin coloring. Next in line in his assets I would list his sense of rhythm, manifest in his movement and his diction alike, and his never failing vitality.

The picture building quality of Negro dialect, its rythmic rise and fall, the earthy quality of Negro folk life; these are things with which the writer of Negro plays may work. They are, I believe, rare thread for his fabric. We have probably seen but the beginning of the Negro play.

I have been deeply interested in what the Negro can do with so-called white plays. Such plays as "Sun-Up" and "Icebound" have been most successfully done by Negro groups. These plays, handled by Negro artists, become a new creation, they take on a new and beautiful quality which comes to them from the Negro's particular dramatic stock. I consider this a valuable contribution. In view also of the great common denominator in all folk plays, I believe that folk plays of all groups can be creditably done by any group which can move freely and sincerely in any folk lore.

I expect that more and more we shall see white groups everywhere doing Negro plays wiht some credit. The exchange should be equally valuable when Negroes undertake to interpret the drama of other groups. While it will probably be true that Irish artists can always do Irish plays best and Russians best interpret Russian plays, and Negroes be most convincing in Negro plays, I believe that in the stimulation and versatility which comes from the exchange of dramatic medium, just as the traveler in a foreign country can sometimes see beauty in surroundings to which the native has become dulled, other dramatic gifts may pick up new high lights which native talent fails to catch. This will probably be the opportunity of the tributary and not the professional theatre.

HAS THE NEGRO A PLACE IN THE THEATRE?

By JULES BLEDSOE

THERE has been a steady growth of interest in the Negro in the Theatre. His histrionic ability is being recognized by the powers that be; not because of benevolence, but because the nature of things has decreed that a new element, a new theme be brought into the Theatre to attract the attention of a public that was fast growing weary of certain forms of entertainment.

Writers, novelists, playwrights and producers are just beginning to appreciate the vast and fertile field of drama existent in Negro life.

The Negro's every move is filled with drama from the time of his inception to the grave. Persecutions, economic slavery and hardships of every nature, all these do strike the chords of pity, remorse and sometimes despair in the heart of the Black Man, and at once set his emotional spirit into play; sometimes expressed in the Spiritual Song of sorrow and religious hope and often he is assailed by that type of melancholia that makes the brother break forth in a fit of that "Indigo song", called the "Blues".

Every creature tries to escape its plight by either fighting within or without. The Negro, by swinging the pendulum in the opposite direction. He tries to outrun his shadow by breaking into frenzied laughter, by wild and tempestuous dancing, as exemplified by the "Charleston" and other break-downs, and very often humor comes to his rescue; the kind that would make the very Fates themselves laugh.

All these characteristics are the materia Theatrical; hence the excursion into our habitat for things native and unexplored.

The Negro as an idiom is and has been an always dependable means of sure fire entertainment. Negro ragtime and dance steps have revolutionized the musical comedy and vaudeville stage. (I mean American). His mannerisms and nuances are employed to great advantage. All a mediocre white comedian has to do is blacken his face and at once he becomes a success in mimicry. Jazz is itself a reversion to primitive African rhythms, having been born in and introduced by the American Negro.

I cite all these instances merely to show that the Black Brother has his place and belongs in the Theatre by the process of natural selection. It is gratifying to see a goodly number of intelligent Negroes emerging into this field. For we must prove by the excellence of the many, rather than that of the few, that we as a race "Got Wings" and expect to use them to fly to the heights of histrionic art.

It is up to the few of us that have gotten past the sentinels at the gate, to fling the gates wide open for our successors.

Once the ambitious educated Negro youth turns his steps toward the Theatre as a profession not to be considered too lightly, and revels in it as he does in the professions of Medicine and law; we shall find ourselves able to run the whole gamut of the Theatre and be thoroughly capable of doing the finer things of the stage, whether it be uttering the classic lines of Shakespeare or chanting the masters of song in a manner befitting only the Gods.

THE THEATRE

A CRITICISM OF THE NEGRO DRAMA
As It Relates to the Negro Dramatist and Artist
By EULALIE SPENCE

YES, we have our colored artists. We have our Robeson, Rose McClenndon, our Wilson and various others who have reached an undeniable place of prominence in the realm of the theatre. And we have had our Florence Mills.

Even the most casual theatre-goer to-day is familiar with one or more of these stars in the theatrical firmament. But alas, the same cannot be said of the Negro dramatist.

Negro drama does not of necessity include the work of the Negro dramatist. Strictly speaking, Negro drama is any drama or theatrical production which essays to portray the life of the Negro. Where, then, is the Negro dramatist?

Who are the writers that have provided the vehicle for Gilpin, Robeson, Rose McClenndon and Bledsoe? Frankly, yet reluctantly, too, we may name them, and never a Negro will be found among them. Suppose there had been no *Emperor Jones*, and no *Porgy*; no *In Abraham's Bosom* and no *Show Boat?* What then? Ask the Negro artist, he knows.

Some there are who have shuddered distastefully at these plays; been affronted by Paul Green, degraded by Du Bose Hayward, and misunderstood by Eugene O'Neill. But ask the Negro artist if he is grateful to these writers. He will tell you. And ask the Negro dramatist what he feels about it. If he is forward-thinking, he will admit that these writers have been a great inspiration; that they have pointed the way and heralded a new dawn.

The drama, more particularly, the American drama, is from twenty to thirty years behind the novel and short story in point of subject matter. There is almost no subject to-day that cannot be discussed with the most revolting detail between the covers of a book. If there are any who doubt this, let them read *Home to Harlem* by Claude McKay. Not so with our drama. Here we have elected to be squeamish, and perhaps advisedly so. Nevertheless, this does not imply that the theatre has not made enormous strides ahead. The drama has developed a new technique, new ways and means, a new genius of mechanism and a new direction.

Unfortunately, almost everyone thinks that he can write a play. Writers will grant the poet his form and the novelist his; the essayist his mould and the writer of short stories his. However, when it comes to the play, why—one merely takes one's pen in hand and presto! we have Dialogue! I have seen plays written by our Negro writers with this caption: To Be Read, Not Played!

A play to be read! Why not the song to be read not sung, and the canvas to be described, not painted! To every art it's form, thank God! And to the play, the technique that belongs to it!

Here it is then that our Negro dramatists have failed to reach a larger and more discriminating public. They have labored like the architect who has no knowledge of geometry and the painter who must struggle to evolve the principles of perspective.

May I advise these earnest few—those seekers after light—white lights—to avoid the drama of propaganda if they would not meet with certain disaster? Many a serious aspirant for dramatic honors has fallen by the wayside because he would insist on his lynchings or his rape. The white man is cold and unresponsive to this subject and the Negro, himself, is hurt and humiliated by it. We go to the theatre for entertainment, not to have old fires and hates rekindled.

Of course, if we have a Shaw or a Galsworthy among us, let him wander at will in the more devious by-paths of race dissection. Let him wander wheresoever he will—provided he has no eye for the box-office. For even as far-famed a dramatist as Galsworthy could not keep his recent play, *The Forest,* more than a very limited time on the London stage. Why? It dealt with propaganda, and as beautifully written and staged as it was, it had to be withdrawn.

What, then, is left to the Negro dramatist? Let him portray the life of his people, their foibles, if he will, and their sorrows and ambition and defeats. Oh, yes, let us have all of these, told with tenderness and skill and a knowledge of the theatre and the technique of the times. But as long as we expect our public, white and colored, to support our drama, it were wise to steer far away from the old subjects.

A little more laughter, if you please, and fewer spirituals!

THE THEATRE

By HARRY S. KEELAN

*P*ORGY is the most artistic creation of the Theatre Guild since Molnar's *Liliom*. Both expressed the same theme—the utter hopelessness of a man with ideals. *Porgy*, the play, was beautiful but *Porgy*, the opera, would be unbearably divine. But where would one find a composer? Coleridge Taylor was the only composer of Porgy's race who understood the orchestra; the others, except perhaps Dett, have been content with ballads and a few instrumental compositions.

Lord, I want to be like Jesus in my heart. That should be the theme of the prelude to the opera *Porgy*. Porgy wanted just that. Bess felt this radiant idealism of Porgy's trying to pierce through her outer armor-plated shell of opportunism and materialism which those of her sex, of all races, have evolved in the struggle for existence. For the first time, she lifted her grubbing face from the ground and looked at the stars, without knowing exactly why. *Lord, I want to be like Jesus in my heart.* Along with this theme must be another similar to the Andante from Beethovan's Seventh Symphony, which would express the beauty and majesty of this ideal, and then fade into a minor of its utter hopelessness—because humanity holds him back. That would be the prelude.

The first act must open with Stravinsky at his most fortzando moments—with every instrument in the orchestra at full blast. *Little David, play on your harp. Hallelu-halleluja, Little David play on your harp, hallelu!* Deems Taylor is needed to portray the crap game. He has a great sense of the grotesque and of musical humor, as displayed in the music which accompanies the appearance of the father-in-law in the last act of the "King's Henchman." But there must be a Wagnerian climax, with the orchestra ascending and ascending faster and faster until, with a crash of the percussion instruments, Serena's husband is killed: Silence. Then a long wail, starting in the flutes, coming through the violins, violas, cellos, and dying in the bass viols as the curtain drops.

The second scene. The orchestral theme should be *Listen to the Lambs*. The sympathetic touch of Dvorak is needed—the Andante of the New World Symphony. *O Death, ain't you got no shame?* Stravinsky again for the discordant note as the detectives enter the mourning chamber and arrest old Peter. Then the undertaker enters. He should be accompanied with the most grotesque of Deems Taylor's music. Suddenly it should change into a sweet tender theme like that of Tschaikowski's in the first movement of the "Pathetique", when the undertaker's heart softens and he tells them to be ready for the funeral tomorrow. As the undertaker goes out amid the silence and soft *God Bless You's* of the Negroes, the orchestra slowly comes to another of those Wagnerian climaxes, when with a shriek—a releasing of pent up fears and emotions—Bess begins *I got a little brother in the new grave yard that outshines the sun!* A concentrated essence of all that is great of the great musicians could not improve this as a vehicle of expression. That is the most superb moment of the play.

The second act portrays the love of Bess and Porgy. In the prelude Wagner's cello is needed. But the Wagnerian cello alone depicts a too conventional love. Debussy must be mixed with Wagner to express its unconventionality, also Deems Taylor. A new instrument must be added to the symphony, as a touch of the saxophone is needed. But throughout, the cello of Wagner plays the dominant theme, showing the sterling qualities of that love, in spite of its unconventionality. The theme should be *Who'll be a witness for my Lord?* Bess was a witness. Love like hers indicates that man might be made of something else beside carbon, hydrogen, nitrogen, phosphorous and a few other chemicals, the total cost of which has been calculated to be ninety-eight cents for a single adult human body. Bess was a witness! Her love was more faithful than Isolde's or Elsa's or Sieglinde's all of which were worthy of Wagner's cello.

How the composer would revel in that scene in the Palmetto forest after the picnic when Bess meets Crown again! The orchestra would start with some rollicking theme of Offenbach's, then as Bess crosses the stage the Mephistophelian theme of Gounod is heard and Crown appears. Bess sees him and stands astounded. *Lord, I want to be like Jesus in my heart* comes from the orchestra as a cry of anguish. As he wooes her roughly with his touch and kisses, the music becomes the sensuous themes of Rimsky-Korsakov. Wagner's cello of love is heard in the beginning but gradually gives way to Rimsky-Korsakov as Bess goes into the thicket. *Lord, I want to be like Jesus in my heart!* This refrain never quite dies out, even after Bess has gone into the thicket with Crown.

Porgy is sitting on his steps with his head bowed, listening to Bess crying out in her delirium. *Nobody knows the trouble I seen!* Will Bess ever get well again. Serena prays and Porgy's head is still bowed. The roustabout is sent to the *conjur woman*. The clock strikes five and Bess appears, cured. Handel would be needed to express the religious fervor that enters Porgy's heart. The return of the roustabout would offer a chance for extremely good music humor.

The men go off in their fishing boats and the storm comes. The Negroes are huddled in Serena's room, singing in their terror. Stravinsky at his best, with a touch of Rossini's storm in *William Tell*. Crown enters. Gounod's Mephistophelian theme. He derides them as cowards. They tell him to fear God. Only the master stroke of Wagner will fit here. As the whole first act of Siegfried leads to a climax when Siegfried pulls his newly forged *Nothung* from the fire, just so the orchestra must come to a Wagnerian climax as Crown says that God has had plenty of chance to kill him as he came through the storm. He beats his breast and cries "Me and God is friends!" A crash of the percussion, then the orchestra starts pianissimo again leading up to a climax as Crown taunts the others about not being men, then rushes out into the storm to rescue the half demented woman on the wharf.

The return of Crown, his struggle with Porgy and the latter's triumph offer great musical possibilities, ending with a hymn of triumph—the excultations of the beast which has successfully defended his mate against attack. a cripple beast with a strong healthy mate—Siegfried after he had broken through the flaming wall and rescued Brunhilde—Lohengrin after his successful defense of Elsa. From the orchestra would come that most heroic of Negro themes—*Go Down, Moses.*

Then strikes the note of tragedy with the entrance of the officers investigating the murder of Crown, and the despairing wails as Porgy is dragged off to view Crown's body. Sporting life enters. Bess is at bay. St. George and the Dragon! Siegfried and Pfafner! The Dragon and Pfafner win. The curtain goes down amid Gluck's *Dance of the Furies* from *Orpheus.*

Lord, I want to be like Jesus in my heart. This theme has changed now from a major to a minor key. Porgy cheerfully gives out the present he has brought back, then calls for Bess. Gradually the story of her departure is unfolded to him. Then would start one of the grandest arias of all opera. King Mark betrayed by Tristan? No. Hunding betrayed by Siegmund? No. Othello dishonored by Iago? No. It is the cry of a soul which has kept its eyes fixed on the stars to avoid seeing the ugliness of humanity, and sees the starlight begin to grow dim. Its body closes the eyes and still cries out how brightly the stars are shining. Tears stream from the tightly closed eyes, as Porgy starts out to find New York and Bess.

Just as Don Juan's mistress, after hearing discussion of the qualities of the Superman and of the parents necessary to produce him, raises her arms toward Heaven and cries, "A father! A father for the Superman!", so might the Du Boise Haywoods, with a far greater qualification, cry out, "A composer! A composer for the opera *Porgy!*" May Deems Taylor hear the cry! Imagine Roland Hayes as Porgy and Paul Robeson as Crown!

[
    JESSIE FAUSET
    The Gift of Laughter
]

THE BLACK man bringing gifts, and particularly the gift of laughter, to the American stage is easily the most anomalous, the most inscrutable figure of the century. All about him and within himself stalks the conviction that like the Irish, the Russian and the Magyar, he has some peculiar offering which shall contain the very essence of the drama. Yet the medium through which this unique and intensely dramatic gift might be offered has been so befogged and misted by popular preconception that the great gift, though divined, is as yet not clearly seen.

Popular preconception in this instance refers to the pressure of white opinion by which the American Negro is surrounded and by which his true character is almost submerged. For years the Caucasian in America has persisted in dragging to the limelight merely one aspect of Negro characteristics, by which the whole race has been glimpsed, through which it has been judged. The colored man who finally succeeds in impressing any considerable number of whites with the truth that he does not conform to these measurements is regarded as the striking exception proving an unshakable rule. The medium then through which the black actor has been presented to the world has been that of the "funny man" of America. Ever since those far-off times directly after the Civil War when white men and colored men too, blacking their faces, presented the antics of plantation hands under the caption of "Georgia Minstrels"

219

and the like, the edict has gone forth that the black man on the stage must be an end-man.

In passing one pauses to wonder if this picture of the black American as a living comic supplement has not been painted in order to camouflage the real feeling and knowledge of his white compatriot. Certainly the plight of the slaves under even the mildest of masters could never have been one to awaken laughter. And no genuinely thinking person, no really astute observer, looking at the Negro in modern American life, could find his condition even now a first aid to laughter. That condition may be variously deemed hopeless, remarkable, admirable, inspiring, depressing; it can never be dubbed merely amusing.

It was the colored actor who gave the first impetus away from this buffoonery. The task was not an easy one. For years the Negro was no great frequenter of the theater. And no matter how keenly he felt the insincerity in the presentation of his kind, no matter how ridiculous and palpable a caricature such a presentation might be, the Negro auditor with the helplessness of the minority was powerless to demand something better and truer. Artist and audience alike were in the grip of the minstrel formula. It was at this point in the eighteen-nineties that Ernest Hogan, pioneer comedian of the better type, changed the tradition of the merely funny, rather silly "endman" into a character with a definite plot in a rather loosely constructed but none the less well outlined story. The method was still humorous, but less broadly, less exclusively. A little of the hard luck of the Negro began to creep in. If he was a buffoon, he was a buffoon wearing his rue. A slight, very slight quality of the Harlequin began to attach to him. He was the clown making light of his troubles but he was a wounded, a sore-beset clown.

This figure became the prototype of the plays later presented by those two great characters, Williams and Walker. The ingredients of the comedies in which these two starred usually consisted of one dishonest, overbearing, flashily dressed character (Walker) and one kindly, rather simple, hard-luck personage (Williams). The interest of the piece hinged on the juxtaposition of these two men. Of course these plays, too, were served with a sauce of humor because the public, true to its carefully taught and rigidly held tradition, could not dream of a situation in which colored people were anything but merely funny. But the hardships and woes suffered by Williams, ridiculous as they were, introduced with the element of folk comedy some element of reality.

Side by side with Williams and Walker, who might be called
the apostles of the "legitimate" on the stage for Negroes, came the
merriment and laughter and high spirits of that incomparable pair,
Cole and Johnson. But they were essentially the geniuses of musical
comedy. At that time their singers and dancers outsang and out-
danced the neophytes of contemporary white musical comedies even
as their followers to this day outsing and outdance in their occasional appearances on Broadway their modern neighbors. Just what
might have been the ultimate trend of the ambition of this partnership, the untimely death of Mr. Cole rendered uncertain; but speaking offhand I should say that the relation of their musical comedy
idea to the fixed plot and defined dramatic concept of the Williams
and Walker plays molded the form of the Negro musical show
which still persists and thrives on the contemporary stage. It was
they who capitalized the infectious charm of so much rich dark
beauty, the verve and abandon of Negro dancers, the glorious fullness of Negro voices. And they produced those effects in the *Red
Shawl* in a manner still unexcelled, except in the matter of setting,
by any latter-day companies.

But Williams and Walker, no matter how dimly, were seeking a
method whereby the colored man might enter the "legitimate." They
were to do nothing but pave the way. Even this task was difficult but
they performed it well.

Those who knew Bert Williams say that his earliest leanings
were toward the stage; but that he recognized at an equally early age
that his color would probably keep him from ever making the "legitimate." Consequently, deliberately, as one who desiring to become a great painter but lacking the means for travel and study
might take up commercial art, he turned his attention to minstrelsy.
Natively he possessed the art of mimicry; intuitively he realized
that his first path to the stage must lie along the old recognized
lines of "funny man." He was, as few of us recall, a Jamaican by
birth; the ways of the American Negro were utterly alien to him and
did not come spontaneously; he set himself therefore to obtaining a
knowledge of them. For choice he selected, perhaps by way of contrast, the melancholy out-of-luck Negro, shiftless, doleful, "easy";
the kind that tempts the world to lay its hand none too lightly upon
him. The pursuit took him years, but at length he was able to portray for us not only that "typical Negro" which the white world
thinks is universal but also the special types of given districts and
localities with their own peculiar foibles of walk and speech and

jargon. He went to London and studied under Pietro, greatest pan-
tomimist of his day, until finally he, too, became a recognized master in the field of comic art.

But does anyone who realizes that the foibles of the American
Negro were painstakingly acquired by this artist, doubt that Williams might just as well have portrayed the Irishman, the Jew, the
Englishman abroad, the Scotchman or any other of the vividly
etched types which for one reason or another lend themselves so
readily to caricature? Can anyone presume to say that a man who
travelled *north, east, south* and *west* and even abroad in order to
acquire accent and jargon, aspect and characteristic of a people to
which he was bound by ties of blood but from whom he was natively separated by training and tradition, would not have been able
to portray with equal effectiveness what, for lack of a better term,
we must call universal rôles?

There is an unwritten law in America that though white may
imitate black, black, even when superlatively capable, must never
imitate white. In other words, grease-paint may be used to darken
but never to lighten.

Williams' color imposed its limitations upon him even in his
chosen field. His expansion was always upward but never outward.
He might portray black people along the gamut from roustabout to
unctuous bishop. But he must never stray beyond those limits. How
keenly he felt this few of us knew until after his death. But it was
well known to his intimates and professional associates. W. C.
Fields, himself an expert in the art of amusing, called him "the fun-
niest man I ever saw and the saddest man I ever knew."

He was sad with the sadness of hopeless frustration. The gift of
laughter in his case had its source in a wounded heart and in bleeding sensibilities.

That laughter for which we are so justly famed has had in late
years its over-tones of pain. Now for some time past it has been
used by colored men who have gained a precarious footing on the
stage to conceal the very real dolor raging in their breasts. To be by
force of circumstances the most dramatic figure in a country; to be
possessed of the wells of feeling, of the most spontaneous instinct
for effective action and to be shunted no less always into the rôle of
the ridiculous and funny,—that is enough to create the quality of
bitterness for which we are ever so often rebuked. Yet that same
laughter influenced by these same untoward obstacles has within the
last four years known a deflection into another channel, still produc-

tive of mirth, but even more than that of a sort of cosmic gladness, the joy which arises spontaneously in the spectator as a result of the sight of its no less spontaneous bubbling in others. What hurt most in the spectacle of the Bert Williams' funny man and his forerunners was the fact that the laughter which he created must be objective. But the new "funny man" among black comedians is essentially funny himself. He is joy and mischief and rich, homely native humor personified. He radiates good feeling and happiness; it is with him now a state of being purely subjective. The spectator is infected with his high spirits and his excessive good will; a stream of well-being is projected across the footlights into the consciousness of the beholder.

This phenomenon has been especially visible in the rendition of the colored musical "shows," *Shuffle Along, Runnin' Wild, Liza,* which livened up Broadway recently for a too brief season. Those of us who were lucky enough to compare with the usual banality of musical comedy, the verve and pep, the liveliness and gayety of those productions will not soon forget them. The medley of shades, the rich colorings, the abundance of fun and spirits on the part of the players all combined to produce an atmosphere which was actually palpable, so full was it of the ecstasy and joy of living. The singing was inimitable; the work of the chorus apparently spontaneous and unstudied. Emotionally they garnished their threadbare plots and comedy tricks with the genius of a new comic art.

The performers in all three of these productions gave out an impression of sheer happiness in living such as I have never before seen on any stage except in a riotous farce which I once saw in Vienna and where the same effect of superabundant vitality was induced. It is this quality of vivid and untheatrical portrayal of sheer emotion which seems likely to be the Negro's chief contribution to the stage. A comedy made up of such ingredients as the music of Sissle and Blake, the quaint, irresistible humor of Miller and Lyles, the quintessence of jazzdom in the Charleston, the superlativeness of Miss Mills' happy abandon could know no equal. It would be the line by which all other comedy would have to be measured. Behind the banalities and clap-trap and crudities of these shows, this supervitality and joyousness glow from time to time in a given step or gesture or in the teasing assurance of such a line as: "If you've never been vamped by a brown-skin, you've never been vamped at all."

And as Carl Van Vechten recently in his brilliant article, *Prescription for the Negro Theater,* so pointedly advises and prophesies, once the spirit breaks through the silly "childish adjuncts of the minstrel tradition" and drops the unworthy formula of unoriginal imitation of the stock revues, there will be released on the American stage a spirit of comedy such as has been rarely known.

The remarkable thing about this gift of ours is that it has its rise, I am convinced, in the very woes which beset us. Just as a person driven by great sorrow may finally go into an orgy of laughter, just so an oppressed and too hard driven people breaks over into compensating laughter and merriment. It is our emotional salvation. There would be no point in mentioning this rather obvious fact were it not that it argues also the possession on our part of a histrionic endowment for the portrayal of tragedy. Not without reason has tradition made comedy and tragedy sisters and twins, the capacity for one argues the capacity for the other. It is not surprising then that the period that sees the Negro actor on the verge of great comedy has seen him breaking through to the portrayal of serious and legitimate drama. No one who has seen Gilpin and Robeson in the portrayal of *The Emperor Jones* and of *All God's Chillun* can fail to realize that tragedy, too, is a vastly fitting rôle for the Negro actor. And so with the culminating of his dramatic genius, the Negro actor must come finally through the very versatility of his art to the universal rôle and the main tradition of drama, as an artist first and only secondarily as a Negro.

Nor when within the next few years, this question comes up,— as I suspect it must come up with increasing insistence, will the more obvious barriers seem as obvious as they now appear. For in this American group of the descendants of Mother Africa, the question of color raises no insuperable barrier, seeing that with chameleon adaptability we are able to offer white colored men and women for *Hamlet, The Doll's House* and the *Second Mrs. Tanqueray;* brown men for *Othello;* yellow girls for *Madam Butterfly;* black men for *The Emperor Jones.* And underneath and permeating all this bewildering array of shades and tints is the unshakable precision of an instinctive and spontaneous emotional art.

All this beyond any doubt will be the reward of the "gift of laughter" which many black actors on the American stage have proffered. Through laughter we have conquered even the lot of the jester and the clown. The parable of the one talent still holds good and because we have used the little which in those early painful days was our only approach we find ourselves slowly but surely

224

moving toward that most glittering of all goals, the freedom of the American stage. I hope that Hogan realizes this and Cole and Walker, too, and that lastly Bert Williams, the inimitable, will clap us on with those tragic black-gloved hands of his now that the gift of his laughter is no longer tainted with the salt of chagrin and tears.

The Negro's Cycle of Song - A Review

By ARTHUR HUFF FAUSET

I'm goin' to heaven on eagle's wing,
All don't see me, goin' to hear me sing.

THE pity of it is that all who read this splendid volume must content themselves with the mere seeing. Negro song is not something to be looked at; to appreciate it and understand it you must hear it.

Odum and Johnson, the compilers of the volume, both heard and saw; better than that, they devoured what came across their paths, and apparently made a good meal of it. Seldom have we had the pleasure of encountering such perfect comprehension of the Negro on the part of white investigators. For say what you will, the Negro is a difficult "problem." Like the Irishman's flea, it's hard to put your finger squarely upon him. Sometimes he seems to defy analysis.

His songs, like himself, are a problem. As I stated above, they must be heard to be fully appreciated and understood. In cold type they are words, ofttimes—and what crude vehicles are words for suggesting the pulsations, the quiverings, and the trippings of the soul! Sometimes in the case of these songs they approach the inanity of nonsense-syllables.

Small wonder. They have arisen from every conceivable condition of mind and body, and from circumstances innumerable. The wonder is not that they are as they are, but that they even exist. What right have Negroes to be singing anyhow! . . . But that's the whole secret.

The songs have their own general characteristics, of course, which make their origin very apparent, but as to classification, they simply defy any method of classifying.

They scan and they don't.

They are full of sense and they are so much nonsense.

They are sad and droll at the same time.

They contain evidences of profound philosophical reflection couched in expressions which have no parallels for naivete.

Depending on your point of view, they might be everything, nothing, more than anything, less than anything.

Now, can you beat that!

This is a choice sample:

I got de blues, but too damn mean to cry.

THE NEGRO AND HIS SONGS, *By Howard W. Odum, Ph.D., and Guy B. Johnson, A.M.* Published by the *University of North Carolina Press.* Price $3.00.

The epitome of dolefulness. Nevertheless I laughed when I read it.

Take this:

When I git to heaven gwine to ease, ease,
Me an' my God goin' do as we please,
Settin' down side o' holy Lamb.

Or this:

Of all de beastes in de woods,
I'd rather be a tick;
I'd climb up roun' my true love's neck,
An' there I'd stick,
Jus' to see her roll dem snow-white eyes.

The following is certainly a jewel:

Someone stole a chicken in our neighborhood,
They 'rested me on suspicion, it was understood.
They carried me 'fo' a jury—how guilty I did flee.
'Cause my name was signed at de head, de jury said was me.

"I couldn't hear nobody pray."   BY DOUGLAS

But then, why try to analyze and classify Negro songs? As well attempt to analyze a spirit. It isn't the words, nor the length of the lines; it isn't even the rhyming—on which Odum and Johnson lay more than necessary stress, I think—none of these are the Negro's song. That song, sir, is an indefinable something which makes you feel it. Negro song . . . feeling . . . that's Negro song. The Negro feels it, you feel it, that's the song. You get the same indefinable something in the glint of a Negro's eyes, the gleam of his teeth, the sway of his body, the lilt of his feet. These are the Negro and his song, and they tell you that the Negro is the soul of his music.

What is the need of dissecting such a stanza as this:

> *Hop right! goin' to see my baby Lou.*
> *Goin 'to walk an' talk wid my honey,*
> *Goin' to hug an' kiss my honey,*
> *Hop right, my baby!*

No mere words make you feel this; it is far from poetry in the conventional sense of that term. But some power from within unquestionably expresses itself in such a song which any man who has ever thought of going to kiss and hug and walk and talk "wid my honey" cannot fail to appreciate.

The song just referred to is among those which Odum and Johnson call Social Songs. In the chapter dealing with these the compilers have the following remarks which very likely will stir up some lively debates:

"It is to be regretted that a great mass of material cannot be published because of its vulgar and indecent content. These songs tell of every phase of immorality and vice and filth; they represent the superlative of the repulsive. Ordinarily the imagination can picture conditions worse than they are, but in the Negro songs the pictures go far beyond the conception of the real. The prevailing theme is that of sexual relations, and there is no restraint in expression. In comparison with the indecency that has come to light in the vulgar songs of other peoples, those of the Negro stand out undoubtedly in a class of their own."

A pretty bald statement and a bold one. Evidently Odum and Johnson have made careful comparisons of the contents of social songs of various peoples. The sympathetic treatment rendered in the whole body of the present work lends weight to the belief that these remarks are not made in the spirit of prejudice against the Negro. At the same time the book has a scientific air about it which suggests, to say the least, that this it not snap judgment. It is up to the Negro to prove his own case based on scientific evidence of the facts.

"An' the stars began to fall."

BY DOUGLAS

It is not a pleasant duty to prolong discussion of an already unpleasant topic, but certainly the scientific investigator must be prepared to give an explanation of this situation in the event that Odum and Johnson have presented the case correctly. The logical question following from such a conclusion as the compilers have come to is this: "Why is this so?" Perhaps the compilers' explanation that "it must be constantly borne in mind that this collection of songs is representative only of what may be called the Negro lower class," is the answer.

--

I believe we can say this with safety: the Negro is never more himself than in his songs. Through them all, religious songs, work songs, social songs, the Soul of Black Folk marches on, restless, dolorous, blithesome, bedewed as with heavenly dew, "sometimes . . . up . . . sometimes . . . down . . ."

Perhaps you are acquainted with the Negro in this mood:

> *Sinner, what you goin' to do*
> *When de devil git you?*
> *What you goin' do*
> *When de devil git you?*
> *What you goin' do*
> *When de devil git you?*
> *Lord, I'm on my way.*

Or in this frame of mind:

> *I was bohn in a mighty bad lan'*
> *For my name is Bad-lan' Stone,*
> *I want you all fer to understan'*
> *I'm a bad man wid my licker on.*

Certainly you haven't missed him as he thus pictures his attitude towards life:

> *Rich folks worries 'bout trouble,*
> *Po' folks worry 'bout wealth.*
> *I don't worry 'bout nuthin';*
> *All I want's my health.*

But if you want to get down to the real soul of the Negro, the part of him that makes all others wonder, wonder about that peculiar faculty of his of being happy when he's sad (or sad when he's happy—which is it?)—ponder over these lines, lines which must have surged more than once through the breast of every Negro who has any sense of the great injustice which he suffers for a "crime" over which he had no control:

> *Ain't it hard, ain't it hard,*
> *Ain't it hard to be a nigger, nigger, nigger?*
> *Ain't it hard, ain't it hard,*
> *For you can't git yo' money when it's due.*

> *Well, it make no difference*
> *How you make out yo' time;*
> *White man sho bring a*
> *Nigger out behin'.*

> *Nigger an' white man*
> *Playin' seven-up;*
> *Nigger win de money—*
> *Skeered to pick 'em up.*

> *If a nigger git 'rested,*
> *An' can't pay his fine,*
> *They sho send him out*
> *To the county gang.*

> *A nigger went to a white man,*
> *An' asked him for work;*
> *White man told nigger;*
> *Yes, git out o' yo' shirt.*

Continued on page 348

The Negro's Cycle of Song

Continued from page 335

> *Nigger got out o' his shirt*
> *An' went to work;*
> *When pay-day come,*
> *White man say he ain't work 'nuf.*

> *If you work all the week,*
> *An' work all the time,*
> *White man sho to bring*
> *Nigger out behin'.*

Song is the Negro's mother. She nurtures him, soothes him, pacifies him, glorifies him. She keeps his heart cheered when the weight of an oppressive world would bend his body to the sod. She exalts him when others would see him abased, and draws his eyes upward to realms of higher achievement when the scoffs of men would crush him and force him into the role of stone-hewer.

Many will be inclined to laugh as they read the words which Odum and Johnson have recorded so faithfully, and interpreted with such evident carefulness. Some will call it gibberish. And nonsense much of it is if naked, cold, physical eyes do the measuring. But visions quickened by a sense of things spiritual cannot fail to perceive that the soul which underlies and permeates these songs of black folk is the same one which in latter years has burst forth into the luxuriant, mellifluous outpourings from the hearts of such children as Dunbar, DuBois and Countee Cullen.

Self-Portraiture and Social Criticism in Negro Folk-Song*

By B. A. BOTKIN

AS one of the recreations of a sociologist, two professors of the University of North Carolina have been quietly and assiduously cultivating one of the richest fields of folk expression in general and of Negro self-expression in particular, furnishing valuable experimental data for the study of folk-song in America. It should be emphasized that their work is of equal importance for both aesthetics and social science, significant alike for the light it throws upon the processes of folk art and for the evidence it presents as to the working of the group mind and the development of a race. Hitherto folk-song has been considered the special possession of folk-lorists, ballad-scholars, and musicians. But in 1925 along came the first volume in the University of North Carolina Social Study Series, entitled The Negro and His Songs, to prove that, since folk art is social in its impulse and inception, if not in expression, the best approach to it is through the medium of sociology. Enough credit has not been given to Dr. Odum as a pioneer in the field. His work was initiated in 1909 when he published his doctoral dissertation at Clark University, under the title Religious Folk-Songs of the Southern Negroes, reprinted from the American Journal of Religious Psychology and Education; and in 1911 when an extensive article on Folk-Song and Folk Poetry as Found in the Secular Songs of the Southern Negroes appeared in the Journal of American Folk-Lore. The fruits of these researches, with the assistance of Mr. Guy B. Johnson, have been made available to the general public in two impressive and highly readable volumes, the full significance of which has yet to be considered. Other collectors, like Natalie Curtis Burlin and H. E. Krehbiel, have concerned themselves chiefly with religious and play songs, due, no doubt, to the traditional association of folk-songs with the religious and play instincts in man, with ritual and the ballad-dance. In the field of play-songs of the nursery, game, and dance, the most important contributions have been Thomas W. Talley's Negro Folk Rhymes, 1922, and Dorothy Scarborough's On the Trail of Negro Folk-Songs, 1925. To a mine of collected material Professor Talley appended an illuminating study of Negro folk-song on the musical, poetic, and ethnological sides, especially with regard to African origins and ante-bellum conditions in America. Miss Scarborough undertook a comprehensive survey of the entire body of Negro folk-song from the point of view of the collector and the scholar, including ballad-relations and textual comparison and annotation. She, too, however, was strongest on the side of game and dance songs. Her chapters on Work-Songs and Blues, suggestive and entertaining as they were, merely laid out the lines for future research. In the blues proper, W. C. Handy's volume in 1926, with introduction by Abbe Niles, filled

the needs of musicians and music-lovers. But there was still room for a scientific study of social backgrounds and sources and the inter-relation of formal and native blues and work and work in general. This has been furnished by Odum and Johnson's two volumes of first-hand collection and authoritative analysis, of which the second fills in the outlines of the former with much additional material and theory, including chapters on types of Negro melodies and phono-photographic records of Negro singers. By means of laboratory experiments which have made possible accurate graphic representation of the most elusive idiosyncrasies of the voice, including slurs and vibrato too subtle for ordinary musical notation, the recording and analysis of folk-tunes and voice-types has been brought definitely within the scope of science.

These various researches point to two interesting conclusions. First, they show as a whole that the task of criticism and interpretation must be shared with white scholars. Collectively, they have the benefit of previous experience. And, individually, they demonstrate the truism that á stranger brings to the study of the literature and society of another race a coolness of detachment and a clearness of perspective vouchsafed only to the outsider. Classic examples, in other fields, are Taine's History of English Literature, De Tocqueville's Democracy in America, and Lord Bryce's American Commonwealth. Secondly, as to the work of Professors Odum and Johnson in particular, their collections of Negro workaday songs prove that the best index to the psychology of a race, paradoxical as it may seem, is what a man thinks about when he is at work.

True, a man is judged by the way he spends his leisure, but, curiously enough, it is work-songs and not play-songs that reflect the preoccupations of leisure.

This follows as a corollary from the axiom that all art originates in a desire to escape from the present situation. Thus, in the game-songs of children, one finds the surplus energy of young bodies still unadapted to the tasks of the grown-up world endeavoring to express itself in imitative action, as, for example, in the well-nigh universal Mulberry Bush. On the other hand, the workaday songs, as distinguished from pastime songs, more often than not concern themselves with the pleasures of leisure: loving and fighting, eating and sleeping, loafing and gaming.

Examination of a few of the dominant types and themes of workaday songs reveals further that, in common with the worker of other races, the mind of the Negro laborer seems to dwell principally on the subjects of comfort and love, which furnish the mo-

*NEGRO WORKADAY SONGS. By Howard W. Odum and Guy B. Johnson. Chapel Hill; The University of North Carolina Press. 1926. $3.

tive of labor. At the same time a racial as well as a social note may be detected in his complaint, the cry, not only of a downtrodden class, but also of an oppressed people.

Psychologically, his imaginative escape is allied to a defense mechanism, as in the following, sung by diggers on a July day:

> Oh, next winter gonna be so cold,
> Oh, next winter gonna be so cold,
> Oh, next winter gonna be so cold,
> Fire can't warm you, be so cold.

All the sorrow and tenderness of love, its bitter and its sweet, are compressed into another pick song with remarkable sureness of dramatic development and an eloquent power of suggestion. "She asked me in de parlor" is perhaps the most finished production of its kind, a perfect example of folk art in the homely natural vigor and directness of its pathos and its beauty, admirably suited at the same time to the psychological purpose of emotional release from the sweat and grime of back-breaking toil.

> Well, she ask me in her parlor,
> An' she cooled me wid her fan,
> An' she whispered to her mother,
> "Mama, I love that dark-eyed man."

> Well, I ask her mother for her
> An' she said she was too young.
> Lawd, I wished I never had seen her
> An' I wished she'd never been born.

> Well, I led her to de altar,
> An' de preacher give his comman',
> An' she swore by God that made her
> That she never love another man.

The note of self-pity struck at the close of the second stanza represents a trait of the Negro, bred in him by centuries of oppression. It is responsible for the plaintiveness and wistfulness of his blues and even the wail and moan of his music. And it is the theme of many of his workaday songs, like the pick song "U—h, U—h, Lawdy":

> U—h, u—h, Lawdy,
> I wonder why
> I got to live
> Fer de by an' de by.

> U—h, u—h, Lawdy,
> Don't you bother me.
> I'm always mighty happy
> When I'm on a spree.

> U—h, u—h, Lawdy,
> U—h, u—h, Lawdy,
> U—h, u—h, Lawdy,
> U—h, Lawdy, u—h, Lawdy, po' me!

Even more typical of the Negro is the ironical or satirical blend of pathos and humor, seen in the chain-gang song "I ain't free":

> De rabbit in the briarpatch,
> De squirrel in de tree,
> Would love to go huntin',
> But I ain't free,
> But I ain't free,
> But I ain't free,
> Would love to go huntin',
> But I ain't free, ain't free.

> De rooster's in de hen house,
> De hen in de patch,
> I love to go shootin'
> At a ol' shootin' match,
> But I ain't free, etc.,
> At a ol' shootin' match,
> But I ain't free, ain't free.

> Ol' woman in de kitchen,
> My sweetie hanging' roun',
> 'Nudder man gonna git 'er,
> I sho' be boun',
> 'Cause I ain't free, etc.,
> 'Nudder man'll git 'er,
> 'Cause I ain't free, ain't free.

> Dig in de road band,
> Dig in de ditch,
> Chain gang got me,
> An' de boss got de switch
> I ain't free, etc.,
> Chain gang got me,

And similarly in the ending of "I don't mind bein' in jail," made familiar in the popular "Jail-House Blues":

> I don't mind bein' in jail
> If I didn't have to stay so long.

In "Better 'n I Has at Home" the prisoner makes light of his trials with ironical resignation, in which self-pity mingles with self-disparagement:

> Cawn pone, fat meat,
> All I gits to eat—
> Better 'n I has at home,
> Better 'n I has at home.

> Cotton socks, striped clothes,
> No Sunday glad rags at all—
> Better 'n I gits at home, etc.

> Rings on my arms,
> Bracelets on my feet—
> Stronger 'n I has at home, etc.

> Bunk for a bed,
> Straw under my head—
> Better 'n I gits at home, etc.

> Baby, baby, lemme be,
> Chain gang good enough for me—
> Better 'n I gits at home, etc.

The strength of his imagination, stimulated by keen longing, often makes the object of his desires vividly real to him. Consider the lively fancy that opens the "Jail House Wail":

> The jail's on fire, Lawd,
> The stockade's burning down.
>
> Well, they ain't got nowhere,
> Lawd, to put the prisoners now.
>
> Taken prisoners out o' jail, Lawd,
> Carried 'em to country road.
>
> Say, I ruther be in chain gang
> Than be in jail all time.

The same process is seen in the child who plays sick because he would rather stay in bed than be in school "all time," or fervently wishes that the school-house would burn down.

And with animal cunning, like the child locked in the closet or the attic, the jail-bird schemes, invoking pleasant visions of escape and vengeance:

> Say, jailer keeps you bound down,
> Lawd, say jailer dog you roun'.
>
> Says if I had my way wid jailer,
> I'd take an' lock him in cell.
>
> I'd take key an' tie it on the door,
> An' go long way from here, Lawd, Lawd.

Because poetry, like religion, in the words of Santayana, gives him another world to live in, the hard-pressed Negro takes naturally to song as prayer and to prayer as song. As the longing for freedom motivates the spirituals and accounts for their universal appeal, so the desire to be where he is not and do what he is not doing explains the blues. The Negro is a roamer, and like all roamers loves to sing the sadness and the weariness of the lonesome road:

> Pity a po' boy
> Stray 'way from home, (bis).
>
> If I ever gits back,
> I sho' never mo' to roam, (bis).

But when he cannot roam, he vents his restlessness in a threat:

> Some o' these days,
> Hit won't be long,
> Mammy gonna call me
> An' I be gone.
>
> Some 'o dese nights,
> An' I don't kere,
> Mammy gonna want me,
> An' I won't be here.
>
> Some o' dese days
> In de by an' by,
> You won't have no'n' t' eat,
> Den you gonna cry.

> Some o' dese days
> While I's here to home,
> Better feed me an' pet me,
> Don't, I's gonna roam.

Perhaps the most frequently encountered symbol of freedom and vicarious experience is the train, which has a powerful fascination for the Negro as for the child mind, whether in the "Chain-Gang Blues"; where its whistle comes to him like the trump of doom:

> Standin' on the road side,
> Waitin' for the ball an' chain.
> Say, if I was not all shackled down
> I'd ketch that wes' boun' train;

or in the free labor gang, where the "Section Boss" improvises his crude poetry, with touching wistfulness and naivete, in the spirit of the child who likes to play engineer or motorman:

> Yonder come the engine
> Ringin' o' the bell:
> Engineer on the right,
> Fireman on the left.
>
> See the engineer makin' time,
> See the engineer gone.
> Fall off the car,
> Throw off the tools.
>
> Throw off the tools,
> Let the engine go by.
> If I could run like he runs,
> I'd run an' never stop.
>
> See the train makin' up speed,
> See the cars go 'long.
> If I had wings like that engine,
> I could run an' fly.
>
> I could pull the bell,
> I could blow the whistle,
> I could pull the bell,
> An' let the engine run.
>
> If I could run like he runs,
> I never would quit,
> I'd always railroad
> I'd always run an' fly.

Trains, of course, have been made familiar to us through the spirituals and the blues. The significance of workaday songs as the basis of these two types of sorrow songs, religious and secular, is attested by the fact that they supply to the latter the homely imagery, concrete symbols, and practical motives of the workaday world, such as those associated with trains.

> Oh, de gospel train's a-comin', etc.
> Oh, she's comin' 'roun' de curve, etc.
> Oh, de train am heavy loaded, etc.
> Oh, sinner have you got your ticket? etc.

Oh, she's boun' straight way to heaven, *etc.*
Oh, Marse Jesus am de captain, *etc.*
Oh, de ride am free to heaven, *etc.*

And in this world the wanderer sings:

I'm gonna ketch dat train, don't know where
　it's from.
Or:

> Longest train I ever saw
> Was nineteen coaches long.
> Darlin' what have I done to you?
> What makes you treat me so?
> An' I won't be treated this-a way.

And Left Wing Gordon moans:

> O Illinois Central,
> What can you spare?
> Fo' my baby's in trouble
> An' I ain't dere.

An inseparable part of the self-portraiture of Negro workaday songs is their social criticism. Out of the Negro's sense of self-pity develops an inevitable conviction of social injustice and an indictment of the existing order. Professor Talley has already given us numerous examples of the slave's smouldering resentment of his treatment at the hands of the whites. And the free laborer still sings:

> Niggers plant the cotton,
> Niggers pick it out,
> White man pockets money,
> Nigger goes without.

And under the ironical title, "Everybody call me the wages man," he concludes:

> White man in starched shirt settin' in shade,
> 　(*three times*),
> Laziest man that God ever made,
> 　Baby, baby.

And this from the Negro whom the white man has always accused of laziness. "Missus" and "Mammy," Marse" and "Nigger," have become charged with new meaning since the Negro worker has had time to contemplate the bondage of liberty:

> Missus in de big house,
> Mammy in de yard.
> Missus holdin' her white hands,
> Mammy workin' hard, (*three ttmes*),
> Missus holdin' her white hands,
> Mammy workin' hard.

> Ol' marse ridin' all time,
> Niggers workin' roun'.
> Marse sleepin' day time,
> Niggers diggin' in de groun', *etc.*

The prisoner also has his grievances:

> When time come to be tried,
> Jail keeper lied on me.

Again:

> Lawd, I went to judge to ask for a fine.
> Judge say, Lawd, he ain't got no time.

The constant threat of the chain-gang hanging over his head (as portrayed in T. S. Stribling's *Birthright*) has bred in the Southern Negro a haunting dread of persecution, thus humorously viewed by the "bad man":

> Went up to 'Lanta,
> Who should I meet?
> Forty-leben blue coats
> Comin' down de street,
> Forty-leben blue boats
> Comin' down de street.
> I ain't done nothin',
> Why dey follerin' me?
> I ain't done nothin',
> Can't dey let me be?

And persecution has also called forth a defense in the nature of a dual personality, one for himself and another for the white man, whom he takes delight in beating at his own game.

> I steal dat corn
> From de white man's barn,
> Den I slips aroun',
> Tells a yarn,
> An' sells it back again . . . .

> I steal de melons
> From his patch.
> It takes a smarter man dan him
> Fer ter ketch,
> An' I sells 'em back again.

Deceit as the defense of the weaker is by no means restricted to the Negro: women and children have also been accused of it.

Out of the oppressiveness of the law grows the necessity of breaking the law; out of the occasional offender develops the "bad man," likewise the boaster, with an offence rather than a defense mechanism, though the latter is still at the root of it, capitalizing his crimes as a means of conquering women, and led to further crime as a result of these troublesome conquests.

> I'm de rough stuff of dark-town alley,
> I'm de man dey hates to see.
> I'm de rough stuff of dis alley,
> But de women's all falls for me.

And this gem, which any poet would be glad to have written, remarkable for its sense of form and plot,—its parallelism and compression, telling a story entirely by suggestion:

I got a gal, you got a gal,
All us niggers got a gal.

He fool 'roun', I fool 'roun',
All us niggers fool 'roun'.

I got a razor, he got a razor,
All us niggers got a razor.

I 'hind de bars, he 'hind de bars,
All us niggers, 'hind de bars.

And it has been left to a "bad man," the pica-resque Left Wing Gordon, to sum up the spirit of the blues in his favorite refrain:

O my babe, you don't know my min',
When you see me laughin',
Laughin' to keep from cryin',

and to strike the keynote of Negro love, typical of the curious inconstancy and hurly-burly of Negro life:

When you think I'm lovin' you.
I'm leavin' you behin',

When you think I'm leavin'
I'm comin' right behin'.

And so we end where we began, with comfort and love, the rewards of labor and the fruits of leisure, which the Negro prizes as only a race with his history can prize them:

De gal love de money
An' de man love de gal;
If dey bofe don't git what dey wants,
It's livin' in hell.

There is scarcely an interest or an activity of the Negro that is not mirrored in these songs, in which he proves himself as much the philosopher as the poet. Unusually direct and concrete even for such a direct and concrete genre as folk-song, and more wise and witty than the folk-songs of most races, these spontaneous snatches exhibit a development of form far in excess of the simplicity and often the crudity of their sentiment.

As to the authors of this volume, they have accomplished their task with completeness and fairness, as impartial observers but not entirely disinterested —with humor and sympathy, with frankness and charm, and, more commendable still, with a reasonable degree of freedom from the besetting sin of collectors; namely, idealization and generalization. And we are told that the end is not yet in sight: songs are still coming in, increasing the importance of the work of collecting and classifying one of the largest and most varied stores of folk-song in existence.

The preponderance of the secular songs of the Negro over his spirituals is indicated by statistics. The composition of spirituals is not dying out, but is undergoing a secularizing process. Within the class of secular songs, the blues, of course, far outnumber any other type. And the need of preserving these native blues grows as the record and sheet-music market is being flooded with an increasing number of worthless imitations.

If any conclusion may be drawn as to the significance of Negro song as a whole, it is that all the western world is feeling the urge of its social rhythm, as the work of man, in field and forest, on ships and docks has felt the impulse of its chant of labor, and as the soul of man has caught the stir of its spirit-cry. Now to the old sorrow songs of the plantation, harking back to the slave ship, must be added these new sorrow songs of the workaday, work-weary world and of the workless lonesome road: the blues. The child-like faith of slave-days is giving way to the worldly cynicism, the disillusionment of freedom, the product of industrial exploitation, migration, and concentration in cities. The free worker or the drifter has his problems and burdens even as the slave had his visions; both take refuge in song. And the sorrow songs of these two ages bear a marked resemblance. For in the end it might be asked if the dominant note of all Negro song is not the homesickness of an alien, homeless folk, "po' boy long way from home," a nostalgia born of a racial, traditional, and ancestral longing for a home that no longer exists, like the Promised Land which the Jews have codified in Zion, and like the Heaven of the Christians to which the Negro has transferred his unsatisfied earthly longings. The Negro is restless and unresting, obsessed with the need of seeking and finding. Appropriately enough, then, his songs, sacred and secular, spirituals and blues, are songs of going home, full of rivers and roads, trains and shoes, arks and chariots "comin' for to carry me home."

Gonna shout trouble over
When I git home,
Gonna shout trouble over,
When I git home.

No mo' prayin', no mo' dyin'
When I git home,
No mo' prayin' an' no mo' dyin'
When I git home.

Meet my father
When I git home.
Meet my father
When I git home.

Shake glad hands
When I git home,
Shake glad hands
When I git home.

Meet King Jesus
When I git home,
Yes, I meets King Jesus
When I git home.

The quartet felt it was making a big impression and then proceeded to exaggerate their gestures and motions. As a result the sacred thought brought out in the words of the song were entirely lost. It was cast aside. Of course the quartet received a thunderous applause at the conclusion of the rendition. At another similar affair, a quartet appeared on the program and they felt it not only necessary to dramatize their songs but also to give the Spirituals a jazz tempo. We all are aware there is a degree of syncopation in our Melodies but this swing should not be carried too far. The singers have now developed a jerky manner coupled with this aforesaid jazz time which has resulted in the roduction of songs altogether different to the ones our forefathers sang inspired by Almighty God Himself.

Quartets are taking these same Spirituals into the theatres and dance halls. A certain quartet was scheduled to sing on one of the previous holiday nights at a "big theatrical ball". One does not have to stretch his imagination very far to judge the types of people present. This particular quartet happens to be one whose repertoire of songs are almost solely Spirituals and Jubilee Songs. It has about three secular numbers. The announcement of this engagement at the ball was received by many as a sign of retrogression for when one becomes so sacriligeous as to take a sacred song to a dance hall—there is something radically wrong with that individual's life and his spiritual downfall is not far distant.

I agree in this Jazz Age, the temptation is very great to put a little "pep" into almost everything. However let us protect our Spirituals—those songs that came from the bleeding hearts of our fore-parents chained in slavery. Those songs that were the outbursts of agonized souls. Let us who realize the importance and worth of these melodies discourage at every opportunity any efforts of singers to entertain their audiences. There should come to the listeners a feeling of inspiration and a heartfelt desire to live a better Christian life after a rendition of a Spiritual.

I once heard a venerable white lady say she always felt a little nearer to heaven whenever she heard a Negro Spiritual. Into these songs was poured the aspiration of a race in bondage whose *religion*, primitive and intense was their whole hope, sustenance and comfort and the realm wherein the soul, at least, soared free. Therefore let us no longer tolerate the profanity of our sacred Spirituals. Let us, who have the opportunity, insist that these songs be used for the Glory of God and not for the amusement of man.

THE PROFANATION OF NEGRO SPIRITUALS

By George A. Webb

Quite recently, the Nordic has condescended to attribute the honor to the Colored Race as the producers of the only real American Music—Negro Spirituals. No sooner had this recognition been given than "Jubilee Choruses" and Quartets galore sprang into existence. All specializing in the singing of these Spirituals. Groups that had ridiculed our Slavery Songs now evince the keenest appreciation. Hardly a concert program is complete without a group of Negro Spirituals as arranged by some of our modern composers.

Were this enthusiasm to stop at this point, all would be well but it has now passed on from the sublime stage down to the ridiculous. I firmly believe the Spiritual should be considered a sacred, serious, song and one no more to be profaned than "Nearer My God To Thee" or "Blest Be The Tie That Binds". It has come to the stage now, especially with these numerous quartets, where they consider it necessary to make the audience laugh at the expense of the sacredness of our beloved Spirituals. Just a few weeks ago, I listened to a quartet, that has a good reputation as to harmonizing, sing a program of Spirituals. There was a number in particular that was disgusting—"Can't Sit Down Sinner". While singing, they dramatized the song and instead of the audience seeing the seriousness of the thought, it was convulsed with laughter.

We wish to pass on to the readers of OPPORTUNITY a letter addressed to them:

Does anyone happen to possess (or to know where they can be found) the words and music of an old song which ran in part:

> 'O run tell Elijah,
>
> To hurry up Pomp
>
> To meet us at the gum tree
>
> Down by the swamp
>
> For to wake Nicodemus today.

> Chorus:
>
> The good time coming
>
> Is almost here.
>
> It was long, long, long on the way.

If any of our readers can help us locate this song we will be glad to relay the information along to our inquirer

by ZORA NEALE HURSTON

T HE real spirituals are not really just songs. They are unceasing variations around a theme.
Contrary to popular belief their creation is not confined to the slavery period. Like the folk-tales,
the spirituals are being made and forgotten every day. There is this difference : the makers of the songs
of the present go about from town to town and church to church singing their songs. Some are printed
and called ballads, and offered for sale after the services at ten and fifteen cents each. Others just go about
singing them in competition with other religious minstrels. The lifting of the collection is the time for
the song battles. Quite a bit of rivalry develops.

These songs, even the printed ones, do not remain long in their original form. Every congregation
that takes it up alters it considerably. For instance, *The Dying Bed Maker*, which is easily the most popular
of the recent compositions, has been changed to *He's a Mind Regulator* by a Baptist church in New Orleans.

The idea that the whole body of spirituals are " sorrow songs " is ridiculous. They cover a wide range
of subjects from a peeve at gossipers to Death and Judgment.

The nearest thing to a description one can reach is that they are Negro religious songs, sung by a
group, and a group bent on expression of feelings and not on sound effects.

359

Spirituals and Neo-Spirituals

There never has been a presentation of genuine Negro spirituals to any audience anywhere. What is being sung by the concert artists and glee clubs are the works of Negro composers or adaptors *based* on the spirituals. Under this head come the works of Harry T. Burleigh, Rosamond Johnson, Lawrence Brown, Nathaniel Dett, Hall Johnson and Work. All good work and beautiful, but *not* the spirituals. These neo-spirituals are the outgrowth of the glee clubs. Fisk University boasts perhaps the oldest and certainly the most famous of these. They have spread their interpretation over America and Europe. Hampton and Tuskegee have not been unheard. But with all the glee clubs and soloists, there has not been one genuine spiritual presented.

To begin with, Negro spirituals are not solo or quartette material. The jagged harmony is what makes it, and it ceases to be what it was when this is absent. Neither can any group be trained to reproduce it. Its truth dies under training like flowers under hot water. The harmony of the true spiritual is not regular. The dissonances are important and not to be ironed out by the trained musician. The various parts break in at any old time. Falsetto often takes the place of regular voices for short periods. Keys change. Moreover, each singing of the piece is a new creation. The congregation is bound by no rules. No two times singing of it is alike, so that we must consider the rendition of a song not as a final thing, but as a mood. It won't be the same thing next Sunday.

Negro songs to be heard truly must be sung by a group, and a group bent on expression of feelings and not on sound effects.

Glee clubs and concert singers put on their tuxedoes,[1] bow prettily to the audience, get the pitch and burst into magnificent song—but not *Negro* song. The real Negro singer cares nothing about pitch. The first notes just burst out and the rest of the church join in—fired by the same inner urge. Every man trying to express himself through song. Every man for himself. Hence the harmony and disharmony, the shifting keys and broken time that make up the spiritual.

I have noticed that whenever an untampered-with congregation attempts the renovated spirituals, the people grow self-conscious. They sing sheepishly in unison. None of the glorious individualistic flights that make up their own songs. Perhaps they feel on strange ground. Like the unlettered parent before his child just home from college. At any rate they are not very popular.

This is no condemnation of the neo-spirituals. They are a valuable contribution to the music and literature of the world. But let no one imagine that they are the songs of the people, as sung by them.

The lack of dialect in the religious expression—particularly in the prayers—will seem irregular.

The truth is, that the religious service is a conscious art expression. The artist is consciously creating—carefully choosing every syllable and every breath. The dialect breaks through only when the speaker has reached the emotional pitch where he loses self-consciousness.

In the mouth of the Negro the English language loses its stiffness, yet conveys its meaning accurately. "The booming bounderries of this whirling world" conveys just as accurate a picture as mere "boundaries," and a little music is gained besides. "The rim bones of nothing" is just as truthful as "limitless space."

Negro singing and formal speech are breathy. The audible breathing is part of the performance and various devices are resorted to to adorn the breath taking. Even the lack of breath is embellished with syllables. This is, of course, the very antithesis of white vocal art. European singing is considered good when each syllable floats out on a column of air, seeming not to have any mechanics at all. Breathing must be hidden. Negro song ornaments both the song and the mechanics. It is said of a popular preacher, "He's got a good straining voice." I will make a parable to illustrate the difference between Negro and European.

A white man built a house. So he got it built and he told the man: "Plaster it good so that nobody can see the beams and uprights." So he did. Then he had it papered with beautiful paper, and painted the outside. And a Negro built him a house. So when he got the beams and all in, he carved beautiful grotesques over all the sills and stanchions, and beams and rafters. So both went to live in their houses and were happy.

The well-known "ha!" of the Negro preacher is a breathing device. It is the tail end of the expulsion just before inhalation. Instead of permitting the breath to drain out, when the wind gets too low for words, the remnant is expelled violently. Example: (inhalation) "And oh!"; (full breath) "my Father and my wonder-working God"; (explosive exhalation) "ha!"

Chants and hums are not used indiscriminately as it would appear to a casual listener. They have

[1] Evening dress.

360

Spirituals and Neo-Spirituals

a definite place and time. They are used to " bear up " the speaker. As Mama Jane of Second Zion Baptist Church, New Orleans, explained to me : " What point they come out on, you bear 'em up."

For instance, if the preacher should say : " Jesus will lead us," the congregation would bear him up with : " I'm got my ha-hands in my Jesus' hands." If in prayer or sermon, the mention is made of nailing Christ to the cross : " Didn't Calvary tremble when they nailed Him down."

There is no definite post-prayer chant. One may follow, however, because of intense emotion. A song immediately follows prayer. There is a pre-prayer hum which depends for its material upon the song just sung. It is usually a pianissimo continuation of the song without words. If some of the people use the words it is done so indistinctly that they would be hard to catch by a person unfamiliar with the song.

As indefinite as hums sound, they also are formal and can be found unchanged all over the South. The Negroised white hymns are not exactly sung. They are converted into a barbaric chant that is not a chant. It is a sort of liquefying of words. These songs are always used at funerals and on any solemn occasion. The Negro has created no songs for death and burials, in spite of the sombre subject matter contained in some of the spirituals. Negro songs are one and all based on a dance-possible rhythm. The heavy interpretations have been added by the more cultured singers. So for funerals fitting white hymns are used.

Beneath the seeming informality of religious worship there is a set formality. Sermons, prayers, moans and testimonies have their definite forms. The individual may hang as many new ornaments upon the traditional form as he likes, but the audience would be disagreeably surprised if the form were abandoned. Any new and original elaboration is welcomed, however, and this brings out the fact that all religious expression among Negroes is regarded as art, and ability is recognised as definitely as in any other art. The beautiful prayer receives the accolade as well as the beautiful song. It is merely a form of expression which people generally are not accustomed to think of as art. Nothing outside of the Old Testament is as rich in figure as a Negro prayer. Some instances are unsurpassed anywhere in literature.

There is a lively rivalry in the technical artistry of all of these fields. It is a special honor to be called upon to pray over the covered communion table, for the greatest prayer-artist present is chosen by the pastor for this, a lively something spreads over the church as he kneels, and the " bearing up " hum precedes him. It continues sometimes through the introduction, but ceases as he makes the complimentary salutation to the deity. This consists in giving to God all the titles that form allows.

The introduction to the prayer usually consists of one or two verses of some well-known hymn. " O, that I knew a secret place " seems to be the favorite. There is a definite pause after this, then follows an elaboration of all or parts of the Lord's Prayer. Follows after that what I call the setting, that is, the artist calling attention to the physical situation of himself and the church. After the dramatic setting, the action begins.

There are certain rhythmic breaks throughout the prayer, and the church " bears him up " at every one of these. There is in the body of the prayer an accelerando passage where the audience takes no part. It would be like applauding in the middle of a solo at the Metropolitan. It is here that the artist comes forth. He adorns the prayer with every sparkle of earth, water and sky, and nobody wants to miss a syllable. He comes down from this height to a slower tempo and is borne up again. The last few sentences are unaccompanied, for here again one listens to the individual's closing peroration. Several may join in the final amen. The best figure that I can think of is that the prayer is an obligato over and above the harmony of the assembly.

The Southern Workman

VOL. LVII   June 1928   No. 6

A FOLK CULTURE IN THE MAKING

BY E. FRANKLIN FRAZIER

ANY development which takes place among the colored people of America possesses significance from two standpoints. First, it indicates a new orientation towards American life as a whole; and second, it signifies a change in the relations and values within the group life of the Negroes themselves. Consequently, from these two standpoints one may view the appearance of the New Negro. By some, this new development has been interpreted as a movement in the direction of cultural autonomy. This immediately raises the question as to how far it is possible for the colored group to develop an autonomous culture; for such development is not only dependent upon the extent ·to which there is created a group tradition, but it is limited by the relationship of the group to .American life. It is the purpose of the writer to indicate some of the limitations placed upon such development, and at the same time to give what seems to him one possible contribution in this direction. Since, however, the idea of cultural self-determination generally implies certain unfounded assumptions concerning the relation of culture to race, something will be said first about this question.

The naive and uncritical assumption generally has been that cultural traits are the expression of the genius or biological characteristics of the race possessing the respective traits. Contributions flowing from many sources have helped to crystallize until lately this belief. For example, when the evolutionary hypothesis was first accepted as explaining the existence of present social as well as physical types, the conditions of so-called savage or primitive peoples were regarded as stages in the progressive development of mankind. These stages in the social development of mankind were not due, according to such theorizing, to external geographic and social factors, but to the internal biological development which was going on. These inferior peoples were supposed, because of inferior brain organization, to lack the power of abstract thought and intellectual concentration; and to show less emotional control than the races which were supposed to stand at the top of the evolutionary process. While this made a very beautiful picture and afforded an easy explanation for an obscure and complex problem, it was upset by patient and extended investigations of native peoples.

These assumptions have proved untenable through the field studies of ethnologists. The languages alone of primitive peoples show them to possess the capacity for abstract thought, and, so far as their ability to reason is concerned, they appear to be able to see relationships as well as modern man. Their lack of the power of intellectual concentration was a belief based upon the tales of travelers who said that these people showed little interest in the questions which were put to them. But trained anthropologists who have studied these peoples have testified that when their interest has been aroused they have shown in some cases intellectual concentration beyond that of the investigator. Likewise with emotional control. It was necessary to appreciate the interests in the lives of uncivilized men in order to realize to what extent they possessed emotional control. The numerous taboos alone to which they were subject furnished ample evidence of emotional control.

While some authorities do not place much credence in the theory of fundamental intellectual differences between races, they hold to the belief of temperamental differences. The Negro is supposed to show a temperamental predilection for music. Even here we are dealing with a highly complex phenomenon which cannot be solved by such a simple explanation. According to the objective, quantitative study of Guy Johnson, a preliminary statement of whose findings has appeared in a previous number of the *Southern Workman*, the Negro does not show any superiority in this regard over the white man.

The reader's attention has been directed to the question of the relation of culture to race because many of those who are urging the Negro to develop along lines of his racial endowment always imply that culture is an expression of biologically inherited traits. Even those who have argued against race purity by showing that the advances in civilization have been made by mixed races have generally overlooked the fact that progress has come with the disruption of old cultural forms. Although this has been accompanied by the mixture of races, the decisive factor has seemingly been social and not biological.

There have been numerous attempts to show that many

of the deviations from American civilization which the culture of the American Negro shows are due to his African social inheritance. Although investigation is now in progress to determine just what the Negro has brought from Africa, it may be asserted without fear of contradiction that when the Negro was brought to America there was a well nigh complete break with his African past. The nature of his subordination in America assured this. The Negro has gradually taken over different elements of the civilization of America, as they have had meaning for him and his knowledge has been funded. The slowness of the process has been due to his relative isolation—proportionate to the extent to which he has participated in the common social heritage. If the Negro were completely isolated, the possibility of his developing an independent culture would be great. But the Negro is forced to participate in the whole gamut of American life.

The Negro, taking over the existing cultural forms in America, is tied up so intimately with the whole fabric of American life that even the cry for economic independence in the sphere of business often becomes futile when we realize to what extent he is subject to the mechanism of credit about him. At the present time, those Negro artists who are supposed by some to be giving expression to the aesthetic emotions of the race are able to make their contributions because of their mastery of the social forms of American culture. In fact it appears that these artists are working on the materials of the Negro's experience in American life. The fact that white writers have made conspicuous contributions by working with these same materials should convince one that the creative power does not lie in any biological inheritance.

The recent outburst of artistic and other forms of expression on the part of the Negro has followed very closely his urbanization and wider contacts as a result of the World War. The breaking up of old habits of thought and participation in a wider world have created what we call a New Negro. This phenomenon has been similar to other movements in which the isolation of a people has been destroyed.

But the Negro has been charged with being only an imitator. Both his well wishers and detractors have always exhorted him to be himself. Does our exposition of the Negro's position in American life exclude the possibility of selection on his part of any of the elements of the culture about him? Must he fall in with every fad of American life? It seems to the writer that while the Negro, because of his intimate relations to American life, cannot develop an autonomous culture, it is possible to consciously direct his energies into those channels which will enrich his life and ac-

celerate the process by which he is becoming civilized. The
Negro is fast building up a tradition which has meaning for
him. Negro boys and girls are learning more each day of
the past through which the group has come. Men and women
of Negro descent are entering into their consciousness as
models. What follows suggests a means by which the Negro
can enter even more into that part of the experience of his
group which has been given artistic expression.

During his teaching experience in the South, the writer
has had many occasions to attend the annual fashion shows
which the schools hold. On these occasions the writer has
remarked the way in which children from all walks of life
have been dressed up in all kinds of clothes and paraded
across the stage. So often the spectacle of these children
bedecked in clothes which were intended for a wealthy lei-
sured class has appeared ridiculous. This has no bearing
on the way in which many of our schools have done valuable
work in teaching Negroes how to dress. The writer is referring to those fashion shows encouraged and sponsored by
manufacturers of clothes which are becoming more popular
each year. Not only does this practice create in the children
false values, but it is letting slip by an opportunity to create
a real appreciation of the folk life of the Negro through
dramatic expression. Suppose instead of such exhibitions
these schools had their students give the plays of Negro life
such as Paul Green has written. Here would be an opportunity to develop dramatic talent. Here would be an opportunity for theatre goers to escape the influence of the idiotic
moving picture. In turning away from the cheap erotic emotions exploited in the films, the Negro would participate in
the deep emotional life of the race. Nothing would be greater
aid to his self-respect than genuine appreciation of the characters of his group. Negro schools in the South would then
mean more to their communities than the exhibitions given
by their athletic teams. Negro schols, which hold a strategic
position in the cultural life of the group, would gain a higher
conception of their role in the community.

All of this appears very theoretical. Probably the writer, who has often thought of, and spoken of, the advantage
of the course which he has suggested, would never have
undertaken to express his ideas in writing had it not been
for an event which he saw in Chicago in November. He had
an opportunity to attend the Tenth Anniversary Celebration
of the Soviet Republic. On that occasion one of the chief
attractions on the program was pantomimes built up on the
life of the workers. Here he saw a group actually creating
artistic forms out of their daily lives. They were attempting

to substitute proletarian for what they called bourgeois art. The writer realized for the first time the artistic possibilities of activities which were normally regarded as routine drudgery. Doubtless many of these people, who had been peasants in Europe, were carrying over from their agricultural lives into industry certain ideas of folk expression. Yet they were actually creating out of their experience in America those forms of artistic expression which had meaning for them. The Negro has an experience which is fertile with possibilities for creating a folk art. Already he has at hand in the plays a form of artistic expression which can enrich his life.

This calls for intelligent direction on the part of his leaders. The leadership which has gone out to the Negro masses has been inclined to look to the more practical things of life. While it is true that those leaders who have sought to make him more efficient economically have not neglected entirely the things pertaining to higher living, they have regarded them more from a utilitarian aspect. A leadership which will lead the Negro into an appreciation of the spiritual values of his experience in America is needed. In this way the artistic creations of the leaders will be made effective in the lives of the masses. A tendency in this direction can be seen in the increasing use of James Weldon Johnson's Negro Anthem in the schools. In this article we have attempted to indicate how a broad-visioned leadership might exploit a rich source of racial experience for the enhancement of the lives of the masses and at the same time bring the masses into communion with the creative spirits of the race. In this way the Negro will be creating a culture that will be unique but not in opposition to his growth and wider participation in American life as a whole.

THE DILEMMA OF THE NEGRO AUTHOR

BY JAMES WELDON JOHNSON

THE Negro author—the creative author—has arrived. He is here. He appears in the lists of the best publishers. He even breaks into the lists of the best-sellers. To the general American public he is a novelty, a strange phenomenon, a miracle straight out of the skies. Well, he *is* a novelty, but he is by no means a new thing.

The line of American Negro authors runs back for a hundred and fifty years, back to Phillis Wheatley, the poet. Since Phillis Wheatley there have been several hundred Negro authors who have written books of many kinds. But in all these generations down to within the past six years only seven or eight of the hundreds have ever been heard of by the general American public or even by the specialists in American literature. As many Negro writers have gained recognition by both in the past six years as in all the generations gone before. What has happened is that efforts which have been going on for more than a century are being noticed and appreciated at last, and that this appreciation has served as a stimulus to greater effort and output. America is aware today that there are such things as Negro authors. Several converging forces have been at work to produce this state of mind. Had these forces been at work three decades ago, it is possible that we then should have had a condition similar to the one which now exists.

Now that the Negro author has come into the range of vision of the American public eye, it seems to me only fair to point out some of the difficulties he finds in his way. But I wish to state emphatically that I have no intention of making an apology or asking any special allowances for him; such a plea would at once disqualify him and void the very recognition he has gained. But the Negro writer does face peculiar difficulties that ought to be taken into account when passing judgment upon him.

It is unnecessary to say that he faces every one of the difficulties common to all that crowd of demon-driven individuals who feel that they must write. But the Aframerican author faces a special problem which the plain American author knows nothing about—the problem of the double audience. It is more than a double audience; it is a divided audience, an audience made up of two elements with differing and often opposite and antagonistic points of view. His audience is always both white America and black America. The moment a Negro writer takes up his pen or sits down to his typewriter he is immediately called upon to solve, consciously or unconsciously, this problem of the double audience. To whom shall he address himself, to his own black group or to white America? Many a Negro writer has fallen down, as it were, between these two stools.

It may be asked why he doesn't just go ahead and write and not bother himself about audiences. That is easier said than done. It is doubtful if anything with meaning can be written unless the writer has some definite audience in mind. His audience may be as far away as the angelic host or the rulers of darkness, but an audience he must have in mind. As soon as he selects his audience he immediately falls, whether he wills it or not, under the laws which govern the influence of the audience upon the artist, laws that operate in every branch of art.

Now, it is axiomatic that the artist achieves his best when working at his best with the materials he knows best. And it goes without saying that the material which the Negro as a creative or general writer knows best comes out of the life and experience of the colored people in America. The overwhelming bulk of the best work done by Aframerican writers has some bearing on the Negro and his relations to civilization and society in the United States. Leaving authors, white or black, writing for coteries on special and technical subjects out of the discussion, it is safe to say that the white American author, when he sits down to write, has in mind a white audience—and naturally. The influence of the Negro as a group on his work is infinitesimal if not zero. Even when he talks about the Negro he talks to white people. But with the Aframerican author the case is different. When he attempts to handle his best known material he is thrown upon two, indeed, if it is permissible to say so, upon three horns of a dilemma. He must intentionally or unintentionally choose a black audience or a white audience or a combination of the two; and each of them presents peculiar difficulties.

If the Negro author selects white America as his audience he is bound to run up against many long-standing artistic conceptions about the Negro; against numerous conventions and traditions which through age have become binding; in a word, against a whole row of hard-set stereotypes which are not easily broken up. White America has some firm opinions as to what the Negro is, and consequently some pretty well fixed ideas as to what should be written about him, and how.

What is the Negro in the artistic conception of white America? In the brighter light, he is a simple, indolent, docile, improvident peasant; a singing, dancing, laughing, weeping child; picturesque beside his log cabin and in the snowy fields of cotton; naïvely charming with his banjo and his songs in the moonlight and along the lazy Southern rivers; a faithful, ever-smiling and genuflecting old servitor to the white folks of quality; a pathetic and pitiable figure. In a darker light, he is an impulsive, irrational, passionate savage, reluctantly wearing a thin coat of culture, sullenly hating the white man, but holding an innate and unescapable belief in the white man's superiority; an everlastingly alien and irredeemable element in the nation; a menace to Southern civilization; a threat to Nordic race purity; a figure casting a sinister shadow across the future of the country.

Ninety-nine one-hundredths of all that has been written about the Negro in the United States in three centuries and read with any degree of interest or pleasure by white America has been written in conformity to one or more of these ideas. I am not saying that they do not provide good material for literature; in fact, they make material for poetry and romance and comedy and tragedy of a high order. But I do say they have become stencils, and that the Negro author finds these stencils inadequate for the portrayal and interpretation of Negro life today. Moreover, when he does attempt to make use of them he finds himself impaled upon the second horn of his dilemma.

II

It is known that art—literature in particular, unless it be sheer fantasy—must be based on more or less well established conventions, upon ideas that have some roots in the general consciousness, that are at least somewhat familiar to the public mind. It is this that gives it verisimilitude and finality. Even revolutionary literature, if it is to have any convincing power, must start from a basis of conventions, regardless of how unconventional its objective may be. These conventions are changed by slow and gradual processes—except they be changed in a flash. The conventions held by white America regarding the Negro will be changed. Actually they are being changed, but they have not yet sufficiently changed to lessen to any great extent the dilemma of the Negro author.

It would be straining the credulity of white America beyond the breaking point for a Negro writer to put out a novel dealing with the wealthy class of colored people. The idea of Negroes of wealth living in a luxurious manner is still too unfamiliar. Such a story would have to be written in a burlesque vein to make it at all plausible and acceptable. Before Florence Mills and Josephine Baker implanted a new general idea in the public mind it would have been worse than a waste of time for a Negro author to write for white America the story of a Negro girl who rose in spite of all obstacles, racial and others, to a place of world success and acclaim on the musical revue stage. It would be proof of little less than supreme genius in a Negro poet for him to take one of the tragic characters in American Negro history—say Crispus Attucks or Nat Turner or Denmark Vesey—, put heroic language in his mouth and have white America accept the work as authentic. American Negroes as heroes form no part of white America's concept of the race. Indeed, I question if three out of ten of the white Americans who will read these lines know anything of either Attucks, Turner or Vesey; although each of the three played a rôle in the history of the nation. The Aframerican poet might take an African chief or warrior, set him forth in heroic couplets or blank verse and present him to white America with infinitely greater chance of having his work accepted.

But these limiting conventions held by white America do not constitute the whole difficulty of the Negro author in dealing with a white audience. In addition to these conventions regarding the Negro as a race, white America has certain definite opinions regarding the Negro as an artist, regarding the scope of his efforts. White America has a strong feeling that Negro artists should refrain from making use of white subject matter. I mean by that, subject matter which it feels belongs to the white world. In plain words, white America does not welcome seeing the Negro competing with the white man on what it considers the white man's own ground.

In many white people this feeling is dormant, but brought to the test it flares up, if only faintly. During his first season in this country after his European success a most common criticism of Roland Hayes was provoked by the fact that his programme consisted of groups of English, French, German and Italian songs, closing always with a group of Negro Spirituals. A remark frequently made was, "Why doesn't he confine himself to the Spirituals?" This in face of the fact that no tenor on the American concert stage could surpass Hayes in singing French and German songs. The truth is that white America was not quite prepared to relish the sight of a black man in a dress suit singing French and German love songs, and singing them exquisitely. The first reaction was that there was something incongruous about it. It gave a jar to the old conventions and something of a shock to the Nordic superiority complex. The years have not been many since Negro players have dared to interpolate a love duet in a musical show to be witnessed by white people. The representation of romantic love-making by Negroes struck the white audience as somewhat ridiculous; Negroes were supposed to mate in a more primeval manner.

White America has for a long time been annexing and appropriating Negro territory, and is prone to think of every part of the domain it now controls as originally—and aboriginally—its own. One sometimes hears the critics in reviewing a Negro musical show lament the fact that it is so much like white musical shows. But a great deal of this similarity it would be hard to avoid because of the plain fact that two out of the four chief ingredients in the present day white musical show, the music and the dancing, are directly derived from the Negro. These ideas and opinions regarding the scope of artistic effort affect the Negro author, the poet in particular. So whenever an Aframerican writer addresses himself to white America and attempts to break away from or break through these conventions and limitations he makes more than an ordinary demand upon his literary skill and power.

At this point it would appear that a most natural thing for the Negro author to do would be to say, "Damn the white audience!" and devote himself to addressing his own race exclusively. But when he turns from the conventions of white America he runs afoul of the taboos of black America. He has no more absolute freedom to speak as he pleases addressing black America than he has in addressing white America. There are certain phases of life that he dare not touch, certain subjects that he dare not critically discuss, certain manners of treatment that he dare not use—except at the risk of rousing bitter resentment. It is quite possible for a Negro author to do a piece of work, good from every literary point of view, and at the same time bring down on his head the wrath of the entire colored pulpit and press, and gain among the literate element of his own people the reputation of being a prostitutor of his talent and a betrayer of his race—not by any means a pleasant position to get into.

This state of mind on the part of the colored people may strike white America as stupid and intolerant, but it is not without some justification and not entirely without precedent; the white South on occasion discloses a similar sensitiveness. The colored people of the United States are anomalously situated. They are a segregated and antagonized minority in a very large nation, a minority unremittingly on the defensive. Their faults and failings are exploited to produce exaggerated effects. Consequently, they have a strong feeling

against exhibiting to the world anything but their best points. They feel that other groups may afford to do otherwise but, as yet, the Negro cannot. This is not to say that they refuse to listen to criticism of themselves, for they often listen to Negro speakers excoriating the race for its faults and foibles and vices. But these criticisms are not for the printed page. They are not for the ears or eyes of white America.

A curious illustration of this defensive state of mind is found in the Negro theatres. In those wherein Negro players give Negro performances for Negro audiences all of the Negro weaknesses, real and reputed, are burlesqued and ridiculed in the most hilarious manner, and are laughed at and heartily enjoyed. But the presence of a couple of dozen white people would completely change the psychology of the audience, and the players. If some of the performances so much enjoyed by strictly Negro audiences in Negro theatres were put on, say, in a Broadway theatre, a wave of indignation would sweep Aframerica from the avenues of Harlem to the canebrakes of Louisiana. These taboos of black America are as real and binding as the conventions of white America. Conditions may excuse if not warrant them; nevertheless, it is unfortunate that they exist, for their effect is blighting. In past years they have discouraged in Negro authors the production of everything but *nice* literature; they have operated to hold their work down to literature of the defensive, exculpatory sort. They have a restraining effect at the present time which Negro writers are compelled to reckon with.

This division of audience takes the solid ground from under the feet of the Negro writer and leaves him suspended. Either choice carries hampering and discouraging conditions. The Negro author may please one audience and at the same time rouse the resentment of the other; or he may please the other and totally fail to rouse the interest of the one. The situation, moreover, constantly subjects him to the temptation of posing and posturing for the one audience or the other; and the sincerity and soundness of his work are vitiated whether he poses for white or black.

The dilemma is not made less puzzling by the fact that practically it is an extremely difficult thing for the Negro author in the United States to address himself solely to either of these two audiences. If he analyzes what he writes he will find that on one page black America is his whole or main audience, and on the very next page white America. In fact, a psychoanalysis of the Negro authors of the defensive and exculpatory literature, written in strict conformity to the taboos of black America, would reveal that they were unconsciously addressing themselves mainly to white America.

III

I have sometimes thought it would be a way out, that the Negro author would be on surer ground and truer to himself, if he could disregard white America; if he could say to white America, "What I have written, I have written. I hope you'll be interested and like it. If not, I can't help it." But it is impossible for a sane American Negro to write with total disregard for nine-tenths of the people of the United States. Situated as his own race is amidst and amongst them, their influence is irresistible.

I judge there is not a single Negro writer who is not, at least secondarily, impelled by the desire to make his work have some effect on the white world for the good of his race. It may be thought that the work of the Negro writer, on account of this last named condition, gains in pointedness what it loses in breadth. Be that as it may, the situation is for the time one in which he is inextricably placed. Of course, the Negro author can try the experiment of putting black America in the orchestra chairs, so to speak, and keeping white America in the gallery, but he is likely at any moment to find his audience shifting places on him, and sometimes without notice.

And now, instead of black America and white America as separate or alternating audiences, what about the combination of the two into one? That, I believe, is the only way out. However, there needs to be more than a combination, there needs to be a fusion. In time, I cannot say how much time, there will come a gradual and natural rapprochement of these two sections of the Negro author's audience. There will come a breaking up and remodelling of most of white America's traditional stereotypes, forced by the advancement of the Negro in the various phases of our national life. Black America will abolish many of its taboos. A sufficiently large class of colored people will progress enough and become strong enough to render a constantly sensitive and defensive attitude on the part of the race unnecessary and distasteful. In the end, the Negro author will have something close to a common audience, and will be about as free from outside limitations as other writers.

Meanwhile, the making of a common audience out of white and black America presents the Negro author with enough difficulties to constitute a third horn of his dilemma. It is a task that is a very high test for all his skill and abilities, but it can be and has been accomplished. The equipped Negro author working at his best in his best known material can achieve this end; but, standing on his racial foundation, he must fashion something that rises above race, and reaches out to the universal in truth and beauty. And so, when a Negro author does write so as to fuse white and black America into one interested and approving audience he has performed no slight feat, and has most likely done a sound piece of literary work.

THE LARGER SUCCESS *

BY JAMES WELDON JOHNSON

Secretary of the National Association for the Advancement of Colored People

MEN may be divided into any number of classes—rich and poor, educated and ignorant, successful and unsuccessful, and so on; but none of these classifications is fundamental. A more vital classification or division of men would be those who live only in the present and those who live both in the present and the future. Having or lacking the power to project oneself into the future is what primarily divides men who move forward and upward from those who remain stationary or slip back.

There is a homely illustration often given to mark this dividing line. It is the difference between a man who plants a tree and a man to whom such an act would never appeal. The man who plants a tree performs an act in the spirit of the Great Creator. He serves not only himself but future generations unknown to him, who will enjoy its fruit and its shade.

---

*Commencement address, Hampton Institute, June 1923

To realize in life the deeper meanings of success one's vision cannot be limited by the circumscribed horizon of the present. It must transcend those bounds and take in the future. This comprehension of the future involves the spirit of altruism, the divine spirit of service to others, and embraces all men and all generations; but it carries not only these abstract and, perhaps to some, vague principles of altruism, but also a very concrete and individual value. For, contrary to the general notion, there is a future which is neither hazy nor unknown. There is a definitely known future, a future which it is possible to know as well as the past is known. This is the future in which those who are today going out from this institution are now probably most interested.

The future is commonly regarded as a mystery in the hands of soothsayers and fortune-tellers. We may grant that this is true of the insignificant details of the future. If a young man is curious to know whether he will marry a girl with light hair and gray eyes or dark hair and brown eyes, let him go to a fortune-teller; but if he desires to know if the sum total of life for him will be a success or a failure, he can find out for himself. For the fundamental and vital facts about the future are subject to governing laws—laws that are as fixed as those we call the laws of nature. No man, unless insane, would jump off the Woolworth Tower and expect to go up. He would know that there is a law called gravitation which never fails to operate. Nor would any scientist put one part of hydrogen with two parts of oxygen and expect to get anything but water.

Following these same principles one may observe himself or others and, depending upon whether he finds diligence or indolence, thrift or shiftlessness, sincerity or hypocrisy, the wasting of time or the improving of opportunities, courage or cowardice, be able to prophesy, and without the aid of a fortune-teller, whether there will be success or failure in life. Here we are reduced to commonplace platitudes, but when we get down to the fundamentals of life, what is there, after all, to stand upon but these same moral platitudes? It is these platitudes, so often sneered at, that contain the wisdom of the human race, proven through ages of experience.

We can foretell the future when we know and understand the past. The future of individuals and nations is all plainly written in history. What man was there familiar with the science of history who could not have foretold the Great War from which the world has not yet recovered? In fact, a number of men did foretell it. The nations of Europe had been doing what nations have done over and over again since the beginning of recorded history, and their acts were followed by precisely the same results.

And so, along these fundamental lines, anyone can tell whether, in the deeper sense, his life is to be a failure or a success. But here I should add that defeat must not be confounded with failure. Many have gone down for the sake of principle and truth. They have been defeated but they have not failed. The crucified Christ on the cross has become the greatest spiritual force in the world.

And now we come back to the larger sense of the future—that sense of the future which comprehends not only the greatest service to self but the greatest service to others, that sense of the future which involves success in its deepest and highest meaning, that which brings not only self-gratification and self-satisfaction but also gratification and satisfaction to our fellows. This is the success to which I wish to point you, and I wish at the same time to impress upon you that this larger success contains within itself the smaller and more concrete success. It is through service in pursuit of the larger success that the smaller success comes unsought.

And what an incentive there is for you into whose faces I am looking for service in the pursuit of the larger success! Millions are waiting upon you—you who are trained and inspired—to bring them light, to bring them hope, to bring them help. You have before you the opportunity to take part in a fight for common humanity and common justice, to have a pioneer's share in building for the future greatness of a race, the opportunity to help in the making of our common country, in deed as well as in name, the greatest democracy under which men have ever lived. These constitute an incentive for service which the white youth of America might well envy you.

And are you familiar with the wonderful background of those you are called upon particularly to serve? Do you realize that you are sprung from and belong to a great race—a race great in numbers, great in physical strength and stamina; and numerical strength and physical strength are prime essentials of racial greatness? And do you also realize that this race from which you are sprung is endowed with many wonderful qualities and gifts: that its historic and prehistoric background is something of which you have no reason to be ashamed and of which you have many reasons to be intensely proud?

Popular opinion has it that the Negro in Africa has been from time immemorial a savage. This is far from the truth. Such an opinion is possible only because there has been and still is an historical conspiracy against Africa which has successfully stripped the Negro race of all credit for what it contributed in past ages to the birth and growth of civilization. Makers of history have taught the world that from the beginning of time the Negro has never been anything but a race of savages and slaves. Anyone who is willing to dig out the truth can learn that civilization was born in the upper reaches of the River Nile: that, in the misty ages of the past, pure black men in Africa were observing the stars, were turning human speech into song, were discovering religious truths, were laying the foundations of government, were utilizing the metals, developing agriculture, inventing primitive tools; in fact, giving the impulse which started man on his upward climb.

The truth is that the torch of civilization was lighted on the banks of the Nile; and we can trace the course of that torch, sometimes flaming, sometimes flickering, and at times all but extinguished,—we can trace it up through Egypt, around the borders of the Mediterranean, through Greece and Italy and Spain, on into Northern Europe. In the hands of each people that held it the torch of civilization has grown brighter and brighter and then died down until it was passed on to other hands. The fact that dark ages fell upon Africa and her people is no more of a discredit than the fact that dark ages fell upon the buried empires of Asia Minor or Asia or ancient Greece. Races and peoples have in their turn carried this torch of civilization to a certain height and then sunk back under the weight of their own exertions.

It seems that there is more truth than mythology in the story of Antæus and Hercules. Hercules, in wrestling with Antæus, found that each time the giant was thrown he arose stronger. The secret lay in the fact that the earth was his mother, and each time he came in contact with her he gained renewed strength. Hercules then resorted to the stratagem of holding him off the earth until his strength was exhausted. So with races and peoples. It seems that after they have climbed to a certain height they must fall back and lie for a period close to Mother Earth. And this reminds us of the truth that all things in the universe move in cycles; so who knows but that, in the whirl of God's great wheel, the torch may not again flame in the upper valley of the Nile?

Nor need you go so far to find a background which will give you confidence and justifiable pride. The record of the Negro in this country constitutes one of the most wonderful pages in American history. Brought here against his will, cut off entirely from the moorings of his native culture, however primitive it may have been, he has, in spite of obstacles, never turned his back to the light. Whatever may be his short-comings, however slow may have been his progress, however disappointing may have been his achievements, he has never consciously sought the downward path. He has always kept his face to the light and has continued to struggle forward and upward, making his humble contribution to the common pros-perity and glory of our land. He has woven himself into the woof and warp of the nation. First setting foot upon the soil of this very State, before the landing of the Pilgrim Fathers, he has, in language, in customs, in mode of thought, and in re-ligion, become thoroughly American.

When this country was plunged into the great World War and we were startled by the thought that perhaps after all we were not a nation but merely a conglomeration of groups as-sembled here under one flag; and when there was distrust and suspicion and even panic, there came the realization that side by side with the original American stocks that landed at Jamestown and at Plymouth stood the American Negro. In-deed, he has every right to say:—

> This land is ours by right of birth,
>   This land is ours by right of toil;
> We helped to turn its virgin earth,
>   Our sweat is in its fruitful soil.
>
> Where once the tangled forest stood,—
>   Where flourished once rank weed and thorn,—
> Behold the path-traced, peaceful wood,
>   The cotton white, the yellow corn.
>
> To gain these fruits that have been earned,
>   To hold these fields that have been won,
> Our arms have strained, our backs have burned,
>   Bent bare beneath a ruthless sun.
>
> That banner which is now the type
>   Of victory on field and flood—
> Remember, its first crimson stripe
>   Was dyed by Attucks' willing blood.
>
> And never yet has come the cry—
>   When that fair flag has been assailed—
> For men to do, for men to die,
>   That we have faltered or have failed.
>
> We've helped to bear it, rent and torn,
>   Through many a hot-breath'd battle breeze;
> Held in our hands, it has been borne
>   And planted far across the seas.
>
> And never yet—O haughty Land,
>   Let us, at least, for this be praised—
> Has one black, treason-guided hand
>   Ever against that flag been raised.

Then should we speak but servile words,
 Or shall we hang our heads in shame?
Stand back of new-come foreign hordes,
 And fear our heritage to claim?
No! stand erect and without fear,
 And for our foes let this suffice—
We've bought a rightful sonship here,
 And we have more than paid the price.

And not only has the American Negro served America, but he has made his contribution to her civilization, especially in art. He has given to America her only great body of folklore and he has likewise given to her her only great body of folk music, that wonderful mass of music which will some day furnish material to Negro composers through which they will voice, not only the soul of their race, but the soul of America.

I have always been glad of the fact that Hampton has made itself the home of that music, that here it has been nurtured and taught and spread, that here your own Nathaniel Dett has developed it in a way to attract the attention of the musicians of the world. This has been an important work because, under a misconception, there has at times been a tendency among Negroes themselves to be ashamed of their greatest contribution to American art. This great gift has sometimes been regarded as a kind of sideshow, something for occasional exhibition, when it is the touchstone, it is the magic thing, it is that by which the Negro can bridge all chasms. No persons, however hostile, can listen to the Negro's singing of this wonderful music without having their hostility melted down.

It is a race with this creditable and even glorious background, with these wonderful potentialities, that you are called upon to serve. This background and these potentialities you ought to study, and from that study you will learn that it is not dead and hopeless material that you have to work with but material waiting to be moulded into an essential element of the future American civilization.

This service has a definite end in view. It is the securing for yourselves and those for whom and among whom you will specifically work the status of full and unlimited American citizenship. I shall not here take the time to re-state the problem of the struggle that is before you. You know the conditions, and evidently you have a knowledge of the favorable and opposing forces that are at work. I shall only say that the problem which is commonly called the Negro Problem but which is, in fact, the American Problem, is not simple; it is complex. It is at the same time economic, social, and sexual. It is complicated by the diverse attitudes taken toward it by white people of various groups. It is further complicated by the fact that for the Negro himself it is compound, in that it is both an individual problem and a group problem.

The compound phase of this question for the Negro is of vital importance because it is the least understood phase of the whole problem, and because it is compound it resolves itself into the two following propositions:—

(1) The Negro must fit himself to the very best of his ability for all the rights and privileges of American citizenship.

(2) He must also find a way to compel a recognition of those rights and privileges when he has fitted himself.

The first proposition is comparatively easy, for it rests almost entirely with the individual and is dependent almost wholly upon his own determination. Thousands and hundreds of thousands of Negroes have achieved individual fitness, but individual fitness, as may be seen at a glance, is not the solution of the whole problem. Study of this first proposition ought to teach us not to make the easy error of believing that our status is due entirely to outside conditions. We must searchingly study ourselves and learn wherein we ourselves fall short, see how much of the blame is our own. One of the first discoveries we shall make is that we are not fully using the powers we already possess.

Perhaps our greatest God-given endowment is our emotionalism, the over-soul in us. But this greatest power in our possession is being recklessly dissipated in loud laughter, boisterous dancing, and a general good time. A pill box of gas with sufficient pressure removed will expand to fill the universe. Steam floating around in the air is no more effective than a whiff of cigarette smoke, but confined in a cylinder is a giant. When we have learned to channel down our emotional power, to run it through a cylinder, it will be transformed into great music, poetry, literature, and drama. It will become an irresistible force in battering down many of the obstacles that now confront us.

I spoke of our wonderful music as being the touchstone, the magic thing, by which the Negro can bridge all chasms. Let me expand that thought. It is through the arts that we may find the easiest approach to the solution of some of the most vital phases of our problem. It is the path of least friction. It is the plane on which all men are willing to meet and stand with us. We might argue in the abstract that the Negro possesses intellect, that he has high ideals, that his soul is sensitive to the most delicate nuances of spiritual reactions, and yet not convince those with whom we argue.   But the production of sublime music, of moving poetry, of noble literature, is that which was to be demonstrated.   There is no argument about it.

A people may become great through many means, but there is only one measure by which its greatness is recognized and acknowledged.   The final measure of the greatness of all peoples is the amount and standard of literature and art they have produced.   The world does not know that a people is great until that people produces great literature or art; and, conversely, no people that has produced great literature or art has ever been looked upon by the world as distinctly inferior.

The status of the Negro in the United States is more a question of mental attitude toward the race than it is a question of actual conditions.   This attitude is based upon a generally accepted estimate of innate intellectual inferiority. There is nothing that will do more to change this mental attitude and raise the status of the Negro than a demonstration by him of intellectual and esthetic parity through the production of literature and art.   And, luckily, his artistic endowment outweighs all his other gifts.

The second proposition of compelling the recognition of rights and privileges which correspond to fitness for them is a far more difficult problem.   It takes group action to solve it. No amount of individual effort has much effect upon it.   We must be able to correlate all of the forces within the group— economic, intellectual, moral, and political—in order to break down the barriers that will not give way to individual effort. These forces can be made to operate effectively only through an adequate machine and that machine is a national organization for this specific purpose.   And the effort which this will take is in no sense selfish; it is in no sense for the exclusive advantage of the Negro.   It is, indeed, for the benefit of true democracy in America.   The Negro stands today demanding of America:—

> How would you have us, as we are—
> Or sinking 'neath the load we bear?
> Our eyes fixed forward on a star—
> Or gazing empty at despair?
> Rising or falling? Men or things?
> With dragging pace or footsteps fleet?
> Strong, willing sinews in your wings?
> Or tightening chains about your feet?

It is upon the answer to these questions that there hangs
the fulfillment or the failure of democracy in America.   It
is for yourselves, and for your particular group, and for your
native land, that you are called upon to see that these questions are answered right.

I say to you, stand firm and unequivocal in your claim for
every right common to American citizenship.   Do not surrender or abdicate a single one.   Assert your claim with
courage and determination.   Make those who withhold these
rights feel constantly that they are committing an injustice.
Do not allow their consciences to go asleep.   Because our
future in this country holds only two choices—full and unlimited
American citizenship, or a permanent secondary status—we
must rise to the one or fall to the other.   It may be a long
time before some of these rights are accorded, but if we keep
our courage we must surely win, for we have God and right
on our side.   The only danger is that we acquiesce, that we
surrender, that we abdicate.   If we ever become Jim-Crowed
in our own souls, God Himself will not be able to save us.
But let me here warn you that for those who serve in this
cause there is a pit into which many may have fallen.   It is
the pit of selfishness, the pit of narrow ambitions.   This pit
is filled with many a man who has conspired with himself to
be a leader of his fellows rather than a server.   Such a one is
always doomed to disappointment.   Such a one must learn
that only to him who serves well will the mass some day say,
"This man serves well; let us follow him."   Sooner or later
it is always found that nothing endures but the truth, that
nothing succeeds but service.

And let me here add one other word of warning.   It is a
sad confession to make that some who have had the advantage of trained minds have used that advantage for the exploitation of their less fortunate fellows.   They have preyed
upon mass ignorance and trustfulness for their own selfish
gain.   I cannot believe that anyone who has been imbued
with the Hampton spirit will be guilty of such practice, but
you must make it your duty to crush out these vultures wherever you find them.   Do it without fear and without mercy.

And now to those who are today to receive their diplomas
from this institution and leave its doors as students: I want
you to take deep into your hearts this truth—the greatest of
all problems lies within yourself, the problem transcending
all differences of race or color or creed or condition, the
problem of your own spiritual and moral development.   Just
how the world will look to you, just what the world will mean

to you,—these lie entirely within yourself. This is the problem which no one can prevent you from working out successfully. Its correct solution depends entirely upon yourself. It is the problem beside which all others sink into insignificance. It is the problem of life itself.

Do you remember those lines in Walt Whitman's "Song of Occupations" in which he makes us understand and feel this fundamental truth? The platitudinarian would say, "Life is what you make it." Whitman in his magic poetry says:—

> "All architecture is what you do to it
>   when you look upon it.
> (Did you think it was in the white or
>   gray stone? or in the lines of arches
>   and cornices?)
> All music is what awakes in you when you
>   are reminded by the instruments.
> It is not the violins and the cornets;
>   it is not the oboe nor the beating
>   drums, nor the score of the baritone
>   singer singing his sweet romanza, nor
>   that of the men's chorus, nor that
>   of the women's chorus.
> It is nearer and farther than they."

I add one more thought to the main theme of these inadequate words which I have been pronouncing. I wish to leave you with a thought of service to God. Perhaps it may be a new thought, for it is common to think of God as all powerful and of service when praying for Him to help. In a degree this idea is erroneous. God is not all powerful and He often needs our help. There are some things which God Himself cannot do: and never yet in the history of the human race has he been able to do anything for any people unless he could find a human heart, a human head, or a human hand to do it through.

And so, whatever plans there may be in the mind of God for us in this land, He cannot realize them, He cannot bring them into being unless we make ourselves the willing instruments through which he may work.

———————

On Writing
About Negroes

WE carry in this is-
sue Miss Brenda
Moryck's discussion of those themes which should
command the attention of Negro writers, not
because we share wholly her point of view, but
because her article is an exceptionally well expressed statement of a view not uncommon
among the Negro literati. For those who still
ponder our insistence in the Contest that themes
should relate directly or indirectly to the Negro, we may state again that along with the development of individual Negro writers it is important that there should be developed a body
of Negro literature. Literature has always been
a great liaison between races, offering up out of
the hidden depths of a spiritually aloof race
the play of their emotions against life, the undeniably human touch which affirms brotherhood both in likenesses and in differences. There
is no contention that Negro writers should not
attempt to treat anything but Negro themes;
rather that it is important *now* that Negro

themes should be treated competently and that Negro writers, knowing them best, should be the ones to do it. The defensive attitude so often expressed in resistance to the exploitation of Negro themes provides an interesting study of the sensitiveness not infrequently encountered among new races. It accounts for the fact that practically the whole of the literature about the Negro, in large part so fervently condemned by the Negroes themselves, so palpably unauthentic, frequently misleading, sometimes criminally libelous, has been written by persons other than Negroes, who have never yet been wholly admitted to the privacy of Negro thots. It is not, of course, impossible for Negro writers to achieve distinguished results with general American themes, and those who know enough about the life to write of it convincingly and entertainingly, are as free to do it as, let us say, Braithwaite and Cullen have been free in the field of poetry. No such demand for racial themes exists in poetry, and our Contest recognized that. But, prose fiction nowadays must carry some conviction of reality. And for Negro writers, at least those who live as Negroes, the handicaps imposed against entrance to the ranks of great literature, are more numerous and restricting in the general themes than the limitations of concentration upon familiar themes can possibly be. The same social barriers behind which rest such gorgeous, even if untouched depths of color and life, keep them out of situations and settings where a great range of their universal stories should carry them. Speculation is a poor substitute for reality. Gossip in imposing Park Avenue mansions, love affairs in Venice, the social habits of millionaires and heiresses, Palm Beach parties, will be told with an unbecoming, even if unintentional bias and tepid unreality by one whose contact with the life has been at best partial, and qualified always by his race. Literary work of the highest order must be honest and sincere. Critics of the prose story are quick to sense the *faux pas* which betray those deeper familiarities with habits and characteristics of the people described. Says one: "Some tales of high society by young persons — and a few older ones — who have evidently never moved in that society illustrate by various ingenious betrayals how perilous it is for an author to step outside of his own experience." Despite this, until recently, the first impulse among many of our aspiring writers has been to attempt these themes, spurning their own environment as uninteresting and unworthy. And where are the great stories which the arguments defend? The point is frequently urged that what Dumas and Pushkin have done in letters is proof of the capacity of Negroes to write about anything—which is true. But Dumas and Pushkin were unqualifiedly a part of European life.

One is not surprised that this sensitiveness should exist about themes. Americans have passed thru the same periods in relation to England. It was Oliver Wendell Holmes who remarked that "it took one hundred and fifty years to lift the English lark out of American poetry." To the early American writers, life in a stern environment meant drudgery and toil and sometimes pain, and when they would write of romance they went as far as possible from their life—to England, from which they had been removed by several generations. No American book was able to raise itself above the snicker of England until these writers began to write out of their own lives and intimate experiences. It requires, as one distinguished critic has well said, "fresh vision to see new beauty for the first time, even when it lies directly in our path."

Again we insist that there is no reason why a Negro should not write of anything under the sun. It should be remembered, however, that present fashions in literature are shifting from the worn out subjects to fresh and unexploited fields. The less glamorous, but more intensely fascinating human types are coming in for treatment. Most significantly, the eyes of our great story tellers and artists are turning slowly upon the Negro as a rich store house of interest. They are at as serious a disadvantage in writing about the subtle intricacies of Negro life and to its peculiar emotional experiences as the Negroes are of writing about them. No less than ten well known writers have stories of Negro life in preparation and the amount of discussion in current publications is constantly increasing. It is, indeed, a renaissance of interest. If Nordic influence wished to be malicious it would adroitly insist that our budding writers release their bolts against the world at large, where competition is keenest, the ground well trodden down, and where they are at their greatest disadvantage,—while they interpret the Negroes and, incidentally, collect the checks.

A Note on the Sociology of Negro Literature

By FRED DE ARMOND

NO people can be understood without some study of their literature and other artistic expression. And the literature of a race, group or nationality, to be rightly appraised and interpreted must be considered with reference to the facts of that people's history, religion and sociology. A failure to appreciate these basic truths is, I believe, a strong contributing cause for the complete ignorance of the Negro on the part of white America, as well as the Negro's lack of conception as to his own powers.

> To understand the literature of the Negro, his life and history must be known. Encrusted attitudes of the South have obscured manifestations of the real character of the Negro and warped them into subtle but socially expedient adaptations, this writer thinks. Slavery blighted artistic expression with the inferior status it conferred. This servile feeling has survived, inhibiting the confident ego associated always with genius. Even Dunbar showed this weakness. The all-consuming tensity of the race struggle is an obstacle both to Negroes and southern whites, the latter calling forth, a few years back, the fierce animadversions of Mencken. The migration has shifted the center of Negro life and brought a new order, new literary themes and forms. Improved relations, he thinks, will release the writers of phillipics for creative work.

The average Nordic, particularly in the South, has become so accustomed to wearing that attitude of lofty superiority and amused tolerance toward blacks that he knows no more about their mental processes than he does about Chinese ideals or Brahman theology. To the rude mind, Negro poetry, art and religion are no more serious than the diverting antics of a favorite pet animal. A great fiction has thus grown up around the Negro character and the Negro himself, with his unusual histrionic ability, has accepted the false conception and fostered it with his feigned burlesque and mimicry. There are few even of our college professors, congressmen and D. D.'s discerning enough to perceive that the "good nigger" is merely a good actor, that all this extravagant deference, feudal manners and Ham Bone humor is merely a form of guile and subtle flattery by which Negroes secure those privileges which other men are expected to stand up and demand as their rights.

To attain the understanding that will straighten all such distorted views, race literature must be studied not by direct comparison, but in the light of the influences that have affected it. American literature proper, not only has a brilliant provincial history of over two hundred years, but it is a direct branch both in blood and tradition, of that stalwart oak, the roots of which go back to the England of Chaucer's day. If I may be excused for using the metaphor still further, I would say that the writing of the American Negro is a healthy sprout that has sprung up within the shade of its mighty progenitor. Sixty-five years ago the race languished in a bondage so hopeless that only by the slyest stealth could any person of color learn to read and write. "Negroes by law are prohibited from learning to read and write," wrote Rev. John Aughey, a Northern clergyman sojourning in Mississippi in 1861. "I had charge of a Sabbath school for the instruction of blacks in Memphis, Tennessee, in 1853. The school was put down by the strong arm of the law, shortly after my connection with it ceased. In Mississippi a man who taught slaves to read or write would be sent to the penitentiary instanter." Frederick Douglass relates in his autobiography how he was deprived of the only real pleasure he ever remembers during his slave days in Maryland, when the school that he was teaching on Sundays was broken up and suppressed by his master. He had previously, by many subterfuges and by the assistance of a kind mistress, succeeded in getting for himself a smattering of the rudiments. At one time he had over forty pupils meeting with the greatest secrecy in a barn, in order that they might taste the delights of knowledge. One of the men who helped to suppress the school by force was a very religious character who had taught the neighboring slaves about the Bible, professing much interest in saving their souls.

But it is not so much the educational development of the Negro under enormous difficulties that constitutes the outstanding feature of his artistic accomplishment, as it is his marvelous adaptability to Caucasian civilization. In reading one of Claude McKay's poems, or listening to Roland Hayes singing, or admiring the pictures of Tanner, one should remind oneself of the vast gulf that the artist has bridged between his art and his savage African ancestry—at most only a few generations away. Wherever the Ethiopian has been transplanted to other parts of the world, he has shown himself remarkably adaptable to foreign civilization.

The record of "America's subject race" has given a flavor of the exotic to our history, an element of color that creates a most enchanting background for literature. Drama and romance are conjured in the imaginative mind by such events as the slave trade, the underground railroad, the gallant dash of colored troops in the war of the rebellion, emancipation and the aftermath of reconstruction with all those bizarre incidents of poetic justice to the former masters. All epochs in the struggle for human liberty have had their interpreters; the Negro people believing as they do that they are still in process of emancipation from the disabilities imposed by race prejudice, have never had such able, eloquent and sincere spokesmen as at this time.

The blighting effect of slavery can hardly be appreciated in its full influence on artistic expression as well as social life. Consciously or unconsciously it imposed on the race a servile feeling of inferiority that centuries will not wipe out. Thus it is only from a feeling of great power that a Negro writer can assert himself with any of that confident ego that we have been wont to expect from genius. There is discernible in Dunbar's poetry a sort of hesitating modesty that causes the reader to feel that some hereditary race consciousness was restraining the highest flights of his genius. It is something of the same inferiority complex that prompted a Negro teacher of an industrial school appearing before a committee of the legislature in a Southern state to apologize for wearing such a good suit. Socially the taint of bondage has exerted a tremendous influence. It should not be forgotten that the institution of marriage properly dates only from Reconstruction. Booker Washington, sitting down to write his autobiography did not even know his father's name. Frederick Douglass could not remember having seen his mother but a few times in his life and then only when she had stolen away at night and walked many miles that she might snatch a few hours with her child. The word "father" was not in the slave child's vocabulary. Many of the first families of Virginia maintained their aristocratic station by the refined and lucrative business of breeding slaves for the southern markets.

White observers have made much of the Negro moral code but said little about these causes that account for a distinction in that respect. In T. S. Stribling's "Birthright," Peter Siner, an educated and refined Negro laments the low standards and the atavism of his race. No such pessimism is justified. It is rather with satisfaction and pride that Negroes should contemplate the progress of sixty years. Most characterizations by white observers are gross exaggerations and caricatures and will be recognized as such by those who see and think for themselves. The lascivious stories set to the familiar Rastus-Liza cast are

an example. As they are related with loud guffaws to groups of male hearers by those verbose gentlemen who know "the niggers" so thoroughly, these anecdotes have about as much realism as the raptures of a California realtor.

James Weldon Johnson, the distinguished colored poet, has called attention to what he considers the greatest obstacle in the way of artistic expression by his race. This is, in the South at least, the all-consuming tensity of the race struggle. Not only does this problem dissipate the intellectual energy of the Negroes, he says, but also in almost equal degree of the Southern whites, accounting for H. L. Mencken's somewhat exaggerated statement: "In all this vast region . . . there is not a single poet, not a serious historian, not a creditable composer, not a critic good or bad, not a dramatist dead or alive." Heywood Broun called the Southern fear of the Negro "an intensified specialization that atrophies the mind of the South."

There has been an absence of objective thought on this subject, either written or spoken, throughout the South; a dogmatism built on such stale repetitions as "The Southern white man is the only person that understands the Negro", "We need no meddling interference from the North", "The Negro is an irresponsible child", etc. The Southern Negroes on their part, while making great strides industrially, have left the intellectual leadership to the North, where the dominant race, instead of hostility, has shown only indifference.

The great migration to the North seems to be one of the practical economic forces working toward a solution of the race problem. This movement, by better distributing the Negro population, is certain to make the question more nearly what it should always have been —national and not sectional in scope and interest. The changing order is already finding expression in the race literature. Bards are singing more of Harlem dance halls and less of Mississippi plantations. The new setting is the big industrial centers of the North which are soon to vie with the cotton belt as the black center of population. Jean Toomer, the new star on the firmament of Negro prose fiction, picks many of his characters from the flotsam of the big city. Miss Fauset scorns precedent by writing a novel of polite Negro society, minus dialect and other thought-to-be indispensable ear-marks of race literature. Poets like Countee Cullen bare their souls and display secret emotions long repressed. A freedom from the inhibitions of the Southland is shown by the Negro press, the pulpit and by publicists, black and white.

Most Southern white men have professed to see in the exodus from the late Confederacy only rainbow-chasing, bound to end in disillusionment for the emigrants. But this opinion is not concurred in by the Negro observers nor by such white writers as Rollin Lynde Hartt and Frank Tannenbaum. Hartt's conclusion is that the principal incentive is the hope of increased security and equal protection of the law. In his new home we see the Negro's facility for adapting himself to changed environment. Every year this quality is enabling thousands to surmount vocational barriers, as it will eventually be the means of overcoming discrimination.

The continuing improvement in inter-racial relations will have the effect of turning Negro thought away from channels of controversy and propaganda. It will release the writers of philippics for more creative work, just as the final abolition of slavery turned Whittier and Lowell from fiery abolition poems to the greater and broader classics on which their fame chiefly rests in our day.

A study of the colored press such as Robert T. Kerlin has made in *The Voice of the Negro*, reveals an undeniably aggressive and bitter feeling against mob-law, disfranchisement, peonage and "Jim-Crowism." Most of the periodicals are strongly pessimistic and cynical. L. M. Hussey writes in *The American Mercury*: "This cynicism distinguishes all his current utterances. It informs and enlivens the propaganda that he prints in his periodicals. These periodicals are seldom naive. They make use of the weapon of irony. To the white brethren seeking civilized amusement, to the Nordic overman a bit soured by the pallid timidities of his accustomed journals, I recommend a trial glance at such Negro papers as *The Crisis*, *The Messenger* and *Opportunity*. Taken after a dose of the usual savorless blather of white journalism, their effect is akin to that of four ounces of ethyl hydroxide."

The bellicosity of those journals like *The Chicago Defender*, *The Black Dispatch* of Oklahoma City and *The Houston Informer* will surprise all those who have been deceived by the stage deference of the blacks into thinking that the race as a whole is quiescent and contented. According to a writer in *World's Work*, in some parts of the black belt of the South the radical Chicago papers are considered as vicious contraband by the authorities, which necessitates their being smuggled in surreptitiously and sold among the Negroes much in the same manner that Garrison's *Liberator* was circulated during slavery. But even in the South there are few of the colored organs that follow the idea of non-resistance. In expressing opinions that are anathema to the orthodox Southerner they seem to encounter less intolerance than would be vented on the white man who gave voice to the same heresies. While we are a long way from having a free press in these United States, it is at least gratifying to reflect on our improvement since the time of Elijah Lovejoy.

Religious fervor is strongly reflected in the literature of the Negro. There is a faith deeply emotional and strictly fundamentalist, imbued with the imagery of a personal Savior, a very real Satan and Hell and a literal construction of the Scriptures. Booker Washington related that he found a pathetic aspiration to learn reading and writing among the older men and women who had spent their youth in slavery. They attended his night schools faithfully and repeatedly told him that they did so solely with the ambition of reading The Bible for themselves before they died.

This strong spiritual craving is traceable to slavery. It was very deliberately cultivated by the masters with the object of providing an emotional outlet that would keep them quiescent. According to Frederick Douglass, drunkenness was encouraged for the same reason. On the Maryland plantations it was customary to give all the field hands a week or two of holiday during the Christmas season, when it was expected that the slaves would waste their time and their money if they happened to have any, in riotous carousing. Then it was certain that no dangerous ideas would occupy their minds and turn their thoughts to freedom.

There is also a close connection between this fervid Christianity inherited by the freedman from the slace, and the Negro spirituals, the most distinctive artistic contribution of the race to our American civilization. Mr. Kerlin in his essay on *Contemporary Negro Poetry* has shown the undoubted kinship between the new Negro poetry and the old spirituals. Both, he says, "bear the stamp of African genius." In the course of evolution we may well expect that the musical theme of the spirituals will be further interpreted in our generation.

In those feeling old hymns, legacy from "Black and Unknown Bards of Long Ago," there is much to provoke the interest of all students of original sources in American life and history. Whether considered as poetry, music or religion, the force and originality of the spirituals are striking. As poetry they symbolized the intense yearning of a people for freedom; as music they were the flight of troubled spirits in spontaneous, melancholy song; as religion they were the primitive appeal of tortured slave souls to a higher power.

Various Negro leaders have charged their people with being too self-conscious and urged them not to exhibit diffidence in displaying their own distinctive qualities, to cease aping white customs and develop themselves in their own way; in short to take a pride in their race and in preserving its entity. They insist that the black race has a very distinct place in the future of America, and in the fullest realization of that future there should be no real clash of interests.

The Advance of the Negro

By V. F. Calverton

THE advance of the Negro is of striking significance to social philosophy. It is the most vigorous and unequivocal proof of the determining effect of environment that history has to herald. In itself, it can serve as a partial basis for a synthetic sociology.

The environmental handicaps of the Negro have been enormous. At the present time, for that matter, the handicaps are still deterring but not annihilating.

DR. ALAIN LOCKE
From a portrait by Winold Reiss.

Before the Civil War Negro education was forbidden in the South and grew like a curious, hot-house plant in the North. Group cooperation was impossible. After the Civil War educational institutions for Negroes developed and multiplied but social fetters tightened, and group progress has been severely limited. With the industrial changes of the twentieth century and the decade preceding, the intensification of the labor problem, and the rise of the proletariat, however, the attitude toward the Negro has been growing steadily more tolerant and appreciative. Unfortunately, this growth has proceeded in such a tardy manner, with mutations that seem so microscopical, that it can but encourage the philosopher and not the plebeian. The internationalization of labor is an important factor in this gradual social change. The labor problem cannot be solved with the exclusion of the Negro. The workers of the United States or of the world cannot unite upon a color or race basis. Color and race must be cancelled eventually if the movement is ever to attain success commensurate with its purpose. A new social state cannot be based upon a color concept. The new changes demand new criteria and new coordinates.

With the development of these social forces, therefore, the Negro, against disadvantage and discouragement, has been able to carve his way into the intellectual life of his time. In a little over two generations—before the Civil War the Negro as a group could make no advance—the Negro is rivalling the white man in fields of endeavor invented and exploited by the latter. The significance of this phenomenon cannot be overestimated. Passing through periods of imitation and self-exaltation, the Negro has now entered a period of acute self-criticism and objective examination of his social assets and aspirations.

It is inevitable that a free class should regard with contempt the capacity of a class that was once enslaved. In every historical episode in which slavery has played a part this reaction has been conspicuous. To overcome this type of prejudice the once enslaved class or people, in common competition, must prove its ability to equal the achievements of the former ruling class. While success in this battle of intellectual and commercial competition may remove the contempt for incapacity, it will not, however, remove the other prejudices that flow immediately from close rivalry. On the other hand, it will intensify these prejudices. The economic rise and competition of the Negro in the South, for instance, was instrumental in the rejuvenation of the Ku Klux Klan. If we turn to another people, the Jews, we can discover, except in the sense that their days of slavery are buried in an ancient past, an excellent illustration of this fact. The Jew has suffered from religious persecution, aggravated by economic causes. The Jew, however, has proven his intellectual genius. Intellectually his work is accepted, and contempt for his capacity is impossible. Contempt for his other qualities, nevertheless, is perpetuated and magnified. Socially, he is still fettered, but in no way as severely as the Negro.

The Negro, however, in the eyes of the old guard has yet to prove his intellectual competence.

The volume entitled *The New Negro*[1], therefore, is significant in that it will help to dispel an old illusion. It projects the work of the contemporary Negro in varied and vivid form. It reveals

[1.] *The New Negro, Edited by Alain Locke.* A. & C. Boni, 1925. $5.00.

his errors and his excellencies, his weakness and his strength. While the achievements of the Negro, as we said in an earlier paragraph, need no defense or justification, none the less this book will proclaim them before a wider audience, and in a manner more consecutive and consistent, more persuasive and poetic, than has been effected in the past.

In sociology, picturesque and profound, the Negro has expressed himself in brilliant if sometimes sentimental style. The work of Booker T. Washington, Burghardt Du Bois, and Charles S. Johnson symbolize three stages of progression in the development of sociological attitudes among the Negro people. Washington represented the period of adaptation and imitation, Du Bois represents the period of defiance and racial exaltation, and Johnson that of criticism and objectification. Washington was the most inspiring leader, Du Bois is the most poetic writer, and Johnson is the most solid thinker. It is in the impartial approach, the dispassionate dissection of materials, the objective evaluation of facts, that the work of Johnson is to be distinguished from that of his two illustrious predecessors. In *The New Frontage on American Life,* one of the most outstanding essays in the volume, as in his studies of the race-riots of a few years ago and his analysis of the Negro migrations, Johnson presents a sound and important study of the changing social life of the Negro. There is no guffawing of glorification or gaudy glitter of phraseology, but an interpretation based upon sound economic facts and social relationships. It is highly unfortunate that nothing of the work of Abram L. Harris, Jr. is included in the book, because in approach his sociological studies are closely akin to those of Johnson and in substance scarcely less significant. Harris is one of the most subtle and scintillating sociologists in the Negro movement of today. Certainly "The Newer Negro" cannot afford his exclusion.

While James Weldon Johnson describes Harlem with color and skill, and Burghardt Du Bois writes illuminatingly of the color-line and the "labor-line" and of the expansion of the Negro mind, and Alain Locke interprets Negro Youth and the Negro Spirituals with genuine sympathy and spirit, it is Walter F. White in *The Paradox of Color* who contributes the most charming and pathetic, the most vivid and touching essay in the volume.

In fiction, Negro writers, on the whole, are groping toward a nebulous maturity. Jean Toomer is an exception. Toomer possesses a style that is at once delicate, subtle and inimitable. His stories *Carma* and *Fern* are fragile forms of loveliness. They quiver with strange, tempting rhythms that captivate and enchant. Eric Walrond, at present a less finished artist than Toomer, in *The Palm Porch* reveals talent that will not remain obscure. Fisher is entertaining but naive, Matheus serious

but sentimental, Hurston clever but crude. Experience, however, may weaken their vices and strengthen their virtues.

Counteè Cullen is the leader of the poets. The last stanza of *To a Brown Boy* is a rich and radiant quatrain. *A Brown Girl Dead* is a quick, tragic thing, possessing a pallid, poignant beauty. *In Memory of Colonel Charles Young* is also an effective poem. Claude McKay is more passionate but a less original poet. Unhappily, several of McKay's best poems are not included in this collection. In *The Tropics of New York*, however, he has created an exquisite poem. Langston Hughes is a spontaneous and spirited poet, but his form needs finish and his substance definiteness.

In conclusion, two things remain; the excellent artistry of Winold Reiss and the inspiring guidance of Alain Locke. Without Winold Reiss the book would lack much of the color and life that it now has, and without Alain Locke the book would lack its orderliness and clarity.

During the coming years we shall wait impatiently for the appearance of *The Newer Negro.*

THE
CAROLINA
MAGAZINE

VOLUME 57   NUMBER 7

The Negro Enters Literature

By CHARLES S. JOHNSON

NEGRO LITERATURE, like early American literature, is more interesting as history than as creative art. The parallel does not stop here: both have been unnaturally influenced by literary patterns alien to their experience; both have been damaged, on the one hand, by rather excessive claims to importance as *Literature,* and on the other, by ruthless sometimes disdainful comparisons, out of their essential social setting and limitations, with older literatures and peoples; both reflect above all else, the violent currents of thought and life in the new world, and, with striking frequency, the very same currents even if from different planes. A discerning writer in one of the southern literary reviews asks, not unwisely, whether, after all, "we should not frankly recognize the fact that American writers have been more successful in mirroring social and economic and political conditions than in creating works of art." There is a certain reasonableness in this point of view for anyone who has actually read the poetry of Anne Bradstreet, Noyes and Oakes, or the fiction of Mrs. Susanna Haswell Rowson, and who recalls that the *Declaration of Independence,* the *Federalist,* and Washington's *Addresses,* nevertheless, rank as the most important literary contributions to the period. Such a point of view is more charitable to Negro literature, and undoubtedly makes its contributions more intelligible, and more significant.

—❦{ 3 }❦—

The
CAROLINA
MAGAZINE

··◇ʟɪᴋ◇··

May
1927

Two other distinctions are important. In a sense not applicable to the American people as a whole, Negro experience has yielded an artistic contribution of a sort, uncounted, perhaps, because unconsciously made. Their years of servitude have left a deposit of rich lore delicately threaded through the pattern of American life, and a strange inimitable music, which, in its vitality and varied forms, grows deeper and wider in influence with the years. They were the subjects of literature long before they began seriously to create it. In their conscious contributions there is a necessary distinction to be made between that writing which is "Negro literature" in the sense of expressing a group consciousness, and that writing by men who happened merely to be Negroes. The not inconsiderable list of theological treatises of such Negroes as Lemuel Haynes, N. C. Cannon, William Catto, and even the verse of Jupiter Hammon, who antedates Phyllis Wheatley, when construed broadly as literature, fall within this class, and are roughly analogous to the theological writings of Jonathan Edwards, the Mathers and the religious doggerel of Wigglesworth. So, also, must be considered the work of such extraordinary persons as William Stanley Braithwaite, lyricist of great charm and anthologist, and Benjamin Brawley who, quite apart from his Negro history has written a textbook of English literature,— free-floating individuals who have appeared occasionally and mingled their contribution, without the distinctive mark of race, to the general fund of American Literature.

Although the saga of the transplanted African has been scarcely more than marginal notes to the drama of America, no wholly intelligent view of the new world development is possible which does not embrace the experiences of these new Cimerii, so intimate and yet so remote in their gloom-world, whose reflections, through their literature are a sort of penumbra of this whole life, softening it into its full beauty.

Slavery as an institution grew, not from a sudden inspiration, but step by step, as economic necessity made peace with conscience. The process required remaking and adjusting of the concepts of race, religion, humanity itself. The periods of change in national and group attitudes have their most poignant reflection in the Negro literature. Phyllis Wheatley, the slave poet who published her first volume of verse at the age of twenty belonged to the colonial period in more than one sense. She came just twenty years after Anne Bradstreet, first American woman poet, with verse which bears up interestingly under comparison. As a Negro writer she is

 4

posited in an almost echoless solitude. She had no followers; her patterns were Ovid and the English classicists who inspired her contemporaries. The vast bulk of her poetry was personal and unracial,—she indited lines "To the King's Most Excellent Majesty," "To His Excellency, General Washington," odes to Neptune, and to Maecenas, and to numerous friends on the death of relatives. A magnificent exception she was, in this period of almost universal Negro illiteracy. When she went to England in 1773 she considered it wise to arm herself with attestations in her book by Governor Hutcherson, John Hancock and some others that she actually wrote the poems ascribed to her. George Horton of North Carolina, near the close of the 18th century, was composing verse which he could not even set down in writing. He nearly bought his freedom with the love lyrics which he composed for students of the University of North Carolina, to be used among the young ladies of the vicinity. Assisted to literacy by some of the professors of the school, he published in 1829 a volume of verse, "The Hope of Liberty," and numerous hymns.

Like strange, broken voices these writers of verse appeared, some thirty or more between Wheatley and Dunbar. Perhaps the most notable of these was Frances E. W. Harper of Baltimore. The institution of slavery and its supporting theories grew. The attempts of the Negroes to express themselves were a struggle, without equipment, against the fast crystallizing philosophy of their sub-humanity, and against the treason of the very religion which they had embraced. They were to learn that their brains were lighter, wrongly placed; that their frontal sutures closed earlier,— always with the same devastating *ergo!* Charles Carroll could argue with finality that "man was made in the image of God and since God, as everyone knows was not a Negro, it followed that the Negro was not a man." Those Negro writers who, after a long silence, followed Phyllis Wheatley, thought in terms of vital rebuttal. When Benjamin Banneker of Maryland, mathematician and astronomer, prepared his Almanac with involved calculations, he sent the manuscript to Thomas Jefferson praying that his accomplishment would help remove the general conceptions about his race. The articulate ones, through every medium at hand were compelled to establish first, their humanity. And so it was that the period just prior to the Civil War by its intensity turned practically all expression into the channel of personal narratives,—those stories based upon the personal experiences of fugitive slaves, which, in themselves held greater immediacy and dramatic power

—⟨ 5 ⟩—

The
CAROLINA
MAGAZINE

..◁ııı▷..

May
1927

than either poetry or fiction. These made valuable material for the Abolitionists, to whose insistence may be accredited the preservation in record of many of these stories. Some are shot through with bright threads, and despite a frequent crudeness, they have moments of real beauty. Jessie Fauset, one of the moderns, was inspired to a poem by this brief paragraph from the autobiography of Sojourner Truth, which seems to catch naively in its lap the vast tragedy and unutterable longing of slavery:

"I can remember when I was a little girl, how my old mammy would sit out of doors in the evenings and look up at the stars and groan, and I would say, 'Mammy, what makes you groan so? And she would say, 'I am groaning to think of my poor children; they do not know where I be and I don't know where they be. I look up at the stars and they look up at the stars!' "

These narratives continued even after emancipation, being in their later form a more sophisticated revolt against the subtler limitations upon status. The Memoirs of Ignatius Sancha, the intrepid African, were published in 1808, *The Story of Richard Allen*, founder of the African Methodist Episcopal Church, appeared even earlier, in 1793. William Wells Brown, both in his personal narrative and in his *Clotel*, an attempt at a novel based upon a dramatic story of real life, revealed an uncannily alert and sensitive mind and command of English; Henry Box Brown, J. W. C. Pennington, the fugitive blacksmith, and Samuel Ringold Ward had stories more powerful than their styles, while Frederick Douglas, the greatest of the fugitives, lacked neither style nor story. These personal narratives steadily broadened from vicarious experiences to attempts to express group aspirations and emotions. They were yet a vital part of this literature when Booker T. Washington's *Up From Slavery*, a story of universal appeal, appeared, and they reached their highest art in the magnificent and bitterly intense *Souls of Black Folk* by W. E. Burghardt DuBois, which appeared in 1902.

Emancipation ushered in a new phase of life and expression. With their "paper freedom" they set out to copy the gloss of their surrounding culture, rebelling against every symbol of their so recent enslavement. Except for the fading light of a few brilliant survivors of the crisis, nothing of any consequence was produced until Dunbar. Coming at that dark period, when, with the release of the working classes, the independent struggle for existence had become more severe, he caught the concept of the more tolerable Negro in his pathetic and contagiously humorous moods, accepted him without apology and without his miserable baggage of a problem, and invested him with a new humanity More, he made him likable,—this simple, kindly, joyous creature, with his softly musical dialect and infectious rhythm. William Dean Howells, in an article in Harpers, hailed Dunbar as the first to feel Negro life aesthetically and express it lyrically. He became a poet of folk life, mentioned in the same breath with Robert Burns. He lifted Negro poetry to a level of critical appreciation, lit new fires of hope among Negroes, then died, broken and disappointed that the world, ignoring his loftier unrestricted verse had "turned to praise a jingle in a broken tongue." The acceptability of his dialect verse, however, inspired a host of followers, few of whom captured the convincing spontaneity of his poetry. Daniel Webster Davis, of Richmond, Virginia, seems to have achieved his style most successfully in his volume of poems published under the title, "Weh Down Souf." This period produced one novelist of competence in Charles W. Chestnut of Cleveland, Ohio. He wrote and published five volumes before 1906, realistic stories and novels of the Reconstruction period, of that highly charged world of mixed blood relations across the line of race; then his pen fell silent, although he still lives. The years between 1900 and 1915 were years of restlessness, uncertainty and transition. Hesitatingly at first and later with greater daring, Negro writers struck a note of frank discontent ranging in temper from bitter resentment to Christian forbearance. Frequently their verse was freighted with racial woes; and occasionally they spoke in terms of universal appeal; they discarded dialect because of its limitations, their technical command improved, their work had the authentic ring of poetry. Joseph S. Cotter, father and son, James Weldon Johnson, Leslie Pinckney Hill, Fenton Johnson, Edward Everett Hawkins, Lucien B. Watkins, Georgia Douglas Johnson, Ann Spencer, Charles Bertram Russell, Alice Dunbar-Nelson, Roscoe C. Jamison, D. Corruthers, William Stanley Braithwaite, Jessie Fauset, and Angelina Grimké, a notable array, began that interesting tradition which blends the expression of the race-mind, with a refined equipment. James Weldon Johnson's *Creation* most vividly symbolizes the gross transition. Aside from being one of the most moving religious poems in American literature, it achieves a rare craftsmanship. In naive, non-dialect speech, it blends the rich imagery of the uneducated Negro minister with the finished skill of a cultured Negro poet. In a curious fashion it bespeaks the meeting and parting of the old and new in Negro life in America:

The
CAROLINA
MAGAZINE

May
1927

The
CAROLINA
MAGAZINE

··◁▱▷··

May
1927

"And God stepped out on space
    And He looked around and said,
'I'm lonely
    I'll make me a world.'

And as far as the eye of God could see
    Darkness covered everything,
    Blacker than a hundred midnights
    Down in a cypress swamp.

Then God smiled,
And the light broke,
And the darkness rolled up on one side,
And the light stood shining on the other,
And God said, 'that's good' . . . ."

The commentators farther removed from the present phase of Negro expression will be able to define more clearly the influence of those social and economic forces shortly after the World War, moving beneath the new mind of Negroes which burst forth with freshness and vigor in an artistic "awakening." With this awakening, probably from the same cause or possibly as a result of it, has come an improved public attitude of acceptance and welcome for these new voices. The first startlingly authentic note was sounded by Claude McKay, a Jamaican Negro living in America. If his was again a note of protest it came clear and unquivering. But it was more than a protesting note; it was one of stoical defiance which held behind it a spirit magnificent and glowing. One poem, "If We Must Die," written at the most acute point of the new industrialism of Negroes, when sudden mass contact in the northern states was flaming into riots, voiced for Negroes where it did not itself create, a mood of stubborn defiance. It was reprinted in practically every Negro newspaper, and quoted wherever its audacious lines could be remembered. But McKay could also write lyrics utterly divorced from these singing daggers. "Spring in New Hampshire" is one of them. He discovered Harlem and found a language of beauty for his own world of color.

"Her voice was like the sound of blended flutes
    Blown by black players on a picnic day."

He left America, spent a while in Russia, moved to France where he now lives.

Jean Toomer flashed like a blazing meteor across the sky, then sank from view. But in that brilliant moment of his flight he illumined the fore-field of this literature. *Cane,* a collection of verse and stories, appeared about two years ahead of its sustaining public mood. It was significantly a return of the son to the Southland, to the stark natural beauties of its life and soil, a life deep and strong, a soil untouched.

The
CAROLINA
MAGAZINE

--◇═◇--

May
1927

> "O land and soil, red soil and sweet gum-tree,
> So scant of grass, so profligate of pines
> Now just before an epoch's sun declines
> Thy son, in time, I have returned to thee,
> Thy son, I have in time returned to thee."

Here was the Negro artist triumphantly detached from propaganda, sensitive only to beauty. Where Dunbar gave to the unnamed Negro peasant a reassuring touch of humanity, Toomer gave to this peasant a passionate charm:

(*Continued on page forty-four*)

277

The
CAROLINA
MAGAZINE

··◁▱▷··

May
1927

The Negro Enters Literature

(*Continued from page nine*)
"Her skin is like dusk on the Eastern horizon,
O can't you see it, O can't you see it,
Her skin is like dusk on the Eastern horizon,
—When the sun goes down."

More than artist he was an experimentalist, and this last quality has carried him away from what was, perhaps, the most astonishingly brilliant beginning of any Negro writer of his generation.

With Countée Cullen came a new generation of Negro singers. Claude McKay had brought a strange geographical background to the American scene which enabled him to escape a measure of the peculiar social heritage of the American Negro. Cullen brought to this scene the fresh view of an American Negro which similarly lacked the impedimenta of an inhibiting tradition. He relied upon nothing but his own sure competence and art. One month found three literary magazines carrying his verse simultaneously, a distinction not to be spurned by any young poet. Then came his first volume, *Color*. He brought an uncannily sudden maturity and classic sweep, a swift grace and an unescapable beauty of style and meaning. The spirit of the transplanted African moved through his music to a new definition—relating itself boldly to its past and present:

—◄{ 44 }►—

> "Lord, not for what I saw in flesh or bone
> Of fairer men, not raised on faith alone;
> Lord, I will live persuaded by mine own.
> I cannot play the recreant to these;
> My spirit has come home, that sailed the doubtful seas."

Thus he spoke, not for himself alone, but for the confident generation from which he came. White gods faded and in their place arose the graces of a race he knew:

> "Her walk is like the replica
> Of some barbaric dance
> Wherein the soul of Africa
> Is winged with arrogance."

and again:

> "That brown girls swagger gives a twitch
> To beauty like a queen."

No brief quotations can describe this power, this questioning of life and even God, the swift arrow thrusts of irony curiously mingled with admiration, the self reliance, the bold pride of race, the thorough repudiation of the double standard of literary judgment. He may have marvelled "at this curious thing to make a poet black and bid him sing," but in his *Heritage* he voiced the half-religious, half-challenging spirit of an awakened generation:

> "Lord, I fashion dark gods too
> Daring even to give to You
> Dark, despairing features where
> Crowned with dark rebellious hair,
> Patience wavers just so much as
> Mortal grief compels, while touches
> Faint and slow, of anger rise
> To smitten cheek and weary eyes.
>
> Lord forgive me if my need
> Sometimes shapes a human creed."

"He will be remembered," says the Manchester *Guardian*, "as one who contributed to his age some of its loveliest lyric poetry."

Langston Hughes, at twenty-four has published two volumes of verse. No Negro writer so completely symbolizes the new emancipation of the

The
CAROLINA
MAGAZINE

--◁▪▷--

May
1927

Negro mind. His is a poetry of gorgeous colors, of restless brooding, of melancholy, of disillusionment:

> "We should have a land of sun
> Of gorgeous sun,
> And a land of fragrant water
> Where the twilight
> Is a soft bandana handkerchief
> Of rose and gold
> And not this land where life is cold.

There are few short poems more beautiful than his *Suicide's Note*:

> "The calm,
> Cool face of the river
> Asked me for a kiss."

Always there is a wistful undertone, a quiet sadness. That is why, perhaps, he could speak so tenderly of the broken lives of prostitutes, the inner weariness of painted "jazz-hounds," and the tragic emptiness beneath the glamour and noise of Harlem cabarets:

> "Does a jazz-band ever sob?
> They say a jazz-band's gay
> Yet as the vulgar dancers whirled
> And the wan night wore away,
> One said he heard the jazz-band sob
> When the little dawn was grey."

His first volume, *The Weary Blues*, contained many moods, the second, *Fine Clothes to the Jew*, marks his final frank turning to the folk life of the Negro, a striving to catch and give back to the world the strange music of the unlettered Negro—his *Blues*. If Cullen has given a classic beauty to the emotions of the race, Hughes has given a warm glow of meaning to their lives.

Each year has revealed new voices. The list of younger poets includes: Arna Bontemps born in Louisiana, now living in New York, Frank Horne of Brooklyn, now living in Georgia, Lewis Alexander of Washington, Helene Johnson of Brookline, Massachusetts, Waring Cuney of Boston, Sterling Brown of Missouri, Clarissa Scott Delaney of Washington and New York, Gwendolyn Bennett of Brooklyn, John Matheus of West Virginia, Donald Hayes of Atlantic City, New Jersey, and Blanche Taylor Dickinson of Pennsylvania. They are, one might say, the newest voices. No one looking for a "school of poetry" will find it here. Bontemps' verse has been characterized by Robert Frost as "the wayward thinking of real poetry"; there is about all of his things a strangely haunting stillness. Gwendolyn Bennett's lyrics have a lithe grace and a precise craftsmanship. Frank Horne is exuberant and hearty. Alexander, interesting enough, has been most successful with his Japanese Hokku poems. Matheus brings what William Rose Benet aptly calls "a wild magic of color." Helene Johnson has a lyric penetration which belies her years, and a rich and impetuous power. Life, their own lives, the full and free emotions of a race, their loves, hates, futility, all that pains to a lyric outcry, is embodied in their song.

Much attention has been given to the poets. The writers of fiction have been few, the writers of drama, fewer. Walter White's, *Fire in the Flint*, was a powerful story of a Negro family in a southern town, balked into a sombre tragedy. *Flight*, a second novel by the same author, was concerned with the vicissitudes of a Negro girl who left her race and returned. W. E. B. DuBois, in 1911 wrote an epic of cotton, *The Quest of the Silver Fleece*, which was obviously fore-timed. It is however, one of the two books by Negro authors translated into the Russian language. The other is René Marau's, *Batuala*. Jessie Fauset's, *There is Confusion*, was an attempt to depict the life and fortunes of the educated Negro middle class. It was a piece of careful competent writing, and has gone through an English printing.

Of the short story writers, Jean Toomer, Eric Walrond, Rudolph Fisher, Arthur Huff Fauset, John Matheus, Zora Neale Hurston, Dorothy West and Eugene Gordon are at the same time the most successful and most promising. In this field, as in poetry, these new writers have abandoned the futile alchemy of trying to correct the outworn stereotypes of Negro characters in fiction through reversing the color of the heroes and villains; they are pointing their plows in the virgin soil of their own people; and, *mirable dictu*, they are beginning to make them interesting. Rudolph Fisher's stories in the *Atlantic Monthly* have breathed life into the migrant Southern and West Indian Negroes in New York. Zora Neale Hurston's stories are slices of life out of the South, realistic and moving. Walrond's first volume of Carribean Stories, *Tropic Death*, reveals him as the most coldly objective Negro writer of this period. In a sense they are not stories

The
CAROLINA
MAGAZINE

··◇■◇··

May
1927

at all, but a series of sense impressions, stark and unforgetable; they are the hot breath and foul tang of the tropics themselves. Fauset's *Symphonesque,* a 1926 *Opportunity* prize winner, was included in two anthologies of the best short stories of the year.

In Drama, Angelina Grimké and Willis Richardson of Washington, Eloise Bibb Thompson of California, and Eulalie Spence of New York, have made the most notable beginnings. The little theatre groups springing up in the culture centers are making more effective plays of Negro life imperative, and they will come!

The almost universal concern with social problems has even to this date precluded direct excursions into the field of *belles lettres.* There has been, however, writing of a marked character with these very problems and group aspirations at the base. One thinks of DuBois' *Dark Water,* of the penetrating essays of Kelly Miller in his two volumes, *Race Adjustment* and *Out of the House of Bondage,* and of the two published volumes of William Pickens.

Unclassified, but of great importance not merely to Negro literature but to the spirit of the new creators of it, is *The New Negro,* a collection of recent poetry, fiction, and essays, edited by Alain Locke. It is, for the stranger to this new Negro life and thinking, the portal to a new world of adventure.

Not without conviction do Negroes refer to this decade as the "renaissance," the period of "the awakening." A brief ten years have developed more confident self-expression, more widespread efforts in the direction of art than the two long, dreary centuries before. And on the gonfalon of this guard, one of them has written this:

> "We have tomorrow
> Bright before us
> Like a flame
> Yesterday, a night gone thing
> A sun-down name.
>
> And dawn today
> Broad arch above the road we came.
> We march!"

RACE PREJUDICE AND THE
NEGRO ARTIST

BY JAMES WELDON JOHNSON

WHAT Americans call the Negro problem is almost as old as America itself. For three centuries the Negro in this country has been tagged with an interrogation point; the question propounded, however, has not always been the same. Indeed, the question has run all the way from whether or not the Negro was a human being, down—or up—to whether or not the Negro shall be accorded full and unlimited American citizenship. Therefore, the Negro problem is not a problem in the sense of being a fixed proposition involving certain invariable factors and waiting to be worked out according to certain defined rules. It is not a static condition; rather, it is and always has been a series of shifting interracial situations, never precisely the same in any two generations. As these situations have shifted, the methods and manners of dealing with them have constantly changed. And never has there been such a swift and vital shift as the one which is taking place at the present moment; and never was there a more revolutionary change in attitudes than the one which is now going on.

The question of the races—white and black—has occupied much of America's time and thought. Many methods for a solution of the problem have been tried —most of them tried *on* the Negro, for one of the mistakes commonly made in dealing with this matter has been the failure of white America to take into account the Negro himself and the forces he was generating and sending out. The question repeated generation after generation has been: what shall we do with the Negro?—ignoring completely the power of the Negro to do something for himself, and even something to America. It is a new thought that the Negro has helped to shape and mold and make America. It is, perhaps, a startling thought that America would not be precisely the America it is to-day except for the powerful, if silent, influence the Negro has exerted upon it—both positively and negatively. It is a certainty that the nation would be shocked by a contemplation of the effects which have been wrought upon its inherent character by the negative power which the Negro has involuntarily and unwittingly wielded.

A number of approaches to the heart of the race problem have been tried: religious, educational, political, industrial, ethical, economic, sociological. Along several of these approaches considerable progress has been made. To-day a newer approach is being tried, an approach which discards most of the older methods. It requires a minimum of pleas, or propaganda, or philanthropy. It depends more upon what the Negro himself does than upon what someone does for him. It is the approach along the line of intellectual and artistic achievement by Negroes, and may be called the art approach to the Negro problem. This method of approaching a solution of the race question has the advantage of affording great and rapid progress with least friction and of providing a common platform upon which most people are willing to stand. The results of this method seem to carry a high degree of finality, to be the thing itself that was to be demonstrated.

I have said that this is a newer approach to the race problem; that is only in a sense true. The Negro has been using this method for a very long time; for a longer time than he has used any other method, and, perhaps, with farther-reaching effectiveness. For more than a century his great folk-art contributions have been exerting an ameliorating effect, slight and perhaps, in any one period, imperceptible, nevertheless, cumulative. In countless and diverse situations song and dance have been both a sword and a shield for the Negro. Take the Spirituals: for sixty years, beginning with their introduction to the world by the Fisk Jubilee Singers, these songs have touched and stirred the hearts of people and brought about a smoothing down of the rougher edges of prejudice against the Negro. Indeed, nobody can hear Negroes sing this wonderful music in its primitive beauty without a softening of feeling toward them.

What is there, then, that is new? What is new consists largely in the changing attitude of the American people. There is a coming to light and notice of efforts that have been going on for a long while, and a public appreciation of their results. Note, for example, the change in the reaction to the Spirituals. Fifty years ago white people who heard the Spirituals were touched and moved with sympathy and pity for the "poor Negro." To-day the effect is not one of pity for the Negro's condition, but admiration for the creative genius of the race.

All of the Negro's folk-art creations have undergone a new evaluation. His sacred music—the Spirituals; his secular music—Ragtime, Blues, Jazz, and the work songs; his folk lore—the Uncle Remus plantation tales; and his dances have received a new and higher appreciation. Indeed, I dare to say that it is

now more or less generally acknowledged that the only things artistic that have sprung from American soil and out of American life, and been universally recognized as distinctively American products, are the folk creations of the Negro. The one thing that may be termed artistic, by which the United States is known the world over, is its Negro-derived popular music. The folk creations of the Negro have not only received a new appreciation; they have —the Spirituals excepted—been taken over and assimilated. They are no longer racial, they are national; they have become a part of our common cultural fund. Negro secular music has been developed into American popular music; Negro dances have been made into our national art of dancing; even the plantation tales have been transformed and have come out as popular bedtime stories. The Spirituals are still distinct Negro folk songs, but sooner or later our serious composers will take them as material to go into the making of the "great American music" that has so long been looked for.

But the story does not halt at this point. The Negro has done a great deal through his folk-art creations to change the national attitudes toward him; and now the efforts of the race have been reinforced and magnified by the individual Negro artist, the conscious artist. It is fortunate that the individual Negro artist has emerged; for it is more than probable that with the ending of the creative period of Blues, which seems to be at hand, the whole folk creative effort of the Negro in the United States will come to a close. All the psychological and environmental forces are working to that end. At any rate, it is the individual Negro artist that is now doing most to effect a crumbling of the inner walls of race prejudice; there are outer and inner walls. The emergence of the individual artist is the result of the same phenomenon that brought about the new evaluation and appreciation of the folk-art creations. But it should be borne in mind that the conscious Afra-merican artist is not an entirely new thing. What is new about him is chiefly the evaluation and public recognition of his work.

II

When and how did this happen? The entire change, which is marked by the shedding of a new light on the artistic and intellectual achievements of the Negro, the whole period which has become ineptly known as "the Negro renaissance," is the matter of a decade; it has all taken place within the last ten years. More forces than anyone can name have been at work to create the existing state; however, several of them may be pointed out. What took place had no appearance of a development; it seemed more like a sudden awakening, an almost instantaneous change. There was nothing that immediately preceded it which foreshadowed what was to follow. Those who were in the midst of the movement were as much astonished as anyone else to see the transformation. Overnight, as it were, America became aware that there were Negro artists and that they had something worth while to offer. This awareness first manifested itself in black America, for, strange as it may seem, Negroes themselves, as a mass, had had little or no consciousness of their own individual artists. Black America awoke first to the fact that it possessed poets. This awakening followed the entry of the United States into the Great War. Before this country had been in the war very long there was bitter disillusionment on the part of American Negroes—on the part both of those working at home and those fighting in France to make the world safe for democracy. The disappointment and bitterness were taken up and voiced by a group of seven or eight Negro poets. They expressed what the race felt, what the race wanted to hear. They made the group at large articulate. Some of this poetry was the poetry of despair, but most of it was the poetry of protest and rebellion. Fenton Johnson wrote of civilization:

I am tired of work; I am tired of building up
    somebody else's civilization.
Let us take a rest, M'lissy Jane.

You will let the old shanty go to rot, the
    white people's clothes turn to dust,
    and the Calvary Baptist Church sink
    to the bottomless pit.

Throw the children into the river; civilization
    has given us too many. It is better to
    die than it is to grow up and find out
    that you are colored.
Pluck the stars out of the heavens. The
    stars mark our destiny. The stars
    marked my destiny.
I am tired of civilization.

Joseph Cotter, a youth of twenty, inquired plaintively from the invalid's bed to which he was confined:

Brother, come!
And let us go unto our God.
And when we stand before Him
I shall say,
"Lord, I do not hate,
I am hated.
I scourge no one,
I am scourged.
I covet no lands,
My lands are coveted.
I mock no peoples,
My people are mocked."
And, brother, what shall you say?

But among this whole group the voice that was most powerful was that of Claude McKay. Here was a true poet of great skill and wide range, who turned from creating the mood of poetic beauty in the absolute, as he had so fully done in such poems as "Spring in New Hampshire," "The Harlem Dancer," and "Flame Heart," for example, and began pouring out cynicism, bitterness, and invective. For this purpose, incongruous as it may seem, he took the sonnet form as his medium. There is nothing in American literature that strikes a more portentous note than these sonnet-tragedies of McKay. Here is the sestet of his sonnet, "The Lynching":

285

Day dawned, and soon the mixed crowds
　　came to view
The ghastly body swaying in the sun:
The women thronged to look, but never a one
Showed sorrow in her eyes of steely blue;
And little lads, lynchers that were to be,
Danced round the dreadful thing in fiendish
　　glee.

The summer of 1919 was a terrifying period for the American Negro. There were race riots in Chicago and in Washington and in Omaha and in Phillips County, Arkansas; and in Longview, Texas; and in Knoxville, Tennessee; and in Norfolk, Virginia; and in other communities. Colored men and women, by dozens and by scores, were chased and beaten and killed in the streets. And from Claude McKay came this cry of defiant despair, sounded from the last ditch:

If we must die—let it not be like hogs
Hunted and penned in an inglorious spot,

Oh, Kinsmen! We must meet the common
　　foe;
Though far outnumbered, let us still be brave,
And for their thousand blows deal one death-
　　blow!
What though before us lies the open grave?
Like men we'll face the murderous, cowardly
　　pack,
Pressed to the wall, dying, but—fighting
　　back!

But not all the terror of the time could smother the poet of beauty and universality in McKay. In "America," which opens with these lines:

Although she feeds me bread of bitterness,
And sinks into my throat her tiger's tooth,
Stealing my breath of life, I will confess
I love this cultured hell that tests my youth

he fused these elements of fear and bitterness and hate into verse which by every test is true poetry and a fine sonnet.

The poems of the Negro poets of the immediate post-war period were widely printed in Negro periodicals; they were committed to memory; they were recited at school exercises and public meetings; and were discussed at private gatherings. Now, Negro poets were not new; their line goes back a long way in Aframerican history. Between Phillis Wheatley, who as a girl of eight or nine was landed in Boston from an African slave ship, in 1761, and who published a volume of poems in 1773, and Paul Laurence Dunbar, who died in 1906, there were more than thirty Negroes who published volumes of verse—some of it good, most of it mediocre, and much of it bad. The new thing was the effect produced by these poets who sprang up out of the war period. Negro poets had sounded similar notes before, but now for the first time they succeeded in setting up a reverberating response, even in their own group. But the effect was not limited to black America; several of these later poets in some subtle way affected white America. In any event, at just this time white America began to become aware and to awaken. In the correlation of forces that brought about this result it might be pointed out that the culminating effect of the folk-art creations had gone far toward inducing a favorable state of mind. Doubtless it is also true that the new knowledge and opinions about the Negro in Africa— that he was not just a howling savage, that he had a culture, that he had produced a vital art—had directly affected opinion about the Negro in America. However it may have been, the Negro poets growing out of the war period were the forerunners of the individuals whose work is now being assayed and is receiving recognition in accordance with its worth.

III

And yet, contemporaneously with the work of these poets a significant effort was made in another field of art—an effort which might have gone much farther at the time had it not been cut off by our entry into the War, but which, nevertheless, had its effect. Early in 1917, in fact on the very day we entered the War, Mrs. Emily Hapgood produced at the Madison Square Garden Theater three plays of Negro life by Ridgley Torrence, staged by Robert Edmond Jones, and played by an all-Negro cast. This was the first time that Negro actors in drama commanded the serious attention of the critics and the general public. Two of the players, Opal Cooper and Inez Clough, were listed by George Jean Nathan among the ten actors giving the most distinguished performances of the year. No one who heard Opal Cooper chant the dream in the "Rider of Dreams" can ever forget the thrill of it. A sensational feature of the production was the singing orchestra of Negro performers under the direction of J. Rosamond Johnson—singing orchestras in theaters have since become common. The plays moved from the Garden Theater to the Garrick, but the stress of war crushed them out. In 1920, Charles Gilpin was enthusiastically and universally acclaimed for his acting in "The Emperor Jones." The American stage has seldom seen such an outburst of acclamation. Mr. Gilpin was one of the ten persons voted by the Drama League as having done most for the American theater during the year. Most of the readers of these pages will remember the almost national crisis caused by his invitation to the Drama League Dinner. And along came "Shuffle Along"; and all of New York flocked to an out of the way theater in West Sixty-third Street to hear the most joyous singing and see the most exhilarating dancing to be found on any stage in the city. The dancing steps originally used by the "policeman" in "Shuffle Along" furnished new material for hundreds of dancing men. "Shuffle Along" was actually an epoch-making musical comedy. Out of "Shuffle Along" came Florence Mills, who, unfortunately, died so young but lived long enough to be acknowledged here and in Europe as one of the finest singing comediennes the stage had ever seen and an artist of positive genius. In 1923 Roland Hayes stepped out on the American stage in a blaze of glory, making his first appearances as soloist with the Boston Symphony Orchestra and later with the Philharmonic. Few single artists have packed such crowds into Carnegie Hall and the finest concert halls throughout the country as has Roland Hayes; and, notwithstanding the éclat with which America first received him, his reputation has continued to increase and, besides, he is rated as one of the best box-office attractions in the whole concert field. Miss Marian Anderson appeared as soloist with the Philadelphia Symphony Orchestra and in concert at the Lewisohn Stadium at New York City College. Paul Robeson and J. Rosamond Johnson and Taylor Gordon sang Spirituals to large and appreciative audiences in New York and over the country, giving to those songs a fresh interpretation and a new vogue.

Paul Robeson—that most versatile of men, who has made a national reputation as athlete, singer, and actor—played in Eugene O'Neill's "All God's Chillun" and added to his reputation on the stage, and, moreover, put to the test an ancient taboo; he played the principal role opposite a white woman. This feature of the play gave rise to a more acute crisis than did Gilpin's invitation to the Drama League Dinner. Some sensational newspapers predicted race riots and other dire disasters, but nothing of the sort happened; the play went over without a boo. Robeson played the title role in a revival of "The Emperor Jones" and almost duplicated the sensation produced by Gilpin in the original presentation. There followed on the stage Julius Bledsoe, Rose McClendon, Frank Wilson, and Abbie Mitchell, all of whom gained recognition. At the time of this writing each of these four is playing in a Broadway production. Paradoxical it may seem, but no Negro comedian gained recognition in this decade. Negro comedians have long been a recognized American institution and there are several now before the public who are well known, but their reputations were made before this period. The only new reputations made on the comedy stage were made by women, Florence Mills and Ethel Waters. In addition there are the two famous Smiths, Bessie and Clara, singers of Blues and favorites of vaudeville, phonograph, and radio audiences. Of course there is Josephine Baker, but her reputation was made entirely in Europe. Nevertheless, these magical ten years have worked a change upon Negro comedy. Before Miller and Lyles brought "Shuffle Along" to New York, managers here could hardly conceive of a Negro musical comedy playing a Broadway house. When Williams and Walker, Cole and Johnson, and Ernest Hogan were in their heyday, people who wanted to see them had to go to theaters outside the great white-light zone. George Walker died before the "new day," and up to his retirement from the stage he kept up a constant fight for a chance for his company to play a strictly Broadway theater. Since "Shuffle Along," hardly a season has passed without seeing one or more Negro musical comedies playing in the finest theaters in New York. In fact, Negro plays and Negro performers in white plays on Broadway have become usual occurrences.

Odd has been the fate of the younger poets who were instrumental in bringing about the present state of affairs. It is a fact that none of them, with the exception of Claude McKay, quite succeeded in bridging over into it. Three of them, Roscoe Jamison, Lucian Watkins, and Joseph Cotter, are dead, all dying in their youth. Fenton Johnson is almost silent. And Claude McKay has for the past four or five years lived practically in exile. However, several of the older writers are busily at work, and there has sprung up in the last three or four years a group of newer creative writers. Countee Cullen and Langston Hughes have achieved recognition as poets. Jean Toomer, Walter White, Eric Walrond, and Rudolph Fisher have made a place among writers of fiction. And Claude McKay, after a period of silence as a poet, has published his *Home to Harlem*, a generally acclaimed novel. These are names that carry literary significance, and they take their places according to individual merit in the list of the makers of contemporary American literature. In addition, there are more than a score of younger writers who are not yet quite in the public eye, but will soon be more widely known. Writers such as these are bound to be known and in larger numbers, because their work now has the chance to gain whatever appreciation it merits. To-day the reagents that will discover what of it is good are at work, the arbiters of our national letters are disposed to regard their good work as a part of American literature, and the public is prepared to accept it as such. This has not always been the case. Until this recent period, the several achievements in writing that have come to light have been regarded as more or less sporadic and isolated efforts, and not in any sense as having a direct relation to the national literature. Had the existing forces been at work at the time, the remarkable decade from 1895 to 1905, which brought forth Booker T. Washington's *Up from Slavery*, W. E. Burghardt Du Bois's *The Souls of Black Folk*, Charles Chesnutt's stories of Negro life, and Paul Laurence Dunbar's poetry, might have signalled the beginning of the "Negro literary renaissance."

During the present decade the individual Negro artist has definitely emerged in three fields, in literature, in the theater, and on the concert stage; in other fields he has not won marked distinction. To point to any achievement of distinction in painting the Negro must go back of this decade, back to H. O. Tanner, who has lived in Europe for the past thirty-five years; or farther back to E. M. Bannister, who gained considerable recognition a half century ago. Nevertheless, there is the work of W. E. Scott, a mural painter, who lives in Chicago and has done a number of public buildings in the Middle West, and of Archibald J. Motley, who recently held a one-man exhibit in New York which attracted very favorable attention. The drawings of Aaron Douglas have won for him a place among American illustrators. To point to any work of acknowledged excellence in sculpture the Negro must go back of this decade to the work of two women, Edmonia Lewis and Meta Warrick Fuller, both of whom received chiefly in Europe such recognition as they gained. There are several young painters and sculptors who are winning recognition. But the strangest lack is that with all the great native musical endowment he is conceded to possess, the Negro has not in this most propitious time produced a single outstanding composer. There are competent musicians and talented composers of songs and detached bits of music, but no original composer who, in amount and standard of work and in recognition achieved, is at all comparable with S. Coleridge-Taylor, the English Negro composer. Nor can the Negro in the United States point back of this decade to even one such artist. It is a curious fact that the American Negro through his whole history has done more highly sustained and more fully recognized work in the composition of letters than in the composition of music. It is the more curious when we consider that music is so innately a characteristic method of expression for the Negro.

IV

What, now, is the significance of this artistic activity on the part of the Negro and of its reactions on the American people? I think it is twofold. In the first place, the Negro is making some distinctive contributions to our common cultural store. I do not claim it is possible for these individual artists to produce anything comparable to the folk-art in distinctive values, but I do believe they are bringing something fresh and vital into American art, something from the store of their own racial genius:

warmth, color, movement, rhythm, and abandon; depth and swiftness of emotion and the beauty of sensuousness. I believe American art will be richer because of these elements in fuller quantity.

But what is of deeper significance to the Negro himself is the effect that this artistic activity is producing upon his condition and status as a man and citizen. I do not believe it an overstatement to say that the "race problem" is fast reaching the stage of being more a question of national mental attitudes toward the Negro than a question of his actual condition. That is to say, it is not at all the problem of a moribund people sinking into a slough of ignorance, poverty, and decay in the very midst of our civilization and despite all our efforts to save them; that would indeed be a problem. Rather is the problem coming to consist in the hesitation and refusal to open new doors of opportunity at which these people are constantly knocking. In other words, the problem for the Negro is reaching the plane where it is becoming less a matter of dealing with what he is and more a matter of dealing with what America thinks he is.

Now, the truth is that the great majority of Americans have not thought about the Negro at all, except in a vague sort of way and in the form of traditional and erroneous stereotypes. Some of these stereotyped forms of thought are quite absurd, yet they have had serious effects. Millions of Americans have had their opinions and attitudes regarding their fellow colored citizens determined by such a phrase as, "A nigger will steal," or "Niggers are lazy," or "Niggers are dirty." But there is a common, widespread, and persistent stereotyped idea regarding the Negro, and it is that he is here only to receive; to be shaped into something new and unquestionably better. The common idea is that the Negro reached America intellectually, culturally, and morally empty, and that he is here to be filled—filled with education, filled with religion, filled with morality, filled with culture. In a word, the stereotype is that the Negro is nothing more than a beggar at the gate of the nation, waiting to be thrown the crumbs of civilization. Through his artistic efforts the Negro is smashing this immemorial stereotype faster than he has ever done through any other method he has been able to use. He is making it realized that he is the possessor of a wealth of natural endowments and that he has long been a generous giver to America. He is impressing upon the national mind the conviction that he is an active and important force in American life; that he is a creator as well as a creature; that he has given as well as received; that he is the potential giver of larger and richer contributions.

In this way the Negro is bringing about an entirely new national conception of himself; he has placed himself in an entirely new light before the American people. I do not think it too much to say that through artistic achievement the Negro has found a means of getting at the very core of the prejudice against him, by challenging the Nordic superiority complex. A great deal has been accomplished in this decade of "renaissance." Enough has been accomplished to make it seem almost amazing when we realize that there are less than twenty-five Negro artists who have more or less of national recognition; and that it is they who have chiefly done the work. A great part of what they have accomplished has been done through the sort of publicity they have secured for the race. A generation ago the Negro was receiving lots of publicity, but nearly all of it was bad. There were front page stories with such headings as, "Negro Criminal," "Negro Brute." To-day one may see undesirable stories, but one may also read stories about Negro singers, Negro actors, Negro authors, Negro poets. The connotations of the very word "Negro" have been changed. A generation ago many Negroes were half or wholly ashamed of the term. To-day they have every reason to be proud of it.

For many years and by many methods the Negro has been overcoming the coarser prejudices against him; and when we consider how many of the subtler prejudices have crumbled, and crumbled rapidly under the process of art creation by the Negro, we are justified in taking a hopeful outlook toward the effect that the increase of recognized individual artists fivefold, tenfold, twentyfold, will have on this most perplexing and vital question before the American people.

The Southern Workman

| VOL. LVII | May 1928 | No. 5 |

THE NEGRO LOOKS AT AN OUTWORN TRADITION

BY ALICE DUNBAR NELSON

THE New Negro—that altogether fascinating and partially mythical creature, conceived by Dr. Alain Locke, and adopted by most of the United States—is living up to the reputation given him by his progenitor. In addition to the usual shibboleths of "seeing life whole," "facing the sun," "expressing himself," he is beginning to think, weigh, consider, analyze. Particularly is he gravely analyzing the dividing line between myth and history, religion and superstition, tradition and fact. He is beginning to learn that much of what he has accepted as Gospel for centuries is nothing but stale and outworn creeds, dogmas, catch-words, slogans, dripping with falsity, and mouldy with senility, not inherent in himself either as a race or as an individual, but foisted upon him by a Caucasian world apprehensive of destruction, and bolstering its supremacy by mental subjugation of the underling.

The Negro has begun to study his own history. Like most of the movements, which we call Renaissance, this study is nothing absolutely new. Since emancipation and the "Autobiography of Frederick Douglass" there have been sporadic books, histories of the Negro, histories of the Negro in war, more or less authentic, more or less written with regard for conventional English, descending to biographical sketches or certain obscure individuals who had contributed to the publication of these volumes.

But this Renaissance has dealt more with historical background. Hardly any other Renaissance has paid so much attention to history. The Negro has learned about his African backgrounds, his African tradition, his African culture. He has learned about his contribution to the culture of this continent. He knows what gifts he has brought to America. He is racially conscious as never before.

But this movement, as with all movements in which the Negro is a component part, is one with a confused objective. He has acquired all the Caucasian's traditions, superstitions, ideas, inhibitions, narrowness. Centuries of slavery had wiped clean the slate of his past. He had nothing of his own. He took on the language, religion, customs of his owners.

Therefore, it is no wonder that he has the white man's idea of history—a chronicle of wars, murders, plots and counterplots, obscure kinglets, stupid rulers, foolish ceremonies. As Voltaire caustically puts it, "History is nothing more than a picture of crimes and misfortunes * * * much like reading the history of highway robbers." So his earlier books chronicle the Negro in war, battles, regiments. It was a generation before the progress of the race meant anything but the story of valor on the battlefield.

This is the one objective. The other is the Negro's own ideal. His definition of contribution to the nation is that of the arts of peace. He is prone to tell you proudly of the first blood shed in the War for Independence. But his pride in that is merely a reflex of the traditions of Massachusetts and the Boston Tea Party. He is actually more proud of Phillis Wheatley's poem to George Washington, of Banneker's Almanac and his friendship with Thomas Jefferson, of the bar sinister on Alexander Hamilton's escutcheon. When he discusses the French and Indian War, because the white American has taught in the histories that that bloody conflict was a moral procedure on account of European conditions, the Negro will boast of the sporadic groups of free and enslaved of his race who helped win the wilderness from France; but in the next breath, he will declaim proudly of the forests he felled, the bridges he built, the streams he dammed, the protection he gave to his owners.

It is a significant fact that the splendid work of Dr. Carter Woodson reflects something of this ideal of a peaceful contribution to the nation. Volume after volume tells of economic progress, scientific strivings, literary ambitions. Dr. W. E. B. DuBois spends a volume to tell of the "Gift of Black Folk" and he is far more interested in the story of the granulation of sugar, of the life of Dr. John Derham, the first Negro physician, and such chronicles, than in the war record of the black man, even at New Orleans with Andrew Jackson.

This confused objective, this dual outlook, is one of the

tragedies of the life of the Negro. Like any other people thrown into an alien civilization with no memories of his own that could have survived his introduction to this continent, he must of necessity, chameleon-like, take on the coloring of his surroundings. When militarism is rampant, he is a militarist. He boasts that the old flag never touched the ground, and hates Indians, Germans, Mexicans, Chinese, anyone who threatens the supremacy of the white American with a fine disregard for personal interests or truth. He has taken on this civilization and he swears by it, even though it destroys his racial life and makes of him a mere adjunct to the pomp and circumstance of his oppressor. He worships a white God, with Nordic angels, and once accepted the Biblical interpretation of the necessity of slavery, even as a certain civilization in an earlier day accepted the Old Testament pronouncement on polygamy. The Negro had taken his ideals of dress, manners, customs, everything from the white man. His superstitions, later research has proved, are not altogether the remnants of African voodoo and *obeah*. The witches of Salem, the "hex" doctors of Pennsylvania, the backwoods rites of the South filtered to the Negro, rather than the Negro giving his rites to the white man.

Nothing is more illustrative of the white man's inhibitions caught and held by the Negro than his attitude on the question of votes for women. He had heard through generations of slavery the Southern ideal of false chivalry, of woman's place in the home, of her constitution too tender and delicate to be exposed to the ruthless gaze of the ballot box. And he gravely advanced like arguments against his own women voting, regardless of the fact that the Negro woman had always had to work, had never had the privilege of staying at home and nursing her delicateness, was pretty strong and capable, and had probably made a more practical contribution to the race than like numbers of males.

Small wonder, then, that the Negro found himself caught in the whirlwind of war. Small wonder, then, that he was confused, floundering; that two ideals presented themselves for his consideration, and that he hesitated to choose, and so hesitating, was all but lost.

For the Negro is by nature a lover of peace. By his own nature, by his deep-seated religious fervor, by his love of home and family, by his gentle and kindly spirit, by the tenderness of his native sympathies, by his centuries of patience and gentleness and forbearance, by his horror of violence and the deeds of violence, he is opposed to war. He will contend and hold on and be stubborn in his moral fight for his rights, privileges, children, religion, racial integrity—but organized warfare is a thing he enters only under the tutelage of the white man. In short, the Negro is brave, but he is not a mass murderer. If rage and hate and the lust of killing make him mad, he kills alone—but he does not lynch the helpless with a mob.

He believes in Christianity. If it were not for the black man in this country, the Christian religion would be at a low point on the graph. And he takes the teaching of the Master literally. If Christianity means the cessation of strife among nations, and he is a Christian, then he believes in his soul that war is wrong.

The New Negro—he who has come of age since 1918—is more firmly convinced even than his elder brother who went overseas, his father who charged up San Juan Hill, or his grandfather who wore the blue in the sixties, that it is all a holocaust of unnecessary carnage. He is weighing skeptically the struggles of that father or uncle who for all his uniform suffered martyrdom in Brownsville and Leavenworth; of that elder brother, who for all his sacrifice in Flanders to make a world safe for democracy, who, in spite of his glorious uniform and medals pinned on his breast for valor, yet has been barred from some of the chapters of the American Legion, and sternly rejected from the coveted "Forty and Eight."

Someone has wittily said that "Old men make wars, young men fight them, women and children suffer from them." A nation is militarized because older men have greed. Grasping for iron and coal and oil, they invent insults, and the flower of the youth of the countries goes forth to avenge fancied wrongs. The Negro is an integral part of whatever nation wherein he happens to be born, and he takes on the customs, languages, wrongs, insults, superstitions, traditions, loyalties, ideals of that land. Therefore the flower of his race, too, went forth for cannon fodder. What it was all about he did not know, did not ask, any more than any other youth. He was fighting the white man's battles, to avenge insults to the white man, given by other white men. And when it was all over, he came home to be kicked around by these same white men. The glorious exception, of course, was the Civil War. There has been no occasion since for the Negro to fight for his own cause. On the other occasions, it seems as if his reward has been a thrill that ceased when the last note of the drum beat had died away.

An age of skepticism toward conventions, a break-down of traditions, has brought with it an attitude of analysis of the clinging to outworn traditions. Just why should the Negro continue in his allegiance toward certain traditional beliefs? Just why shall he acecpt certain ready-made convictions, slogans, Babbitries? Why send him to school for sixty years, and spend billions upon his education if it were not to develop within him the faculty of reasoning, of weighing, considering, judging for himself? So he turns the white light of his focus upon the vital questions touching life : Religion, Society, Politics, War. And in this last he finds matter for profound consideration. Peace against War. Christ against cannon. Lincoln, Sherman, and Grant against Bismarck. Kant and the great philosophers against Nietsche and Hearst and the jingoes. With the Quaker in Voltaire's "Dictionaire Philosophique" he says, "Our God, who has bidden us love our enemies and suffer evil without complaint, assuredly has no mind that we should cross the sea to go and cut the throats of our brothers because murderers in red clothes and hats two feet high enlist citizens by making a noise with two sticks on an ass's skin."

The Negro has been misunderstood so much himself that he sympathizes most deeply with those who are misunderstood. He therefore can look most deeply into the causes of war. He can clearly visualize it as the result of misunderstanding, noncomprehension of the essentials of *meum* and *teum*. Rather than murder in cold blood the robber of his hen roost or wood yard, he would apprehend the intruder, and hale him before a court of law there to be given a punishment to fit the crime. Then there is no murder on his soul, no widow to call down curses upon his hasty temper, no orphans whose lives are changed from opportunity to bitterness.

This does not mean that the Negro, whose thoughts are turning to the peaceful solution of the world's maladjustments, is disloyal to his country and his flag. There is no group in this land more passionately loyal or patriotic. The favorite boast of the race is that in its hands "the old flag never touched the ground." The favorite peroration of the Negro spell-binder, and one which always evokes the most sustained applause is the recital of his patriotic devotion to the nation in time of war, his readiness when the country calls. He is none the less ready. But he does not want the land of his birth to plunge itself into unnecessary and avertable conflicts.

But looking around him, the Negro is aghast at the implications and perhaps imprecations hurled upon the simple believer in the teachings of Christ, the clear thinker who sees the futility of carnage to settle disputes, the member of a race who believes with Washington that it were better to keep free of entangling alliances. "Pacifist" is a term of contempt in time of peace, of opprobrium in time of war. And there are some organizations of peace and amity and goodwill in which a Negro is not wanted any more than in some war organizations. Small wonder then, if the Negro sadly concludes that peace is ofttimes a white man's peace, as war is ofttimes a white man's war—until time of dire emergency.

Negro Authors and White Publishers

By JAMES WELDON JOHNSON

NEGRO writers, like all writing folks, have many things to complain about. Writers have always felt and many of them have plainly said that the world did not fully appreciate their work. This attitude has seldom been justified. The great or good writers who have not been acknowlsistance which I do not think is based on the facts and which reacts to the injury of the writers uttering it. This complaint is: that the leading white publishers have set a standard which Negro writers must conform to or go unpublished; that this standard calls only for books depicting the Negro in a manner which tends to degrade him in the eyes of the world; that only books about the so-called lower types of Negroes and lower phases of Negro life find consideration and acceptance.

Now, in the first place, there is a certain snobbishness in terming the less literate and less sophisticated, the more simple and more primitive classes of Negroes as "lower". At least as literary material, they are higher. They have greater dramatic and artistic potentialities for the writer than the so-called higher classes, who so closely resemble the bourgeois white classes. The vicious and criminal elements—and we must admit that even in our own race there are such elements—are rightly termed "lower", but even they have more accessible dramatic values than the ordinary, respectable middle-class element. It takes nothing less than supreme genius to make middle-class society, black or white, interesting—to say nothing of making it dramatic. But I am jotting down this brief essay with the prime purpose of pointing out the dangers, especially to young writers, in complaining that publishers refuse to consider their work because it portrays Negro life on too high a level. When a writer begins to say and then believe that the reason why he cannot get published is because his work is *too good* he is in a bad way. This is the way that leads to making a fetish of failure. It is a too easy explanation of the lack of accomplishment. It is this "superior work—sor-

edged as such by the generation in which they lived are rare. And where such acknowledgement has not been accorded by the generations which touched an author's life, posterity has hardly ever revoked the unfavorable judgment.

Nevertheless, writers have many did publishers—low brow public" complex that gives rise to the numerous small coteries of unsuccessful writers, white as well as colored; the chief function of the members of these coteries being the mutual admiration of each other's unpublished manuscripts. This attitude brings its adherents to a position of pathetic futility or ludicrous superiority.

Within these seven or eight years of literary florescence I doubt that any first class publisher has turned down a first rate work by any Negro writer on the ground that it was *not on a low enough level.* Now, suppose we look at the actual facts as shown by the books published in these recent years by leading publishers. Let us first take fiction and list the books depicting Negro life on the "upper" levels or shedding a favorable light on the race that have been published:

There Is Confusion.......Jessie Fauset
Fire In the Flint........Walter White
Flight ....Walter White
The Prince of Washington Square ....Harry F. Liscomb
Quicksand ....Nella Larsen
Dark Princess......W. E. B. Du Bois
Plum Bun ....Jessie Fauset
Passing ....Nella Larsen

Now, those depicting Negro life on the "lower" levels:

Cane ....Jean Toomer
Tropic Death ....Eric Walrond
Home to Harlem......Claude McKay
Walls of Jericho......Rudolph Fisher
The Blacker the Berry,
                    Wallace Thurman
Banjo ....Claude McKay

The score is eight to six—with "Tropic Death", "Walls of Jericho" and "Cane" on the border line. In non fiction the "upper level" literature scores still higher. In that class we have:

good reasons for complaining; for their lot is a hard one. And it may be that Negro writers have some special good reasons for complaining; I am not sure that at the present time this is so. However that may be, there is one complaint that some younger Negro writers are uttering with greater and greater in-

A Social History of the
    American Negro..Benjamin Brawley
Negro Folk Rhymes.Thomas W. Talley
The Book of American Negro
    Poetry...Ed James Weldon Johnson
The New Negro......Ed Alain Locke
The Book of American Negro
    Spirituals. Ed. James Weldon Johnson
The Second Book of American Negro
    Spirituals. Ed. James Weldon Johnson
Color ....Countée Cullen
Caroling Dusk .....Ed. Countée Cullen
Darkwater ....W. E. B. Du Bois
Gift of Black Folk..W. E. B. Du Bois
Plays of Negro Life,
            Ed. Locke and Gregory
God's Trombones,
            James Weldon Johnson
Copper Sun...........Countée Cullen
Negro Labor in the United States,
            Charles H. Wesley
A Bibliography of the Negro in Africa
    and America.......Monroe N. Work
What the Negro Thinks...R. R. Moton
Rope and Faggot........Walter White
An Autumn Love Cycle,
            Georgia Douglas Johnson

In the other column, in non fiction, we have only:

The Weary Blues.....Langston Hughes
Fine Clothes to the Jew,
            Langston Hughes

And it must be said that although Mr. Hughes shows a predilection for singing the "lower" and "humbler" classes of Negroes, these two volumes contain many poems that are highly inspirational.

In non fiction the score is nineteen to two. I do not see how any one who looks at these figures can fail to see that the complaint against the publishers is not in consonance with the facts. I believe that Negro writers who have something worth while to say and the power and skill to say it have as fair a chance today of being published as any other writers.

Negro Authors Must Eat

By GEORGE W. JACOBS

NOT long ago a Negro author addressed an audience of which I was a member. For no reason beyond the possible squeamishness of his own conscience, he apologized for certain unwholesome nuances in one of his latest works; and in doing so he uttered these three words: "Authors must eat."

My mind drifted back to the childhood of man. I gazed upon a hairy fellow poised upon a crag, playing a lute. Unconscious of an audience, oblivious of possible audiences, he played. For the moment he was enchanted by the sublime fact of nature. Suddenly the fellow stopped, leaped from the crag, and with his lute tucked under an arm raced toward a glade in the jungle where a dinosaur had just been slain. As the hunters hacked away at their respective portions of the kill, the lutist struck up a wanton tune that he had heard in a certain fancy cave. One of the hunters winked at him knowingly; then tossed him a luscious dinosaur ear. When the lutist had eaten, he trudged away in the direction of his crag. From time to time he held his lute up before his eyes, focusing upon it a gaze both apologetic and caressing. Finally he said in a tone of resignation not untinged with remorse: "Oh well, lutists must eat."

In spite of the efforts of the lecturer I remained unconvinced that even the Negro author is justified in burdening his interpretation of nature with the servilities of a steward. Other men have shunted the burden of their support into channels separate from their art. Aeschylus was a soldier and public official. Sophocles was a general and the commander of a fleet. Cervantes was a naval commissary and tax collector. Art to them was more than a mere purveyor of groceries. "The literature of a people," wrote Lowell, "should be the record of its joys and sorrows, its aspirations and its shortcomings, its wisdom and its folly, the confidant of its soul."

One of the opportunities which presented itself to the Negro writer at the close of the late war was that of destroying the racial stereotypes, the perpetuation of which now precludes the possibility of any immediate "literature of a people." Ten years ago the passion for a candid and comprehensive delineation of every phase of Negro life was such that the literate world clamored for the Negro of artistic ability as it had clamored at no previous time since the emancipation of the race. In response to those clamors, the Negro writers of New York, to whom I shall confine this discussion, plunged beneath the surface of their environment; they hoisted the sewer system to one's very nose and, amid the jingling of many shekels, insisted that this was all that there was of black Harlem.

Almost from the beginning certain white writers saw in the Negro writers' efforts to respond to these demands a politer form of amusement than that afforded by any of the Harlem night clubs. They trekked up to Harlem to show the little colored boys and girls the path to Parnassus; they redefined "the literature of a people" as "the record of a people's shortcomings and its follies." However, now that the clamors have become less insistent, one discovers with

more regret than surprise that those Negro writers who had the privilege of being patronized along the way to Parnassus have ebbed with the tide of interest. Many of them had passionately and honestly sought escape through art. They found new shackles in artistic patronage. The public ceased to accept the summary disposal of two hundred thousand Harlem Negroes in the words: idiotic, amoral, hyper-sexual.

The present Negro fiction writers of Harlem fall into two general types. One type subscribes unapologetically to the sensational. The other type subscribes no less unapologetically to a solitary contemplation of a black savage dropped bodily into a white culture. The prostitute is the high priestess of the first type. Negro primitivism is the creed of the second. Extremists both.

Harry Hansen in reviewing Maxwell Bodenheim's "Georgie May" objected to the chief character on the ground that prostitutes as a whole are so free from inhibitions or nuances that their portrayal is unworthy of a writer capable of describing complex characters. There is merit in that criticism. Nevertheless, even among the Georgie Mays there are many individuals who, despite their flouting of conventional morality, possess personal codes of ethics, anti-social though they may be, which present a fascinating bundle of contradictions. If I object, then, to the role that the prostitute plays in latter-day fiction by Negroes, it is not on the ground that she lacks complexity of character, but on the ground that she is portrayed out of the depths of ignorance. She is, with scarce an exception, endowed with a physical hideousness, born of the ancient superstition that only the good should be presented as beautiful. She is endowed with a bestiality possible only to the vulgar rich.

Regarding the second type of Harlem fiction, this cult, like the harlotesque, was born along the path to Parnassus. One of the white apostles of the bizarre had chanced to see an "over-ginned" Negro girl "get loose" in a Harlem Honky Tonk. "What perfect abandon! How delightfully primitive!" that apostle had exclaimed. Once in Buffalo I saw a white woman similarly alcoholic and similarly voluptuous in her dancing. Somehow it never occurred to me that the woman might be anything other than pathetically drunk. This is no rash dismissal of all the primitivists as frauds. No doubt many of them are sincere. However, one does not go to pre-Druid England to delineate a Broadway character of English descent. Why, then, this insistence on returning to Africa to understand the Harlem black? I am not unmindful of the centuries which separate the white from pre-Druid England. I simply remind the reader that today, granted the same environmental conditions, the Harlem black and the Broadway white fit not dissimilarly into the mold of our mechanized American culture. This preoccupation with the primitive, therefore, belongs more properly to the fields of anthropology and archaeology than to fiction. It no more interprets Harlem than it does Broadway.

The sort of perspective I am advocating does not pay immediate dividends on the American mart. We must look for the Negro writer who is prepared to endure the rejection of his work long enough to starve the taste for sewer sensationalism and misguided primitivism. There are two women novelists in Harlem who are delightful exceptions to the prevailing vogue. Nella Larsen and Jessie Fauset have always had as their primary purpose the presentation of aes-

thetic truth. We look cheerfully toward an increasing skill
and vision in these writers; and toward novels which will
augment that public in which their art has created "the
willing suspension of disbelief."

The question of the immutability of the types which
the Negro author is to use in portraying the lives of colored
folk is of such magnitude that I am forced to consider evidence on the question. In an article in the *American Mercury* for December, 1928, by way of apology for this continuation of the stereotypes, James Weldon Johnson said:
"It would be straining the credulity of white America to the
breaking-point for a Negro writer to put out a novel dealing
with the wealthy class of colored people." He continues:
"American Negroes as heroes form no part of white America's concept of the race." Again, he says: "So that whenever an Aframerican writer addresses himself to white
America and attempts to break away from or break through
these conventions and limitations, he makes more than an
ordinary demand upon his literary skill and power."

Granted. But tell me, of what use are creative powers
that cannot meet this demand? A Flaubert could choose
and reject, choose and reject, until he found the precise, the
only word to express his exact meaning. An Ibsen could
revise a play again and again until he achieved the perfection
that his mind demanded. Are we concerned in this matter
with artists—be those artists ever so embryonic—or are we
concerned with plowboys who, though transplanted from
clod to concrete, still plod on mentally behind their mules,
remaining one with their mules, looking ever and only toward sundown, and food and beds of dry straw?

Negro authors, once they free their art of the necessity of
furnishing the means of life, will drop the stereotypes into
limbo with the assurance that real art will finally create in
their readers a demand for honest treatment of every grada-
tion of Negro life.

Our Literary Audience

By STERLING A. BROWN

WE have heard in recent years a great deal about the Negro artist. We have heard excoriations from the one side, and flattery from the other. In some instances we have heard valuable honest criticism. One vital determinant of the Negro artist's achievement or mediocrity has not been so much discussed. I refer to the Negro artist's audience, within his own group. About this audience a great deal might be said.

I submit for consideration this statement, probably no startling discovery: that those who might be, who should be a fit audience for the Negro artist are, taken by and large, fundamentally out of sympathy with his aims and his genuine development.

I am holding no brief for any writer, or any coterie of writers, or any racial credo. I have as yet, no logs to roll, and no brickbats to heave. I have however a deep concern with the development of a literature worthy of our past, and of our destiny; without which literature certainly, we can never come to much. I have a deep concern with the development of an audience worthy of such a literature.

"Without great audiences we cannot have great poets." Whitman's trenchant commentary needs stressing today, universally. But particularly do we, as a racial group need it. There is a great harm that we can do our incipient literature. With a few noteworthy exceptions, we are doing that harm, most effectually. It is hardly because of malice; it has its natural causes; but it is none the less destructive.

We are not a reading folk (present company of course forever excepted). There are reasons, of course, but even with those considered, it remains true that we do no read nearly so much as we should. I imagine our magazine editors and our authors if they chose, could bear this out. A young friend, on a book-selling project, filling in questionnaires on the reason why people did not buy books, wrote down often, with a touch of malice—"Too much bridge." Her questionnaires are scientific with a vengeance.

When we do condescend to read books about Negroes, we seem to read in order to confute. These are sample ejaculations: *"But we're not all like that." "Why does he show such a level of society? We have better Negroes than that to write about." "What effect will this have on the opinions of white people."* (Alas, for the ofay, forever ensconced in the lumber yard!) . . . *"More dialect. Negroes don't use dialect anymore."* Or if that sin is too patent against the Holy Ghost of Truth—*"Negroes of my class don't use dialect anyway."* (Which *mought* be so, and then again, which *moughtn't*.)

Our criticism is vitiated therefore in many ways. Certain fallacies I have detected within at least the last six years are these:

We look upon Negro books regardless of the author's intention, as representative of all Negroes, i.e. as sociological documents.

We insist that Negro books must be idealistic, optimistic tracts for race advertisement.

We are afraid of truth telling, of satire.

We criticize from the point of view of bourgeois America, of racial apologists.

In this division there are, of course, overlappings. Moreover all of these fallacies might be attributed to a single cause, such as an apologistic chip on the shoulder attitude, imposed by circumstance: an arising snobbishness; a delayed Victorianism: or a following of the wrong lead. Whatever may be the primary impulse, the fact remains that if these standards of criticism are perpetuated, and our authors are forced to heed them, we thereby dwarf their stature as interpreters.

ONE of the most chronic complaints concerns this matter of Representativeness. An author, to these sufferers, never intends to show a man who happens to be a Negro, but rather to make a blanket charge against the race. The syllogism follows: Mr. A. shows a Negro who steals; he means by this that all Negroes steal; all Negroes do not steal: Q.E.D. Mr. A. is a liar, and his book is another libel on the race.

For instance, *Emperor Jones* is considered as sociology rather than drama; as a study of the superstition, and bestiality, and charlatanry of the group, rather than as a brilliant study of a hard-boiled pragmatist, far more "American" and "African," and a better man in courage, and resourcefulness than those ranged in opposition to him. To the charge

From the jacket of Mamba's

that I have misunderstood the symbolism of Brutus Jones' visions, let me submit that superstition is a human heritage, not peculiar to the Negro, and that the beat of the tom-tom, as heard even in a metropolitan theatre, can be a terrifying experience to many regardless of race, if we are to believe testimonies. But no, O'Neill is "showing us the Negro race," not a shrewd Pullman Porter, who had for a space, a run of luck. By the same token, is Smithers a picture of the white race? If so, O'Neill is definitely propagandizing against the Caucasian. O'Neill must be an East Indian.

All God's Chillun Got Wings is a tract, say critics of this stamp, against intermarriage; a proof of the inferiority of the Negro (why he even uses the word Nigger!!! when he could have said Nubian or Ethiopian!) ; a libel stating that Negro law students all wish to marry white prostitutes. (The word prostitute by the way, is cast around rather loosely, with a careless respect for the Dictionary, as will be seen later.) This for as humane an observation of the wreck that prejudice can bring to two poor children, who whatever their frailties, certainly deserve no such disaster!

This is not intended for any defense of O'Neill, who stands in no need of any weak defense I might urge. It is to show to what absurdity we may sink in our determination to consider anything said of Negroes as a wholesale indictment or exaltation of all Negroes. We are as bad as Schuyler says many of "our white folks" are; we can't admit that there are individuals in the group, or at least we can't believe that men of genius whether white or colored can see those individuals.

Daughters by DuBose Heyward

Of course, one knows the reason for much of this. Books galore have been written, still are written with a definite inclusive thesis, purposing generally to discredit us. We have seen so much of the razor toting, gin guzzling, chicken stealing Negro; or the pompous walking dictionary spouting malapropisms; we have heard so much of "learned" tomes, establishing our characteristics, "appropriativeness," short memory for joys and griefs, imitativeness, and general inferiority. We are certainly fed up.

This has been so much our experience that by now it seems we should be able to distinguish between individual and race portraiture, i.e., between literature on the one hand and pseudo-science and propaganda on the other. These last we have with us always. From Dixon's melodramas down to Roark Bradford's funny stories, from Thomas Nelson Page's "Ole Virginny retainers" to Bowyer Campbell's *Black Sadie* the list is long and notorious. One doesn't wish to underestimate this prejudice. It is ubiquitous and dangerous. When it raises its head it is up to us to strike, and strike hard. But when it doesn't exist, there is no need of tilting at windmills.

In some cases the author's design to deal with the entire race is explicit, as in Vachel Lindsay's *The Congo,* subtitled "A Study of the Negro Race"; in other cases, implicit. But an effort at understanding the work should enable us to detect whether his aim is to show one of ours, or all of us (in the latter case, whatever his freedom from bias, doomed to failure). We have had such practice that we should be rather able at this detection.

We have had so much practice that we are thin-skinned. Anybody would be. And it is natural that when pictures of us were almost entirely concerned with making us out to be either brutes or docile housedogs, i.e., infra-human, we should have replied by making ourselves out superhuman. It is natural that we should insist that the pendulum be swung back to its other extreme. Life and letters follow the law of the pendulum. Yet, for the lover of the truth, neither extreme is desirable. And now, if we are coming of age, the truth should be our major concern.

This is not a disagreement with the apologistic belief in propaganda. Propaganda must be counter checked by propaganda. But let it be found where it should be found, in books explicitly propagandistic, in our newspapers, which perhaps must balance white playing up of crime with our own playing up of achievement; in the teaching of our youth that there is a great deal in our racial heritage of which we may be justly proud. Even so, it must be artistic, based on truth, not on exaggeration.

Propaganda, however legitimate, can speak no louder than the truth. Such a cause as ours needs no dressing up. The honest, unvarnished truth, presented as it is, is plea enough for us, in the unbiased courts of mankind. But such courts do not exist? Then what avails thumping the tub? Will that call them into being? Let the truth speak. There has never been a better persuader.

Since we need truthful delineation, let us not add every artist whose picture of us may not be flattering

to our long list of traducers. We stand in no need today of such a defense mechanism. If a white audience today needs assurance that we are not all thievish or cowardly or vicious, it is composed of half wits, and can never be convinced anyway. Certainly we can never expect to justify ourselves by heated denials of charges which perhaps have not even been suggested in the work we are denouncing.

To take a comparison at random. Ellen Glasgow has two recent novels on the Virginia gentry. In one she shows an aging aristocrat, a self appointed lady killer, egocentric, slightly ridiculous. In another she shows three lovely ladies who stooped to "folly." It would be a rash commentator who would say that Ellen Glasgow, unflinching observer though she is, means these pictures to be understood as ensemble pictures of all white Virginians. But the same kind of logic that some of us use on our books would go farther; it would make these books discussions of *all* white Americans.

Such reasoning would be certainly more ingenious than intelligent.

The best rejoinder to the fuming criticism "But all Negroes aren't like that" should be "Well, what of it. Who said so?" or better, "Why bring that up?" ... But if alas we must go out of our group for authority, let this be said, "All Frenchwomen aren't like Emma Bovary but *Madame Bovary* is a great book; all Russians aren't like Vronsky, but *Anna Karenina* is a great book; all Norwegians aren't like Oswald but *Ghosts* is a great play. Books about us may not be true of all of us; but that has nothing to do with their worth.

A S a corollary to the charge that certain books "aiming at representativeness" have missed their mark, comes the demand that our books must show our "best." Those who criticize thus, want literature to be "idealistic"; to show them what we should be like, or more probably, what we should like to be. There's a great difference. It is sadly significant also, that by "best" Negroes, these idealists mean generally the upper reaches of society; i.e. those with money.

Porgy, because it deals with Catfish Row is a poor book for this audience; *Green Thursday,* dealing with cornfield rustics, is a poor book; the *Walls of Jericho* where it deals with a piano mover, is a poor book. In proportion as a book deals with our "better" class it is a better book.

According to this scale of values, a book about a Negro and a mule would be, because of the mule, a better book than one about a muleless Negro; about a Negro and a horse and buggy a better book than about the mule owner; about a Negro and a Ford, better than about the buggy rider; and a book about a Negro and a Rolls Royce better than one about a Negro and a Ford. All that it seems our writers need to do, to guarantee a perfect book and deathless reputation is to write about a Negro and an aeroplane. Unfortunately, this economic hierarchy does not hold in literature. It would rule out most of the Noble prize winners.

Now Porgy in his goat cart, Kildee at his ploughing, Shine in a Harlem poolroom may not be as valuable members of the body economic and politic as "more financial" brethren. (Of course, the point is debatable.) But that books about them are less interesting, less truthful, and less meritorious as works of art, is an unwarranted assumption.

Some of us look upon this prevailing treatment of the lowly Negro as a concerted attack upon us. But an even cursory examination of modern literature would reveal that the major authors everywhere have dealt and are dealing with the lowly. A random ten, coming to mind, are Masefield, Hardy, Galsworthy in England; Synge and Joyce in Ireland; Hamsun in Norway; O'Neill, Willa Cather, Sherwood Anderson, Ernest Hemingway in America. Not to go back to Burns, Crabbe, Wordsworth. The dominance of the lowly as subject matter is a natural concomitant to the progress of democracy.

This does not mean that our books must deal with the plantation or lowly Negro. Each artist to his taste. Assuredly let a writer deal with that to which he can best give convincing embodiment and significant interpretation. To insist otherwise is to hamper the artist, and to add to the stereotyping which has unfortunately, been too apparent in books about us. To demand on the other hand that our books exclude treatment of any character other than the "successful Negro is a death warrant to literature.

Linked with this is the distaste for dialect. This was manifested in our much earlier thrice told denial of the spirituals. James Weldon Johnson aptly calls this "Second Generation Respectability."

Mr. Johnson is likewise responsible for a very acute criticism of dialect, from a literary point of view, rather than from that of "respectability." Now much of what he said was deserved. From Lowell's *Bigelow Papers* through the local colorists, dialect, for all of its rather eminent practitioners, has been a bit too consciously *"quaint,"* too *condescending.* Even in Maristan Chapman's studies in Tennessee mountaineers there is a hint of "outlandishness" being shown for its novelty, not for its universality.

Negro dialect, however, as recorded by the most talented of our observers today, such as Julia Peterkin, Howard Odum, and Langston Hughes, has shown itself capable of much more than the "limited two stops, pathos and humor." Of course, Akers and Octavus Roy Cohen still clown, and show us Negroes who never were, on land or sea, and unreconstructed Southrons show us the pathetic old mammy weeping over vanished antebellum glories. But when we attack these, we do not attack the medium of expression. The fault is not with the material. If Daniel Webster Davis can see in the Negro "peasant" only a comic feeder on hog meat and greens, the fault is in Davis' vision, not in his subject.

Lines like these transcend humor and pathos:

"I told dem people if you was to come home cold an' stiff in a box, I could look at you same as a stranger an' not a water wouldn' drean out my eye."

Or this:

"Death, ain't yuh got no shame?"

Or this:

"Life for me ain't been no crystal stair."

Or:

"She walked down the track, an' she never looked back,
I'm goin' whah John Henry fell dead."

Julia Peterkin, Heyward, the many other honest artists have shown us what is to be seen, if we have eyes and can use them.

There is nothing "degraded" about dialect. Dialetical peculiarities are universal. There is something about Negro dialect, in the idiom, the turn of the phrase, the music of the vowels and consonants that is worth treasuring.

Are we to descend to the level of the lady who wanted Swing Low, Sweet Chariot metamorphosed into "Descend, welcome vehicle, approaching for the purpose of conveying me to my residence?"

THOSE who are used only to the evasions and reticences of Victorian books, or of Hollywood (!) (i.e. the products of Hollywood, not the city as it actually is) are or pretend to be shocked by the frankness of modern books on the Negro. That the "low" rather than the "lowly" may often be shown; that there is pornography I do not doubt. But that every book showing frankly aspects of life is thereby salacious, I do stoutly deny. More than this, the notions that

white authors show only the worst in Negro life and the best in theirs; that Negro authors show the worst to sell out to whites, are silly, and reveal woeful ignorance about modern literature.

Mamba and Hagar are libellous portraits say some; *Scarlet Sister Mary* is a showing up of a "prostitute" say others. "Our womanhood is defamed." Nay, rather, our intelligence is defamed, by urging such nonsense. For these who must have glittering falsifications of life, the movie houses exist in great plenty.

The moving picture, with its enforced happy ending, may account for our distaste for tragedy; with its idylls of the leisure class, may account for our distaste for Negro portraiture in the theatre. Maybe a shrinking optimism causes this. Whatever the reason, we do not want to see Negro plays. Our youngsters, with some Little Theatre Movements the honorable exceptions, want to be English dukes and duchesses, and wear tuxedoes and evening gowns. Our "best" society leaders want to be mannequins.

Especially taboo is tragedy. Into these tragedies, such as *In Abraham's Bosom* we read all kinds of fantastic lessons. "Intended to show that the Negro never wins out, but always loses." "Intended to impress upon us the futility of effort on our part." Some dramatic "critics" say in substance that the only value of plays like *Porgy, In Abraham's Bosom* is that they give our actors parts. "Worthwhile," "elevating" shows do not get a chance. They are pleading, one has reason to suspect, for musical comedy which may have scenes in cabarets, and wouldn't be confined to Catfish Row. With beautiful girls in gorgeous "costumes;" rather than Negroes in more but tattered clothing.

"These plays are depressing," say some. Alas, the most depressing thing is such criticism. Should one insist that *In Abraham's Bosom* is invigorating, inspiring;

A scene from the Theatre Guild production of Porgy

showing a man's heroic struggle against great odds, showing the finest virtue a man can show in the face of harsh realities,—enduring courage; should one insist upon that, he would belong to a very small minority, condemned as treasonous. We seem to forget that for the Negro to be conceived as a tragic figure is a great advance in American Literature. The aristocratic concept of the lowly as clowns is not so far back. That the tragedy of this "clown" meets sympathetic reception is a step forward in race relations.

I SINCERELY hope that I have not been crashing in open doors. I realize that there are many readers who do not fit into the audience I have attempted to depict. But these exceptions seem to me to fortify the rule. There are wise leaders who are attempting to combat supersensitive criticism. The remarks I have seen so much danger in are not generally written. But they are prevalent and powerful.

One hopes that they come more from a misunderstanding of what literature should be, than from a more harmful source. But from many indications it seems that one very dangerous state of mind produces them. It may be named—lack of mental bravery. It may be considered as a cowardly denial of our own.

It seems to acute observers that many of us, who have leisure for reading are ashamed of being Negroes. This shame make us harsher to the shortcomings of some perhaps not so fortunate economically. There seems to be among us a more fundamental lack of sympathy with the Negro farthest down, than there is in other groups with the same Negro.

To recapitulate. It is admitted that some books about us are definite propaganda; that in the books about us, the great diversity of our life has not been shown (which should not be surprising when we consider how recent is this movement toward realistic portraiture), that dramas about the Negro character are even yet few and far between. It *is* insisted that these books should be judged as works of literature; i.e., by their fidelity to the truth of their particular characters, not as representative pictures of all Negroes; that they should not be judged at all by the level of society shown, not at all as good or bad according to the "morality" of the characters; should not be judged as propaganda when there is no evidence, explicit or implicit, that propaganda was intended. Furthermore those who go to literature as an entertaining building up of dream worlds, purely for idle amusement, should not pass judgment at all on books which aim at fidelity to truth.

One doesn't wish to be pontifical about this matter of truth. "What is truth, asked Pontius Pilate, and would not stay for an answer." The answer would have been difficult. But it surely is not presumptuous for a Negro, in Twentieth Century America, to say that showing the world in idealistic rose colors is not fidelity to truth. We have got to look at our times and at ourselves searchingly and honestly; surely there is nothing of the far fetched in that injunction.

But we are reluctant about heeding this injunction. We resent what doesn't flatter us. One young man, Allison Davis, who spoke courageously and capably his honest observation about our life has been the target of second rate attacks ever since. George Schuyler's letter bag seems to fill up whenever he states that even the slightest something may be rotten on Beale Street or Seventh Avenue. Because of their candor, Langston Hughes and Jean Toomer, humane, fine grained artists both of them, have been received in a manner that should shame us. This is natural, perhaps, but unfortunate. Says J. S. Collis in a book about Bernard Shaw, "The Irish cannot bear criticism; for like all races who have been oppressed they are still *without mental bravery*. They are afraid to see themselves exposed to what they imagine to be adverse criticism. . . . But the future of Ireland largely depends upon *how much she is prepared to listen to criticism* and how far she is capable of preserving peace between able men." These last words are worthy of our deepest attention.

WE are cowed. We have become typically bourgeois. Natural though such an evolution is, if we are *all* content with evasion of life, with personal complacency, we as a group are doomed. If we pass by on the other side, despising our brothers, we have no right to call ourselves men.

Crime, squalor, ugliness there are in abundance in our Catfish Rows, in our Memphis dives, in our Southwest Washington. But rushing away from them surely isn't the way to change them. And if we refuse to pay them any attention, through unwillingness to be depressed, we shall eventually, be dragged down to their level. We, or our children. And that is true "depression."

But there is more to lowliness than "lowness." If we have eyes to see, and willingness to see, we might be able to find in Mamba, an astute heroism, in Hagar a heartbreaking courage, in Porgy, a nobility, and in E. C. L. Adams' Scrip and Tad, a shrewd, philosophical irony. And all of these qualities we need, just now, to see in our group.

Because perhaps we are not so far from these characters, being identified racially with them, at least, we are revolted by Porgy's crapshooting, by Hagar's drinking, by Scarlet Sister Mary's scarletness. We want to get as far away as the end of the world. We do not see that Porgy's crapshooting is of the same fabric, fundamentally, psychologically, as a society lady's bridge playing. And upon honest investigation it conceivably might be found that it is not moral lapses that offend, so much as the showing of them, and most of all, the fact that the characters belong to a low stratum of society. Economically low, that is. No stratum has monopoly on other "lowness."

If one is concerned only with the matter of morality he could possibly remember that there is no literature which is not proud of books that treat of characters no better "morally" than Crown's Bess and Scarlet Sister Mary. But what mature audience

(*Continued on page 61*)

would judge a book by the morality of its protagonist? Is *Rollo* a greater book than *Tom Jones* or even than *Tom Sawyer?*

Negro artists have enough to contend with in getting a hearing, in isolation, in the peculiar problems that beset all artists, in the mastery of form and in the understanding of life. It would be no less disastrous to demand of them that they shall evade truth, that they shall present us a Pollyanna philosophy of life, that, to suit our prejudices, they shall lie. It would mean that as self respecting artists they could no longer exist.

The question might be asked, why should they exist? Such a question deserves no reply. It merely serves to bring us, alas, to the point at which I started.

Without great audiences we cannot have great literature.

The Burden of Credulity

By H. L. MENCKEN

THE Negroes of the United States, taking one with another, probably constitute the poorest racial group in the country. Even the Indians, despite expropriation and oppression, show a higher average wealth, for not a few of them, in late years, have got rich from oil lands, and white philanthropists have not yet managed to pick them clean. Maybe the Mexicans are as poor as the Negroes, but I doubt it. Many of them have worked their way into high positions, both private and public. There is prejudice against them so long as they are in poverty, but as soon as they get money they may aspire to anything. But the overwhelming majority of Negroes are still doomed to dull and profitless toil. Not many of them do well in business, and even fewer succeed in the professions. A really successful Negro lawyer, physician, banker, engineer or man of science is still a sort of miracle. Nor are Negro artists much better off. The more meretricious sort often make money, but not the good ones. I can think of no Negro painter or writer who makes $10,000 a year. A few musicians perhaps—but that is about all.

Part of this lack of success is due, plainly enough, to the prejudice of the dominant white. He still thinks of the Negro as congenitally inferior, and is thus loath to employ him in situations calling for unusual skill. Not many white men, even in New England, go to Negro doctors when they are ill, or seek the advice of Negro lawyers when they are in trouble, or engage Negro teachers to teach their children. Even when a Negro does manifestly superior work there is a disposition to decry it. Every time I print an article by a Negro in *The American Mercury* certain readers send me word that it is bad, and ought not to have been printed. Similarly, when I sat lately to a Negro portrait painter, a number of friends assured me that the painting would be a botch, though they had not seen it and did not know the artist. Along with this hostility, of course, there goes, at least in certain quarters, a dis-

> *The challenge of Mr. Mencken, distinguished editor of "The American Mercury," will not go unanswered. In the March issue of* OPPORTUNITY *Rev. A. Clayton Powell, pastor of the Abyssinian Baptist Church of New York City, one of America's leading Negro clergymen, will reply in behalf of the Negro church.*
>
> THE EDITOR.

position to excessive friendliness. It is enough to give the Negro writer or painter his chance, but it is seldom enough to make him really secure. The common run of whites do not share it. They suspect everything that is black, whether it be free verse or pathology.

This burden is matched by another: there is little apparent tendency among Negroes themselves to support and encourage their genuinely salient men. Normally, they seem to follow only two kinds of leaders: those who try to make them satisfactory to white people and those who try to make monkeys of them. In the former class (along with many palpable frauds), are a number of honest men, and some of them are my friends. But I believe they are all on the wrong track. No matter how much Negroes come to be like white men they will still be Negroes, and white men will continue to notice the fact. Perhaps the problem thus presented is intrinsically insoluble. I do not pretend to answer. But I am sure that very little is accomplished for the race by following leaders who associate so much with whites that they have come to think white themselves. Once they got social equality for all Negroes of their own class, as they have got it for themselves, they would apparently be content. But great races are never satisfied with equality. What they always try to demonstrate is superiority.

That Negroes, in more than one way, are superior to most American whites is something that I have long believed. I pass over their gift for music (which is largely imaginary) and their greater dignity (which Dr. Eleanor R. Wembridge has described more eloquently than I could do it), and point to their better behavior as members of our common society. Are they, on the lower levels, somewhat turbulent and inclined to petty crime? Perhaps. But that crime is seldom anti-social. It gets a lot of advertising when it is, but that is not often. Professional criminals are rare among Negroes, and, what is more important, professional reformers are still rarer. The horrible appetite of the low-caste Anglo-Saxon to police and harass his fellow-men is practically non-existent among them. No one ever hears of Negro wowsers inventing new categories of crime, and proposing to jail thousands of their own people for committing them. Negro Prohibitionists are almost as rare as Catholic Prohibitionists. No Negro has ever got a name by pretending to be more virtuous than the rest of us. In brief, the race is marked by extraordinary decency. Even the hog-wallow Christianity that it commonly patronizes has not sufficed to degrade it to the cannibalistic level of the white cracker.

I wish I could add that this Christianity is otherwise worthy of a self-respecting people, but I fear that I cannot. As a matter of fact, it is extraordinarily stupid, ignorant, barbaric and preposterous. Almost I am tempted to add that it is downright simian. Borrowed at the start from the lowest class of Southern whites, it has been so further debased by moron Negro theologians that, on its nether levels, it is now a disgrace to the human race. These theologians constitute a body of bold and insatiable parasites, and getting rid of them is a problem that will daunt all save the bravest of the future leaders of black America. They fill their victims with ideas fit only for the jungle, and for that office they take a toll that is cruel and debilitating. What it amounts to annually I don't know, but it undoubtedly makes up the heaviest expenditure of the Negro people. All they get for it is continued subjugation to the superstitions of the slave quarters. They are kept in a bondage to credulity and fear that is ten times as degrading as any political bondage could ever be.

Some time ago an eminent Baptist ecclesiastic was boasting that, among all the Negro Baptists in America, there was not one who was not a Fundamentalist. I daresay that the Methodists might plausibly echo that boast. It is a shameful thing to say of any people who aspire to advance in the world. Fundamentalism is not a body of doctrine that rational men may take or leave; it is a body of doctrine for ignoramuses exclusively; it is the negation of every intellectual decency. To spread it among simple folk is as immoral as it would be to teach them that a horse-hair put into a bottle will turn into a snake. It may be that many of the black racketeers who preach it believe in it themselves. If so, that only proves that they should be chased out of their pulpits as public nuisances, and put to useful work.

I see no reason why Negroes should be such heavy patrons of these dunghill varieties of Christianity. If their nature demands the consolations of religion, then there is plenty of room for them on more decorous levels. In Baltimore my friend, Dr. George F. Bragg, Jr., shepherds a flock of Episcopalians: they are intelligent and civilized people, and he himself is respected as a scholar and as a man. There are in the same town many Negro Catholics— quiet, devoted, self-respecting men and women, to whom a Methodist revival would be as horrifying as it would be to the president of Harvard. But four-fifths of the more pious Negroes of Baltimore are still under the hooves of evangelical theologians, and it is these gentry who get their hard-earned money and keep them dumb and hopeless. Within half a mile of my home in the town there are dozens of grotesque chapels, each radiating anthropoid superstitions, each supporting an oily go-getter, and each pumping dollars out of poor people. Further on are huge churches almost without number—most of them foisted on the ignorant by whites eager to clear out, and each with its mortgage. Meanwhile, the 150,000 Negroes of Baltimore are unable to support their one small hospital, and when they are ill most of them have to turn to the whites.

The curse of this barnyard theology lies over the whole of America. It is responsible for the worst corruptions of our politics, and the generally uneasy and uncomfortable tone of American life. It gave us Prohibition. It put Hoover into the White House. In the South it is solidly behind Ku Kluxery, and is hence mainly to blame for the exploitation and ill-usage of the Negro. Yet there are so-called Negro leaders who argue gravely that it is a boon to their own people—that there is something mysteriously refining and uplifting about it—in other words, that it is a merit to keep Negroes ignorant. I only hope that this appalling doctrine finds no customers among the young Negroes who now pour out of the colleges, eager to find some way to help their own. If they come out Methodists and Baptists, then the situation of the Negro in America is indeed hopeless. But if they emerge with some share of sound knowledge and a decent respect for their own minds, then they will apply themselves to combatting this last and worst vestige of slavery. There can be no real and general progress in the race until it is disposed of. So long as Negroes believe in rubbish they will never get beyond the level of the Southern poor whites. In other words, they will never get beyond the level of the most ignorant and degraded white men now known on earth.

H. L. Mencken Finds Flowers In a "Dunghill"

By A. Clayton Powell

NEGROES of the United States! Stop boasting about your economic progress. You have scarcely made any. You are poorer than the Indians or the Mexican greasers. All the presidents of the United States, from Harrison to Hoover, with other outstanding men and women of the world, who declared your progress during the past sixty-five years could not be matched by any other group in America, were "kidding" you.

Your success in business is hardly worth mentioning, and your supposed hundreds of successful physicians and lawyers are, in fact, so few that when you stumble upon one you have seen a miracle. Your hundreds of Negro teachers in the mixed schools of New York and New England are so inconsequential that they are not selected by white boards, as you imagine, for "white men" in these regions, "do not engage Negro teachers to teach their children."

Get it out of your head at once that Bert Williams, Florence Mills, Jules Bledsoe, Paul Robeson and Richard B. Harrison will ever be enrolled among the successful artists, for your "Negro artists are not much better off than your professional men." Your painters are botchers. They can not earn a living.

You had thought that W. E. Burghardt Du-Bois, Countee Cullen, James Weldon Johnson, Walter White, Langston Hughes, Carter G. Woodson, Kelly Miller, and a dozen others, dead and living, were good writers. You are mistaken. The most critical magazine in America has to apologize to the reading public everytime it prints an article from the pen of a Negro. Your leaders are either trying to transform the Negroes into white people or turn them into monkeys. "They are all on the wrong track."

Your musical gift of which you have been proud from the days of the original Fisk Jubilee Singers to these glorious days of Harry Burleigh, Roland Hayes and Marian Anderson, "is largely imaginary."

> With characteristic vigor Rev. A. Clayton Powell of the Abyssinian Baptist Church, New York City, replies to Mr. H. L. Mencken's "Burden of Credulity," an attack on Negro Fundamentalism, which was published in the February number of OPPORTUNITY.

Your Church, good God! If you ever muster courage to enter another one, put on a gas mask. The preacher you thought was preaching the pure gospel, with what little light he could get in the spiritual darkness of America, is a "barnyard theologian," and the Church you thought was a pile of salt to save you is a "dunghill." If you have any respect for your Sunday-go-to-meeting clothes leave them at home, for once inside of your Church you will find a "hog-waller Christianity."

The foregoing statements do not misrepresent in the least, an article in February OPPORTUNITY by Mr. H. L. Mencken, the most distinguished, and learned iconoclast on the American continent.

Mr. Mencken in his Baltimore "Dunghill Varieties of Christianity" finds at least two flowers. He calls one Episcopalian and the other Catholic. Small favors thankfully received, but, beware of the Greeks bearing gifts, for this scholarly discoverer knows that the same flowers can be found in a thousand other spots in all parts of this country, and many of them are growing in Negro Methodist and Baptist churches.

The eminent Baptist ecclesiastic, who boasted that "among all the Negro Baptists in America there was not a one who was not a Fundamentalist," is woefully ignorant of the present trend of the Negro Methodist and Baptist ministry. R. R. Wright, L. H. King, J. W. E. Bowen, W. Y. Bell, Bishop Matthew Wesley Clair, and scores of other Methodist clergymen are as far removed from the "barnyard theologian" as Mr. Mencken is from the most mental and morally warped Nordic who declares that the poorest, lowest and most ignorant white man is superior to the wealthiest and most cultured Negro.

I can point to hundreds of modern progressive Negro Baptist ministers, like Mordecai Johnson, Vernon Johns, J. Raymond Henderson, Horatio S. Hill, C. H. Pearson, W. P. Hayes and Miles Fisher.

I know the preachers from coast to coast, and, as I dictate this article, I can not think of a young Negro minister of training who is contending for the "tradition of the elders." Even in many of the churches presided over by men who are hovering around three score years and ten, like the 19th Street Baptist Church of Washington, D. C., where Walter Brooks has been the shepherd for forty-five years, Mr. Mencken will find the same decorum, dignity and intelligent seriousness he finds in the isolated Baltimore church.

I agree that the doctrine of Fundamentalism, as believed and practiced in certain sections, is not only "a negation of every intellectual decency," but of every other kind of decency, and especially respect for the sacredness of human personality. I will bet Mr. Mencken a year's subscription to the *American Mercury* against a contribution to our Free Food Kitchen, that the mob which went on a rampage in Maryville, Mo., while the OPPORTUNITY press was turning off his article, was 95 per cent Fundamentalist. These Fundamentalists were not poor "white trash" either, unless those composing the executive, legislative and judicial departments of that state are considered in that class. Hardly.

These Fundamentalists roasted an innocent man, for under our system of jurisprudence every man is presumed innocent until his guilt is proven. They not only burnt up a schoolhouse, the symbol of American progress, but the judicial prerogative, the state and federal constitution, the decency and self-respect of their own women who stood looking at the nude body of a man writhing in flames, without the slightest shock to their modesty. If the Fundamentalist white pulpit or press has uttered a single word of protest against this act, a thousand times redder than the reddest acts of the Russian Communists, a wistful eye has not seen it nor a listening ear heard it. Even the February *American Mercury* is as silent as the Sphinx.

On the other hand, it would be hard to find in these United States, a single Negro preacher who has not, with the most vigorous English, thundered against this un-Christian, inhuman, anarchistic carnival. The Negro Church is the only church that has persistently opposed lynching and the Negro pulpit is the only pulpit that has unceasingly preached the brotherhood of man.

The Negro Church from its beginning until now, has valiantly fought for freedom, justice and every principle of Christianity. In 1832 the first Anti-Slavery Society was organized in the basement of a colored Baptist church in Boston, by Wm. Lloyd Garrison and twelve others, including the Negro pastor of that church. Mr. Garrison went to that old ecclesiastical "dunghill" because it was the only church or place in the environs of the "cradle of liberty" (?) which would allow him to start a campaign against the most colossal crime ever committed on this or any other continent.

Nearly every school established for Negroes or by Negroes grew out of the earnest advocacy and fervent prayers of these old "barnyard" preachers. While old Pastor Qualls was on his knees praying in the basement of the Friendship Baptist Church of Atlanta, Ga., for God to send someone to enlighten the young Negroes who had just emerged from the darkness of Christian slavery, two noble white women from the North, knocked at the door, and then and there Spelman Seminary, the most noted School for women and girls in the Southland, was born.

All Negro publishing houses in this country were not only started by Negro preachers, but they are run by Negro preachers.

Dr. George E. Haynes is not merely the Secretary of the Commission on Race Relations of the Federal Council of Churches of Christ in America, but his wisdom is sought by men of all races more than the wisdom of any other member of the Commission.

Dr. Eugene Kinckle Jones, the organizing and directing genius of the National Urban League, one of the most efficient social service organizations in the nation, gladly admits that he received his inspiration from his father, who was an honored Baptist preacher. Ninety per cent of the business and professional men and women of the race would be happy to testify that they owe their success to the publicity and patronage of the Negro pulpit.

Let us look for some more flowers. Mr. Mencken says that he believes that Negroes are superior to American whites in more ways than one. To justify this belief he places special emphasis upon the "extraordinary decency" of the race.

Had Mr. Mencken gone a little farther, he would have discovered that the average Negro is also superior to the average white American in long suffering, patience, meekness, veracity and love. The Negro has almost destroyed the white man's ethical standards, and especially his sense of veracity.

Let a Negro attempt to register at a decent

hotel, purchase a Pullman or a theatre ticket, and the white man will look him straight in the eye, without the slightest compunction of conscience and say, "Not a room left; house sold out; every berth reserved."

I wish I could say that this careless veracity had not crept into the average white pulpit. When a Negro attempts to join a white church nine out of ten times, the preacher says to him, with the greatest theatrical kindness and sympathy, "I have not a spark of prejudice, and I would like to fellowship you, but my parishioners would not stand for it. Your presence would disrupt my church." A white preacher without prejudice could not remain in a congregation with prejudice six months, as demonstrated recently in Detroit.

Now, this Negro knows that the hotel clerk, the theatre and Pullman agents and the preacher are not telling the truth, but he doesn't turn away with any bitterness in his heart for the white man, but pity. He loves the white man who hates him, and the one who loves is always superior to the one who hates.

Where did the Negro get his superior decency, patience, meekness, veracity and love? He certainly did not get these qualities in the school house. Neither did he receive them in the white man's home, for they were not there to receive. They were drilled into him in the Negro Church Sunday School and Christian home. God only knows what would have been the history of the race in this country if these superior Christian qualities had not been pounded into the Negro by the Negro preacher and church, which Mr. Mencken so mercilessly slanders, and so ruthlessly attempts to read out of the race.

Are the Negro preachers and churches perfect, or have they always given a good account of their stewardship? I am the last preacher to give an affirmative answer to these questions. All close observers will say with Mr.

Mencken that too much of the Negro's energy, money and time have been used in buying and building churches and too little in race building. We have enough church houses. It would be a godsend if we would cease church building and buying, except in rare cases, for the next twenty-five years, and devote our energy, money and time to the economic, social, intellectual, moral and spiritual advancement of the race.

All honest men will further agree with Mr. Mencken that there are too many "parasites, moron theologians, oily go-getter racketeers, pumping dollars out of the poor people" in the Negro pulpit. But neither Mr. Mencken nor his "future leaders of black America" need waste any literary shot on these ecclesiastical rascals. The rising tide of intelligence and the deepening sense of a true God in the Negro Church will soon solve this grave problem. Healing, to be permanent, must come from within—not from without. These fake shepherds, who are shearing the sheep without feeding them, are already on the run. The expulsive power of a new religious affection, will, in the next ten or fifteen years, make them a shameful memory.

When I think that the Negro was brought out of a jungle religion in Africa, into a worse jungle American Christianity; when I recall that the Negro was not only brought here by racketeers, but that he existed for two hundred and forty years in the most damnable racket known to the United States, and that he has lived for the past sixty-five years in the racket of peonage, chain gang labor, and industrial exploitation, it is a miracle that he has made any appreciable progress toward genuine religion.

A greater miracle still, is that the Negro believes in any sort of a religion or any kind of a God presented to him by the white American. Had it not been for his ignorance he would have cursed God and died.

ART IS NOT ENOUGH

BY BENJAMIN BRAWLEY

THE reader of books today, perusing the ordinary work fresh from the press, is often taken aback. He has a vague feeling that something is wrong. He is often loath to express his feeling for fear of running into a fallacy; but he knows that he is not satisfied. Sometimes he has a sense of being cheated. It is the endeavor of this article to see just what there is in the temper of the poetry and fiction of today to account for such an effect, and to some extent at least to note the influences that have brought us where we are. The study began in a consideration of the work of recent Negro writers in the United States, but more and more this appears as simply one part of the main stream of American literature.

In order to have the proper perspective it may be necessary for us to go back at least two hundred years. By the second quarter of the eighteenth century, it will be recalled, religion in England had developed into mere formalism. It had no message for the man in the street, and for the gentry a minister might simply read from a book of sermons on a Sunday. Reaction was bound to come; but the impulse that represented it and that became known as romanticism offered strange contradictions. On one hand, in the work of Wesley, it gave a new meaning to faith. On the other hand, with its inducement to freedom in thinking, it led to infidelity. It was in connection with this latter result that there took place one of the profound shifts in the history of modern thought. Formerly philosophers had been primarily concerned with the greatness of God; henceforth their chief interest was to be the dignity of Man. Under the new impulse Rousseau spoke of a return to nature, Blake of the free play of desire, and Paine of the Rights of Man. Mary Wollstonecraft also spoke in meeting for the Rights of Woman; and the work of all such writers crystallized in the French Revolution.

Within the next fifty years the practical view of life and society was strongly assisted by the Industrial Revolution, and only in part could the Oxford Movement stay the rising tide of unbelief. Then came Darwin, a quiet scholar exploding a bomb in the camp of the orthodox; and Herbert Spencer applied the idea of evolution to all departments of knowledge. As never before, Economics and Sociology began to ask for recognition as sciences. Each was in its point of view largely materialistic. Not unnaturally there developed in line with them the so-called Institutional Church, the failure of which makes a notable chapter in recent history.

All of this has much more to do with literature than appears on the surface. By the close of the nineteenth century men's minds had been taken off the other world and fixed upon the world that is, and the more they pondered this present world the more they found it to be in rather bad condition. A profound pessimism settled upon men's thinking; in literature as in science there was emphasis on the analytical method, and realism passed into naturalism. George Eliot wrote novels of sombre hue, and Thomas Hardy and George Gissing flourished, not to mention Zola in France. This naturalist tendency we wish to remark as the first of several great influences that are still to be felt among us.

Very close to it at times, however, was another principle that had been developing throughout the century—aestheticism or the "art for art's sake" heresy. Mr. Chesterton has called DeQuincey "the first and foremost of the decadents." Characterization could hardly be more apt, for it was DeQuincey who so elevated style as to make it not simply the dress of thought but perhaps even something suggesting thought itself. The principle was further seen in the paganism of Keats; and the sensuousness of this great poet was reflected in Rossetti and the other Pre-Raphaelites. In America there was Poe; and seldom has there been an author who has written more beautifully and who had so little to say. It was he who contended that Art had nothing to do with Science, the search for truth, on one hand, or with Religion, the basis of conduct, on the other. Technically this divorce of art and morality may have been justified, but for all practical purposes it was fatal, and it was the secret of many of the wasted lives strewn like wrecks over the reign of Victoria. Aestheticism is today the second of the large influences that affect us. We are asked to accept almost anything provided it poses as art.

A third influence is the mood of abandon that was incident to the war and that still lingers. The intense living of a few brief months led to indifference as to the future, and meanwhile there was the coarsest hedonism. New and exotic forms of entertainment were demanded; cabarets in Harlem became popular; and the reign of jazz began. There was a new cult of the primitive; the old plantation Negro gave way to the city Negro; and the flash-light Negro of the city cultivated the mood of the jungle. It was this phase of the matter that was admirably set forth in the article "The Negro Fad," by Miss Helene Magaret, in the *Forum* for last January. In the everyday life of our cities in the East the air of abandon, of utter recklessness, has been seen in the fascination of the so-called "numbers" game for hosts of people. In its issue for August 13 the *New York Age* stated that the Negroes of Harlem alone spend every day on this form of gambling not less than $28,000. Men who are out of work and who may not even have had a breakfast will somehow find fifty cents or a dollar to spend in the hope of getting a "break." In other places along the Atlantic seaboard even some ministers and school teachers have indulged in the game.

These three influences have been dominant—first, naturalism, or undue emphasis on the sordid aspects of life; second, aestheticm, or the concern with artistic to the exclusion of other values; and third, extreme hedonism with its consequent mood of abandon. In connection with these things, however, it may not be amiss to note two or three individuals who in one way or another have been representative. First is Walt Whitman, who has now been elevated to a place in American literature undreamed-of sixty years ago. Whitman has had influence in two ways: first, in his frank absorption in things physical, and second, in his invention of new rhythms for the expression of his ideas. He assumed of course a strong position when he said that the temper of American life called for new forms of writing—that this America of the stock-yards and the sweat-shops, of Niagara and the Sierras, could not be encased in a sonnet. He was in line with the most radical tendencies of modern thought, and we were undoubtedly in need of some degree of radicalism. It will be observed, however, that Whitman's theory practically involved for every phase of art the destruction of all the forms that the experience of mankind had justified. To him not only would Poe and Tennyson and Longfellow be out of date, but Shakespeare and Michelangelo, Bach and Beethoven as well. In a literary sense Amy Lowell, Carl Sandburg, and Edgar Lee Masters were his children, and most of our young Negro poets are his grandchildren. A second figure of extraordinary significance has been Sigmund Freud, who has aptly been termed one of the false prophets of the age. Freud's emphasis on psychoanalysis and our "unconscious urges" is perfectly in line with the "self-expression" of which we have heard so much in recent years —the "self-expression" that seeks only its own and that has wrought havoc in the American home. In connection with it we find little attention given to self-control; and it is obvious that any organism, even any machine, can fulfil its destiny only in proportion as it holds in complete subjection all of its powers. A locomotive can not go right or left as it pleases; it must harness its steam and go on the track before it if it would arrive at the goal. An athlete, if he would win the race, can not indulge himself as self-expression might suggest, but must have the mastery of all the resources of his being. So it is with a writer; he must control rather than be controlled by his thoughts and emotions; and ultimate control consists only in doing the will of God. This is what Dante meant in his famous sentence, "In His will is our Peace." A third important figure and another false prophet is George Bernard Shaw, who has affected our criticism perhaps more than any one else. Shaw's principle is very simple; it is always to be on the opposing side or to hurl a stone at any existing institution. If it is good, say it is bad; and by all means tell little children that their elders are stupid. Once the trick is exposed, the method does not seem very brilliant; and once at least, when Shaw jesed at England's effort in the war, the British public informed him that it was not amused. In the United States, nevertheless, we have had the *American Mercury*. In the last analysis the method is that of the cynic, and cynicism is cowardice. It is much easier to throw a stone than to carry a difficult task through to the end.

This all means that what Matthew Arnold called "high seriousness" has been noticeably lacking in our recent literature, and especially in our Negro literature. Arnold, some one may say, was a Puritan; and then comes the question, Is it the business of art to preach? Certainly not, but art increases in significance according as it has some meaning for humanity. Concerned chiefly with form, it is thin or weak until it also has content. The Beautiful is like a lovely but haughty lady who will fall into a pit if she disdains the company of the Good and the True. Let us take an illustration. In recent years we have had numerous novels on the order of *Black April*, *Nigger Heaven*, and *Home to Harlem*, and plays such as *Porgy* and *Goat Alley*. Many Negro people are offended by these productions and experience a sense of personal affront when they see them or read them. "Why should you be offended?" asks the modern and sometimes the sympathetic critic; "these people portrayed are not you; they are simply striking individuals that the author has chosen to use, and you go out of the way when you bring in the race question." To this we reply frankly that we are offended and feel that we have reason to be, that the race question insists on being present, and that the presentation gives a distorted view of life. If we read of one coarse and ignorant Negro, then of another coarse and igno-

314

rant Negro, then of another and another and another, it is by a very simple induction that we conclude that all Negroes are coarse and ignorant. It is on this basis that the Catholics object to any portrayal of a priest on the stage that is not dignified; and there is no such thing as putting a character named Shylock into a play, calling him a Jew, and at the same time saying that he has nothing to do with the Jews. A few years ago the French dramatist, M. Brieux, visited Atlanta. After being taken to various clubs and special points of interest for three days, he said, "But what about the Negro? I have heard much of him but have not seen him." "Oh! you would like to see the Negro?" smiled his hosts; "we will show him to you"; and they took their guest down Decatur Street by some of the lowest dens in the city. "I see," said M. Brieux as he returned to his hotel. We submit that he had not seen; at best he had seen some Negroes but not the Negro. The colleges on the west side of the city and the business houses in the fourth ward were as unknown to him as when he came to town; and so far as the Negro is concerned our literature of today is treating the American public just as M. Brieux was treated in Atlanta.

That, however, is not all. Several writers of today, some Negroes among them, have taken the greatest of the Negro's gifts and degraded and mutilated it almost beyond recognition. From time immemorial the highest aspiration of the human soul has been in the field of the religious. The very heart of the Jewish people is in the Old Testament. In both Greek and Norse literature the gods were prominent, and the Indian was most uplifted when he prayed to the Great Spirit. In Shakespeare and Dante, Wordsworth and Coleridge alike the principle holds. The Negro also has this supreme gift, some have thought in unusual measure; and never was there a people that passed through greater tragedy. What, however, has happened? Our Sorrow Songs have been degraded into coarse dance rhythms, and our preaching has been made a burlesque. Our writers have grasped the tinsel on the surface, ignoring the gold that lay beneath it. Just here it is that John Jasper of Richmond was a figure of notable significance. In his crude way he was an artist and an orator of superb power. His preaching was not strong in the moral element; but he could dazzle a congregation by the conceptions of his imagination, and he did what he attempted better that any other speaker of whom we have record. Our literature has capitalized him; but it has not yet appreciated the earnest work of Andrew Bryan, Richard Allen, and Daniel A. Payne, and it will not fulfil its purpose until it reflects our noblest striving.

Just a few days ago I came again upon a book of old addresses, and I found that a Negro man gave this warning fifty years ago. It was Alexander Crummell and he was speaking to the young men at Lincoln. Some of his sentences come to us today with startling pertinence. "It is this mastery of our faculties," he said, "which is one half of achievement in life. . . . . The process by which this is effected is discipline." Further: "You have got to train a people to solid, sober, and persistent thought." Again: "One marked and dangerous peculiarity constantly betrays itself; the stream of tendency among cultivated colored Americans is too exclusively *aesthetical.* There is a universal inclination to that which is pleasing, polished, and adorning. Where there is cultivation, it is mainly in poetry, music, fiction, private theatricals, the opera. . . . This love of the beautiful among our people shows all the signs of being but a mere possession. It is mere unrestrained spontaneity; and spontaneity, valuable as it is, requires the restraints and limitations which can only be furnished by the imperial faculties of the moral and mental nature, the Conscience and the Reason."

If literature were an end in itself, such a word might not be necessary. It has, however, aims that reach far beyond itself. It is of the warp and woof of life. We turn to it not only for entertainment, but also for inspiration and hope. We cherish it because of its vast possibilities. A single poem has been known to change a career. If literature is as important as this, it has an obligation to the public. Accordingly we have the right to expect that when we turn to it for bread we shall not be given a stone.

———————

Claude McKay to Nancy Cunard 9/18/32, from Tangier, Morocco.
[MS Cunard/recip/McKay,Claude. Harry Ransom Humanities Research Center,
University of Texas at Austin.]
[The original is handwritten. Ellipses appear in the original manuscript.]

Dear Miss Cunard,

Hope I don't bore you to death asking favors but this stupid cheque drawn on N.Y.
will take 25-30 days before I can cash it there (the first time sent like this) and I need the
money now. My bank will not cash it spot because I have no funds left–will collect only
which will take an even longer time. So will you put it through yours for me and send
the equivalent in francs–preferably *mandat* which is the safest? Since both my friends who
could do this are out of France you're about the quickest person I know who can fix me
up.

I have finished the chapter! Now typing all I hand-wrote when the machine was in
pawn–100 pages nearly. After that revision and ought to have all done by the middle of
next month.

And please *don't* worry about my contribution. It will be a real relief and joy to turn
to something else after a year's hard work on my peasant saga. Since you won't have
fiction I am going to do an authentic bit of personal history–a travelogue and perhaps a
poem and you can choose the most fitting.

I am very buoyant about my three months more lease of life–I am sending you
Santori's letter–also Reides's so that when you go to Paris you will have all the
necessary details in approaching him. I don't expect a whole lot from them–the French
pay so little for writing–last year I got 200 francs for a short story–but whatever they
give will help even out Harper's.

No, I dislike Eric Walrond. And he does me too. Think he is very pretentious light-
weight. Knew him when I was on the Liberator with Max Eastman & he on the Negro
World with Garvey. 1922. Garvey had given me hell and more in his paper (he had a
grudge about me for showing up the preposterous side of his movement in the Liberator)
because the police had broken up a Liberator affair and beaten some guests on account of
my dancing with a white woman–Crystal Eastman & the N.Y. papers had made quite a
scandal of it. Eric came to see me and give some inside dope on Garvey's character for me
to make a comeback attack –the crassest moral stuff & besides he was working for the
man. . . . Next time I heard from him was 1925 in France *he wrote* asking me to read
stories for a competition in the Negro magazine "Opportunity" for which he was assistant
editor & offered to place some stuff for me. I was glad to do it for I was quite broke. The
stories and poems I sent in did not take the prize, but because I was known a little the
magazine proceeded to print them without paying me. And so I had my agent on them to
collect. The Negro magazines and papers are almost all pirates paying no attention to the
ordinary journalistic procedure such as recognizing the source of reprinted stuff and
payment. I find most of them have a way of making people pay for "write-ups" and their
mug on the page.

But my ultimate success with "Home to Harlem" after years of struggling brought
all the black venom out against me. I was told that Walrond said "I knew how to exploit
people." And my friends of the "enemy race" whom I have shamefully exploited have

1

never to my knowledge complained. I was called every damned thing. (Schomburg especially amazed me. Because he was always a young old dog. Full of naughty tales. Couldn't imagine him sitting well with Du Bois. But I suppose he slated me to curry favor with the Aframericans, being West Indian. Moreover when I was broke in Marseilles, he wrote me asking that I should copy my book of verse by hand for which he would pay 50 dollars. I put my novel aside & started the job just to have the ready cash & after I had begun it he said he didn't want it–had changed his mind). Schomburg who I always counted a close friend called me (in a review) a buzzard a hog and what not? Walrond (in a widely reprinted article) said I had been invited to Russia by the Soviet government and the impression was that I had become a bolshevik agent. A lie. I had to peddle autographed copies of poems, burn my friends, & work as a fireman from New York to Liverpool to get to Russia. And although the bolsheviks tried to *make* me represent the Negro race, I let them know I was a free spirit, a poet although politically my sympathies were communist.

What maddened the American [indecipherable word] was my making money out of my novel, because the whole intelligentsia crowd have a wards-of-charity mentality–a helpless looking to the powerful philanthropist for awards and scholarships. I told Walrond he ought to have use[d] his scholarship to try and achieve liberty of mind and freedom of expression. I have gone carefully through his stories and stripped of their journalistic verbiage they reveal nothing but the average white man's point of view towards Negroes. The "Palm Booth," the best one is just a "White Cargo" written by a black man.

Of the Negro writers today I think Langston Hughes is the real thing, also Wallace Thurman once he finds his stride. Rudolph Fisher, a nice humorist, Locke a kindly Professor.

2

Claude McKay to Nancy Cunard 9/29/32, from Tangier, Morocco.
[MS Cunard/recip/McKay,Claude. Harry Ransom Humanities Research Center,
University of Texas at Austin.]
[The original is handwritten. Ellipses appear in the original manuscript.]

Dear Nancy Cunard

Mille Mercis for the mandat which I finally cashed today after some delay. By some mistake in the French post office I received instead of the usual slip of notification the entire mandat and when I presented it the functionnaires from controleur to facteur were not interested in paying the money but in knowing how I got it. I got the money after three days' delay the functionnaires trying to blame the perfectly innocent Spanish Post Office for their own carelessness.

Now that you have suggested to me what you want for your book and something that suits me exactly I have been already outlining the outstanding notes under three major headings, viz.: Jamaica, America, Europe. . . . Also I want to give you a *new* poem. And I hope I shall be able to compose it in time. I haven't written a line for about ten years and since I have always felt a desire to work in more elastic frames than those in which I have set my earlier poetry.

Max Eastman thinks I should try. He arrived here last Wednesday on a short visit with his Russian wife. They came from Istanbul (and Palestine) where they had gone to see Trotsky. Lovely people and I still love them more than ever. He was my first American-white friend and has remained the most faithful–since 1918. Last time I saw him was in the Spring of 1927 when he left Southern France to return to America. He wrote the preface for my American book of poems "Harlem Shadows" published in 1922. Did you ever see it? If not I shall send you my only copy if you let me have it back some time–no hurry. It is out of print.

He is very sorry he did not meet you when you went to America last Spring. He sailed from N.Y. the first of June, I am so sure that if you had stayed for a couple of more days with them at Croton (about one hour's rail from N.Y.) you would have been in *one* congenial atmosphere at least in America. I lived all over America, South, West(Middle) and East and it was the only place I ever really felt happy–as I used to be sometimes in Jamaica. I went to live in this little house with black friends, white friends and a Chinese friend. The people who frequented it were of all kinds: communists, socialists, liberals, artists–nearly all free spirits. And there may have been little prejudices lurking among them (where are they not found?) But the atmosphere was too rare for them to flourish. It was too bad Eastman had to give up the magazine and the group was scattered. It was the *only* thing of its kind in all of that mammoth vast America. And it was not really understood even by the people who appreciated it. They characterized Eastman as a hedonist and simply because he was not doctrinaire nor moral of attitude about the difficult art of living.

And I have found Socialists, Communists too and Negroes fighting for social equality more bigoted than some of the bourgeoisie in their intellectual and moral outlook. Of course I subscribe to the Communist economic programme, but man does not live by bread alone. My main objection to the Communists is their attitude towards art and artists. I don't believe in proletarian art nor bourgeois art nor all the other loose

1

social definitions of art. To me authentic art is just there, whatever its origin, racial, national or any kind of social, transcending its cadre and becoming a possession of all humanity and I don't give a hoot for the pedantic divisions and names except as a means of identification. The Communists rant about proletarian art and artists. True art is too rare a thing to be dictated to by politics. For Communism is politics like Socialism, Republicanism, Monarchism—the science of governing people and regulating their social and economic life. The artist who is a communist in politics should be at least as free to express himself in a Communist society as his confrere in a bourgeois society who is a Republican or Monarchist in politics. I think the Communist theory of proletarian art is wrong. It means really propaganda art and while I believe in organized political propaganda I don't in organized propaganda art. About art I am romantic. I salute it everywhere. I don't expect artists to be angels full of brotherly and universal love, even though I rate them so much the higher *if* they possess such qualities.

This brings me to your mention of literary animosities. Happily I am free of that. I am so romantic about creative art that I really get a kick out of an artist's success—a live one. That kind of success thrills me more than any. But I loathe insincerity in art and pretentious artists. And there are so many of them—the fake ones who make the most noise and do their damndest to spoil and cheapen the genuine.

I was thinking of a short article (I think your original limit was 260 words) but now I will be able to let myself go. The thing right now is to finish the book and knuckle down to your stuff. Max Eastman has a car here and wants to carry me off to Seville. Thinks I need a vacation and it is lonely here a little and the fish factory [??]. But I wish he had come at the end of October instead. It is imperative I should finish. And the loneliness is good for working. After that I hope we meet and spend some days talking a little about everything. I am going to tell Max and Eliena to go to see you in Paris. They are shocked to death over what happened to you in America and Cuba. Eliena likes America—but in the same way you do and also myself—the eye something to look at—and the energy. Only she likes the picture enough to live with it and for me it is one to admire but not to live with. I was never happy in Harlem, but I was always excited, restless, and enjoyed the excitement.

Must stop now. Thanks again for the cheque put through.

2

"Writers, Words and the World." Langston Hughes. Speech at the Paris Meeting of the International Writers Association for the Defense of Culture, July 25, 1938.
[MS Cunard/Misc/Hughes,Langston/Lecture,Writers, Words and the World ccms. Harry Ransom Humanities Research Center, University of Texas at Austin.]

Words have been used too much to make people doubt and fear. Words must now be used to make people *believe and do*. Writers who have the power to use words in terms of belief and action are responsible to that power *not* to make people believe in the wrong things. And the wrong things are, as surely everyone will agree, death instead of life, suffering instead of joy, oppression instead of freedom, whether it be freedom of the body or of the mind.

Words put together beautifully, with rhythm and meaning, are as the branches and roots of a tree—if that meaning be a life meaning—such words can be of more value to humanity than food to the hungry or garments to the cold. For words big with the building of life rather than its destruction, filled with *faith* in life rather than doubt and distress, such words entering into the minds of men last much longer than today's dinner in the belly or next year's overcoat on the back. And such words, even when forgotten, may still be reflected in terms of motives and actions, and so go out from the reader to many people who have never seen the original words themselves.

Writers have power. The better the writer the greater that power to impel people toward the creation of a good life. We know that words may be put together in many ways: in beautiful but weak ways having meaning only for the few, worldly-wise and capable of understanding; or in strong and sweeping ways, large and simple in form, like yesterday's Walt Whitman or today's Theodore Dreiser.

The best ways of word-weaving, of course, are those that combine music, meaning and clarity in a pattern of social force.

One's own creative talents must supply the music of the words, one's background and experience, the meaning, and one's ability to study, simplify and understand, the clarity. To understand being the chief of these.

To understand! In one way the whole world situation today is very simple: greed against need. But within that simplicity there are many complexities and apparent contradictions. The complexities of race, of capital and labour, of supply and demand, of the stock exchange and the bowl of rice, of treaties that lie and bombs that tell the truth. And all these things are related to creative writing, and to the man or woman who writes. The shortest poem or story—let us say about a child playing quietly alone in a courtyard—and such a poem or story will be a better one if the author understands the relationship of his child to the Tokio war-machine moving against China. Why? Because the Tokio war-machine—if its lines be traced clearly back to Paris or London or Berlin or New York—the Tokio war-machine touches that very child in our simple little story, no matter in whose yard the child may be playing.

Because our world is like that today, so related and inter-related, a creative writer has no right to neglect to understand clearly the social and economic forces that control our world. No matter what his country or what his language, a writer, to be a good writer, cannot remain unaware of Spain and China, of India and Africa, of Rome and Berlin. Not only do the near places and the far places influence, even without his knowledge, the

1

very subjects and material of his books, but they affect their physical life as well, their actual existence and being. For there are two depositories for books today: on democratic shelves or in reactionary bonfires. That is very simple. Books may live and be read, or be burned and blown away.

So there may still be those who use words to make people doubt and wonder, to remain inactive, unsure of the good in life, and afraid to struggle for it. But we must use words to make them believe in life, to understand and attempt to make life better. To use words otherwise, as decent members of society, we have no right.

2

Democracy, Negroes, and Writers by Langston Hughes
[5/13/41 as sent to: League of Am. Writers]
[JWJ/Hughes/MSS. James Weldon Johnson Collection, Beinecke Rare Book Library, Yale University.]

Writing is the urge to tell folks about it. About what? About what hurts you inside. Colored folks, through the sheer fact of being colored, have got plenty hurting them inside. You see, we, too, are one of those minority races the newspapers are always talking about. Except that we are here in America, not in Europe, fourteen million of us— a rather large minority, but still minority.

Now, what's hurting us? Well, Jim Crow is hurting us. Ghettos, and segregation, and lack of jobs is hurt[ing] us. Signs up: COLORED TRADE NOT DESIRED, and dirty names such as the Jews know under Hitler hurt us. So those of us who are writers have plenty to tell the world about.

To us democracy is a paradox, full of contradictions. Sure, in the North Negroes can vote, but we can't work in airplane factories and various other defense industries supported with *our* tax money as well as that of other citizens. In the South we can't vote, but we can howl to high heaven about it in our newspapers—and run the risk of lynching and the Ku Klux Klan for howling. In Mississippi the state spends nine times as much for the education of each white child as it does to educate a Negro child, yet the Negro population equals the white, and the wealth of the state is based on the labor of Negroes in the sun of the cotton fields. We give and others take. That's what makes us mad. So we feel bad and have to write about it.

The color line runs right on down from capital through labor, although labor is waking up a bit. But in many industries today the factories won't hire us because they say the unions won't admit us, and the unions won't admit us because they say the factories won't hire us: a vicious circle into which a swastika fits perfectly. We can sweep a floor almost anywhere if a white man doesn't need the job, but even if we graduate from Massachusetts Institute of Technology, we still are not permitted to run a machine in the average American Factory. A great many Negroes work, study, and learn, and then are frustrated by the blind alley of color-segregation in American industry. That color line runs all the way through culture and the arts, as well. There are world-famous and very great American Negro singers, some of whom have appeared in opera abroad, but not one had been asked to appear at the Metropolitan. And in many cities where they sing, their own people, the Negro concert goers, are Jim Crowed and segregated. There are some excellent Negro writers in this country, too, but, to my knowledge, none is employed at present in Hollywood where the real money for writers lies. All along the line, we suffer economic discrimination of a discouraging and arbitrary sort, be we artisan or artist.

The League of American Writers, meeting in their Fourth Writer's Congress in New York on June 6th, has been one of the few cultural organizations to take up the fight for the artistic and economic equality of the Negro writer. Another stand of equal importance to Negro, and all writers, is the League's position on freedom of speech and publication. To colored people in the United States this is of particular importance as the trend toward suppression and censorship is growing and already there is a tendency to attempt to prevent Negro newspapers, with their editorials against discrimination in

1

323

defense industries and the Jim Crow set-up of our army and navy, from being read by Negro soldiers and draftees in the army camps. From this it is but a step to the actual suppression of Negro papers, or else the censorship of their articles and editorials.

Negroes, like all other Americans, are being asked at the moment to prepare to defend democracy. But Negroes would very much like to have a little more democracy to defend. And democracy is achieved only through constant vigilance, struggle, and the educational processes of the written and spoken word. For Negro writers it is vital that the channels of free press and publication be kept open. It is necessary to the well-being of the creative soul that the harsh and ugly aspects of our life be exposed to public view in order that they might be changed and remedied in accordance with the democratic ideals for which we are urged to be ready to die. But ideals on paper mean very little. They must be put into practice. Writers must be free to call for and work toward the realization of full democracy in regard to peoples of all colors, else the light will rapidly go out for everyone of us, white or Negro, gentile or Jew, for if we wish to preserve democracy, we must not only defend it but *extend* it.

2

PHYLON

THIRD QUARTER, 1947   VOL. VIII, NO. 3

By **LANGSTON HUGHES**

My Adventures as a Social Poet

POETS WHO write mostly about love, roses and moonlight, sunsets and snow, must lead a very quiet life. Seldom, I imagine, does their poetry get them into difficulties. Beauty and lyricism are really related to another world, to ivory towers, to your head in the clouds, feet floating off the earth.

Unfortunately, having been born poor — and also colored — in Missouri, I was stuck in the mud from the beginning. Try as I might to float off into the clouds, poverty and Jim Crow would grab me by the heels, and right back on earth I would land. A third floor furnished room is the nearest thing I have ever had to an ivory tower.

Some of my earliest poems were social poems in that they were about people's problems — whole groups of people's problems — rather than my own personal difficulties. Sometimes, though, certain aspects of my personal problems happened to be also common to many other people. And certainly, racially speaking, my own problems of adjustment to American life were the same as those of millions of other segregated Negroes. The moon belongs to everybody, but not this American earth of ours. That is perhaps why poems about the moon perturb no one, but poems about color and poverty do perturb many citizens. Social forces pull backwards or forwards, right or left, and social poems get caught in the pulling and hauling. Sometimes the poet himself gets pulled and hauled — even hauled off to jail.

I have never been in jail but I have been detained by the Japanese police in Tokyo and by the immigration authorities in Cuba— in custody, to put it politely — due, no doubt, to their interest in my written words. These authorities would hardly have detained me had I been a writer of the roses and moonlight school. I have never known the police of any country to show an interest in lyric poetry as such. But when poems stop talking about the moon and begin to mention poverty, trade unions, color lines, and colonies, somebody tells the police. The history of world literature has many examples of poets fleeing into exile to escape persecution, of poets in jail, even of poets killed like Placido or, more recently, Lorca in Spain.

My adventures as a social poet are mild indeed compared to the body-breaking, soul-searing experiences of poets in the recent fascist countries or of the resistance poets of the Nazi invaded lands during the war. For that reason, I can use so light a word as "adventure" in regard to my own skirmishes with reaction and censorship.

My adventures as a social poet began in a colored church in Atlantic City shortly after my first book, *The Weary Blues,* was published in 1926. I had been invited to come down to the shore from Lincoln University where I was a student, to give a program of my poems in the church. During the course of my program I read several of my poems in the form of the Negro folk songs, including some blues poems about hard luck and hard work. As I read I noticed a deacon approach the pulpit with a note which he placed on the rostrum beside me, but I did not stop to open the note until I had finished and had acknowledged the applause of a cordial audience. The note read, "Do not read any more blues in my pulpit." It was signed by the minister. That was my first experience with censorship.

The kind and generous woman who sponsored my writing for a few years after my college days did not come to the point quite so directly as did the minister who disliked blues. Perhaps, had it not been in the midst of the great depression of the late '20's and early '30's, the kind of poems that I am afraid helped to end her patronage might not have been written. But it was impossible for me to travel from hungry Harlem to the lovely homes on Park Avenue without feeling in my soul the great gulf between the very poor and the very rich in our society. In those days, on the way to visit this kind lady I would see the homeless sleeping in subways and the hungry begging in doorways on sleet-stung winter days. It was then that I wrote a poem called "An Ad for the Waldorf-Astoria," satirizing the slick-paper magazine advertisements of the opening of that de luxe hotel. Also I wrote:

PARK BENCH

I live on a park bench.
You, Park Avenue.
Hell of a distance
Between us two.

I beg a dime for dinner —
You got a butler and maid.

But I'm wakin' up!
Say, ain't you afraid

That I might, just maybe,
In a year or two,
Move on over
To Park Avenue?

In a little while I did not have a patron any more.

But that year I won a prize, the Harmon Gold Award for Literature, which consisted of a medal and four hundred dollars. With the four hundred dollars I went to Haiti. On the way I stopped in Cuba where I was cordially received by the writers and artists. I had written poems about the exploitation of Cuba by the sugar barons and I had translated many poems of Nicholas Guillen such as:

CANE

Negro
In the cane fields.
White man
Above the cane fields.
Earth
Beneath the cane fields.
Blood
That flows from us.

This was during the days of the dictatorial Machado regime. Perhaps someone called his attention to these poems and translations because, when I came back from Haiti weeks later, I was not allowed to land in Cuba, but was detained by the immigration authorities at Santiago and put on an island until the American consul came, after three days, to get me off with the provision that I cross the country to Havana and leave Cuban soil at once.

That was my first time being put out of any place. But since that time I have been put out of or barred from quite a number of places, all because of my poetry — not the roses and moonlight poems (which I write, too) but because of poems about poverty, oppression, and segregation. Nine Negro boys in Alabama were on trial for their lives when I got back from Cuba and Haiti. The famous Scottsboro "rape" case was in full session. I visited those boys in the death house at Kilby Prison, and I wrote many poems about them. One of these poems was:

CHRIST IN ALABAMA
Christ is a Nigger,
Beaten and black —
O, bare your back.

Mary is His Mother —
Mammy of the South.
Silence your mouth.

God's His Father —
White Master above,
Grant us your love.

Most holy bastard
Of the bleeding mouth:
Nigger Christ
On the cross of the South.

Contempo, a publication of some of the students at the University of North Carolina, published the poem on its front page on the very day that I was being presented in a program of my poems at the University in Chapel Hill. That evening there were police outside the building in which I spoke, and in the air the rising tension of race that is peculiar to the South. It had been rumored that some of the local citizenry were saying that I should be run out of town, and that one of the sheriffs agreed, saying, "Sure, he ought to be run out! It's bad enough to call Christ a *bastard*. But when he calls him a *nigger,* he's gone too far!"

The next morning a third of my fee was missing when I was handed my check. One of the departments of the university jointly sponsoring my program had refused to come through with its portion of the money. Nevertheless, I remember with pleasure the courtesy and kindness of many of the students and faculty at Chapel Hill and their lack of agreement with the anti-Negro elements of the town. There I began to learn at the University of North Carolina how hard it is to be a white liberal in the South.

It was not until I had been to Russia and around the world as a writer and journalist that censorship and opposition to my poems reached the point of completely preventing me from appearing in public programs on a few occasions. It happened first in Los Angeles shortly after my return from the Soviet Union. I was to have been one of several speakers on a memorial program to be held at the colored branch Y. M. C. A. for a young Negro journalist of the community. At the behest of white higher-ups, no doubt, some reactionary Negro politicians informed the Negro Y. M. C. A. that I was a Communist. The secretary of the Negro Branch Y then informed the committee of young people in charge of the memorial that they could have their program only if I did not appear.

I have never been a Communist, but I soon learned that anyone visiting the Soviet Union and speaking with favor of it upon returning is liable to be so labeled. Indeed when Mrs. Roosevelt, Walter White, and so Christian a lady as Mrs. Bethune who has never been in Moscow, are so labeled, I should hardly be surprised! I wasn't surprised. And the young people's committee informed the Y secretary that since the Y was a public community center which they helped to support, they saw no reason why it should censor their memorial program to the extent of eliminating any speaker.

Since I had been allotted but a few moments on the program, it was my intention simply to read this short poem of mine:

> *Dear lovely death*
> *That taketh all things under wing,*
> *Never to kill,*
> *Only to change into some other thing*
> *This suffering flesh —*
> *To make it either more or less*
> *But not again the same,*
> *Dear lovely death,*
> *Change is thy other name.*

But the Negro branch Y, egged on by the reactionary politicians (whose incomes, incidentally, were allegedly derived largely from gambling houses and other underworld activities), informed the young people's committee that the police would be at the door to prevent my entering the Y on the afternoon of the scheduled program. So when the crowd gathered, the memorial was not held that Sunday. The young people simply informed the audience of the situation and said that the memorial would be postponed until a place could be found where all the participants could be heard. The program was held elsewhere a few Sundays later.

Somebody with malice aforethought (probably the Negro politicians of Uncle Tom vintage) gave the highly publicized California evangelist, Aimee Semple McPherson, a copy of a poem of mine, "Goodbye, Christ." This poem was one or my least successful efforts at poetic communication, in that many persons have misinterpreted it as an anti-Christian poem. I intended it to be just the opposite. Satirical, even ironic, in style, I meant it to be a poem against those whom I felt were misusing religion for worldly or profitable purposes. In the poem I mentioned Aimee Semple McPherson. This apparently made her angry. From her Angelus Temple pulpit she preached against me, saying, "There are many devils among us, but the most dangerous of all is the red devil. And now there comes among us a red devil *in a black skin!*"

She gathered her followers together and sent them to swoop down upon me one afternoon at an unsuspecting and innocent literary luncheon in Pasadena's Vista del Arroyo Hotel. Robert Nathan, I believe, was one of the speakers, along with a number of other authors. I was to have five minutes on the program to read a few poems from my latest collection of folk verses, *Shakespeare in Harlem,* hardly a radical book.

When I arrived at the hotel by car from Los Angeles, I noticed quite a crowd in the streets where the traffic seemed to be tangled. So I got out some distance from the front of the hotel and walked through the grounds to the entrance, requesting my car to return at three o'clock. When I asked in the lobby for the location of the luncheon, I was told to wait until the desk clerk sent for the chairman, George Palmer Putnam. Mr. Putnam arrived with the manager, both visibly excited. They informed me that the followers of Aimee McPherson were vehemently picketing the hotel because of my appearance there. The manager added with an aggrieved look that he could not have such a commotion in front of his hotel. Either I would have to go or he would cancel the entire luncheon.

Mr. Putnam put it up to me. I said that rather than inconvenience several hundred guests and a half dozen authors, I would withdraw — except that I did not know where my car had gone, so would someone be kind enough to drive me to the station. Just then a doorman came in to inform the manager that traffic was completely blocked in front of the hotel. Frantically the manager rushed out. About that time a group of Foursquare Gospel members poured into the lobby in uniforms and armbands and surrounded me and George Palmer Putnam, demanding to know if we were Christians. Before I could say anything, Mr. Putnam lit into them angrily, saying it was none of their business and stating that under our Constitution a man could have any religion he chose, as well as freedom to express himself.

Just then an old gentleman about seventy-two who was one of the organizers of the literary luncheon came up, saying he had been asked to drive me to the station and get me out of there so they could start the luncheon. Shaking hands with Mr. Putnam, I accompanied the old gentleman to the street. There Aimee's sound truck had been backed across the roadway blocking all passage so that limousines, trucks, and taxis were tangled up in all directions. The sound truck was playing "God Bless America" while hundreds of pickets milled about with signs denouncing Langston Hughes — atheistic Red. Rich old ladies on the arms of their chauffeurs were trying to get through the crowd to the luncheon. Reporters were dashing about.

None of the people recognized me, but in the excitement the old gentleman could not find his car. Finally he hailed a taxi and nervously thrust a dollar into the driver's hand with the request that I be driven to the station. He asked to be excused himself in order to get back to the luncheon. Just as I reached out the door to shake hands in farewell, three large white ladies with banners rushed up to the cab. One of them screamed, "We don't shake hands with niggers where we come from!"

The thought came over me that the picketing might turn into a race riot, in which case I did not wish to be caught in a cab in a traffic jam alone. I did not turn loose the old gentleman's hand. Instead of shaking it in farewell, I simply pulled him into the taxi with me, saying, "I thought you were going to the station, too."

As the pickets snarled outside, I slammed the door. The driver started off, but we were caught in the traffic blocked by the sound truck lustily playing "God Bless America." The old gentleman trembled beside me, until finally we got clear of the mob. As we backed down a side street and turned to head for the station, the sirens of approaching police cars were heard in the distance.

Later I learned from the afternoon papers that the whole demonstration had been organized by Aimee McPherson's publicity man, and that when the police arrived he had been arrested for refusing to give up the keys to the sound truck stalled midway the street to block the traffic. This simply proved the point I had tried to make in the poem — that the church might as well bid Christ goodbye if his gospel were left in the hands of such people.

Four years later I was to be picketed again in Detroit by Gerald L. K. Smith's Mothers of America — for ever since the Foursquare Gospel demonstration in California, reactionary groups have copied, used and distributed this poem. Always they have been groups like Smith's, never known to help the fight for democratic Negro rights in America, but rather to use their energies to foment riots such as that before Detroit's Sojourner Truth housing project where the Klan-minded tried to prevent colored citizens from occupying government homes built for them.

I have had one threatening communication signed *A Klansman.*

And many scurrilous anonymous anti-Negro letters from persons whose writing did not always indicate illiteracy. On a few occasions, reactionary elements have forced liberal sponsors to cancel their plans to present me in a reading of my poems. I recall that in Gary, Indiana, some years ago the colored teachers were threatened with the loss of their jobs if I accepted their invitation to appear at one of the public schools. In another city a white high school principal, made apprehensive by a small group of reactionary parents, told me that he communicated with the F. B. I. at Washington to find out if I were a member of the Communist Party. Assured that I was not, with the approval of his school board, he presented me to his student body. To further fortify his respectability, that morning at assembly, he had invited all of the Negro ministers and civic leaders of the town to sit on the stage in a semi-circle behind me. To the students it must have looked like a kind of modern minstrel show as it was the first time any Negroes at all had been invited to their assembly.

So goes the life of a social poet. I am sure none of these things would ever have happened to me had I limited the subject matter of my poems to roses and moonlight. But, unfortunately, I was born poor — and colored — and almost all the prettiest roses I have seen have been in rich white people's yards — not in mine. That is why I cannot write exclusively about roses and moonlight — for sometimes in the moonlight my brothers see a fiery cross and a circle of Klansmen's hoods. Sometimes in the moonlight a dark body swings from a lynching tree — but for his funeral there are no roses.

A Note on *Contempo* and

Langston Hughes

EVERYONE knows the further South you go the worse the prejudice (with a few exceptions here and there, such as the town of San Antonio, Texas, which was Mexican until a few decades ago—latin therefore, non-"nordic." A Texan Negro friend said the degree of prejudice and race hatred varied surprisingly in regions as close as thirty miles from each other). Sometimes the barriers get broken down, by determined people, as at Chapel Hill, in North Carolina, the seat of an important (white) University, where, amongst others, Paul Green, sympathetic author of several fine plays on Negro life, is professor. There used also to be there a lively, straight-speaking and active periodical, called *Contempo*.[1] In December 1931 Langston Hughes, the most famous of the younger Negro poets, was on a lecture tour through the States. The students of Chapel Hill invited him to speak, *Contempo* printed him. Langston Hughes denounced the *Scottsboro* case and flayed the Southern *crackers*.[2] The effect was of course like wildfire. The North Carolina crackers had never seen the like before. *The Southern Textile Bulletin*, Charlotte, N.C., December 3, 1931, wrote:

> Langston Hughes, a Negro, while participating in the communist effort to create interest in nine Alabama negroes convicted of assaulting two white girls, wrote an article containing the following:
> " For the sake of american justice (if there is any) and for the honor of southern gentlemen (if there ever were any) let the south rise up in press and pulpit, home and school, senate chambers and rotary clubs and petition the freedom of the dumb young blacks so indiscreet as to travel unwittingly on the same freight train with two white prostitutes. . . ."
> In spite of the fact that this Negro deliberately and intentionally made the above and many more insulting remarks about the people of the south both his statement and his poetry were published with gusto and approval by Contempo, a publication issued by the students of the university of N.C., and that publication also said:
> " Langston Hughes, prominent poet and novelist, is soon to be the guest of the editors of Contempo."
> We had hoped the swallowing of the insults of this Negro was limited to the editors of Contempo, which is not

---

[1] At present published in Snow Building, Durham, North Carolina ; editor, Anthony Buttita, (author of *Negro Folklore in North Carolina*, see previously).
[2] The rabidly offensive Southerner crazed with race-prejudice.

A Note on *Contempo* and Langston Hughes

an official publication of either the students of N.C. university or the university itself, but we note the following editorial in the daily Tar Heel, the official student publication:
" Langston Hughes, prominent Negro poet and novelist, spoke before various groups of the student body during the latter part of last week. His poetry as well as his speaking is the expression of a clear and sincere spirit."

We have no doubt that Langston when he said that there were never

The editors of *Contempo* enter-them, Buttita, sent me this photo-" daily discrimination " (I had Chapel Hill):

Buttita and Abernethy, editors of Contempo, *standing on each side of Langston Hughes in front of the U.S. Post Office, main street, in Chapel Hill, North Carolina.*
On this occasion the breaking of the prejudice in this Southern State lies in the fact that black and white together could be seen by the townsfolk on an equal footing !

Negroes are not allowed to eat in get any service at all in large places with a pale shame on their faces. they are quickly gotten rid of, and soda in the place, sandwiches can be and buses, the Negro always gets crowded, bus wont stop for Negro, that particular occasion we had snappiest cafeteria in town . . . surprise, and what was the idea and waitresses were particularly comment arose. We were going to this; some people even threatened cafeteria explain . . . of course, Langston to a white drug store for soda jerker took Hughes for a at that, but since he found out that had given him service the way he angry and attempted to catch us the jaw . . . told his friends about cheap vengeance for some days. in our bookshop for a day or so the University came around to talk color line, race question and other

Hughes meant to be very clear any southern gentlemen. . . .

tained Langston Hughes—one of graph and wrote me this note on asked him what this was like in

same places as whites; they do not unless they wait around for a while In drug stores and soda fountains, do not get to eat cream or drink taken out . . . in cars and trains the lousiest back seat . . . and if but will for white man. . . . On Langston Hughes for dinner at the everyone looked and looked for of it all . . . the Negro waiters pleased in seeing the event. Much be boycotted for carrying on like to make the manager of the he didnt know . . . then we took a drink . . . the cheap, southern mexican or something and let it go Hughes was a " nigger " and he would have a white man, he got in a place or two and sock us in it and we were looked at with That is not all. We had Langston . . . ladies of the courtly order of and argue with Hughes on the such stuff . . . a certain wife of a

certain nephew of good old Woodrow Wilson—she can't have kids, by the way—thought Hughes was darling, cute, and wanted to have him out to dinner in her Dreamshop . . . her home in the Buttons, a section in Chapel Hill, . . . think she forgot it or changed her mind. . . .

142

Alfred A. Knopf to Langston Hughes, 7/29/30.
[JWJ/Hughes/Corres. James Weldon Johnson Collection, Beinecke Rare Book Library,
Yale University]

[letter from Bernard Smith, Knopf publicity Dept]

You may be interested in the following comment on "Not Without Laugher" from
Benjamin Brawley.

A few days ago you were so good as to send me for review "Not Without Laughter",
by Mr. Langston Hughes. I regret after an examination that I cannot review this book, at
least not without calling attention to its very unpleasant tone, and that I should prefer not
to do. The book is being returned to-day. I have sometimes had to wonder how such an
excellent firm as yours brings out such books as this, but I guess you know best what
you want to publish.

What can we do with a mind like Professor Brawley's?

1

Langston Hughes to Carl Van Vechten, 9/4/30.
[JWJ/Hughes/Corres/Langston Hughes to Carl Van Vechten. James Weldon Johnson
Collection, Beinecke Rare Book Library, Yale University]

[portion of a letter]

Dear Carlo,

    Benj. Brawley refused to review my novel at all, and sent his free copy back to
Knopfs saying that it was crude and immoral. But otherwise the Negro comments have
been grand, and the white press amazingly nice. Thanks to you, Carlo, for the splendid
blurb you wrote me . . . .[ellipses in the manuscript] The southern press have been
swell and mostly sympathetic. I guess it's selling a little, too

1

Alfred A. Knopf, Inc to Langston Hughes, 3/2/31.
[JWJ/Hughes/Corres. James Weldon Johnson Collection, Beinecke Rare Book Library,
Yale University]

[letter by Bernard Smith]

This letter is probably an act of impertinence. I can excuse it only by saying that it is being written at the request of Walter White.

I met White about a week ago at a party. We talked about your work in general and "Not Without Laughter" in particular, and I happened to mention your new volume of poems. Naturally, he wanted to know my opinion of it. I told him, frankly, that I was rather disappointed, and after explaining why, he urged me to write to you about it. This is the result. You will understand that I am doing so only after much hesitation. My opinion will no doubt be of little significance to you, but White evidently thinks otherwise.

There are several poems in your new collection which seem to me to be among the very best you have ever written. They are all in the section devoted to racial protest. This fact leads me to conclude that it is not so much the poetic quality they may possess that gives them value, but rather their intensity of feeling, their meaning, their strength and vigor. These latter qualities also characterized your New Masses Christmas poem, unfortunately omitted from this collection.

The other poems, lyrics of love and loneliness, seem to me to be neither distinguished nor important. So many poets have treated these emotions!

It appears that, however intensely you may experience these moods, in the process of objectifying them into poetry you lose something, because subconsciously you suspect they are minor. But in the process of rendering your racial feelings into poetry you lose nothing, because subconsciously you know they are major.

Finally, with "Not Without Laughter" you have entered a new phase. It is certainly the most important piece of work you have done. To publish this volume of poems now would be an act of retrogression. There is no need for it. I am impressed, too, with the fact that the best ingredients in your new poems can best be put into prose. I think you have, artistically, intellectually and emotionally, reached a point at which it would be sheer waste to recall past moods and methods.

Blame this letter on Walter White, if you will, or on my sincere interest in and appreciation of your work.

1

Carl Van Vechten to Blanche Knopf, April 3, 1933.
[Knopf, Inc./recip/ Hughes, Langston. Harry Ransom Humanities Research Center,
University of Texas at Austin]

Langston's book I have read carefully *twice*. I am sorry to say I do not think much of it. It is very weak, the revolutionary poems on which it is supposed to stand firmly are more hysterical than lyrical and I think it would hurt his reputation to have the book published where it stands. I wish, once & for all, he would decide whether he is a revolutionary or a poet. I think in ten years from now, were he a poet, whatever the social outcome, he would be heartily ashamed of the puerile sentiments disclosed in commonplace phrases in these poems.

In its title section, the first poem is bunk, stale stuff, stalely expressed: we are hungry and we are going to have a revolution; Park Bench, ditto; Advertisement for the Waldorf-Astoria: I particularly dislike this one and this cheap way of thinking–there are, as you know, more people gainfully employed at this hotel than there are guests.

Tired, on the other hand, is an oasis, a little gem of poetic thought. In To the Little Fort and Sh-Ss-Ss we get back to the good old blah again.

The next section is considerably better. In fact I liked everything but the one called The Dame. However, it should be remembered that the three strongest poems, Justice, Scottsboro, and Christ in Alabama have already appeared in magazines & in Langston's pamphlet, Scottsboro Limited.

The next section, Mingled Breath, is all right save for the piece called Ph.D. which I find trite & poisonous. A House in Taos again has made plenty of previous appearances.

The section called Broke contains a couple of swell blues, very moving, but the long poem called Broke reads like a Bert Williams lyric & is unworthy of a book of this (presumably) caliber.

The section called Our Spring brings us back to the revolution. The first two poems are not so bad and the Ballad of Lenin is gorgeous. I also like Moscow. But I cannot see anything in the chart for Tom Mooney and May Day except cheap Masses stuff. And where is A New Song, Langston's best revolutionary lyric, recently published in Opportunity? Why hasn't he included that?

You can see I am not very enthusiastic about this book and I am writing Langston to the same effect.

2

Blanche Knopf to Langston Hughes, August 21, 1933.
[Knopf, Inc./recip/ Hughes, Langston. Harry Ransom Humanities Research Center,
University of Texas at Austin]

[excerpt from the letter]

Frankly I do not think there is anything that you should do with the book of poems
until you have a prose book ready to come out with it. If you publish a book of verse
today & it doesn't sell you will have to climb uphill again for the prose book.
Publishing them together will give you the breaks. At least that is the way I feel about it
and I think I am right.

1

Langston Hughes to Blanche Knopf, February 27, 1934.
[Knopf, Inc./recip/Hughes, Langston. Harry Ransom Humanities Research Center,
University of Texas at Austin]

[excerpt from the letter]

[Hughes informs Knopf that he is sending a revision of his poetry manuscript, now entitled *A New Song*, and that he has shown the poems to Lincoln Steffens and other friends in California, and read them at public readings].

As I wrote to you, I believe there is definitely a public for such a volume of poems. . . . If the manuscript is acceptable to you I would appreciate an advance of One Hundred Dollars. And, if you should not care to publish it, I would like to know soon, so I can place it elsewhere.

1

Carl Van Vechten to Blanche Knopf, March 12, 1934.
[Knopf, Inc./recip/Hughes, Langston. Harry Ransom Humanities Research Center,
University of Texas at Austin]

There seem to be some slight changes in this Langston manuscript, but that does not alter my opinion of the book as a whole. I think the revolutionary poems are pretty bad, more revolutionary than poetic; all this has been done a million times better. And the centre part of the book is not nearly as good as Langston's other books of poetry. I think, as a matter of fact, that he has gone as far as he ever will go as a poet, and except for casual magazine appearances, he might be well advised to leave this Muse alone henceforth.

Of course, there can be no talk of his going elsewhere with the book. He should be written that of course you will print it if he insists upon it. I think stress should be laid on the fact that he has another book coming out and that it is impossible for a publisher to produce two books at once and that it is advisable to put this off for a time. And that if he still wants to publish this next year, why of course you will do it. If further arguments are necessary, it might be brought forward that it is bad policy to publish a book which is such a letdown from his previous work in this direction, that communists do not buy books and few others will want to buy a book in which the communist sentiment is stronger than the art. If he wants to let his radical friends know how he feels, he has already done so when these verses have appeared in magazines.

However, at all times, it should be stressed that you will print the book of course, if he wants it done. Langston is never unreasonable and I don't think he will be in this case. However, as you are going away, you'd better talk this situation over pretty thoroughly with Alfred, as many letters & telegrams may go through about this.

1

Blanche Knopf to Langston Hughes, March 12, 1934.
[Knopf, Inc./recip/Hughes, Langston. Harry Ransom Humanities Research Center,
University of Texas at Austin]

March 12, 1934

Dear Langston,

I am sailing the end of this week and therefore this letter. I have given the question of your book of poetry a good deal of thought and have come to the following conclusion, which I write you because I think we know each other well enough to be completely frank and have no pretense as a barrier.

I don't think that this is the moment for you to publish a book of poems–I think that you have become much more important than this poetry is and that the publication of such a book now would tend to hurt your name rather than help it. This in my very humble opinion, is not as good a book of poetry as your earlier ones. Definitely I think the place for these poems is between magazine and not book covers, now. By this I don't mean that ultimately at some future time the poetry should not and cannot be published; but I don't believe that a propaganda book in verse is wise for you nor do I think that the communists would back you up and buy it. From a publishing point of view I would much rather not do your poems now and do your next prose book when it comes along if we both agree on that.

Now that I have written my worst I want to add that if you still feel definitely that you want us to publish the book of poetry, we are your publishers and I would not want to let you go elsewhere so if you insist on publication of the poetry of course we will do it. I am merely giving my best advice and my opinion and I hope you will take it in the way that I mean, which is in deepest friendship.

I am going to be abroad for about six or seven weeks to see publishers, etc. and should be back at the latest by May 1. In the meantime I hope sincerely that you agree with me. But if you don't, we will do whatever you say.

With my best regards and very good wishes, I am
Yours always,

Langston Hughes Esq.
Box 1582
Carmel, California

1

Langston Hughes to Blanche Knopf, nd [1934].
[Knopf, Inc./recip/Hughes, Langston. Harry Ransom Humanities Research Center,
University of Texas at Austin]

[excerpt from the letter]
[Regarding the book of short stories, *The Ways of White Folks*]:

Please try to get a good display of it in Harlem, possibly at A.G. Dill's shop on 135th
Street. He is an old friend of mine, formerly on THE CRISIS, and would probably give it
a good break in his place.

{Hughes notes that his agent, Maxim Lieber, thinks that it is possible to sell one of the
stories, "Rejuvenation through Joy" to the movies, and he asks Blanche Knopf to help in
this].

[Regarding the poetry manuscript, A New Song]:

I would not like to have you publish it merely to please me, since you do not like it. I do
feel that it is important however that the proletarian poems therein be published soon,
and that they be published in a form available to a working class audience, that is, in a
cheap edition. . . . [Hughes asks Knopf to release the manuscript to him so that he can
give it to International Publishers] or some others who cater to a workers public and who
will distribute it through workers' bookshops, unions, etc. throughout the country. I
have written Carl Van Vechten of this plan, and he thinks it is a good one."

1

Memo, HS [Harold Strauss]to Mr. Knopf 3/1/40.
[Knopf/uncatalogued/permanent title folders. Hughes, Langston. Harry Ransom
Humanities Research Center, University of Texas at Austin]

I have re-read the 102 pages of Hughes' autobiog. that I held in question in my first reading, and that we asked H. to revise.

He has cut 50 pages from the book, and rewritten other sections, making them more personal. He has done 75% of what I would have liked to have seen him do; but then, Mrs. Knopf and Mr. Van Vechten were not as exacting as I.

For myself, I am satisfied with the book as it stands. I will not bicker about the lists of petty Harlem celebrities that H. literally forces into the text. He and Van Vechten wand them there, and although they slow up the story, they will not materially damage a book as fine as this.

A good test of a book is whether it stands up in second reading. I can say that I am still as enthusiastic about it as I was the first time.

1

Memo HS [Harold Strauss] to Mrs. Knopf, 4/8/40.
[Knopf/uncatalogued/permanent title folders. Hughes, Langston. Harry Ransom
Humanities Research Center, University of Texas at Austin]

Re HUGHES:

The two short missing chapters were promised by Hughes "when I get to New York shortly," in his letter of 2/8/40.

We asked H. to cut down, not to eliminate the long poem entitled WALDORF ASTORIA. He has done this. In my first report I said that one of the things I liked particularly was the way H. works his poems into his autobiography.

What we did ask that he cut out was the *reviews* of his poetry, and his own comments on those reviews, which got involved in the theories of literature. These have been virtually eliminated.

Regarding the total amount of cuts, my memo of 3/1/40 summarizes my position.

The ending is memorable! The last two paragraphs are word for word as they stood in the previous version. The paragraphs before may have been slightly sharpened in phraseology, but they are not changed in substance. They are good, and I hope that you will let the last line stand. It will explain to people who know H. why he has not told the rest of the story in this volume.

1

Langston Hughes to Mrs. Blanche Knopf, 2/8/40 [from Monterey California].
[Knopf/uncatalogued/permanent title folders. Hughes, Langston. Harry Ransom
Humanities Research Center, University of Texas at Austin]

Dear Blanche,

THE BIG SEA has been sent off to you again Monday by express from San Francisco,
complete except for two short chapters to be inserted when I get to New York shortly, as
the material to complete them is there.

I went over the book very carefully, cutting and polishing in the light of yours, Carl's,
and Ben Lehman's comments and criticisms. It has been shortened some 50 pages, and I
think thereby improved.

The portion which you liked least has been cut one third, about thirty five pages out of a
hundred in the Harlem Renaissance section. Carl, as you know, felt that most of that
material was important historically and had not been written before. But I have tried to
speed it up, and make it more personable, and more readable. I hope I have
succeeded. . . . . [ellipses in the manuscript] My own feeling about that section is this:
That it was the background against which I moved and developed as a writer, and from
which much of the material of my stories and poems came. Also the people to whom
most of the space is devoted there, Carl Van Vechten, Wallace Thurman, Zora Hurston,
Rev. Becton were people who were certainly very much a part of that era, their names
known to thousands of folks. And since, I believe, a large part of the sale of my books is
to readers who sort of specialize in Negro literature and backgrounds, and to schools and
colleges, sociology classes, etc., it would seem to me that that material would be of
interest. And to Negro readers as well, who would certainly give me a razzing if I wrote
only about sailors, Paris night clubs, etc., and didn't put something "cultural" in the
book–although the material is not there for that reason, but because it was a part of my
life. And the fault lies in the writing if I have failed to make it live. But I hope in the
revision that I have bettered it. . . . . [ellipses in the manuscript] Many of the
superfluous names have been cut, as have the excerpts from reviews of my early poems,
and the portions of the WALDORF ASTORIA, and the chapter PATRON AND
FRIEND, as you suggested. Most of the abstractions have been cut, too. So I hope you
will find the whole thing somewhat better. Certainly, I have greatly appreciated yours and
Carl's help and advice.

One other observation regarding some of the material in the book and some of the names
mentioned that are widely known to Negro readers (and I suppose to students of Negro life
and literature): I have a large Negro reading and lecture public (as witness my annual
lecture tours largely to Negro schools, clubs, etc.) For instance one could not write about
life in Negro Washington without including the names I mention therein who are
nationally known to most colored people and who are very much a part of the literary and
social life of colored Washington—which is, as I point out, a segregated life. I mention
this so that you won't think they're being included as a "courtesy gesture," they being as

1

much as part of Negro life as Dorothy Parker would be if a white writer were writing of literary life in New York. I give you this as an example because, although I hope most of my book will be interesting to the general public regardless of color, some small portions of it may have vital meaning only to my own people. But that, it seems to me, would only add to the final integrity and truth of the work as a whole. And I am trying to write a truthful and honest book.

A few minor details:

Do you think there should be an appendix of names and places? [handwritten "No–HS"]

Do you think there should be dates beneath the sub-titles of each section indicating the period covered therein, as for instance:

I. TWENTY-ONE

(1902-1923)

Do you think it will be possible (as you asked me to bring to your mind later) to get out a cheaper edition (perhaps paper bound even) that might be sold exclusively by myself at lectures limited, if you wish, to Negro organizations and audiences—since many places where I speak have no book shops in town anyhow, and most colored people cannot buy the more expensive books—but will buy them if they fall within their price range and are brought *directly to* them, as I do when I lecture. For several years past now, as you know, I've taken all my royalties in books anyhow—and probably will continue to purchase a great many of my own books to sell at the lectures as long as I continue to lecture—which I guess will be a long time, as it certainly helps to sustain life.

Thanks for returning the manuscript of the poems. And for my copy of the Stevens contract.

I'll be in New York, I think, around the 25th or 28th at the latest. Kindly ask Miss Rubin to send all mail for me from now on to me at 634 St. Nicholas Avenue, c/o Harper, Apt. 1-D, New York, as I leave the coast day after tomorrow.

I plan to return to the coast in the early summer and write the second volume of the autobiography, and I hope a new novel. (But you have heard about that novel for a long while now haven't you?) Well, all things get done in time! And it's surely coming up.

With my best to you,
Sincerely,

Langston
Langston Hughes

2

[Knopf/uncatalogued, permanent title folders, Hughes, Langston. Harry Ransom Humanities Research Center, University of Texas at Austin.]

H. Synopsis. I like enormously all but 102 pages of the 430 or so (including interleavings) of the MS. Paramount is its human interest and sheer story-telling power. It is full of emotion; unassuming, nostalgic. Hughes as a person makes a strong bid for our sympathies in a natural and unaffected manner. Besides himself, a dozen or so personalities spring vividly and memorably to life. For the most part these are obscure and unknown people about whom Hughes feel [sic] free to write frankly, such as his mother and father, the seamen and stewards with whom he shipped, the cooks, waiters, dancers and singers in French restaurants, etc. etc. Hughes goes wrong only where he deals with celebrities – and in the weak 102 pages, the pages concerning Harlem in the twenties, he apparently has succumbed to a false sense of obligation, for he has included a thumbnail sketch of every well known Harlemite, *whether or not they entered Hughes' own story.*

This MS is an autobiography; but Hughes forgets that occasionally. When he writes about what he saw and did and felt, and what happened to him, he is good. When he makes courtesy gestures to this person and to that institution, he is beside the point and out of order – not to say a little boring.

The objectional section runs from page 257 to page 358, inclusive, although there are occasional passages that might be retained. The only bit in this section that I really like is pp 293-297, about A'Leila Walker. The rest is too full of "I met so and so. . ."; too full of dull details about Hughes' first literary contacts, and the reception of his poems (including, of all things, lengthy quotations from the reviews he got); too full, with all due respect, of Mr. Van Vechten, as well as Thurman, Toomer, Hurston, etc. (although Hughes' later adventures with Miss Hurston are good, for they are probably autobiographical); also too full of quotations from Hughes' own short stories and articles, which attempt a theoretical interpretation of the Negro Renaissance. In short, here the book departs from its autobiographical purpose, and becomes a "Harlem Cavalcade." This is wrong.

The rest of the MS I find highly exciting, and would print almost as it stands. I like particularly the Mexican episodes, and the Italian episodes. My only criticism is that there is too much about Hughes' "patron" (pp. 389-394); the remaining section about her is excellent) in view of the fact that he cannot name or identify her. Here the familiar criterion should be used: whatever deals with the relationship between her and him should be retained; but whatever deals with her other affairs, her charities, her philosophies, her contacts, should be boiled down to a sentence or two.

I like the way the poems are introduced, for they are, in a way, autobiographical, reflecting Hughes' mood at the time. I think, however, that the long poem on the Waldorf, p, 400-402, could be quoted merely in part. And I definitely take exception to discussions of the theory of poetry, such as are to be found on pp. 322-325.

*** ***

1

I have the strongest possible feeling that this book should be published by itself, without waiting for Volume II (1930-40). In the first place, it has a natural ending in the coming of the depression. In the second place, Hughes is best when he writes about old memories; I am afraid that he will be hampered in writing about more recent material now, first because of the feelings of the people about whom he writes, and second because his emotions are still too much bound up in events. In the third place, physically there is plenty here for one book. In the fourth place, *the pre-1930 material has strong claims on the public interest*; *this may be nullified* by the more recent material, such as passages on Spain, that Hughes intends to include. Perhaps five years from now public interest will be ripe for the story of Hughes' life during the thirties; and he certainly will be able to write more freely than now. But my final reason is strongest of all: IF VOLUME II IS DONE WELL AND HAS "SALES ANGLES", IT WILL MAKE A BOOK BY ITSELF. BUT IF VOLUME II SHOWS THE PERSISTENCE OF THE TENDENCY OF VOLUME I TO WEAKEN AS THE TIME NEARS THE PRESENT, IT MAY RUIN THE APPEAL OF VOL I. I suggest that, reworked according to suggestion, Vol. I. be published alone. I am convinced that it will sell upwards of 10,000 copies. It has the appeal of "Only Yesterday", plus superb story telling, plus the portrait of a highly sympathetic personality.

2

THE NEGRO AND RADICAL THOUGHT

MR. CLAUDE McKAY, one of the editors of *The Liberator* and a Negro poet of distinction, writes us as follows:

"I am surprised and sorry that in your editorial, 'The Drive', published in THE CRISIS for May, you should leap out of your sphere to sneer at the Russian Revolution, the greatest event in the history of humanity; much greater than the French Revolution, which is held up as a wonderful achievement to Negro children and students in white and black schools. For American Negroes the indisputable and outstanding fact of the Russian Revolution is that a mere handful of Jews, much less in ratio to the number of Negroes in the American population, have attained, through the Revolution, all the political and social rights that were denied to them under the regime of the Czar.

"Although no thinking Negro can deny the great work that the N. A. A. C. P. is doing, it must yet be admitted that from its platform and personnel the Association cannot function as a revolutionary working class organization. And the overwhelming majority of American Negroes belong by birth, condition and repression to the working class. Your aim is to get for the American Negro the political and social rights that are his by virtue of the Constitution. the rights which are denied him by the Southern oligarchy with the active co-operation of the state governments and the tacit support of northern business interests. And your aim is a noble one, which deserves the support of all progressive Negroes.

"But the Negro in politics and social life is ostracized only technically by the distinction of color; in reality the Negro is discriminated against because he is of the lowest type of worker. . . .

"Obviously, this economic difference between the white and black workers manifests itself in various forms, in color prejudice, race hatred, political and social boycotting and lynching of Negroes. And all the entrenched institutions of white America,—law courts, churches, schools, the fighting forces and the Press,—condone these iniquities perpetrated upon black men; iniquities that are dismissed indifferently as the inevitable result of the social system. Still, whenever it suits the business interests controlling these institutions to mitigate the persecutions against Negroes, they do so with impunity. When organized white workers quit their jobs, Negroes, who are discouraged by the whites to organize, are sought to take their places. And these strike-breaking Negroes work under the protection of the military and the police. But as ordinary citizens and workers, Negroes are not protected by the military and the police from the mob. The ruling classes will not grant Negroes those rights which, on a lesser scale and more plausibly, are withheld from the white proletariat. The concession of these rights would immediately cause a Revolution in the economic life of this country."

We are aware that some of our friends have been disappointed with THE CRISIS during and since the war. Some have assumed that we aimed chiefly at mounting the band wagon with our cause during the madness of war; others thought that we were playing safe so as to avoid the Department of Justice; and still a third class found us curiously stupid in our attitude toward the broader matters of human reform. Such critics, and Mr. McKay is among them, must give us credit for standing to our guns in the past at no little cost in many influential quarters, and they must also remember that we have one chief cause,—the emancipation of the Negro, and to this all else must be subordinated—not because other questions are not important but because to our mind the most important social question today is recognition of the darker races.

Turning now to that marvelous set of phenomena known as the Russian Revolution, Mr. McKay is wrong in thinking that we have ever intentionally sneered at it. On the contrary, time may prove, as he believes, that the Russian Revolution is the greatest event of the nineteenth and twentieth centuries, and its leaders the most unselfish prophets. At the same time

THE CRISIS does not know this to be true. Russia is incredibly vast, and the happenings there in the last five years have been intricate to a degree that must make any student pause. We sit, therefore, with waiting hands and listening ears, seeing some splendid results from Russia, like the cartoons for public education recently exhibited in America, and hearing of other things which frighten us.

We are moved neither by the superficial omniscience of Wells nor the reports in the New York *Times;* but this alone we do know: that the immediate work for the American Negro lies in America and not in Russia, and this, too, in spite of the fact that the Third Internationale has made a pronouncement which cannot but have our entire sympathy:

"The Communist Internationale once forever breaks with the traditions of the Second Internationale which in reality only recognized the white race. The Communist Internationale makes it its task to emancipate the workers of the entire world. The ranks of the Communist Internationale fraternally unite men of all colors: white, yellow and black—the toilers of the entire world."

Despite this there come to us black men two insistent questions: What is today the right program of socialism? The editor of THE CRISIS considers himself a Socialist but he does not believe that German State Socialism or the dictatorship of the proletariat are perfect panaceas. He believes with most thinking men that the present method of creating, controlling and distributing wealth is desperately wrong; that there must come and is coming a social control of wealth; but he does not know just what form that control is going to take, and he is not prepared to dogmatize with Marx or Lenin. Further than that, and more fundamental to the duty and outlook of THE CRISIS, is this question: How far can the colored people of the world, and particularly the Negroes of the United States, trust the working classes?

Many honest thinking Negroes assume, and Mr. McKay seems to be one of these, that we have only to embrace the working class program to have the working class embrace ours; that we have only to join trade Unionism and Socialism or even Communism, as they are today expounded, to have Union Labor and Socialists and Communists believe and act on the equality of mankind and the abolition of the color line. THE CRISIS wishes that this were true, but it is forced to the conclusion that it is not.

The American Federation of Labor, as representing the trade unions in America, has been grossly unfair and discriminatory toward Negroes and still is. American Socialism has discriminated against black folk and before the war was prepared to go further with this discrimination. European Socialism has openly discriminated against Asiatics. Nor is this surprising. Why should we assume on the part of unlettered and suppressed masses of white workers, a clearness of thought, a sense of human brotherhood, that is sadly lacking in the most educated classes?

Our task, therefore, as it seems to THE CRISIS, is clear: We have to convince the working classes of the world that black men, brown men, and yellow men are human beings and suffer the same discrimination that white workers suffer. We have in addition to this to espouse the cause of the white workers, only being careful that we do not in this way allow them to jeopardize our cause. We must, for instance, have bread. If our white fellow workers drive us out of decent jobs, we are compelled to accept indecent wages even at the price of "scabbing". It is a hard choice, but whose is the blame? Finally despite public prejudice and clamour, we should examine with open mind in literature, debate and in real life the great programs of social reform that are day by day being put forward.

This was the true thought and meaning back of our May editorial. We have an immediate program for Negro emancipation laid down and thought out by the N. A. A. C. P. It is foolish for us to give up this practical program for mirage in Africa or by seeking to join a revolution which we do not at present understand. On the other hand, as Mr. McKay says, it would be just as foolish for us to sneer or even seem to sneer at the blood-entwined writhing of hundreds of millions of our whiter human brothers.

SOVIET RUSSIA AND THE NEGRO

CLAUDE MCKAY

MR. McKAY SPEAKING IN THE THRONE ROOM OF THE KREMLIN

THE label of propaganda will be affixed to what I say here. I shall not mind; propaganda has now come into its respectable rights and I am proud of being a propagandist. The difference between propaganda and art was impressed on my boyhood mind by a literary mentor, Milton's poetry and his political prose set side by side as the supreme examples. So too, my teacher,—splendid and broadminded though he was, yet unconsciously biased against what he felt was propaganda—thought that that gilt-washed artificiality, "The Picture of Dorian Gray", would outlive "Arms and the Man" and "John Bull's Other Island". But inevitably as I grew older I had perforce to revise and change my mind about propaganda. I lighted on one of Milton's greatest sonnets that was pure propaganda and a widening horizon revealed that some of the finest spirits of modern literature— Voltaire, Hugo, Heine, Swift, Shelly, Byron, Tolstoy, Ibsen—had carried the taint of propaganda. The broader view did not merely include propaganda literature in my literary outlook; it also swung me away

from the childish age of the enjoyment of creative work for pleasurable curiosity to another extreme where I have always sought for the motivating force or propaganda intent that underlies all literature of interest. My birthright, and the historical background of the race that gave it to me, made me very respectful and receptive of propaganda and world events since the year 1914 have proved that it is no mean science of convincing information.

American Negroes are not as yet deeply permeated with the mass movement spirit and so fail to realize the importance of organized propaganda. It was Marcus Garvey's greatest contribution to the Negro movement; his pioneer work in that field is a feat that the men of broader understanding and sounder ideas who will follow him must continue. It was not until I first came to Europe in 1919 that I came to a full realization and understanding of the effectiveness of the insidious propaganda in general that is maintained against the Negro race. And it was not by the occasional affront of the minority of civilized

353

fiends—mainly those Europeans who had been abroad, engaged in the business of robbing colored peoples in their native land—that I gained my knowledge, but rather through the questions about the Negro that were put to me by genuinely sympathetic and cultured persons.

The average Europeans who read the newspapers, the popular books and journals, and go to see the average play and a Mary Pickford movie, are very dense about the problem of the Negro; and they are the most important section of the general public that the Negro propagandists would reach. For them the tragedy of the American Negro ended with "Uncle Tom's Cabin" and Emancipation. And since then they have been aware only of the comedy —the Negro minstrel and vaudevillian, the boxer, the black mammy and butler of the cinematograph, the caricatures of the romances and the lynched savage who has violated a beautiful white girl.

A very few ask if Booker T. Washington is doing well or if the "Black Star Line" is running; perhaps some one less discreet than sagacious will wonder how colored men can hanker so much after white women in face of the lynching penalty. Misinforma-

tion, indifference and levity sum up the attitude of western Europe towards the Negro. There is the superior but very fractional intellectual minority that knows better, but whose influence on public opinion is infinitesimal, and so it may be comparatively easy for white American propagandists—whose interests behoove them to misrepresent the Negro—to turn the general indifference into hostile antagonism if American Negroes who have the intellectual guardianship of racial interests do not organize effectively, and on a world scale, to combat their white exploiters and traducers.

The world war has fundamentally altered the status of Negroes in Europe. It brought thousands of them from America and the British and French colonies to participate in the struggle against the Central Powers. Since then serious clashes have come about in England between the blacks that later settled down in the seaport towns and the natives. France has brought in her black troops to do police duty in the occupied districts in Germany. The color of these troops, and their customs too, are different and strange and the nature of their work would naturally make their presence irritating and unbearable to the inhabitants

AN INTERNATIONAL GROUP INCLUDING A CHINESE, RUSSIAN JEW, NEGRO, RUSSIAN GENTILE, BULGARIAN, HINDU, AMERICAN MULATTO, ALGERIAN, JAPANESE, ARMENIAN, KOREAN, AND WHITE AMERICAN

HOLITSCHER, THE GERMAN NOVELIST; CLARA KETKIN, VETERAN GERMAN COMMUNIST; CLAUDE McKAY, POET.

whose previous knowledge of Negroes has been based, perhaps, on their prowess as cannibals. And besides, the presence of these troops provides rare food for the chauvinists of a once proud and overbearing race, now beaten down and drinking the dirtiest dregs of humiliation under the bayonets of the victor.

However splendid the gesture of Republican France towards colored people, her use of black troops in Germany to further her imperial purpose should meet with nothing less than condemnation from the advanced section of Negroes. The propaganda that Negroes need to put over in Germany is not black troops with bayonets in that unhappy country. As conscript-slave soldiers of Imperial France they can in no wise help the movement of Negroes nor gain the sympathy of the broad-visioned international white groups whose international opponents are also the intransigent enemies of Negro progress. In considering the situation of the black troops in Germany, intelligent Negroes should compare it with that of the white troops in India, San Domingo and Haiti. What might not the Haitian propagandists have done with the marines if they had been black instead of white Americans! The world upheaval having brought the three greatest European nations—England, France and Germany—into closer relationship with Negroes, colored Americans should seize the opportunity to promote finer inter-racial understanding. As white Americans in Europe are taking advantage of the situation to intensify their propaganda against the blacks, so must Negroes meet that with a strong counter-movement. Negroes should realize that the supremacy of American capital today proportionately increases American influence in the politics and social life of the world. Every American official abroad, every smug tourist, is a protagonist of dollar culture and a propagandist against the Negro. Besides brandishing the Rooseveltian stick in the face of the lesser new world natives, America holds an economic club over the heads of all the great European nations, excepting Russia, and so those bold individuals in Western Europe who formerly sneered at dollar culture may yet find it necessary and worth while to be discreetly silent. As American influence increases in the world, and especially in Europe, through the extension of American capital, the more necessary it becomes for all struggling minorities of the United States to organize extensively for the world wide propagation of their grievances. Such propaganda efforts, besides strengthening the cause at home, will certainly enlist the sympathy and help of those foreign groups that are carrying on a life and death struggle to escape the octuple arms of American business interests.

And the Negro, as the most suppressed and persecuted minority, should use this period of ferment in international affairs to lift his cause out of his national obscurity and force it forward as a prime international issue.

Though Western Europe can be reported as being quite ignorant and apathetic of the Negro in world affairs, there is one great nation with an arm in Europe that is thinking intelligently on the Negro as it does about all international problems. When the Russian workers overturned their infamous government in 1917, one of the first acts of the new Premier, Lenin, was a proclamation greeting all the oppressed peoples throughout the world, exhorting them to organize and unite against the common international oppressor — Private Capitalism. Later on in Moscow, Lenin himself grappled with the question of the American Negroes and spoke on the subject before the Second Congress of the Third International. He consulted with John Reed, the American journalist, and dwelt on the urgent necessity of propaganda and organizational work among the Negroes of the South. The subject was not allowed to drop. When Sen Katayama of Japan, the veteran revolutionist, went from the United States to Russia in 1921 he placed the American Negro problem first upon his full agenda. And ever since he has been working unceasingly and unselfishly to promote the cause of the exploited American Negro among the Soviet councils of Russia.

With the mammoth country securely under their control, and despite the great energy and thought that are being poured into the revival of the national industry, the vanguard of the Russian workers and the national minorities, now set free from imperial oppression, are thinking seriously about the fate of the oppressed classes, the suppressed national and racial minorities in the rest of Europe, Asia, Africa and America. They feel themselves kin in spirit to these people. They want to help make them free. And not the least of the oppressed that fill the thoughts of the new Russia are the Negroes of America and Africa. If we look back two decades to recall how the Czarist persecution of the Russian Jews agitated Democratic America, we will get some idea of the mind of Liberated Russia towards the Negroes of

America. The Russian people are reading the terrible history of their own recent past in the tragic position of the American Negro to-day. Indeed, the Southern States can well serve the purpose of showing what has happened in Russia. For if the exploited poor whites of the South could ever transform themselves into making common cause with the persecuted and plundered Negroes, overcome the oppressive oligarchy —the political crackers and robber landlords—and deprive it of all political privileges, the situation would be very similar to that of Soviet Russia to-day.

In Moscow I met an old Jewish revolutionist who had done time in Siberia, now young again and filled with the spirit of the triumphant Revolution. We talked about American affairs and touched naturally on the subject of the Negro. I told him of the difficulties of the problem, that the best of the liberal white elements were also working for a better status for the Negro, and he remarked: "When the democratic bourgeoisie of the United States were execrating Czardom for the Jewish pogroms they were meting out to your people a treatment more savage and barbarous than the Jews ever experienced in the old Russia. America", he said religiously, "had to make some sort of expiatory gesture for her sins. There is no surfeited bourgeoisie here in Russia to make a hobby of ugly social problems, but the Russian workers, who have won through the ordeal of persecution and revolution, extend the hand of international brotherhood to all the suppressed Negro millions of America".

I met with this spirit of sympathetic appreciation and response prevailing in all circles in Moscow and Petrograd. I never guessed what was awaiting me in Russia. I had left America in September of 1922 determined to get there, to see into the new revolutionary life of the people and report on it. I was not a little dismayed when, congenitally averse to notoriety as I am, I found that on stepping upon Russian soil I forthwith became a notorious character. And strangely enough there was nothing unpleasant about my being swept into the surge of revolutionary Russia. For better or for worse every person in Russia is vitally affected by the revolution. No one but a soulless body can live there without being stirred to the depths by it.

I reached Russia in November—the month

THE PETROGRAD HOME FOR CHILDREN RENDERED DESTITUTE BY THE FAMINE

of the Fourth Congress of the Communist International and the Fifth Anniversary of the Russian Revolution. The whole revolutionary nation was mobilized to honor the occasion, Petrograd was magnificent in red flags and streamers. Red flags fluttered against the snow from all the great granite buildings. Railroad trains, street cars, factories, stores, hotels, schools—all wore decorations. It was a festive month of celebration in which I, as a member of the Negro race, was a very active participant. I was received as though the people had been apprised of, and were prepared for, my coming. When Max Eastman and I tried to bore our way through the dense crowds, that jammed the Tverskaya Street in Moscow on the 7th of November, I was caught, tossed up into the air, and passed along by dozens of stalwart youths.

"How warmly excited they get over a strange face!" said Eastman. A young Russian Communist remarked: "But where is the difference? Some of the Indians are as dark as you." To which another replied: "The lines of the face are different, the Indians have been with us long. The people instinctively see the difference." And so always the conversation revolved around me until my face flamed. The Moscow press printed long articles about the Negroes in America, a poet was inspired to rhyme about the Africans looking to Soviet Russia and soon I was in demand everywhere—at the lectures of poets and journalists, the meetings of soldiers and factory workers. Slowly I began losing self-consciousness with the realization that I was welcomed thus as a symbol, as a member of the great American Negro group—kin to the unhappy black slaves of European Imperialism in Africa—that the workers of Soviet Russia, rejoicing in their freedom, were greeting through me.

(*Concluded in the January* CRISIS)

SOVIET RUSSIA AND THE NEGRO

(Concluded)

 Claude McKay

RUSSIA, in broad terms, is a country where all the races of Europe and of Asia meet and mix. The fact is that under the repressive power of the Czarist bureaucracy the different races preserved a degree of kindly tolerance towards each other. The fierce racial hatreds that flame in the Balkans never existed in Russia. Where in the South no Negro might approach a *"cracker"* as a man for friendly offices, a Jewish pilgrim in old Russia could find rest and sustenance in the home of an orthodox peasant. It is a problem to define the Russian type by features. The Hindu, the Mongolian, the Persian, the Arab, the West European—all these types may be traced woven into the distinctive polyglot population of Moscow. And so, to the Russian, I was merely another type, but stranger, with which they were not yet familiar. They were curious with me, all and sundry, young and old, in a friendly, refreshing manner. Their curiosity had none of the intolerable impertinence and often downright affront that any very dark colored man, be he Negro, Indian or Arab, would experience in Germany and England.

In 1920, while I was trying to get out a volume of my poems in London, I had a visit with Bernard Shaw who remarked that it must be tragic for a sensitive Negro to be an artist. Shaw was right. Some of the English reviews of my book touched the very bottom of journalistic muck. The English reviewer outdid his American cousin (except the South, of course, which could not surprise any white person much less a black) in sprinkling criticism with racial prejudice. The sedate, copperhead "Spectator" as much as said: no "cultured" white man could read a Negro's poetry without prejudice, that instinctively he must search for that "something" that must make him antagonistic to it. But fortunately

MR. McKAY FLYING FROM PETROGRAD TO THE FORT OF KRONSTADT

Mr. McKay did not offend our susceptibilities! The English people from the lowest to the highest, cannot think of a black man as being anything but an entertainer, boxer, a Baptist preacher or a menial. The Germans are just a little worse. Any healthy looking black coon of an adventurous streak can have a wonderful time palming himself off as another Siki or a buck dancer. When an American writer introduced me as a poet to a very cultured German, a lover of all the arts, he could not believe it, and I don't think he does yet. An American student tells his middle class landlady that he is having a black friend to lunch: "But are you sure that he is not a cannibal?" she asks without a flicker of a humorous smile!

But in Petrograd and Moscow, I could not detect a trace of this ignorant snobbishness among the educated classes, and the attitude of the common workers, the soldiers and sailors was still more remarkable. It was so beautifully naive; for them I was only a black member of the world of humanity. It may be urged that the fine feelings of the Russians towards a Negro was the effect of Bolshevist pressure and propaganda. The fact is that I spent most of my leisure time in non-partisan and anti-bolshevist circles. In Moscow I found the Luxe Hotel where I put up extremely depressing, the dining room was anathema to me and I grew tired to death of meeting the proletarian ambassadors from foreign lands, some of whom bore themselves as if they were the holy messengers of Jesus, Prince of Heaven, instead of working class representatives. And so I spent many of my free evenings at the Domino Café, a notorious den of the dilettante poets and writers. There came the young anarchists and menshevists and all the young aspiring fry to read and discuss their poetry and prose. Sometimes a group of the older men came too. One evening I noticed Pilnyak the novelist, Okonoff the critic, Feodor the translator of Poe, an editor, a theatre manager and their young disciples, beer-drinking through a very interesting literary discussion. There was always music, good folk-singing and bad fiddling, the place was more like a second rate cabaret than a poets' club, but nevertheless much to be enjoyed, with amiable chats and light banter through which the evening wore pleasantly away. This was the meeting place of the frivolous set with whom I eased my mind after writing all day.

The evenings of the proletarian poets held in the Arbot were much more serious affairs. The leadership was communist, the audience working class and attentive like diligent, elementary school children. To these meetings also came some of the keener intellects from the Domino Café. One of these young women told me that she wanted to keep in touch with all the phases of the new culture. In Petrograd the meetings of the intelligentzia seemed more formal and inclusive. There were such notable men there as Chukovsky the critic, Eugene Zamiatan the celebrated novelist and Maishack the poet and translator of Kipling. The artist and theatre world were also represented. There was no communist spirit in evidence at these intelligentzia gatherings. Frankly there was an undercurrent of hostility to the bolshevists. But I was invited to speak and read my poems whenever I appeared at any of them and treated with every courtesy and consideration as a writer. Among those sophisticated and cultured Russians, many of them speaking from two to four languages, there was no overdoing of the correct thing, no vulgar wonderment and bounderish superiority over a Negro's being a poet. I was a poet, that was all, and their keen questions showed that they were much more interested in the technique of my poetry, my views on and my position regarding the modern literary movements than in the difference of my color. Although I will not presume that there was no attraction at all in that little difference!

On my last visit to Petrograd I stayed in the Palace of the Grand Duke Vladimir Alexander, the brother of Czar Nicholas the Second. His old, kindly steward who looked after my comfort wanders round like a ghost through the great rooms. The house is now the headquarters of the Petrograd intellectuals. A fine painting of the Duke stands curtained in the dining room. I was told that he was liberal minded, a patron of the arts, and much liked by the Russian intelligentzia. The atmosphere of the house was theoretically non-political, but I quickly scented a strong hostility to bolshevist authority. But even here I had only pleasant encounters and illuminating conversations with the inmates and visitors, who freely expressed their views against the Soviet Government, although they knew me to be very sympathetic to it.

During the first days of my visit I felt that the great demonstration of friendliness was somehow expressive of the enthusiastic spirit of the glad anniversary days, that after the month was ended I could calmly settle down to finish the book about the American Negro that the State Publishing Department of Moscow had commissioned me to write, and in the meantime quietly go about making interesting contacts. But my days in Russia were a progression of affectionate enthusiasm of the people towards me. Among the factory workers, the red-starred and chevroned soldiers and sailors, the proletarian students and children, I could not get off as lightly as I did with the intelligentzia. At every meeting I was received with boisterous acclaim, mobbed with friendly demonstration. The women workers of the great bank in Moscow insisted on hearing about the working conditions of the colored women of America and after a brief outline I was asked the most exacting questions concerning the positions that were most available to colored women, their wages and general relationship with the white women workers. The details I could not give; but when I got through, the Russian women passed a resolution sending greetings to the colored women workers of America, exhorting them to organize their forces and send a woman representative to Russia. I received a similar message from the Propaganda Department of the Petrograd Soviet which is managed by Nicoleva, a very energetic woman. There I was shown the new status of the Russian women gained through the revolution of 1917. Capable women can fit themselves for any position; equal pay with men for equal work; full pay during the period of pregnancy and no work for the mother two months before and two months after the confinement. Getting a divorce is comparatively easy and not influenced by money power, detective chicanery and wire pulling. A special department looks into the problems of joint personal property and the guardianship and support of the children. There is no penalty for legal abortion and no legal stigma of illegitimacy attaching to children born out of wedlock.

There were no problems of the submerged

lower classes and the suppressed national minorities of the old Russia that could not bear comparison with the grievous position of the millions of Negroes in the United States to-day. Just as Negroes are barred from the American Navy and the higher ranks of the Army, so were the Jews and the sons of the peasantry and proletariat discriminated against in the Russian Empire. It is needless repetition of the obvious to say that Soviet Russia does not tolerate such discriminations, for the actual government of the country is now in the hands of the combined national minorities, the peasantry and the proletariat. By the permission of Leon Trotsky, Commissar-in-chief of the military and naval forces of Soviet Russia, I visited the highest military schools in the Kremlin and environs of Moscow. And there I saw the new material, the sons of the working people in training as cadets by the old officers of the upper classes. For two weeks I was a guest of the Red navy in Petrograd with the same eager proletarian youth of new Russia, who conducted me through the intricate machinery of submarines, took me over aeroplanes captured from the British during the counter-revolutionary war around Petrograd and showed me the making of a warship ready for action. And even of greater interest was the life of the men and the officers, the simplified discipline that was strictly enforced, the food that was served for each and all alike, the extra political educational classes and the extreme tactfulness and elasticity of the political commissars, all communists, who act as advisers and arbitrators between the men and students and the officers. Twice or thrice I was given some of the *kasha* which is sometimes served with the meals. In Moscow I grew to like this food very much, but it was always difficult to get. I had always imagined that it was quite unwholesome and unpalatable and eaten by the Russian peasant only on account of extreme poverty. But on the contrary I found it very rare and sustaining when cooked right with a bit of meat and served with butter—a grain food very much like the common but very delicious West Indian rice-and-peas.

The red cadets are seen in the best light at their gymnasium exercises and at the political assemblies when discipline is set aside. Especially at the latter where a visitor feels that he is in the midst of the early revolutionary days, so hortatory are the speeches, so intense the enthusiasm of the men. At all these meetings I had to speak and the students asked me general questions about the Negro in the American Army and Navy, and when I gave them the common information, known to all American Negroes, students, officers and commissars were unanimous in wishing that a group of young American Negroes would take up training to become officers in the Army and Navy of Soviet Russia.

The proletarian students of Moscow were eager to learn of the life and work of Negro students. They sent messages of encouragement and good will to the Negro students of America and, with a fine gesture of fellowship, elected the Negro delegate of the American Communist Party and myself to honorary membership in the Moscow Soviet.

Those Russian days remain the most memorable of my life. The intellectual Communists and the intelligentzia were interested to know that America had produced a formidable body of Negro intelligentzia and professionals, possessing a distinctive literature and cultural and business interests alien to the white man's. And they think naturally, that the militant leaders of the intelligentzia must feel and express the spirit of revolt that is slumbering in the inarticulate Negro masses, precisely as the emancipation movement of the Russian masses had passed through similar phases.

Russia is prepared and waiting to receive couriers and heralds of good will and interracial understanding from the Negro race. Her demonstration of friendliness and equality for Negroes may not conduce to promote healthy relations between Soviet Russia and democratic America, the anthropologists of 100 per cent pure white Americanism may soon invoke Science to prove that the Russians are not at all God's white people. I even caught a little of American anti-Negro propaganda in Russia. A friend of mine, a member of the Moscow intelligentzia repeated to me the remarks of the lady correspondent of a Danish newspaper: that I should not be taken as a representative Negro for she had lived in America and found all Negroes lazy, bad and vicious, a terror to white women. In Petrograd I got a like story from Chukovsky, the critic, who was on intimate terms with a high worker of the American Relief Administration and his southern wife. Chukovsky is himself an intellectual "westerner", the term applied to those Russians who put Western-European civilization before Russian culture and believe that Russia's salvation lies in becoming completely westernized. He had spent an impressionable part of his youth in London and adores all things English, and during the world war was very pro-English. For the American democracy, also, he expresses unfeigned admiration. He has more Anglo-American books than Russian in his fine library and considers the literary section of the New York *Times* a journal of a very high standard. He is really a maniac of Anglo-Saxon American culture. Chukovsky was quite incredulous when I gave him the facts of the Negro's status in American civilization.

"The Americans are a people of such great energy and ability," he said, "how could they act so petty towards a racial minority?" And then he related an experience of his in London that bore a strong smell of *cracker* breath. However, I record it here in the belief that it is authentic for Chukovsky is a man of integrity: About the beginning of the century, he was sent to England as correspondent of a newspaper in Odessa, but in London he was more given to poetic dreaming and studying English literature in the British Museum and rarely sent any news home. So he lost his job and had to find cheap, furnished rooms. A few weeks later, after he had taken up his residence in new quarters, a black guest arrived, an American gentleman of the cloth. The preacher procured a room on the top floor and used the dining and sitting room with the other guests, among whom was a white American family. The latter protested the presence of the Negro in the house and especially in the guest room. The landlady was in a dilemma, she could not lose her American boarders and the clergyman's money was not to be despised. At last she compromised by getting the white Americans to agree to the Negro's staying without being allowed the privilege of the guest room, and Chukovsky was asked to tell the Negro the truth. Chukovsky strode upstairs to give the unpleasant facts to the preacher and to offer a little consolation, but the black man was not unduly offended:

"The white guests have the right to object to me," he explained, anticipating Garvey, "they belong to a superior race."

"But," said Chukovsky, "*I* do not object to you, *I* don't feel any difference; we don't understand color prejudice in Russia."

"Well," philosophized the preacher, "you are very kind, but taking the scriptures as authority, I don't consider the Russians to be white people."

Garvey and Garveyism—An Estimate

By A. F. ELMES

A CLOSE-UP view of a picture frequently exaggerates elements out of all proportion to their true importance. This principle should also be borne in mind in estimating all human movements. History cannot be written fairly and dispassionately nor a just interpretation given to events in the midst of the ferment of such events, nor yet at a time, nor by a person that stands too near the stage of such events.

The British Parliament has recently decided to give publicity to all the documents relating to the recent war. The world will look with more than ordinary interest and expectancy to such publications, and now seven. years after the Armistice, judgment as to where full responsibility for the war should be placed, what were the causes primary and secondary—in a word, the interpretation of the facts in full fairness would do well to wait on these documents.

No one will refuse to admit this principle—the principle that human movements cannot be viewed in their true perspective at close range. History must have time to justify itself.

Lest there be any prejudice as to the identity of the writer, he wishes to say of himself at the outset, that he is not, nor ever was a Garveyite, nor has he at any time shown a disposition to become an orthodox disciple of Garvey. He has no stock in the defunct Black Star Line, nor in any of the enterprises fostered by the movement. He claims no particular fitness to declare himself on the subject except that of an outsider, a student of human movements, a sympathetic observer of Garvey and the workings of the colossal and unwieldy program he inaugurated.

In Harlem and in other parts of the country the writer has had the experience of personal encounters, unaccompanied however by any physical violence, with ardent disciples of Garvey and he numbers among these some of his friends who themselves have been puzzled as to his (the writer's) inability, perhaps more frankly his mental obtuseness, in not being able to recognize this savior of his race.

His contacts have been wide and he has watched and studied the movement, read with' avidity the *Negro World* and he has before him as he pens this article "The Constitution and Book of Laws, made for the Government of the Universal Negro Improvement Association, Inc., and African Communities' League, Inc., of the World. Revised and Amended Aug. 1920."

Newspaper and magazine articles have appeared on both sides and the language of some of these have been poignantly sarcastic and many of them have descended to the plane of abuse and personal vilification of the man Garvey. And they have all had a wide circulation.

Now that the "tumult and the shouting" is about to subside in both pro- and anti-Garvey camps, now that Garvey himself has passed into the shadows of the Federal Prison and open opposition to him has necessarily been rendered futile, it were well for some sympathetic outsider whose state of mind thus characterized would fit him eminently to present the case, frankly and openly to do so.

Let it be observed that no man could stand in one of those teeming Liberty Hall audiences, see one of Garvey's ostentatious parades, hear Garvey's magnetic voice, read his *Negro World,* watch the sweep of his ideas and then say there was nothing to it. Let him do this and he would cast a serious doubt on his mental integrity. This is apart entirely from the goodness or the badness of Garveyism. There is something to it; all reasonable men will readily admit.

And how does this come to be? It is the personality of Garvey himself. Call him what you will: a visionary, impossible idealist, fanatical reformer, unprincipled opportunist; behind these epithets lie the unconquerable fact of Garvey, the personality of the man who has dramatically attracted the attention of the world.

Contrary to much of what has hitherto been published, I believe the man was not fundamentally insincere. What he saw, he saw and there was no make believe in his own mind. True, many of his followers have been disappointed, they were duped, bewildered and surrendered reason as well as ready money. The thing has not worked out as they expected; but in Garvey's own mind there was a close fit between what he gave forth and what he held in his mind. I think he was substantially and in the main sincere.

If I understand his program correctly he was sound in his basic contention for his people. Above I gave a passing characterization to his program as being unwieldy. The objects of the U. N. I. A. as given in its Constitution and Book of Laws make me smile as I read them over. They go from reclaiming the fallen and assisting the needy to the establishing of a Negro nation in Africa, from helping backward tribes in Africa to the foundering of Universities, Colleges, Academies and a world-wide commercial enterprise . . . Comprehensive, colossal, topheavy and impossible! No one man is wise nor powerful enough to sit astride so many horses at one and the same time.

Interpreting these manifold objects synthetically and as Garvey sought to have them carried out in practice, what do we find? He is contending for the principle of a self-sustaining, self-propagating group life, that as a race the Negro will not rise into the fulness of racial self-hood until his group becomes fully competent and adequate in resources for the demands of his economic, political, moral and spiritual life. What is there against this? All Negro organizations vote its full adoption with both hands up. In principle; yes, we do.

No man who is content to remain poor, who for his normal needs seeks dependence on others, merits much respect. No race comes into the place of dignified self-hood that stays poor. Marcus Garvey argues when the colored man needs a suit of clothes, there should be a colored tailor competent to fit him, a colored wholesale store from which the goods can be procured, colored factory for the preparation of the raw material, colored producers for this raw material and ships manned and owned by men of his race to transport the goods. He would close up the whole economic circle with agents and agencies of his own people. Thus he carried the doctrine in the other aspects of Negro life. Is not this principle valid for a program of uplift and advance for any people?

Marcus Garvey while fundamentally sincere, unhappily failed to realize his limitations, and the tremendous sweep of his mind was not balanced by adequate penetrating power. While he dreamed the emotional content of those dreams, the showy fabric of his visions bore him away in method from the immediate or remotely practicable. In short, for the carrying out of such universal aims there seemed wanting in the leader many of the intellectual prerequisites.

No estimate of Garveyism as a social movement can ignore the fact that his personality plus the mere size of the things he attempted to do gave him a good measure of the power of his appeal. He thought in terms large and universal and would in one organization compass the Alpha to Omega of his people's progress. Such a mind is usually "short" in analytic power and penetrative capacity. Garvey's was eminently so. His very inability for clear-cut, analytical reasoning made him intolerant of interference and made him assume at times the investiture of divine rightness and supernatural inspiration for his scheme.

Garvey was a prophet. He was possessed of a great and noble passion. The fervor with which he believed in himself and his message, the full measure of his devotion to what he held to be right cannot be successfully gainsaid. He missed the mark in method and procedure. Like other reformers that went before him, this passion for redemption of his people led him beyond the bounds of discretion and his inability to sense his limitations was really a dire element in his psychology. Garveyism came to be regarded by a number of well-thinking Negroes as a gospel of hate for white people and all that appertains to this group. This was worse than unfortunate. No program of permanent uplift for the Negro can successfully proceed on such an issue. Breathing out threatenings and slaughter against the dominant element among whom we live and move and have our being was common among the disciples of Marcus Garvey. Foolish and worse. Teach Negroes to hate white people and it will soon be impossible to teach them to love and think

well of their own. Garveyism lost much of the intelligent sympathy, if not open avowal, it might have gained by the fiery ebulitions of its ardent ambassadors. Nevertheless, our judgment of Garvey and his movement, I will say, should not be given on this count only. It is meet to observe that reformers and seers are prone to deliver themselves in such manner. It is also true that the excesses to which a movement goes should not necessarily bias judgment in this direction. Reformers, prophets and human movements that would rectify an existing order have this habit.

"Liberty, equality, fraternity" are the accepted bulwarks of democracy. Turn to the story of the French Revolution and see the extravagance out of which these ideas were salvaged. They would tear down everything; yea, and religion also. On the corner of a street in Paris a red republican was heard to declare how they were going to destroy churches, crucifixes and shrines, all that stood for the perpetuation of religion. Yet history points proudly to that event as marking the birthday of the modern democratic movement.

Garvey's was a great idea. It had in it a remarkable power of appeal and contagion. When a great idea deeply lays hold of the minds of a group with other suggestive elements in its mental and social atmosphere co-operating, it is liable to cause commotion and as a result throw up to attention much frothy and extraneous matter.

The phenomenal spread of Garveyism, further, must be attributed to the leader's knowledge of the psychology of his people joined to the fact—and this is most significant—of the time and circumstances in which the movement was inaugurated. Mark the elements in Negro psychology which he took cognizance of and marshalled to his service. Garvey proves a conviction of my own that only the Negro can properly interpret the Negro. The love of symbols, the craving for power, titles, etc., plumed knights in showy parades—all these Garvey took and exploited for the U. N. I. A. All the gorgeous periphery in dress, court display, fantastic titles were very relevant to his aim—the capture of the heart (if not the head) and the imagination of the masses of his people, and it worked. He captured moreover, some of the intellectuals. This was a splendid achievement. If only the leader had had the good sense to bind this latter class to himself for counsel, executive direction and business management in the special lines of his manifold enterprises the crash might have been postponed and made much less dramatic. I am not convinced that some crash would have been altogether avoided, for Garvey flattered by success grew dogged and impatient of the counsel of others.

After-the-war psychology was most potent in the success of Garvey and his endeavor. I think that this after-the-war psychology plus the personality of this Negro Moses contributed more than anything to his conquests. Garveyism unlocked the hopes long-imprisoned of thousands of Negro young men who had been drafted or seen service on the battle fields of Europe. Like the Ku Klux Klan this movement cannot be fully accounted for apart from due regard to the extreme susceptibility of the social atmosphere that followed the World War. Was Garvey a cunning opportunist in his ready seizure of this? Was not self-determination one of the cardinal principles in the settlement of the war?

The thousands who followed Marcus Garvey drank deeply the draughts of this new freedom as he offered it, to satisfy their half-conscious cravings for such freedom, and so he swept the Negro world, and to many his word became the law of their life.

The movement has suffered not only by Garvey's unproductive schemes, indiscreet financial ventures and poor business management; but also from the chicanery and cupidity of a number of those whom he drew around him and to whom offices of responsibility were given.

And now, Marcus Garvey is behind the bars convicted of using the mails to defraud and the most pertinent question is what of the U. N. I. A.? Orthodox disciples of his give the answer to the satisfaction of those within the fold. It could well be put: "Garvey's body lies. . . But his soul goes marching on." But for the masses of Negroes outside of the fold who do but ill to rejoice in the downfall of Garvey, it were well to discover if there is anything in this wreck of hopes and enterprise that may well be salvaged.

Here is one thing. Set this down to the eternal credit of Marcus Garvey that before him there has not been a man who stirred into expression the consciousness of the Negro peoples to the extent that he succeeded in doing,—extent both in degree and geographical area over which his ideas swept. Negroes all over the world have come to think of themselves as a Race—one in hope and destiny, as never before. Now this I count to be a thing of high value. This consciousness of race has been perhaps more vocal in America than anywhere else among Negroes, and was there before Garvey, you will say; but Garvey gave to it larger proportions and doubtless a height to which it had never risen. Under the spell of his propaganda it was amplified to an extent that gives justification to the name of his organization, Universal Negro Improvement Association. Thus the present state into which Garveyism has fallen offers a new challenge; that new challenge is for some new leader of equal breadth of sympathy, more practical intellect and of sober counsel to give himself to the task of the conservation of this race consciousness for the future good of this people. Much as this great spiritual product has come to be regarded as a thing greatly needed, it would be a pity to see it lost under the crash of Garvey's fall. Perhaps this leader can be found in the ranks of the U. N. I. A.

Further, the basic principle of Garveyism as mentioned before, that is, a self-supporting group life has in it something for the present and future good. There are of course, some dangers in the over-emphasis of independence. Independence is a rela-

tive term and pushed too far becomes a ludicrous impossibility. All that is bad in the civilization we characterize as Nordic is not bad because it is Nordic, but rather as it represents an imperfect stage in the cultural development of a people. It were better that while we encourage this self-competent group life we do not isolate ourselves so as to be inaccessible to something good or better than we ourselves have yet attained.

The Negro in America will never consent to be completely isolated economically, politically nor socially. And it is open to question whether white people want this isolation for themselves, that is, leaving out the color-haters and propagandists among them. Negroes should want a measure of independence and self-competence with proportionate co-operation, they should want to see multiplied all the profitable and friendly points of contact to the end that they might assimilate all that is highest and best in the civilization around them. Garveyism neglecting this principle gave to its program a revolutionary aspect in contrast to an evolutionary method of advance.

But even this revolutionary aspect was not wholly its leader's responsibility. The social forces that had been playing on the life of his people and more especially during the years of the Great War were outside of his control. Revolutions are almost without exception born in the breasts of the submerged class. When the mental, moral and spiritual energies of a people have been long imprisoned and have been denied opportunity to work themselves out along paths of constructive normal advance they are prone to break out and explode and it is not easy to hold their onward surge within the limitations of the usual conventions. Garveyism flowed true to form. In the spring of 1919 I was one of a number of colored men in one of those regional schools conducted by the National War Work Council of the Y. M. C. A. The director from one of the States of the far South.

He told of the fears voiced by certain white people lest the Negroes of this country should catch the contagion of Russian Bolshevism which was just then running its riotous career. "It would raise hell over here!" one white man had said to him. It has since been pointed out with becoming pride that the race has shown no signs of being influenced by the Red propaganda. But why this fear? Analyze it and see that it was a significant way of recognizing that Negroes like the peasants of Russia represent this submerged class with similar political and social forces allied against them.

This is the vital place for sober, intelligent leadership.

Finally, it does not do to treat Garveyism with detached indifference; it does not do to blame, decry nor vilify in any sweeping, indiscriminate manner, nor yet "without sneering, others teach to sneer". Many an outsider like myself may be brought sooner or later to admit: after all there was something to it!

The Garvey Movement

E. Franklin Frazier

GARVEY, himself, could not have planned a more strategic climax to his career in America than his imprisonment in Atlanta. The technical legal reason for his incarceration is obscured by the halo that shines about the head of the martyr. There is a sort of justice in this; for if the government were to punish all those who use the mails to defraud, it would round up those energetic business men who flood the mails with promises to give eternal youth and beauty to aging fat matrons, to make Carusos and Galli Curcis of members of church choirs, and to make master minds of morons. Garvey's promises were modest in comparison. And, indeed, what does one ship, more or less, matter in an imaginary fleet of merchantmen?

There are aspects of the Garvey Movement that can not be treated in this cavalier fashion. It is those aspects we propose to set forth here. The writer recalls that when he was a child one could still hear Negroes express the hope that some Moses would appear among them and lead them to a promised land of freedom and equality. He has lived to see such hopes displaced by more prosaic and less fanciful efforts towards social betterment. When Booker Washington first appeared on the scene he was hailed as a Moses. This was chiefly an echo of the white man's appraisal and soon died down when the Negro heard a message of patient industry, unsweetened by any prospect of a glorious future. What has distinguished the Garvey Movement is its appeal to the masses. While Negroes have found a degree of self-magnification in fraternal orders and the church, these organizations have not given the support to their ego-consciousness that whites find in the Kiwanis and especially the Klan. Garvey re-introduced the idea of a Moses, who was incarnate in himself, and with his masterly technic for dealing with crowds, he welded Negroes into a mass movement.

Before considering Garvey and his work, something should be said of the people he had to work with. The social status of the Negro in America should make them fertile soil for a mass movement to spring up in. They are repressed and shut out from all serious participation in American life. Not only does the Negro intellectual feel this repression, but the average Negro, like all mediocre people whose personalities must be supported by empty fictions, must find something to give meaning to his life and worth to his personality. One has simply to note how the superficial matter of color raises the most insignificant white man in the South to a place of paramount importance, in order to appreciate how much support a fiction gives to one's personality. Yet American Negroes have been relatively free from mass movements. This fact should not be regarded as a further testimony to the Negro's reputation for a policy of expediency in his present situation. There have been other factors to take the place of mass movements.

Many American Negroes have belittled the Garvey Movement on the ground that he is a West Indian and has attracted only the support of West Indians. But this very fact made it possible for him to contribute a new phase to the life of the American Negro. The West Indian Negroes have been ruled by a small white minority. In Jamaica, the Negro majority has often revolted and some recognition has been given to the mulattoes. This was responsible for Garvey's attempt, when he first came to this country, to incite the blacks against those of mixed blood. He soon found that there was no such easily discernible social cleavage recognized by the whites in this country. Yet his attempt to draw such a line has not failed to leave its effect. The fact that the West Indian has not been dominated by a white majority is probably responsible for a more secular view of life. The Garvey Movement would find the same response among the Negroes of the South as among the West Indians were it not for the dominating position of the preacher, whose peculiar position is symtomatic of an otherworldly outlook among the masses. Even in the face of this situation foreign Negroes have successfully converted hard-shelled Baptists to the Movement in spite of the opposition of their ministers. This secular influence in the life of the Negro attains its true significance when viewed in relation to the part that preparation for death plays in the life of the black masses.

The Garvey Movement afforded an asylum, as all mass movements, for those who were dissatisfied with life for many reasons, which could in this case be attributed to their status as Negroes. Although most of his followers were ignorant, we find among them intellectuals who had not found the places in the world that their education entitled them to. Instead of blaming themselves,—and they were not always individually responsible—they took refuge in the belief that in an autonomous black Africa they would find their proper place. The black rabble that could not see its own poverty, ignorance, and weakness vented its hatred upon obscure "traitors" and "enemies," who generally turned out to be Negro intellectuals who had achieved some distinction in American life. There is good reason to believe that Garvey constantly directed the animosity of his followers against the intellectuals because of his own lack of formal education.

We have noted how the Garvey Movement turned the Negro's attention to this world. This was accomplished not only by promising the Negro a paradise in the future in Africa; but through the invention of social distinctions and honors, the Negro was made somebody in his present environment. The humblest follower was one of the "Fellowmen of the Negro Race," while the more distinguished supporters were "Knights" and "Sirs." The women were organized into the Black Cross Nurses and the men into the Great African Army. "A uniformed member of a Negro lodge paled in significance beside a soldier of the Army of Africa. A Negro might be a porter during the day, taking his orders from white men, but he was an officer in the Black Army when it assembled at night in Liberty Hall. Many a Negro went about his work singing in his heart that he was a member of the great army marching to 'heights of achievements'."[1] Yet these extravagant claims were based upon the deep but unexpressed conviction in the minds of most Negroes that the white man has set certain limits to their rise in this country.

In his half acknowledged antagonism towards Negro preachers and the soporific religion they served the masses, Garvey did not ignore its powerful influence. In fact he endeavored to fuse the religious experience of the Negro with his own program. The symbolism associated with Christmas was made the sign of the birth of a Negro nation among the nations of the earth; while Easter became the symbol of a resurrected race. Nor did he overlook the opportunity to make his position appear similar to that of Jesus. According to him, his own people, especially the recognized Negro leaders, had incited the American authorities against him just as the Jews had incited the Roman authorities against Jesus. In this connection the idea of gaining a lost paradise appears as it does in most mass movements. The "Redemption of Africa" became the battle cry. To his followers he trumpeted: "No one knows when the hour of Africa's redemption cometh. It is in the wind. It is coming one day like a storm. It will be here. When that day comes, all Africa will stand together."[2]

The messianic element in this movement is not altogether lacking, although it does not stand out prominently. When Garvey entered the prison in Atlanta, besides commending his wife to the care of his followers, he spoke of the possibility of his death as only a messiah would speak. Under the caption, "If I Die In Atlanta," he bade his followers:

"Look for me in the whirlwind or the storm, look for me all around you, for, with God's grace, I shall come and bring with me the countless millions of black slaves who have died in America and the West Indies and the millions in Africa to aid you in the fight for liberty, freedom and life."[3]

By this promise Garvey raised himself above mortals and made himself the Redeemer of the Black World.

Many people are at a loss to understand how Garvey was able to attract supporters to a scheme which was manifestly infeasible and has been discredited by continued exposés of corruption and

bickering within the organization. But such tests of reasonableness can not be applied to schemes that attract crowds. Crowds, it has been said, never learn by experience. The reason is clear, for the crowd satisfies its vanity and longings in the beliefs it cherishes. Not only because of their longing for something to give meaning to their lives, but because of the scepticism about them, Negroes do not find the satisfaction that their fathers found in the promise of heavenly abode to compensate for the woes of this world. They therefore offer a fine field for charlatans and fakirs of every description. This Movement has attracted many such men who give the black crowds the escape they are seeking. The work carried on by the National Association for the Advancement of Colored People, which has been the subject of so many attacks by Garvey, has never attracted the crowd because it does not give the crowd an opportunity to show off in colors, parades, and self-glorification. The Association appeals to intelligent persons who are trying to attain tangible goals through cooperation. The same could be said of the Urban League. Dean Kelly Miller, it is said, once made the shrewd observation that the Negro pays for what he wants and begs for what he needs. This applies here as elsewhere. Those who support this Movement pay for it because it gives them what they want—the identification with something that makes them feel like somebody among white people who have said they were nobody.

Before concluding this brief interpretive sketch, we must add a few observations. Doubtless the World War with its shibboleths and stirrings of subject minorities offered a volume of suggestion that facilitated the Garvey Movement. Another factor that helped the Movement was the urbanization of the Negro that took place about the time. It is in the cities that mass movements are initiated. When the Negro lived in a rural environment he was not subject to mass suggestion except at the camp meeting and revival.

One of the most picturesque phases of the Movement has been the glorification of blackness which has been made an attribute of the celestial hierarchy. To most observers this last fact has been simply a source of merriment. But Garvey showed a knowledge of social psychology when he invoked a black god to guide the destiny of the Negro. The God of Israel served the same purpose. Those whites who said they would rather go to hell than to a heaven presided over by a black god, show what relation the average man's god must bear to him. The intellectual can laugh, if he will; but let him not forget the pragmatic value of such a symbol among the type of people Garvey was dealing with.

The question is often asked, "Is Garvey sincere?" The same question might be asked of the McGee brothers of the Kentucky Revival and of evangelists in general. Although Garvey's appeal has been more permanent, his methods have been

---

[1] Garvey: A Mass Leader, The Nation, Vol. CXXIII. No. 4189 by the writer.
[2] Ibid

[3] The Negro World, February 14, 1925.

in many respects those of the evangelist. Just because evangelists as a rule are well fed and free from material wants, it would be uncritical to put them all down as common swindlers. Likewise, with the evidence we have, we can not classify Garvey as such. He has failed to deal realistically with life as most so-called cranks, but he has initiated a mass movement among Negroes because it appealed to something that is in every crowd-minded man.

his name now four years after his conviction, as that of a mere criminal and exploiter of ignorant Negroes. It would be worth the inquiry to learn why this lone black figure, bumptious and flamboyant as he is, can call forth in such concert the interests of those governments with black subjects, in protecting them from his doctrine. There are faint flashes of irony in the solicitude. Most important in the philosophy which he preached were these:

The black peoples of the world are entitled to a country and government of their own where they can develop their own culture, industry and commerce, and elevate themselves to an equal status with the white races of the world.

Africa is their ancestral home and the most natural place for them to go.

The acceptance by black people of the standards of white people is an anomaly. Rather than accept white gods they should conceive them as being of their own image, and things black be given the same virtue for Negroes that things white have for white persons.

Now these principles, apart from the practical difficulties of accomplishment, are not very different from the advice of a large part of the white race to Negroes:

They should be deported to Africa.

They should not imitate white people, but do something themselves for which they will feel proud.

They should not expect to share completely the culture which the white races have developed themselves for themselves. And so on.

It must be concluded, it seems, that it is not so desirable even as a vague and unrealizable dream that Negroes should desire to go back to Africa. That, in the final analysis, it is unflattering to descry effectively that trait of "imitation" which for so many years has been regarded supercilliously by the "superior white races" Garvey, we fear, is more the symbol of a peculiar mood in Negroes than inspirer of it. He has succeeded in articulating some of the long crushed and unformed desires of the black masses, and he has done it with the usual glamor and arrogance of mass leaders. Only by considering these desires and their possible embarrassment to those governments with interests into which they cannot com-

MARCUS GARVEY has been released from the Federal Prison in Atlanta and deported to Jamaica, his home. Nothing has been lacking in the *Garvey and* precautions taken to guard *the "Garvey* him, not only from escape, *Movement"* but from the demonstrations of his followers. He was sent to prison on the technical charge of using the mails to defraud, a circumstance with but slight relationship to the important facts of his activities, and by a legal conviction which did not destroy that influence which seems to be uncommonly irritating to the authorities of several governments, including his own. No one dismisses

fortably fit, does Garvey and what he represents become dangerous. It was as right as it was legal to send him to prison; but this neither touched the movement which bears his name, nor the mood of the least advantaged of the suppressed peoples the world over, of which this movement was an expression.

The Social Philosophy of Booker T. Washington

By CHARLES S. JOHNSON

IT has now been thirteen years since Booker T. Washington died, and thirty-five years since a lightning flash across the brooding South illumined the social philosophy which made him great. The battle of the two "schools of Negro thought" waged bitterly and long, has had the effect of reducing the tenets of both to commonplace politics and rhetoric, and of obscuring, at least for the present generation, the vast interplay of social forces of a period just past, which are so interesting now to the student of race and of societies. The case of the "leaders" who insist upon prompt and unqualified recognition of Negroes upon an equalitarian basis, is relatively simple, and can be established by the Declaration of Independence, the Constitution, the principles of Christianity and abstract ethics. In this country, perhaps the only qualifying condition in the principles sustained has been the fact that the protagonists have been, by the very nature of things, the articulate ones who have not themselves been wholly certain whether they meant to include all Negroes or merely all Negroes sufficiently well educated and cultured to argue for their rights. And while the aspect of race and rights held by the resisting white population has been of the unpalatable mass, that of the indignant Negroes has been most frequently of those Negroes merely who were indignant. Their course has been more direct, requiring less strategy, tolerance and patience, and indeed, less compromising, temporarily or permanently either with ideals or with the ordinary privileges of citizenship. But this does not yield the story of the battle of cultures in that section of the country where most of the Negroes have been and still are; where emotions, by no means favorable to the ultimate doctrines of the equalitarians, have been whirling at white heat; and where traditions required to be dismantled in the same orderly manner that they were built up. In this setting Mr. Washington was important; not because he became a great man, or a great Negro, or rose from slavery, but because he embodied the survival elements of the Negro race in an environment hostile to its ultimate objectives.

The strategies which he employed, consciously or unconsciously, are only now finding their most pronounced effect in the self-concern of Negroes and in the attitudes of white persons with respect to them. His social philosophy, where it has been recognized at all, has been taken too personally. Inevitably the ones who objected to it most were the articulate Negroes who needed it least, and who have merely seen the directness of his principles without considering the logic of their implications. It is possible, with a great freedom, to view this philosophy in the light of the very nature of human nature.

If the coldly dispassionate judgment of a philosopher or social psychologist, with no racial theories at stake, were sought in advice as to the calculating diplomacy required to establish a submerged group of former slaves on a plane of equality with their former masters, who both hated and despised them, he would quite reasonably argue thus:

In the first place, passions cannot be argued with; the meeting of defiant passion with resistant passion never brings peace but conflict which ends inevitably without conviction.

Beliefs disparaging to the weaker group which have grown up over hundreds of years until they crystallized into traditions, cannot be swept away by mere assertions of their falsity, however false they may be. They must be proved objectively, and this proof can best proceed when the emotional resistance to proof is is diverted.

When there is fear that the weaker group will destroy the integrity of the stronger or threaten its self-interest if freely admitted to equality with it, this fear more than any other passion, will lead to desperate measures, and no movement of the weaker group, however exalted in its principles can succeed rapidly until the fears are by some means quieted, or entirely dissipated.

This philosopher would probably advise, as a first step, the allaying of these fears by any means at hand which did not compromise manhood. He would advise taking hold of those strangely effective "symbols" and "myths" which have been most potent in promoting an aggressive racial solidarity in the stronger group, stripping them of their most horrid features when these features are not immediately required, and retaining those features which are required, to give them most acceptable content. A force is a force by whatever name it is called. And if to the stronger group "social equality" in its most obnoxious sense means a matter of eating together, and to the weaker group means the acquirement of a status which if carried out would make eating together a simple matter of course, it is the surer wisdom to expend energy on the status and let human nature take its inevitable course. This philosopher would reasonably argue that since men hold passionately to opinions which are founded upon intangible emotions, the wiser strategy would shift proof from a subjective to and objective plane, from immaterial belief to visual reality. Such a diplomacy would select from the "emotional clusters", the most favorable features and extend their implications, and it would spare itself the energy of combatting unfavorable features futilely by the expedient of pointing out, to the strong group, the self-destructive qualities inherent in them. It would as frequently as possible divert unpleasant attention from itself, by directing attention to greater "menaces". It would deprive the stronger group of the satisfaction it might get through insults, by developing the defensive coating of a sense of humor; it would rid the inferior position of that debasement which engenders scorn, by deliberately rationalizing this position into one which gave its enemy no satisfaction. It would constantly divert attention from abstract and undefinable theories while it laid an unmoveable foundation at the base of this scorn.

And of what should such a foundation consist:

1. Security in the possession of land
2. Security in the possession of wealth
3. Security in the possession of skill
4. Security in the possession of health
5. Security in the possession of a sound education
6. Sensitiveness to beauty and order.

These, when they are analyzed are precisely the foundations of abiding culture ond civilization. The end, if carried through, would be a radically improved status and acceptance, and in the effort, the weaker group would have the greater spur of deliberate design and intention. The passions conserved might burst forth in creative art and intellectual employments; command of emotions could bring superiority to the silent conflict; security of wealth, by all the economic laws which we worship today, brings respect; security of health brings strength and resistance. This, in its principal outline was actually the social philosophy of Washington.

The setting. Washington was born in slavery, a fact which gave a certain dramatic value to his life and philosophy, as did the similar birth of Douglas and his subsequent flight from the institution. Following his various experiences to manhood now well known through his autobiography, which has been translated into some seventy languages, he emerged from Hampton in 1875. And although his important social career did not begin immediateyl, the significance of all that was to follow lay in the position of Negroes at that period and their relation to the vast national and sectional changes in process. De Toqueville pointed out a subtle truth when he observed that the difference between the ancient slave masters and those of the South was that the former kept the bodies of their slaves in bondage but placed no restraint upon their minds, while the Americans employed their despotism and their power against the human mind itself, depriving the slave even of the desire for freedom. Not only had the slave been denied education, but the duration of the system required that he be stripped of his humanity for conscience sake. Theories of an eternal and inescapable inferiority in mind and soul had been established from science, philosophy and Biblical literature. Their ignorance was taken as proof of the eternal fitness of their status. Sympathies for the slave in his hopeless position were dulled by the assurances that the slave neither wanted nor could sustain anything different. The literature painted his happiness and contentment. Even the slave be-

lieved. Then came the Civil War, which with a blow swept away the institution without touching the habits of mind which supported it. The revolution of a reconstruction period followed with the sudden rise to power of the despised blacks supported in office by the guns of the North. Passions had been whipped into a delirium of hatred and desire for revenge. However wrong the South had been it had suffered defeat and had had heaped upon its head the bitterest of insults. And when the Army was removed there came the inevitable and cataclysmic recoil. The Ku Klux Klan arose bringing in a reign of terror; the freed Negroes were without property or education or protection; the poor whites who had been held in a poverty and debasement even worse than that of the slave, began to emerge and vent their long suppressed hatred—a hatred stirred deeper by the fear of the competition of Negroes. They began to make laws, repressive laws, beginning first with attempts to render useless the hand of the emancipated slave in competition in the open labor market. The revulsion against the former slaves was electric. They were pushed not only out of office but out of politics. The slogans "White domination", white supremacy and "The Solid South", had their birth. Passions were directed against every symbol of association. Then it was that most talk was heard of deportation, annihilation, segregation. Demagogues like Tillman in South Carolina and Vardaman in Mississippi arose, and rode to power on the inflamed hatred of illiterate whites. Tillman told them what they wanted to hear:

"The Negro bears about him a birthright of inferiority that is as unalterable as eternity. He who in the morning of Creation set the shifting sands as a barier to the mad waves of the mighty deep and said thus far, has also set his seal upon the Negro forever in his black skin, kinky hair, thick lips, flat nose, double layer of skull, different anatomy as well as analogy from white men. His stupid intellect is fulfilled in prophesy, uttered thousands of years ago, but no less true today, "A servant of servants shalt thou be".

The breaking up of slavery had forced a change in the agricultural economy; fertile lands were being exhausted and the population was moving toward new lands. The North, now beginning to feel contrite, was insisting less and less upon interfering with the South in its handling of what was termed its own "peculiar problem", and, moreover offered little economic opportunity for the Negroes outside the South. It was instead, looking to the South as a field for investments when the fires of anger should finally die down sufficiently to permit them to enter. The Negroes' struggle was fourfold: against a new economic system, against the revenge of the poor whites, against the scorn of their former masters and against their own ignorance. This struggle was registering in increasing ill feeling, repressive legislation and a terrific mortality. Underneath the whole fabric was one surging passion—that of fear: fear of the competition of Negroes, fear of an enforced social equality, fear of political domination, and fear of losing the black labor, so necessary to the rebuilding of the South. It was then that there appeared also the book called *Ariel;* which attempted to prove that a Negro was the snake who tempted Eve in the Garden of Eden. And it was admitted into the libraries.

Into this picture Washington came. It is entirely possible that had it not been for his famous Atlanta speech, delivered before the Cotton States Exposition in 1895, he would not have been known for more than the successful school principal that he was, nor had either the influence or prestige to give weight to his ideas, however worthy; nor to have faced situations demanding the vital judgments and practice which went into his later career. He had addressed but one other important Southern body and then for only five minutes. He was not known nationally, although he had been working in the South some fourteen years. But Atlanta was making a bid for Northern capital, and to make a show of cosmopolitanism, invited Washington to appear on the program. No one expected him to do anything unusual. Such occasions, however, present at times, the opportunity for the projection of a fortunate philosophy if one has a philosophy to offer. By just such chance incidents are men made.

The author of a recent volume, *Men and Portents* recalls the power of chance, clear-cut philosophies in public utterance. The philosophy of Lincoln comes down to us embalmed in the famous sentence, "No nation can long continue to exist, half slave, half free." It was a clarification of a great impending issue. Aristide Briand in London at the signing of the Locarno pact arose to international fame overnight by a fortunate remark which challenged the thought of the world on the action taken there. He gave an ideal plain and unequivocal utterance. Similarly, Coolidge emerged from obscurity by a phrase, while the nation was in the midst of panic over a local situation of vast national implications. He settled fears that were agitating the public mind even tho these fears were as illusory as the racial fears that obsessed the south. In the Boston police strike, when the bugbear of Bolshevism terrified, and there was alarm, lest, not merely Boston but the country would find itself forced to change its concepts of social order, he brought in the militia, broke the strike and made a speech in which he said: *"There is no right to strike against the public safety by anybody, anywhere, anytime."* The author, quoting a commentator says, of the speech. "It struck fire from the Americanism of the entire country. Wires relayed it to the remotest regions and it thrilled the United States." He was rewarded with the vice-presidency and moved on up. The same circumstance surrounded Booker Washington in Atlanta. Fears were rampant, segregation laws were the expression of these fears; they were widening in their reach—the schools, transportation, intermarriage laws, and finally they were reaching out for industry threatening the life as well as the manhood of the race. The major part of his philoso-

phy is embodied in that speech. But the phrase that rang over the south and country was this: *"In all things that are purely social we can be as separate as the fingers of the hand, yet one as the hand in all things essential to mutual progress."*

The effect was electric. It was a solution. Clarke Howell of the Atlanta *Constitution* wired to New York that it was one of the most notable speeches ever delivered to a southern audience; "a revelation, a platform upon which blacks and whites can stand with full justice to each other."

This is as good a point as any to begin a rough classification of his full philosophy and it is stated descriptively and briefly.

He advocated conciliatory rather than aggressive tactics in race relations. The principle has been confused both by his critics and his imitators of less vision and courage. It is not for us to determine whether he was less manly, or wanted less than those who insisted on their full rights immediately. The fact remains that no power within the control of Negroes could have quieted the fears of the white south now gaining the sympathies of the north in its dilemma over the Negro problem, nor saved them from the injury of these fears exploded. Altho the white south received this as a solution for all time, nowhere is it evident that Washington stated this as more than a temporal adjustment. These results were immediate: For the first time the south found itself listening seriously to the voice of the Negro, it was a demonstration of acumen from an unexpected and disarming source; it called attention to Negro progress; it killed the spectre of a fictitious social equality and began the destruction of the vague and mysterious connotations of the other myths and symbols that had been troubling the south, it strategically reversed the position of Negroes in the south from that of a menacing burden to that of a possible ally, and linked the fortunes of Negroes publicly with the fortunes of the south.

All of us are familiar with the interpretations placed upon these doctrines by white persons. Let us consider some of the implications: Social psychologists recognize now the tremendous potency of symbols and illusions. One of the items in the rift between the two sects of Quakers is on the trivial matter of whether or not the hat should be worn in church. Difference is heavily charged with emotion. Wars have been fought over symbols of faith in religion. We are aware how during the World War, men were stirred to cast away their lives on the symbolism of a vague and meaningless phrase "Saving the world for Democracy." Just such a symbol is "Social Equality," and the wisest social strategy recognizes this as a symbol and treats it so. The inevitable result has been the laying of a foundation beneath tradition for the very social equality which was feared. The paradox is clear when it is observed that Washington, himself came to be accorded, in recognition of the position to which his power entitled him, a social recognition attained by no rank of his Atlanta audience below that of the Governors.

He advocated the ownership of land and homes

and the development of business. The difference between the American Negro and the European peasant is in the ability to own land. It is on the security of income of the masses that the talented tenth must rest. He urged remaining on the farms because whites were leaving them. He urged the establishment of business thus to combine with labor the contribution of capital to their resources. And wisely he refrained then from exploiting the political aspects of economic principles inherent in this program, and from giving it the spectre of a name. In ths respect he was more subtle than the Socialists who, by emphasizing the differences in theories without attempting to live their own into execution, surrounded themselves with a conscious resistance which in the end defeated their hopes.

He emphasized the dignity of work. To Negroes this was a kind of treachery, an attitude which had developed from the association of work with the former status of slavery. This, however, was a prop for the broad economic platform which Washington attempted to lay. In this way the tides were turned which were pushing Negroes from their old traditional trades and permitting the revengeful poor whites to come too precipitously to power. The masses of men without philosophy could be stimulated to harder effort when prosaic work itself, so vastly necessary, was surrounded by glamour. One expedient was a fortune phrase, oft repeated, which had the effect of drawing from the work an element of pride which it lacked for so many. "There is a difference between working and being worked."

He advocated beginning boldly at the beginnings with the elements of education. His most effective method of emphasis was ridicule of the thin and crackly veneer of the half-educated. It was the emphasis which developed into the schism between the schools of higher and industrial education. When disgusted with the inadequacies of public provision for elementary training for Negroes in the south, he did not content himself with the virtuous feeling of indignation over the difference per capita spent for white and Negro children in the States. In the mood of the south it was a proportion, which befitted the situation of the two classes —"one civilized; the other incapable of civilization." He interested philanthropy in planting a seed of Negro training which gradually drew white and Negro support and raised the level to a point that would not have been attained in fifty years of distant agitation. The wisdom of this lies in the fact that people, contented in their ignorance can never be expected to want seriously to be educated until a first interest has been stirred. No one can say how much the quiet dissemination of training thruout the rural south was responsible for the discontent which registered in the migration. On the industrial phase, we are just beginning to appreciate the value of the substitutes for apprenticeship which his type of institution provided, now that it has been incorporated into this educational policy of the country.

A recent study of industrial training by Dr. May of the University of Illinois points out the absolute absence of any formal method in our present industrial system for men to move from unskilled to skilled trades, since the break-up of the apprentice system a hundred years ago. Those who have contact with Negro labor know how hopeless is this progression for Negroes where no emergency forces the experiment with Negro labor in new lines. Eighty per cent of the Negro population depends upon labor for its sustenance, and the other twenty per cent is measured in its advance by the stability and competence of the base.

He was an objectivist. People believe what they can see whether they will to believe or not. Instead of giving his whole emphasis to arguing that Negroes are capable of being educated he helped Negroes educate themselves. His vast institution at Tuskegee was indisputable evidence of the capacity of Negroes for managing their own affairs. The principle carried thru his educational practice and the finer elaborations of this practice which have since been developed independently by Dewey and Montessori. His work constituted a contribution to educational theory and practice.

He refused to stress politics. On this point he has received the most persistent criticism from Negroes. But he would have been less astute than his other policies indicate if he had not seen that the agitating for ballots was merely another of the meaningless appurtenances which even the white voters did not take advantage of when the novelty had worn off. As has already happened in many of the southern cities, the enfranchisement of Negroes was forced by the logic of events when it became apparent that there were Negroes who wanted elected men who in character were superior to those who rose to power thru ignorance and chance. And a man who is broad enough to be fair to Negroes is most likely to be the one most social minded, and capable of administering the affairs of a community.

He diverted attention from Negroes by comparing them with other races and cultures—i.e., he lifted them to a new level by finding someone lower. This was the burden of his book *"The Man Lowest Down,"* and the comparison was made with an extraordinary sympathy. He rationalized his own status when he said, "You can beat me being a white man but I can beat you being a Negro." It was no different from the present course of the Negro writers and artists who, in their new representations of Negro life are deing the very thing for which he found a phrase.

There is another apt example of his philosophy which would bear quoting: "No man can drag me down by making me hate him. If you hold me in the gutter you must remain there with me." In this there is the subtle directing of attention to the intelligent self-interest of the stronger group. It is an irresistable reminder that the strong cannot abuse the weak without suffering consequences as debasing to itself as it creates for others.

Effort has been made to state this philosophy in the light of its implications for the general development of Negroes in this country. The tre-

(Continued on page 115)

THE SOCIAL PHILOSOPHY OF BOOKER T. WASHINGTON

(Continued from page 105)

mendous advances in understanding evidenced in the south would suggest that many of these policies have worked. Whether this advance would have come without it is worth speculating upon, but there is no pressing indication that it would. Human nature has changed and the response has been to a process of molding, it would seem, rather than to shock. There is still need of a doctrine of work, of self-respect, of creative inspiration, of material development, of friendships that will progressively dispel the fears of one group of what the full manhood status of the other will do to it.

The most effective interest of the present is art, and even of this it may be said that it is but an elaboration of Washington's principles of stressing work rather than the rewards of work. And in any estimate of this philosophy, it should be evident that there is no virtue in the hand that withholds the rewards so that they must be acquired thru strategy even after they are earned.

There is a view which may be taken of this whole setting, which conceives the white south itself as the object of education, and, since it must be untaught the traditions of hundreds of years, and new principles instilled, the Negroes conceived as the teachers. Here then might apply to the Negroes an adage, as aptly as to the martyred old philosopher of whom it was said:

"Woe to him who would teach men faster than they can learn."

Acknowledgments

Johnson, Charles S., ed. *Ebony and Topaz: A Collectanea* (New York: Opportunity, 1927): 1–166.

Schuyler, George S. "The Negro-Art Hokum." *Nation* 122, No. 3180 (June 16, 1926): 662–63. Reprinted from *The Nation* magazine. Copyright the Nation Company, L.P.

Hughes, Langston. "The Negro Artist and the Racial Mountain." *Nation* 122, No. 3181 (June 23, 1926): 692–94. Reprinted from *The Nation* magazine. Copyright the Nation Company, L.P.

Johnson, Charles S. "Editorial: American Negro Art." *Opportunity* 4, No. 44 (August 1926): 238–39.

Johnson, Charles S. "Editorial: Gambling the Lyre." *Opportunity* 4, No. 46 (October 1926): 302–3.

"Editorial: Some Perils of the 'Renaissance'." *Opportunity* 5, No. 3 (March 1927): 68.

Hurston, Zora Neale. "Characteristics of Negro Expression." In Nancy Cunard, ed., *Negro: Anthology Made by Nancy Cunard 1931–1933* (London: Wishart & Co., 1934): 39–46.

Cunard, Nancy. "Harlem Reviewed." In Nancy Cunard, ed., *Negro: Anthology Made by Nancy Cunard 1931–1933* (London: Wishart & Co., 1934): 67–75.

"A Negro Art Exhibit." *Southern Workman* 51, No. 12 (December 1922): 542–43. Reprinted with the permission of the Hampton University Archives.

Locke, Alain. "To Certain of Our Phillistines." *Opportunity* 3 (May 1925): 155–56.

"Editorial: Negro Art." *Opportunity* 4, No. 41 (May 1926): 142–43.

Barnes, Albert C. "Negro Art, Past and Present." *Opportunity* 4, No. 41 (May 1926): 148–49.

Buermeyer, Laurence. "The Negro Spirituals and American Art." *Opportunity* 4, No. 41 (May 1926): 158–59, 167.

"Editorial: More About African Art." *Opportunity* 5, No. 5 (May 1927): 126.

Herskovits, Melville J. "The Art of the Congo." *Opportunity* 5, No. 5 (May 1927): 135–36.

Potamkin, Harry Alan. "African Plastic in Contemporary Art." *Opportunity* 5, No. 5 (May 1927): 137–39.

O'Neil, Raymond. "The Negro in Dramatic Art." *Crisis* 27 (1924): 155–57. Reprinted with the permission of the Crisis Publishing Company.

Jelliffe, Rowena Woodham. "The Negro in the Field of Drama." *Opportunity* 6, No. 7 (July 1928): 214.

Bledsoe, Jules. "Has the Negro a Place in the Theatre?" *Opportunity* 6, No. 7 (July 1928): 215.

Spence, Eulalie. "A Criticism of the Negro Drama: As It Relates to the Negro Dramatist and Artist." *Opportunity* 6, No. 6 (June 1928): 180.

Keelan, Harry S. "The Theatre: A Review of *Porgy*." *Opportunity* 6, No. 6 (June 1928): 180–81.

Fauset, Jessie. "The Gift of Laughter." In Addison Gayle Jr., ed., *Black Expression: Essays By and About Black Americans in the Creative Arts* (New York: Weybright and Talley, 1969): 159–65.

Fauset, Arthur Huff. "The Negro's Cycle of Song—A Review." *Opportunity* 3 (November 1925): 333–35, 348.

Botkin, B.A . "Self-Portraiture and Social Criticism in Negro Folk-Song." *Opportunity* 5, No. 2 (February 1927): 38–42.

Webb, George A. "The Profanation of Negro Spirituals." *Opportunity* 6, No. 6 (June 1928): 182.

Hurston, Zora Neale. "Spirituals and Neo-Spirituals." In Nancy Cunard, ed., *Negro: Anthology Made by Nancy Cunard 1931–1933* (London: Wishart & Co., 1934): 359–61.

Frazier, E. Franklin. "A Folk Culture in the Making." *Southern Workman* 57, No. 6 (June 1928): 195–99. Reprinted with the permission of the Hampton University Archives.

Johnson, James Weldon. "The Dilemma of the Negro Author." *American Mercury* 15, No. 60 (December 1928): 477–81.

Johnson, James Weldon. "The Larger Success." *Southern Workman* 52, No. 9 (September 1923): 427–36. Reprinted with the permission of the Hampton University Archives.

"On Writing About Negroes." *Opportunity* 3 (August 1925): 227–28.

De Armond, Fred. "A Note on the Sociology of Negro Literature." *Opportunity* 3 (December 1925): 369–71.

Calverton, V.F. "The Advance of the Negro." *Opportunity* 4 (February 1926): 54–55.

Johnson, Charles S. "The Negro Enters Literature." *The Carolina Magazine* 57, No. 7 (May 1927): 3–9, 44–48.

Johnson, James Weldon. "Race Prejudice and the Negro Artist." *Harper's Monthly* (November 1928): 769–76. Reprinted with the permission of *Harper's Monthly*.

Nelson, Alice Dunbar. "The Negro Looks at an Outworn Tradition." *Southern Workman* 57, No. 5 (May 1928): 195–200. Reprinted with the permission of the Hampton University Archives.

Johnson, James Weldon. "Negro Authors and White Publishers." *Crisis* 36 (July 1929): 228–29. Reprinted with the permission of the Crisis Publishing Company.

Jacobs, George W. "Negro Authors Must Eat." *Nation* 128, No. 3336 (June 12, 1929): 710–11. Reprinted from *The Nation* magazine. Copyright the Nation Company, L.P.

Brown, Sterling A. "Our Literary Audience." *Opportunity* 8, No. 2 (February 1930): 42–46, 61.

Mencken, H.L. "The Burden of Credulity." *Opportunity* 9 (February 1931): 40–41.

Powell, A. Clayton. "H.L. Mencken Finds Flowers in a 'Dunghill.'" *Opportunity* 9 (March 1931): 72–74.

Brawley, Benjamin. "Art Is Not Enough." *Southern Workman* 61, No. 12 (December 1932): 489–94. Reprinted with the permission of the Hampton University Archives.

"Claude McKay to Nancy Cunard, September 18, 1932, from Tangier, Morocco." Transcribed copy. Original is handwritten. [MS Cunard/recip/McKay, Claude. Harry Ransom Humanities Research Center, University of Texas at Austin.] Reprinted with the permission of the Harry Ransom Humanities Research Center and The Archives of Claude McKay, Carl Cowl, Administrator.

"Claude McKay to Nancy Cunard, September 29, 1932, from Tangier, Morocco." Transcribed copy. Original is handwritten. [MS Cunard/recip/McKay, Claude. Harry Ransom Humanities Research Center, University of Texas at Austin.] Reprinted with the permission of the Harry Ransom Humanities Research Center and The Archives of Claude McKay, Carl Cowl, Administrator.

Hughes, Langston. "Writers, Words and the World." Typed manuscript of a speech given at the Paris meeting of the International Writers Association for the Defense of Culture, July 25, 1938. Transcribed copy. [MS Cunard/Misc/ Hughes, Langston/Lecture Writers, Words and the World ccms. Harry Ransom Humanities Research Center, University of Texas at Austin.] Reprinted with the permission of the Harry Ransom Humanities Research Center and the Estate of Langston Hughes.

Hughes, Langston. "Democracy, Negroes, and Writers." Typed manuscript of an address to the League of American Writers dated May 13, 1941. Transcribed copy. [JWJ/Hughes/MSS/286. James Weldon Johnson Collection, Beinecke Rare Book Library, Yale University.] Reprinted with the permission of the Estate of Langston Hughes.

Hughes, Langston. "My Adventures as a Social Poet." *Phylon* 8, No. 3 (September 1947): 205–12. Copyright 1947 by Clark Atlanta University, Atlanta, Georgia. Reprinted with permission.

"A Note on *Contempo* and Langston Hughes." In Nancy Cunard, ed., *Negro: Anthology Made by Nancy Cunard 1931–1933* (London: Wishart & Co., 1934): 141–42.

"Alfred A. Knopf to Langston Hughes, July 29, 1930." Transcribed copy. [JWJ/Hughes/ Corres. James Weldon Johnson Collection, Beinecke Rare Book Library, Yale University.] Reprinted with the permission the Estate of Alfred Knopf.

"Langston Hughes to Carl Van Vechten, September 4, 1930." Transcribed copy. [JWJ/ Hughes/Corres/LH to CVV. James Weldon Johnson Collection, Beinecke Rare Book Library, Yale University.] Reprinted with the permission of the Estate of Langston Hughes.

"Alfred A. Knopf to Langston Hughes, March 2, 1931." Transcribed copy. [JWJ/ Hughes/Corres. James Weldon Johnson Collection, Beinecke Rare Book Library, Yale University.] Reprinted with the permission of the Estate of Alfred Knopf.

"Carl Van Vechten to Blanche Knopf, April 3, 1933." Transcribed copy. [Knopf, Inc/ Recip/Hughes, Langston. Harry Ransom Humanities Research Center, University of Texas at Austin.] Reprinted with the permission of the Harry Ransom Humanities Research Center and the Estate of Carl Van Vechten.

"Blanche Knopf to Langston Hughes, August 21, 1933." Transcribed copy. [Knopf, Inc./recip/Hughes, Langston. Harry Ransom Humanities Research Center, University of Texas at Austin.] Reprinted with the permission of the Harry Ransom Humanities Research Center and the Estate of Langston Hughes.

"Langston Hughes to Blanche Knopf, February 27, 1934." Transcribed copy. [Knopf, Inc./recip/Hughes, Langston. Harry Ransom Humanities Research Center, University of Texas at Austin.] Reprinted with the permission of the Harry Ransom Humanities Research Center and the Estate of Langston Hughes.

"Carl Van Vechten to Blanche Knopf, March 12, 1934." Transcribed copy. [Knopf, Inc./recip/Hughes, Langston. Harry Ransom Humanities Research Center, University of Texas at Austin.] Reprinted with the permission of the Harry Ransom Humanities Research Center and the Estate of Carl Van Vechten.

"Blanche Knopf to Langston Hughes, March 12, 1934." Transcribed copy. [Knopf, Inc./recip/Hughes, Langston. Harry Ransom Humanities Research Center, University of Texas at Austin.] Reprinted with the permission of the Harry Ransom Humanities Research Center and the Estate of Langston Hughes.

"Langston Hughes to Blanche Knopf, nd [1934]." Transcribed copy. [Knopf, Inc./ recip/Hughes, Langston. Harry Ransom Humanities Research Center, University of Texas at Austin.] Reprinted with the permission of the Harry Ransom Humanities Research Center and the Estate of Langston Hughes.

"Memo, HS (Harold Strauss) to Mr. Knopf, March 1, 1940." Transcribed copy. [Knopf/uncatalogued/permanent title folders/Hughes, Langston. Harry Ransom Humanities Research Center, University of Texas at Austin.] Reprinted with the permission of the Harry Ransom Humanities Research Center and the Estate of Alfred Knopf.

"Memo, HS (Harold Strauss) to Mrs. Knopf, April 8, 1940." Transcribed copy. [Knopf/ uncatalogued/permanent title folders/Hughes, Langston. Harry Ransom Humanities Research Center, University of Texas at Austin.] Reprinted with the permission of the Harry Ransom Humanities Research Center and the Estate of Alfred Knopf.

"Langston Hughes to Mrs. Blanche Knopf, February 8, 1940 [from Monterey, California]." Transcribed copy. [Knopf/uncatalogued/permanent title folders/ Hughes, Langston. Harry Ransom Humanities Research Center, University of Texas at Austin.] Reprinted with the permission of the Harry Ransom Humanities Research Center and the Estate of Alfred Knopf.

"Reader's Report, November 27, 1942, Langston Hughes, *The Big Sea*, H. Strauss." Transcribed copy. [Knopf/uncatalogued/permanent title folders/Hughes, Langston. Harry Ransom Humanities Research Center, University of Texas at Austin.] Reprinted with the permission of the Harry Ransom Humanities Research Center.

Du Bois, W.E.B. "The Negro and Radical Thought." *Crisis* 22 (July 1921): 102–04. Reprinted with the permission of the Crisis Publishing Company.

McKay, Claude. "Soviet Russia and the Negro." *Crisis* 27 (December 1923, January 1924): 61–65, 114–18. Reprinted with the permission of the Crisis Publishing Company.

Elmes, A.F. "Garvey and Garveyism—An Estimate." *Opportunity* 3 (May 1925): 139–41.

Frazier, E. Franklin. "The Garvey Movement." *Opportunity* 4 (November 1926): 346–48.

"Garvey and the 'Garvey Movement.'" *Opportunity* 6, No. 1 (January 1928): 4-5.

Johnson, Charles S. "The Social Philosophy of Booker T. Washington." *Opportunity* 6, No. 4 (April 1928): 102–05, 115.